BURLINGTON COUNTY

(NEW JERSEY)

MARRIAGES

COMPILED BY
H. STANLEY CRAIG

Southern Historical Press, Inc.
Greenville, South Carolina

This volume was reproduced from
An 1932 edition located in the
Publisher's private Library
Greenville, South Carolina

All rights reserved. No part of this publication may be reproduced,
stored in a retrieval system, transmitted in any form, posted
on to the web in any form or by any means without
the prior written permission of the publisher.

Please direct all correspondence and orders to:

www.southernhistoricalpress.com
or
SOUTHERN HISTORICAL PRESS, Inc.
PO Box 1267
375 West Broad Street
Greenville, SC   29601
southernhistoricalpress@gmail.com

Originally published: Merchantville, NJ, 1932
Copyright 1932 by H. Stanley Craig
ISBN #0-89308-315-1
All rights Reserved.
Printed in the United States of America

KEY TO SOURCES

[1]Marriage Licenses, from the New Jersey Archives 1683-1790.

[2]Records of Trinity P. E. Church, Mount Holly, 1860-1900.

[3]County Clerk's Records, recorded from 1795 to 1840.

[4]Records of St. Andrew's P. E. Church, Mount Holly, 1785-1892.

[5]Records of Chesterfield Friends' Meeting, 1682-1845.

[6]Records of Burlington Friends' Meeting, 1678-1806.

[7]Records of Upper Springfield Friends' Meeting, 1788-1827.

[8]Records of St. Mary's P. E. Church, Burlington, 1738-1832.

[9]Records of Evesham Friends' Meeting, 1703.1769.

[10]Records of Upper Evesham Friends' Meeting, 1798-1930.

[11]Records of Little Egg Harbor Friends' Meeting, 1715-1859.

[12]Chester Friends' Meeting, 1804-1826.

[13]Mount Holly Friends' Meeting, 1778-1826.

[14]Docket of William Stockton, J. P.

BURLINGTON COUNTY MARRIAGES

Aaronson, Aaron—Rebecca Scattergood, Dec. 11, 1730.[1]
   Benjamin—Hope Folwell, 3-13-1767.[1]
   Benjamin—Mary Ann Bozorth, 10-22-1873.[2]
   Benjamin—Sarah Etta Page, 6-16-1898.[2]
   Caleb—Lydia Harvey, 11-18-1819.[3]
   Ephriam—Amy T. Black, 1-9-1823.[3]
   Ezra—Hope Folwell, 12-8-1811.[3]
   Frederick—Sarah Chew, 3-27-1897.[2]
   George—Mary Hancock, 5-1-1800.[3]
   George—Maria Page, 8-18-1830.[3]
   John—Esther Perkins, 2-27-1823.[3]
   Joseph—Hannah Folwell, Aug. 25, 1736.[1]
   Joseph—Anne Marriott, Mar. 39, 1749.[1]
   Joseph—Achsah Black, 10-9-1782.[1]
   Joseph—Margaret Renear, 4-22-1801,[3]
   Joseph—Mary VanHorn, 8-15-1818.[3]
   Nathan—Eliza Gaskell, 12-31-1822.[3]
   Theodore Risden—Florence Mills, 12-26-1895.[2]
   Thomas—Sarah Black, 7-24-1787.[1]
   Thomas—Ann Foster, 1-18-1821.[3]
   Thomas—Sarah P. Aaronson, 5-20-1836.[3]
Aayre, Thomas W.—Sarah Stretch, 2-1-1830.[4]
Abbott, John—Anne Mauliverer, May 26, 1696.[5]
   John (s. Timothy and Anne)—Susanna Eullock, 9-1-1778.[5]
   Joseph (s. John and Susanna)—Ann Rickey (d. John and Ann) 3-7-1805.[5]
   Timothy (s. Timothy and Anne)—Anne Newbold (d, Joshua and Rebecca), Trenton, 5-9-1822.[5]
   William (s. Timothy and Anne)—Helena Lawrie, 3-13-1782.[5]
   William—Rebecah Holloway, 1-11-1787.[5]
   Zacariah—Kitty Simons, 8-16-1804.[6]
Abelea, Melchesidee—Mary Power, 10-30-1780.[1]

Acabel, Tab—Vilet Still, 6-8-1817.³
Acey, James—Elizabeth Gaskill, 9-13-1823.⁸
Ackley, Julius B.—Susannah Hunt, 10-26-1811.³
Acton, Benjamin—Mary Satterthwaite, 1720.⁶
  Benjamin—Sarah Miller, 4-24-1808.⁷
  Samuel— ——— Hall, 3-28-1796.⁷
Adair, John—Martha Crossley, 12-5-1774.¹
Adeir, Robert—Rebecca Huddleston, 5-21-1768.⁸
Adams, Abraham—Susan Hankins, 9-28-1825.³
  David—Mary Ryner, 5-22-1786.¹
  Elijah—Eliza Warren, 2-28-1824.³
  Humphrey—Ann Falkingburgh, 8-2-1837.³
  Isaac—Abigail Kelley, 10-17-1819.³
  Jacob—Hannah Hammel, 5-22-1784.¹
  Jacob—Eliza Jones, 3-7-1819.³
  James—Eliza Fortiner, 8-24-1837.³
  James, Jr.—Jane Bass, 9-16-1815.³
  Jeremiah—Ann Land, 3-7-1796.⁸
  Jesse L., D.D.S.—Emily F. Deacon, 3-19-1884.⁸
  John—Rachel Burr, 1732.⁶
  John—Judith Pettitt, Aug. 15, 1737.¹
  John—Margaret Flint, 11-10-1769.¹
  John—Ann Marter, 6-28-1803.⁸
  John—Sarah Hance, 4-22-1810.⁸
  John—Mary Pippett, 1-4-1829.³
  Jonathan—Mary Holland, 4-7-1814.³
  Joseph—Mary Littlejohn, 1687.⁶
  Joseph—Mary Elmor, 10-6-1755.⁸
  Joseph—Sarah Pitman, 9-27-1810.³
  Joseph—Ann Brush, 8-8-1822.³
  Joseph—Rebecca Lewis, 8-3-1829.³
  Joseph—Lydia Austin, 3-19-1835.⁴
  Moses—Elizabeth Ingler, 9-12-1772.¹
  Reuben—Anna Reily, 5-17-1818.⁸
  Samuel—Amelia Gaskill, 10-2-1824.³
  Samuel—Margaret Smith, 3-23-1828.³
  Samuel—Ann McIlvaine, 10-5-1837.³
  Stephen—Sarah Rogers, 9-1-1773.¹
  Stephen—Lorina Brush, 12-14-1832.³
  Thomas—Elizabeth Bowker, 8-9-1771.¹
  Thomas—Sarah Shaw, 12-24-1781.¹
  Thomas—Ann Eyres, 5-30-1785.¹

BURLINGTON COUNTY MARRIAGES

Adams, Thomas—Mary Lucas, 4-2-1809.³
  William—Mary Smith, 11-12-1812.³
  William—Sarah Fort, 9-26-1816.³
  William—Elizabeth, Taylor, 3-14-1819.³
  William—Sarah Higbee, 9-16-1827.³
  William H.—Sarah Ann Wright, 12-3-1835.³
Adare, William—Mary Backster, 10-24-1805.³
Addams, John—Sarah Smith, Gloucester co., May 26, 1729.¹
  John—Mary Toal, 8-21-1821.³
  John—Sarah T. Newbold, 16-30-1823.³
  Joseph—Ann Newton, 9-17-1801.³
  Nathan—Sarah Oldale, Oct. 16-1745.⁸
Addis, Thomas—Ann English, July 10, 1749.¹.
Ager, Hugh—Ruth Parker, 6-5-1818.³
Agor, Hugh—Margaret Maham, 1-6-1811.³
Agnue, Samuel—Sarah Dorce, 12-14-1800.³
Aiker, Richard—Hannah Keeler, 1-22-1804.³
Aikins, Thomas—Sarah Bishop, 6-18-1808.³
Aikman, Thomas—Franklina E. Craft, 4-24-1821.³
  Thomas—Jane Lazilere, 10-7-1802.³
Airs, Vincen—Jane Ingland, 3-20-1830.³
Akely, William—Charlotte Cunningham, 12-28-1795.³
Akerman, Philip—Hannah Stockton, 11-12-1771.¹
Akin, Thomas—Hope Farrow, 8-1-1802.³
Akly, Adam—Mary Parker, 2-17-1766.¹
Albertson, Benjamin—Bersheba Gibbs, 2-1-1834.³
  Josiah—Ann Austin, 1727.⁹
  Levi, Gloucester co.—Keziah Roberts, 4-24-1756.¹
  Samuel—Sarah Barret, 12-27-1797.⁴
Albison, John—Mary Boyd, 6.16-1821,³
Allbright, John—Mary Marpole, 1-28-1831.³
  Philip—Ann Prickett, 11-8-1832.³
Alcott, Anthony—Elizabeth Scroggy, 12-26-1809.³
  Job—Catherine Hufty, 6-26-1816.⁸
  Jonathan—Ann Lake, 4-30-1813. ³
  Josiah—Tabitha O'Neal, 10-29-1782.¹
  Thomas—Martha Brannin, 12-25-1780.¹
  William—Harriet Platt, 4-26-1826.³
Aldrich, George Wells—Sallie Sleeper, 5-8-1862.⁸
Ajexander, Joseph—Mary Sevill, 3-22-1774.¹
Alisworth, Philip—Phebe Seamons, 3-27-1803.³
Allcut, Thomas—Margaret Hoopper, 10-26-1811.³

Allen, Aaron—Lydia Garkin, 1-30-1823.³
Abraham—Sarah Pitman. 10-26-1782.¹
Benjamin—Elizabeth Allen, Mar. 27, 1730,¹
Benjamin—Patience Borden, Dec. 8, 1737.¹
Benjamin—Deborah Sharp, Oct. 25, 1744.¹
Behjamin—Rebecca Sherwin, Dec. 7, 1749.¹
Benjamin—Sarah Middleton, 12-29-1804.³
Benjamin—Rachei Joyce, 4-3-1830.³
Charles—Jemima Lovland, 2-26-1821.³
Charles—Jane Riiey, both Bucks co., Pa., 9-90-1829.³
Charles Tennet—Miriam Epley Gaskill, 12-28-1831.²
David—Sarah Boreen, 5-8-1820.³
George—Elizabeth, Pearson, 11-24-1885.³
Isaac—Martha Hugg, 10-18-1800,³
James—Martha C. Cowperthwaite, 10-29-1831.³
James, Jr.—Ann King, 3-20-1817.³
Jedediah—Sarah Austin, 6-24-1810.⁷
Jedediah—Hannah Abbot, 3-28-1827.⁷
Jeremiah—Margaret Mairs, 1-5-1760.¹
John—Rebecca Gibbs, 1746.⁶
John—Anne Herbert, 4-13-1774.¹
John—Hannah Lippincott, 1-14-1814.¹⁰
Joseph—Sarah Iredell, 1-6-1768.¹
Joseph—Rachel Cline, 1-12-1783.¹
Joseph—Sarah Crammer, 12-12-1783.¹
Joseph—Sarah Bodine, 2-15-1818³
Joseph—Lydia Patterson. No date given.³*
Joseph Warren—Sarah Barns Norcross, 11-27-1837.³
Josiah—Ann Cowpertewaite, 1-1-1829.³
Ner—Hope Test, 11-28-1791.¹⁰
Peter—Elizabeth Wheeler, Aug. 16. 1751.¹
Ralph (s. Josiah). Shrewsbury—Ann Wright (d. Mahlon and Mary), 10-21-1782.⁵
Robert, Shrewsbury—Edith Andrews (d. Edward), 6-5-1717.¹¹
Robert—Margaret Anderson, 11-17-1810.³
Semuel—Martha Braning, 11-12-1760.¹
Samuel—Elizabeth Jones, 8-31-1772.¹
Samuel—Margaret Borden, 4-6-1785.³
Samuel—Kitty V. Cox, 9-5-1799.³
Samuel—Sarah Carr, 11-22-1799.³

---

*Married by Samuel Wright, J. P.

Allen, Samuel (s. Judia and Ann—Mary G. Taylor (d. Cumberland and Isabel, 10-6-1831.[5]
  Thomas—Mary Prickett, 1-14-1783.[1]
  Thomas—Elizabeth Jameson, 2-16-1796.[3]
  Thomas—Anna Cramer, 6-1-1823.[3]
  William—Hannah Wooster, 9-12-1796.
  William—Ann Tulley, 2-28-1811.[3]
  William—Rebecca Sesrs, 12-6-1813.[3]
  William—Mary Burton, 4-2-1815.[3]
  William—Mary Ellis, 4-6-1825.[6]
  William—Elizabeth Adams, 7-12-1835.[3]
Allinder, Joshua—Mary Nixon, Dec. 17, 1733.[1]
Allinson, David—Beulah Zanes, 4-24-1824.[3]
  Thomas—Mary Shinn, 1745.[6]
Allison, Joseph—Elizabeth Scattergood, 1721.[6]
Alloway, Elijah—Susanna Carson, 6-1-1799.[3]
  Jacob, Jr.,—Mary Taylor, 4-30-1798.[8]
  Joshua—Nancy Smith, 4-14-1814.[3]
  William—Mary Thompson, 9-7-1822.[3]
Alloways, Abraham—Hannah Lanning, 7-29-1773.[1]
  Edward—Mary Birn, 2-9-1824.[3]
  Isaac—Christian Davidson, 11-20-1773.[1]
  Isaac—Ann Nottaway, 12-7-1830.[3]
  Idrael—Levinia Powell, 1-1-1824.[3]
  John—Dorothy Hughes, Jan. 1, 1740.[1]
  John—Elizabeth Shinn, 6-13-1774.[1]
  John—Hannah Alkut, 5-24-1802.[3]
  John—Emily W. Rinear, 12-9-1852.[4]
  Joseph—Sarah Starkey, 11-19-1807.[3]
Anderson, Aaron—Elizabeth Williamson, 7-2-1786.[1]
  Abraham—Theodosia Denton, 10-31-1835.[3]
  Andrew—Martha Brock, 2-1-1762.[1]
  Andrew—Patience Stockton, 4-9-1791.[1]
  Andrew—Betsey Allen, 1-4-1819.[3]
  David—Emelia Briggs, 9-5-1783.[1]
  Edward—Susan Donielly, 2-3-1821.[3]
  Ezekiel—Mary Miller, 12-28-1797.[3]
  Israel—Lorena Rigans, 7-3-1810.[3]
  James—Elenor Toy, 10-17-1777.[1]
  James—Mary Whodo, 2-15-1802.[7]
  James—Margaret Raynels, 11-20-1825.[3]
  James—Susanna E. Thomas, 4-11-1853.[3]

Anderson, James K.—Henrietta Southwick, 12-17-1838.³
  John—Priscilla Stokes, Glouce3ter co., 9-20-1817.³
  John—Mary Ann Brethwaite, 1-13-1855.⁴
  Joseph—Sarah Stackhouse, 3-5-1810.³
  Joshua, Trenton—Mary Wood, Nov. 27, 1745.¹
  Josiah—Sarah Anderson, 11-26-1769.¹
  Mordecai, Jr.—Mary Taylor. 1723.¹¹
  Samuel—Tabitha Waterman, 1-2-1817.³
  William—Rebecca Leeds, 5-5-1815.³
  William—Isabella Carr, 3-28-1831.³
Andrews, Chester—Sarah Thomas, 4-16-1820.³
  Ebenezer—Patience Lippincott, 1742.⁹
  Bdward—Sarah Ong, Feb. 8, 1694.¹
  Edward—Tabitha Richar4son, 1756.⁹
  Jacob—Keziah Rider, 3-10-1764,¹
  John—Hannah Parker, 2-7-1776.¹
  Nathan—Dorcas Mathis, 6-22-1834.⁵
  Nehemiah—Elizsbeth Lippincott, 1739.¹¹
  Nelson—Salina Hartman, 3-12-1836.⁰
  Peter—Esther Butcher, 1721.⁶
  Peter—Esther Butcher, 1728.¹¹
  Peter, Jr. (s. Samuel)—Hannah Somers, 1755.¹¹
  Samuel—Elizabeth Ridgway (d. Thomas, Sr., 1726.¹¹
  Thomas—Catharine Webstcr, 1752.⁹
  William—Susanna Estalow, 6-6-1797.³
Anthony, George W.—Annetta D. Woodingtou, 11-5-1872.⁸
Antram, Daniel—Susanna Weaver, 1-30-1758.¹
  David—Rebecca Bryan, 2-8-1773.¹
  Isaac—Jana Ridgua, 1721.⁶
  Isaac—Ruth Wehb, 1-26-1773.¹
  Isaac—Mary Briant, 10-20-1809.³
  James—Anna Milton, 2-17-1801.³
  John—Frances Butcher, 1682.⁶
  Jossph—Anna Merret, 11-18-1773.¹
  Joseph—Hannah Stretch, 4-10-1796.⁸
  Thomas, Jr.—Margaret Lamb, 3-25-1757.¹
  William—Rachei Briant, 12-8.1805.³
  William—Eleaor Johnson, 4-7-1808.³
Artrim, Aaron—Amisa Ann Reeve, 10-4-1835,³
  Caleb—Martha Antrim, 9-5-1802.³
  David—Mary Faikingburgh, 1709.¹¹
  David—Rebecca Bryant, 2-8-1773.⁸

Antrim, Isaac—Ann Crusher, 1742.[6]
  John (s. John)—Priscilla Haines (d. Daniel), 10-1-1743.[6]
  John—Hannah Stockton, 8-20-1801.[3]
  John—Maria Cook, 4-30-1815.[3]
  John—Mary Warrick, 2-3-1832.[3]
  Samuel—Charlotta Hawk, 11-10-1781.[1]
  Thomas—Sarah Zelley, 1715.[6]
  Thomas—Ann Mason, 1-19-1812.[3]
Aply, Aron—Sarah Miles, 8-16-1806.[3]
Appleby, John—Phebe Leek, 8-25-1803.[3]
Applegate, George—Sarah Fenton, 11-14-1763.[1]
  John—Sarah Johnston, 10-22-1785.[1]
  John—Sarah Tayror, 11-23-1826.[1]
  Liscom—Eliza Erwin, 2-3-1856.[8]
  Neweil—Sarah Ann Bowers, 1-21-1836.[3]
  Perine—Bath Tidiagot, 11-26-1806.[3]
  Samuel—Jane Scroggins, 1-20-1777.[1]
  Samuel—Lydia Thorn, 4-25-1802.[3]
  Samuel—Elennor Robbins, 11-14-1829.[3]
  Silas—Lydia Ivins, 9-18-1777.[1]
  William—Phebe Clinton, 10-13-1808.[3]
  Zachariah T.—Mary A. Goff (d. Wllliam and Sarah), 9-2-1870.[4]
Archer, Amos—Rebecca Archer, 2-25-1828.[3]
  Isaac—Sarah Stokes, 11-24-1799.[3]
  John—Phebe Mount, 3-21-1823.[3]
  Joseph—Martha Tuly, 10-3-1769.[8]
  Joseph—Prudence Baldin, 8-18-1814.[3]
  Samuel—Ann Eliza Hancock, 2-7-1835.[3]
Arden, Edward—Elizabeth Morton, Sept. 5, 1730.[1]
  George—Rachel D. Young, 7-5-1823.[3]
  John—Margaret Keen, Pennsylvania, 6-4-1774.[1]
Armstrong, Alexander—Elizabeth McClean, 9-10-1828.[3]
  Anthony—Vinice Marshall, 12-31-1807.[8]
  Enoch,—Susan Coal, 8-20-1821.[3]
  Floyd—Clara V. Risdon, 9-30-1874.[2]
  Franklin—Mary Longstreth (d. William and Mary), 7-3-1867.[4]
  George—Anne Hamilton, 5-14-1826.[8]
  Isaac—Sarah Ann Caffary, 2-1-1821.[3]
  John—Elizabeth Shinn, 7-11-1764.[1]
  John—Hannah Entosh, 2-8-1798.[3]
  John—Hannah Kelle, 5-12-1800,[3]
  John Henry—Sarah Lizzie Rapp, 2-15-1890.[4]

Armstrong, Peter—Elizabeth Wilkins, 9-24-1803.[3]
　Robert—Mary Wildman, 4-30-1798.[3]
　Robert—Mary Ann Clanagan, 8-4-1825.[3]
　Samuel—Maria Fox, Nov., 1824.[3]
　Thomas—Hannah Stockton, 5-10-1810.[3]
　William—Joannah London, 3-26-1776.[1]
Arnell, James—Mary Mott, Jan. 3, 1739.[1]
Arney, Daniel (s. Joseph and Margaret)—Elizabeth Wright (d. Israel and Alice), 12-3-1794.[5]
Arnold, Fred McKenzie—Esther Sharp Whitaker, 6-32-1929.[7]
　James—Phebe Inman, 1795.[11]
　James—Elizabeth Bartlett (wid. John), 1826,[11]
　Levi (s. John and Rachel)—Hannah Wright (d. John and Han-Hannah), 11-3-1802.[5]
　Samuel—Pamy Cox, 1785.[11]
　William—Kesiah Woodard, 11-21-1812.[3]
Arnoll, Richard—Sarah Chamberlin, 1681.[6]
Arnolt, Jacob—Priscilla Down, 5-1-1802.[3]
Arthur, William—Sarah Briggs, Nov. 23, 1741.[1]
Asoy, Jacob—Charity Lambert, 12-5-1805.[3]
　Michael—Bethenie Simons, 12-16-1783.[1]
　Samuel—Sarah Atkinson, 8-3-1779.[1]
　Samuel—Mary Morris, 9-29-1812.[3]
　Samuel—Ann Croshaw, 2-20-1831.[3]
　Thomas—Martha Stiles, 1-23-1819.[3]
　William—Rachel Shinn, 1-19-1808.[3]
Ash, George—Sarah Bates, 9-24-1759.[1]
　Jacob—Elizabelh Lee, 2-12-1780.[1]
Ashard, Caleb—Mary Stockton, 4-21-1808.[3]
Ashbridge, Aaro—Elizabeth Sullivan, 1846.[6]
Ashburn, William—Hannah Hugg, July 21, 1750.[1]
Ashard, Amos—Cecelia Cheesman, Aug. 14- 1728,[1]
　Amos—Sarah Butcher, 12-26-1811.[70]
Ashmore, Daniel M.—Hannah Garrison, 11-11-1830.[3]
　James—Matilda C. Rose, 3-25-1828.[3]
　Joseph—Elizabeth Ware, 1-21-1810.[3]
　Robert—Plovine Cook, Trenton, 10-4-1812.[3]
　William—Frances D. Chambers, 11-7-1831.[3]
Ashten, Andrew—Elizabeth Brannin, 2-19-1804.[10]
　John—Patience Taylor, both Shackamaxon, Dec. 7, 1679.[6]
　John, Bucks co., Pa.—Mary Fenton, 2-13-1765.[1]
　Joseph—Anne Helson, 6-19-1770.[1]

Askin, Thomas—Sarah Butterfield, 12-9-1796.³
Assay, Thomas—Deborah Pitman, 7-30-1808.³
Assen, Charles—Letitia Fort, 6-9-1810.³
Asson, William—Mary Platt, Feb. 9, 1746.¹
Asy, Jacob—Sarah Foster, 12-24-1806.³
Atkins, John—Hannah Parmer, 12-26-1805.³
Atkinson, Aaron—Robecca Bunting, 11-2-1820.⁸
Atkinson, Aaron—Sarah Rockhill, 5-12-1796.⁸
  Amos—Mary Bishop, 11-17-1779.¹
  Amos—Emaline R. Stedfold, 9-9-1838.³
  Benjamin—Rebecca Lee, 8-3-1829.³
  Benzamin—Phebe Ann Aaronson, 11-26-1831.³
  Benjamin S.—Ann Gibson, 5-25-1835.³
  Caleb C.—Hannah Griscome, 1-7-1826.³
  Clayton (s. Henry and Ann)—Margaret Hendrickson (d. Joseph and Elizabeth), 2-10-1814.⁵
  Clayton—Abigail Antrim, 9-24-1818.³
  Collin—Ann Adams, 1-16-1806.³
  Edward Bentley—Florence Coleman Parker, 11-18-1882.²
  Emptson—Sarah Ridgway, 4-9-1783.¹³
  George (s. Samuel and Rebecca)—Carrie R. Lemas (d. Clayton and E.), 12-27-1881.⁴
  Isaac—Elizabeth Reeves, Jan. 12, 1736.¹
  Isaac—Rosity Beats, 9-17-1784.¹
  James—Sarah Arison, 5-11-1756.¹
  James—Theodocia Lee, 1-24-1823.³
  Job—Mary Arison, 9-21-1761.¹
  Job, Gloucester co.—Esther Sharp, 8-17-1780.¹
  Job—Elizabeth Estell, 4-28-1827.³
  John—Hannah Shinn, 1716.⁶
  John—Sarah Folwell, 1-21-1754.¹
  John—Sarah Berry, 2-25-1761.¹
  John—Mary Cooper, 11-12-1761.¹
  John—Elizabeth Clevenger, 2-8-1764.¹
  John—Mary Platt, 10-9-1828.³
  John P.—Abigail Atkinson, 11-14-1822.⁸
  Jonathan—Mary Hillyer, 12-7-1767.⁸
  Jonathan—Mrs. Margaret Peacock, 8-7-1837.
  Joseph—Sarah Aaronson, Feb. 10, 1731.¹
  Joseph—Jennett Cowgill, 1743.⁶
  Joseph—Rebecca Garwood, 12-20-1780.¹
  Joseph—Rebecca McGowan, 12-15-1827.³

Atkinson, Mahlon—Sarah Smith, 11-28-1791.[7]
  Michael—Hope Shinn, 1720.[6]
  Moses—Rachel Shreve, 2-22-1761.[1]
  Moses—Elizabeth Powell, 10-21-1784.[1]
  Moses—Priscilla Martin, 9-27-1826.[3]
  Phineas—Keziah Leeds, 1-4-1796.[3]
  Samuel—Esther Evans, 1746.[9]
  Samuel—Hannah Chester, 12-1-1767.[1]
  Samuel—Elizabeth Lippincott, 4-22-1771.[1]
  Samuel—Marian Norton, 5-25-1775.[1]
  Stacy—Kesiah Johnson, 1-14-1799.[3]
  Thomas—Susanna Shinn, 1739.[6]
  Thomas (s. Caleb and Sarah)—Rebecca Fisher (d. Shomas and Elizabeth), 2-17-1814.[12]
  Thomas—Elizabeth Smith, 5-1-1831.[3]
  Walker—Rachel Wallis, Sept. 10, 1746.[1]
  William—Elizabeth Curtis, 1686.[6]
  William—Mary Bishop, Feb. 3, 1731.[1]
  William—Mary Allison, 11-6-1783.[13]
  William—Elizabeth Elton, 12-26-1799,[3]
  William—Theodosia Wright, 12-3-1830.[3]
  Wiiliam E.—Mary Ann Aaronson, 12-19-1831.[3]
  William H—Aiice A. Yarnall, 9-10-1866.[2]
Atmore, Robert—Sarah Benneworth, 8-15-1836.[3]
Auner, Peter—Margaret White, both Philadelphia, 10-19-1797.[3]
Austin, Abel—Prudence Stratton, 2-10-1798.[3]
  Amos—Esther Hainea, Sept. 27, 1730.[1]
  Amos—Judith Austin, 11-27-1836.[3]
  Amos—Emma Clevenger, 1-9-1868.[2]
  Caleb—Lydia Mason, 1758.[9]
  Caleb—Hannah Marter, 3-16-1815.[3]
  Francis—Deborah Allen, May 7, 1748.[1]
  Francis—Rachel Wilmerton, 2-17-1805.[3]
  Hezekiah—Rebecca Peak, 6-17-1814.[3]
  Hosea—Elizabeth Smith, 8-14-1808.[3]
  Jacob—Handah Austin, 9-20-1764.[1]
  Jacob—Hannah Green. 8-3-1816.[3]
  Jonathan—Rebecca Mason, 1747,[9]
  Joseph—Elizabetq Ballenger, 4-19-1782.[1]
  Joseph—Ruth Crane, 5-9, 1805.[5]
  Joseph—Amanda Eastland, 1-3-1838.[3]

BURLINGTON COUNTY MARRIAGES

Austin, Joshua (s. Jonathan and Elizabeth)—Priscilla Dudley (d. Jacob and Mary), 2-23-1815.[12]
  Mahlon—Hannah Borton, 9-8-1814.[3]
  Nathan—Beulah A. Rogers, 9-4-1828.[3]
  Porpupy—Ann C. Baker, 4-26-1815.[3]
  Richard M.—Rebecca L. Elkinton, 10-28-1913.[3]
  Samuel—Jemima Sharp, 9-13-1798.[3]
  Samuel—Achsah Busson, 7-12-1810.[3]
  Seth—Lydia Nailor, 3-9-1771.[1]
  Seth—Sarah Pippit, 2-26-1799.[3]
  William—Mary Robeson, 1741.[9]
  William—Hannah Thomas, 1749.[0]
  William—Hannah Claypool, 3-1-1770.[8]
  William—Elizabeth Lippincott; 1-13-1802.[60]
  William—Mary Shepherd, 7-7-1838.[3]
Averill, Henry—Louisa Griffith, 12-12-1815.[3]
Ayars, Addi—Mary Severs, 3-22-1815.[3]
Ayers, Obediah—Susannah Thomas; 5-12-1803.[1]
Ayrs, Valentine—Elizabeth Parker, Apr. 3, 1749.[1]
Babcock, Nathaniel—Lovina Bishop, 11-12-1760.[1]
Bachelor, George—Hannah Munyan, 1-8-1789,[4]
  James—Bathsheba Gibbs, 9-7-1817.[3]
Backster, Thomas—Nancey Hilberson, 9-9-1804.[3]
  Thomas—Hannah King, 3-30-1800.[3]
Baester, Robert—Mary Doren, 7-23-1774.[1]
Bacon, Daniel—Rebecca Borrodail, 1741,[5]
  Job—Ruth Thompson, 2-24-1800.[7]
  John—Rebecca Pearson, 1749.[6]
  John—Mary Tyler, 6-26-1813.[7]
  Mark Balderston—Jane Eves Haines, 10-10.1907.[10]
  Rufas—Ann Good, 4-1-1819.[3]
  Thomas—Eliz. Wright, 10-26-1807.[7]
Bailey, Elijah—Sarah Ford, 9-10-1810.[3]
  John—Rachel Harris, 8-31-1759.[1]
  Richard—Martha Reeves, 7-20-1837.[3]
  Samuel—Jane Thomas; 2-2-1822.[3]
  William—Sarah Bishop, 1-1-1835.[3]
Baily, Elias—Ann Gibbs, 3-28-1829.[3]
Baird, Paul Potter—Elizabeth Peterson, 10-10-1819.[8]
  Samuel—Charity Brown, 1-12-1820.[6]
Baker, Anthony—Eliza Cammel, 9-3-1829.[8]
  Looe—Elizabeth Wardell, 7-1-1805.[3]

Baley, John—Jane Leonard, 8-25-1807.³
Balienta. Louis—Msrgaret Berryman, Trenton, 5-7-1812.³
Ballanger, Samuel—Alice Parker (d. Joseph, Sr.), 1745.¹¹
   William—Dorothy Stockton, 3-24-1781.¹
Ballenger, Aaron (s. Thomas and Mary)—Sarah Evans (d. William and Rachel), 4-14-1814.¹²
   Edward—Prudence Murry, 5-25-1809.³
   John—Hannah Carll, 4-2-1792.⁷
   Richard—Mary Ann Haines, 10-2-1823.¹³
   Samuel—Mary Shinn, 5-8-1788.¹³
   Thomas—Brazilla Carson, 5-28-1768.¹
   Wm.—Amy Borden, 2-27-1792.⁷
Ballinger, Amariah—Elizabeth Garwood, 1726.⁹
   Amazea—Ruth Collins, 1744.⁹
   Amaziah—Mary Ashbrook, 1751.⁹
   Henry—Mary Harding, 1684.⁶
   Isaac—Esther Shinn, 5-22-1799.¹⁰
   Job—Susanna Troth, 11-13-1823.¹⁰
   John—Mary Ridgua, 1718.⁶
   John—Mary Andrews (wid.), 1753.¹
   John—Mary Edwards, 1-7-1802.³
   Joshua—Ruth Haines, 2-13-1823.¹⁰
   Joshua—Martha Stratten, 1741.⁹
   Richard—Mary Ann Haines, 10.9-1823.¹³
   Samuel—Ann Walker, 11-13-1795.³
   Thomas—Elizabeth Elkinton, 1713.⁶
Banks, Alexander A.—Mary Louisa Hoppnagle, 1-30-1855.⁴
   Richard—Catherine Gifford, 2-21-1818.⁰
   Thomas—Meribah Rossell, 4-3-1817.³
Bankson, Peter—Mary Wills, 12-17-1798.³
   William—Elisabeth Evans, 2-11-1816.⁸
Barber, Burtis (s William and Ann)—Mercy Allen (d. Henry and Lydia). No dane given.⁵
   Henry—Rachel Morford, 3-2-1775.⁸
   Henry—Mary Williams. 10-3-1805.⁸
   Joseph—Lydia Scott, 3-5-1803.³
   Joseph J.—Martha Staffon, 9-25-1806.³
   William—Ann Burr, 10-7-1784.⁵
   William—Ann Rinold, 12-7-1826.³
Bardine, Samuel—Parnel Sooy, 8-6-1813 ³
Bareford, Joseph—Hester Mathews, 2-9-1826.
   Thomas—Rhoda Jennings, 3-19-1812.³

Bareford, William—Ann Sutts, 12-23-1821.[3]
  Wm. Ann Leeds, 12-24-1826,[3]
Barkelow, Geo.—Meriah Seed, 5-24-1810.[3]
  Barker, Joseph—Hannah Wright, 1704.[6]
  Joseph, Pennsylvenia—Elizabeth Morford, 7-24-1772.[8]
  Joshua—Martha Raper, 1730.[6]
Barkley, Moses—Elizabeth Fowler, 10-21-1719.[3]
Barnes, Charles—Patience Scott, 9-20-1818.[3]
  Charleston—Rebecca Kindle, 8-23-1803.[3]
  Dasiel—Rachel Wood, 10-4-1838.[3]
  Ephraim—Basheba Morgan, both Salem co., 11-15-1798.[3]
  John—Christiana Dotson, 12-3-1807.[3]
  John—Catherine Ebert, 12-17-1771.[1]
  Joseph, Atlantic co.—Sophia Wilsey, 8-30-1838.[3]
  Samuel, Wilmington—Han. Woodnutt, 11-26-1792.[7]
  Thomas, Jr.—Saran Watson, June 10, 1732.[1]
  William—Martha Bromley, Feb. 13, 1672.[1]
Barnet, John—Mary Conaro. 3-20-1788.[1]
Barnhart, Henry—Ann Estelo, 7-18-1810.[3]
  Jacob—Mary Eslon, 1-30-1773.[1]
  William—Sarah Brown, 5-23-1798.[3]
Barras, Samuel—Isabella Freeman, 9-10-1813.[3]
Barrickstaller, Joseph—Suzanna Sullyvan; 9-15-1774.[8]
Barrett, James—Sarah Ivins, 11-10-1796.[3]
Barrington, John—Edith Burr, 11-4-1811.[3]
  Richard Colcott (s. William and E. D.)—Bessie Fort (d. William and R. A.), 8-31-1862.[4]
Barronhart, Isaac—Ann Smith, 1-8-1800.[3]
Barry, John— Mary Cramer, 8-13-1825.[3]
  John—Jane Bond, 9-11-1788.[4]
  Joseph—Matilda Woolston, 4-3-1837.[3]
Barth, Job—Julia Ann Thompson, 11-27-1833,[3]
Bartholomew, Benjamin—Mary Murrell, 12-10-1777.[1]
Bartlett, Edmund—Mercy M. Ridgway, 12-10-1831.[3]
  James—Phebe Ann Barnes, 1835.[11]
  John—Elizabeth Sooy, 4-5-1801.[3]
  Joseph—Ann P. Willits (d. Thomas, Jr), 1326.[11]
  Nathan, Sr.—Judith Somers, 1760.[11]
  Nathan, Jr.—Hannah Willits)d. John, Jr.),1819.[11]
Bartley, Jacob—Dinah Stile, 1-30-1808.[3]
Barton, Aaron—Bathsheba Antram, 1750.[6]
  Charles D.—Emily S. Whitacre, 10-19-1905.[10]

Barton, Edward—Sarah Day, 1706.[6]
  John—Ann Butcher, 1709.[6]
  Jonathan—Mary Schooly, 1740.[5]
  Joseph—Rachel B. Evans, 12-25-1828.[10]
  Joshua—Anna M. Stokes, 2-14-1878.[10]
  William—Sarah Borden. 8-13-1805.[8]
  William—Susanna Mason, 11-5-1828.[8]
Bass, George—Ann Appleton, 8-3-1767.[8]
  William—Rebecca Ewan, 4-13-1784.[1]
Basse, Pitman, Butler co., Pa.—Ann Rogers, 9-21-1816.[8]
Bassett, Daniel, Jr.—Ruth Miller, 4-25-1791.[7]
  David S, (s. Samuel and Mary), Gloucester co.—Hope Hollingshead (d. Hugh and Eleanor), 4-23-1807.[12]
  Elisha—Mary Nicholson, 3-30-1810.[7]
  Josiah—Sarah Ellet, 4-28-1788.[7]
  Nathan—Sarah Saundes, 5-26-1788.[7]
Bassonett, John—Mary Cronin, 11-26-1805.[8]
Bates, Benj.—Ann Edwards, 4-24-1819,[8]
  Benjamin, Sarah Hammell, 10-5-1777.[1]
  Charles— ——— Johnston, 5-10-1804.[3]
  Daniel—Sarah Ann Brooks, 1821.[14]
  Daniel W., Philadelphia—Jane Plummer, 6-16-1836.[8]
  Gideon—Mary Toy, 3-24-1795.[8]
  John—Sarah Collins, Gloucester co., Sept. 19, 1747.[1]
  John—Abigail Stratton, 3-20-1782.[1]
  Joseph—Priscilla Prickett, 10-9-1831.[8]
  Josiah—Priscilla Cooper, 3-12-1799.[3]
  Josiah—Rebecca Haines, 2-3-1814.[8]
  Josiah—Elizabeth Weeks, 6-10-1814.[8]
  William—Rebecca Stone, 10-22-1818.[8]
Batten, James—Ann Mannington, 8-1-1822.[8]
  John, Gloucester co.—Ann Scott, 3-23-1766.[1]
Batterson, John—Hannah Penn, 9-23-1821.[8]
Battis, John—Catharine Coates, 9-16-1804.[8]
Battison, Wm.—Lydia Gardiner. 1-10-1803.[8]
Baumbach, Henry—Lena Greenwood. 7-27-1894.[2]
Bavis, John—Abigail Norcross, 10-3-1777.[1]
Baxter, Joseph—Priscilla Sharp, 3-12-1882,[3]
Bayard, Helany—Charlotte Shaffer, 6-10-1811.[3]
Bayles, John V. D.—Anna B. Hughes, 12-24-1868.[2]
Bayley, Samuel—Deborah Sulcey, 10-10-1829.[8]
Baynton, Peter—Mary Carpenter, Jan. 8, 1739.[1]

Bazier, Charlez, Philadelphia—Elizabeth Mitchell, 8-6-1833.[3]
Bazzel, George—Catherine Hopkins, 12-31-1835.[3]
Beaumont, John—Sarah Pancoast (d. William), May 17, 1744.[5]
  John A.—Catharine A. Bass, 10-3-1843.[4]
Bean, John—Rebecca Crispin, 4-25-1813.[3]
Beard, William—Katherine Murfin, 1679.[6]
Beatty, John, Jr., Maria Burr Budd, 9-5-1816.[3]
Beats, Charles—Sarah Crammer, 7-6-1800.[3]
Bechtel, Jonas—Effy Wood, 10-21-1827.[3]
Beck, Aaron—Hope Shinn, 7-11-1774.[1]
  George—Mary Griffith, Nov. 2, 1750.[1]
  Henry—Mary Pancoast, 3-25-1802.[8]
  James—Hannah Antrim, 1-7-1808.[3]
  James—Charlotta C. Watkinson, 12-31-1838.[3]
  John—Deborah Wood, Feb. 22, 1747.[1]
  John—Polly Ferris, 6-20-1780.[1]
  John D.—Susanna Hammell, 3-26-1804.[3]
  Joseph—Sarah Scattergood, 4-24-1779.[1]
  Raworth—Hannah Gibbs, Apr. 8, 1743.[1]
  Samuel—Elizabeth McGallard, 8-22-1777.[1]
Beckly, Adam—Rebecca Johnston, 12-4-1805.[3]
Beers, James—Susan Benezet, 7-24-1810.[8]
Beesley, Joseph—Susannah Crossby, 11-20-1766.[1]
  Theophilus—Hannah Wistar, 12-6-1820.[7]
  William G.—Rachel Pettitt, 9-27-1826.[7]
Belanger, Eve, Jr.— ———— ————, 1724.[11]*
  James, Sr.—Marjorie Smith, 1727.[11]
Bell, Ezra C.—Priscilla M. Evans, 11-15-1883.[10]
  Jeremiah—Hannah Hance, 4-25-1799.[3]
  Reason, Gloucester co.—Ann Peterson, 12-1-1827.[3]
  Richard Moore—Julia Black, 12-4-1873.[2]
  Robt. W.—Sarah Hance, 9-22-1838.[3]
  William—Elizabeth Philips, 8-6-1775.[8]
  William—Melinda Haywood, 8-30-1826.[8]
Belcher, Joseph—Hannah Woolston, 5-31-1754.[1]
Belford, Samuel—Mary Adams, both Pennsylvania, 12-2-1819.[3]
Bennet, Elige—Susannah Everet, 1-30-1813.[2]
  Henry—Abigail Borden, 1-29-1874.[1]
  Henry—Ann Williamson, 11-15.1890.[3]

*Married out of Meeting.

Bennet, Jacob—Hannah Hogeland, Bucks co., Pa., 8-14-1768.[8]
  James—Susannah Danally, 11-21-1770.[1]
  John—Mary Kindel, June 8, 1741.[1]
  Joseph—Martha Rogers, 3-21-1764.[1]
  Joshua—Matilda Edwards, 7-3-1825.[3]
  Joshua—Catherine Quinn, 4-24-1833.[3]
  Michael—Charity FitzRandolph, 11-14-1774.[1]
  Samuel—Mrs. Sarah Shinn, 1-18-1809.[4]
  William—Elizabeth Sweem, 10-9-1786.[3]
  Wm.—Mary Peterson, 12-30-1815.[3]
Bennett, Alfred—Anna Maria Anderson, 9-22-1831.[3]
  Jeremiah—Rebecca Brown, Jan. 27, 1746.[1]
  Job—Hannah Lear, 1-9-1803.[3]
  John—Sarah Gaskell, 5-30-1772.[1]
  Samuel—Mary Harrison, 4-7-1832.[3]
  Samuel—Msry A. Allen, 12-4-1836.[3]
  Thomas—Rebecca H. Pearce, 6-15-1837[3]
  Uriah—Elizabeth Gilman' 2-28-1808.[3]
Benstead, Daniel—Rachel McCollin, 8-25-1801.[3]
Bentil, Charles—Effe Forman, 4-10-1806.[3]
Berkinshaw, Thomas—Margaret Bliss, Nov. 11, 1738.[1]
Berry, John—Mrs, Cilance Loveland, 4-6-1806.[3]
Bessnott, Charlea—Sarah Green, 12-10-1818.[3]
Bethune, Nathaniel—Elzy Hewson, 10-10-1803.[8]
Betts, Joseph—Elizabeth Fort, 1-23-1768.[1]
Bevan, Charles, Philadelphia—Mary Kemble, 7-9-1772.[1]
  Charles, Pennsylvenia—Elizabeth Morford, 7-29-1772.[1]
  Charles—Mary Lippincott, 3-4-1805.[1]
  Samuei—Susanna Carter, 1747.[6]
Bevis. Denmore—Bloomey Garrish, 2-21-1784.[1]
  George—Mary Sooy, 1-6-1771.[4]
  Thomas—Mary Draper, Nov. 18, 1737.[1]
  Thomas—Elizabeth Brackney, June 24, 1711.[1]
Bevy, John—Prudence Andrews, 2-6-1764.[1]
Bibby, Richard—Mary Radford, May 11, 1730.[1]
Bickham, John—Deriah Jolley, 8-5-1761.[7]
Bickley, Abraham—Elizabeth Gardiner, 1695.[6]
  Adam—Dorothy Smith, 1719.[9]
  William—Mary Wills, July 18, 1734.[1]
B,ddle, Isaac—Sarah Tallman, 2-4-1813.[2]
  Joel—Mary Walling, Jan. 4, 1748.[1]
  Joseph—Sarah Rogers, Jan. 6, 1745.[1]

BURLINGTON COUNTY MARRIAGES

Biddle, Joseph, Jr.—Sarah Shreve, 11-7-1763.[1]
  Thomas—Mary Antrum, Oct. 20, 1728.[1]
  William—Elizabeth Berry, 4-3-1771.[8]
Bidgood, William—Esther Burroughs, Feb. 5, 1733.[1]
Biel, Alexander—Hannah Rogars, 1737.[6]
Bigalow, Thomas—Sarah Clevenger, 1-28-1808.[3]
Bigelow, Ssmuel—Edith Peterman, 12-26-1799.[3]
Biggins, John—Rachel McVay, 6-28-1765.[1]
Biglow, Samuel—Eleanor Conrow, 8-28-1767.[1]
Biles, George—Mary Walton, both Hunterdon co,, 1-17-1824.[3]
Bill, John—Mary Gardiner, 11-2-1815.[3]
Billings, George—Sarah B. Keeler, 5-26-1837.
Bim, John—Mary Sile, 9-12-1763.[1]
Bingham, John—Elizabeth Stratton, 7-24-1815.[3]
Binn, Cyro—Rebecca Coward, 8-1-1836.[8]
  John—Margaret Wright- 8-5-1838.[3]
Blad, John W.—Ann Pes, 3-17-1805.[3]
  Joseph—Ann French, 1822.[14]
  Richard—Ann McGuire, 12-16-1804.[8]
  William—Abigail Lanning, 1-26-1825.[1]
  Zebedee—Hannah Giberson, 1-7-1825.[8]
Birdsal, Uriah—Elizabeth Webb, 10-29-1767.[1]
Birdsall, Edward—Grace M. Collins, 8-31-1828.[3]
  Gideon—Palmyra Osborn (d. Thomas), 1818.[11]
  Stephen—Deliverance Willits, 1738.[11]
  Stephen, Jr.—Desire Mott, 1770.[11]
Birkey, John—Elizaabelh Quicksal, 9-7-1826.[8]
Bischoff, Robert Albert—Emma Louisa Donnelly, 6-8-1896.[2]
Bishop, Ahab—Sarah R. Sharp, 1-6-1833.[3]
  Allen—Lydia Peacock, Jr., 2-11-1826.[3]
  Andrew—Margaret Sutton, Oct. 20, 1338.[8]
  Barzilla—Ann Jess, 9-2-1776.[1]
  Charles—Mary Plumb, 5-31-1834.[8]
  Daniel—Ann Frazer, 9-5-1837.[3]
  Ever—Mary Crispin, 2-23-1782.[1]
  Oodfrey—Priscllla Sharp, 6-8-1811.[3]
  Isaiah—Rebecca Cathcart, 3-10-1821.[3]
  Japhed—Rachel Haines, 4-12-1804.[3]
  Job (s. Isaac and Mary)—Hannah Durell (d. Da—— and Elizabeth), 3-2-1809.[12]
  Job—Hannah E. Moore, 6-6-1836.[3]

Bishop, John—Rebecca Matlock, Oct. 22, 1737.[1]
  John—Mary Stockton, 12-24-1783.[1]
  John—Rebecca Hackney, 3-2-1804.[3]
  Jonathan—Elizabeth Knox, 9-31-1837.[3]
  Joseph—Ann Reeves, 5-28-1754.[1]
  Joshua—Sarah Estlow, 2-10-1780.[1]
  Joshua—Elizabeth Malsbury, 9-5-1812.[3]
  Noah—Thankful Bennet, 11-3-1772.[1]
  Peter, Ann Wetherill, Sept. 15, 1731.[1]
  Robert—Mary Hall, Aug. 19, 1727.[1]
  Robert, Jane Hanes, 1-18-1759.[1]
  Robert M.—Edith Deacon, 3-11-1824.[3]
  Robert W.—Lucy Ridgeway, 1-3-1793.[1]
  Stokes—Mary Emma Hatcher, 8-29-1872.[8]
  Thomas—Hannah Lanning, Aug. 1, 1730.[1]
  Thomas—Elisha (?) Prickett, Dec. 20, 1732.[1]
  Thomas—Sarah Garwood, 3-5-1754.[1]
  Thomas—Lucretia Furnace, 5-18-1779,[1]
  Thomas—Deborah Prickett, 3-1-1793.[3]
  Thomas—Sabina Schenk, 3-24-1827.[3]
  Timothy—Sophia Brock, 3-13-1764.[1]
  William—Mary Indicott, Nov. 19, 1729.[1]
  William—Ann Richards, Sept. 9, 1734.[1]
  William—Lavina Jones, 6-5-1788.[13]
  William—Elizabeth Thompson, 11-28-1811.[3]
  William—Mary Woolston, 2-20-1812.[3]
  William—Sarah Bowers, 5-12-1827.[3]
Bishopp, Thomas—Sarah Smith, Dec. 29, 1730.[1]
Bispham, Benjamin—Zilpha Viscombe, 10-6-1779.[13]
  John—Margaret Reynolds, 9-16-1754.[1]
  John—Margaret Budd, 10-9-1732 [13]
  John E.—Sally Ann Budd, 10-7-1831.[4]
  John E.—Sally Ann Budd, 12-7-1831.[3]
  Jordan—Jane Alcott, 11-18-1798.[3]
  Joseph—Rebecca Elton, 10-24-1799.[3]
  Joseph, Jr.—Susan R. Tucker, 10-22-1828.[4]
  Joshua—Abigail Foster, 1-27-1817.[3]
  Josiah H. (s. Thomas and Hannah)—Jerusha Haines (d. John and Elizabeth), 1812.[12]
  Samuel, Philadelphia—Elizabeth Bispham, 8-21-1781.[1]
  Samuel, Philadelphia—Maria Stokes (d. John), 12-25-1823.[3]
  Thomas—Sarah Hinchman, Gloucester co., 2-18-1754.[1]

Bispham, Thomas—Hannah Haines, 9-21-1784.[1]
  William—Mary Ann Roberts, 1-4-1827.[3]
  William—Laura Wistar, 1865.[2]
Black, Ezra—Regina Rockhill, 1-30-1800.[3]
  Henry—Johanna Ripp; 5-28-1807.[3]
  James, Philadelphia—Judith Seal, Bucks co., Pa., 5-26-1804.[3]
  John—Sarah Rockhill, Dec. 4, 1706.[5]
  John, Philadelphia—Amye Borden, Sept. 3. 1746.[1]
  John—Mary Lippincott, 9-22-1770,[1]
  John—Lydia Newbold, 2-10-1784.[1]
  John—Sarah Newbold, 12-21-1816.[3]
  John—Ella Hankinson, 10-13-1884.[2]
  John. Jr.—Sarah Ann Barton, 9-29-1831.[3]
  Samuel—Charlotta Biddle, 10-17-1816.[3]
  Thomas—Mary Barton, 1746.[6]
  Thomas—Mary Wood, 12-29-1814.[3]
  William—Mary Gibbs, 8-14-1754.[1]
  William T.—Charlotte B. Black, 3-9-1843.[4]
Blackham. Josiah—Elizabeth Stoakes, Feb, 1, 1729.[1]
Blackmore, George—Mary Merrit, July 26, 1728.[1]
Blackwood, Evaul—Mary Burr, 12-1-1825.[3]
Blair, Abraham—Elizabeth Leech, 5-22-1781.[1]
  Robert—Ann Walker, 11-4-1780.[1]
  William W.—Nancy Burdin, 9-6-1804.[3]
  William N., Jr.—Henrietta Reeve, 11-3-1830.[3]
Blake, James—Mary Hutchinson, 4-4-1811.[3]
  John—Phebe Hambleton, 9-28-1808.[3]
  Price—Sarah J. Pancoast, Jr., 5-4-1799.[3]
  Samuel—Mary Allen, both Monmouth co., 11-3-1809.[3]
  Thomas—Anne ———, July 29, 1728.[1]
  Thomas—Rebecca Robbins, 4-1-1804.[3]
Blakely, James—Hannah Scott, 3-22-1828.[3]
  John Stites—Rachel English. 2-18-1826.[3]
Blaker, Peter—Sarah Harvey, both Bucks co., Pa., 5-4-1811.[3]
  Lewis—Eliza Weldon. 3-3-1836.[3]
Bleyler, Thomas—Rebecca R. Radford, 5-25-1836.
Bliss, George—Elizabeth Wills (d. Daniel), Apr. 17, 1712.[6]
  George—Susanna Preston; June 26, 1751.[1]
Blond, Gabriel—Susanna Yard, Apr. 18, 1739.[1]
Bloom. John M—Frances D. Jaques, 12-1-1804.[3]
Bloomfield, Jeremiah—Elizabeth Cawen, 8-28-1773.[1]
  Joseph Eliis—Mary Frances Barbarouse, 9-15-1819.[4]

Bloust. Landelin—Amy Shinn, 7-27-1831.³
Bodine, Daniel B.—Elizabeth S, Lamb, 9-5-1838.³
   Dewitt Clinton—Ida Page Shinn (d. Job and Jane), 12-10-1878.⁴
   Francis—Mary Rose, 3-20-1768.¹
   Jesse E.—Grace Mathis, 6-7-1825.³
   Joel—Sarah Gale, 11-12-1818.⁸
   Joel—Elizabeth Nixon, 11-18-1820.³
   Joel—Phebe Forman, 2-19-1821.³
Bogar, Francis—Hester Foard, 9-30-1819.³
   Joseph—Grace Denniss, 8-24-1808.³
   Wiiliam—Lydia Lippincott, 1-10-1804.³
Boggley, Charles—Elizabeth Stevens, May 27, 1682.¹
Boggs, Isaac—Sarah Lanning, 8-13-1768.¹
   John, Rev.—Eliza Hopkins, 1-3-1806.³
Boker, Joseph—Ann Nailor, 5-20-1824.³
Bokhorn, Jessee—Mary Edmond, 1-14-1808.³
Bolton, Edward—Sarah Pancoast, 1696.⁶
   John—Beulah Shinn, 4-14-1805.¹³
   Joseph—Rachel Matson, 11-6-1771.¹
   Joseph—Beulah Shinn, 4-4-1805.¹³
   Joseph—Mary Haines, 5-10-1810.¹³
   Reuben—Alice Stratton, 1-21-1821.³
   William—Mary Jones, 9-1-1810.³
   William—Jane Gibbs, 10-9-1828.³
Bomen, George—Mary Thompson, 6-9-1760.¹
   Henry—Elizabeth Moore, 9-3-1825.³
Bond, Jesse—Elizabeth Phillips, 10-16-1805.¹⁰
Bone, Robert—Matildy Ann Anthony, 5-3-1827.³
Bonham, Samuel—Ruth Bowyer, Philadelphia, May 29, 1747.¹
Boody, Smith—Margaret Kemble. 1-20-1827.³
Boolock, David (s. Amos)—Abigail Ridgway (d. Joseph), 4-3-1813.¹³
Boothe, Albert—Agnes Braithwaite, both Trenton, 11-5-1772.⁸
Boozey, Joseph—Rachel Fenimore, 1-1-1805.³
Boradail, William—Harriet Bispham, 3-2-1814.³
Boradell, John—Sarah Frampton, 1701.⁶
Borden, Apollo—Hannah Karlin, 1-20-1831.³
   Asa—Ann Ward, 11-16-1814.⁶
   Benj.—Mary Haines, 7-27-1805.³
   Charles—Effe Norcross Earl, 6-5-1813.³
   Daniel—Tabitha Redman, 5-18-1798.³
   David—Mary Eldridge, 1-4-1803.³

Borden, Ebenezer—Amy Andrews, Oct. 18, 1748.[1]
  Edward—Hannah Zelly, 5-8-1806.[3]
  George—Susan Robbins, 9-19-1824.[3]
  Jacob—Margaret Barbiss, 6-26-1775.[3]
  John—Content Clayton, 1-19-1783.[1]
  John, Jr.—Nancy Smith, 1-16-1823.[3]
  Jonathan, Monmouth co.—Mary Earle, Nov. 26, 1730.[1]
  Jonathan—Lydia Mason, 1-4-1791.[4]
  Jonathan, Jr.—Rebecca Horner, Sept. 14, 1743.[1]
  Joseph—Rebeckah Middleton (d. Thomas and Prudence), 2-15-1759.[5]
  Joseph—Sarah Baker, 2-13-1762.[1]
  Joseph—Elizabeth Lippincott, 9-22-1783.[1]
  Richard—Catherine Taylor, 9-21-1772.[1]
  Richard—Catherine Deberd, 11-23-1780.[1]
  William—Ann Jacobs, 4-14-1806.[3]
Bordman, Joseph—Catherine Departeone, 1-6-1753.[3]
Boreadil, Arthur—Martha Davis, 12-9-1866.[3]
Borradaile, Arthur—Margery Addams, Apr. 27, 1731.[1]
  William—Jerusey Jordan, 9-14-1782.[1]
Borraidell, William—Sarah Rockhill. Date not given.[1]
Borton, Abraham—Margery Kirkbride, 9-15-1764.[1]
  Abraham (s. John and Hannah), Pbiladelphia)—Mary Dudley (d. Joshua and Rachel). 4-28-1808.[12]
  Bethune—Mary Butcher, 3-15-1834.[3]
  Charles Hains—Annie M. Winkelspecht, 5-2-1896.[3]
  Edward—Mary Braddock, 9-19-1804.[10]
  Ephraim—Mary Burrows, 1-15-1814.[3]
  Isaac—Mary Hooten, 1761.[9]
  Isaac—Harriet Heaton, 1-4-1832.[3]
  Jacob—Jemimah French, 4-21-1790.[1]
  Jacob—Jemimah Kay, 10-10-1799.[13]
  Jesse P.—Elizabeth Hunt, 7-29-1812.[3]
  John—Hester Alcot, 9-16-1754.[1]
  John—Jemima Braddock, 5-14-1800.[10]
  Joseph H.—Henrietta Haines, 2-11-1855.[13]
  Joshua—Rachel Borton, 9-24-1781.[1]
  Nerr—Ruth H. Peacock, 11-11-1824.[3]
  Obadiah—Susannah Butcher, 1732.[6]
  Obadiah—Mary Driver, 1794.[9]
  Richard—Rachel Braddock, 1-16-1801.[9]
  Samuel—Mercy Owen, 4-7-1796 [1]

Borton, Samuel—Mary Borton, 8-16-1829.³
  Thomas—Ann Borton, 1681.⁶
  Uriah—Mary Collins, 9-121-798.¹⁰
  William—Hannah Cole, 1699.⁶
  William—Deborah Hedge, 1731.⁹
  William—Martha Owen, 4-7-1760.¹
  William—Elizabeth Edwards, 1-27-1803.³
Bosah, William—Rebecca Pettit, 1-13-1839.⁵
Bosser, Christopher—Anne Masson, 10-30-1774.⁸
Boswick, Francis—Priscilla Pacock, Feb. 19, 1682.¹
Bosworth, John—Innocent Borden, July 13, 1734.¹
  Samuel—Sarah Symonds, July 14, 1747.¹
Bottomly, Francis—Betsey Geer, 8-18-1856.⁴
Bough, Francis—Elizabeth Taylor, 5-1-1798.³
Bouker, Michael—Mary Collins, Sept. 9, 1741.¹
Boulton, Benjamin—Jane Ellis, 8-18-1831.³
  Edward—Alice Stratton, 10-25-1797.¹⁰
  Henry—Hannah Davis, Nov. 3, 1746.¹
  Henry—Elizabeth Richardson, 1-14-1819.³
  Isaac—Sarah Applegate, July 15, 1745.¹
  Isaac—Mary Warrick, 8-6-1773.¹
  Samuel—Susanna Brown, 4-16-1812.³
  Thomas—Hannah Scott, 3-31-1774.¹
  Thomas—Mary Richardson, 3-28-1819.³
  William—Hannah Campbell, 5-28-1766.¹
  Zebedee D.—Rebeeca Bryan, 12-4-1834.⁰
Boun, Elias—Abigail Smith, 11-1-1804.³
Bound, Cato—Sarah Currey, 3-11-1801.³
  Samuel—Mary Louisa Bunting, 10-29-1825.⁸
Bounds, James—Louisa Day, 9-20-1828.³
Bowden, John—Margaret Shepherd, 7-27-1789.⁴
Bowen, Edw. Emerson—Mary Bowman Woodington, 4-17-1876.⁸
  John—Susanna Britain, July 19, 1744.¹
  William—Hannah Durell, 4-4-1822.³
Bower, Daniel—Elizabeth W. Smith, 1-5-1818.³
  Edmond—Mary Foster, 10-22-1765.¹
  William—Bathsheba Brown, 12-11-1797.³
Bowers, Edward—Elizabeth Woodward, 2-6-1834.³
  Elijah—Mrs. Deoshe Robins, 12-6-1799.⁸
  Elijah—Eliza Sears, 3-24-1823.³
  William, Salisbury, N. C.—Hannah E. Coppuck, 9-26-1833.⁸
Bowker, Bsrzillai—Hester Mingen, 3-4-1774.¹

Bowker, Charles—Alice Folks, 10-5-1770.[1]
  Charles—Amey Springer, 2-28-1830.[3]
  Elisha—Hannah Lawrence, 9-5-1835.[3]
  Isaiah—Martha Allcot, 3-5-1789.[4]
  Isaiah—Mary Lee, 11-12-1826.[3]
  Japhett—Elizabeth Sharp, 9-25-1828.[3]
  John—Jemima Mills, Aug. 28, 1838.[1]
  John—Ane Cramer, 2-2-1814.[3]
  Joseph—Grace Garwood, May 15, 1746.[1]
  Joseph—Mary Lame, 1-5-1784.[1]
  Joseph—Lucrecy Moore, 8-20-1797.[3]
  Joseph—Kesiah Johnson, 8-1-1821.[1]
  Joseph C. (s. Japhet and Elizabeth)—Lizzie M. Prickett, (d. Randolph and Ann), 8-15-1865.[4]
  Laban—Rhoda Gaskill, 2-24-1784.[1]
  Levi—Annie Mount, 10-16-1773.[1]
  Michael—Esther Richardson, Feb., 1815.[3]
  Richard—Joanna James, May 13, 1741.[1]
  Richard—Esther Gwin, Sept. 26, 1750.[1]
  Thomas—Ann Foulks, 2-25-1837.[3]
  William—Letis Wills, 8-25-1796.[3]
Bowlby, George—Elizabeth Tonkin, Aug. 17, 1737.[1]
  Thomas, Morris co.—Mary Tuley, June. 12, 1749.[1]
Bowlen, Peter—Lettice Hugg, 6-4-1816.[3]
Bowman, Henry—Ellen Mitchell, 6-28-1835.[3]
  Nathaniel—Ann Williams, 10-30-1812.[3]
Bown, Philip—Mary Taylor, 3-11-1765.[1]
Bowne, Philip—Sarah Wilson, 1-10-1778.[1]
Box, Aaron—Ann Southwick, 4-28-1804.[3]
Boyd, James—Mary Boger, 1-14-1807.[3]
  John—Mary Dunum, 11-25-1824.[3]
  Thomas, Rhoda Reed, 9-2-1806.[5]
  William—Elizabeth Anderson, 11-8-1775.[1]
Boyden, James—Miriam Ridley, 1695.[6]
Boye, Patrick—Betsy Barrenhart, 2-2-1802.[3]
Boyer, Joshua Fennimore—Amy Matilda Smith—4-27-1859.[6]
Boyes, Richard—Mary Dodson, Nov. 1, 1683.[1]
Bozerth, Andrew—Mercy Smith, 2-9-1798.[3]
  William—Rebecca Gant, 4-6-1831.[3]
Bozorth, Aaron—Jane Nailor, 1-24-1799.[3]
  Andrew—Mary Bishop, 5-21-1756.[1]
  Joseph—Elizabeth Griffith, 8-13-1835.[3]

Bozorth, William—Mary Ann Ross, 1-1-1835.[3]
  Zebulon—Margaret Regions, 4-11-1768.[8]
Brachman, Mathias—Isabella Wair, 5-9-1760.[1]
Brackncy, Isaac—Mary Lippincott, 6-9-1825.[3]
  John—Mary Cheeseman, 1758.[9]
  Joseph—Abigail Borden, 2-24-1747.[1]
  Joseph—Rachel Middleton, 5-6-1782.[1]
  Joseph—Elizabeth Smith, 3-10-1787,[1]
Braddock. Charles W.—Rebecca Ann Alcutt, 1-7-1837.[3]
  Daniel—Sarah Rodgers, 1-31-1799.[8]
  David—Priscilla Wills, 10-7-1806.[3]
  Jacob B.—Sarah Ann Austin, 1-31-1833.[3]
  Job—Hope Garwood, 1-26-1819.[3]
  Jonathan—Ann Crispin, 2-27-1806.[3]
  Joseph—Rhoda Johnston, 11-12-1812.[3]
  Josiah—Elizabeth Shinn, 9-20-1821.[3]
  Ner—Sylvia Crispin, 9-12-1797.[3]
  Robert—Elizabeth Bates, Nov. 24, 1737.[1]
  Samuel—Judith A. Bates, both Gloucester co., 1-19-1823.[8]
  William—Ann Rogers, 10-27-1803.[3]
  William R.—Sarah Shreve, 2-30-1823.[3]
Bradford, William, Philadelphia—Rachel Budd, Aug. 18, 1742.[1]
Bradshaw, Samuel—Jane Newell, 3-26-1776.[1]
Bradway, David—Hannah Bradway, 5-26-1788.[7]
  David—Hannah Fogg (wid,), 1-25-1808.[7]
  ———— —Mary Stretch, 1-5-1820.[7]
Brady, Isaac—Deborah Howell, 6-30-1796.[3]
  Isaac—Mary Clutch, 3-2-1801.[3]
  John—Leah Wehronz, 5-11-1797.[3]
Bragg, Benj. C.—Ruth Lippincott, 5-30-1821.[3]
Braily, Isaac—Ester Ashwood, 3-22-1809,[3]
Braman, Jonathan—Anna Starkey, 1-11-1779.[1]
Brandt, Richard—Ann T. Ruder, 2-13-1823.[3]
Branin, Abijah—Ann Smith, 10-12-1823.[3]
  Brazilla!—Taressa Alloway, 5-15-1831.[3]
  Francis—Ann Penquite, 5-11-1802.[3]
  John Curtis—Tacy Thorn, 12-27-1817.[3]
  Nathaniel—Elizabeth Porter, 4-14-1813.[3]
  Robert—Elizabeth Norcross, Nov. 24, 1730.[1]
  William—Elizabeth Brooks, 10-1-1771.[1]
  William—Lydia Phillips; 2-24-1805.[3]
  William—Rebecca A. Shinn, 1-21-1833.[3]

Branin, William (s. John and Rachel), New York—Achsah Gaunt
 (d. Samuel and Achsah), Pilesgrove, 12-6-1826.⁵
Brannin, Benjamin—Elizabeth Pointzell, Sept. 14, 1741,¹
 Cornelius—Amelia Neven, 11-30-1773.¹
 Elihu—Rachel Fenimore, 6-16-1821.³
 Ezra—Rachel Shinn, 9-12-1811.¹⁰
 Gershom—Jemima Braddock, 1-8-1835.³
 John—Abigail Ann Jones, 11-29-1832.⁸
 John, Jr.—Rachel Vanderbeck, 10-5-1791.⁵
 William—Abigail Rogers, 2-3-1779.¹³
 William—Lydia Bates, 5-30-1799³
Branning, George—Hannah Haines, 1-30-1810.³
Branson—Charles—Harriet Stratton, 10-20-1826.³
 James—Rebeckah Bishop, 3-14-1796.¹³
 John—Martha Osborn, 1748.⁶
 Jonathan—Alice Atkinson, 1745.⁹
 Joseph—Mary Edge, Mar. 18, 1745/6.¹
 Joseph—Ruth Ann Haines, 3-21-1821.³
 Lyndall—Rebecca Rogers, 1749.⁶
 Moses—Sara Borrodail, 12-5-1766.¹
 Sam—Susanna Farley, 6-9-1786.⁸
 Thomas (s. David and Sarah)—Ann Hendrickson (d. Joseph and
  Elizabeth), 3-4-1804.⁵
 William White, Rev.—Mary Isabelle Clark, 8-5-1355⁸
Brantingham, George B.—Phebe Boulton, 3-9-1801.¹⁰
Bras, William—Mary Gingling, 10-28-1815.³
Brass, Elias—Rachel Ony, Jan. 24, 1742.¹
Brazenton, Samuel—Lydia Andrews, 4-15-1824.¹⁰
Brayman, Jonathan—Sarah Wilson, Nov. 1, 1742.¹
 Samuel—Elizabeth Lycans, 1-14-1783.¹
 William—Abigail Rogers, 2-3-1779.¹³
Brelsford, Abraham—Elizabeth Mayhew, 2-18-1833.⁷
Brewer, Aaron—Martha Taylor, 3-17-1818.³
 Elias—Rebecca Wickers, 9-25-1786.¹
 Isaac—Sarah Meredith, 2-27-1806.³
 James—Acsah Carter, 12-7-1807.³
 John—Levise Adams, 3-10-1805.³
 Robert—Mary Atkinson, 9-14-1837.³
Breyan, Joseph—Mary White, Aug. 16, 1746.¹
Brian, John—Mary Manus, Dec. 6, 1733.¹
 Richard—Hannah Crockford, 1-23-1754.¹
 Thomas—Elizabeth Scattergood, 1687.⁶

Brian, William—Elizabeth Connaro, 3-25-1782.[1]
Briant, Horon—Hannah Engle, 6-18-1813.[3]
   Jonathan—Sarah Carson, Pennsylvania, 6-4-1829.[3]
   Thomas—Hannah Frazier, 8-26-1809.[3]
Brick, John W.—Margaret Allen, 11-5-1832.[3]
Brientnall, John—Hannah Sharpe, 1724.[6]
Briest, John—Drucilla Probasco, 4-20-1834.[3]
Briggs, Abel—Lettice Woolston, 1-26-1773.[1]
   David—Hannah Ong, 12-14-1759.[1]
   David—Mary Stapleton, 12-16-1788.[4]
   David—Martha Grover, 10-20-1807.[3]
   George—Anne Woolston, 9-14-1734.[1]
   Henry—Atlantic Willshire, 12-9-1824.[3]
   John—Hannah Briggs, 8-9-1766.[1]
   William—Dasey Parker, 5-21-1803.[3]
   William—Mary Asay, 9-18-1808.[3]
   William—Amy Reeves, 9-20-1822.[3]
   William—Ann Ashmore, 7-20-1831.[3]
Brighton, William—Mary Williams, 1-29-1837.[3]
Brightwell, Benjamin—Diadame Adams, 1-18-1764.[1]
Bringingham, Thomas—Elinor Sullivan, Nov. 3, 1740.[1]
Brinton, Joseph—Hannah Gordon, 9-19-1801.[3]
Britan, Richard—Rhoda Woodward, 7-23-1767.[1]
Brittain, Ephraim—Jane Quigley, 12-28-1820.[3]
Britton, Daniel—Rachel Purdy, 10-15-1818.[3]
   Enoch—Eliza Smith Coxe, 3-27-1831.[3]
   Lazarus—Mary Adams, 8-31-1802.[3]
   Samuel—Hagar Johnson, 3-24-1828.[3]
Brock, Daniel—Deborah Deacon, 3-16-1784.[1]
   Daniel—Martha Shreve, 1-5-1817.[3]
   Deacon—Rebecca Creely, 1-9-1836.[3]
   James—Elizabeth Marlin. Date not Given.[3]
   John—Mary Brockney, 2-9-1779.[1]
   John—Rebecca Singer, 10-12-1799.[3]
   Mathias—Rachel Reeves, Sept. 19, 1750.[1]
   Oddy—Amelia Hammett, 4-5-1803.[3]
   Oddy—Lydia Lippincott, 10-22-1829.[3]
   Samuel—Susan Thompson, 11-10-1824.[3]
   Samuel—Susan Thompson, 11-19-1824.[3]
   Thomas—Agness Sharp, 10-21-1802.[3]
   Uriah—Sarah Marter, 1-7-1810.[3]
Broderick, Thomas—Parthenia Potter, 11-12-1756.[1]

BURLINGTON COUNTY MARRIAGES

Brognard, John—Sarah Smith, 1-7-1784.¹
  John S.—Sarah Burr, 1-2-1809.³
Bronson, William—Mercy Marriot, 4-9-1801.³
Brooks, Bowyer—Lydia Shinn, 7-10-1794.¹³
  Daniel—Grace Burrough, 9-1-1811.³
  Edward—Keziah Woolman, 1-23-1823.³
  Isasc—Margaret Parker, 11-26-1778.⁷
  Isaac—Ann Bowker, 11-9-1826.³
  Isaiah—Marietta Hackney, 1-3-1837.³
  James—Elizabeth Anderson, 10-15-1804,³
  John—Susannah Garwoed, 9-7-1781.¹
  John—Macy Woolman, 1-8.1818.³
  Samuel—Mary Parker, 12-7-1782.¹
  Samuel—Ann Striker, 3-18-1802.⁵
  Samuel, Jr.—Rachel Shute, 3-1-1827.³
  Seth—Martha Alloway, 7-9-1830.³
  Stephen—Ann Elkinton, Aug. 19, 1740.¹
  Thomas—Elizabeth Thomas, 5-26-1800.³
  Thomas—Hepsibah Evsns, 3-1-1811,³
  Thomas—Lydia Borton, 5-9-1814.³
  William—Hannah Guinnell, 9-20-1758.¹
Brothers, Eli—Mary Kindle, 4-25-1824.³
  Ferdinand—Martha M. Lukens, 12-21-1865,⁶
Brotherton, David—Phebe Gibbs, 12-2-1831.⁸
  Thomas—Margt. Cannon, 12-19-1853.⁸
Brown, Aaron—Elizabeth Vanhise, 1-30-1830.³
  Abia—Margaret Sharp, 3-12-1765.¹
  Abraham—Phebe Adams (d. John), 1712.⁶
  Abraham—Susanna Richardson, Joly 26, 1749.¹
  Abraham—Jane Ridgway, 8-22-1774.¹
  Abraham—Ann Eakin, 9-4-1823.³
  Alexander, Trenton—Anne Bickham, 6-8-1774.¹
  Allen—Rachel Warren, 2-1-1827.³
  Asa—Nancy Carragerm, 10-10-1802.³
  Asher—Elizabeth Reed, 2-5-1811.³
  Benjamin—Elizabeth Ridgway, 1750.⁶
  Benjamin—Elizabeth Williams, 8-19-1808.³
  Benjamin—Emeline Warren, 9-18-1824.³
  Benjamin H.—Alice P. Stevenson, 5-7-1833.³
  Benjamin H.—Eliza Ann H. Woolston, 12-31-1846.⁴
  Caleb—Levine Wallen, 5-17-1814.³
  Charles—Jane Boys, 6-4-1837.³

Brown, Charles—Hannah E. West, 10-6-1858.[4]
  Clayton—Mary Robins, Mar. 8, 1749/50.[1]
  Clayton—Esther Ballinger, 11-10-1816.[10]
  Daniel—Katharine Lynch, 2-10-1789.[4]
  Eber—Sarah Ann Ritchie, 1-30-1836.[3]
  Edward—Anne Wilkinson, May 30, 1750.[1]
  Enoch W.—Sarah Ann Newell, 10-17-1833.[3]
  George—Rachel Lippincott, 2-6-1803.[3]
  George—Rachel Lippincott, 12-2-1802.[3]
  Henry—Mary Miskelly. 8-15-1796.[3]
  Henry—Jane McMinn, 3-29-1821.[3]
  Isaac—Sarah Lippincott, 2-20-1812.[3]
  James—Honour Clayton, 1679.[6]
  James—Letty Harsems, 9-20-1797.[8]
  James—Jane Cromell, 1-30-1828.[5]
  Japhet—Rachel Brayman, 11-27-1773.[1]
  Job—Elizabeth Allen, 5-31-1790.[7]
  Joel—Ann Eliza Keeler, 1-16-1832.[8]
  John—Ann Stancie, 1681.[6]
  John—Mary Brock, 1707.[6]
  John—Mary Gordon, Middlesex co., July 9, 1729.[1]
  John—Margaret Robins, Monmouth co., Dec. 4, 1750.[1]
  John—Alice Coward, 2-7-1759.[1]
  John—Deborah Claypoole, 10-13-1760.[1]
  John—Sarah Esdall, 6-20-1775.[8]
  John—Mary Norcross, 7-25-1775.[1]
  John—Mary Page, 3-27-1780.[1]
  John—Sarah Hughes, 5-13-1799.[3]
  John—Ann Murray, 12-17-1804.[3]
  John, Milford, Pa.—Ann Reynolds, 6-7-1810.[8]
  John—Sarah Vanhorn, 4-6-1811.[3]
  John—Deborah Brock, 10-28-1813.[6]
  John—Mary Early, 10-27-1815.[3]
  John—Margaret Buffin, 5-16-1829.[3]
  John—Mary Atkinson, 4-10-1834.[3]
  John H.—Hannah Clair, 6-8-1869.[2]
  John M.—Elizabeth Kele, 2-1-1823.[8]
  John T.—Susan Vernon, 6-29-1819.[3]
  Jonathan—Hannah Bulong, Apr, 13, 1748,[1]
  Jonathan—Sarah Cross, 9-3-1808.[3]
  Joseph—Anne Higgs, 8-14-1759.
  Joseph—Hannah Tucker, 4-15-1773.[1]

BURLINGTON COUNTY MARRIAGES

Brown, Joseph—Jane Esdel, 3-15-1786.[1]
  Joseph—Ann Allen, 8-26-1793.[7]
  Joseph—Sarah Chasey, 8-30-1820.[8]
  Joseph, Jr.—Harriet Cole, 1-2-1818.[3]
  Joshua—Rebecca B. Pancoast. 9-21-1865.[10]
  Lewis T.—Martha Elliott, both Philadelphia, 1-25-1868.[4]
  Nicholas—Amy Thorne, 10-3-1830.[3]
  Preserve—Mary Dawson, Nov. 3, 1742.[1]
  Preserve, Philadelphia—Mary Sykes (d. John and Joanna), Oct. 21, 1747.[5]
  Preserve, Jr., Philadelphia—Mary French (d. Richard), Oct. 15, 1724.[5]
  Randle—Rebecca Morton, 1-11-1801.[3]
  Richard—Elizabeth Powell, 1720.[6]
  Richard—Sarah Taylor, 5-15-1755.[5]
  Richard—Lydia Woolston, 6-3-1825.[3]
  Richard E.—Susan Godly, 3-4-1865.[2]
  Robert—Susan Parker, 7-12-1834.[3]
  Samuel—Ann Buffin, 1750.[6]
  Samuel Biles (s. William and Rebecca), Philadelphia—Ann Klimpton (d. Moses and Eliza), 7-22-1797.[3]
  Samuel—Catharine Newman, 9-23-1802.[3]
  Samuel—Elizabeth Thompson, 8-17-1823.[3]
  Thomas—Rebecca Buffin, 10-3-1829.[3]
  William—Elizabeth Haines, 1738.[6]
  William—Phillis Williams, 6-2-1816.[3]
  William—Abigail Pippit, 10-6-1816.[3]
  William—Mary Jones, 11-5-1825 [3]
  Zabulon—Bathsheba Moll, 1-17-1759.[1]
Browne—Alexander—Anne Bickham, 6-9-1774.[3]
  Caleb, Eastern Divison—Mary Browne, Nov. 17, 1731.[1]
  Frank W.—Laura A. Lippincott (d. Morgan and E. R.), 11-15-1877.[4]
  James—Sarah Lindon, Jan. 25, 1737.[1]
  James—Priscilla Boulton, 4-16-1812.[3]
  Philip—Elizabeth Hancock, 11-26-1836.[3]
  Thomas—Mary Nutt, 9-19-1768.[8]
  William—Elizabeth Burrodail, 3-11-1758.[1]
  William—Catharine Loten, 8-20-1718.[3]
Brownell, Ezekiel- Martha Mason, 7-10-1822.[4]
Browning, Edward, Gloucester co.—Grace Oldale, July 8, 1751.[1]
  George—Mary Clement, 10-3-1805.[3]

Browning, George T.—Esther T. Engle, 12-26-1834.³
  Joseph—Mary Vandergrift, 10-9-1782.¹
  Samuel—Sarah Newton—1-8-1824.³
  William—Grace Fish, 4-4-1811.³
Bruce, James—Winefred Franklin, 9-20-1768.⁸
Bruer, Richard—Elizabeth Waln, 6-7-1821.³
Bruere, John H.—Sarah E. Holmes, 3-8-1827.³
  Jonathan—Thomasin Imlay, 2-26-1833.³
Bromby, Joseph—Hannah Clark, 12-26-1777.⁷
Bruson, Aaron—Euphemia Cromwell (colored), 9-2-1809.⁸
  Gilbert—Deborah Cromwell, 1-12-1817.³
Bryan, Aaron—Martha Hopewell, 12-26-1783.¹
  Abraham—Mary Fenimore, 1728.⁶
  Benjamin—Nancy Richardson, 10-18-1780.¹
  Charles—Rebecca Ervin, 9-20-1821.³
  Charles—Merab. Shreve, 12-14-1833.²
  Guy—Rebecca S. Burr, 4-12-1837.⁴
  Haran—Johannah Sikes, Aug. 21, 1751.¹
  Heron—Mary Eldridge, 1732.⁶
  Heron—Jane Pratt, 7-24-1758.¹
  Heron—Rebecca Green, 11-28-1761.¹
  Jacob—Mary Ritchie, Allentown, 5-26-1758.¹
  James—Ann Wilson, Oct. 14, 1741.¹
  John—Mary Ann Knight, 9-25-1831.³
  Joseph—Deborah Budden, 3-24-1839.⁴
  Samuel—Mary Pancoast, 12-18-1764.¹
  Thomas—Rebecca Collins, 1698.⁶
  Thomas—Sarah Cox, Nov. 22, 1730.¹
  Thomas—Mary Haines, July 17, 1745.¹
  Thomas—Fanny Coxe, 12-31-1761.¹
Bryant, Joseph—Mary White, Oct. 14, 1746.²
  Joseph—Keziah Mullen. 1-29-1815.³
  Samuel—Elizabeth Carty, 5-13-1796.³
  Thomas—Amey Garwood, 1-29-1797.³
  William—Mary Bishop, 9-28-1823.³
Buck, Joshua—Elizabeth Weatherby, 1-17-1830.³
Buckhard, David—Mary McGuire, Oct. 29, 1749.¹
Buckingham, John, Connecticut—Josephine S. Duby, Canada, 11-14-1881.⁴
Buckley, Elton James—Mabelle Aucker. 12-7-1872.²
  John, Rev.—Abigail S. Monrow, 4-21-1835.³
  Thomas—Martha Chubb, 8-4-1789.⁴

Buckman, Benjamin—Ann Robbins, 12-19-1822.³
Budd, Benj. S., Dr,—Sarah Dobbins, 1-12-1803.⁸
   David—Catharine Allen, Feb. 6, 1738.¹
   Eli—Anne Carman, 4-2-1774.¹
   Isaac—Ruth Woolston, 12-6-1755.¹
   James—Susan VanWyck, 6-4-1827.³
   John—Hannah King, Dec. 31, 1750.¹
   John—Hannah Lippincott, 7-28-1764.¹
   John D.—Caroline M. Striker, 11-26-1844.⁴
   Jonathan—Ann Saxton, 10-15-1777.¹
   Joseph—Abigail Shinn, 8-6-1778.¹
   Joseph—Mary Fox, 10-27-1781.¹
   Joseph—Mary Gooldy, 1-24-1830.³
   Joseph J.—Sarah R. Earl, 3-7-1834.³
   Levi—Mary Woolston, 9-1-1774.¹
   Levi—Mary Wilkins, 9-26-1833.³
   Stacy—Sarah Munrow, 5-20-1763.¹
   Samuel—Hannah Gile, 4-14-1766.¹
   Samuel—Hannah Pippitt, 1-20-1831.³
   Thomas—Rebecca Atkinson, 1739.⁹
   Thomas—Ann Irick, 2-27-1811.³
   Thomas J.—Ann Haines, 3-23-1829.³
   Wesley—Cumberland co.—Sarah Budd, 5-16-1799.³
   William—Susanna Coles, Gloucester co., Jan. 5, 1735.¹
   Wiliiam—Lititia Hoff, 7-18-1767.¹
   William—Sarah Croshaw, 9-25-1796.³
   William—Elizabeth Zelley, 1-14-1808.³
   William—Mary Ann Gaskill, 2-26-1829.³
Buddell, William—Hannah Clarke, Mar. 13, 1731.¹
Budden, Hosea—Deborah Simmons, 5-14-1818.³
   James—Elizabeth Crammer, 8-25-1830.⁵
   James, Jr.—Mary Bishop, 11-11-1810.³
   William—Elizabeth Carter, May 10, 1746.¹
Buddin, Joseph—Rebecca Packer, Mar. 27, 1741.¹
Buffin, John—Ann Woolman, 1712.⁶
   Michael—Christian Chipman, 1677.⁶
   Michael—Rebecca White, 1-28-1813.³
   Richard—Hannah Falkenburg (d. Henry, Jr.), 1769.¹¹
Bullas, Samuel—Mary Toy, 8-13-1775.¹
Bulling, George—Hepzibah Asey, 5-27-1801.³
   William W.—Mary C. Davis, Monmouth co., 11-3-1837.³
Bullock, Amos—Margaret Butcher, 10-4-1780.¹³

Bullock—Amos (s. Isaac and Elizabeth)—Elizabeth Sharp (d. Anthony and Anne), 6-20-1816.[12]
Anthony (s. Joseph and Elizabeth)—Hannah Wood (d. William and Hannah), 5-10-1789.[5]
Edward (s. Isaac and Elizabeth)—Hannah Laning (d. Samuel and Esthdr), 10-18-1804.[12]
George (s. Joseph and Elizabeth)—Edith Wood (d. William and Hannah), 2-7-1766.[5]
John—Rachel Griscom, 2-7-1820.[7]
John—Elizabeth Quigley, 9-28-1837.[3]
Joseph—Esther Boynton, both Philadelphia, 12-6-1770.[5]
Joseph, Jr. (s. Joseph and Elizabeth)—Lydia Lawrie (d. James and Mary), 3-15-1780.[6]
Nathan—Matilda French, 3-3-1817.[8]
Nathan—Elizabeth Lee, 5-8-1827.[3]
Thomas—Elizabeth Stewart, 2-14-1767.[1]
Thomas—Acsah Rockhill, 12-19-1772.[1]
Bullus, Francis—Elizabeth Winnick, 1-8-1791.[1]
Bunting, Adam—Ann Stephenson, 2-21-1770.[1]
Benj.—Jane Rite, 1-24-1815.[3]
Benjamin—Elizabeth Steward, 9-8-1772.
Gharles (s. Samuel and Elizabeth)—Phebe M. Burdsall (d. Richard and Fanny), 4-7-1830.[5]
Daniel—Nancy Lovit, 7-22-1779.[1]
Isaac (s. Benj. and Sarah)—Mary Wynn (d. John and Ann), 10-27-1807.[12]
Israel—Susan Bennet, 2-22-1816.[3]
John—Mary Carter, 2-24-1757.[1]
John—Lydia Bunting; 9-24-1795.[3]
John—Rebecca Taylor, 6-29-1816.[3]
John—Phebe Ann Ayres, 12-12-1838.[3]
John, Jr.—Patience Tilton, 3-5-1768.[1]
Joseph, Bucks co., Pa.—Latice Pancoast, 9-19-1830.[8]
Joshua—Amy Nutt, 9-23-1768.[1]
Joshua—Mary Large, 11-17-1785.[5]
Marmaduke—Deborah Herbert, 8-9-1817.[3]
Phineas T.—Anna M. Antrim. 12-24-1828.[3]
Samuel—Msry Folkes (d. Thomas), Nov. 18, 1684.[5]
Samuel—Mary Willitts, Monmouth co., May 11, 1739.[1]
Samuel—Elizabeth Zilley, 11-30-1815.[3]
Samuel, Jr.—Mary Wolston, 1713.[9]
Thomas—Sarah Harvey, 4-17-1755.[1]

BURLINGTON COUNTY MARRIAGES

Bunting, William—Abigail Horseman (d. Marmaduke), Oct. 11, 1716.[5]
  William—Sarah Terry, Feb. 29, 1743.[1]
  William—Anne Stewart, 11-15-1779.[1]
Burch, James—Hannah Little, 2-16-1811.[2]
  Jeremiah—Sarah Wilkinson, 6-4-1811.[3]
Burcham, Henry—Margaret Haines, 1685.[6]
  James—Elizabeth Woodhouse, 1705.[6]
Burdsal, Aaron—Nancy Charlton, 8-11-1804.[3]
  Elijah—Mary Wills, 6-18-1765.[1]
  Burdsall, Elijah, Jr.—Esther Prickett, 1-13-1796.[8]
  Jacob—Jane Buzby, 1727.[6]
  Jacob—Elizabeth Coles, Apr. 4, 1730
Burdsall, John—Mary Mullen, 1-24-1805.[3]
  Samuel—Abigail Wilson, 1822.[14]
  William—Theodosia H. Turner, 10-19-1835.[3]
  Willis—Dorothy Crispin, 2-3-1796.[3]
Burges, Moses, Pennsylvania—Ann Hancock, 1-18-1810.[3]
Burgess, Thomas—Jane Large, 1748.[6]
Burgis, Benjamin—Abigail Eassland, Nov. 20, 1731.[1]
  Daniel—Mary Wood, 8-4-1808.[3]
Burk, Alexander—Mary McDonald, 2-6-1765.[1]
  Miles—Ella Lemon, 9-26-1868.[2]
  Ruth—Mary Roe, 1-16-1776.[1]
Burling, John D.—Mary Githens, 7-14-1831.[5]
Burkitt, Thomas—Sarah Roydhouse, 10-29-1839.[4]
Burne, William—Mary Robertson, 1-18-1765.[1]
Burnett, William—Ada Malone, 10-21-1897.[2]
Burnside, James—Mary Hendricks, July 19, 1727.[1]
  James—Mary Seed, Oct. 22, 1729.[1]
Burr, Barzillai—Mary Smith, Jr., 1-4-1787.[13]
  Charles—Lucy Ann Troth, 5-29-1826.[3]
  Edmund W.—Parthemia R. Burr, 2-5-1815.[13]
  George W.—Elizabeth Blackwood, 11-26-1818.[3]
  Henry—Mary Owen, Jan. 10, 1736.[1]
  Henry—Elizabeth Foster, 1753.[9]
  Henry—Abigail Bishop, 11-16-1793.[1]
  Henry—Mary Thomas, 4-24-1808.[3]
  Henry—Elizabeth Inskeep, 1819.[14]
  Henry—Margaret Quick, 11-13-1861.[2]
  Hudson—Martha Hancock, 10-28-1829.[3]
  Israel—Susan B. Flinn, 12-5-1837.[2]

Burr, Jas.—Margaret Bispham, 11-15-1804.[2]
   John—Elizabeth Davidson, Sept. 4, 1738.[1]
   John—Jean Woolston, 12-7-1800.[8]
   John B.—Mary H. Tash, 1-1-1821.[1]
   Joseph (s. Henry and Elizabeth)—Jane Abbott (d. John and Anne), 12-16-1766.[5]
   Joseph (s. Robert), Pennsylvania—Elizabeth Wills (d. Moses) 5-4-1785.[6]
   Joseph—Margaret Bispham, 11-15-1804.[3]
   Joseph F.—Sarah C. Newbold, 11-11-1848.[4]
   Joseph, Jr.—Mary Mnllen, May 15, 1749.[1]
   Joshua S.—Mary Newbold, 2-20-1817.[3]
   Marmaduke—Martha Bispham, 12-4-1782.[13]
   Robert—Christiana Gregory. 9-25-1770.[1]
   Samuel—Elizabeth Lippincott, 6-23-1798.[3]
   William—Merium Fenemore, 3-20-1808.[2]
   William Hudson—Ann Ridgway, 1-7-1790.[13]
Burridge, Thomas—Hannah Pall, 7-25-1822.[8]
Burrough, Benj.—Ann Armstrong, 12-17-1810.[1]
   Irie, Gloucester co.—Anne Hollinshed, 2-9-1797.[8]
   Joseph—Anner Lippencott, 11-11-1824.[10]
   William—Achsah Burr, 3-5-1789.[13]
Burroughs, Aaron—Patience Cox, 12-18-1800.[3]
   David—Sarah Amy Marjoram, 11-4-1830.[5]
   Jefferson, Richmond, Va.—Mary Anna Hart, 10-3-1870.[4]
   Samuel—Priscilla Moore, 3-3-1808.[3]
   Samuel, Waterford—Keturah Haines, 2-23-1826.[3]
Burrows, Michael—Mary Carter, 5-1-1764.[1]
   Michael—Isabel Jack, 5-28-1784.[1]
Burtis, Abner, Monmouth co.—Rachel Shinn, 3-14-1810[3]
   David W.—Lucy Ann Longstreet, 11-1-1838.[6]
   Francis—Charlotte Kirby, 11-27-1813.[3]
   Joseph—Elizabeth Waters, 11-24-1796.[3]
   Samuel—Martha R. Dobbins, 4-10-1855.[4]
   William—Lucy Tilton, 11-8-1804.[3]
   William—Mary Davis, 6-19-1834.[3]
Burton, Charles—Anne Medcalf, Sept. 17, 1731.[1]
   Charles (s. David and Catharine)—Lydia Moore, wid. (d. John and Hannah Taylor), 10-8-1800.[5]
   David—Ann Butler, 3-5-1830.[3]
   George—Elizabeth Thompson, 8-26-1826.[2]
   Geo. Henry—Rebecca R. Roth, 3-19-1874.[8]

Burton, Phineas—Mary Parker, 6-17-1833.³
William—Emelia Trouth, 8-24-1821.³
William—Agnes Higgins, 11-4-1833.³
Busby, Isaac—Rachel Sharp, Apr. 5, 1743.¹
John—Sarah Ellis, 5-9-1758.¹·
Robert C.—Rebecca Costill, 3-12-1829.³
Bush, Platt—Elizabeth Treat, 9-8-1803.³
Busson, James—Mary Bodine, 1-11-1810.³
Joseph—Elizabeth Cunningham, 12-31-1766.¹
Bustill, William—Elizabeth Tonkan, Jan. 3, 1687.¹
Butcher, Benajah—Rachel Shinn, 2-5-1784.¹³
  Benajah (s. Benajah and Rachel)—Abigail Roberts (d. William and Amey), 10-17-1822.¹²
  James—Mary Kimble, 9-24-1788.⁴
  Job—Margaret Barton, 1750.⁶
  John—Mary Harvey, 1709.⁶
  John—Elizabeth Hatkinson, Jr., 11-9-1788.¹³
  John, Jr.—Mary Ridgway, Feb. 23, 1738.¹
  Joseph—Prudence Rogers, 1747.⁹
  Samuel—Eleanor Ashead, 5-24-1849.¹⁰
  Thomas—Elizabeth Harvey, 1713.⁵
  Thomas—Hannah Stockton, 10-20-1803.³
Butler, Abel—Sarah Marett, 2-14-1776.¹
  Abel—Edith Sleeper, 4-9-1795.³
  B)njamin—Hannah Webster, 4-13-1796.¹⁰
  Daniel—Lydia Tindal, 10-18-1810.³
  John—Susannah Kimpson, 10-6-1767.¹
  John— —— Higgins, 7-30-1802.³
  John—Diademia Thorn, 6-2-1821.³
  Joseph—Ann Gibberson, 10-30-1808.³
  Peter—Anna Mitchell, 8-29-1813.
  William—Buley Johnson, 11-1-1810.³
  William—Adeline Mathis, 2-1-1818.³
Butterfield, John—Rebecca Wood, July 29, 1740.¹
  John—Ann Carter, 9-2-1819.³
Butterworth, Benjamin—Ann Ogburn, Sept. 11, 1729.¹
  Benjamin—Ann McCarty, Nov. 18, 1736.¹
  Benjamin—Sarah Likins, 7-26-1757.¹
  Benj.—Rachal Shinn, 3-31-1804.³
  Edward—Lettice Dungan, 6-19-1828.³
  Job—Elizabeth Wells, 8-26-1826.³
  John, Jr.—K. Stockton, 2-6-1827.³

Butterworth, Joseph—Elizabeth Lippincott, 3-1-1801.[3]
   Samuel—Ann Ridgway, 3-26-1805.[3]
   William—Hannah Lippincott, 2-19-1829.[3]
Buttle, Charles—Deborah E. Wetherill, 4-2-1866.[10]
Buxton, John—Hannah Tallman, 5-20-1773.[1]
Buzby, Amos, Jr.,—Mary Vanhorn, 3-23-1806.[8]
   Asher—Ruth Wright, 5-5-1819.[7]
   Charles—Esther Pedrick, 8-16-1818.[8]
   Daniel—Mary Wells, 8-9-1764.[1]
   Daniel—Hannah Buzby, 9-22-1826.[3]
   Daniel—Hannah Stockton, 3-21-1832.[3]
   Isaac—Hannah Tomlin, 2-17-1801.[3]
   Jabez—Grace Lippincott, 7-17-1768.[1]
   John—Hannah Cripps, 1733.[6]
   John (s. Jabez and Sarah)—Ann Roberts (d. Joseph and Susannah), 3-29-1810.[10]
   John—Mary King, 12-24-1825.[3]
   Joseph (s. William and Susannah)—Margaret Haines (d. John and Mary), 3-25-1813.[12]
   Joseph—Hannah Smith, 1-5-1826.[3]
   Nathan—Mary Moore, 1-23-1836.[3]
   Nichalas—Mary French, 1695.[5]
   Nicholas—Hannah Haddon, 9-6-1798.[3]
   Richard—Hannah French, 1695.[6]
   Thomas—Margaret Haines, 1727.[6]
   Thomas—Hannah Austin, 3-2-1795.[1]
   William (s. Nicholas)—Mary Wills (d. Daniel), Oct. 25, 1739.[6]
   William (s. Jabus and Sarah)—Guilelma Haines (d. Darling and Mary), 10-11-1804.[12]
Bye William B.—Frances Smith, 9-2-1820.[6]
Byrne, Joseph—Mary Dobson, 3-4-1778.[1]
   Patrick—Mary Ballenger, May 5, 1727.[1]
   Patrick—Mary Murrell, Aug. 13, 1741.[1]
Cafferty, William—Mary Bowen, 11-7-1771.[1]
Caffrey, George—Mary Lane, 1-18-1824.[3]
Cahill, James—Jane Taylor, 6-29-1768.[1]
Cail, Daniel—Thankful Fanning, 6-1-1770.[1]
Cain, William, Trenton—Mary Dennett, 5-31-1832.[3]
Calkitt, James—Sarah Lippincott, 3-5-1812.[3]
Call, Lawrence—Ann Anthony, 11-3-1831.[3]
Callender, William—Catharine Smith, 1731.[6]
Calvin, Bartholomew—Hester Hammitt, 5-9-1801.[3]

BURLINGTON COUNTY MARRIAGES

Camblos, George W.—Susan D. Budd, 4-11-1832.[4]
Camborn, Joseph—Sarah McGlocklin, 5-22-1807.[3]
   Joseph—Theodotia Loper, 8-24-1833.[3]
Camel, Barzillai—Beulah King, 8-9-1806.[3]
   Robert—Ann Clayton, 2-2-1828.[3]
Cameron, John—Hester McMullen, 10-3-1803.[3]
Cammerer, Henry, Jr., Philadelphia—Sarah Croner, 12-4-1796.[1]
Camp, Charles—Leuraney Estel, 4-23-1795.[3]
   Daniel—Maria White, 5-3-1832.[3]
Campbell, Arthur, Philadelphia—Mary Esdall, 9-13-1764.[1]
   Benjamin—Bersheba Gibbs, 2-1-1834.[1]
   Charles—Jemima Acey, 4-26-1806.[3]
   Colin, Rev.—Mary Martha Bard, 1742.[8]
   Jeremiah—Unity Thomas, 3-15-1798.[3]
   John—Mary Eyre, 6-10-1765.[1]
   Jonathan—Rachel Bogart, 2-5-1776.[1]
   Michael—Harriet Bond, 3-17-1820.[3]
   Robert—Mary Reed, 6-15-1807.[3]
   Thomas—Elizabeth Baker, 1-8-1797.[3]
   William, Philadelphia—Rebecca Dougherty, 7-6-1879.[4]
Campion, Charles—Keturah L. E. Jones, 2-11-1829.[1]
   John—Sarah Hall, 1-31-1804.[3]
   Joseph Jr.—Sarah Woolston, 3-2-1825.[3]
   Stacy B.—Maria Dungan, 1-20-1820.[3]
Camrin, Daniel—Vashti Lippincott, 11-15-1826.[3]
Canfield, Isaac W.—Eliza N. Lawrie, 12-14-1824.[3]
   Josiah F., Morris co.—Sarah Campion, 3-31-1835.[3]
Caregon, John—Mary Joice, 3-23-1823.[3]
Carly, Owen, Gloucester co.—Esther Watson, Aug. 20, 1742.[1]
Carlile, Amos—Sarah Williams, 3-20-1814.[3]
   John—Ann Smith, 1744.[6]
Carlisle, John—Mary Glading, 1704.[6]
Carman, Aaron—Elizabeth Stevenson, 4-7-1759.[1]
   Jacob—Sarah Heritage, 10-5-1771.[1]
   James—Margaret Harrison, 8-2-1798.[3]
   John—Anne Stockdon, Feb. 15, 1744.[1]
   John—Mary Jones, 1-25-1783.[4]
   John—Ann Carr, 6-28-1807.[3]
   William—Hannah Warren, 12-24-1829.[3]
Carmon, Caleb—Ann Warren, 11-6-1808.[3]
   Elias B.—Sarah Brown, 3-17-1830.[4]
   Elias B.—Susan Brown, 3-17-1830.[3]

Carpenter, Thomas—Mary Tonkin, 4-13-1774.¹
  Richard—Mary Tilton Krantz, 6-17-1886.²
Carper, John Deacon—Sarah Price, 5-6-1802.³
Carr, Adam—Elizabeth Yard, Sept. 25, 1740.¹
  Barzillai—Mary Forman, 10-18-1817.³
  Caleb, Rhode Island—Sarah Ridgway (d. Thomas, Jr.), 1748.¹¹
  James—Mary Calvert, both Bristol, Pa., 11-23-1771.³
  John—Deborah Bird, 11-8-1827.³
  John H.—Hannah Kinsey, 12-4-1811.³
  John L.—Ruth Bennet, 9-3-1818.³
  Solomon C.—Elizabeth Cliver, 11-4-1826.³
  Thomas—Latitia Nucles, 7-24-1797.³
  Thomas—Hannah Colket, 12-31-1825.³
Carrigas, William—Catharine Phillips, 10-8-1824.³
Carrol, George—Mary Grey, 6-1-1834.³
Carslake, William—Abigail Rockhill, 11-28-1782.¹
  William, Jr. (s. William and Abigail)—Ann Middleton (d. David and Elizabeth), 11-8-1821.⁵
Carson, Charles—Sarah Perine, 1-29-1800.³
  Charles—Rebecca Russell, 8-25-1810.³
  Daniel—Eliz. Clinton, 8-28-1824.³
  Thomas, Philadelphia—Rebecca Hays, 10-16-1831.³
  William—Priscilla Baxter, 9-9-1838.³
Carstlake, David—Anne Thomas, 1-29-1774.¹
Carter, Clayton—Sarah Webb, 1-15-1837.³
  Franklin S.—Ellen H. Woolman, 9-23-1875.²
  George—Hannah Atkinson, 12-24-1834.³
  Hudson—Achsah Harris. 1-9-1804.³
  John—Zeiruiah Rainar, 12-10-1829.³
  Joseph—Mary Gaskill, 1-2-1757.¹
  Joseph—Lavinia Still, 10-23-1826.³
  Josiah—Hannah Higgins, 2-7-1826.³
  Josiah—Elizabeth S. Beaman, 4-26-1829.³
  Micajah—Elizabeth Saint, Nov. 7, 1741.¹
  Micajah—Susannah Ewan, Feb. 22, 1744.¹
  Samuel—Margaret Stoutenburge, 6-11-1815.³
  Samuel—Rachel Brown, 4-2-1827.³
  William—Hester Pitt, 7-10-1819.³
Cartey, Charles—Hannah Caskey, 9-18-1756.¹
  Daniel—Hope Shivers, Gloucester co., 11-10-1775.¹
  Daniel—Ann Shivers, 11-4-1777.¹

Carty, Asa—Rebecca Briant, 2-19-1800.⁵
　Carrel—Bathsheba Ann Jelley, 7-29-1830.³
　John—Ann Newell, 7-3-1808.³
　John—Sarah Grant, 1-3-1825.³
　Josiah—Mary Githens, 5-29-1803.³
　Josiah—Ann Ruddorow, 2-13-1801.³
　Owen, Gloucester co.—Esther Watson, Aug. 20, 1842.¹
　Thomas—Lydia Gibbs, 10-18-1827.³
Carven, John—Margaret Taylor, 3-2-1821.³
Casler, Joseph C.—Elizabeth Higgins, 9-20-1833.³
Cassaday, William—Ann Doughty, 1-2-1834.³
Casseday, James—Rachel Dennis, 5-23-1758.¹
Cassell, Nicholas—Debarah Satterthwaite, 1726.⁶
Cassgroves, James, Philadelphia—Mary Ann Bell, 7-5-1830.³
Casselen, David—Mary Buffin, 1742.⁶
Cathcart, Caleb—Hester Vaunn, 10-3-1812.³
　Elijah—Elizabeth Gibson, 2-9-1836.³
　William—Rachel Gibson, 2-25-1833.³
Catlen, Thomas—Lydia Pettit, 7-5-1813.³
Caton, Robert—Ann Truckniss, 12-9-1760.¹
Cattell, James—Ann Rogers, May 18, 1738.¹
　James—Mary Pratt, Jan. 19, 1740.¹
　William—Rebecca Malsbury, 8-15-1801.³
Cattle, John—Mary Pearce, 1714.⁶
　John—Hannah Garret, 1-25-1826.³
　William—Thomasine Malsbury, 2-7-1796.³
Cauley, Geo. Henry—Sarah Eliz. Dillon, 7-7-1885.²
Caulket, Samuel—Jane Pedrick, 4-25-1795.³
Causter, Paul—Elizabeth Moore, 1-24-1798.³
Cavalier, David—Mary Cramer, 9-19-1782.¹
　John—Elizabeth Weeks, 2-28-1811.³
　Peter—Ann Tearney, Feb. 11-1739.¹
Cavilier, Charles—Elizabeth Weatherby, 12-2-1804.³
Cawley, Jonathan—Hannah Bsssett, 3-19-1813.⁷
　Joseph—Hannah Coal, 9-26-1838.³
　Samuel—Lydia Shreve, 9-31-1830.³
Cayler, Henry—Charity Southwick, 8-25-1767.¹
Cerrier, John—Elizabeth Richardson, 9-2-1805.³
Chadwick, John—Elizabeth Light, May 10, 1688.¹
Chafey, Thomas—Mary Buzby, 4-10-1834.³
Chafis, Samuel—Mary Edwards, 10-9-1803.³
Challender, Samuel—Rebecca Steward, 2-16-1826.³

Challener, Richard—Elizabeth Powell, Nov. 13, 1728.[1]
Chambers, David—Margaret Crocket, 12-10-1805.[3]
  Henry, Ann Woolston, 8-27-1807.[3]
  Job—Elizabeth Hubbs, Gloucester co., 1-10-1797.[3]
  Joel M.—Keziah Sweet, 5-6-1833.[3]
  John—Anne Burk, Gloucester co., 19-8-1767.[1]
  John—Hannah Hubbs. 11-1-1798.[3]
  John—Eliza Haines (d. Samuel), 1829.[14]
  Joseph—Sarah Shores, Nov. 17, 1730.[1]
  Joseph—Mary Webb, 10-21-1761.[4]
  Lewis—Elizabeth Willguss, 7-29-1798.[3]
  Richard—Anna Bispham, 5-12-1814.[3]
  Samuel—Margaret Bowers, 10-13-1813.[3]
  Samuel—Ann Keziah Simons, 12-5-1829.[3]
  William—Mary Kain, 5-23-1805.[3]
  William—Ann Rodgers, 5-15-1806.[3]
  William—Hannah Cesar, 10-26-1822.[3]
  William—Julian Sweet, 8-12-1829.[3]
Chambless, Allen—Sarah Nicholson, 4-29-1816.[7]
Champion, Benjamin W.—Anna M. Fromberger, 11-3-1856.[4]
  Mathew—Catherine Bard, 1691.[6]
  Thomas—Elizabeth Ciger, 6-10-1814.[3]
Channen, Isaac—Elizabeth Furniss, 3-11-1780.[1]
Channely, Joel—Rebecca Ann Doughty, 6-24-1837.[3]
Chapman, Abraham—Margaret Imlay, 8-1-1767.[1]
  Benj'm—Hannah Rogers, 2-7-1805.[3]
  Edward—Bathsheba Heulings, Oct. 22, 1741[1]
  Elijah—Achsah Borden, 3-27-1783.[1]
  John, Jr. (s John and Rebecca)—Lydia Middleton (d. Joseph and Avis), 6-4-1828.[5]
  Joseph—Martha Stewart, 3-24-1757.[1]
  Joseph—Elizabeth Mount. 1-10-1835.[3]
  Lewis—Hannah Giberson, 4-10-1777.[1]
  Lewis G.—Ann Dye, 2-17-1821.[3]
  Mathew—Sarah Goddas, 1-10-1835.[3]
  Robert—Harriet Harris, 11-14-1819.[3]
  Robert, Jr.—Susanna Ireton, Jan.14-1728.[1]
  William—Mary Ann Rossell, 3-16-1836.[4]
Chapple, Thomas—Mary Stevenson, 8-23-1806.[4]
Charles, Simon—Martha Fann, 1688.[6]
Charmelee, John, Jr.—Amalia Falkinburg, 11-15-1823.[8]
Chase, Joshua—Julianna Phillips, 8-29-1798.[3]

Chase, Robert G., Rev.—Susan A. Dobbins, July, 1858.[4]
Chaunt, James—Lydia Catharine Steele, 3-28-1866.[4]
Cheesman, Nathan—Rebecca Ford, 3-30-1799.[3]
   William—Hope Ward, 5-13-1814.[5]
Chemaly, Michael—Judith Alloways, 8-28-1783.[1]
Cheshlre, Samuel—Ann Robins, Sept. 13, 1740.[1]
Chew, Benjamin—Ann Branson, 4-24-1836.[3]
   Israel—Hannah Worster, 10-19-1817.[3]
   Joshua—Abigail Branin, 11-18-1827.[3]
   Robert—Elizabeth Penn, 9-25-1817.[3]
   William, Gloucester co.—Elizabeth Allinson, 4-21-1774.[1]
Chllds, John—Esther Foster, 2-9-1837.[8]
   Joshua—Ann Wilkins, 10-14-1825.[3]
Chipman, John—Jane Curtis, 1688.[6]
Chivers, James— Rebecca Doster, Apr. 1, 1641.[1]
Chloe, Edward—Rachel Hagerman (colored), 3-22-1801.[8]
Cholloner, John—Ann Lucking, 5-9-1762.[1]
Christian, John—Tamar Bowker, 3-13-1778.[1]
Christianman, Christian—Rebecca Ann Gunnels, 11-17-1831.[7]
Christopher, Charles—Rebecca Lippincott, 10-29-1815.[8]
Chubb, Thomas—Susanna Owen, 4-12-1758.[1]
Chulemela, William—Phebe Gardner, 1-31-1804.[3]
Chumard, George—Mary Allen, 11-21-1762.[1]
   William—Jane Kendall, 10-4-1773.[1]
   William—Mary Winton, Monmouth co., 1-12-1776.[1]
Church, Richard—Charlotte Cramer, 2-4-1800.[8]
   William—Margaret Stockton, 6-22-1797.
Cintoine, James, Jr.—Mary Newbould, 1725.[6]
Cirkuit, John—Hannah Woolston, 1705.[6]
Clain, Joseph—Rebecca Dudley, 1-5-1815.[3]
Clauson, Cornelius—Annie Burcham, Nov. 21, 1728.[5]
Clap, John—Martha Grimes, 12-19-1782.[1]
   William—Rebecca Wright, 1-30-1768.[1]
Capp, George—Rebecca Shinn, 9-23-1761.[1]
   John—Martha Burr, 3-17-1779.[1]
Clark, David—Elizabeth Betts, 9-16-1756.[1]
   Elisha—Martha Fenimore, 6-24-1816.[8]
   Ephraim Olden (s. Elisha and Ann), Somerset co.—Emily Shinn
     (d. Joseph and Elizabeth), 3-4-1824,[5]
   George A.—Hannah L. Jones, 12-23-1863.[2]
   Gideon T.—Ella Compton, 5-9-1865.[8]
   James—Ann Lipsay, 12-31-1796.[5]

BURLINGTON COUNTY MARRIAGES

Clark, James C. (s. Joseph)—Rebecca A. Chapman, 11-30-1860.⁴
  John—Elizabeth Green, Dec. 22, 1747.¹
  John, Bucks co., Pa.—Amy Merriott, 12-13-1774.¹
  John—Sarah Hamilton, 1-29-1778.¹
  John—Rebecca Miller, 2-2-1807.⁸
  John—Jane Cooper, 4-29-1820.³
  John—Mary Huston, 8-5-1822.³
  John L.—Sophia Ross, 8-1-1797.³
  Joseph C.—Elizabeth Coppuck, 12-27-1820.³
  Joseph C.—Cornelia Vandyke, 1-1-1852.⁴
  Reuben—Olive Clark, both Gloucester co., 9-21-1811.³
  Richard—Elizabeth Flanagan, 1728.⁹
  Robert F.—Lydia W. Osborn, 11-3-1836.³
  Samuel—Elizabeth Bennet, May 14, 1747.¹
  Thomas—Rebecca Pierson, 10-30-1788.⁴
  Thomas—Rachel Redman, 1-27-1817.⁷
  Thomas—Sarah Wright, 12-4-1874.⁸
  Thomas Cullen, Philadelphia—Abbie May Haverson, 4-22-1891.⁴
  William—Elizabeth Punner, 4-10-1778.¹
  William—Mary Donnell, 12-16-1779.¹
Clarke, Benjamin (s. Benjamin)—Hannah Lawrie (d. William), Monmouth co., 12-13-1764.⁵
  Benjamin (s. Elisha and Anne) Somerset co.—Rachel Clarke (d. Charles and Mary), Middlesex co., 3-7-1822.⁵
  Charles (s. John) Middlesex co.—Mary Skrim (d. Abraham), Salem co., 3-5-1794.⁵
  David (s. Benjamin and Hannah), Middlesex co.—Annie Olden (d. Joseph and Achsah), 4-10-1806.⁵
  Elisha (s. Benjamin), Somerset co.—Hannah Ann Olden (d. Joseph and Ann), Middlesex co., 1-9-1793.⁵
  Elisha (s. Benjamin and Hannah), Somerset co.—Sarah Hewes (d. James and Ursilla) Middlesex co., 11-7-1811.⁶
  Elisha L. (s Elisha and Ann)—Meribah F. Ellis (d. Barzilla and Mary), Middlesex co., 12-7-1826.
  Enoch (s. Benjamin asd Hannah)—Elizabeth Wood (d. William and Hannah), 2-15-1792.⁶
  Isaac (s, James), Middlesex co.—Mary Lawrie (d. William) Monmouth co., 11-9-1767.⁵
Clauts, Jacob—Sarah Farmer, 6-3-1779.¹
Clay, Samuel—Mary Ann Phillips, 10-4-1825.³
Claypool, Abraham—Hope Fennimore, 12-7-1774.¹
  Abraham—Elizabeth Higgins, 5-21-1829.³

Claypool, Abraham—Emeline Hartman, 11-30-1830.²
  David—Rebecca Ward, 11-28-1780.¹
  Wingfield—Mary Pool, 2-21-1782.¹
Claypoole, Edward Abram—Nellie Blanche Letts, 7-9-1893.²
  Jacob—Mary Kirby, 11-26-1804.³
  Joseph—Jane Killingham, 2-20-1836.²
  Joseph—Mary Bonnalt, 12-21-1837.⁸
Clayton, Bennet—Lavinia Sharp (colored), 11-11-1832.³
  Cooper—Elizabeth E. Haines, 11-15-1860.¹⁰
  James—Rebecca Hutchins, 8-8-1771.¹
  James—Ann McClong, 1-17-1835.³
  James—Mary Ann McClary, 1-14-1835.³
  John—Elizabeth Breton, June 21-1746.¹
  John—Ann Hisler, 2-15-1817.³
  Joseph—Ann Stevenson, 1-4-1769.¹
  Joseph—Amelia Gaskill, 3-16-1832.³
  Parnell—Constant Wooley, Shrewsbury, Dec. 9, 1731.¹
  Samuel—Jemima Thorn, 2-24-1796.³
Cleaveland, George—Hannah Rogers, 9-20-1756.¹
Clegg, Walter O.—Augusta Allen, 9-29-1862.³
Clement, Evan, M.D. (s. Samuel), Gloucester co.—Ann Wills (d. James and Elizabeth), 4-8-1795.⁶
  John—Haney Page, 1795.⁶
Clemer, Conrad—Mary White, Mar. 2, 1735.¹
Clevenger, Abraham—Jane Platt, July 26, 1742.¹
  Barzillai—Meribah Alcott, 3-5-1823.³
  Caleb—Margaret Hyle, 9-2-1798.³
  Daniel—Mary Logan, 12-31-1835.³
  Elias—Lydia Soper, 11-23-1826.³
  George, Deliverance Horner, July 19, 1739.¹
  Isaac R.—Mary Wright, 2-12-1828.³
  Job—Margaret Brown, 3-4-1772.¹
  Job—Sarah Alcott, 2-19-1828.³
  John—Hannah Baker, Mar. 17, 1742.¹
  John Combs—Dority Goldy, 1-8-1807.³
  John—Sarah Haley, 3-18-1826.³
  Jonathan—Mary Mills, 7-28-1803.³
  Jonathan—Kiturah Fort, 10-28-1832.³
  Richard—Hester McCoy, 3-14-1829.³
  Thomas—Hannah Renner, 3-7-1811.³
  Thomas—Priscilla Gale, 10-20-1833.³
  Samuel—Mercy Asson, Aug. 15, 1750.¹

Clevenger, William—Elizabeth Inman, 9-5-1812.[3]
    Zachariah—Mary Gaskill, 11-9-1778.[1]
Clifford, Thomas—Anna Shires, 1730.[6]
    Thomas—Ann Guest, 1740.[6]
Clifton, Henry—Jane Engle (wid.), 1703.[9]
    Hugh—Mary Wood, 1738.[6]
    Nathan—Mary Robinson, 11-21-1780.[1]
    Samuel- Susannah Castle, 2-6-1761.[1]
Cline, Isaiah—Maria Taylor, 2-20-1830.[3]
    John—Edith Jonson, 2-14-1807.[3]
    Joshua—Hepsibah Willits, 9-24-1799.[3]
    Joshua—Mary Howell, 12-25-1825.[3]
    Richard—Rebeckah Bass, 3-7-1815.[3]
    Samuel—Hannah Prickett, 9-23-1808.[3]
Clinhuff, Ephraim—Rebecca Strallein, 1-13-1762.[1]
Cliver, Benj.—Deborah Gamble, 9-6-1823.[3]
    David—Anna Rodman, 11-2-1826.[3]
    Joel—Rachel Atkinson, 1-13-1810.[3]
    Joel—Elizabeth Fort, 1-1-1815.[3]
    John—Elizabeth Harthorn, 5-8-1798.[3]
    Peter—Sarah Collins, 8-26-1781.[1]
    Samuel—Ellen Johnson, 11-30-1812.[3]
    Samuel—Esther Jane Mathis, 12-2-1837.[3]
    William—Ann Allen, 11-22-1823.[3]
Cloin, John—Ann Fuffmon, 6-26-1825.[3]
Clothier, Caleb—Elizabeth Jones, 3-15-1800.[10]
    Caleb (s. James and Mary)—Elizabeth Warrington (d. John and Mary), 12-19-1811.[5]
    Henry—Abigail Rigua, 1717.[6]
Cloud, Edward H.—Emily Haines, 12-28-1873.[10]
Clouts, Jacob—Susannah Chemilly, 4-15-1782.[1]
Clowes, Joseph—Patience Barker, 1740.[6]
Clunn, John—Elizabeth Johnson, 1-4-1816.[3]
Clutch, James—Achsah Wilkerson, 10-18-1821.[3]
    Samuel—Ella Johnson, 11-31-1812.[3]
    Uriah—Hannah Sinclear, 10-25-1821.[3]
Coahlan, Patrick—Catharine Sill, July 23, 1750.[1]
Coale, Thomas S.—Margaret Haines, 12-31-1831.[3]
Coate, Daniel—Sarah Mills, 11-8-1766.[4]
    Henry—Rachel Jones, 1-14-1783.[1]
    Marmaduke—Susan Mathis (d. John, Sr.), 1747.[11]
    Thomas—Sarah Leek, 1-2-1754.[1]

Coates, Barzillai—Mary Irick, 2-19-1812.³
  George Morrison—Anna Troth, 11-1-1840.⁴
  Joseph H.—Elizabeth W. Hornor, 10-31-1838.⁴
  Thomas—Mary Stiles, 10-2-1806.⁵
  William—Rebekkah Sharp, 1727.⁶
  William—Mary Stockton, 3-6-1817.³
Coats, Daniel—Esther Troth, 11-15-1823.³
Cob, Jacob—Catherine Mitchel, Nov. 23, 1741.¹
Cobb, Amos—Mrs. Ann Brewer, 3-7-1831.³
  Joseph, Rebecca Smith, 6-29-1835.⁶
  Oliver—Ann Brewer, 3-7-1831.³
Cobberly. Westley—Rachel Ann Horner, 6-8-1825.³
  Cobourn, John—Elizabeth Cramer, 10-6-1816.³
Cobson. James—Harriet Stevensen, 3-2-1803.³
Coer, George B.—Elizabeth Ann Darby, 8-12-1854.⁴
Coffey, Joseph—Patience Tatem, Gloucester co., 1-20-1768,¹
Coffin, William—Ann Bodine, 9-19-1798.³
  Jacob—Hannah Wilkind. 1721.⁹
Coil, Neal—Elizabeth Wills, 3-1-1804.³
Colcot, Joseph—Sarah Zelley, 12-15-1800.³
Colcott, Robert—Mary Ewing, 1-7-1771.¹
Cole, Andrew—Mary Mitchell, 7-20-1773.¹
  Chalkley—Meribah Gale, 9-29-1837.⁸
  Ezra—Mariah Mathis. 8-16-1835.³
  Henry, Jr.—Mary Hays, 1-3-1799.³
  Job—Hannah Braddock, 1815.¹⁴
  Job—Hannah Ann Lippincott, 9-5-1821.³
  John—Rebecca Lippincott, 1-7-1767.¹
  Joseph—Sarah Heulings, 2-26-1796.³
  Nathan—Rebecka Peace, 3-25-1807.³
  Samuel—Mary Lippincott, 1731.⁹
  William—Rebecca Allen, 3-8-1804.³
Coleman, Jacob (s. Samuel and Deborah)—Hannah E. Hurley (d
  Dennis and Deborah), 2-5-1824.⁵
  Jesse—Esther Cranmer, 1-25-1827.³
  John—Mary Carter, 4-19-1805.³
  Wilson A.—Martha Youngs, 11-30-1820.³
Coles, David B.—Mary Deacon, 2-26-1825.
  Ezra—Maria Mathis, 10-25-1835.³
  Job—Hannah Braddock, 10-19-1815.³
  John—Rachel Wills, 3-8-1804.³
  Joseph—Catharine Haines. 1-10-1801.³

Coles, Joseph H., Gloucester co.—Hannah N. Woolston, 9-17-1839.[3]
  Kendle, Gloucester co.—Sarah Engle, 10-20-1796.[1]
  Kemble—Neziah Lippincott, 3-17-1798.[3]
  Samuel—Mary Matlack, 5-4-1767.[1]
  Samuel W.—Mary Ann Deacon, 11-1-1821.[3]
  Thomas—Gloucester co.—Hannah Stokes, July 29, 1733.[1]
Colkett, James—Josephine R. Crammer, 5-28-1873.[4]
  Samuel—Hannah Chumelea, 3-7-1802.[5]
  William—Mary Ann Cranmer, 3-10-1829.[3]
Colkitt, James—Mary Doltin, 1-10-1819.[3]
Collet, Mark—Susan B. Wallace, 4-15-1817.[3]
Collier, Samuel—Elizabeth Bunting, 1-4-1818.[3]
Collings, Barzillai—Jemima Gifford, 5-1-1817.[3]
  Charles (s. Isaac and Rachel), New York City—Margaret Bullock (d. George and Edith), 4-8-1801.[5]
  Francis—Mary Gosling, 1687.[6]
  Joseph—Katherine Huddleston, Sept. 8, 1698.[5]
  Thomas (s. Isaac and Rachel), New York City—Ann Abbott (d. John and Susan), 9-10-1812.[5]
Collins, Abraham—Alley Smart, 3-19-1787.[1]
  Alfred—Frances Stokes, 1859.[14]
  Charles—Ruth Starkey, Sept. 29, 1748.[1]
  Charles—Elizabeth Kirkland, 3-18-1830.[3]
  Clayton—Esther Evens, 3-30-1837.[10]
  Daniel—Ann Woolston, 5-5-1833.[3]
  David—Ann Harding, 12-16-1775.[1]
  Francis—Ann Haines (wid.), 1746.[9]
  George—Joanna Roche, Oct. 30, 1731.[1]
  George—Mary Ann Parker, 1847.[11]
  James—Elizabeth Burdsall, 1774.[11]
  James—Sykes Pharo, 1804.[11]
  Job—Mary Haines, 3-17-1774.[1]
  Job—Ann Reed, 1-25-1837.[3]
  John—Ruth Burdsell, 4-4-1771.[1]
  John—Hope Wainright, 12-15-1795.[3]
  John—Annie Willits, 1804.[11]
  John—Mary Douglass, 6-1-1815.[3]
  Jonathan—Mary Cole, 5-31-1781.[1]
  Joseph—Elizabeth Mullen, 1-31-1788.[4]
  Joseph—Sarah Edwards, 2-27-1812.[4]
  Joseph—Elizabeth Norcross, 11-26-1826.[3]
  Richard—Sarah Griffith, 8-27-1759.[1]

Collins. Richard—Beulah Ivins (colored), 12-23-1826.⁶
  William—Rebecca Ann Gardner, 4-28-1821.³
  Zebedee—Hannah Atkins, both Monmouth co., 5-28-1820.³
  Zebedee, Jr.—Rebecca Rouse, 5-23-1824.³
Collock, Isaac, Elizabethtown—Elizabeth Cox, 8-31-1811.³
Colsit, Joseph—Ann Sager, 3-2-1837.³
Colson, Caleb—Sarah Bradway, 2-24-1812.⁷
  David—Jane R. Harris, 9-12-1827.³
Colston, David, Susanna Sweeney, 1-3-1817.³
Colton, Chauncy, Rev.—Anne Coxe, 10-15-1832.⁸
  Stacy—Rachel D. Mathews, 1-30-1836.³
Coltson, David—Sarah Bull, 8-26-1806.³
Colvan, John—Martha Brown, 3-15-1818.³
Colwell, William—Lucretia Mary Marling, 2-11-1771.⁸
  William—Susan Winan, 9-17-1808.³
Combs, Amos (s. Isaac and Euphemia)—Ann Woodmansee (d. Daniel and Miriam), Hunterdon co. 3-10-1808.⁵
  Benjamin (s. John and Rebecca)—Charity Craft (d. George and Mary), both Monmouth co., 12-12-1798.⁵
  David—Mary W. Cushman, 6-10-1829.³
  John, Jr.—Mary Ashton, both Monmouth co., 11-4-1795.⁵
Comfort, Jonathan, J.—Hannah Haines, 10-12-1865.¹⁰
Comley, John—Rebecca Budd (colored), 6-9-1803.
Compton, Jacob, Princeton—Elizabeth Brittain (wid.), Kingston, 4-27-1819.³
Conart, Thomas—Mary Antram, 1748.⁶
Conaroe, Job—Rebecca Tolbert, 11-28-1796.³
Conarro,'Joseph—Valeria Moore, 11-9-1760.¹
Conarrow, Andrew, Jr.—Keziah Johnston, 5-10-1756.¹
Conditt, Stephen—Mary E. Groom, 1-23-1834.³
Cundon, James—Isabella Pittman, 1-21-1762.¹
Condrick, John—Sarah Alton, 5-5-1763.¹
Condy, Jonathan W—Elizabeth Hopkins, 10-12-1797.³
Conerow, Andrew—Rebecca Arnold, Mar. 29, 1727.¹
Congo, Thomas—Hope Thomas (colored), 5-8-1824.⁸
  William—Juliana Hawkins, 11-20-1838.³
Conklin, John—Eliza Louman, 3-11-1824.⁸
Conkling. Boas—Anna Budd. 3-21-1816.³
Conn, Gilbert—Sarah Plumby, 6-27-1816.³
  Samuel—Parmelia Carter, 4-6-1771.¹
Connarow, Isaac—Rachel Hiles, 5-15-1809.³
Connel, Amos—Hannah Whitehouse, 3-10-1806.³

Conner, Thomas—Achsah Burr, 1-7-1816.[3]
Connor, Edward—Elizabeth Milligan, 3-8-1825.[3]
  John—Mary Roberts, 1-11-1773.[8]
  William—Rody Brown, 12-22-1801.[3]
Conover, David Vandeveer—Charlotte Black Read, 5-25-1864.[2]
  Elias—Rachel Gillingham, 3-7-1837.[3]
  Harvey G.—Augusta S. Rogers, 5-16-1865.[8]
  Jacob—Grace Cranmer, 1731.[11]
  John—Annie Baughman, 12-15-1885.[2]
Conrad, Solomon White (s. John and Sarah), Philadelphia—Elizabeth Abbott (d. John and Susannah), 9-9-1802.[5]
Conrew, John—Rebecka Antrim, 4-15-1812.[3]
Conrow, Andrew—Jane Antrim, 1745.[6]
  Charles—Hannah Seed, — -14-1795.[3]
  Darling—Sarah Elkinton, 8-24-1778.[1]
  Darling (s. Darling and Sarah)—Esther Hunt (d. John and Esther), 4-25-1805.[12]
  Darnel—Deliverance Stokes, Mar. 16, 1733.[1]
  Eber—Lucy Ann Shephard, 11-27-1816.[3]
  George—Naomy Tomlinson, 6-11-1788.[1]
  Isaac—Elinor Wright, 1730.[6]
  Jacob—Hope Haines, 11-5-1812.[3]
  Joel—Ann Sutton, 7-27-1820.[3]
  Samuel—Mary Hunter, 4-5-1797.[3]
  Wm.—Margaret Edmunds, 9-4-1812.[6]
Consolly, Barney A.—Harriet Smith, 4-25-1833.[8]
Cook, Daniel—Martha West, 3-22-1810.[3]
  David—Cloe Coones, 6-2-1814.[3]
  George W.—Sarah Ann Rudderow, 12-24-1835.[8]
  Israel—Abigail Bodine, 12-2-1820.[3]
  Jacob—Elizabeth Swem, 6-18-1812.[3]
  Job—Mary Warrick, 5-17-1772.[1]
  John—Sarah Crammer, 11-23-1809.[3]
  John—Ann Pharo, 1849.[11]
  John M.—Rebecca Clevenger, 2-28-1801.[3]
  John M.—Mary Richardson, 2-5-1815.[3]
  Josiah—Mary Mason, 11-22-1827.[3]
  Samuel—Mary Vansciver, 3-30-1817.[3]
  Stacy—Ann Deacon, 4-9-1782.[1]
  Thomas (s. Ebenezer and Sarah), Monmouth co.—Rebecca Coombs (d. John and Rebecca), 5-5-1814.[5]
  Thomas—Maria Ann Stockton, 12-6-1821.[3]

BURLINGTON COUNTY MARRIAGES

Cook, Wellington—Letitia Johnson, 7-4-1835.³
  William—Kitty Cox, 6-25-1807.³
  William—Martha Fenimore, 9-21-1812.³
  William—Sarah Lame, 4-4-1825.³
  William—Sarah Gooldy, 2-1-1827.³
  William—Hannah P. Bryan, 12-27-1837.³
  William B.—Eleanor Taylor, 10-1-1815.³
  William, Jr.—Mariam Mason, 9-24-1807.³
Cooke, Benjamin—Elizabeth Webb, 5-31-1759.¹
  David—Mary W. Cushman, 5-6-1829.³
  William, Philadelphia—Sarah Driver, May 12, 1730.¹
  William, Jr.—Ann Cooke, 2-21-1811.³
Cooms, Charles—Phillis Bristow, 8-28-1803.³
  Charles—Sarah Davis, 11-27-1821.³
  Isaiah—Robert (?) Squan, 3-5-1803.⁸
  Sapio—Rachel Murry, 12-8-1804.³
Cooper, Benjamin, Gloucester co.—Elizabeth Hopewell, 3-6-1759.¹
  Benjamin—Elizabeth Rowand, 10-2-1813.³
  Benjamin—Lydia Evans, 2-17-1859.¹⁰
  Benjamin W.—Elizabeth Lippincott, 2-11-1830.¹⁰
  Daniel—Deborah Middleton, 8-21-1797.³
  David E.—Elizabeth H. Wills, 11-4-1822.¹⁰
  Henry—Elizabeth Curtis, May 13, 1735.¹
  Isaac—Hannah Coate, 1726.⁶
  Jacob—Rachel Pippit, 3-10-1767.¹
  James—Elizabeth Hoiles, 12-24-1802.¹⁰
  James (s. William and Sarah), Gloucester co.—Lucy Middleton (d. Samuel and Sarah), 11-23-1837.⁵
  John—Gloucester co.—Anne Clark (d. Benjamin and Ann), Somerset co., Mar. 18, 1712/13.⁵
  John—Rebecca Eayre, 5-1-1783.¹
  Nathan— ——Pancoast, 1-22-1797.⁷
  Peter K., Esther Johnson, 6-19-1831.³
  Richard—Henrietta Jones (colored), 3-23-1833.³
  Samuel, Gloucester co.—Prudence Brown, 2-7-1767.¹
  Samuel R.—Rebecca Lippincott, 3-18-1897.¹⁰
  Thomas—Elizabeth Cooper, 9-13-1758.¹
  William, Gloucester co.—Ann Folwell, 5-4-1768.¹
  William, Pennsylvania—Elizabeth Fenimore, 11-12-1774.¹
  William—Ann Miller, 1-27-1800.⁷
  William—Maria Jackson, 8-9-1838.⁴
Copner, Hugh—Matilda Anderson, 3-10-1824.³

Copp, Elliphaif, Dr,—Deborah Copperthwaite, 1821.[14]
Copperthwaite, Hugh—Keziah Atkinson, 1734.[6]
  Hugh—Hannah Atkinson, Apr. 19, 1737.[1]
  Jonathan, Monmouth co.—Elizabeth Richardson, 1-27-1810.[3]
  Thomas—Mary Borden, Feb. 19, 1733.[1]
Coppock, Bartholomew—Amy Cox, Aug. 4, 1730.[1]
  Daniel K.—Esther K. Hughes, 1-26-1820.[3]
  James—Emeline Allen, 2-18-1834.[3]
  James D.—Rebecca S. Clark, 12-14-1847.[4]
  Peter V.—Eleanor Hollingshead, 12-12-1827.[4]
Corey, Peter—Martha Walker, 4-29-1784.[1]
Corkford, James—Jane Rymar, 11-13-1798.[8]
Corlis, William—Ann Cox, Middlesex co., 6-3-1756.[1]
  William—Elizabeth Davis, 2-5-1809.[3]
Corliss, George—Mary Branson, 9-19-1803.[3]
Corncan, John A.—Rebecca H. Gibbs, 3-2-1837.[3]
Cornelius, James—Sarah Bennet, 4-30-1827.[3]
  Joseph—Rebecca Ludy (colored), 6-27-1835.[8]
Cornell, William—Hannah Mott, 9-17-1834.[3]
Cornew, John—Rebekah Antrim, 4-15-1812.[3]
Cornwell, Emerson B.—Ruth Ann Brown, 12-20-1821.[3]
Corry, William—Martha Roy, 1-11-1766.[1]
Corson, Daniel—Ann Hebbarn, 8-11-1786.[3]
Cosseboom, Nathaniel—Anne Venables, 8-24-1861.[1]
Costill, Benj.—Rachel Morris, 3-6-1803.[3]
  Hugh—Hannah Hilliar, 4-2-1787.[1]
  Hugh—Sarah Ayres, 8-27-1833.[3]
  Joseph—Hannah Ridgway, 5-27-1816.[7]
  Josiah—Elizabeth Austin, 10-13-1825.[10]
  Okie H.—Mary Ann Eayre, 3-2-1825.[8]
  Samuel—Mary Spachus, 4-16-1829.[8]
Costroe, Joseph—Anna Sharp, 8-29-1759.[1]
Cotman, William—Bridgett Stewart, 5-11-1800.[3]
Cotton, George—Hannah Polk, 7-12-1869.[2]
  Isaac—Charity Bennett, 12-1-1805.[3]
Couch, Isaac—Sarah Brittin, 1-13-1839.[3]
Coughlin, Samuel—Ann Weber, 5-22-1861.[8]
Courtland, Samuel, Island of Jamaica—Sarah Norris Tallman, 1-19-1800.[3]
Courtney, Francis—Mary Ross, 8-16-1801.[3]
Coward, Clayton—Elizabeth Darby, 12-18-1825.[3]
Cowen, Michael—Margaret Brian, 8-10-1763.[1]

BURLINGTON COUNTY MARRIAGES

Cowgill, Aaron—Sarah Kelley, 3-31-1814.³
  Edmund—Mary Johnson, Aug. 3, 1736.¹
  Edward—Ann Osborne, 1707.⁶
  George—Elizabeth Sowden, 1-24-1776.¹
  Henry—Mary Batton, 1724.⁶
  Jacob—Parthena Imley, 11-15-1777.¹
  John—Elizabeth Ridgway, 11-12-1761.¹
  Nehemiah—Joyce Smith, 1717.⁶
  Nicholas—Esther Davis, 11-12-1761.¹
  Ralph—Susannah Pancoast, 1697.⁶
  Stephen—Ally Simmons, 11-11-1804.³
  Thomas—Diana Edwards, 12-25-1834.³
Cowperthwaite, Job S.—Frances Maria Shinn, 12-17-1835.
  John—Mrs. Ann Chapman, Monmouth co., 3-15-1821.³
  Stacy (s. Job and Anna)—Rebecca Burrough (d. Reuben and Mary), 1-15-1824.¹²
  William—Hope Shreve, 2-4-1767.¹
  William—Martha Stratton, 2-2-1797.³
  William (s. Job and Ann)—Martha W. Justice (d. Joseph and Esther), 10-1-1818.¹²
  William—Elizabeth R. Jones, 1-24-1836.³
  William H.—Rebecca Sterling—12-5-1821.³
Cox, Abraham Beekman (s. Abram B. and Levantia), Albany—Augusta McBlair TenEyck (d. John C. and Julia), 4-30-1873.⁴
  Benj.—Rebecca Lamb—2-11-1802.³
  Benj.—Keziah Eayres, 9-16-1812.³
  David—Sebiney Rogers, 1-16-1816.³
  Edward—Frances Hill, 4-4-1816.³
  Jacob—Hannah Havens, 1-16-1819.³
  James—Hannah Brock, 2-6-1798.³
  James—Elizabeth Pope, 8-8-1822.³
  Jesse—Susan Deacon, 11-8-1832.³
  John—Abigail Ellis, Sept. 30, 1744.¹
  John—Elizabeth Ambruster, 12-3-1778.¹
  John—Hannah Smith, 10-25-1780.¹
  John—Eliza Heivin, 2-21-1813.³
  John—Elizabeth Lamb, 8-11-1806.³
  Joseph—Hannah Haines, 8-31-1761.¹
  Joseph, Trenton—Elizabeth Monrow, 11-9-1826.³
  Joseph B.—Lydia Seaman, 12-27-1836.³
  Joseph S.—Mary Jane Brown, 11-1-1855.⁴
  Leuza A.—Mary A. Thompson, 9-5-1829.³

Cox, Richard—Elizabeth Newbury, June 18, 1730.[1]
   Richard, Rachel Bradshaw, 10-12-1775.[1]
   Richard—Ann Elton, 6-11-1805.[3]
   Richard S.—Susan Griffith, 1-23-1816.[8]
   Richard S.—Ann Leeds, 4-21-1828.[3]
   Richard S.—Mary Deacon, 2-26-1835.[3]
   Samuel—Barbara Salar, 12-10-1756.[1]
   Samuel—Elizabeth Hopewell, 11-2-1775.[1]
   Samuel—Mary Sutts, 12-20-1780.[1]
   Samuel, Jr.—Sarah Emley, 10-17-1774.[1]
   Samuel W.—Mary Gyberson, 10-27-1833.[3]
   Silvanus—Mary Burtall, 9-8-1811.[3]
   Thomas—Sarah Ward, Mar. 21, 1750.[1]
   Uz—Diademia Witcraft, 4-16-1824.[3]
   William—Rachel Mason, 12-15-1761.[1]
   William K.—Mary Belange, 12-25-1832.[3]
   William W.—Mary R. Southwick, 3-28-1836.[3]
Coxe, Richard—Susannah Matson, 4-18-1799.[3]
   William, Jr.—Rachel Brockhay, 1-25-1810.[3]
   William S., Dr.—Eliza Barbarouse, 11-3-1825.[3]
Coxton, Joel—Mary Boody, 12-11-1829.[3]
Craddock, David—Sarah Nummock, 12-17-1759.[1]
Craft, Abel—Mary Stille, 10-8-1824.[3]
   Emlen—Ann Garrison, 5-16-1833.[3]
   George—Mary Lanning, 1-14-1760.[1]
   George—Ann Troth, 3-23-1820.[10]
   George—Mary S. Norcross, 5-7-1835.[3]
   Gershom—Lydia Hancock, Nov. 25, 1741.[1]
   James—Margaret Rockhill, 7-19-1758.[1]
   James, Jr.—Mary English, Oct. 21, 1740.[1]
   John—Sarah Rockhill, 3-19-1772.[1]
   Joseph—Esther Ridgway (d. Job), Barnegat, 1786.[11]
   Samuel—Hannah Lanning, 12-29-1763.[1]
Craig, John—Elizabeth Parrott, 1725.[6]
Craine, Ervin—Sarah Pippitt, 10-23-1832.[3]
Cramer, Azariah—Rachel Cooper, 6-19-1831.[3]
   Caleb, Jr.—Ann Darby, 12-18-1831.[3]
   Charles—Mary Gaskill, 4-6-1809.[3]
   Clerkson—Harriet Ridgway, 6-20-1824.[3]
   Courtney—Catharine M. Deacon, 2-7-1823.[3]
   Darius—Sarah Cramer, 1-3-1833.[3]
   David—Rachel Allen, 6-8-1767.[1]

C ramer—George—Lucy Cole, 1-7-1807,³
  Gideon—Mary Giberson, 3-25-1826.³
  Isaac—Rebecca Jones, 7-1-1765.¹
  Job—Sarah Cramer, 7-15-1824,³
  John—Margaret Smith, 7-23-1757.¹
  John L.—Latisha Leeds, 3-15-1822.³
  Jonathan—Ann Brewer, 3-31-1814.³
  Joseph B.—Ann Mathis, 10-2-1825.³
  Joshua B.—Sarah S. Thompson, 3-14-1830.³
  Levi—Susannah Fiffer, 5-21-1815.³
  Levi—Esther Horn, 1743.¹¹
  Richard—Sarah Perkins, 10-10-1757.¹
  Samuel—Lydia Corin, 6-16-1784.¹
  Seemon—Phebe Devinney, 6-12-1766.¹
  Seemor—Mary Smith, June 23, 1737.¹
  Stephen—Sarah Little, Oct. 31, 1749.¹
  Stephen—Ruth Loveland, 10-1-1761.¹
  William—Hannah Leeds, Gloucester co., 3-14-1774,¹
  William—Mary Adams, 3-15-1818.³
 Cranmer, Abraham—Abigail Birdsall, 1758.¹¹
  Bornt S.—Anna Haines, both Manahawkin, 3-20-1861.⁴
  Caleb, Sr.—Phebe Mathis (wid. of Job, Sr.), 1792.¹¹
  Jacob (s. John)—Phebe Valentine, 1756.¹¹
  John—Mary Andrews, 1721.¹¹
  John—Rebecca Stout, Shrewsbury, 1726.¹¹
  Josiah—Susan Earlin, 8-1-1807.³
  Stephen—Nancy Robbins, 4-7-1803.³
  Stephen W.—Mary H. Penpuite, 2-15-1835.³
  Thomas—Abigail Willits, 3-10-1716.¹¹
  Thomas—Mary Ridgway, 1728.¹¹
  William—Ruth Southwick, 1716.⁶
  Willits—Hannah Pharo, both Monmouth co., 10-8-1809.³
 Cramp, John—Martha Fenei, 1-1-1798.³
 Crane, Nathan L.—Mary Buzby, 3-3-1827.³
  Samuel—Mary Mick, 3-27-1835.³
 Craven, Thomas—Elizabeth Sydenham, 2-7-1771.⁵
 Crawford, David—Susan McAlpin, 11-2-1799.³
  Robert—Mary Page, 11-18-1798.³
  Uz—Mary Donley, 4-14-1821.³
  William—Charlotte Read, 9-27-1808,³
  William—Maria Sharp, 6-28-1835.³
  Crawley, Samuel—Amy Pettit, 1787.¹¹

Crayne, John—Mary Ellwell, Feb. 19, 1727.[1]
Creby, Hugh—Abigail Smart, 6-19-1765.[1]
Creely, Nelson—Hannah Hancock, 2-14-1835.[3]
Crider, Jacob—Mary Ann Coleman, 11-9-1829.[3]
Crim, William—Mary Breeds, 6-21-1835.[3]
Cripps, Benjamin—Mary Hough, 1734.[6]
  John—Mary Eves, 1731.[9]
  Samuel—Hannah Lawrie, 1744.[6]
Crispin, Abel—Hannah Evans, 3-10-1796.[3]
  Benjamin—Margaret Owen, 1722.[9]
  Benjamin—Rachel West, 2-16-1784.[1]
  Benjamin—Agnes Hutchinson, 10-29-1817.[3]
  Caleb—Mary Buzby, 4-10-1834.[3]
  Charles—Hannah Sage, 11-24-1825.[3]
  George—Elizabeth Reeve, 9-22-1807.[3]
  Jacob—Ann Chub, 7-18-1781.[1]
  Jonathan— ——— Hewlings, 5-14-1770.[1]
  Joshua—Rachel Lippincott, 5-10-1779.[1]
  Joshua—Abigail Hackney, 6-16-1807.[3]
  Micajah—Rachel Conner, 10-3-1811.[3]
  Paul—Hannah Wright, 10-30-1831.[3]
  Seth—Hannah Strattan, 12-8-1789.[1]
  Silas—Patience Haines, 1745.[6]
  Thomas—Hester Hueston, 3-14-1812.[3]
Croak, Nicholas—Elizabeth Kirkpatrick, 11-14-1812.[3]
Crocket, Benj.—Rebecca Wiltsey, 10-18-1808.[3]
  John—Hannah Whiley, 12-30-1802.[3]
Crockett, John—Catherine Grapevine, 9-20-1773.[1]
Crombwell, Lewis—Elizabeth Thompson, 4-23-1836.[3]
Crompton William—Elizabeth Neale, 10-31-1797.[3]
Crowell, Sibarton—Martha Foard, 1-25-1811.[3]
Cronders, Nathan—Dorothy Easely, 11-30-1786.[1]
Crooks, John—Hannah Smith, 4-20-1796.[3]
  Richard—Sarah Voto, 2-26-1783.[1]
Crosby, John—Mary Shinn, 1686.[6]
  John—Elizabeth Wilson, 1737.[6]
Croshaw, George—Meribah T. Warren, 12-13-1387.[3]
  Isaiah—Ann Leeds, 4-2-1779.[1]
  Isaiah—Anna Stockton, 9-7-1801.[3]
  John—Rebecca Briggs, 4-25-1774.[1]
  John—Elizabeth Stockton, 3-6-1800.[3]
  John—Eleanor Stillwell, 2-15-1829.[3]

BURLINGTON COUNTY MARRIAGES

Croshaw, Josiah—Jarasa Gooldy, 4-5-1804.²
   Thomas—Hannah Whitton, 3-18-1783.¹
Crosher, John—Sarah Antrom, 1735.⁶
Croskey, Joseph—Maria Thernsa Macomb, 7-4-1833.⁸
Crosley, Edward—Mary Nelson, 8-18-1810.³
   William—Sarah Ann Buzby, 8-23-1835.³
Cross, Caleb—Levina Witcraft, 10-15-1818.³
   Caleb—Rebecca Randall, 9-25-1856.⁴
   George O.—Rachel Barklay, 8-2-1839.³
   John—Anne Butterworth, 12-5-1784.¹
   Joseph—Hester Williams, 9-1-1827.³
   Joseph—Martha Jane Garwood, 10-3-1833.⁴
   Joseph—Florence Zelley, 12-16-1874.²
   Samuel—Sarah Nickels, 4-8-1820.³
Crosson, Charles, Jr.—Fanny Reed, 12-26-1824.³
Crosthan, Thomas—Dorothy Weaver, 3-7-1765.¹
Crosthwaite, Harrison—Abigail Corwine, 5-2-1818.³
Crowner, George H.—Grace A. Woolman, 8-21-1825.³
Crues, James—Sarah Forsyth (d. Matthew and Rebecca), May 23, 1734.⁵
Crumble, Jacob—Rhoda Boulton, 1-3-1808.³
Crusher, John—Rachel Antrum, 1742.⁶
Crutzell, Thomas A.—Levinia Carman, 1-7-1813.³
Cubberly, Isaac—Anne Hooper, Middlesex co., Dec. 7, 1749.¹
   James—Anne Minging, Oct. 31, 1745.¹
   James—Anne Ford, 11-8-1777.¹
   Samuel—Ruth Stanhope, 5-10-1827.³
Cullen, Thomas F. Rev., Tioga, Pa.—Mary Jane Clark, 10-30-1860.⁴
Culver, John—Catharine Stout, 10-3-1835.³
Cummings, John—Nancy Warris, 1-29-1809.³
   Obediah—Ann Pidgion, 6-10-1824..
   Thomas—Mary Craig, 1753.⁹
   William—Hannah Gifford, 9-10-1821.³
Cundy, William—Sarah Jane Clothier, 1-3-1834.³
Cunningham, Andrew—Ann Brown, 6-12-1754.¹
   Bernhard—Jane McDowell, 5-11-1798.³
   George—Patty Gaskill, 5-6-1803.³
   George—Sarah Vandergrift, 2-20-1788.¹
   John—Elizabeth Ervine, 12-31-1781.¹
   Joseph, Trenton—Mary Ann Raum, 11-19-1824.³
   Thomas—Sarah Bowles, Mar. 15, 1748.¹
   Thomas—Sarah Meyers, 11-23-1826.⁸

Cunningham, William—Elizabeth Ridgway, 4-29-1757.[1]
Curly, Joel—Hannah Hill.   Recorded 2-7-1829.[3]
Currey, William—Martha Rogers, Dec. 8, 1749.[1]
Curry, Henry—Elizabeth Fowler, 8-28-1818.
  Thomas—Tabitha Frieze, 8-10-1802.[3]
Curtis, Asa—Elizabeth Ridgway.   No date given.[3*]
  Clark—Maria Hay, 11-7-1805.[3]
  David—Charlotte Tilton, 2-28-1802.[3]
  John, Capt. Bowman's Co.—Sarah Wood, 2-5-1781.[1]
  John, Jr. (s. John and Rebecca)—Sarah Taylor (d. John and Sarah), 3-10-1785,[5]
  Joseph—Elizabeth Kelley, 10-21-1795.[3]
  Nathaniel—Eliz. Heulings, 7-10-1712.[8]
  Robert—Jane Carter, 2-5-1776.[1]
  Thomas (s. John)—Elizabeth Ellis (d. Thomas), Nov. 21, 1694.[5]
  Thomas—Abigail Conrow, 9-1-1767.[1]
  Thomas—Nancy Kelly, 2-28-1803.[3]
  Thomas—Ann L. Hughes, 6-22-1826.[3]
  William—Kesiah Cox, 6-8-1795.[3]
  William—Mary Lippincott, 2-8-1821.[3]
Curty, William—Rebecca Atkinson, 1-11-1827.[3]
Cush, Jacob—Sarah Abraham, 10-15-1800.[3]
Custer, Samuel—Elizabeth Ellis, 1-5-1800.[3]
Cutler, Thomas—Martha Thomson, 4-29-1766.[1]
Dagy, John, Philadelphia—Harriet Norcross, 1-4-1817.[3]
Dalton, Henry—Hannah Hammock, 12-13-1777.[1]
Daly, Charles—Margaret Hamilton, 9-18-1808.[3]
Dancer, John D.—Mary Ann Robbins, 10-20-1830.[3]
Danford, Samuel—Mary Groom, Sept. 12, 1737.[1]
  William—Esther Foster, 4-6-1778.[1]
Dangner, Peter—Elizabeth Lannen, 7-27-1808.[3]
Darbyshire, John—Elinor Gregg, Aug. 12, 1731.[1]
Dare, John—Mary Crawford, 7-30-1819.[3]
Darley, Recompense—Sarah Allen, 6-7-1812.[3]
Darnell, Charles—Lydia Haines, 1-15-1852.[10]
  David,—Mary C. Evans, 2-11-1806.[10]
  Edward—Jane Driver, 1754.[9]
  Howard—Elizabeth Haines, 3-10-1868.[10]
  Isaac—Sarah B. Saunders, 1-13-1825.[10]

---

*Married by Samuel Wright, J. P.

Darnell, John—Hannah Borton, 1722.[9]
Joshua—Elizabeth Lippincott, 10-21-1812.[10]
Josiah (s. Josiah and Susan)—Mary L. Haines (d. **Darling and Mary**), 12-20-1821.[9]
William—Rachel Holland, 3-20-1827.[3]
Daton, Joseph—Mary Shealds, 3-7-1824.[3]
Daugherty, Lawrence M.—Mary Ann Reeve, 2-3-1826.[3]
Daughton, Wm.—Unity Folwell, 4-20-1806.[3]
Davenport, Francis (wid.)—Rebecca Decow, Oct. 12, 1692.[5]
George W.—Anna B. McNeill, 9-18-1831.[3]
Joseph—Elizabeth Gibbs, 5-11-1757.[1]
Samuel—Ruth Price, 1-10-1765.[1]
Davids, James—Elizabeth Guyan, 12-10-1818.[3]
Davidson, Benjamin—Hannah Brewer, 6-5-1817.[3]
James—Hannah Newell, 1-3-1802.[3]
James—Ann Jones, 8-25-1827.[3]
John—Amy Hay, 4-23-1772.[1]
John—Ann Shinn, 12-7-1778.[1]
John—Minnie Emma Bryant, 3-23-1890.[2]
William—Lacy Holden, Oct. 4, 1746.[1]
William—Elizabeth Eastlack, 8-4-1777.[1]
Davies, David—Jane Stackhouse, Pennsylvania, Aug. 9, 1731.[1]
John—Hannah Carter, May 11, 1736.[1]
John, Martha Ward, 9-10-1765.[1]
Davis, Andrew—Mary Hatkinson, 7-1-1781.[1]
Andrew—Margaret Stackhouse, 9-13-1812.[3]
Benj.—Jemima Brown, 6-7-1802.[3]
Benjamin—Mary Haines, 5-9-1822.[13]
Curtis—Mary Hornor, 11-15-1858.[4]
David—Mary Musgrove, 1733.[9]
David—Jane Philips, 9-14-1754.[1]
David—Mary Haines, 11-16-1798.[10]
Edward—Experience Lathbury, 1-14-1804.[1]
Gabriel—Sarah Ballinger, 1743.[9]
Gabriel, Jr.—Sarah Garwood, 4-29-1883.[3]
George—Elizabeth Vanzant, Pennsylvania, 2-10-1828.[3]
Grant (s. John J. and Mary)—Mary Jane Plasket (d. John and Charlotta), 4-18-1889.[4]
Hewet—Mary Pearson, 7-6-1809.[3]
Howell—Margaret Antrum, 4-18-1761.[1]
Howell—Sarah Cliver, 11-16-1816.[3]
Isaac—Mary Wistar, 4-26-1813.[7]

Davis, Israel—Rebecca Hains, 7-13-1826.²
Jacob—Mary Stratton, 9-24-1792.⁷
James—Jane Richardson, 5-9-1774.¹
Job—Mary Ann Smith, 11-25-1818.²
John—Sarah Forsyth, 9-28-1826.³
John—Diadema Bishop, 3-8-1762.¹
John—Elizabeth Beatty, Trenton, 10-6-1795.³
John—Mary Johnson—9-7-1803.³
John—Rebecca Nixon, 10-24-1812.³
John—Nancy Ann Whye, 7-25-1835.³
John—Ann Jane McFarland, 10-13-1866.²
Jonathan, Chester, Pa.—Martha Garwood, Mar. 31, 1737.¹
Jonathan—Esther Haines, 1742.⁹
Joseph—Abigail Havens, 9-23-1753.¹
Joseph—Mary Cook, 3-18-1824.³
Joseph—Rebecca King, 2-12-1826.²
Joshua—Susanna Lamb, 3-22-1801.³
Josiah—Charlotte Britton, 1-12-1832.³
Samuel—Mary Kelly, 11-7-1783.¹
Samuel C.—Mary Prickett, 6-15-1826.³
Sampson—Susan Freeman, 6-1-1839.³
Sheldon H.—Sarah A. Fenimore, 11-27-1862.²
Thomas—Rebecca Conrow, 11-9-1797.³
Thomas—Ann Weatherby, 5-15-1830.²
Thomas—Sarah Higgins, 3-5-1831.²
Thomas—Sarah Wooley, 2-24-1838.³
William—Sarah Stockton, 1-9-1761.¹
William—Lydia Connaroe, 6-1-1788.⁴
William—Mary Evans, 2-22-1803.²
William—Rachel Ivins, 12-10-1803.³
William, Jr. (s. William)—Ann Vincomb (d. William), June 24 1735.⁶
Dawson, Francis—Rachel Jesse, 1729.⁶
Jeremiah—Anne King, 7-29-1778.¹
John—Grace Searle, Pennsylvania, 4-5-1768.⁸
Richard—Lydia Silvers, 1743.⁶
Day, Augustus—Abigail Smith, 6-28-1799.³
Walter—Sarah Cubberly, 6-14-1806.³
Daymond, Samuel—Elizs Cole, 12-5-1832.³
Dayton, William—Rebecca Pharo, 6-25-1834.³
Deacon, Allen N.—Margaret Dunlap, 9-9-1852.⁴
Amos H.—Rebecca Perkins, 12-15-1831.²

BURLINGTON COUNTY MARRIAGES

Deacon, Barzillai—Lydia Swame, 1-21-1802.³
  Barzillai—Mary Hancock, 11-8-1832.³
  Benajah—Elizabeth Budd, 12-15-1836.³
  Benjamin—Hannah Hewlings, 12-19-1816.³
  Benjamin H. (s. Joseph and Rebecca)—Annie S. Zelley (d. Clayton and Mary) 5-21-1879.⁴
  Charles—Rebecca D. Buzby, 11-13-4837.³
  Charles H.—Catharine Wright, 1-1-1838.³
  Charles Henry—Louisa Peacock, 12-31-1867.²
  Daniel—Beulah Woolston, 9-24-1829.³
  David—Sarah Hutchinson, 5-4-1809.³
  George—Martha Charles, 1693.⁵
  George—Joan Fennimore, Jan. 1, 1728.¹
  George—Ann Burr. 1-29-1757.¹
  George—Achsah Hutchins, 9-19-1805.³
  George—Hannah Woolman, 2-16-1815.³
  Henry C.—Elizabeth Stokes, 3-1-1832.³
  Jeremiah Haines—Hannah Ann Gilbert, 10-21-1898.²
  Job—Mary Atkinson, 3-14-1784.¹
  Job—Mary Adeir, 2-22-1810.³
  John—Esther Wills, 1726.⁶
  John—Hannah Eayres, 11-20-1787.¹
  John B.—Caroline R. Smith, 11-16-1880.⁴
  John, Jr—Hannah Elton, Mar. 16, 1748.¹
  Joseph—Mary Chambers, 11-30-1808.²
  Joseph P.—Emily Ann Schuyler, 11-25-1824.³
  Joseph R—Elizabeth Busby, 10-5-1826.³
  Samue—Mehitabel Rogers, 3-20-1762.¹
  Samuel, Tuckerton—Eliza Allen, Bass River, 11-23-1818.³
  Thomas—Mercy Stiles, 3-17-1796.³
  Thomas—Mary Haines, 1-3-1798.³
  W. Budd—Wilhelmina Lintz, 10-4-1865.²
  Wilbert—Sarah French, 12-19-1803.³
  William—Elizabeth Rogers, 1-25-1764.¹
  Wm.—Sarah Garwood, 4-27-1804.³
Deals, George—Hannah Lee, 6-20-1811.³
Dean. Peter—Catherine Stout, 10-14-1809.³
Deaton, Joseph—Lydia Ridgway, 11-21-1802.³
Decker, Nicholas—Lydia Minion, 11-7-1765.¹
Decou, Charles—Rachel Barton, 2-14-1867.¹⁰
    Eber—Sarah Eves, 1743.⁹
    Isaac—Mary Cripps, 1737.⁹

Decou, Isaac, Jr.—Hannah Nicholson, 1733.[6]
Thomas H.—Martha H. Moore, 4-1-1831.[3]
Decow, Daniel (s. Isaac and Mary)—Margaret Taylor (d. James and Abigail), 4-9-1801.[5]
Francis—Sarah Walsh, Nov. 26, 1734.[1]
Isaac—Anne Davenport, Apr. 24, 1705.[5]
Isaac (s. Daniel and Margaret)—Miriam H. Taylor (d. William and Ann), 1-7-1836.[5]
Jacob—Jane Duncan, Sept. 20, 1736.[1]
Joseph (s. Eber)—Achsah Taylor (d. John), 10-15-1778.[5]
Nathan (s. Isaac and Mary)—Deborah Coleman (d. Samuel and Deborah), 12-6-1832.[5]
Robert—Jane Gibbs, 2-18-1813.[3]
Samuel (s. Isaac and Mary)—Mary Lawrie (d. Thomas and Anne), 12-8-1796.[5]
Stacy (s. Isaac and Mary)—Helena Abbott (d. William and Rebecca), 10-12-1820.[3]
Wesley—Keziah Ewen, 5-17-1832.[3]
William (s. Stacy and Helena), Mercer co.—Cathrin Middleton (d. Allen and Cathrin), 11-14-1844.[5]
Dehart, Henry—Dority Story, 11-11-1805.[3]
Dehony, Nicholas—Jane Jennings, 5-23-1808.[3]
Delaplaine, John—Sarah Johnson, 1739.[11]
John—Mary Bustill, 1745.[6]
Nicholas—Sarah Ong (d. John, Sr.), 1731.[11]
Delatush, Henry—Rebecca Thompson, 12-15-1761.[1]
John—Elizabeth Garwood, 4-18-1759.[1]
Delavane, Joseph—Rosanna Pinear, 4-11-1825.[3]
Dell, Richard—Elizabeth Decow, June 5, 1695.[1]
Richard—Elizabeth Bennett, Aug. 11, 1698.[1]
Delzell, Thomas—Elizabeth Jacoby, 8-8-1803.[3]
Dempsey, William—Amey Whitaker, 12-11-1787.[4]
Deney, William—Patience Bolsworthy, Monmouth co., 7-11-1761.[1]
Denight, Joseph—Martha Brown, 12-31-1788.[4]
Dennis, Aaron—Mary Carter, 12-6-1817.[3]
Alfred Samuel (s. John W. and Angeline)—Martha Smith Grosvenor (d. John and Jane), 10-13-1887.[4]
Anthony—Eliza Ann Preston, 11-15-1823.[3]
Burton—Rhoda Crawford, 4-28-1834.[3]
Charles—Ann Matilda Starkey, 8-23-1837.[3]
Edmond—Mary Johnston, 9-12-1797.[3]
James—Sarah Elmore, Mar. 20, 1738.[1]

Dennis, James Barton (s. Barton and Lydia)—Mary English Hughes (d. William and Ann), Philadelphia, 12-24-1874.[4]
    John, Jr.—Elizabeth Taylor, 1-19-1826.[3]
    Lippincott F.—Emma R. Stiles, 12-13-1862,
    Philip—Elizabeth Skirm, 11-27-1761.[1]
    Thomas—Eliza Butler, 1-27-1839.[3]
    William—Mary Rogers, June 1, 1737.[1]
Denton, Robert—Jane Moon, Feb. 12, 1738.[1]
Depuy, John—Hannah Sutton, both Bucks co., Pa., 9-18-1819.[3]
    Tolbot W. C.—Frances Craig Moffett, 4-19-1865.[8]
Deveney, John—Mary Humpner, 6-13-1779.[3]
    John—Mahala Mathis, 8-10-1800.[3]
Deveny, John—Sarah Brown, 7-30-1815.[3]
Devenney, Richard—Martha Helverton, 2-24-1798.[3]
Deviney, William, Jr.—Elizabeth Peters, 9-17-1795.[3]
Devinne, William—Mary Flitcraft, 1-21-1797.[3]
Divinney, Clayton—Susan Asey, 3-1-1831.[3]
    Michael—Ann Ridgway, 8-23-1817.[3]
    William—Lydia Robinson, 4-27-1829.[3]
Devinny, Clayton—Charlotte Haines, 12-13-1814.[3]
Devo, Conrad—Sarah Stratton, 10-23-1765.[1]
Dewall, Garret—Annie M. Tyler, 9-26-1828.[2]
Dewell, John—Hannah Pearce, 1730.[6]
Dey, Jno. V.—Anna R. Kingdon, 10-29-1872.[8]
Dezelles, David—Deborah Kelley, 3-21-1811.[3]
Dick, James—Lucia Richardson, 10-29-1772.[5]
    Joseph B.—Rhoda Witcraft, 10-8-1828.[3]
Dickards, Peter—Salamy Lawrence, 2-6-1759.[1]
Dicker, Michael—Catharine Sutphine, 9-9-1771.[8]
Dicks, Curtis—Elizabeth Bennett, 3-26-1797.[3]
Dickson, Thomas—Ann Cavaleer, 1-7-1817.[3]
Dikes, Thomas—Sarah Burkee, June 18, 1731.[1]
Dilks, George—Sarah M. Pancoast, 2-20-1829.[3]
Dillen, Archibald—Ann Shields, 1-21-1802.[3]
    William—Mary Gaugh, 11-25-1808,[3]
Dillon, James—Catherine Vaughan, 6-5-1779.[1]
    James—Mary Ann Hutchinson, 4-12-1831.[8]
Dilwin, James—Lydia Gillingham, 9-18-1819.[3]
Dilworth, William Skinner—Ida Josephine Crevier, 12-15-1886.[2]
Dingwell, Philip—Mary Daily, Nov. 7, 1750.[1]
Dinner, Septimus—Mary Gaskill, 3-24-1808.[3]
Dinsmore, James—Martha McComb, 5-13-1829.[3]

Disbery, Robert—Mary Kimber, 8-4-1820.[3]
Diviney, Jesse—Rebecca Piper, 10-30-1803.[3]
Divinney, William—Lydia Robinson, 4-2-1829.[3]
Divinny, Charles—Susanna Thomas, 10-9-1823.[3]
Dix, Curtis—Hannah Elsden, 10-2-1827.[3]
Dixon, Thomas—Catherine Myers, 4-28-1778.[1]
Dobbins, Edward T.—Martha Read, 12-14-1826.[3]
  George W.—Abigail Fowler, 1-13-1831.[3]
  Hillman—Mary Lippincott, 7-27-1834.[3]
  Isaac—Mary Ann Brown, 3-1-1830.[3]
  James—Anne Fox, 9-7-1767.[1]
  James—Lydia Prickett, 1-24-1814.[3]
  James, Jr.—Sarah Carty, 1-12-1779.[1]
  Joab—Elizabeth Iredell, 8-4-1777.[1]
  Joab—Mary Cline, 3-8-1809.[3]
  John—Susannah Ridgway, 2-7-1796.[3]
  John, Jr.—Mary Murrel, 12-23-1779.[1]
  John, Jr.—Sarah B. Read, 5-6-1829.[4]
  Mycajah—Hannah Eayres, 6-25-1781.[1]
  William—Mary Eldridge, 3-24-1774.[1]
  William—Sarah Leeds, 3-18-1804.[3]
  William—Rebecca Crushaw, 2-29-1806.[3]
  William—Abigail Brock, 2-1-1816.[3]
Doble, Benj.—Hester Lucas, 12-11-1823.[3]
Dodd, Joshua—Rebecca Scott, 1-11-1818.[3]
  Thomas—Ann Boone, May 8, 1734.[1]
  William—Mary Fowler, 3-24-1804.[3]
Doldy, Isaac—Pamela Martin, 4-1-1808.[3]
D'Olier, William—Anne Woolman, 6-8-1875.[8]
Doltin, Joseph—Ann Atkinson, 2-12-1818.[3]
Donald, Thomas M.—Josephine Prickett, 10-28-1861.[8]
Donally, Daniel—Mary Thomas, 4-4-1777.[1]
Donley Daniel—Susannah Davis, 8-2-1818.[3]
Donnelly, William—Catherine Johnson, 4-11-1775.[1]
Donnolly, Bryan—Susanna Collins, May 10, 1738.[1]
Donoly, Joseph—Rebecca Lippincott, 11-25-1809.[3]
Dorinward, Robert—Elizabeth Otway, 10-5-1767.[1]
Dorel, Samuel—Mary Gale, 1-20-1816.[3]
Doron, Charles Henry—Rachel Ellis Woodward, 4-16-1891.[2]
  John—Mary Steward, 9-7-1773.[1]
  John—Rebecca Hartgrove, 10-19-1822.[3]
  Joseph—Mary Johnston, 11-1-1805.[3]

BURLINGTON COUNTY MARRIAGES

Doran, Joshua—Elizabeth Bugbie, 12-54-1801.[3]
  Stacy, Jr.—Eliza Morgan, 1-29-1836.[3]
  Thomas—Sarah Leeds, 12-13-1777.[1]
  William—Roxanna Pricket, 9-2-1836.[2]
Dorton, William—Martha Garrottel, 7-9-1798.[1]
Dorvat, John—Elizabeth English, 7-14-1817.[3]
Dory, James—Ann McIlvaine, 12-9-1778.[1]
Dotey, Ebenezer—Mehitable Shinn, 7-10-1778.[1]
  Ebenezer—Margaret Woolston, Sept. 21, ——.[1]
  William—Rachel Murphy, 1-8-1776.[1]
Doty, Whitehead—Mary Jameson, 10-2-1796.[3]
Doubty, Daniel—Hannah Johnston, 8-23-1808.[1]
Doughaday, Thomas—Hannah Stout, 5-2-1829.[3]
  William—Sarah Platt, 4-7-1803.[3]
Dougherty, Cornelius—Susannah Shaw, 7-24-1802.[1]
  James—Elizabeth Ridgway, 5-5-1815.[3]
  Samuel—Mary Hay, 3-22-1821.[3]
Doughton, George F—Susanna Stokes, 12-21-1839.[3]
  John—Ann Adams, 4-20-1762.[1]
Doughty, Thomas—Hannah Wells, 3-24-1831.[3]
Douglas, Charles—Mary Ann Vandergrift, 2-1-1834.[1]
  George—Atlanah Wood, Sept. 28, 1741.[1]
  Joseph—Benjamina Walker, 9-23-1768.[1]
  Thomas, Monmouth co.—Elizabeth Borden, Jan. 9-1734.[1]
Douglass, Harry—Cora Anna Atkinson, 9-15-1900.[2]
  James—Charity Emmons, 9-4-1813.[3]
  John—Rachel Pearson, Sept. 24, 1730.[1]
  Joseph—Caroline Luke, 12-5-1811.[3]
  Robert—Lucy Stout, 11-16-1778.[1]
Dowd, William—Mary Knapp, 8-2-1832.[3]
Dowell, Henry—Phebe Taylor, 10-20-1816.[3]
Downe, William—Mary Cassida, 1-4-1801.[3]
Downing, Timothy—Sarah Little, 12-30-1783.[1]
Downs, James—Elizabeth Earl, 1-27-1759.[1]
  Robert—Elizabeth Bevington, 12-18-1817.[1]
  Samuel—Abigail Austin, 11-24-1783.[1]
  William—Elizabeth Morse, 4-21-1804.[3]
Downy, William—Ann Dayton, 12-14-1817.[3]
Draper, Alfred John—Agnes Holman, 7-4-1892.[2]
Driver, John—Mary Sparks, May 13, 1749.[1]
Drindy, John—Lucida Trusty, 9-10-1825.[3]
Duble, Abraham—Ann H. Stackhouse, 12-23-1824.[1]

Dable, James—Elizabeth Burtin, 2-28-1819.³
   James—Mrs. Ann Rockhill, 11-11-1834.³
Duche, Andrew, Philadelphia—Hannah Shords, June 21, 1731.¹
Duckworth, John—Sarah Hankins, Mar. 20, 1734.¹
   Joseph—Esther Ong, June 1. 1737.¹
   William—Hannah Clevenger, Aug. 21, 1731.¹
   William—Mary Wright, Dec. 6, 1731.¹
Dudley, Charles—Martha Morris, 3-5-1812.³
   Francis—Rachel Wilkins, 1733.⁹
   Francis—Susan Lippincott, 2-16-1832.³
   Isaac—Mary Borton, 12-4-1801.³
   John—Rachel Braddock, 11-14-1804.¹⁰
   Nathan—Anna B. Haines, 2-9-1837.³
   William—Lydia Carns, 1-31-1828.⁵
Dueate, Enoch—Flora Plumby, 11-8-1811.³
Duel, John—Lydia Lippincott, 3-31-1794.⁷
Duffee, William—Hannah Jones, both Monmouth co., 12-5-1820.³
Dugdale, Thomas—Sarah West, 10-7-1815.¹³
Dulcy, Thomas—Hannah Ann Lacal, 4-13-1838.³
Dunfee, William—Elizabeth Jervis, 9-6-1763.¹
Dungan, Joseph D.—Theodosia B. Keeler, 11-3-1844.⁴
Dunham, Benjamin—Jane Ogden, 6-27-1772.⁸
   Kimble—Jane Land, 3-28-1821.³
Dunlap, Thompson—Sarah Morrow, 7-31-1815.³
Dunn, Miller—Mary Latas, 4-20-1836.³
   William—Mary Wheat, 1715.⁶
Durell, Abner—Abigail Marter, 2-20-1834.³
   Henry—Ann Birdsill, 5-9-1830.³
   Jeremiah (s. Johathan and Grace)—Harriet Lippincott (d. Jehu and Achsah), 4-8-1824.⁵
   John—Elizabeth Fenimore, 8-21-1777.¹
   Jonathan—Ann Sogers, 12-1-1825.³
   Martin—Sybilla Leeds, 1-13-1784.¹
   Samuel—Ann Linsey, 12-19-1802.³
   Samuel—Catharine Marter, 12-6-1832.³
   William—Jemima Brown, 2-8-1821.³
Durnell, Isaiah—Mary Haines, 1787.¹¹
   Isaiah—Sarah Bartlett (d. Nathan, Sr.), 1794.¹¹
Durr, John Jacob—Sarah Ann Grooms, 12-31-1836.³
Dury, James—Ann Eldridge, 10-12-1829.³
Dusser, Florimund Joseph—Elizabeth Mortimer, 5-25-1797.⁸

Dutcher, Peter—Rebecca Gale, 2-18-1808.³
Dutton, Abraham—Hannah White, 12-28-1817.³
Duvell, William—Thaney Wills, 1-8-1801.³
Dyer, John—Margaret Glass, July 28, 1730.¹
  Joseph. Rachel Prickett, 10-21-1803.³
Eames, Daniel Henry—Mary Greenleaf Cole, 3-31-1852.⁴
Earl, Anthony S.—Elizabeth Budd, 8-30-1801.³
  Caleb—Hester Gardiner, 5-5-1779.¹³
  Daniel—Hannah Shinn, 7-10-1798.³
  John—Ester Hall, 11-16-1761.¹
  John—Abigail Smith, 5-5-1785.¹³
  John—Mary Tulley, 9-14-1811.³
  John—Keziah Shreve, 2-18-1813.³
  John P.—Mary Wetherill, 2-14-1817.³
  Samuel—Hannah Folwell, 11-4-1778.¹³
  Samuel W.—Anna Wetherill, 10-14-1822.³
  Taunton, Martha Newbold, 4-25-1830.³
  Thomas—Mary Cripps, 1727.⁶
  Thomas—Judith Bostido, Monmouth co., Sept. 30, 1736.¹
  Thomas—Mary McLeary, 2-5-1785,¹
  William—Mary Sharp, 1739.⁹
  William,—Mary Warren, 9-12-1783.¹
  William L.—Harriet Harvey, 10-4-1814.³
Earle, John, Sr.—Abigail Haines, 1-9-1798.³
  Thomas (s. Taunton and Mary)—Edith Sykes (d. Anthony and Mary, 4-15-1778.⁵
Earling. Daniel. Rebecca Herber, 2-23-1768.¹
Early, George—Sarah Norcross, 1-14-1830.³
  Jacob—Hannah Prickett, 4-16-1757.¹
  Jacob—Mary Burr, 3-11-1832.³
  James—Eliza Lutts, 10-16-1818.³
  John—Mary Cawman, 2-8-1810.³
  William (s. James and Eliza)—Mary Adelaide Crammer (d. Zadock and Martha), 6-5-1872.⁴
Earrick, John—Sarah Gibson, 9-15-1776.¹
Ears, Obediah—Rachel Fields, 12-25-1805.³
Eastburn, Cyrus—Aseneth S. Haines, 3-21-1861.¹⁰
  Jonathon—Beulah Gaskill, 10-11-1816.¹³
Eastlack, Edwin, Philadelphia—Margaret Holland, Princeton, 3-1. 1836.³
Eaton, Thomas, Huntingdon co—Sarah A. Anderson, 2-3-1830.³
Eayre, Habakkuk—Mary Jones, May 24, 1747.¹

Eayre, John—Rebecca Rogers, 9.20-1756.[1]
    Joseph—Charity Ballenger, 9-5-1767.[1]
    Richard—Sarah Garwood, Dec. 2, 1732.[1]
    Samuel—Elizabeth Eayre, 2-26-1829.[3]
    Stacy—Sarah Nixon, 2-9-1837.[3]
    Thomas W.—Sarah H. Stretch, 2-1-1830.[3]
Eayres, Abraham—Sarah Lamb, 3-13-1806.[3]
    Edward—Lisa ——— (colored), 3-23-1801.[3]
    Hosea—Hannah Leeds, 9-2-1773.[1]
    Samuel—Sarah Ann Eayres, 5-5-1836.[3]
Eberline, Gotleib—Mary Carty, 7-30-1875.[2]
Eckman, John Lewia Prescott—Susan Barrington (d. William and Eliza), 12-20-1876.[4]
Ecret, Isaac—Lydia Bogart, 8-24-1776.[1]
Edgman, William—Elizabeth Thimble, 1-7-1754.[1]
Edman, William—Dorothy Powell, 8-12-1779.[1]
    Thomas—Bulah Ewan, 11-10-1825.[3]
Edmond, William—Agness Bozough. 7-25-1825.[3]
Edwards, Abel—Ann McDevitt, 3-24-1829.[3]
    Alexander—Matilda Higgins, 1-3-1803.[3]
    Asa—Eliza Newton, 11-20-1828.[3]
    Benjamin H.—Mary Lutts, 2-3-1826.[3]
    John—Mary Ingram, 1700.[6]
    John—Susannah Bennet, May 6, 1746.[1]
    John—Letitia Moon, 8-17-1756.[1]
    John—Jane Wood, 9-13-1801.[3]
    John, Jr.—Sarah Briant, 5-29-1799.[3]
    Josiah—Claria Pippett, 2-3-1799.[3]
    Moore—Nancy Thorn, 5-26-1810.[3]
    Noah—Hannah Downs, 5-12-1832.[3]
    Owen—Sasannah Farnsworth, Apr. 11, 1732.[1]
    Samuel—Sarah Ptule, 8-27-1827.[3]
    William P.—Susan Wilkins, 8-30-1827.[3]
Egbert, Elisha—Sarah Filer, 8-12-1833.[3]
    John C.—Ann W. Stewart, 2-9-1834.[3]
Egee, Joseph—Mary Clark, both Bucks co., Pa. 3-2-1836.[3]
Eggleston, Reuben—Elizabeth Shamaley, 8-5-1796.[3]
Elberson, Daniel—Mary Cline, 12-21-1825.[3]
    Griffith—Hannah Shinn, 12-14-1826.[3]
    Jacob—Sarah Johnson, 10-14-1810.[3]
    Jacob—Margaret Babcock, 8-19-1813.[3]
    Samuel—Hannah Scott, 6-6-1815.

Elbertson, William—Rebecca Zane, 6-9-1831.³
Eldridge, Abraham—Mary Lippincott, 1757.⁹
  Jabez—Hannah Forker, 1-7-1771.¹
  Jabus—Esther Reeve, Nov. 12, 1746.¹
  Jabus—Mary Hopewell, 12-30-1776.¹
  James—Esther Rogers, June 4, 1739.¹
  James—Mary Haywood, 6-4-1796.³
  Jesse—Mary Reese, 5-2-1778.¹
  Job—Rebecca Smith, 3-9-1805.³
  Job—Jane Lippincott, 3-8-1816.¹⁰
  John—Abigail Watson, 8-19-1802.³
  Jonathan—Mary Antrum, Sept. 12, 1744.¹
  Jonathan—Abigail Atkinson, 1750.⁶
  Noah—Margaret Haines, Sept. 31, 1739.¹
  Obadiah—Achsah Haines, 11-28-1764.¹
  Obadiah—Hannah Smith, 3-2-1796.³
  Obadiah—Rachel Peters, 5-9-1798.³
  Obadiah—Rachel H. Atkinson, 11-29-1804.³
  Obadiah—Elizabeth Farrow, 12-8-1816.³
  Obadiah, Jr—Ann Wilson, Apr. 21, 1740.¹
  Reuben—Ann Endicott, Apr. 29, 1751.¹
  Solomon—Elizabeth Fort, Dec. 31, 1744.¹
  William—Sarah Crispen, 1-20-1772.¹
  William—Elizabeth Hooten, 12-16-1818.³
Elkincton, George—Mary Bingham, Jan. 13, 1683.¹
Elkington, George—Mary Core, 1688.⁶
Elkinton, Asa—Letitia Lippincott, 11-24-1788.⁷
  Fenton—Elizabeth H. Hewling, 3-27-1817.⁴
  George—Sarah Perrine, Feb. 18, 1748,¹
  George—Bulah Wells, 7-21-1783,¹
  Joseph—Elizabeth Antrum, 1713.⁶
  Joseph—Elizabeth Haines, 9-14-1815.³
Ellemor, George—Elizabeth Miller, 9-30-1824.⁸
Ellenberger, William Martin—Bertha Risdon, 10-15-1896.²
Ellett, John—Mary Smith, 4-11-1792.⁷
Elliot, John—Sarah English, 3-14-1809.³
Ellis, Aaron—Susannah Ellison, 5-7-1754.¹
  Barzillai (s. John and Elizabeth), Monmouth co.—Mary Wright (d. Ebdnezer and Elizabeth), Middlesex co., 2-5-1807.⁵
  Benj—Sarah Bishop, 3-11-1802,¹
  Benjamin, Philadelphia—Mary Abbott (d. John and Anne), Nov. 24, 1720.⁵

Ellis. Charles, M.D.—Elizabeth Anna Byles, 7-14-1869.[8]
    Charles (s. Wright and Agnes)—Mary Stella Kelly, 9-8-1892.[4]
    David (s. John and Elizabeth)—Ann Middleton (d. Jacob and Hannah), 3-10-1808.[5]
    Francis--Elizabeth Hunt, 1733.[6]
    Francis—Leah Brown, 10-7-1754.[1]
    Job—Mary Gard. 3-25-1769.[1]
    John (s. Francis)—Lucia Ridgway (d. Richard), 5-12-1762.[5]
    John, Monmouth co.—Elizabeth Fowler, 10-17-1776.[5]
    Joseph—Ann Bullers, 1-17-1785.[1]
    Peter—Miriam Middleton, 4-18-1771.[5]
    Peter (s. John)—Abigail Stockton (d. Samuel, 5-7-1812.[13]
    Rowland—Sarah Allison, 4-17-1815.[8]
    Samuel—Meriam Cox, 1-6-1814.[3]
    Samuel—Mary Earl, 3-4-1819.[13]
    Thomas—Margery Hutchins, July 12, 1740.[1]
    Thomas, Gloucester co.—Anna Humphries, 4-9-1765.[1]
    William—Mary Taylor, 10-15-1779.[1]
Ellison, David—Rhoda Carr, 5-4-1824.[3]
    James—Ann Addis, 2-11-1758.[1]
    James—Hannah Ireton, 4-19-1778.[1]
    Jesse—Lydia Hayne, 3-19-1787.[4]
    John, Monmouth co.—Catharine Vandyke, 3-1-1756.[1]
    John—Elizabeth Doughty, 3-23-1758.[1]
    Samuel—Ruth Smith. 12-31-1792.[7]
Elmer, Lucius Q. C.—Emeline Clark, 7-4-1852.[4]
Elton, John—Elizabeth Williams (wid. of Col. William), Philadelphia, 11-27-1800.[3]
    Robert—Sarah Woolman, Apr. 18, 1737.[1]
    Samuel—Mary Fetters, 4-29-1821.[3]
    Thomas—Margaret Griffin, 7-7-1769.[1]
Elverton, Nicholas—Phebe Taylor, 12-9-1777.[1]
Elwell, David—Mary Haines, 1740.[9]
Ely, Gervas—Mary Briggs, 12-28-1825.[3]
    Henry P.—Mary Reeves, 2-15-1844.[10]
    Hugh B. (s. Jesse and Rachel), Bucks co., Pa.—Sarah M. Olden (d. Joseph and Achsah), 10-13-1814.[5]
    John, Hunterdon co.—Phebe Allison, May 3, 1731.[1]
Embly, William—Hannah Piper, 6-23-1808.[3]
Emond, Isaac—Rebecca Vanhorn, 11-25-1837.[3]
Emlay, Richard (s. William and Mary), Hartford, Conn.—Maria Milnor (d. Joseph and Sarah), Trenton, 10-12-1811.[5]

Emlay, Solomon—Sarah Satherwaite, 1-31-1802.³
Emlen, George, Jr. (s. George), Philadelphia—Ann Reckless (d. Joseph), Dec. 5, 1740.⁵
Emley, Cyrus—Elizabeth Miller, 1-14-1800.³
  Daniel—Hannah Nutt, 12-3-1801.³
  Daniel—Jane Poinsett, 12-3-1807.³
  Henry—Mary Chamberlain, 9-9-1838.³
  James—Sarah Divinny, 11-24-1810.³
  James—Achsa Horner, 10-22-1814.³
  John—Elizabeth Emley, 2-15-1806.³
  Joseph—Sarah Steward, Monmouth co., 2-13-1767.¹
  Joseph—Phebe Mills, 11-23-1772.¹
  Joseph, Monmouth co.—Martha Emley, 10-29-1818.⁸
  Samuel—Ann Kirby, 11-21-1775.¹
  Samuel—Elizabeth Hutchinson, 1-5-1811.³
  Samuel—Charlotte DeCamp, 1-27-1831.³
  Samuel, Jr., Catharine Andries, 5-21-1763.¹
  Thomas—Elizabeth Wardell, 11-14-1753.¹
  William—Elizabeth Saxton, Freehold, July 15, 1746.¹
  William—Susan Decamp, 2-20-1822.³
  William T.—Elizabeth Willits, 12-8-1810.³
Emmery, Samuel—Anna Looker, 1-16-1813.³
Emmons, Benjanin—Sarah King, 1824.¹⁴
  Isaac—Rhoda Johnson, 9-30-1834.³
  Jesse—Elizabeth Fraser, 6-15-1811.³
  Jesse—Abigail Rogers, 11-26-1831.³
  Jeremiah—Mary Cheeseman, 12-17-1835.³
  Julius—Margaret Haines, 1-24-1817.³
  Samuel—Elizabeth Taylor, 5-6-1809.³
Endicot, John—Ruth Matlock, Oct. 19, 1749.¹
Endicott, Barzilla—Anne Norton, 4-12-1779.¹
  Thomas—Sarah Welsh, 6-19-1759.¹
England, Abraham—Catharine Wright, 3-28-1838.⁸
  Edward—Elizabeth Moran, Nov. 4, 1741.¹
Engle, Abraham W.—Elizabeth Peacock, 3-1-1826.⁸
  Abraham—Sarah Engle, 6-18-1835.³
  Arthur—Elizabeth Engle, 12-7-1820.³
  Eber W.—Aliceina B. Peacock, 3-10-1825.³
  George C.—Acksa Cook, 1-5-1826.³
  Ikshua*—Hope Small, 5-3-1802.³

---

*Joshua in index.

Engle Job C.—Louisa Caroline Forman, 12-31-1825.³
  John—Mary Ogborn, 1707.⁹
  John—Hannah Middleton, Nov. 11, 1737.¹
  John—Hannah Weatherby, 8-19-1802.³
  Joseph—Mary Borton, 1760.⁹
  Joseph—Mary Haines, 6-7-1810.¹³
  Morris—Rosanna McIntosh, 5-23-1829.²
  Robert—Rachel Ann Engle, 1-8-1827.³
  Samuel—Sarah Myers, 8-21-1775.¹
Englehart, John—Mary Marian. 9-23-1779.¹
English Abraham, Mary Eddis, Aug. 11, 1744.¹
  Abraham—Elizabeth Price, 9-22-1874.¹
  Abraham—Hannah Richardson, 2-23-1815.³
  Amos—Mary Craft, 3-7-1765.¹
  Amos—Ann Brown, 10-25-1801.³
  Asa—Mary Leviné, 9-27-1804.²
  Benjamin—Lydia Vandyke, 10-5-1761.¹
  Daniel S.—Elizabeth Severn, both Bucks co., Pa. 5-12-1836.³
  Enoch—Elizabeth Sedgwick, 3-17-1821.³
  George—Eliza Hance, 2-18-1824.³
  George—Mary Ann Walton, 9-18-1862.⁸
  Isaac—Rebecca Warner, 1-13-1764.¹
  Isaac—Susannah Thomas, 6-27-1805.³
  James (s. Joseph and Abigail)—Thomesin Wright (d. Isaac and Sarah), 2-16-1804.⁵
  James—Abigail English, 4-7-1822.³
  Jesse—Rebecca Prior, 3-29-1804.³
  John—Margaret Barris, Bucks co., Pa., Sept. 10, 1744.¹
  John—Anne Inskeep, Sept. 20, 1749.¹
  John—Leah Ellis, 1-6-1796.²
  John—Lurania Zanes, 5-4-1822.³
  John, Jr.—Elizabeth Andrews, 12-31-1809.²
  Joseph—Abigail English. 8-2-1770.¹
  Joseph (s. Joseph and Elizabeth)—Triphena Wilson (d. William and Abigail), 4-16-1783.⁵
  Joseph—Elizabeth Pope, 1-8-1795.¹³
  Joseph—Ruth Fenimore, 1-11-1816.³
  Joseph, Jr.—Mary Butler, 10-27-1769.¹
  Moses—Margaret Fisher, 8-24-1805.²
  Moses—Sarah Rockhill, 7-1-1831.³
  Nathaniel—Margaret Tully, 3-4-1810.³
  Samuel—Elizabeth Hammel, 11-13-1762.¹

English, Samuel—Elizabeth Rockhill, 8-28-1783.[1]
Samuel—Elizabeth Hornor, 11-1-1834.[3]
Squire—Ann Gaskill, 4-17-1800.[3]
Thomas—Ann Smith, Feb. 17, 1733.[1]
Thomas, Jr.—Ann Rockhill, 3-10-1768.[1]
William—Catherine Davison, 12-3-1785.[1]
William—Rebecca Folwell, 1-9-1800.[3]
Enoch, Thomas—Mary Haines, 10-16-1759.[1]
Epley, William—Charlotte Hewit, 11-15-1835.[3]
Ernest, Daniel—Sarah Lame, 3-13-1779.[1]
Ervein, Robert—Ann Eliza Curtis, 9-15-1845.[4]
Ersan, Julius—Elizabeth Wright, 1752.[9]
Esdall, Edward—Mary Kinison, 3-14-1744.[1]
John—Sarah Ellis, 1-3-1768.[3]
Samuel—Abigail Vansciver, 12-29-1797.[3]
Thomas—Elizsbeth Palmer, July 1, 1738.[1]
Thomas—Rachel Mollikan, 6-28-1764.[1]
Eslow, John—Susannah Battison, 10-9-1807.[3]
Estal, Nicholas—Elizabeth Johnson, 10-30-1803.[3]
Estell, Daniel—Hannah Fort, 11-3-1761.[1]
Samuel—Anne Fort, 12-26-1759.[1]
Estello, John—Jane Gamble, 4-14-1824.[3]
Estelow, Benj.—Mary Haley, 1-1-1816.[3]
James—Phebe Hews, 9-23-1831.[3]
Esthouser, Ludwick. Cathrine Garret, 5-5-1799.[3]
Estill, Joseph—Meribah Morton, 10-6-1831.[3]
Richard—Rebecca Fenimore, 2-8-1829.[3]
Estilow, Christopher—Sarah Lowden, 12-26-1826.[4]
Estle, Joseph—Sarah Tash, 11-9-1800.[3]
Lewis—Rebecca Veal, 5-1-1834.[3]
Estlow, Charles—Hannah Jacobs, 3-29-1817.[3]
Estow, Godfrey—Lottie Symons, 1-9-1785.[1]
Etris, John—Esther Morton, 1-14-1812.[3]
Ettinger, John—Theodosia Watson, 11-18-1775.[1]
Evans, Absalom—Hannah Gaskin, 1738.[6]
Amos—Elizabeth Gant, 12-18-1823.[10]
Beriah—Rebeckah Jones, 3-22-1810.[3]
Charles H., Jr.—Alice John, 4-12-1922.[10]
Darling (s. William and Rachel)—Rachel Matlack (d. William and Letetia), 1-19-1826.[3]
David—Sarah E. Roberts, 4-14-1836.[10]
David—Sarah Warner, 12-15-1836.[3]

Evans, Eli—Mariah Barrett, 10-8-1829.[30]
  Elwood—Sarah Evens, 3-27-1873.[1]
  Enoch (s. William and Rachel)—Rebecca Tomlinson (d. Samuel and Mary), Waterford, 3-24-1814.[3]
  Evan—Mary Collins, 1823.[14]
  Isaac—Bathsheba Stokes, 1740.[9]
  Isaac—Esther Collins, 4-1-1782.[1]
  Isaac—Hester Bishop, 8-23-1810.[3]
  Isaac, Jr.—Mary Smith, 4-23-1777.[7]
  Jacob—Rachel Eldridge, 1749.[9]
  Jacob—Mary Cherrington, 1756.[9]
  Jacob—Meribah Jones, 11-25-1830.[3]
  James—Barbary McKenny, 1-28-1810.[3]
  James—Ann Hedley, 5-12-1832.[3]
  James, New Orleans—Sarah Peacock, 8-24-1836.[3]
  John—Abigail Lippincott, 10-22-1903.[10]
  John C.—Kezia Hackney, 8-18-1875.[2]
  John W.—Martha E. Gibbs, 6-6-1839.[3]
  Joseph—Elizabeth Bishop, 2-9-1789.[13]
  Joseph—Lydia Barnes, 10-28-1800.[3]
  Joseph—Elisabeth Bishop, 3-25-1813.[3]
  Joseph—Rebecca Wills, 11-2-1816.[3]
  Joseph—Lydia Wills, 4-16-1868.[10]
  Joseph B.—Priscilla Haines, 3-20-1862.[10]
  Joseph G.—Sarah F. Wills, 5-11-1882.[10]
  Latham—Elizabeth Cooper, 4-25-1804.[3]
  Levi—Parham Lippincott, 1-23-1809.[3]
  Lott—Lydia Channell, 8-18-1756.[1]
  Lott—Basheba Chester, 10-10-1809.[3]
  Miles—Rebecca Sharp, 11-1-1810.[3]
  Nathan—Hannah French, 3-7-1792.[1]
  Nathan—Rebecca Griffin, 3-31-1831.[3]
  Robert—Rachel Sulcey, Philadelphia, 1-6-1820.[3]
  Robert T., Chester co., Pa.—Elizabeth Ridgway, 10-8-1803.[3]
  Samuel I.—Lydia S. Wilkins, 2-21-1832.[3]
  Thomas—Esther Haines, 1715.[9]
  Thomas—Rebekkah Owen, 1730.[6]
  Thomas—Diana Cassel, 7-4-1738.[8]
  Thomas (s. Enoch and Mary)—Abigail Bispham (d. Thomas and Hannah), 12-20-1804.[12]
  Thomas—Sarah Burrough, 3-13-1815.[10]

BURLINGTON COUNTY MARRIAGES 77

Evans, Thomas B. (s. William and Rachel)—Mary Matlack (d. George and Sarah), 2-13-1823.³
   Uriah—Rachel F. Sanders, 2-17-1831.¹⁰
   Walter—Rebecca T. Antrum, 5-27-1823.³
   William—Sarah Roberts, 1738.⁹
   William—Susan Evans, 3-20-1834.¹⁰
   William, Jr.—Elizabeth B. Evens, 11-14-1867.¹⁰
Evarts, Edward—Eliza King, 8-7-1829.³
Evelman, Joseph—Jemima Rockhill, 1-3-1821.³
Evens, Eby—Rebecca Eavs, 11-25-1798.³
   Evan—Sarah Middleton, 6-30-1777.¹
   Howard—Helen Lippincott, 9-1-1898.¹⁰
   Jacob L.—Elizabeth L. Evens, 10-11-1877.¹⁰
   Jesse—Ann Camp, 5-28-1818.³
   Joshua R.—Rebecca Evans, 11-18-1922.¹⁰
   Thomas—Elizabeth L. Saunders, 3-18-1852.¹⁰
Evergan, John—Rachel Gale, 4-17-1831.³
Everham, Adam—Anne Mathews, 3-5-1818.³
   Isaac—Evaline Conrad, 8-24-1815.³
   John—Elizabeth Harvey, 11-9-1804.³
   Joshua—Ann I. Taylor, 2-1-1827.³
   William C.—Sarah Gibbs, 7-2-1854.⁴
Everingham, Benj.—Elizabeth English, 10-17-1805.³
   Joseph—Mary Gilbert, Apr. 19, 1751.¹
   William—Abigail Sherrard, 2-2-1773.¹
   William—Lydia Jones, 9-30-1777.¹
   William—Susannah Bennet, 1-4-1810.³
   William—Mary Horner, 2-10-1814.³
Eves, George—Mary Conrow, 11-3-1835.³
   John—Mary Hudson, Aug. 10, 1710.⁶
   John—Jane Evans, 1752.⁹
   Robert—Mary Olive, 1696.⁶
   Samuel—Jane Wills (d. John), Dec. 2, 1713.⁶
   Samuel—Mary Shinn, 1721.⁶
   Samuel—Hannah Gardiner, 4-10-1828.³
   Samuel—Jane E. Haines, 4-11-1861.¹⁰
Ewall, Isaac—Ann Vansciver, 1-8-1814.³
Ewan, Absalome—Rachel Grant, 7-1-1764.¹
   Alexander—Mary White, 12-25-1826.³
   Ambrose—Anne Trenton, Apr. 30, 1729.

Ewan, Charles Henry (s. Job and Mary)—Mary Augusta Sharp
(d. Job and Mary), 3-5-1889.[4]
  David—Hannah Small, 4-7-1814.[3]
  Evan—Mehitable Weaver, 6-5-1770.[1]
  Job—Mary Parker, 1-16-1835.[3]
  John—Martha Enocks, Nov. 23, 1737.[1]
  John—Susannah Burtis, 2-28-1770.[1]
  Julius—Anna Motte, May 23, 1733.[1]
  Levi—Sarah Shaver, 3-29-1784.[1]
  Moses—Rebecca Stokesberry, 5-1-1782.[1]
Ewans, Barzilla—Elizabeth Hays, 3-2-1764.[1]
Ewen, Job—Mary C. Parker, 2-14-1835.[3]
  Joseph—Martha Edmonds, 1-9-1817.[3]
Ewin, Charles—Levinia Jones, 2-19-1819.[3]
Ewing, Absalom—Kesiah Taylor, 3-6-1773.[1]
  Alexander—Susan Little, 4-1-1829.[3]
  Daniel—Sabilla Willets, 3-17-1827.[3]
Eyer, John H.—Margaret Jones, 11-9-1817.[3]
Eyre, George—Rebecca Shreve, 4-10-1754.[1]
  George—Mary Lippincott, 9-30-1789.[1]
  James—Margaret Hays, 1-22-1818.[3]
  Thomas—Elizabeth Lippincott, 1751.[9]
Eyres, Asa—Anne Wilkins, 1-17-1797.[3]
  George—Mary Smith, May 15, 1729.[1]
Ezdall, James—Elizabeth Fordham, 9-27-1764.[1]
Fagan, Robert—Mary Gray, 10-8-1809.[3]
  William—Lydia Chambers, 10-31-1822.[3]
Fagen, James—Mary Asey, 12-23-1769.[1]
  James—Mary Quigley, 6-27-1772.[1]
Fagins, William—Patience Jervis, 1-7-1768.[1]
Fairholm, Joseph—Sarah Loper, 10-27-1816.[3]
Fairland, John—Mary Schenck, 11-10-1829.[3]
Fairman, Thomas—Elizabeth Kinsey, 1680.[6]
Falkenburgh, Timothy, Tuckerton—Elizabeth Parker, 9-19-1838.[3]
Falkinbridge, David—Faith Cook, Shrewsbury, 3-18-1767.[1]
Falkinburg, Hezekiah—Ann Rochelle, 3-27-1834.[3]
  Samuel—Hannah Truax, 6-13-1834.[3]
  Samuel C., Jr.—Sarah Monrow, both Tuckerton, 5-11-1834.[3]
Falkingburgh, Henry Jacob, Jr.—Penelope Stout, Shrewsbury,
1731.[11]
  Jacob—Phebe Southard, 2-8-1764.[1]
Falkner, Jess—Isabell Jones, Pennsylvania, Aug. 25, 1741.[1]

Fammage, Daniel—Suffiah Head, 8-18-1813.[3]
Farehollen, Isaac—Mary Pindel, 7-27-1822.[3]
Farguson, John—Elizabeth Dagworthy. Feb. 10, 1730.[1]
  Shadrack—Lydia Nicholas, 11-3-1786.[1]
  Robert—Abigail Enocks, 10-9-1784.[1]
Farmer, Andrew—Jemima Cunningham, 12-17-1763.[1]
  George—Theadosia C. Long, 5-17-1819.[3]
Farnsworth, Amariah—Elizabeth Whitecraft, 6-4-1776.[1]
  Daniel—Rachel Pearce, 1714.[6]
  Samuel—Demaris Howard, Jan. 19, 1709.[1]
Farnum, Allen—Tobitha Jobs, 10-19-1815.[3]
  Samuel—Rebecca Marls, 11-10-1818.[3]
Farquhar, Benajah (s. Adam aed Elizabeth), Philadelphia—Elizabeth Wright (d. Jonathan and Elizabeth), 7-4-1805.[5]
  John—Hannah Clark, July 28, 1750.[1]
Farr, George—Eliza Jane Wilson, 9-30-1853.[4]
  Robert—Anne Stewart, 10-21-1861.[2]
Farrell, George—Elizabeth Atkinson. 9-23-1766.[1]
  Robert—Rebecca Lucus, Apr. 20, 1734.[1]
Farrington, Abraham, Somerset co.—Phebe Bunting (d. Samuel and Mary), Oct. 21, 1725.[5]
  Joseph—Rebecca Alcott, 2-24-1761,[1]
Farroe, Patrick—Elizabeth O. Gilmore, 6-19-1830.[3]
Farrow, Gideon—Mary Ann Crachow, 7-21-1825.[6]
Faves, John Davis—Adrianne D'Olivares, 7-31-1831.[3]
Feagan, James—Alice Kirby, Feb. 6, 1740.[1]
Fearguson, William,—Elizabeth Curel, 5-3-1833.[3]
Fearon, Peter—Susanna Marriott, 1714.[6]
Feldon, Jeremiah—Nancy Dowers, 8-4-1816.[3]
Fenimore, Abraham—Merion H. Lippincott, 1-30-1802.[3]
  Abraham—Rebecca Bishop, 11-1-1810.[3]
  Benjamin—Mary Hutchins, 3-4-1774.[1]
  Caleb—Elizabeth Fenimore, 4-28-1774.[1]
  Caleb—Jane Potter, 9-19-1802.[3]
  Caleb—Lidya Buzby, 1-1-1818.[3]
  Charles—Ann Laquard, Gloucester co., Sept. 20, 1744.[1]
  Charles H.—Martha M. Pitman, 6-¨-1836.[3]
  Daniel—Sarah Fenimore, 4-11-1816.[3]
  David—Ruth Bispham, 1-22-1801.[3]
  Enoch—Hope Lippincott, Mar. 1799.[3]
  Isaac—Martha Moore, 2-23-1800.[3]
  Isaac—Hannah Marter, 1-19-1826.[3]

Fenimore, Isaac—Hannah Wiegand, 1-29-1826.²
  James—Mary Severns, 5-24-1809.³
  Japhet—Charity Parker, 10-23-1780.¹
  John—Elizabeth Humphreys, 1729. ⁶
  John—Rebecca Fenimore, 5-24-1773.¹
  John—Sarah Bayley, 1-23-1811.³
  John—Ann Adams, 11-24-1816.³
  John, Jr.—Rachel Carson, 10-1-1775.¹
  John W.—Elizabeth Stevenson, 9-12-1801.³
  Joseph—Ann Perkins, 7-22-1766.¹
  Joseph—Sarah Vanhorne, 9-3-1777.¹
  Joseph—Nancy Calvert, 2-2-1800.³
  Joshua—Ann Davis, 6-9-1836.³
  Joshua—Mary Pittman, 8-10-1834.³
  Pierson—Mary Williamson, 10-24-1775.¹
  Pearson—Ruth Woodington, 5-23-1812.³
  Richard—Mary Crosby, 1711.⁶
  Richard—Sarah Newell, Nov. 2, 1736.¹
  Richard—Hannah Allen, 11-13-1759.¹
  Thomas, Jr.—Ann Gaskill, 4-3-1800.³
  Washington—Priscilla Stephenson, Gloucester co., 2-24-1825.³
  William—Rachel Humphreys, Sept. 18, 1742.¹
  William—Mary Wilkinson, 8-22-1757.¹
  William S.—Elizabeth Bodger, 6-16-1824.³
  William—Abigail Fort, 3-3-1831.³
  William—Jane Pitt, 9-11-1831.³
  William—Sarah Fenton, 5-15-1834.³
Fennimore, James—Elizabeth Scattergood, 7-30-1775.¹
  John—Sarah Bryant, Dec. 3, 1730.¹
  Jonathan—Elizabeth Cox. 10-18-1798.³
  Joseph—Mary Newton, 12-11-1800.³
  William—Joyce McFaulin, July 16, 1739.¹
Fenton, George, Jr.—Elizabeth Scroggy, 3-12-1777.¹
  Joel—Elizabeth Fenimore, 2-11-1819.³
  Joseph—Phebe Fowler, 1-24-1829.³
  Joseph—Mary Ann Reed, 9-7-1833.
  Robert—Grace Boyer, 1-19-1762.¹
  Robert—Sarah English, 9-19-1813.²
  Samuel—Rebecca Kent, 11-17-1769.¹
  Samuel—Ann Wilson, 11-6-1823.³
  Samuel B.—Mary R. Taylor, 8-15-1833.³
  Thomas—Elizabeth Barns, 5-17-1798.³

Fenton, Thomas—Lydia Ann Rainear, 9-18-1813.[3]
  Thomas,—Isabella Ferguson, 1-28-1825.[3]
  Thomas—Susan Patterson, 10-4-1838.[3]
  William—Hannah Hughes, 7-29-1773.[1]
  William—Elizabeth Kindall, 8-9-1773.[1]
Fenwick, James A.—Mary T. Coshell, 11-13-1843.[4]
Fenymore, John—Mary Meyers, 3-20-1800.[3]
Ferguson, Alexander—Mary Barry, 4-13-1757.[1]
  Charles—Eliza Hart, 4-24-1830.[3]
  Charles G.—Elizabeth Bunting, 5-19-1835.[3]
  Gideon—Ruth Schull, 11-17-1798.[3]
  John—Eleanor Willson, 12-8-1768.[1]
Fetters, Charles, Jr.—Mary Haines, 12-6-1807.[3]
  Jonathan—Bettina Adams, 1-21-1821.[3]
  Michael—Elizabeth Bennett, 9-12-1807.[3]
Field, Ambrose—Susan Decow, Apr. 24, 1705.[5]
  Benjamin—Mary Barton, 1734.[6]
  Benjamin (s. Benjamin)—Tobitha Rockhill (d. Edward), 11-18-1772.[5]
  Benjamin—Martha Tallman, 11-1-1801.[3]
  Caleb—Mary Thomas, 10-5-1817.[3]
  Elijah—Mary Gibbs, 1-28-1771.[1]
  Edward (s. Benjamin and Tabitha)—Mary Tilton (d. Jeremiah and Hannah), 4-8-1802.[5]
  Isaac—Mary Archer, 4-10-1772.[1]
  Isaac—Mrs. Mary Bates, Philadelphia, 6-8-1837.[3]
  Job, Philadelphia—Mary Lyons, 7-2-1770.[1]
  Job—Nancy Morris, 6-8-1814.[3]
  Robert—Mary Taylor (d. Samuel), Apr. 12, 1722.[5]
  Thomas—Leah Lippincott, 7-27-1804.[3]
  Thomas—Rebeccah Woodward, 2-28-1805.[3]
  Thomas S.—Mary L. Reeves, 5-29-1838.[3]
  Timothy T.—Julia P. Davison, 12-23-1830.[3]
Fifer, John—Mary Taylor, 8-7-1808.[3]
  John—Sarah Applegate, 1-21-1823.[3]
Filer, John—Ann Mires, 2-19-1807.[3]
  William H.—Mary Ann Griscom, 3-12-1887.[2]
Filson, John—Nancy Worrel, 2-16-1802.[3]
Fish, Benjamin—Elizabeth Lee, 6-25-1797.[3]
  Fish, Jeremiah—Ann Rudderow, 2-21-1822.[3]
  John—Elizabeth Gaunt, 11-4-1830.[3]
  Obadiah—Jane Collins, 1-21-1830.[3]

Fisher, Abraham—Achsa Streatrer, 9-3-1831.[3]
  James—Jane Borden, 5-2-1803.[3]
  Job—Elizabeth Malsby, 4-27-1814.[3]
  John—Grace Mason, 1747.[9]
  John, Monmouth co.—Martha Coles, 12-27-1836.[3]
  Michael—Sarah Wright, 12-11-1802.[3]
  Redwood (s. Miers and Sarah), Philadelphia—Rebecca Wells (d. Gideon and Hannah), 12-10-1821.[5]
  Robert—Elizabeth Elberson, 12-9-1837.[3]
  Samuel—Sarah Lane, 1721.[6]
  Samuel—Elizabeth Hinchman, 3-8-1820.[7]
  William—Mary Hunter, both Monmouth co., 8-29-1819.[3]
Fistar, William Henry (s. Robert and Kitty), Trenton—Lucy Virginia Harris (d. Andrew and Maggie), 12-12-1876.[4]
Fistman, Isaac—Cybelah Bozorth, 9-24-1797.[3]
Fitchild, William—Bridget McMann, Lancaster, Pa., 7-22-1832.[3]
Fitzsimmons, Daniel—Hope Bowker, 12-5-1796.[3]
Flennard, Henry—Susannah Fenimore, 11-18-1813.[3]
  Jacob—Hannah Fenimore, 1-26-1815.[3]
Flint, Samuel—Deborah Bennett, 12-1-1796.[3]
Flitcraft, Abraham—Susan Cotton, 3-30-1802.[3]
  Isaiah—Elizabeth Snuff, 4-2--1795.[3]
  William—Rhoda Dicks, 12-12-1832.[3]
Foard, James W.—Martha Fenimore, 11-1-1819.[3]
Folkes, Thomas (s. Thomas)—Elizabeth Curtis (d. John), Feb. 21, 1688.[5]
Follwell, John—Mary Gibbs, 9-13-1771.[1]
  John—Susannah Gardiner, 4-7-1796.[13]
  Joseph—Mary Warren, 6-16-1766.[1]
  Nathan—Jane Chalmer, July 21, 1748.[1]
  Nathan—Catharine Spike, 4-5-1761.[1]
  Nathan—Hope Atkinson, 2-4-1785.[1]
  Nathan—Rebecca Cook, 8-19-1803.[3]
  Twineing—Esther Barker, 11-7-1822.[3]
  William—Anne Potts, Dec. 6, 1727.[1]
  William—Nancy White, 10-27-1802.[3]
  William—Abigail Land, 5-28-1826.[3]
Forbes, Charles—Caroline Fowler, 3-3-1827.[3]
  Joseph—Rebecca Lippincott, 6-12-1803.[3]
  William—Phebe Noble. No date given.[3]
Force, Jacob—Mary Darling, 6-21-1774.[1]
  Jacob—Sarah Marriel, 1-1-1799.[3]

Force, James W.—Catharine Larn, both Berks co., Pa., 1-12-1837.[2]
  John—Betsey Arnold, 4-27-1781.[7]
  John—Harriet Vansciver, 1-18-1824.[3]
  Joseph—Mercy Adams, 1-11-1774.[1]
  Levi M.—Ann Gosling, 4-8-1813.[2]
  Matthew—Jane Sidmans, 8-15-1772.[1]
  William—Mary Window, 5-2-1804.[3]
Ford, Charles—Elizabeth Shinn, 12-12-1768.[1]
  Charles—Margaret Ann Adams, 4-25-1818.[3]
  George—Phebe Hutchinson, 9-2-1830.[2]
  John—Bathsheba Tyler, 9-17-1796.[3]
  Thomas—Rachel Leek, July 3, 1742.[1]
  Thomas—Mary Drummond, 2-19-1782.[1]
  Thomas, Jr.—Nancy Cramer, 4-19-1817.[1]
  William—Sarah Wills, 4-19-1783.[1]
Forest, Jacob—Rebecca Stiles, 5-22-1800.[3]
Forgison, John—Margaret J. Sapp, 2-13-1834.[2]
Forker, Adam—Hannah Gaskill, Aug. 25, 1749.[1]
  Daniel—Juliana Risdon, 8-9-1813.[3]
  George—Rebecca Crammer.[3]
  Henry—Deborah S. Bride, 6-10-1839.[3]
  Samuel—Sarah Knight, 3-17-1781.[1]
  Samuel C.—Lilla Beatty, 10-3-1848.[4]
Forman, Isaac—Kitturah Cock. No date given.[3*]
  John, Jr.—Phebe Mather, 11-25-1783.[1]
  Thomas—Susan Mount, 9-17-1823.[2]
Forrester, John—Elizabeth Delatush, 3-16-1776.[1]
Forsith, John—Alice Herd, 12-31-1756.[4]
Forster, William—Experience Whildon, 1712.[9]
Forsyth, John—Lucretia Taylor, 1-6-1768.[1]
  John—Elizabeth Antram. No date given.[3*]
  Joseph—Margaret Middleton, Monmouth co., June 9, 1722.
  Joseph—Deborah Ivins, 2-3-1814.[3]
  Joshua—Ann Stillwell, 1-16-1827.[3]
  Matthew—Rebecca Oldling, Mar. 15, 1696.[5]
  Samuel—Elizabeth Stewart, 11-28-1804.[3]
  Thomas—Margaret Hodson, 11-6-1813.[3]
  ———— —Anna Gaunt, 1786.[11]
Forsythe, Jacob, Monmouth co.—Anna B. Brown, 9-4-1836.[4]

---

*Married by Samuel Wright, J. P.

Forsythe, Matthew—Mercy Smith, 1741.[6]
Fort, Abraham—Elizabeth Edmond, 9-7-1761.[1]
  Abraham—Rachel Pippet, 12-9-1827.[3]
  Andrew—Ann Platt, 3-10-1808.[3]
  Andrew—Sarah King, 11-29-1837.[3]
  Daniel—Grace Rossell, 3-26-1831.[3]
  Frank G.—Mary Lowden, 5-16-1872.[4]
  Frederick W.—Laura F. R. Depuy, 4-14-1864.[8]
  George F., Monmouth co.,—Ann Maria Bodine, 6-30-1831.[3]
  John—Mary Allen, 9-23-1812.[3]
  John, Jr.—Elizabeth Woolston, 12-27-1756.[1]
  John, Jr.—Martha Gaskill, 7-5-1772.[1]
  Joseph—Hester Nailer, 1-2-1784.[1]
  Joseph—Mary Morris, 2-28-1811.[3]
  Levi—Sarah Anderson, 2-4-1819.[3]
  Levi—Elizabeth Rossell, -29-1819.[3]
  Marmaduke—Mary Cousins, Dec. 9, 1738.[1]
  Marmaduke—Elizabeth Marriot, 10-23-1775.[1]
  Marmaduke—Achsah Bates, 5-29-1777.[1]
  Roger—Joanna Libby, Apr. 12, 1733.[1]
  Samuel—Avis Burdsal, 8-29-1768.[1]
  Samuel—Ann Kimble, 12-26-1825.[3]
  Stephen S.—Tharza Lamb, 6-2-1832.[3]
  William—Ann Allen, 2-9-1823.[3]
Fortiners, Ebenezer—Johannah Pettitt, 2-3-1813.[3]
Forward, William—Sarah Watson, 10-14-1832.[3]
Foster, Amariah—Mary Prickett, July 15, 1748.[1]
  Arnold—Martha Adams, 1-10-1828.[3]
  Edmond—Elizabeth Havelon, 3-10-1823.[3]
  George F.—Mercy L. Gibbs, 3-15-1832.[3]
  George W., Philadelphia—Sarah B. Rhodes, 3-26-1802.[3]
  Isaac—Eleanor Knight, 4-6-1800.[3]
  Jeremiah—Sarah Peterson, 11-16-1782.[1]
  Job—Rachel Campbell, 10-20-1808.[3]
  John—Anna Gibbs, 5-27-1776.[1]
  John—Hope Cammel, 6-21-1800.[3]
  John, Jr.—Mary Havens, 3-29-1823.[3]
  John W.—Lucy Ann Lippincott, 3-7-1838.[3]
  Jonathan, Gloucester co.—Elizabeth Southwick, 3-19-1820.[3]
  Joseph R.—Mariah Ann Hoy, 11-29-1832.[3]
  Josiah, Jr.—Elizabeth Wilkins, 3-7-1799.[2]
  Hugh—Mary Oakley, 10-16-1803.

Foster, Miles—Hannah Shinn, 7-10-1798.³
  Nicholas—Martha Arnold, 11-19-1754.¹
  Samuel H.—Achsa Richardson, 3-4-1821.³
  Thomas,—Margaret Parke, 1-2-1796.³
  Thomas—Analiza McChever, 12-11-1829.³
  Uriah—Anne Lord, 11-12-1770.¹
  William—Hannah Core, 1729.⁹
  William—Sarah Bishop, 10-11-1779.¹
  William—Mary Cross, 12-9-1779.¹
  William—Anna Haines, 1-17-1788.¹
  William—Hester Harker, both Philadelphia, 10-8-1803.³
  William—Mary Custer, 11-15-1813.³
  William—Sarah Hewlings, 10-2-1828.³
  William—Marian Haines, 12-1-1831.³
  William Henry—Lizzie North, 8-20-1884.²
  William, Jr.—Elizabeth Steelman, 3-24-1809.³
Foulkes, Joseph—Susan Green, 6-22-1827.³
Foulks, Isaiah—Keturah Chamberlain, 1-19-1804.³
  Obadiah—Ann Buck, 10-5-1815.³
Fowler, Abel—Amy Ellis, 3-25-1820.³
  Ahab—Ann Holland, 3-31-1829.³
  Asa—Elizabeth Blake, 2-9-1807.³
  Chester—Mary Brooks, 7-8-1804.³
  Jacob—Sarah Jorman, 12-14-1781.¹
  Jonathan—Hannah Lawrence, Sept. 20, 1742.¹
  Joseph—Hannah Wilsey, 1-25-1806.³
  Joseph (s. John)—Meribah Middleton (wid of Jonathan), Oct. 27, 1748.⁵
  Joshua—Phebe Herbert, 1-2-1803.³
  Joshua—Tobitha Jobs, both Bucka co., Pa., 11-11-1829.³
  Nathan—Abigail Hotten, 1-19-1812.³
  Samuel—Rachel Innion, 8-23-1809.³
  Thomas—Lucy Elberson, 6-3-1803.³
Fox, Barton—Sarah Parmer, 4-21-1803.³
  David—Ann Borton, 2-27-1820.³
  George—Susannah Hackney, 1696.⁶
  Isaac—Prudence Peterman, 1-24-1796.³
  Isaac—Eliza Lane, 1-21-1826.³
  John—Alice Hutchins, 7-15-1770.⁸
  John—Rebecca Borden, 4-7-1774.⁸
  Jonathan—Sarah Forman, 5-12-1763.¹
  Jonathan—Ann Crusher, 2-14-1796.³

Fox, Patrick—Hannah Baker, 6-19-1772.¹
  Samuel—Sarah Conklan, 3-13-1823.³
  William Budd—Mary Haines, 2-4-1832.³
Foy, Thomas—Elizabeth Sabborne, both Monmouth co., 7-16-1829.³
Frake, John—Elizabeth Holeman, 3-11-1825.²
  Joseph Henry—Mary Elizabeth Bain, 4-12-1883.⁴
Frambus, David—Clarissa Addams, 9-24-1804.³
Frampton, Aaron—Eliza Ann Emmins, 11-21-1830.³
Francis, Robert—Ann Wilsey, 8-19-1804.³
Franklin, Benj.—Elizabeth Whitcraft, 9-3-1815.³
  Henry—Frances Parker (colored), 1-22-1834.³
  Joseph—Sarah Franklin, 11-24-1808.³
Fraser, Joseph—Lydia White, 9-11-1811.³
Frazer, David—Margaret King, 12-19-1827.³
  Edward—Maria Wood, 10-17-1833.³
  John—Susanna West, 4-15-1800.³
  Joseph, Philadelphia—Elizabeth Foster, 1-23-1780.¹
  Nathan—Mary N. Johnson, 2-8-1837.³
  Richard Saunders—Esther Ann Miller, 5-8-1828.³
  Robert—Margaret Carr, 3-9-1767.¹
  Robert—Mary Bowker, 10-14-1809.³
  William, Rev.—Hannah Stockton, 8-9-1768.⁸
Frazier, Benj.—Beuley Norcross, 9-18-1813.³
  Caleb—Ann Loverman, 1821.¹⁴
  Charles—Elizabeth King, 3-11-1838.³
  Daniel—Hannah Phiilips, 1819.¹⁴
  Job—Sarah Bates, 12-3-1801,³
  William—Susan Rainere, 4-6-1826.³
  William—Sarah Jane Towey, 2-16-1898.²
Freeing, Thomas—Hannah Adams, 7-20-1778.¹
Freeman, David—Julian Sharp, 4-8-1820.³
  Francis—Phillis West, 8-20-1814.³
  Isaac—Susannah Riley (colored), 5-2-1819.³
  N. A.—Maria Ross Parker, 8-4-1859.⁸
  William—Elizabeth Hews, 9-25-1758.¹
French, Benjamin—Martha Hall, Jan. 29, 1742.¹
  Charles (s. Uriah), Philadelphia—Rebecca Taylor (d. Jacob), 4-7-1773.⁵
  Charles—Hannah E. Moore, 1-17-1820.³
  Charles H.—Mary Moore, 1-7-1826.³
  Edward—Judith Scattergood, 11-30-1834.³
  George—Beulah Kelley, 3-23-1815.³

French, Hiram—Eliza Headley, 9-35-1836.³
  Isaac—Theodocia Lippincott, 1-12-1804.³
  Jackson Brown—Catherine Lawrence, 10-1-1790.¹
  Jacob—Phebe Glesen, 9-27-1819.³
  James—Sarah Ferguson, 10-12-1779.¹
  James (s. Thomas and Mercy)—Ann Rogers (d. William and Ann), 5-17-1801.³
  Joseph—Martha Newton, 9-2-1804.⁸
  Joseph—Mary Stokes, 12-9-1813.³
  Joshua—Elizabeth M. Beck, 10-23-1817.³
  Richard—Sarah Scattergood, 1693.⁶
  Richard—Mary King (d. Hermanus), Jan. 13, 1701.⁵
  Richard—Hannah Lippincott, 4-12-1861.¹⁰
  Thomas—Mary Cattel, 1732.⁹
  Thomas—Jemimah Elkenton, May 8, 1846.¹
  Thomas—Mercy Coxe, 4-22-1769.¹
  Uriah—Rachel Ingersoll, 6-29-1771.¹
  Uriah—Isabella Peacock, 8-6-1800.³
  William—Lydia Taylor, Sept. 20, 1748.¹
  William, Jr.—Levina Cramer, 6-23-1822.³
  William—Eliza Decker, 12-18-1824.³
  William—Phebe Mathis, 1-28-1827.³
Frost, John—Hannah Moss, 4-25-1809.³
Fry, Daniel—Rebecca Platt, 1-25-1798.⁸
  John—Ann Simson, 1-20-1807.³
Fuller, James—Hannah Mathis, 4-29-1837.³
Fullingsby, John—Olive Brazington, 12-5-1774.¹
Fulton, Joseph (s. Thomas and Hannah), Chester co., Pa.—Ester Cowperthwaite (d. Job and Anna), 2-10-1809.⁵
  Robert—Catherine Sparburn, 10-4-1756.¹
  Robert—Mary Rogers, 7-19-1765.¹
Furman, Berzillai (s. Josiah and Ruth), Trenton—Elizabeth Middleton (d. George and Hannah), 9-4-1775.⁵
  George Middleton (s. Richard W. and Hannah—Margaret Kelly, (d. David and Hannah), 3-10-1803.⁵
  Isaac—Sarah H. Gaskill, 4-20-1835.³
  Richard Way (s. Josiah), Trenton—Hannah Middleton (d. George and Hannah), 1-21-1773.⁵
  Samuel—Ann Miller, 11-25-1808.³
Furnes, Benjamin—Dorothy Higginbottom, Aug. 23, 1745.¹
Furniss, Benjrmin—Elizabeth Gardiner, 1707.⁶

Gabitas, William—Rachel Marshall, 1696.⁶
Gable, Daniel—Rebecca Kelley, 4-18-1816.³
   William—Jane Young, 12-30-1815.³
Gage, Nathan—Anna Platt, 6-5-1808.³
Gail, Abell—Mary Gale, May 19-1749.¹
Gaines, Josiah—Rebecca Shreve, 11-29-1796.³
Gale, Abel—Lydia Cramer, June 16, 1740.¹
   Alexander—Susanna Uncle, 2-20-1808.³
   David—Mary Wainwright, 7-3-1741.¹
   Enoch—Margaret Brown, 10-24-1830.³
   Hazleton—Martha Bennett, 10-27-1837.³
   Isaac, Bucks co., Pa.—Elizabeth Powell, Nov. 4, 1747.¹
   Jacob—Hester Cavaleer, 10-16-1815.³
   James—Hannah Gaunt, 3-3-1784.¹
   Joseph—Massey Allen, 3-16-1783.¹
   Joseph, Jr.—Hannah Drexall, 7-2-1822.³
   Thomas—Elizabeth Kille, Oct. 8, 1739.¹
   William—Hannah Stringer, 10-3-1818.³
   William—Elizabeth Sherman, 6-19-1831.³
Galigan, John—Mrs. Mary Quickmire, 8-12-1835.³
Gallagher, Wm. B.—Ann Wright, 2-18-1812.⁸
Gamble, James—Hope Crammer, 9-2-1798.³
   James—Hellen Orr, 1-2-1821.⁸
   Patrick—Elizabeth Eldridge, 5-12-1771.¹
   Samuel—Rachel Johnson, 9-13-1765.¹
   Warren—Ann Early, 2-5-1837.³
   William—Elizabeth Tolman, 7-15-1776.¹
Gammel, Samuel—Jane Deacon, Apr. 10, 1734.¹
Gard, William—Margaret Bowker, 1-29-1779.¹
Gardiner, Benjamin—Phebe Borden, Hunterdon co., May 18, 1737.¹
   John—Sarah Rydan, 1689.⁶
   John—Mary Lucas, 9-8-1803.⁸
   John, Jr.—Margaret Small, 2-12-1824.³
   Joseph—Catharine Ridgway, 1724.¹¹
   Joseph—Martha Haines, 11-12-1840.¹⁰
   Robert—Rebecca W. Fort, 5-3-1830.³
   S. Harrison—Elizabeth Haines, 11-20-1902.¹⁰
   Thomas—Elizabeth Basnett, 1701.⁶
   Thomas—Susannah Elton, June 16, 1748.¹
   Thomas M.—Patience Lippincott, 12-21-1797.³
   William—Mary Jourdan, 3-17-1779.¹
   William—Ann Eliza Borden, 1-14-1836.³

BURLINGTON COUNTY MARRIAGES 89

Gardner, Charles—Lydia Whitecraft, 6-23-1800.³
  John—Margaret Wilder, 3-22-1821.⁸
  Joshua—Mary Cline, 2-25-1808.³
  Stacy—Meribah Whiticraft, 12-27-1838.³
  Thomas—Hannah Mathews, 1684.⁶
Garner, Benjamin—Catharine Peterson, 3-4-1812.³
  Chas. P.—Sarah Vansciver Horn, 12-24-1867.⁸
  Daniel—Mary Cline, 1-14-1813.³
  Stephen—Hannah Miller, 9-19-1816.³
Garnier. John W.—Mary Dawson, 6-10-1819.³
Garon, Samuel—Lavinia T. Morton, 4-6-1876.²
Garren, John—Ann Platt, 5-4-1823.³
Garret, James—Elizabeth Hammell, 10-19-1823.³
  John—Elizabeth Stevenson, 1-18-1818.³
Garrett, Thomas, Darby, Pa.—Rebecca Sykes (d. Jno. and Joanna),
    Apr. 25, 1744.⁵
  Walter Stillwell—Mary Rambo McDonald, 12-8-1898.²
Garrison, David. Salem co.—Rebecca Coperthwaite, 3-17-1770.¹
  John William (s. John J. and Frances A.). Detroit, Mich.—Mary
    Sykes Earl (d. John and Harriet), 10-22-1890.⁴
Garron, James—Sarah Farley (d. George), 9-22-1822.³
Garwood. Abraham—Amey Haines, 9-25-1776.¹
  Asa—Mary McConacal, 11-14-1803.³
  Benj.—Keturah Hackney, 11-28-1811.³
  Daniel—Susanna Collins, 1737.⁹
  George—Elenor Smith, 1-20-1809.³
  Hezekiah—Gartree Hammel, 1-11-1765.¹
  Jacob—Elinor Ostler, 1720.⁶
  Jacob—Rhoda Rato, 10-10-1776.⁵
  James—Hannah Horner, 5-22-1756.¹
  James—Bethiah Webb, 3-4-1766.¹
  James—Elizabeth Horner, 1-29-1818.³
  John—Charity Wright, 1746.⁹
  John—Hester Haines, 3-6-1764.¹
  John—Mary Scott, 11-7-1805.¹³
  John—Martha Zanes, 5-27-1813.³
  John—Rachel Dillon, 5-22-1817.³
  Joseph B.—Ida Eliz. Cox, 10-16-1878.²
  John, Jr.—Sarah Williams, 4-8-1801.³
  John P.—Sarah Clutch, 7-16-1815.³
  John, Sr.—Elizabeth Hackney, 10-22-1801.³
  Joseph—Elizabeth Antrum, Mar. 27, 1732.¹

Carwood, Joseph—Mary Pancoast, Gloucester co., 6-9-1706.¹
  Joseph J.—Leah Devinney, 10-20-1757.¹
  Obadiah—Mary King, 8-17-1756.¹
  Samuel—Phebe Hubbs, 3-12-1825.³
  Samuel—Rebekka Crosby, 1878.⁶
  Samuel—Mabel Bartram Evans, 5-10-1930.¹⁰
  Thomas—Mary Ballinger, 1733.⁹
  Thomas—Mary Sharp, 11-12-1763.¹
  Thomas—Sarah Ann Wilkins, 11-12-1820.³
  William—Jane Troth, 1725.⁹
  William—Charity Gaskill, 5-17-1766.¹
  William—Bridget O'Donley, 8-7-1787.¹
  William—Ann Felton, 2-31-1814.³
  William—Rachel Prickett, 1-7-1836.³
  William—Sarah Wiegan, 2-8-1838.³
Gascoigne, Larner—Peggy Johnson, 7-19-1802.³
Gash, Martin—Ann Johnson, 12-27-1766.¹
Gaskel, Josiah—Mary Weaver, 8-19-1754.¹
Gaskell, Forman—Eliza Leek, 11-5-1837.³
  Josiah—Rebecca Lippincott, 1704.⁶
  Samuel—Mary Enoch, 1745.⁶
Gaskill, Aaron—Susanna Marriott, 1749.⁶
  Aaron—Rachel Malsbury, 3-17-1810.³
  Aaron W. (s. Josiah and Elizabeth)—Martha Middleton (d. Jediah and Anna), 10-7-1830.⁵
  Abel—Hannah Clayton, 7-9-1797.³
  Abraham—Ann Crammer, 8-18-1784.¹
  Abraham—Mary Dicks, 3-28-1827.³
  Abraham—Eliza Taylor, 2-16-1832.³
  Absalom—Phebe Pippitt, 2-26-1812.³
  Benjamin—Mary Dennis, Monmouth co., Jan. 16, 1738.¹
  Benjamin—Sarah Husted, 1756.⁹
  Benjamin, Jr.—Sarah Endicott, 6-18-1767.¹
  Bloomfield—Rebecca Haines, 12-7-1821.³
  Caleb—Hope Rossel, 7-15-1765.¹
  Caleb—Hannah V Antrim, 3-9-1832.³
  Charles—Bathsheba Stackhouse, 10-31-1805.³
  Charles—Beulah Kirby, 3-26-1807.³
  Charles—Eliza Huff, 2-5-1832.³
  Charles R.—Mary B. Warner, 11-14-1822.³
  Daniel—Mary Davenport, 12-1-1812.³
  David—Sarah Ernest, 11-9-1764.¹

BURLINGTON COUNTY MARRIAGES 91

Gaskill, Ebenczer—Elizabeth Wood, June 21, 1731.[1]
  Ebenezer—Hester Gould, 1-14-1769.[1]
  Ebenezer—Elizabeth Ridgway, 6-21-1795.[3]
  Ebenezer—Susanna Grant, 12-30-1800.[3]
  Edward—Elizabeth Harker, 9-23-1766.[1]
  Edward, Jr.—Elizabeth Lippincott, Aug. 1, 1732.[1]
  Elijah—Rachel Ludrick, 9-19-1799.[3]
  Elijah—Frances Frazer, 1-8-1832.[3]
  Enoch—Mary Adams, 3-8-1801.[3]
  Isaac—Mary Devinny, 9-21-1820.[3]
  Jacob—Ruth Donally, 5-13-1779.[1]
  Jacob—Esther Rudrow, 4-20-1797.[3]
  Jacob—Ann Hooper, 7-16-1797.[3]
  James—Abigail Stockton, 10-30-1754.[1]
  Jennings—Elizabeth Whitehouse, 11-7-1812.[3]
  Joab—Anna Hooper, 7-16-1797.[4]
  Job—Elizabeth Haines, 3-6-1758.[1]
  Job—Lois Prickett, 6-9-1768.[1]
  Job—Mary Scroggy, 1-10-1805.[3]
  Job—Ellen McClang, 3-28-1835.[3]
  John—Martha Parker, 6-7-1764.[1]
  John—Rachel Grant, 8-4-1767.[1]
  John—Ann Kindle, 12-24-1807.[3]
  John—Sarah Lamb, 12-3-1812.[3]
  Jonathan—Jane Shinn, 1732.[6]
  Jonathan—Jane Southwick, 3-12-1787.[4]
  Jonathan—Rebecca Smith, 2-2-1832.[3]
  Joseph—Grace Powell, 1744.[6]
  Josepn—Ann Pointset, 1-4-1777.[7]
  Joseph—Sarah Stockton, 2-19-1804.[3]
  Joseph—Sarah Bass, 1-15-1808.[3]
  Josiah—Amy Sreve, 1737.[6]
  Josiah—Mary Griffith, 1748.[5]
  Josiah—Martha Gaskill, 1-9-1760.[1]
  Josiah (s. Josiah and Beulah)—Eliza Wright (d. Aaron and Elizabeth), 3-6-1806.[5]
  Levi—Lydia Powell, 12-11-1767.[1]
  Mahlon—Mary Lippincott, 1-11-1798.[3]
  Moses—Lydia Budd, 9-1-1774.[1]
  Moses—Abigail Kelley, 6-29-1817.[3]
  Nathan—Hannah Owen, 11-1-1797.[3]
  Nathaniel—Hannah Cope, 1-80-1811.[3]

Gaskill, Richard—Rebecca Sailor, 11-19-1829.[3]
    Samuel—Mary Enochs, Nov. 16, 1748.[1]
    Samuel—Sybella Collins, 12-19-1759.[1]
    Samuel—Susannah Garvey, 1-6-1784.[1]
    Samuel—Rebecca Warren, 2-15-1801.[3]
    Samuel—Margaret Thorn, 12-17-1805.[3]
    Samuel—Theophila Cripps, 1827.[6]
    Stephen—Lavinah Gaskill, Jan. 30, 1748.[1]
    William—Rhoda Johnson, 12-19-1816.[3]
    William—Ann Hork, 7-24-1821.[3]
    Zorobabel—Ann Lippincott, 1723.[6]
Gaskin, Daniel—Martha Shinn, 1735.[6]
Gates, Ezekiel—Harriet Bowker, 11-22-1824.[3]
    Michael—Nancy Oen, 7-15-1815.[3]
Gaunt, Amariah—Elizabeth Rose, 9-21-1822.[3]
    Elisha—Drusilla Norcross, 12-7-1826.[3]
    Samuel—Hannah Woolman, 1749.[6]
    Samuel—Hannah Austin, 3-16-1815.[3]
    Samuel W., Dr.—Hannah Longstreth, 1-14-1817.[3]
Gauntt, Asher—Mary Stockton, 6-26-1787.[1]
    Benjamin H., D.D.S.—Josephine Coate, 11-4-1869.[2]
    Hananiah—Ann Ridgway, 1730.[11]
    John—Jean Sattherwaite (d. Samuel and Jean), 11-24-1756.[5]
Geffries Staten—Ann Trout, 11-20-1827.[3]
Geiger, William C.—Anna Maria McCloskey, 6-5-1831.[8]
Gelbert, George—Hannah Hays, 9-10-1783.[1]
George, Ira Nelson (s. George W. and Clara B.)—Lizzie Stephenson (d. William and Sarah S.), 8-8-1892.[4]
    John—Sarah Durell, 3-2-1765.[1]
    John—Sarah Perry, 12-31-1773.[1]
    Jonathan—Margaret Barber, 9-22-1804.[3]
    Samuell—Rachel Matlock, 11-24-1796.[3]
Gerlach, Richard Francis—Mary Leeds Slack, 10-4-1899.[2]
Gethens, Daniel—Elizabeth Proud, 3-25-1784.[1]
Gewell, George—Lydia Ann Fenton, 9-3-1838.[3]
Gibbon, Zephaniah—Nancy Smyrun, 1-30-1799.[3]
Gibbs, Aaron—Mary Ann Emmons 1-24-1830.[3]
    Abraham—Mary Ann Arison, 8-26-1856.[4]
    Amos—Nina Slack, 2-28-1878.[4]
    Andrew Eckard—Rachel Shemar Gardner, 5-4-1899.[4]
    Barzillai—Mary Haverland, 12-25-1822.[3]
    Benjamin—Phebe Ridgeway, Sept. 7, 1748.[1]

Gibbs, Benjamin—Ann Kerlen, 8-8-1836.[3]
  Caleb—Isabella Brannin, 4-29-1799.[3]
  Elias—Phebe Fowler, 11-2-1813.[3]
  Francis—Martha Hall, Oct. 22, 1748.[1]
  Isaac—Hannah Pope, 1716.[6]
  Isaac, Jr.—Susannah Davis, 1739.[6]
  John—Ann Lucas, 1729.[6]
  John—Sarah Brown, 8-19-1765.[1]
  John—Theodosia Brannen, 4-26-1798.[3]
  Joseph—Mary Clark, 6-18-1757.[1]
  Joseph—Rhoda Harker, 8-28-1770.[1]
  Joseph—Hannah Ann Atkinson, 10-30-1828.[3]
  Joshua—Hannah Burrough, 1757.[9]
  Josiah—Elizabeth Wilkins, 3-4-1795.[8]
  Lucas—Mary Hanse, 8-29-1796.[7]
  Mahlon—Mary Wilson, 9-30-1776.[1]
  Martain, Jr.—Hannah Beck, 4-22-1809.[3]
  Martin (s. John)—Rebecca Forsyth (d. Matthew), 10-17-17?1.[5]
  Martin—Sarah Shinn, 11-26-1827.[3]
  Mathias—Rebeccah Unkel, 8-21-1802.[3]
  Richard—Rebecca Cowgill, Mar. 17, 1725.[5]
  Robert—Catherine Fatchett, 4-15-1776.[1]
  Samuel—Mercy Earl, 4-17-1764.[1]
  Samuel—Sarah Burroughs, 7-5-1823.[3]
  Seth—Alice Stevenson, 10-20-1788.[1]
  Stacy—Ann Hilderman, 8-2-1807.[3]
  William—Martha Goforth, 2-13-1805.[3]
  William—Elizabeth Phagens, 1-16-1781.[1]
Giberson, Benjamin—Rebecca Reeves, 11-23-1826.[2]
Gibson, Asa—Sarah Ridgway, 1-21-1816.[3]
  Claton—Ann Test, 10-15-1814.[8]
  Isaac—Hannah Ashbrook, 1-8-1768.[1]
  Jacob—Hannah Ford, 1-30-1817.[3]
  John—Sarah Hunt, 1719.[6]
  John—Ann Morton, Nov. 23, 1841.[1]
  John—Sarah Marriott, Apr. 8, 1749.[1]
  John—Keziah Matlack, 6-2-1831.[1]
  John—Ann Read, 4-20-1833.[3]
  Joseph—Mary Ballinger, 1766.[9]
  Luke—Sarah Clark, 1721.[9]
  Merit—Margaret Alloways, 9-14-1800.[3]
  Oliver—Mary Read, 1-18-1834.[3]

Gibson, Samuel—Catharine Clayton, 3-3-1782.[1]
  Samuel—Mary Wallin, 1-18-1801.[3]
  William Z.—Lydia H. Paul, 1-16-1869.[2]
Gifford, Abraham—Catherine Fury, 10-16-1771.[1]
  Eli—Susannah Stiles, 12-31-1815.[3]
  Isaac—Rachel Evins, 3-23-1796.[3]
  Jonathan—Esther Mathis (d. Eli, Jr.), 1826.[11]
  Johathan, Jr.—Matilda Andrews, 7-19-1801.[3]
  Joshua—Elizabeth Mott, 4-2-1805.[3]
  Joshua—Eveline Augburn, 12-30-1822.[3]
  Martin—Mary Morton, 8-28-1832.[3]
  Mordica—Mary Ann Swanson, 9-22-1835.[3]
  Thomas—Mary Soper (wid. of Reuben, Sr.), 1789.[11]
  Thomas—Esther Gifford, both Tuckerton, 4-10-1836.[2]
  William—Catherine Taylor, May 16, 1734.[1]
  William—Elizabeth Smith, 4-12-1774.[1]
  William—Hannah Braddock, 1-27-1797.[3]
  William—Ann Brock, 12-10-1810.[3]
Gilbert, Benjamin—Mary Smith, 8-16-1761.[1]
  Benjamin—Sarah Bunting, 3-14-1772.[1]
  Benjamin—Lydia Vaun, 8-27-1832.[3]
  David—Mary Tulley, 12-3-1817.[3]
  Ellis—Hannah Stephens, 12-30-1838,[3]
  George—Sarah Ann Briggs, 12-19-1822.[3]
  Henry—Susan English, 3-18-1819.[3]
  Jesse—Lavinia Buffin, 3-2-1826.[3]
  Joseph—Bulah Martin, 5-7-1806.[3]
  Joseph—Christian Macpherson, 8-20-1824.[3]
  Joseph—Margaret Rodman, 1-16-1834.[4]
  Samuel—Nancy Fowler, 10-10-1807.[3]
  William—Lydia Kirby, 12-11-1806.[3]
  William—Susan Hale, 12-20-1832.[3]
Giles, Lewis—Margaret Wissing, 8-18-1771.[1]
Gilham, Robert—Mary Foster, Aug. 10, 1737.[1]
Gill, John, Jr.—Anne Smith, 1-10-1788.[13]
  John—Prudence Thompson, 5-27-1799.[7]
  Robert, Philadelphia—Grace Pearson, 7-7-1811.[3]
  Silas—Mary Allen, 2-26-1804.[3]
  Thomas—Hannah Hollinshead, Jan. 9, 1743/4.[1]
  Thomas—Ann Githens, 4-27-1809.[3]
  Thomas, Jr.—Ann Vansciver, 5-18-1805.[3]
  William H.—Phebe A. Shreve, 7-6-1858.[4]

Gillam, Robert—Grace Pedrick, Mar. 21, 1745.[1]
  Mathew—Elizabeth Adams, 3-25-1815.[3]
Gillham, Lucas—Ann Indicott, Feb. 19, 1740.[1]
Gillingham, Frank G.—Charlotte Matthews, 3-20-1862.[2]
  Mahlon (s. Yeamans), Philadelphia—Susan Clark (d. Isaac and Mary), 10-6-1808.[5]
Gilman, Charles—Martha Hilliard, 1819.[14]
  Daniel—Mary Higgings, 12-18-1762.[1]
Gilmore, Daniel—Mary Farnum, 11-28-1815.[3]
  Joseph—Ellen Carter, 2-13-1832.[3]
Gilpin, Richard A.—Mary C. Watmongh, 8-5-1854.[8]
Ginglin, Daniel—Marrietta Allen, 10-1-1836.[3]
Ginkins, Benjamin—Susannah Wright, 10-10-1754.[1]
Girham, John—Catharine Fleanard, 2-10-1823.[3]
Girvin, Martin Hortrick—Mary Lavina Corr, 7-29-1884.[4]
Githens, Frank Smith—Carrie Edna Nack, 12-11-1894.[2]
  Joseph—Susannah Winner, 12-20-1827.[3]
  Samuel—Mary Dobbins, 2-18-1808.[3]
  William—Sophia Pike, 5-7-1827.[3]
Githings, Thomas—Mary Delaplain, 4-2-1768.[1]
Giverson, John—Lydia Giverson, 2-3-1759.[1]
Gladden, William—Hope Lippincott, 1701.[6]
Glenn, James— Emeline Lewis, 2-25-1838.[3]
Glew, Richard—Ann Mills, 1-10-1778.[1]
Glisson, William—Sarah Delatush, 1-14-1778.[1]
Glover, Eli—Margaret Clear, 10-16-1825.[3]
  Eli S.—Sarah B. Billing, 3-23-1835.[3]
  Elwood—Emeline Jones, 11-4-1836.[3]
  John Ogden—Ann Ridgway, 11-13-1817.[10]
  William—Hannah Stiles, 10-14-1802.[3]
Glymm, William—Ann Abbey, 6-1-1854.[4]
Godafray, Jean Maximilien Maurice—Eliza Crawford, 12-29-1808.[1]
Goelet, James—Sarah Lawrence, June 20, 1752.[1]
Goforth, Thomas, Gloucester co.—Martha Stratton, 10-9-1762.[1]
Goldy, Curlis—Rachel Morton, 2-15-1812.[3]
  Daniel—Sarah Pippitt, 9-13-1832.[3]
  Elijah—Rhoda Dutton, 1-14-1828.[3]
  Isaiah P.—Mary Estill, 8-28-1823.[3]
  John—Mary McCulley, 10-16-1784.[1]
  John— Amelia Wright (d. Samuel), 12-11-1800.[2]
  Joseph—Rachel Atkinson, 12-6-1798.[3]
  Joseph—Eliza Childs, 3-26-1825.[3]

Goldy, Samuel—Jerusha Curtis, 2-2-1765.[1]
  Samuel—Ann Toy, 9-29-1770.[1]
  William—Mary Bennet, 2-17-1825.[3]
  William C.—Hannah Peacock, 3-29-1816.[3]
Goldsmith, Stephen—Sarah Baxter, 7-20-1831.[3]
Gonnigal, Samuel—Elizabeth Reed, 3-3-1821.[3]
Goodher, Thomas—Elizabeth Zane, 5-5-1830.[3]
Goodrich, Alex Wright—Mary Emma Morris, 2-9-1875.[8]
Goodwin, Charles Lloyd (s. Samuel D. and Mary), Gloucester co.—Rebecca Borden Grover, 11-24-1886.[4]
Goorley, John (s. Samuel and Priscilla)—Rachel H. Morgan (d. Adam and Bathey), Gloucester co., 9-21-1820.[12]
Gordon, Charles—Edith Nixon, 9-25-1823.[3]
  Daniel—Izilah Pedrick, 7-31-1787.[4]
  Lewis, Monmouth co.—Sarah Chambers, 1-21-1837.[3]
  William—Martha Eyre, 8-17-1765.[1]
  William—Mary Wood, 5-26-1801.[3]
Gormley, John—Jane Calvin, 8-22-1809.[3]
Goslin, Henry—Elizabeth Goheen, 4-7-1836.[3]
  James—Rachel Frazier, 11-8-1838.[3]
  John, Jr.—Lydia Malsbury, 5-19-1821.[3]
  William—A. Wagoner, 9-13-1813.[3]
Gosling, Jacob—Mary Gale, Bristol, Pa., 4-24-1786.[8]
  John—Sarah Budd, Dec. 13, 1736.[1]
Gough, Benj.—Sarah Hopkins, 2-15-1823.[3]
Govett, Joseph—Esther Welsh, 1737.[6]
Grandon, Bernard—Sarah Pointsway, Dec. 29, 1740.[1]
Grans, William—Jane Ashmore, 5-14-1832.[3]
Grant, Elihu—Phebe Inman, 12-27-1820.[3]
  Henry—Maria Smith, 2-16-1830.[3]
  James—Marjorie Smith, 1776.[11]
  James—Elizabeth Mahan, 9-15-1806.[3]
  James—Rhoda Harris, 9-29-1806.[3]
  James—Hannah Moore, both Monmouth co., 6-25-1837.[3]
  John—Ann Gibson, 1-26-1801.[3]
  Joseph—Susanna Gaskill, 12-22-1770.[1]
  Joseph—Mary Mick, 6-18-1804.[3]
  Josiah—Mary Letts, 4-18-1778.[1]
  Josiah—Martha Coxe, 10-15-1822.[3]
  Larner—Charlotte Clayton, 2-12-1815.[3]
  Lewis—Hannah Holl, 5-29-1804.[3]
  Thomas—Hannah Harber, 10-14-1778.[1]

BURLINGTON COUNTY MARRIAGES

Gravatt, Asher— Sarah Pierce, 12-27-1809.³
  William—Elizabeth Mann, 2-11-1809.³
Graves, Richard—Dorothy Sattherwaite, 1721.⁶
Gray, David—Sarah McMullen, 12-25-1836.³
  James—Sophia West, 7-8-1812.³
  William—Hannah Davis, 3-26-1760.¹
  William—Achsah Applegate, 2-7-1807.³
Greaves, Robert—Elizabeth Martin, 3-17-1778.¹
Green, Alfred D.—Elizabeth McClurg, both Hunterdon co , 11-29-1837.³
  Charles—Martha Harris (colored), 10-28-1824.³
  Daniel—Mary Johnston, June 1, 1740.¹
  Daniel—Polly Rizar, 11-30-1811.³
  Daniel—Mary S. Reeve, 1-17-1827.³
  Ephraim—Susan Penier, Nov. 1771.⁸
  George—Ann Thompoon, Oct. 15, 1750.¹
  George—Mary Anderson, 3-11-1812.³
  George—Elizabeth McClain, 10-5-1833.³
  Gilbert—Rosanna Parks, 10-9-1771.¹
  James—Lydia Cromwell, 12-30-1811.³
  Jesse—Elizabeth Musgrove, 3-6-1815.³
  John—Catharine Husted, 1745.⁹
  John—Rebecca West, 2-5-1776.¹
  John—Rachel Mannery, 12-4-1800.³
  John— Sarah Cook, 11-10-1803.³
  John—Rachel Crozier, 11-5-1829.³
  Joseph—Sarah Reubant, 11-21-1802.³
  Joseph—Fanny Rolly, 3-18-1826.³
  Pompey—Phebe Hugg, 2-22-1805.³
  Richard—Elizabeth Cunningham, 7-2-1764.¹
  Richard—Jane Ann Applegate, 7-21-1827.³
  Silas—Sarah King, 8-17-1800.³
  Thomas—Hannah Arnal, 1743.⁶
  Thomas—Mary Stockton, 4-27-1786.⁸
  Thomas—Lydia Hilliard, 5-14-1788.⁴
  Thomas—Rebekah Hilliard, 2-19-1801.³
  Thomas, Jr.—Abigail Shreve, 1-18-1821.³
  Thomas, Sr.—Elizabeth Custer, 3-20-1825.³
Greeves. John—Lydia Brown, 3-22-1821.³
Gregg, Amos—Eliza Monkton Macolm, 8-17-1806.³
Gregory, James—Elizabeth Willson, 9-8-1776.¹
Greverson, John—Mary Ann Horner, 8-7-1836.³

Grey, Hugh— ——— Mulligan, 11-19-1797.³
   Jesse—Sarah Budd, 4-5-1827.³
   John—Hannah Beck, 10-22-1797.³
Grieg, Cato—Mary Anderson (colored), 1-21-1818.⁸
Griffee, Benj.—Elizabeth Wiltshire, 8-19-1819.³
Griffin, James—Bridget Maxfield, Jan. 21, 1740.¹
   Moses—Mary Duffle, 11-26-1801.³
   Norman—Eliza Rose, 4-8-1828.³
Griffith, Charles—Eliza Aaronson, 8-17-1826.³
   Joseph—Rebecca F. Craft, 11-12-1801.³
   Matthew—Isabella Reeves, 12-15-1830.³
   Morgan—Mary White, Aug. 7, 1746.¹
Griffiths, Amos—Hannah Tuley, 12-11-1817.³
   Thomas—Emily Dark, 12-17-1892.²
Grigory, Richard—Mary Southwick, 12-14-1800.³
Grinslade, John—Reb. Moore, 12-26-1790.⁷
Grimes, George, Salem—Mary Rodgers, Aug. 29, 1743.¹
Grinage, Jonathan—Lydia Steel, 11-23-1795.³
Griscom, Benjamin—Susannah Adams, 12-31-1798.⁷
   Benjamin—Rebecca Thompson, 10-28-1811.⁷
   David—Rachel Stuart, 4-28-1817.⁷
   John—Abigail Hoskins, 9-3-1800.³
   Robert Roscoe—Sarah Lyida Cameron, 5-12-1787.²
   Thomas—Elizabeth Sutphin, 7-26-1830.³
   Tobias—Deborah Gabitas, 1711.⁶
   William—Ann Stewart, 12-29-1800.⁷
Groff, Garret, Salem co.—Amy Stratton, 11-15-1764.¹
   Joseph—Elizabeth Jones, 3-16-1807.³
Grogg, Samuel—Mary Ewing, 12-23-1798.³
Gromden, William—Elizabeth Cornelius, 6-10-1836.³
Gronbeck, Herman (s. Christian and Katherine)—Christine Baggesgaard (d. Jans and Sophia), Viele, Denmark, 8-21-1887.⁴
Groom, Edward—Martha Watkinson, 3-9-1836.³
   Peter, Jr.—Hannah Smith, 2-11-1830.³
Grow, John—Rachel Raker, Gloucester co., 1-1-1812.³
Grubb, Charles Ross—Florence Reynolds, 7-10-1873.⁸
   Henry G.—Mrs. Annie Odenheimer Ball, 3-13-1875.⁸
   Robert—Maria Sherman, 2-15-1837.³
Gruff, Henry—Mary Perkins, 1683.⁶
Guerrat, Joseph—Ann Burgess, 7-4-1765.¹
Guest, George—Elizabeth Marshall, 1701.⁶
Guffy, Jonathan—Maria Perrin, 12-29-1810.³

BURLINGTON COUNTY MARRIAGES

Guiberson, Reuben—Sarah Pain, 8-20-1809.³
Gulick, Cornelius—Sallie J. Marshall, 12-25-1873.²
  Gideon—Rebecca Coombes, 8-23-1817.³
Gunnel, Charles W.—Keturah Quicksall, 12-1-1830.³
Gunnin, Dennis—Eleanor Connar, 12-16-1770.⁸
Gunyan, James—Elizabeth White, 1-30-1800.³
Guy, Benj.—Diana James (colored), 8-24-1824.³
  Elwood—Laomia Thompson, 12-3-1846.⁴
  Noah—Elizabeth Brown, 8-26-1821.³
  William—Elizabeth Green, 9-7-1816.³
Haas, John—Mary Klingle, 9-28-1853.⁸
Hackbury, Josiah—Allis Hunter, 7-9-1826.³
Hackinson, John—Rhoda Leonard, 4-27-1813.³
Hackney, Edmund—Rachel Ivins, 5-4-1789.¹
  Obediah—Hannah Cox, 6-11-1807.³
  Thomas— —— Albertson, Sept. 19, 1748.¹
  Thomas—Elizabeth Tomlinson, 4-16-1788.¹
  William—Sarah Ingle, 4-16-1770.¹
  William—Rebecca Reed, 2-16-1812.³
  William—Elizabeth Bishop, 5-12-1814.³
Hageman, Jesse—Mary Ann Havens, 4-28-1827.³
Hagerly, Lewis F.—Ann Ellis, 10-7-1809.³
Hagerman, John—Catherine Grant, 8-9-1821.³
Haggins, George—Eliza Smith, 8-25-1821.³
Haily, Hezekiah—Beulah Sharp, 5-6-1827.³
Haines, Aaron—Anne Eayres, 1-14-1776.¹
  Aaron—Sarah Haines, 10-1-1807.³
  Aaron, Jr.—Martha Stokes, 10-29-1795.³
  Aaron N.—Priscilla Gardiner, 6-22-1843.¹⁰
  Abel—Elizabeth Stokes, 10-30-1800.³
  Abel—Nancy Moore, 3-2-1808.³
  Abraham—Hannah Rakestraw, 12-28-1772.¹
  Abraham—Mary Jones, 2-9-1804.³
  Abraham—Ann Evans, 11-10-1831.³
  Allen—Rebecca Doron, 12-13-1828.³
  Allen—Rebecca Ann Biddle, 3-22-1855.⁴
  Alphonso—Rachel Price Croshaw, 12-11-1878.⁴
  Amos—Rebecca Troth, 1731.⁹
  Arthur E.—Marion D. Whitacre, 12-15-1917.¹⁰
  Benjamin—Marjorie Balanger (d. James, Sr.), 1772.¹¹
  Benjamin—Mary Smallwood, 8-6-1789.⁴
  Benjamin—Elizabeth Kirby, 5-14-1795.³

Haines, Benjamin—Hannah Hunter, 1-5-1807.[3]
 Benjamin—Elizabeth King, 1-23-1812.[3]
 Benjamin—Mary Haines, 10-15-1891.[10]
 Caleb (s. John)—Sarah Burr (d. Henry), 1719.[6]
 Caleb (s. Josiah and Abigail)—Mary Eldridge (d. Jonathan), 11-15-1781.[6]
 Caleb—Mary Stockton, 4-21-1808.[3]
 Caleb—Hope Lippincott, 11-15-1811.[10]
 Caleb (s. Job and Sarah)—Lydia Warrington (d. Henry and Rebecca), 4-15-1824.[12]
 Caleb—Ann C. Braddock, 10-3-1830.[3]
 Carlile—Sarah Matlack, 1721.[9]
 Charles—Mary Troth, 10-14-1813.[10]
 Charles, Gloucester co.—Rachel Moore, 12-11-1817.[3]
 Charles—Margaret Woolston, 11-25-1830.[3]
 Charles—Mary Atkinson, 5-17-1849.[10]
 Charles A.—Mary Ann Middleton, 2-28-1833.[3]
 Charles A. (s. Isaac, Jr.)—Mary E. Kay (d. Jacob and Rachel), 10-31-1876.[4]
 Clayton—Mrs. Hannah Worrell, 11-7-1828.[3]
 Core—Mary Haines, 10-12-1794.[10]
 Daniel—Elizabeth Bryan, 1719.[6]
 Edmund—Charlotte Leeds, 12-17-1782.[1]
 Edmund—Sarah Coxe, 12-25-1822.[3]
 Edward—Grace Stites, 6-9-1813.[3]
 Elwood—Elizabeth Evans, 3-31-1836.[10]
 Enoch—Priscilla Eayre, 4-6-1767.[1]
 Ezekiel—Abigail Kemble, 1745.[6]
 Forman—Pamelia Ann Duley, 2-11-1837.[3]
 Francis—Hester Hoff, 9-20-1801.[3]
 George—Margaret Lamb, June 7, 1731.[1]
 George—Elizabeth Sharp, 6-4-1773.[1]
 George—Ruth Gaskill, 1-10-1789.[4]
 George (s. Thomas and Eliza)—Edith Woolman (d. Asher and Rachel), 4-13-1796.[6]
 George—Mary Hungerford, 10-27-1816.[3]
 George—Sarah Wills, 2-17-1825.[10]
 George—Elizabeth M. Wilson, 11-4-1837.[3]
 George—Edith T. Engle, 5-16-1861.[10]
 George E.—Mary Coate, 1-24-1829.[3]
 Habakuk Eayres—Charlotte Fleet, 5-9-1830.[3]
 Ira—Sarah Smith, 2-8-1827.[3]

Haines, Isaac—Keziah Woolman, 1-15-1778.[1]
Isaac—Elizabeth Austin, 2-17-1801.[3]
Isaac—Alice Anna Mason, 3-30-1814.[2]
Isaac—Edith Haines, 2-13-1839.[3]
Isaac—Hannah Costille, 12-12-1839.[3]
Isaac Charles (s. Charles and M.)—Rebecca Zelley Deacon (d. W. H. and Hope), 6-8-1890.[4]
Isaac H.—Rachel Evans, 11-14-1844.[10]
Isaiah—Lydia H. Miller, 3-12-1837.[3]
Isaiah, Jr.—Rachel Peacock, 12-28-1799.[3]
Jacob—Sarah Austin, 4-6-1770.[1]
Jacob (s. Samuel and Lydia)—Hannah Stokes (d. John and Hannah), 4-9-1784.[6]
Jacob—Elizabeth Bowker, 7-18-1798.[3]
Jacob (s. Jacob and Bathsheba)—Rebecca Warrington (d. John and Mary), 3-15-1804.[12]
Jacob—Mary Githens, 3-14-1830.[3]
James—Vashty Rogers, 8-24-1817.[3]
Jeremiah—Hannah Booy, 1736.[6]
Jeremiah—Elizabeth Bispham, 1-21-1802.[3]
Jeremiah—Ann Stokes, 12-1-1804.[3]
Jervis—Elizabeth Reeve, 9-21-1826.[3]
Jesse—Mary Armstrong, 8-2-1783.[1]
Job—Esther Hammitt, 1749.[9]
Job—Sarah Carr, 10-9-1788.[13]
Job—Sarah Briggs, 6-20-1802.[3]
Job—Ann Stiles, 1-23-1823.[3]
Job—Mary S. Reeves, 10-18-1849.[10]
Joel—Hope Lippincott, 12-3-1810.[3]
John (s John)—Elizt'h Satterthwaite, Nov. 13, 1709.[5]
John—Ann Ashard, 1734.[9]
John—Mary Shreve, 1758.[9]
John—Martha Eayres, 7-29-1765.[1]
John—Ann Taylor, 10-6-1781.[1]
John (s. Ephraim and Hannah)—Mary Wills (d. Moses and Margaret), 3-11-1789.[6]
John—Martha Taylor, 6-25-1792.[7]
John (s. Isaac)—Jemima Brown, 1-31-1803.[3]
John—Martha Philips, 3-24-1803.[3]
John—Ann Lippincott, 9-19-1812.[3]
John—Eleanor Bacon, 4-26-1813.[7]
John—Sarah Evens, 3-29-1827.[10]

Haines, John H.—Elizabeth Howell, 7-7-1798.³
John O.—Sarah Wills, 3-24-1864.¹⁰
John S.—Mary Ann Woolston, 4-12-1821.³
Jonathan—Hannah Sharp, 1740.⁹
Jonathan—Sarah Goldy, 11-17-1775.¹
Jonathan—Mary Haines, 10-6-1800.³
Jonathan—Neomy Stratton, 2-19-1807.³
Joseph—Patience Prickett, Aug. 25, 1740.¹
Joseph—Hope Reeves, Nov. 2, 1749.¹
Joseph—Mary Reeves, 3-19-1771.¹
Joseph—Izabella Middleton, 1-14-1802.³
Joseph—Ann Jones, 8-1-1802.³
Joseph—Phebe Braddock, 12-24-1802.³
Joseph—Mary Haines, 7-15-1803.³
Joseph—Marian Brown, 7-8-1811.³
Joseph—Deborah Engle, 11-16-1815.¹⁰
Joseph (s. Caleb and Mary)—Hannah Middleton (d. Nathaniel and Sarah), 2-11-1819.¹²
Joseph, Philadelphia—Achsah Bidelle, 1-25-1821.³
Joseph—Lucy Ann Engle, 10-4-1822.³
Joseph—Mary Evens, 2-15-1838 ¹⁰
Joseph, Jr.—Eliza Alcutt, 2-28-1826.³
Josiah—Ann Burk, 3-23-1800.³
Josias (s. John)—Martha Burr (d. Henry), Apr. 25, 1723.⁶
Levi—Elizabeth Andrews, 9-7-1767.¹
Levi—Mary Jenkins, 1-21-1774.¹
Levi—Abigail Devenny, 7-31-1814.³
Mahlon—Mary Leonard, 10-29-1814.³
Mark—Ann Haines, 2-15-1827.¹⁰
Moses—Patience Antram, Dec. 11, 1747.¹
Nathan—Sarah Austin, 1725.⁹
Nathan—Rebecca Ballanger, 5-21-1756.¹
Nathan—Esther Buzby, 1825.¹⁴
Nathaniel (s. William)—Mary Harvey (d. John), Mar. 23, 1739.⁶
Ner—Elizabeth Jones, 1-1-1801.³
Ner—Ann Eliza Hunter, 10-17-1833.³
Peter M. (s. William M.)—Anna Droew, 3-17-1874.⁴
Richard—Deborah Peak, 8-27-1807.³
Richard—Elizabeth Crammer, 8-13-1828.³
Robert—Rachel Venicomb, 5-17-1760.¹
Robert P.—Sarah L. Hewlings, 5-25-1831.³
Samuel—Elizabeth Buzby (d. William), 5-13-1767.⁶

Haines, Samuel (s. Samuel and Lydia)—Mary Stevenson (d. Cornell), 10-16-1788.[6]
Samuel—Mary Pettit, 7-26-1799.[3]
Samuel—Mary Wisham, 7-26-1803.[3]
Samuel—Elizabeth Brown, 4-10-1806.[3]
Samuel—Hannah Eyres, 2-21-1811.[3]
Samuel—Edith Coats, 3-6-1817.[3]
Samuel— ——— LeMunion, 6-22-1832.[3]
Samuel B.—Rebecca Garwood, 9-21-1836.[3]
Samuel S.—Elizabeth C. Stokes, 11-11-1869.[10]
Simeon—Mary Stratton, 5-28-1766.[7]
Simeon—Ann Cole, 1-8-1797.[3]
Solomon—Rebecca Sharp, Oct. 17, 1749.[1]
Solomon—Rachel Curtis, 12-13-1797.[10]
Spencer Lincoln (s. Joel and Martha)—Adelaide Peterson (d. James and Hannah), 12-4-1889.[4]
Stokes—Lydia Ann French, 1818.[14]
Stokes—Mary S. Sloan, 11-10-1879.[2]
Tailor—Ann Wilson, 12-5-1822.[3]
Thomas—Elizabeth Austin, 1692.[6]
Thomas—Rebekkah Foster, 1726.[6]
Thomas—Elizabeth Mullin, 10-10-1761.[1]
Thomas—Lucretia Pettit, 11-23-1761.[1]
Thomas—Mary Cattell, 11-12-1766.[1]
Thomas—Sarah Conrow, 3-23-1778,[1]
Thomas—Mary French, 2-24-1803.[3]
Thomas—Sarah Coal, 12-31-1818.[3]
Thomas—Sarah Coates, 1818.[14]
Thomas—Elizabeth Sharp, 3-14-1827.[3]
Thomas—Elizabeth Love, 6-6-1827.[3]
Thomas P.—Theodocia Wilkins, 3-4-1829.[3]
Timothy—Rebecca Fenimore, 11-8-1801.[3]
Uriah—Sarah R. Stokes, 8-4-1825.[3]
Wesley—Sarah Lippincott, 9-20-1835.[3]
William—Sarah Paine (d. John), 1695.[6]
William—Frances Bonney, 1732.[6]
William—Elizabeth Ballinger, 1748.[9]
William—Mary Earley, 1-8-1778.[1]
William B.—Mary T. Haines, 3-19-1857.[10]
William E.—Sarah B. Haines, 11-14-1833.[10]
William E.—Sarah Ann Coles, 3-5-1835.[3]
Wm.—Susan Silver, 2-25-1788.[7]

Haines, Wm R.—Mary S. Mullen (d. Samuel), 10-24-1822.³
Halbert, William—Penniah Branin, 1-22-1818.³
   William—Peniah Warren, 1818.¹⁴
Hale, Edward—Susanna Mulford, 3-2-1837.³
   Robert—Rebecca Reves, both Bristol, Pa., 1-29-1835.³
Haley, Benj.—Phebe Clark, 10-30-1805.³
   Ezekiah—Mary Carty, 12-8-1810.³
   Jacob—Elizabeth Mauris, Mar. 7, 1746.¹
   John—Abigail Marice, 3-7-1782.¹
   John—Rachel Deacon, 3-13-1831.³
   William—Lucy Brewer, 11-2-1826.³
Hall, Daniel—Jane French, 1697.⁶
   George, Cumberland co—Ann Elkinton, 6-20-1775.¹
   Francis—Naomi Middleton, June 9, 1740.¹
   James—Elizabeth Stockton, 4-6-1784.¹
   John—Rachel Cogall, 9-3-1764.¹
   John—Mary Davis, 8-27-1807.³
   John E.—Mary Taylor, 7-11-1809.³
   Joseph—Sibilla Pearson, 6-30-1808.³
   Joseph—Ruth Clement, 9-1-1808.³
   Joseph—Sarah Carty, 12-17-1718.³
   Joseph—Olivia Gardon, 1-3-1822.³
   Maurice—Eliz. Woodnutt, 12-28-1812.⁷
   Morris—Lydia Potts, 3-30-1788.⁷
   Samuel—Elizabeth Newbury, Apr. 29, 1746.¹
   Samuel—Julian Truax (colored), 3-21-1824.³
   Stephen—Elizabeth Smith, 4-29-1799.⁷
   Thomas—Mable Shoemaker, Dec. 17, 1750.¹
   Washington—Mary Ann Stockton, 9-7-1836.⁴
   William—Abigail Lear, 2-8-1823.³
   Rev. Mr.—Sarah Lucas, 3-2-1824.⁸
Hallam, Thomas—Jane L. Cooper, 2-26-1856.⁸
Hallet Richard (s. Israel and Naomi), NewYork City—Sarah
   Clarke (d. Isaac and Mary), Middlesex co., 5-4-1791.⁵
Hambleton, John—Meriah Cranmer, 4-7-1827.³
   Pierson—Mercy Ireton, 2-5-1804.³
   Samuel—Elizabeth Thompson, 8-30-1817.³
Hamilton, Benjamin M.—Anna L. Reeves, 3-16-1867.²
   Joseph A.—Mary W. Longstreth, 10-30-1823.³
   Thomas—Sarah Cox, 6-17-1804.³
   Thomas H.—Barbara Bozarth, 12-13-1876.²
   William—Catharine Conover, 9-7-1782.³

Hamilton, William—Ruth Ireland, 1-11-1806.[3]
Hammel, Enoch—Hope Mintle, 10-25-1795.[3]
   Felix—Elizabeth Langley, 4-26-1770.[1]
   James—Elizabeth Peake, 3-13-1799.[3]
   John—Jane Hancock, 9-26-1811.[3]
Hammell, Butler—Hester Austin, 6-3-1798.[3]
   Enoch—Eleanor Harris, 10-13-1825.[3]
   Israel—Hannah Hudson, 11-12-1829.[3]
   James—Sarah Butler, Oct. 23, 1742.[1]
   John—Elizabeth Kelly, 8-5-1778.[1]
   Laban—Rebecca Brock, 3-9-1837.[3]
   Moses, Jr.—Jerusa P. Holland, 2-10-1829.[3]
Hammet, John—Mary Reeves, Jan., 1809.[3]
Hammett, George—Rhoda Packer, Feb. 21, 1731.[1]
Hammit, John—Rachel Eves, 2-1-1774.[1]
Hammitt, Charles—Sarah Anderson, 9-4-1806.[3]
   Elias—Anna Lippincott, 1-6-1779.[1]
   George, Gloucester co.—Sarah Sharp, 4-28-1757.[1]
   George—Margaret Coverly, 12-22-1798.[3]
   Jacob—Rebecca Crispen, 4-11-1795.[3]
   Thomas—Mary Bodine, 3-26-1810.[3]
Hammack, Samuel—Esther Sharp, 1747.[9]
Hempfield, Solomon—Mary Ann Cornish, 3-27-1837.[3]
Hamps, Jonah—Rebeccah Lippincott, 10-4-1798.[3]
Hance, Charles—Deborah W. Redford, 11-9-1835.[3]
   David, Jr.—Mary Updike, 1-17-1799.[3]
   Edward—Sarah Potts, 1-19-1814.[3]
   Jomes— Hannah Stratton, 11-24-1817.[7]
   Jediah—Sarah Burr, 1791.[3]
   Jeremiah (s. David and Hannah)—Mary Thorn (d. John and Tacy), 2-6-1812.[5]
   John—Grace Webb, 8-18-1838.[3]
Hancock, Asa—Amy Richardson, 7-19-1811.[3]
   Benjamin Deacon—Mary T. Richardson, 9-6-1826.[3]
   Benjamin R.—Anna Fennimore, 9-26-1857.[8]
   Caleb— Beulah Brown, 1-20-1828.[3]
   Daniel—Rhoda Lippincott, 3-1-1774.[1]
   Daniel—Hannah Hains, 2-20-1812.[4]
   Edward—Sarah English, Jan. 23, 1742.[1]
   Edward—Susan Rose, 1-25-1823.[3]
   Elijah—Maria Scattergood, 1-4-1821.[3]
   Elisha—Bethia Antrim, 3-12-1812.[3]

Hancock, Ephraim—Louisa E. Aaronson, 3-3-1831.³
  George—Ann Tuly, 6-25-1754.¹
  Godfrey—Charity Cole, 11-21-1847.³
  Isaac—Mary English, 2-6-1782.¹
  Pearson—Meriam Deacon, 9-8-1779.¹
  Robert L.—Martha B. Foster, 6-2-1836.³
  Samuel—Lydia Gilbert, 10-29-1807.³
  Thomas—Martha Deacon, 3-6-1796.³
  Thomas—Prudence L. Micholson, 12-21-1826.³
  Thomas—Mercy Atkinson, 12-1-1836.³
  Timothy—Rachel Sirman, Nov. 6, 1684.¹
  William—Hester Curtis, 6-5-1782.¹
  William—Maria Mason, 6-11-1818.³
Handcock, John—Martha Richardson, Jan. 1, 1739.¹
Hangon, John—Mary Eliza Bragg, 7-27-1837.³
Hank, John—Rebekkah Bryant, Jr., 1737.⁶
  Martin—Hannah Foster, 3-31-1802.³
Hankerson, John—Elizabeth Risdon, 7-16-1820.³
Hankins, George—Martha E. Dudley, 9-9-1824.³
  Isaac—Mathew (? Martha) Griffy, 9-23-1771.¹
  John—Mary Signet, 9-3-1754.¹
  John—Hannah Burden, 10-23-1778.¹
  Zachariah—Ann Hankins, 6-10-1803.³
  Zackeriah—Sarah Folwlen, 3-16-1802.³
Hankinson, Charles—Rachel Filers, 5-12-1832.³
Hannoydatt, John—Mrs. Rhody Nugent, 7-14-1799.³
Harbert, Isaac—Tabitha Bell, 8-15-1765.¹
Harden, John—Sarah Bowen, 10-23-1806.³
Hardiman, Abraham—Rebekka Wilsford, 1698.⁶
Harding, Thomas—Elizabeth Nichols, 1693.⁶
  William—Bridget Killday, 6-14-1784.¹
  William—Margaret Crockfort, 10-8-1815.³
Hardman, Josiah—Mary Miller, 4-9-1835.³
Hargrove, John—Catherine Miller, 9-10-1763.¹
Harker, Aaron—Rachel Ann Earlin, 1-23-1883.²
  Abel—Damaris Zelley, 12-23-1782.¹
  Benjamin—Mary Harris, 12-19-1804.³
  Benjamin—Elizabeth Pitman, 11-24-1819.³
  Benjamin—Catharine Horner, Monmouth co., 10-13-1836.³
  Edmond—Eliza Anderson, 12-5-1816.³
  Isaac—Martha Berryman, 2-11-1796.⁶
  Joseph—Sarah Marrow, 11-29-1779.¹

Harker, Joseph, Jr.—Martha Parker, 11-3-1832.[3]
  Samuel—Pheby Kithcart, 7-6-1804.[3]
  Thomas, Mary Ecret, 3-23-1826.[3]
  Whittam—Rebecca Four. No date given.[3]*
  ———— — ———— Whitcraft, 11-30-1899.[2]
Harman, Lot—N. Williams, 10-1-1812.[3]
Harmer, Joshua L.—Rebecca W. Haines, 11-17-1864.[10]
Harmon, Peter—Anna Woodward, 2-15-1834.[3]
Haronson, Samuel—Mercy Rockhill, 12-29-1825.[3]
Harriott, Samuel—Jane Gardiner (certificate), Feb. 3, 1690.[6]
Harris, Abraham—Rebeckah Hollingshead, 1-7-1788.[4]
  Abram R.—Ann Howell, 2-1-1832.[3]
  Benjamin—Catherine Tarker, 8-24-1806.[3]
  David—Elizabeth Horner, 1-5-1816.[3]
  Francis—Rejoice Burge, 10-17-1774.[1]
  Francis—Harriet Herbert, 1-25-1806.[3]
  George—Mary Verree, 1745.[6]
  George—Mary Burr, 5-2-1772.[1]
  Henry—Elizabeth Herbert, 6-2-1802.[3]
  Isaac—Jane Applegate, 4-6-1818.[3]
  ~~Jeremiah~~—Rebecca Powell, 11-4-1802.[13]
  Joel S., Philadelphia—Anna Longcusp, 3-5-1834.[3]
  John—Sarah Eldridge, Mar. 24, 1737.[1]
  John—Jemima Ashton, Apr. 2., 1750.[1]
  Joseph—Mary Lamb, 8-21-1796.[3]
  Joseph—Sarah Coates, 1822.[4]
  Otis—Jemima Braddock, 8-23-1818.[3]
  Robert—Mahaley Scoby, 2-26-1835.[3]
  Samuel—Charlotte Ranier, 1-9-1811.[3]
  Samuel—Esther Miller, 12-20-1818.[5]
  Samuel—Sarah Monyon, 6-23-1832.[3]
  Thomas—Christian Wilson, 3-18-1798.[3]
  Thomas—Elizabeth Ellis, 3-18-1830.[3]
  Thomas—Delia Johnson, 6-20-1839.[4]
  Thos.—Mary Jones, 12-24-1801.[3]
  William—Sarah Atkinson, Jan. 5, 1731.[1]
  William—Jane Richardson, 3-18-1772.[1]
  William—Hannah Wilson, 4-9-1783.[1]
Harrison—Alexander—Sarah Moore, 1823.[14]

---

*Married by Samuel Wright, J. P.

Harrison, Benj.—Harriet Parker, 10-19-1822.³
  George—Elizabeth Schuyler, 8-12-1839.³
  Joseph—Martha Walton, 2-7-1776.¹
  Richard—Ruth Buckman, May 4, 1687.⁵
  Richard—Rachel Everingham, June 21, 1736.¹
  Richard—Edith Wright, 8-14-1765.¹
  Thomas—Rebecca Hodson, 3-25-1804.³
  William—Mary Gale, 9-28-1813.⁸
  Wright—Sarah Murdock, 12-31-1832.³
Harry, Aubrey—Sarah Bonsall, 1-14-1754.¹
Harsfull, John—Hannah Kunlass, 2-10-1836.³
Hart, Benj.—Elizabeth Shemerwas, 12-8-1814.³
  Gasper—Martha Reed, 12-25-1806.³
  Jacob—Mary Read, 10-29-1801.³
  James. H.—Elizabeth Bennett, 1865.⁸
  John—Silva Daniels, 5-17-1817.³
  William—Jane Coney, 1-9-1823.³
Hartgrove, William—Sarah Goaldy, 10-19-1815.³
  Joseph—Mary Armstrong, 8-30-1834.³
Hartley, Hugh—Mary Duckworth, Dec. 29, 1740.¹
  James—Elizabeth Bispham, 3-24-1796.³
Hartman, Caleb—Mary Brown, 4-21-1821.³
  Enoch—Caroline Borden, 2-28-1817.³
  George—Bernice Stevenson, 12-4-1831.³
  John—Sarah Radford, 4-6-1761.¹
  John—Sabillah Elkinton, 4-6-1771.¹
  John—Mary Hutchinson, 7-29-1832.³
Hartshorn, Epson—Mary Hodson, 9-6-1806.³
  John—Achsah Warren, 3-6-1806.³
  John, Jr. (s. John and Lucy), Union co.—Elizabeth Field (d. Elijah and Mary), 6-5-1799.,
  Samuel—Abigail Shinn, 10-9-1823.³
  William, Monmouth co.—Lydia DeCamp, 6-15-1836.³
Hartshorne, Enoch, Monmouth co.—Elizabeth Salter, 11-22-1761.¹
  Hugh—Hannah Pattison, 1741.⁶
  Samuel W.—Ann Mount, 5-8-1779.¹
  William—Elizabeth Jones. No data given.*
Harvey, Daniel—Sarah Folwell, 8-11-1777.¹
  David—Margaret Epley, 11-16-1801.³

---

*Married by Samuel Wright, J. P.

Harvey, Job (s. John)—Mary Satterthwaite (d. Samuel), 5-25-1768.[5]
  Job—Sarah Bunting, 7-12-1821.[3]
  John—Elizabeth Hun, 1718.[6]
  Jno.—Harriet Curtis, 2-12-1806.[3]
  Peter—Mary Hancock, Apr. 8, 1748.[1]
  Samuel D.—Rebecca Schofield, 12-12-1852[4]
  Thomas—Lydia W. Wainwright, 10-6-1829.[3]
  William—Phebe Austin, 3-9-1796.[3]
Hase, John—Sarah Wilson, 10-12-1798.[3]
Hazelwood, George—Margaret Butcher, 1681.[6]
Hatcher, William—Bulah Sutvin, 1-29-1826.[3]
Hatfield, George—Mary Moses, July 6, 1739.[8]
Haton, Robert—Susan Hunter, 1-20-1825.[3]
Havens, Cyrus—Margaret Ford, 9-30-1826.[3]
  Daniel—Amy Harker, 2-13-1823.[3]
  Edward—Sarah Parker (d. Joseph, Sr.) 1749.[11]
  Joseph—Susannah Vreeland, 9-13-1757.[1]
  Joseph—Mary Young, 2-4-1805.[3]
  Stephen—Sarah Ellison, 6-1-1784.[1]
  Thomas—Sarah Cramer, 1737.[11]
  Thomas—Sarah Taylor, 1751.[11]
  Thomas—Ann Allen, 7-8-1797.[3]
  Thomas—Fanny Bowker, 1-21-1829.[3]
  William—Ann Anderson, 12-31-1831.[3]
Haviland, Thomas Joshua—Phebe Eliz. Ballinger, 5-8-1929.[10]
  William—Alexa Swemm, 11-11-1815.[3]
Hawk, Joseph—Margaret McKilley, 6-5-1780.[1]
Hawkins, Harry, Jr—Clara King Gaskill, 10-20-1897.[2]
  Robert Henry—Emma E. Hopkins (d. John), 3-17-1880.[4]
  Roger—Eliz. Holman, 7-14-1812.[8]
  Thomas—Polly Kinsey, 4-20-1799.[3]
Hay, Morris—Eleanor Hutton, 9-13-1768.[1]
  Thomas—Mary Thorne, May 20, 1746.[1]
  William—Mary Curtis, 8-3-1770.[1]
  William—Charlotte Ramsey, 5-16-1815.[3]
Hayburn, James, Philadelphia—Mary Hopewell, 12-24-1781.[1]
Haydock, Eden—Mary Ash West, 10-6-1803.[13]
Hayes, Jacob—Deborah Westervelt, Nov. 1, 1744.[1]
  Stacy—Harriet Hammell, 2-22-1816.[3]
  William—Lydia Meyer, Dec. 12, 1740.[1]
Haynes, John—Esther Bourton, Dec. 10, 1684.[6]

Hays, Abraham—Elizabeth Whitcraft, 9-18-1836.³
  Addis—Mary Hancock, 2-21-1830.³
  Charles—Sarah Adinson, 11-9-1834.³
  Jacob—Mary Lippincott, 12-25-1812.³
  John—Rhody Vaughn, 11-19-1782.¹
  Oswell—Rebecca Mingin, 11-12-1815.³
  Speachus—Jane Jones, 9-2-1821.³
  Thomas—Elizabeth Borden, 6-11-1818.³
  William—Rebecca King, 5-19-1777 ¹
  William Jr.—Harriet Hays, 2-26-1818.³
  William—Hannah Earl, 9-28-1814 ³
Haywood, George—Abigail Bowne, 9-17-1828.⁴
Haze, Michael—Elizabeth Hammel, 12-26-1811.³
Hazlehurst, Ambrose—Isabella Johnson, 4-16-1825.³
Hazelton, Abraham—Susanna Burroughs, 6-7-1756.¹
Hazleton, Thomas—Mary Wilson, 5-22-1831.³
  William—Abigail Wright, 4-22-1775.¹
  William—Jane Elberson, 3-14-1822.³
  Samuel—Martha Paine. No date given.³ ⁵
Headley, Jesse—Mary Rockhill, 10-23-1837.³
Henly, Joseph—Ann Burton, 7-7-1833.³
Heard, Richard—Mary Rulins, 2-25-1777.¹
Heartly, Roger, Pennsylvania—Rebecca Parker, June 21, 1727.¹
Heaton, Abraham, Bucks co., Pa.—Mary Bowman, 11-16-1826.³
  David—Mary English, 11-30-1826.³
  Joseph—Lydia Hunter, 1-9-1831.³
  Robert—Ann Horner, 1-8-1795.¹
Heavens, Daniel—Rebecca Wainright, 2-2-1759.¹
Heaviland, William—Sarah Farren, 1-8-1802.³
Heavlin, Charles—Emily Hutchinson, 5-14-1829.³
Hedger, Joseph— —— Webb, 8-17-1814.³
  Joseph—Sarah Stephenson, 1742.⁶
Hedgson, Joseph—Mary Davis, 12-23-1831.³
Heisler, Daniel—Mary Carman, 9-23-1779.¹
  George—Rachel Sharp, 3-5-1831.³
  George M.— Anna Stainbrook, 9-12-1877.⁴
  John—Amey Simons, 12-16-1821.³
  Westley—Susan Grant, 3-9-1823.³
Heiss, Joseph—Jannet Taylor, 3-18-1811.³

---

*Married by Samuel Wright, J. P.

Hellson, Richard—Catharine Clayton, Jan. 12, 1831.[1]
Helms, William—Letitia Brailsford, 11-7-1802.[3]
Henderson, Charles Dilworth (s. Davis and Helen), Detroit, Mich.,
—Helen Earl Newbold (d. Joseph and Harriet), 5-15-1889.[4]
  George—Elizabeth Shemely, 7-25-1818.[3]
  Jonathan, Monmouth co.—Mary Brownson, 12-26-1816.[3]
Hendrickson, Daniel Jr.—Mary Lippincott, 2-19-1807.[3]
  David—Hannah Middleton, 12-2-1800.[3]
  James—Susan Ann Harris, 6-29-1833.[3]
  John—Anne Cox, 11-14-1763.[1]
  Joseph—Elizabeth Forsyth, 1-14-1796.[5]
  Joseph—Rebecca Atkinson, 2-23-1831.[3]
  Joseph—Hannah Sweet, 2-11-1837.[3]
  Thomas—Edith A. Wall, 11-20-1834.[3]
Hendry, John—Sarah Lovett, 11-24-1764.[1]
  Samuel—Elizabeth Anderson, 3-2-1785.[1]
  Samuel—Mary Hough, 3-13-1806.[3]
  Shadrack—Elizabeth Johnston, 8-30-1834.[3]
Hengrickson, Jacob—Ruth Fregam, 11-23-1800.[3]
Henry, Charles—Louisa Johnson Stockton, 9-3-1863.[8]
  John—Susanna Gibbs, 1-6-1764.[1]
  Moses—Lucretia Smith, 1822.[14]
Henton, George—Abigail Rodgers, Sept. 23, 1743.[1]
Hemmingsworth Isaac—Deborah Cloin, 6-26-1825.[3]
Herbert, Benajah—Sarah Starkey—10-7-1817.[3]
  George—Elizabeth Coward, 8-30-1835.[3]
  Jacob, Shrewsbury—Hannah Allen, 9-14-1797.[3]
Herd, Samuel—Eliza Brayman, 2-23-1768.[1]
  Thomas—Alice Smith, Jan. 18, 1741.[1]
Heritage, John—Ann Hugg, Gloucester co., Aug. 22, 1741.[1]
  John W., Gloucester co.—Ruth Hains, Oct. 14, 1746.[1]
  Thomas—Elizabeth Higgins, 10-24-1813.[3]
Herkins, John—Mary Whitaker, 5-3-1765.[1]
Herman, John—Margaret Boyes, 7-28-1804.[8]
Herriott, Barnibas—Sarah Webb, 1-27-1798.[9]
Herritage, Joseph—Sarah Whiteall, Gloucester co. Mar. 17, 1730.[1]
Herts, Franklin B.—Eliza Wilson, 1-31-1881.[2]
  William—Mary Gifford, 5-1-1828.[3]
Hervey, James—Harriet Frake, 5-2-1829.[3]
  Samuel—Elizabeth Murphy, 7-21-1816.[3]
Hervy, George—Grace Math's, 2-11-1811.[3]
  Silvester—Mary Ireland, 11-12-1808.[3]

Heslip, David—Catherine Garkins, 6-18-1788.[1]
Hess, Charles—Hannah Fowler, 11-13-1824.[3]
Heulings, Abraham—Sarah Perkins, 8-15-1757.[1]
  Isaac—Ruth Snowden, Dec. 15, 1752 [8]
  Israel—Ann Tantum, Oct. 10. 1740.[1]
  Jacob—Elizabeth Eves, 1-16-1775.[1]
  Joseph—Hannah Wood, Gloucester co., May 12. 1741.[1]
  Joseph—Elizabeth Hammick, Gloucester co., 6-14-1756.[1]
  Samuel—Rosamond Garwood, 6-22-1763.[1]
Heustis, Barzilla—Hope Stockton, 2-7-1804.[3]
  John—Mary Higbey, 1-29-1765.[1]
Heuston, William—Lavinia Cox, 3-23-1826.[3]
Hewitt, Chas. Barrington—Mary Eliz. Giterson, 5-9-1872.[8]
  Francis K.—Emma Churchman, 12-25-1872.[8]
Hewit, Samuel—Ruth Page, 2-5-1802.[3]
Hewlings, Abraham—Anne Mary Hay, 7-29-1758.[1]
  Abraham—Elizabeth Burr, 9-5-1774.[1]
  Abraham—Sarah Collins, 12-4-18'9.[3]
  Abram—Mary Vandeveer, 8-3-1825.[3]
  Amos—Lydia Hollingshead, 1-26-1797.[3]
  Amos—Mary Haines, 2-5-1829.[3]
  Isaac—Ann Ware, 10-19-1763.[1]
  Jacob L.—Mary C. Butterworth, 12-3-1829.[3]
  James—Edith Earl, 3-9-1816.[3]
  Mark—Catharine Holt, 4-10-1829.[3]
  Samuel—Ann L. Eyres, 11-1-1810.[3]
  Samuel—Hannah Coates. 11-18-1824.[3]
  Thomas H.—Sarah L. Burroughs, 12-19-1833.[3]
  William—Dorothy Eves (certificate), 9-7-1680.[6]
  William (s. Jacob)—Esther Wright (d. Jonathan), June 2, 1743.[6]
  William—Lydia Lamb, 9-21-1797.[3]
Hewlins, Nathaniel—Mary Leech, 12-12-1821.[8]
Hews, William—Prudence Thomas, 10-10-1757.[1]
Hewson, John—Jane Erwin, 5-14-1779.[1]
  Joseph—Rachel Haines, 4-5-1770.[1]
Hickman, Francis—Jane Moon, Nov. 3. 1743.[1]
Higbee, William—Ruth Middleton, 6-21-1756.[1]
  Samuel—Ann Robbins, 5-14-1815.[3]
Higgbee, Hugh Hollinshed. Dr.—Rebecca Lippincott, 12-10-1829.[3]
Higgins, Benjamin—Mary Jobs, 9-18-1832.[3]
  Bryan—Sarah Warrick, Aug. 17, 1737 [1]
  Cornelius—Anna Jane Thimbless, 9-9-1830.[3]

Higgins, Goldy—Sarah Bennett, 2-24-1805.³
Jackson—Martha Covenhoven, 9-16-1802.³
Jodia—Mary Newbold, May 12, 1684.¹
Jonathan—Mercy Adams, 3-16-1798.³
William—Catherine Walberth, 8-13-1809.³
William—Catherine Hebberth, 9-13-1809.³
Highflinger, Joseph—Elizabeth Cross, 1-1-1833.³
Hight, John—Mary Roberts, 4-12-1855.⁸
Hilborne, Thomas—Mary Shreve, 1739.⁶
Hill, Henry—Martha Thompson, 7-24-1819.³
James A., Trenton—Mary Ann Ashmore, 12-15-1830.³
Jeremiah—Lydia Davis (colored), 10-23-1803.³
John, Pennsylvania—Elizabeth Smith, 12-15-1756.⁵
John—Ann Hodgins, 6-2-1770.¹
John—Mary Gongo, 9-18-1819.³
John—Sally Riley (colored), 6-9-1833.³
Peter—Tina Lewis, 9-9-1795.³
Robert—Anne Gillman, Nov. 1, 1749.¹
Seth—Mary Grubb, May 8, 1685.¹
William—Elizabeth Ashton, Sept. 9, 1749.¹
William—Mary Burns, 1-1-1810.³
William Nutt—Euphemia Howell, 9-12-1832.³
Hiller, Edward—Sarah Haines, Jan. 21, 1733.¹
Uriah—Sarah Eayres, July 21, 1745.¹
Hillhouse, Thomas—Julia Ten Eyck, 6-3-1884.⁴
Hilliard, Edward—Nancy Stockton, 8-5-1813.³
Hollingshead—Ann Mullen, 5-14-1788.⁴
Joshua—Martha R. Oliphant, 5-8-1838.³
Uriah—Elizabeth Wirt, 2-14-1796.³
William H. I.—Martha Virginia Woolston, 3-21-1871.²
Hillier, Jacob—Martha Robinson, 4-17-1762.¹
John—Elizabeth Green, Pennsylvania, 1-9-1772.¹
Hillman, Daniel—Grace Haines, 1-16-1806.³
Joseph, Haddonfield—Ann Parker, Tuckerton, 11-8-1833.³
Samuel—Sarah Allingbury, 5-20-1813.³
Hillyard, William—Mary Alcutt, 11-9-1817.³
Jonathan—Emeline C. Haines, 2-11-1847.¹⁰
William—Ann Reeve, 9-20-1821.¹⁰
Hilyer, Samuel—Mary Atkinson, 8-22-1816.³
Hinchman, John—Elizabeth Weiley, 12-30-1789.¹
Lot—Catherine Newman, 1-17-1798.³
Hinds, Jeremiah—Mary Fitzhugh, May 29, 1739.¹

Hines, Thomas—Elly Stuart, 7-31-1784.[1]
    William—Jane Reeve, 1-11-1818.[3]
Hinkle, Hiram (s. William and Catharine), and Adeline Gibbs (d. Samuel), 11-13-1873.[4]
    Thomas—Rachel Husbands, 6-19-1799.[3]
Hirby, William—Ann Taylor, Apr. 18, 1735.[1]
Hireborn, John (s. Amos and Ruth), Pennsylvania—Mary B. Smith (d. Thomas and Latitia), 10-17-1822.[12]
Hires, William D., Rev.—Eleanor I. Mott, 5-20-1835.[3]
Hireton, Obediah—Mary King, July 29, 1723.[1]
Hite, Ralph, Philadelphia—Charlotte Sharp, 12-15-1832.[3]
Hoagland, Oaky—Hannah Price, 12-26-1805.[3]
    Okey—Eleanor Field, 6-1-1795.[3]
Hodge, Wm., Jr.—Elizabeth Mount, 1-14-1813[3]
Hodgson, Joseph—Mary Davis, 12-23-1831.[3]
Hodson, George—Harriet Gibson, 2-7-1811.[3]
    John—Anne Whittiker, Sept. 27, 1716.[5]
    Levi—Jane B. Wright, 6-6-1833.[3]
    William—Elizabeth Taylor, 9-2-1777.[1]
Hoff, William—Mary Force, 10-4-1833.[3]
Hoffe, Daniel—Mary Worley, Mar. 4, 1741.[1]
Hoffee, George—Margaret Brandenburg, 9-21-1775.[1]
Hoffman, Jonathan—Amanda Elizabeth Holland, 7-9-1852.[4]
Hoge—Joseph, Elizabeth Fenton, 1-15-1763.[1]
Hogeland, D. V.—Ester Gilkinson, 8-3-1831.[8]
Hoggins, Timothy—Katharine Hamilton, Aug. 21, 1745.[1]
Hoile, Nicholas—Priscilla Bell, 12-14-1777.[1]
    Nicholas—Increase Middleton, 3-20-1828.[10]
Hoiles, George—Gartrightefredris Mathis, 1-19-1826.[3]
    Nicholas—Phebe Gaunt, 10-10-1811.[13]
Holbert, Thomas—Mary Cline, 12-25-1797.[3]
Holder, John—Joanna Tindall, Feb. 9, 1736.[1]
    Samuel—Tacey Jones, Nov. 1, 1736.[1]
Holeman, Elsworth—Elizabeth Parson, 10-11-1838.[3]
    Joel—Ann Curtis, 4-8-1816.[3]
    John—Nancy Hufman, 2-10-1803.[3]
Holland, Daniel—Mary Smith, Aug. 20, 1730.[1]
    James—Hannah Reeves, 4-14-1803.[3]
    Jeremiah—Deborah Kelley, 10-19-1826.[3]
    John—Elizabeth Venaball, 3-31-1790.[1]
    Joshua—Margaret Matthews, Philadelphia, 10-22-1800.[3]
    Samuel A.—Rachel Stinmitz, 1-16-1817.[3]

Hollings, Charles— Nancy Brown, 7-26-1799.³
  Lawrence—Mary Conrow, 7-18-1818.³
Hollingshead, Andrew (s. Morgan and Rebecca)—Susannah French
  (d. George and Rachel), 1811.¹²
  Benjamin—Jerusha Oliphant, 11-27-1759.¹
  Charles—Esther Haines, 11-17-1825.³
  Charles Ellis—Mary Shaw Sterling, 10-20-1813.³
  Enoch—Martha Austin, 3-23-1797.³
  Hugh, Jr.—Mary Mallen, 9-11-1782.¹
  Jacob (s. Josiah and Mary)—Mary Haines (d. Samuel and
    Elizabeth), 7-15-1789.⁶
  John—Agnes Hackney, 1693.⁶
  John—Sarah Dobbins, 8-25-1767.¹
  John—Martha Boston, 3-18-1782.¹
  John—Zelas Hollingshead, 12-5-1787.¹
  Joseph—Sarah Pearson, 1740.⁶
  Joseph—Jerusha Hollingshead, 8-30-1759.¹
  Joseph—Mary Buttler, 3-1-1787.¹
  Joshua—Ann French, 6-20-1811.⁴
  Morgan—Rebecca Matlock, 9-30-1775.¹
  Morgan (s. Edmund and Mary)—Jane Lippincott (d. Joshua
    and Rachel), Woolwich, 5-11-1809.¹²
  Samuel—Ann Russell, July 9-1736.¹
  Samuel—Elizabeth Hancock, 2-26-1809.³
  William—Hannah Ruderon, Apr. 1, 1727.¹
Hollins, Samuel— Sarah Wilson, 9-21-1809.³
Holloway, Benj.—Abigail Robins, 11-27-1814.³
  George, Hunterdon co.—Ruth Wood, Nov. 10, 1731.⁵
  George—Mary Emley, 7-25-1761.¹
  George R.—Sarah Ann Ferguson, 9-10-1839.³
  Isaac—Mary Haines, 1758.⁹
  James—Ann Kirby, 6-15-1803.³
  James—Mrry Burtis, 1-15-1835.²
  John—Constant Handcock, 3-28-1758.¹
  Peter—Margaret Forgison, 2-20-1824.³
  Peter—Ann Stackhouse. No date given.³*
  William—Ann Martin, 4-21-1756.¹
Holman, Daniel—Rachel Reeves, 1-14-1815.³
Holmes, James Shreve (s. James and Hannah)—Mary Louisa
  Oliphant (d. Jon. and Louisa), 12-18-1867.⁴

---

*Married by Samuel Wright, J. P.

Holmes, Aaron—Sarah Austin, 3-7-1799.[3]
 Joseph L.—Ann Lawkie, 11-12-1800 [3]
 Levi C.—Mary Ann VanMartyr, 12-10-1836.[3]
 Rozel—Anne Bruce, 11-11-1822 [3]
 Thomas—Elizabeth Alkman, 3-31-1832.[3]
 William—Mary Venable, 2-25-1768.[1]
 Zebulon—Sarah Higgins, 12-3-1807.[3]
Holton, John—Ann Cline, 9-25-1796.[3]
Homan, John—Gloucester co.—Mary Johnson, 3-1-1812.[3]
 Peter—Mercy Harding, Oct. 25, 1730.[1]
Honeyman, Samuel D.—Mary James, 3-31-1805.[3]
Hoock, Samuel, Trenton—Hannah Mount, 6-25-1764.[1]
Hood, John M.—Louisa Steenberg, 4-24-1823.[3]
Hooker, Jacob—Sarah Darets, Oct. 10, 1744.[1]
Hooper, Abram—Priscilla Southwick, 9-28-1767.[1]
 Abraham—Phebe Spacius, 5-10-1832.[3]
 Jacob—Elizabeth Armstrong, 2-3-1829.[3]
 Samuel—Ann Baxter, 9-9-1799.[3]
 William—Margaret French, Dec. 24, 1744.[1]
 William—Elizabeth Goldy, 3-22-1801.[3]
 William—Theodosia Morris, 12-31-1826.[3]
Hooten, Benj.— Baulah Mullen, 12-21-1809.[3]
 Thomas—Rebecca Conrow, 2-6-1812.[3]
 Thomas—Jane Dorman, 1-1-1778.[1]
Hooton, William—Rebecca Stretch, 1-14-1806.[3]
Hootton, John—Sarah Kay, Apr. 22, 1737.[1]
Hoover, Wm. Dier, Jr.—Ray Irick Sailer (d. Samuel), 12-24-1888.[4]
Hopewell, Daniel—Mary Becket, 7-27-1754.[1]
 Joseph—Sarah Briggs, 1733.[9]
Hopkins, Davis—Susan Cole, 4-16-1839.[3]
 Isaac—Mary Ackley, 8-24-1795.[3]
 John—Louisa Mott, 5-21-1834.[3]
 Joseph—Ann Shippey, Mar. 20, 1745.[1]
 Robert—Dinah Thompson, 1726.[6]
 Willard—Lucy Ann Read, 12-6-1836.[3]
Hopper, John, Gloucester co.—Ann Garwood, Dec. 5, 1737.[1]
 Samuel—Mary Johnson, 1734.[3]
Horn, James—Mary Smick, 10-2-1802.[3]
 John—Lydia Hart, Dec. 27, 1736 [1]
Horner, Bartholomew (s. Isaac)—Elizabeth Wills (d. John), Jan. 25, 1729.[6]
 Benjamin—Hannah Hammel, 3-6-1800.[3]

Horner, Caleb R.—Catherine Brown, 8-30-1834.³
  Charles—Elizabeth Toy, 12-11-1831.³
  Daniel—Elizabeth Durell, 1-21-1802.³
  David—Martha Stockton, 8-22-1836.³
  Dillon—Priscilla Palmer, 3-31-1833.³
  Edward—Lydia Anderson, 10-30-1818.³
  Edward—Lydia Mullen. 3-14-1824.³
  Elias—Sarah Bogar, 2-18-1827.³
  Ephraim—Rachel Rakestraw, 10-22-1805.³
  Fuller—Mrs. Penelope Dunphy, 12-18-1827.³
  Heath—Pleasant Haigue, Feb. 25, 1728.¹
  Isaac—Elizabeth Sykes, May 19, 1709.⁵
  Isaac—Eleanor Bowne, Sept. 4, 1718.⁵
  Isaac—Agnes Sesen, Aug. 4, 1730.¹
  Isaac (s. David and Mary—Keziah Pharo (d. Caleb and Silence)
    2-11-1813.¹²
  Isaac, Jr.—Mary Potts, Trenton, 11-6-1757.⁵
  James—Elizabeth Clymer, 1-2-1831.³
  John—Mary Harker, 3-14-1805.³
  John—Matilda Platt, 3-3-1807.³
  John—Elizabeth Lines, 12-16-1815.³
  John—Elizabeth Deacon, 1-9-1823.³
  John—Ann Vansciver, 4-19-1829.³
  John H.—Elizabeth Ford, 7-11-1835.³
  Joseph—Sarah Taylor, 1-3-1763.¹
  Joseph—Mary Cotten, 12-5-1798.³
  Joseph—Amy Page, 1-17-1818.³
  Richard—Juliann McMullen, 9-11-1824.³
  William—Sarah Campion, 1-2-1802.³
  William—Elizabeth Lucas, 10-11-1812.³
  William—Abigail Taylor, 1-12-1814.³
  William—Mary Mingen, 8-11-1825.³
  William—Maria Jackson, 7-7-1831.³
Hornor, Job—Levisa W. Wright, 11-23-1826.³
  John—Mary Butler, 7-8-1758.¹
  Richard—Patience Morris, 2-6-1800.³
Hornsetter, Joshua—Weightstell McMurren, 12-7-1829.³
Horsell, William—Phebe Hooper, 12-27-1807.³
Horsepull—Richard, Margaret Page, 11-10-1802.³
Horsley, Anderson—Rachel Mc Lealand, 5-15-1808.³
Hosier, Wm. Robart—Sarah Peake, 9-3-1881.²
Hoskins, John—Martha Treat, 12-12-1803.³

Hoskins, John—Mary Raper, 1750.[6]
 John, Jr.—Sarah Haines, 6-11-1809.[10]
 Thomas, Philadelphia—Elizabeth Richards, 4-5-1799.[3]
Hoskinson, Thomas Julius (s. William and Elizabeth), Erie, Pa.—Blance E. Williams (d. James and Mary), Waterford, Pa,, 12-18-1889.[4]
Hough, Jonathan—Mary Bryan, May 30, 1741.[1]
 Thomas—Euphemia Brown, 3-4-1817.[3]
 William—Elizabeth Tindell, 12-7-1825.[3]
Housler, Joseph—Sarah Ranier, 8-29-1781.[1]
 Thomas—Margaret Jackson. 10-20-1810.[3]
Houston, Paul—Naomi Cox, 10-6-1814.[3]
How, John—Mary Ann Blanchard, 11-16-1782 [1]
 Micajah, Hunterdon co.—Sarah Field, 1-22-1770.[1]
Howard, Benjamin—Ann Fenimore, 12-29-1796.[3]
 Frank—Susannah Bartlett, 5-30-1865.[8]
 John—Elizabeth Smith, 9-28-1811.[3]
 Levi D.—Anna Maria Miller, 3-31-1829.[3]
 Michael—Catherine Roche, July 24, 1731.[1]
 Michael—Lydia Bittle, 9-9-1756.[1]
 Peter—Elizabeth Middleton, 11-2-1784.[1]
 Robert H.—Anna M. Fromberger, 11-13-1856.[4]
 Robert Hill—Annie Eyre Walcott, 7-3-1884.[4]
Howell, Abel—Euphamia Miller, 6-16-1799.[3]
 Arthur R.—Ann Eliza Hise. 12-21-1837.[3]
 Daniel—Mary Chambers, 6-27-1833.[3]
 Edward L —Rachel Nolton, 10-2-1814.[3]
 Henry B., Trenton—Hannah Curlis, 1-2-1812.[3]
 Jeremiah—Catharine Megonagle, 3-19-1818.[3]
 John—Philay Valentine, 3-15-1817.[3]
 John Richardson—Mrs. Susan Deacon Slack, 4-28-1886.[4]
 Lemuel—Tamar Heustis, 1-15-1804.[3]
 Richard—Rebecca Stockton, 9-21-1818.[8]
 Stacy—Sarah Taylor, 2-22-1821.[3]
 Thomas—Rebecca Church, 3-11-1797.[3]
 William—Elizabeth Starkey, 12-17-1814.[3]
 William A.—Sarah Ann Carman, 4-18-1833.[3]
 William C.—Eva Lawrence, Trenton, 11-11-1828.[3]
 William C.—Hannah H. Borden, 3-13-1822.[3]
Howey, Robt.—Naomi Coulson, 12-26-1791.[7]
 William—Anne Hewit, 8-4-1783.[1]
Hoy, James—Ella Nora Howell, 9-5-1832.[3]

Hoy, John—Achsah Kindell, 3-31-1783.[1]
Hoyle, Andrew—Pheby Nichols, 6-25-1783.[1]
Hubbard, John—Elizabeth Maddocks, May 13, 1732.[1]
  Lucius V.—Mary R. Peacock, 10-19-1840.[4]
Hubbs, Charles—Phebe Anderson, 3-26-1807.[3]
  Edward—Hannah Cohn, 3-3-1800.[3]
  Edward—Rebecca Vandergrift, 9-5-1816.[3]
  Joseph—Rebecca Stockton, 9-14-1797.[3]
  Philip K.—Rebecca Brick, 4-4-1821.[7]
  Samuel C.—Priscilla Garwood, 12-13-1831.[3]
  Snowden—Achsah Ivins, 11-15-1808.[3]
Hudd, Thomas—Sarah Blantley, 1689.[6]
Huddy, Hugh—Martha Hunloke, May 6, 1701.[1]
Hudson, Abimelech—Priscilla Beswick, Mar. 25, 1690.[1]
  John—Mary Stokes, 1696.[6]
  John—Elizabeth Moore, 11-3-1817.[3]
  William—Jane Evans (d. William), 1717.[9]
Huesson, Josiah—Ann Hammell, 12-18-1813.[3]
Huestis, Joseph—Euphamia, 8-6-1776.[1]
  Moses—Ann Rogers, 12-17-1771.[1]
Huff, Charles Lawrence—Charlotte Evelyn Randall, 9-25-1889.[4]
  Isaac—Mercy Leeds, 12-2-1771.[1]
  John—Rhoda Stockton, 3-22-1821.[3]
  Richard—Alice Herd, 12-29-1793.[8]
Hufman, Samuel—Sarah Prickett, 1-8-1839.[3]
Huffnagle, Allen—Mary McHenry, 4-5-1866.[2]
Hugg, George—Mary Williams, 6-22-1823.[4]
  Jacob—Hope Powell, Aug., 1793.[3]
  James—Lydia Emley, 10-18-1818.[3]
  John—Mary Middleton, 1730.[6]
  John—Elizabeth White, 3-24-1822.[3]
  John—Fanny Still, 2-1-1827.[3]
  Knight—Martha Reeve (wid.), 2-3-1803.[3]
  Samuel—Dorothy Jonnson, 5-13-1819.[3]
  Socrates—Frances Jackson, 3-24-1818.[3]
  Wm.—Margaret Shinn, 1-22-1801.[3]
Huggin, John—Hannah Martin, Nov. 30, 1736.[1]
Hughes, James—Rachel Lord, Mar. 7, 1737.[1]
  James—Ann Hemp, 8-26-1798.[3]
  James—Tryphena Tyler, 1-10-1803.[3]
  James—Hannah Engle, 3-19-1804.[3]
  Mathias—Eliza Smith, 3-3-1831.[3]

Hughes, William Evan—Sarah Antram, 10-28-1775.[1]
Hughston, John, Gloucester co.—Martha Austin, Nov. 1, 1740.[1]
Hulin, George, Jr.—Elizabeth Stokes, 1-22-1834.[3]
Hulings, Aully McCalley—Margaret Peacock, 3-21-1821.[3]
Hulme, George—Ann Butler, 5-31-1774.[1]
   George—Tennel Neale, 11-8-1781,[1]
   James S.—Hannah S. Lippincott, 10-5-1826.[13]
   Joseph M.—Margaret B. Oliphant, 4-9-1856.[4]
Huls, David—Mary Cassada, 1-25-1810.[3]
Hulse, Benjamin, Gloucester co.—Susan King, 9-11-1836.[3]
   Clayton—Martha Baird, Gloucester co., 2-14-1837.[3]
   Clifford—Alice Emley, 7-14-1898.[1]
   James—Rachael Gibbins, 5-13-1769.[1]
   John—Mary Fisher, 9-3-1808.[3]
   Samuel—Elizabeth Odell, 1-25-1821.[3]
Hultz, William—Ann Gifford, 4-7-1802.[3]
Hultze, William—Edith Clear, 2-6-1836.[3]
Hume, Joseph R.—Mary E. Shreve, 4-8-1819.[13]
   Robert—Elizabeth Paul, 1708.[6]
Humphreys, John—Elizabeth Wells, 1716.[6]
   John—Sarah Doughty, 5-8-1758.[1]
   Joshua—Encrease Lippincott, 1737.[6]
Humphries, Jonathan—Sarah Doughty, 1724.[6]
   Joshua—Rachel Horner, 1711.[6]
   Wm.—Mary Cary, 11-6-1805.[3]
Hunloke, Thomas—Sarah Bunting (d. Samuel), June 21, 1711.[3]
   Thomas—Mary Bard, 4-11-1771.[8]
Hunsinger, George—Alice Jennet, 6-4-1764.[1]
Hansman, John—Rachel Bishop, 2-14-1799.[3]
Hunt, Abram, Hunterdon co.—Theodosia Pierson, 2-21-1764.[1]
   Azariah—Elizabeth Salter, 3-8-1806.[3]
   Benjamin (s. John and Esther)—Phebe Cowperthwaite (d. Hugh and Rebecca), 2-20-1806.[12]
   Isaiah—Hester Stratton, 5-28-1766.[1]
   Jesse—Mary Carman, 11-19-1797.[3]
   Robert—Abigail Wood, Gloucester co., Dec. 19, 1733.[1]
   Samuel—Mary Gardner, 1739.[6]
   Samuel—Deborah Bennett, 12-1-1796.[4]
   William—Margaret Pearson, 1687.[6]
   William—Mary Woolman, 1720.[6]
Hunter, Adam—Mrs. Elishaba Severns, 11-20-1831.[3]
   Charles—Mary Hammell, 10-2-1811.[3]

Hunter, George—Sarah Taylor, 9-27-1804.³
James—Rachel Murphy, 11-21-1775.⁸
John—Mary Stratton, 11-3-1773.¹
John, Philadelphia—Jane Rickey, 8-28-1809.³
John—Rebecca Fish, 2-17-1831.³
Joseph—Mary Gilmer, Hunterdon co., 9-15-1764.¹
Thomas—Mary Pearson, 1-17-1799.³
William—Caroline S. King, 3-16-1837.³
William Washington—Mary McMasters, 5-9-1805.³
Huntley, Asher—Mary Parker, 11-12-1800.³
Joseph—Rebecca Hane, 8-24-1826.³
Hurley, Daniel—Atlantic Stokes, 1-1-1826.³
Edward—Frances Warwick, Monmouth co., Nov. 3, 1729.¹
Huse, Joseph—Mary Cline, 4-5-1806.³
Husted, Eli—Esther Haines, 1-11-1798 ³
Huston, Caleb—Priscilla Crispin, 3-8-1804.³
Jacob—Mary Backster, 7-1-1802.³
John—Mary Davison, 10-19-1799.³
Josiah—Maria Ward, 6-28-1828.³
Hutch, William—Maria Williams, 7-2-1814.³
Hutchens, Alfred—Susan Edgar, 12-17-1835.³
Hutchin, Amos—Elizabeth Luffbury, 10-25-1821.⁸
Hugh—Elizabeth Baker, July 6, 1730.¹
Hugh—Rebecca Underhill, Mar. 3, 1708.⁵
John—Sarah Gibbs, Nov. 9, 1742.¹
Samuel—Sarah Tucker, Oct. 10, 1738.¹
Hutchins, Aaron—Elizabeth Myers, 11-18-1830.³
Abraham—Martha Ann Amish, 3-16-1899.²
Amos—Hannah Fenimore, 4-4-1772.¹
George—Elizabeth Hall, Oct. 6, 1746.¹
Hugh—Ann Nutt, 1-23-1769.¹
Joseph—Grace Richards, May 1, 1745.¹
Hutchinson, Isaac—Mary Allison, 1723.⁶
John, Middlesex co.—Elizabeth Pearson, Mar. 24, 1730.¹
John—Mary Hutchinson, 1-27-1825.³
John Palmer—Alice Newbold, 11-12-1885.⁴
Jonathan—Elizabeth Hill, 2-25-1771.¹
Robert—Sarah Clutch, 4-3-1769.¹
Robert—Phebe Ann Johnson, 5-4-1831.³
William—Ann McCabe, 11-12-1770.¹
William B.—Sarah Oliver, 2-22-1837.³
Hutson, Henry, Philadelphia—Abigail Bodine, 2-22-1817.³

Hutson, John—Mary Benton, 12-11-1794.¹
Hutton, Harry (s Henry), Philadelphia—Cora Lucinda Dillon (d Hester), 8-13-1890.⁴
  Joseph—Mary Orr, 12-4-1852.⁴
  William—Ann Glynn, 8-17-1853.⁸
Hynds, Silvester—Catherine Kearns. 2-8-1759.¹
Hyres, Stephen—Mary Jones, 8-4-1805.³
Hyrlin, Peter—Mary Smith, Sept. 29, 1740.¹
Hyson, William—Ann Burcalow, 3-14-1813.³
Imlay, Nathaniel—Ann English 4-5-1771.¹
Indicott, John- Mary Gosling. Mar. 22, 1728.¹
  Joseph—Ann Gillam, May 12, 1736.¹
Ingall, Robert—Joan Horne, July 4, 1684.¹
Ingar, Adam—Sarah Rogers, 8-3-1816.³
Ingland, Jacob—Rachel Taylor, 11-4-1809.³
Ingle, Robert—Rachel Vinicomb, 1728.⁶
Inglin. Content—Susanna Kerlin, 10-18-1804 ³
  William—Rebecca Connarroe, 9-7-1810.³
Ingling, Jacob—Jane Green, 10-28-1826.³
Inglish. Benjamin—Sarah Wetherill. May 10, 1741.¹
Inman, Abel—Sarah Connarro, July 23, 1750.¹
  Barzillai—Sarah Frazier, 9-18-1813.³
  Benjamin—Jemima Brundidge. Sept. 11, 1739.¹
  Thomas—Charity Bounds, 1-22-1818 ³
Inskeep, John—Elizabeth Buchanan, 6-26-1758.¹
  Joseph—Mary Matlack, Dec. 19, 1728.¹
Ireland, Amaza—Jane Burrey, 2-13-1806.³
  Hugh—Rebecca Jones, 3-28-1835.³
  Joseph—Mary A. Andrews, 2-11-1837.³
  Richard—Phebe Crispin, 1-1-1833.³
  William—Anne Chamberlane, 12-24-1801.³
  Charles—Rebecca Giberson, 1-27-1827.³
Ireton, Guy—Rhodia Bennet, 4-14-1803.³
  John—Hannah Stockton, 5-23-1762.¹
  Joseph—Rebecca Lear, 7-6-1831.³
  Obadiah—Vashti Fenton, 1-21-1754.¹
  Samuel—Achsah King, 4-3-1779.¹
  Samuel, Trenton—Hannah Boyd, 8-23-1821.³
  William—Anne Reynolds, 10-1-1764.¹
  William—Ann Curtis, 12-10-1820.³
Irick, Henry C.—Lydia Hewlings, 5-11-1825.³
  Job—Matilda Burr, 1-18-1827.³

Irick, John—Mary Sailor, 2-28-1761.[1]
John—Mary Shinn, 2-26-1781.[1]
John S.—Emeline S. Bishop, 5-17-1832.[4]
William H.—Sallie S. Eayre, 3-10-1863.[4]
William, Jr.—Sarah C. Hewling, 2-9-1822.[3]
Irwin, James, Gloucester co.—Sarah Chambers, Nov. 1, 1744.[1]
Islow, Isaac—Anne Shinn, 9-15-1781.[1]
Ivins, Aaron—Ann Cheshire, 5-7-1767.[1]
    Aaron Bucks co., Pa.—Hope Aaronson, 10-19-1826.[3]
    Amos—Hannah Nippins, 4-23-1826.[3]
    Anthony—Sarah Wallen, 3-15-1806.[3]
    Barzillai—Mary Decow, 1-20-1801.[3]
    Barzillai—Rebecca Stokes, 10-24-1816.[3]
    Barzillai—Lydia Morris, 8-15-1832.[3]
    Barzillia—Margaret Treadwell, Oct. 8, 1767.[1]
    Charles—Elizabeth L. Shinn, 5-1-1823.[3]
    Daniel—Theodosia Hammell, 7-25-1777.[1]
    Daniel—Deleh Conover, 1-8-1783.[1]
    Isaac—Sarah Johnson, Apr. 26, 1711.[1]
    Isaac—Dolly A. Joyce, 1-21-1813.[3]
    Isaac—Rebecca Brown, 1-13-1838.[3]
    Isaac, Jr.—Mary Hopkins, 1737.[6]
    James—Ann Schooley, 12-23-1824.[3]
    John—Mary Lovett, 3-26-1776.[1]
    John—Elizabeth Ivins, 1-23-1819.[3]
    John, Jr.—Elizabeth Toner, 8-21-1808,[3]
    John P.—Mary Chequvine, 9-5-1837.[3]
    Joseph—Hannah Everingham, Oct. 22, 1741.[1]
    Joseph—Hannah Carty, 12-30-1798.[3]
    Samuel—Sarah Platt, 12-20-1766.[1]
    Samuel—Sarah Applegate, 1-11-1779.[1]
    Samuel—Rebecca Gibbs, 1-3-1798.[3]
    Samuel—Rachel Harker, 3-10-1803.[3]
    Samuel—Phebe Lannin, 7-12-1825.[3]
    Solomon—Elizabeth Everingham, Nov. 22, 1742.[1]
    Solomon—Susanna Rockhill, 5-25-1770.[1]
    Theodore—Elizabeth Inman, 12-16-1815.[3]
    Thomas—Mary Cliver, 10-27-1827.[3]
    William—Priscilla Page, 8-1-1767.[1]
    William—Mary French, 4-7-1773.[1]
    William—Elizabeth Emley, 10-15-1821.[3]
Ivory, Mathew—Mary S. Cox, 9-30-1830.[3]

Jack, Abraham—Margaret Jupiter, 3-21-1797.³
Jackson, Benjamin—Rachel Cole, 4-12-1812.³
   Benjamin—Mahala ——— (colored), 2-21-1837.³
   Charles—Hannah Jolly (colored), 12-15-1835.³
   George—Sarah M. Souder, 7-29-1838.³
   Hugh—Rachel Matlock, 1-14-1813 ³
   John—Mary Moreton, Jan. 10, 1748.¹
   John—Julian Lockinson, 12-30-1802.³
   John—Mary James, 1-8-1825.³
   Joseph—Margaret Moone, Oct. 10, 1734.¹
   Josh—Clara Taylor (colored), 9-5-1799.³
   Omer—Margaret Mills, 10-6-1797.³
   Richard—Ann Okelay, 2-19-1802.³
   Richard—Sarah Hancock, 12-6-1802.³
   Timothy—Ann Chambers, 3-12-1788.¹
   William—Anne Kennedy, 6-3-1773.¹
   William, Gloucester co.—Jane Loveland. 12-25-1824.³
Jackway, Robert—Issabel Carr, 1-31-1802.³
Jacobs, Hugh—Catharine Decker (alias Dilks), 1-29-1781.¹
   Jacob—Elizabeth Vandegrift, 2-26-1796.³
   Job—Charlotte Squan, 6-28-1797.³
   John—Catherine Decker, 3-26-1774.¹
   Joseph—Sarah Burns, 2-25-1819.³
   Levi—Abigail Dobbins, 2-1-1798.³
   Samuel—Sarah Vsnsciver, 5-18-1811.³
Jacques, Peter L.—Maria Hale, 3-16-1836.³
James, Benjamin Lloyd, Anne Lindsey Lonstow, 8-22-1860.⁸
   Hiram—Sarah Richardson, 12-13-1803.³
   John—Priscilla Dutton, 12-22-1778.¹
   John—Ann Fenimore, 10-4-1821.³
   Thomas—Thirza Reed, 12-26-1824.³
   William—Rebecca Bellford, 12-18-1803.³
   William A —Sarah Higgbee, 9-16-1827.³
Jameson, Clayton—Mary Shinn, 9-11-1836.³
   Robert—Elizabeth Chapman, 4-27-1796.⁵
Jannit, James—Anna Ireland, 9-23-1819.³
Jarvis, James—Edith Hunt, 9-26-1811.³
   John—Catharine Clackberen, both Trenton, 10-15-1798.³
Jearman, Howard, New York City—Eliza Tucker, 10-13-1811.³
Jefferies, Samuel—Mary Cramer, 6-5-1804.³
Jefferis, Benj.—Charlotte Buson, 9-14-1809.³
   Elijah W.—Mary Griscom, 10-2-1825.⁷

Jefferson, William H., Newcastle, Del.—Eliza L. McMichael, 11-18-1873.[8]
Jeffreys, James—Sarah Webb, 8-22-1827.[3]
Jenings, Peter—Anne Nott, Mar. 20, 1683/4.[1]
Jenkin, Henry—Margaret Harris, Feb. 26, 1728.[1]
Jenkins, Richard—Hester Franklin, 4-18-1829.[4]
Jenks, Daniel T.—Mary Ann Stockton, 10-14-1819.[3]
Jennings, Thomas—Ann Borton, 1731.[9]
Jervis, Francis, Philadelphia—Catharine King, Dec. 28, 1737.[1]
    William—Rebecca Fagins, 6-18-1808.[3]
Jess, David—Ruth Silver, 1742.[6]
    Zachariah—Hannah Southwick, 1750.[6]
Jesse, Zachariah—Rachel Lippincott, 1714.[6]
Jessup, John—Elizabeth Ballinger, 1762.[9]
    William—Mary Roberts, 11-12-1835.[10]
Jewell, William—Rachel Baker, 12-12-1763.[1]
    William—Mary Shields, 10-25-1801.[3]
Jobbs, Thomas—Mary Ann Giles, 12-16-1827.[3]
Jobes, Ezekiel—Rebecca Smith, 5-18-1779.[1]
    William—Mary Bowker, 2-4-1813.[3]
Jobs, Ezekiel—Mary Lucas, 2-20-1823.[3]
    George, Jr.—Sarah Johnston, 8-20-1759.[1]
    Isaac—Hannah Hance, 1-19-1775.[1]
    John—Beauler Hunt, 4-5-1825.[3]
    Richard—Mrs. Marche Freaze, 1-5-1800.[3]
John, William—Elizabeth Jones, 8-16-1797.[3]
Johnson, Aaron—Eliza Crumwell, 10-31-1825.[3]
    Abner—Lydia Quigley, both Pennsylvania, 8-22-1819.[3]
    Abner, Jr.—Ann Osborn, 7-25-1824.[3]
    Anthony—Rebecca Fowler, 5-2-1829.[3]
    Benjamin—Sarah Cooms, 8-28-1827.[3]
    Caleb—Anna Scott, 7-22-1819.[3]
    Charles—Rachel Day, 12-20-1834.[3]
    Charles—Sophia Butterworth, 10-27-1835.[3]
    Charles—Rebecca Wilson, 7-6-1862.[4]
    Clayton—Mary Ann Crusher, 4-15-1797.[3]
    Cornelius—Ann Jobes, 7-10-1833.[3]
    Edward—Mary Heaton, 10-29-1815.[3]
    Ezekiel—Hester Scott, 4-1-1782.[1]
    Ezekiel Cooper—Hope Wanderlin, 3-10-1808.[3]
    Isaac—Harriet Page, 10-4-1812 [3]
    Jacob—Sarah Fenton, July 19, 1733.[1]

Johnson, James—Joanna Clayton, 5-11-1802.[3]
    James—Ann Bruson, 6-2-1804.[3]
    James—Hannah Wills, 4-24-1808.[3]
    James—Mary Lewis, 12-12-1833.[3]
    John—Hannah Fenton, 11-9-1779.[1]
    John—Margaret Sterling, 6-5-1805.[3]
    John—Pamelia Brown, 10-2-1809.[3]
    John—Mary Newton, 11-9-1815.[3]
    John—Rebecca Core, 12-19-1822.[3]
    John—Phebe Butler, 4-3-1829.[3]
    John—Elizabeth Houston, 4-19-1832.[3]
    John— Margarette Cramer, 12-31-1835.[3]
    John—Leah Cox, 8-30-1838.[3]
    Jonathan—Mary McCollum, 5-29-1779.[1]
    Jonathan—Cynthia Sawyer, 9-23-1821.[3]
    Jonathan W.—Abigail Lee, 10-25-1835.[3]
    Joseph—Gertrude Lykens, July 25, 1745.[1]
    Joseph—Mary Ellis, 1753.[9]
    Joseph—Letitia Ewan, 11-27-1775.[1]
    Joseph—Sarah Nixon, 11-24-1810.[3]
    Joseph—Mary Atkinson, 3-24-1831.[3]
    Joseph—Mary Dutton, 9-23-1837.[3]
    Joseph P.—Sarah Ann Charmelee, 7-28-1827.[3]
    Levi—Susan Dubal, 3-3-1825.[3]
    Levy—Sarah Cole, 7-6-1805.[3]
    Mark A.—Lavinia Morton, 6-11-1815.[3]
    Mathias—Dorothy Parker, 2-18-1779.[1]
    Oliver—Lettice Gooby, 12-25-1817.[3]
    Othniel—Lydia Applegate, 11-8-1813.[3]
    Peter—Martha Small, 6-13-1797.[3]
    Peter—Sarah Wilson, 11-17-1807.[3]
    Philip—Rhoda Estill, 8-10-1776.[1]
    Samuel—Ann Vanneman, 1-2-1813.[3]
    Samuel—Ann Lincum, 6-16-1832.[3]
    Samuel—Hannah Holloway, 1-8-1837.[3]
    Thomas—Mary Jones, Manasquan, 1723.[11]
    Thomas—Mary Shemely, 6-14-1783.[1]
    Thomas—Ann Brackney, 2-21-1822.[3]
    Thomas R.—Adelaide Robinson, 9-16-1874.[8]
    William—Phebe Conover, 5-10-1807.[3]
    William—Lydia L. Letts, 2-26-1833.[3]
    William—Elizabeth Vanderbeck, 5-25-1833.[3]

Johnson, William G.—Esther Sooy, 6-2-1836.[3]
Johnston, Charles R.—Bathsheba Deacon, 12-25-1828.[3]
  David—Abigail Shinn, 11-3-1779.[13]
  Even—Elizabeth Cox, 12-26-1804.[3]
  Isaac—Sarah Brown, 10-22-1803.[3]
  James—Lucy Saltar, Aug., 1739.[8]
  James—Elizabeth Lukemire, 12-2-1785.[1]
  John—Priscilla Lane, 1688.[6]
  John, Philadelphia—Margaret Sterling (d. James) 6-5-1805.[3]
  John—Jane Babbleton, 7-15-1810.[3]
  John—Hannah Ann Saylor, 2-24-1831.[3]
  Jonathan—Jerusha Mullen, 4-13-1805.[3]
  Joseph—Lydia Gaskill, 3-19-1809.[3]
  Samuel—Harriet Howard, 6-4-1818.[3]
  Thomas—Phoebe Haely, 5-22-1813.[3]
  William—Fanny Lippincott, 8-18-1796.[3]
Johnstone, Isaac—Elizabeth Wetherill, 1727.[6]
Jolly, John, Bucks co., Pa.—Dinah Quest, Aug. 28, 1746.[1]
  Robert—Hannah Hunter, 9-9-1832.[3]
  Soll—Abigail Ward, 4-3-1803.[3]
Joice, Clayton—Margaret Snyder, 11-23-1815.[3]
  Hurr—Ann Walton, 1-11-1810.[3]
  Joseph—Theodotia Gaskill, 2-16-1814.[3]
  William—Mary Gragery, 12-27-1820.[3]
Jones, Aaron—Rebecca Harris, 1-12-1815.[3]
  Aaron, Monmouth co.—Ann Bustil, 2-4-1837.[3]
  Abraham—Elizabeth Bolton, 8-31-1773.[1]
  Abraham—Sarah Lewis, 2-23-1815.[3]
  Allen—Marian Pope, 1825,[14]
  Amos—Abigail Scroggy, 9-19-1799.[3]
  Anson—Sarah Quinn, 5-26-1829.[3]
  Anthony—Mary Fenton, 4-9-1835.[3]
  Benj.—Elizabeth Eldridge, 12-20-1804.[3]
  Benjamin—Elizabeth Butler, 1-16-1759.[1]
  Benjamin—Elizabeth Miller, 11-23-1823.[3]
  Benjamin, Jr.—Jane Atkinson, 1727.[6]
  Benjamin, Jr.—Elizabeth Carter, 1746.[6]
  Caleb—Sarah Smith, 12-31-1801.[3]
  Chalkley—Abigail Sharp, 4-4-1806.[3]
  Charles—Sarah Eayre, 12-28-1803.[3]
  Charles—Jane Thorn, 1-3-1826.[3]
  Charles—Elizabeth Shinn, 11-23-1833.[3]

Jones, Charles M.—Elizabeth Brooks, 5-2-1822.³
  Daniel—Sarah Harding, 10-16-1754.¹
  Daniel—Elizabeth Sharp, 1-29-1781.¹
  David—Rebecca Foster, 9-13-1797.¹⁰
  David—Mary Clevenger, 7-3-1835.³
  Edward B.—Ellen Virginia Coppuck, 11-27-1872.²
  Eli S.—Hester Webster, 10-18-1835.³
  Francis—Jane Wallis, Nov. 27, 1729.¹
  George W., Philadelphia, Elizabeth Bishop, 11-28-1836.³
  Hezekiah—Lavina Shinn, 1749.⁶ *also Lavinia*
  Hezekiah—Barbary Lear, 11-29-1796.³
  Hezekiah—Mary Woolston, 8-28-1817.³
  Hezekiah, Jr.—Lettis Rogers, 4-3-1872.¹³
  Ira—Elma Haines, 11-9-1831.³
  Isaac—Margaret Frasher, 11-26-1801.³
  Isaac, Jr.—Elizabeth Severs, 10-8-1815.³
  Isaiah—Catherine Wilson, 10-23-1834.³
  Israel—Hannah Hilsee, 10-17-1821.³
  Jacob—Dinah Steinson, 9-28-1763.¹
  Jiles—Ann Wetherby, 6-7-1798.³
  Josiah—Mary Lewis, 12-17-1757.¹
  Job—Sarah Campion, 11-23-1775 ¹
  Job B.—Hannah K. Evens, 10-13-1870.¹⁰
  John (s. Edward), Pennsylvania—Mary Doughty (d. Jacob)' Nov. 12, 1717.⁵
  John, Philadelphia—Mary Brown (d. Preserve), 8-12-1756.⁵
  John—Elizabeth Field, 5-3-1789.⁴
  John—Sarah Clutch, 4-25-1795.³
  John—Catherine Inger, 2-3-1796.³
  John—Jane Fort, 5-10-1818.³
  John—Abigail Harris (colored), 11-7-1819.³
  John—Susan Brown, 6-22-1839.⁴
  John Jr.—Martha Staples, 12-28-1763.¹
  Jonathan, Walton co., N. Y.—Lydia Shinn, 7-13-1801.³
  Jonathan (s. Joseph and Elizabeth), Pennsylvania—Mary Cowperthwaite (d. Job and Anna), 2-12-1824.¹²
  Joseph—Sarah Shinn, 8-3-1764.¹
  Joseph—Ann Weister, 10-26-1800.³
  Joseph—Rebecca Burr, 2-18-1813.³
  Josiah—Abigail Reed, 4-17-1828.³
  Josiah—Patience Lee, 7-26-1832.³
  Josiah F.—Deborah T. Haines, 10-20-1870.¹⁰

Jones, Lamberton—Mary Tilton (wid.), 6-17-1830.[3]
  Miles—Anna Atkinson, 3-30-1815.[3]
  Nathaniel B.—Emilie L. Lippincott, 3-1-1900.[10]
  Obediah—Rebecca Price, 10-18-1780.[1]
  Patrick—Martha Chambers, Feb. 16, 1741.[1]
  Paul—Deborah C. Vansciver, 12-28-1828.[3]
  Richard—Sarah E. Gibbs, 6-13-1833.[3]
  Richard—Elizabeth Price. No date given.[1]
  Samuel—Abigail Rogers, June 1, 1750.[1]
  Samuel—Mary Garwood, 4-18-1775.[1]
  Samuel—Eiizabeth Read, 4-9-1799.[3]
  Samuel—Jane Hollins, 9 5-1818.[3]
  Samuel—Elizabeth Quig, 11-18-1827.[3]
  Samuel—Mary Woolston, 1-21-1828.[3]
  Samuel—Sabilla Webb, 7-31-1830.[3]
  S. Herbert—Hannah B. Wills, 5-16-1912.[10]
  Thomas—Sarah Page, Apr. 17, 1738.[1]
  Thomas—Elizabeth Cox, 1-7-1789.[4]
  Thomas—Ann Middleton, 12-21-1813.[3]
  Timothy—Elizabeth Worth, 2-12-1831.[3]
  William—Elizabeth Atkinson, 1747.[6]
  William—Mary Birdsell, Aug. 10, 1749.[1]
  William—Elizabeth Powell, 1750.[6]
  William—Elizabeth Terry, 12-16-1796.[3]
  William—Hannah Lukemires, 3-13-1806.[3]
  William—Sarah Dolton, 1-24-1828.[3]
Jonson, Jonas—Sarah Evans, 8-6-1814.[3]
  Thomas—Ann Stratton, 8-17-1799.[3]
Jorden, John—Mary Kemble, 12-21-1822.[3]
Joyce, Allen—Ann Prickett, 10-11-1801.[3]
  Clayton—Margaret Snyder, 1815.[14]
  James—Margaret Ofttar, 11-1-1817.[3]
  Samuel—Hepsebee Taylor, 12-22-1796.[3]
  Samuel—Mary Wooster, 2-5-1329.[3]
  Thomas—Mary Woodrow, 9-2-1789.[4]
  William—Hannah Phillips, 12-26-1797.[3]
Joyes, William—Abigail Peacock, 1-10-1833.[3]
Juliat, Romeo—Fame Pendergrass, 8-24-1802.[3]
Jusman, Abel—Sarah Ponarro, July 23, 1750.[1]
Justice, George (s. John and Mary)—Phebe Middleton (d. George and Hannah), 11-13-1777.[5]
  James—Martha Norton, 10-31-1871.[8]

Kahn, George—Martha Meyers, 10-14-1830.[8]
Kaighn, Charles—Sarah Stern, 11-24-1814.[3]
  Joseph—Susanna Evans, 2-16-1837.[10]
Kaign, John—Elizabeth Hill, 1710.[6]
Kain, John—Eva Snow, 7-19-1874.[5]
  Richard B.—Patience S. Haines, 12-2-1821.[3]
  William—Ann Lippincott, 3-8-1804.[3]
Kalbe, John Cooper—Elizabeth Atkinson Cline, 6-5-1828.[3]
Kale, Chris—Lydia Atkinson, 3-5-1767.[1]
  Jacob—Mary Ann Fish, 3-19-1825.[3]
  Richard—Ann Severs, 12-15-1835.[3]
Kanney, Thomas—Mrs. Nancy Wright, 12-25-1799.[3]
Karge, Adam—Mary Coyne, 12-22-1873.[4]
Karlin, Charles—Charity B. Pedrick, 1-1-1838.[3]
Kay, David M.—Rachel Walton. Recorded 9-20-1828.[3]
  Isaac, Jr.—Mary Sharp, 9-7-1815.[3]
  Josiah, Gloucester co.—Rebecca Davenport, May 14, 1713.[5]
Kays, William—Barbara Smith, May 11, 1743.[1]
Kean, William S.—Sarah Emmand, 8-7-1838.[3]
Kearney, Michael, Amboy—Elizabeth Lawrence, 6-30-1774.[8]
Keating, John—Hannah Myers, 2-21-1764.[1]
Keegan, William—Mary Gilbert, 1-19-1818.[3]
Keeler, Amos—Elizabeth Hodge, 8-10-1812.[3]
  Edward—Mary Parker, 8-26-1809.[3]
  Jacob—Janet Brackney, 4-17-1777.[1]
  John—Hannah Hartshorne, 2-27-1817.[3]
  Samuel—Fanny Kempton, 4-5-1807.[3]
  Samuel—Rebecca Runyan, 6-21-1808.[3]
  William—Theodosia Budd, 1-17-1785.[1]
  William H.—Achsa R. Stout, 4-10-1834.[3]
Keen, Charles—Ann Lofton, 1-14-1828.[3]
  Peter—Elmina Paiste, 6-27-1839.[3]
Keene, John—Hannah Foster, 11-10-1802 [3]
Keenan, William—Louisa Bunting, 9-15-1799.[3]
Kein, James M.—Rachel Green, 3-19-1827.[3]
Keler, John—Ann Bowker, 4-27-1815.[3]
Keller, William—Mary Norcross, 9-23-1813.[3]
Kelley, Abraham—Deborah Hammell, 3-23-1786.[8]
  Asa—Ann Eliza Hays, 3-12-1818.[3]
  David, Jr.—Lydia English, 5-25-1808 [3]
  Frederick William (s. William J. and Mary E.)—Keziah S. Plummer (d. Benjamin and Mary), 1-10-1868.[4]

Kelley, Isaiah—Lydia K. Foster, 12-16-1816.³
  Israel—Hannah Thomas, 6-26-1821.³
  James—Ann Len, Nov. 5, 1736.¹
  James—Lettice Fort, 11-4-1777.¹
  James D., Salem co.—Ann Willits, 10-27-1823.³
  John—Rebecca Martin, 9-30-1778.¹
  John—Rachel Smith, 4-12-1804.³
  John—Mary Bennet, 6-29-1826.³
  Joseph—Mary Roberts, 3-12-1799.³
  Joseph—Hannah C. Clevenger, 7-7-1834.³
  Levi—Hannah Stillwell, 1-23-1800.³
  Lucas W.—Elizabeth A. Fenimore, 5-19-1825.³
  Richard—Eliza Williams, 3-12-1822.³
  Richard M.—Eleanor Birdsall, 2-25-1836.³
  Samuel—Elizabeth Robbins, 12-24-1812.³
  Samuel—Elizabeth Story, 3-31-1831.³
  William E.—Susan W. Jones, 7-18-1833.³
Kelly, Abraham—Rachel Atkinson, 1739.⁶
  Cornelius—Penelope McDaniel, Aug. 1, 1739.¹
  Isaiah—Elizabeth Kempton, 2-11-1826.³
  Joseph—Phebe Buckman, both Bucks co., Pa., 4-13-1768.⁸
  Patrick—Susan Quigmore, 4-22-1806.³
  Richard—Sarah Ivins, 2-28-1776.¹
  Richard—Ann Howell, 1-21-1800.³
  William—Katharine Sharoe, Aug. 12, 1745.¹
Kelsey, Thomas—Sarah Butler, 10-16-1782.¹
Kemble, Abel—Mary Bolten, 3-14-1768.¹
  Benjamin—Lydia R. Deacon, 9-27-1827.³
  Edward—Leonia Atkinson, 5-22-1768.⁸
  Edward—Hannah Wright, 10-3-1777.¹
  Edward—Elizabeth Frazier, 10-31-1830.³
  Elton—Sarah Steverson, 9-14-1761.¹
  John—Charity Stevenson, 9-24-1778.¹
  Peter—Louise Reeves, 7-3-1797.³
  Samuel—Priscilla Scott, 6-9-1811.³
  Samuel, Jr.—Polly Ross, 1-3-1782.¹
  Thomas—Ruth Garwood, 3-5-1772.¹
  Thomas—Priscilla Burr, 11-5-1773.¹
  Vaspasian—Rachel Haines, Mar. 15, 1746.⁶
  William—Beulah Cattle, 11-1-1827.³
Kemings, James—Anne Hodson, July 21, 1727.¹
Kempton, James H.—Mary Antrim, 9-30-1830.³

Kempton, Moses—Lucy M. Dobbins, 4-17-1823.⁴
  Moses, Jr.—Mary Coppuck, 3-29-1810.³
  Samuel—Harriet Watson Budd, 1-1-1806.³
  William—Levina Merritt, 10-18-1783.¹
  William—Nancy Branson, 2-21-1813.³
Kendall, Thomas—Mary Elton, Dec. 25, 1684.¹
Kendel, Joseph—Mary Rogers, 2-7-1806.⁶
Kendell, Joseph, Salem—Elizabeth Jones, 2-2-1803.³
Kendle, Isaiah—Mary Stiles, 5-23-1834.³
Kenney, Philip—Sarah Bryan, Feb. 3, 1736.¹
  Michael—Sarah Kendle, 9-10-1824.³
  Richard—Ann Remer, 12-17-1815.¹
Kent, Ishmeal—Elizabeth Collins, Dec. 26, 1731.¹
  Luke—Letitia Dougherty, 11-23-1797.³
Kenton, John—Elizabeth Shubb, 2-9-1757.¹
Kerlin, Isaac—Elizabeth Gibbs, 5-2-1805.³
  Israel—Ann Carslake, 1-6-1814.³
  Joseph—Abigail Hazelton, 12-20-1763.¹
  Matthias—Elizabeth Thomas, 11-18-1772.¹
  Samuel—Hannah Phares, 2-26-1829.³
  William—Elizabeth Gibson, 7-13-1807.³
Kerr, James—Louisa S. Johnston, 6-29-1828.³
  Job—Edith Carman, 6-11-1831.³
Kester, Joseph—Hannah Steward, 2-17-1826.³
  John—Mary Arnell, 2-3-1827.³
  Pearson—Mary Holloway, 3-30-1802.³
  Peter—Theodosia Hickman, 12-4-1773.¹
Key, Samuel, Jr.—Sarah Moore, 11-15-1814.³
Kiffcart, Elijah—Charlotte Gibbon, 1-26-1828.³
Kille, Abraham—Mary Powell, 12-20-1768.¹
  George M.—Esther Haines, 7-21-1831.³
  Robert H.—Hannah W. Lippincott, 2-3-1842.⁴
  Robert N.—Annie F. Stockton, 10-12-1870.⁴
  Samuel H.—Nancy Clark, 6-20-1848.⁴
Killey, Aaron—Mercilah Harris, 1-28-1766.¹
  David, Monmouth co.—Hannah Middleton, 2-14-1771.⁵
Killgore, James—Neomy Brown, Dec. 14, 1720.¹
Killpatrick, Foster—Phebe Steward, 7-14-1820.³
  Thomas—Ann Palmer, 9-9-1761.¹
Kilroy, John—Mary Engham, 4-5-1818.³
Killy, Samuel—Bathsheba Richards, May 23, 1733.¹
Kimball, Aaron S.—Matilda Laning, 4-21-1833.³

BURLINGTON COUNTY MARRIAGES

Kimball, Benjamin—Elizabeth Leeds, May 20, 1732.[1]
George—Mary Elton, Nov. 27, 1739.[1]
John—Ann Leeds, Aug. 24, 1738.[1]
Kimble, Able—Sarah Chamberlain, 4-18-1822.[3]
George—Sarah Sargible, 10-30-1836.[4]
John—Anna Leeds, 8-27-1738,[8]
John—Martha Prince, 9-7-1820.[3]
John—Rhoda Smith, 11-18-1830.[3]
Joseph—Barbara Adams, 9-2-1788.[4]
Joseph—Elizabeth Schuyler, 12-11-1828.[3]
Lewis—Rachel Fairholm, 3-4-1830.[3]
Samuel—Mary Meek, 1-24-1796.[3]
Kimpton, John—Elizabeth Victory, Feb. 25, 1731.[1]
Kinard, Samuel—Elizabeth Linsey, 6-22-1796.[3]
Kindall, George—Rebecca Gardiner, Dec. 25, 1740.[1]
Job—Anne Dotey, 9-28-1775.[1]
John—Phebe Stevens, Aug. 3, 1741.[1]
John—Susanna Adams, 9-26-1810.[3]
Kimsey, Abraham—Rhoda Stockton, 9-27-1779.[1]
Kindell, Thomas—Rachel Brass, Sept. 19, 1750.[1]
Kindle, Alexander—Susan Powell, 11-26-1820.[3]
Gilbert—Hannah Bates, 3-3-1831.[3]
John—Mary Rossil, 11-26-1806.[3]
Robert—Frances Pitman, Oct. 22, 1750.[1]
Robert—Emeline Grissom, 5-20-1832.[3]
Thomas—Mary Lutts, 3-25-1834.[3]
William—Hope Wilkins, 1-28-1816.[3]
Smith—Fanny Franks, 9-18-1828.[3]
Kiner, Edward Pole—Mary Taylor Balm (d. William), 6-12-1778.[4]
John Frederick—Kate Saturday, 7-4-1878.[4]
John Frederick—Mary Emma Rapp, 1-20-1886.[4]
Joseph Warren (s. William and Ann)—Mary Laura Sailer (d. Samuel and Sarah), 5-31-1876.[4]
King, Abraham—Phebe Faulkenburg, 3-12-1826.[3]
Anthony—Ellen Hambleton, 5-10-1811.[3]
Benajah—Mary Britten, 1-29-1784.[1]
Charles—Beulah Ann Childs, 12-25-1828.[3]
Charles Elliot, Germantown, Pa.—Josephine Kille Clark, 6-30-1880.[4]
Daniel S.—Lydia S. Stokes, 2-22-1838.[3]
Isaac—Mary Boulton, 11-4-1768.[1]
Israel, Jr.—Helenah Kirby, 10-26-1822.[3]

King, James—Mary Williams, 9-4-1829.³
   Jesse—Sheba Small, 9-17-1789.⁴
   John—Elizabeth Woodward, Monmouth co , Nov. 13, 1706.⁵
   John—Sarah Carman, 10-8-1765.¹
   John—Mary Ann Wilson, 11-3-1832.³
   John Elliott—Lucretia Haines, 1-16-1839.³
   Joseph—Elizabeth Stockton, 2-10-1803.⁸
   Miles—Sarah Simons, 10-2-1798.³
   Moses—Rebecca Cathcard, 10-22-1815.³
   Moses—Parthena Garret, 7-24-1824.³
   Peter—Melissa Githens, 12-20-1821.²
   Peter—Vashti Buzby, 9-3-1829.³
   Samuel—Theodocia Briggs, 1-28-1757.¹
   Stacy—Rebecca S. Gamble, 8-22-1818.³
   Thomas—Elizabeth Simons, 9-10-1764.¹
   Wllliam—Mary West, 6-6-1778.¹
   William—Margaret Pippit, 12-23-1827.³
   William—Mary Ann M. Marter, 2-18-1836.³
Kingdon, Jabez—Naomi T. Carr, 11-23-1837.³
   James—Adaline Bates, 11-7-1838.³
Kingsland, Albert A.—Florence E. Binney, 12-12-1876.⁸
Kingston, Thomas—Sarah Cripps, Mar. 23, 1741.¹
Kinkead, David—Mary Land, 5-5-1787.⁸
Kinsey, Charles—Elizabeth Keene, 4-9-1812.⁸
   Clement—Mary Plum, 1-2-1787.⁴
   Warner—Ann French, 3-28-1839.³
   William—Hope Cattle, 3-19-1801.³
Kinsinger, Samuel—Mary Loveman, 10-1-1835.³
   William—Sarah Mullen, 4-27-1809.³
Kinsolving, Lucien Lee—Alice Brown, 1-7-1892.²
Kirby, Benj.—Elizabeth Lewis, 1-25-1810.³
   Benjamin—Margaret Dougherty, 11-19-1836.³
   Caleb—Allice Asson, 9-19-1802.³
   ьimpson—Ann Allen, 1-11-1781.⁵
   Farnsworth—Charlotte Parker, 7-21-1805.³
   John—Rebecca Pettit, 5-20-1776.¹
   John—Alice Brown, 5-4-1801.³
   Jonathan—Ame Black, 6-11-1768.¹
   Joseph—Sarah Carter, 3-3-1783.¹
   Richard—Elizabeth Foulks, Jan. 30, 1749/50.¹
   Robert (s. Job and Mary), Monmouth co.—Maria Middleton (d. Jediah and Anna), 10-9-1823.⁵

Kirby, Samuel—Lenah Hartshorne, 4-19-1766.¹
Thomas—Rebecca Bigelow, 12-20-1799.²
Kirk, James—Ann Oldman, Sept. 19, 1732 ¹
Samuel (s. William)—Margaret Little Bain, 1-25-1871.⁴
Kirkbride, Jacob—Jane R. Woolman, 1-31-1839.³
John (s. Joseph and Mary)—Hannah Sykes (d. John and Joanna), Mar. 16, 1731.³
John—Elizabeth Prickett, 12-18-1813.³
John—Priscilla Stricker, 12-27-1835.³
Jonathan (s. Mahlon) Pennsylvania—Elizabeth Curtis (d. Joseph) 11-18-1767.⁵
Joseph—Mary P. Collins, 5-14-1828.³
Mahlon—Ann Hillier, 6-5-1814.³
Phineas—Mary Rogers, 7-22-1779.¹
Phineas R.—Cornelia Hendrickson, 5-11-1838.³
Phinehas—Rebecca Watson, 12-30-1809.³
Samuel—Abigail Stackhouse, 8-23-1827.²
Stacy—Sarah Hammitt, 12-29-1814.³
William Elizabeth Rogers, 6-8-1799.³
Kirkoff, Christopher—Sarah Barber, 12-3-1814.³
Kiser, Samuel—Sarah Stevenson, 10-13-1818.³
Kitchens, John—Ann Nordyke, 2-23-1758.¹
Kite—Henry B.—Jane Hancock, 7-17-1831.³
Kithcart, Jacob—Hannah Reeve, 7-31-1826.³ ·
Kline, J. Newton—S. Lavinia Thompson, 1-10-1861.²
Knaps, Daniel—Lydia Earley, 8-16-1817.³
Knight, Daniel—Mary Ridgway, 1-3-1796.³
Jonathan— Elizabeth Borden, 2-1-1798.³
Joseph, Philadelphia, (s. Thomas and Hannah, Gloucester co.)— Edna Wooley (d James and Hulda), Trenton, 3-9-1814.⁵
Thomas—Elizabeth Browne, Aug. 12, 1686.¹
Walter—Elizabeth Roberts, 4-13-1843.¹⁰
Knowles, John—Ann Phillips, both Hunterdon co., 3-22-1828.³
Kobbs, Conrad—Margaret Plasket (d. William), 7-27-1757.⁵ -
Kroop, John—Rebecca Williams, 7-30-1824.³
Kuhn—George—Lucy Ann Keen, 5-30-1817.⁸
Kyrlin, Thomas—Grace Buffln, Mar. 29, 1741.¹
Lacky, Stokes Haines—Ann French, 12-17-1818.³
Lacy, Thomas—Susanna Newbold, 10-26-1803.³
Israel C.—Sarah Quigley, 11-18-1830.³
Ladd—Jonathan—Ann Wills, 1723.⁹
Laing, James—Phebe Onge, July 22. 1731.¹

Laing, Walter (s. William and Katharine)—Anna W. Lukens (d. David and Esther), both Pennsylvania, 6-5-1845.[5]
Lake, Henry—Rhoda Flitcraft, 1814.[14]
Lakie, Henry—Rhodia Whitcraft, 8-1-1814.[3]
Lamb, Isaiah—Susanna Warren, 1-21-1796.[3]
  Jacob—Sarah Haines, 1732.[6]
  Jacob—Lydia Haines, 1750.[6]
  Jacob—Mary Shinn, 4-19-1768.[1]
  Jacob—Elizabeth Shinn, 3-3-1777.[1]
  Jacob—Sarah Inskeep, 4-26-1777.[1]
  Jacob—Ann Merritt, 3-11-1805.[3]
  Jacob—Phebe Horner, 4-9-1816.[3]
  Jacob—Margaret Watkinson, 5-10-1832[3]
  Jacob—Mary Ann Ann Ganfac, 12-31-1837.[3]
  Joseph—Rebecca Budd, Mar. 28, 1738.[1]
  Joseph—Edith Taylor, 5-27-1782.[1]
  Joseph—Bula Gilbert, 3-15-1825.[3]
  Joseph—Lucy Ann Troth, 5-29-1826.[3]
  Joseph, Jr.—Mary Earl, 5-7-1777.[13]
  Joseph L —Louisa B. Rosel, 6-23-1835.[3]
  Martin—Catharine Shinn, 11-25-1824.[3]
  Nehemiah—Lettice Foster, 9-12-1772.[1]
  Nehemiah—Ann Patterson, 11-29-1829.[3]
  Samuel—Nancey Starkey, 4-25-1798.[3]
  Samuel—Mariah Warren, 6-8-1826.[3]
  Samuel—Hope Abliven, 12-5-1833.[3]
Lambert, E. Coles—Emma Wager, 3-16-1852.[4]
  George—Charlotte Knox, 9-23-1837.[3]
  Samuel—Rhoda Bailey, 5-22-1813.[3]
  Thomas—Margaret Scott, 1695.[6]
  Thomas—Anne Wood (d. William), Jan. 31, 1710.[5]
  Thomas—Mary Gardiner, 1724.[9]
  Thomas—Anna Stevenson, 1731.[6]
  William—Elizabeth Carry, 1-1-1818.[3]
Lamborn, Richard—Phebe Gibbs, 8-29-1796.[7]
Lame, John—Anne Ewing, 4-26-1758.[1]
  John—Dinah Turner, 5-1-1780.[1]
  John—Grace Forcyth, 3-28-1804.[3]
  John, Jr.—Anna Web, 11-21-1822.[3]
  Joshua—Lydia Ann Taylor, 10-2-1828.[3]
Lanagin, Charles—Rhoda Estill, 8-7-1837.[3]
  William—Hannah Roberts, 1-1-1835.[3]

Land, John—Catherine Hoar, 2-5-1778.[1]
 Thomas—Alice Higbee, 11-28-1763.[1]
 Thomas—Lydia Patterson, 8-24-1817.[3]
 William—Sarah Morris, 5-9-1781.[1]
Lane, Jacob—Charlotte Adams, 5-4-1822.[3]
 John, Sr.—Hannah Atkinson, 9-22-1819.[3]
 Stephen—Ann Edward, 9-8-1777.[1]
 William—Ellen Wilkinson, 11-18-1813.[3]
Lang, Alexander—Sarah Little, 4-7-1834.[3]
Langercan, Richard—Mary Bozworth, Apr. 29, 1741.[1]
Langford, John—Isabelia Bowman, Oct. 30, 1686.[1]
Langstaff, George—Charlotte Bishop, 2-3-1808.[3]
 James—Harriet Haines, 4-20-1830.[4]
Laning, Asa—Lydia Ford, 2-10-1824.[3]
 John V.—Sarah Tamper, 6-18-1836.[3]
 Joseph—Susannah Rouse, 5-16-1812.[3]
 Paul—Rachel Porter, 3-4-1813.[3]
 Samuel, Jr.—Sarah Humphreys, 2-18-1814.[3]
Lankins, Jonathan—Mary Bennett, Monmouth co., 12-17-1779.[1]
Lanmaster, Henry—Elizabeth Stiles, 7-23-1837.[3]
Lannen, Samuel—Esther Palmer, 12-1-1808.[3]
Lanrin, William—Esther Campbell, 1-6-1783.[1]
Lanning, John—Grace Craft, 11-11-1761.[1]
 John—Amey Arnel, 11-12-1777.[1]
 Joseph—Mary Jaquatt, Jan. 2, 1741.[1]
 Joseph—Marcy Lounsberry, 12-7-1756.[1]
 Samuel—Ann Elkinton, Sept. 20, 1732.[1]
 William B.—Rachel Margerum, 6-25-1837.[3]
Lanningham, Neal—Rachel Bareford, 1-10-1807.[3]
Larew, David—Sarah Larzalere, both Bucks co., Pa., 6-2-1768.[8]
Large, Ebenezer—Dorothy Bickley, 1727.[6]
 Ebenezer, Jr.—Anne Field (d. Matt and Patience), Oct. 14, 1742.[5]
 Jacob, Monmouth co.—Eliza Field, June 11, 1719.[5]
 Samuel, Jr. (s. Samuel H. and Rebecca), Huntingdon co.—Mary Murfin (d. William and Sarah), May 24, 1744.[5]
Larkins, John—Catherine Kille, 7-31-1780.[1]
Larren, Daniel, Bucks co., Pa.—Elizabeth Sutton, 5-21-1763.[1]
LaRue, George Milton—Mary Lippincott Kille, 7-5-1882.[4]
Larzalere, John—Mary Anne Annan, 12-14-1828.[8]
 Morris—Mary Kinsey, 12-16-1810.[8]
Larzelere, Benjamin—Mary Daymond, 1-21-1835.[3]
 Nicholas—Isabella McEvarry, 8-11-1823.[3]

Larzelere, Thomas—Mary H. Hancock, 5-26-1836.³
Lataurette, Paul—Sarah Shourds, 7-17-1800.³
Laurence, John—Anne Leonard, Middlesex co., 7-18-1753.¹
   John—Martha Tallman, 11-14-1759.¹
Laurie, John—Ann Ridgway, 4-4-1816.³
Laurinson, Jacob—Mary Bowker, 11-25-1800.³
Lavenner, John—Lydia Atkinson, Aug. 20, 1729.¹
Lawrence, Andrew—Sarah Wallace, 2-3-1774.¹¹
   Cesar—Jane Smith, 7-27-1813.³
   Charles—Elizabeth Lowden, 10-8-1809.³
   Christopher—Elizabeth Vandeveer, 12-15-1799.³
   David—Acsah Shreve, 12-12-1807.³
   Jacob—Elizabeth Feorigin, 10-14-1767.¹
   James, Monmouth co.—Catherine Waters, 10-29-1765.¹
   John, Monmouth co.—Hannah Borden, Apr. 26, 1731.¹
   John—Elizabeth Gardiner, 9-23-1811.³
   Joseph, Monmouth co.—Rachel Curtis, Dec. 18, 1712.⁵
   Newton—Mary Ann G. Evans, 6-30-1838.³
   Samuel—Hannah Shinn, 10-17-1807.³
   Samuel—Sarah Kelts, 1-20-1836.³
   Thomas—Hannah Bunting (d. Timothy), 10-8-1788.⁵
Lawrenson, Joseph—Rachsl Malsbery, 8-16-1809.³
Lawrie, James, Monmouth co.—Mary Borden, 11-15-1759.⁵
   Thomas, Monmouth co.—Ann Murfin, 6-19-1760.⁵
Lawyer, Joseph—Rebecca Stewart, 2-29-1812.³
   William—Mrs. Mary Luckmiers, 6-3-1799.³
Layton, Israel—Anne Lippincott, 1-1-1820.³
   William—Mrs. Sarah Rogers, 12-1-1838.³
Lazelere, John—Sarah Robbins, 5-15-1836.⁴
Leader, Nathaniel—Barbara Cox, 9-12-1775.⁸
Leach, Thomas—Rachel Borden, 12-27-1808.³
Leake, George—Mary Bass, 8-7-1808.³
Leap, Henry—Mary Willis, 3-1-1777.¹
Leason, John—Mary Cross, 7-8-1805.³
Leconard, Nicholas, Gloucester co.—Mary Cardiffe, Aug. 8, 1743.¹
Leconey, William—Abigail Crispin, 10-31-1787.¹
Lee, Andrew—Mary Green (colored), 3-12-1803.³
   George—Ann Haines, 4-25-1829.³
   George—Martha B. Rogers, 12-25-1842.⁴
Lee, Hooper—Lavinia Lee (colored), 4-9-1826.³
   Hooper—Mary Washington, 10-1-1831.³
   Hope—Rachel Lee (colored), 11-27-1834.⁴

BURLINGTON COUNTY MARRIAGES 139

Lee, James C.—Rachel R. Stockton, 8-28-1834.[4]
John—Johanna Fort, Jan. 4, 1727.[1]
Joseph P.—Dorothy B. Taylor, 2-9-1826.[3]
Thomas—Theodocia Powell, 11-6-1759.[1]
William—Joan Smith, Sept. 23 1689.[1]
William—Mary Wright, 9-19-1802.[3]
Leebinger, Martin—Sarah King, 4-17-1802.[3]
Leech, Jesse—Elizabeth Parker, 6-21-1780.[1]
Uz—Eiizabeth Tallman, 5-22-1781.[1]
Leeds, Abraham—Anne Lamb, Mar. 14, 1750.[1]
Abraham—Mary Wells, 3-10-1808.[3]
Azariah—Mary Morris, 6-8-1801.[3]
Daniel—Ann Stacey, 1681.[6]
Daniel—Rebeckah Sooy, 8-24-1814.[3]
David—Beulah Sharp, 11-7-1795.[3]
Henry—Hannah Pharo, 1833.[11]
Isaac—Rebecca Moore, 2-7-1805.[3]
Isaac—Elizabeth Johnson, 4-16-1821.[3]
Isaiah—Elizabeth Jones, 6-3-1778.[1]
Jacob—Abigail Lippincott, 6-18-1818.[3]
John—Rebecca Corelery, June 7, 1737.[1]
John (s. Japhet, 1st)—Sarah Coate (wid. Marmaduke), 1751.[11]
John—Hannah Niglee, 12-23-1804.[3]
John—Elenor Toy, Gloucester co., 1-27-1820.[3]
Joseph—Margaret Jones, 10-5-1775.[1]
Josiah—Martha Wright, 11-4-1803.[3]
Moses—Rachel Cramer, 3-24-1812.[3]
Nehemiah—Elizabeth Eayre, 4-4-1774.[1]
Nehemiah—Mary Little, 3-4-1802.[3]
Philo—Sarah Shinn, Nov. 1, 1740.[1]
Robert (s. Japhet, 1st)—Abigail Higbee (d. John), 1732.[11]
Samuel—Eliza Phillips, 11-2-1828.[5]
Samuel—Sarah B. Stokes, 9-23-1847.[10]
Solomon, Gloucester co.—Martha Farrow, 1-30-1765.[1]
Stacy—Elizabeth Rockhill, 3-1-1810.[3]
Thomas—Margaret Collier, 1678.[6]
Titan—Hope French, 1-31-1759.[1]
Titan—Mary Warrington, 2-26-1782.[1]
Vincent—Hannah Stockdon, 1736.[6]
William—Mary Osborn (d. Richard, Sr.), 1768.[11]
Leek, George—Hannah Mathis, 1-8-1816.[3]
John—Rose Pincock, 1-27-1807.[3]

Leek, Samuel—Sarah Mathis, 3-25-1784.[1]
   Samuel—Harriet McGowan, 9-7-1826.[3]
   William G.—Phebe Adams, 5-14-1826.[3]
   William Jr.—Mary Caveleer, 4-8-1827.[3]
Lefuse, William—Elizabeth Johnson, 11-29-1775.[1]
LeMunion, David—Mary Fisher, 4-13-1828.[3]
Lennon, Samuel—Jane Johnston, 10-3-1811.[3]
   Lenox, James C.—Amy P. Adams, 6-23-1836.[3]
   William Moore—Susan R. Wooley, 12-2-1835.[3]
Leonard, Elias—Mary Ervin, 2-18-1779.[1]
   John, Monmouth co.—Frances Schooly, 5-26-1769.[1]
   Michael—Ann Brigs, 6-20-1782.[1]
   Nicholas—Catharina Scheriper, 5-12-1761.[1]
   William—Artis Smith, 4-25-1801.[3]
Lester, John—Ann Williams, 4-30-1839.[3]
Letts, Aaron—Rhoda Pearce, Jr., 8-27-1797.[3]
   Samuel—Eliza Cook, 9-14-1822.[3]
   William—Isabella Horner 11-30-1829.[3]
Leuallen, Samuel—Lydia Warren, 11-2-1826.[3]
Leukins, Jonathan—Kesiah Antram, 12-10-1807.[3]
Leverans, Lewis—Patience Garwood, 3-1-1798.[3]
Leverly, John—Sarah Gibson, 1738.[6]
Levie, James—Alice Corey (colored), 11-27-1823.[3]
Levis, Edward Hulme—Theodora Bryan Risdon, 1-12-1892.[2]
Levy, Frederick Harrington—Mary Chetwood Bispham, 2-6-1872.[2]
   William—Anne Allen, May, 1823.[8]
Lewallen, Abraham—Lettice Dobbins, 3-2-1799.[3]
   Isaac—Sarah Gaskill, 2-26-1801.[3]
   Jacob—Sarah Eldridge, 8-4-1796.[3]
   Rheuben—Sarah Gaunt, 9-17-1799.[3]
   Samuel—Hannah Middleton, 11-1-1821.[3]
Lewellen, Isaac—Elizabeth England, Philadelphia, 11-24-1815.[3]
Lewis, Asher—Elizabeth Helberson, 5-18-1815.[3]
   Clayton—Mary Sweem, 11-26-1810.[3]
   Ellis, Holmesburg, Pa.—Esther Griffiths, Philadelphia, 10-7-1822.[3]
   Franklin B.—Rebecca B. Coppuck, 10-14-1857.[4]
   Gideon—Kesiah Cole, 1-6-1809.[3]
   Jacob—Rachel Green, 11-2-1815.[3]
   James—Rebecca Eslick, 10-12-1815.[3]
   James—Fanny Rogers, 5-11-1822.[3]
   Job—Sarah Zane, 3-3-1814.[3]

BURLINGTON COUNTY MARRIAGES

Lewis, John—Lydia Sharp, 8-3-1784.¹
John—Abigail Still (colored), 1818.¹⁴
Joseph—Mary Stratton, Oct. 18, 1733.¹
Joseph—Martha Cox, 2-3-1800.³
Joseph—Sarah Parker, 12-24-1804.³
Joseph—Hannah Adams, 4-13-1829.³
Nathaniel—Sarah Cooper, 12-7-1831.³
Richard Earl—Sarah Glover Risdon, 7-15-1885.⁴
Robert—Elizabeth Scott, 1703.⁶
Samuel—Hannah Pattin, 12-21-1801.³
Samuel—Mary Woodward, 8-31-1837.³
Thomas—Catharine Bishop, 11-16-1809.³
William— Ursilla Clevenger, 11-7-1799.³
Zadig—Maria Minnick, 11-12-1809.⁸
Libbet, Joseph, Bucks co., Pa.—Rachel Swift, 10-25-1821.³
Lidden, James—Anne Lane, both Bucks co., Pa, 5-30-1771.⁸
Light, Daniel—Elizabeth Nebb, 1711.⁶
Lightfoot. Thomas—Mary Smith, 1744.⁶
  Thomas (s. Samuel and Mary), Pennsylvania—Rachel Hunt (d. Elijah and Esther), Middlesex co., 1-5-1785.⁵
Like, Richard—Rebecca Hulse, 4-8-1829.³
Linard, Benjamin Ralph—Sarah Anderson Jones, 10-23-1872.⁸
Lincoln, Gideon—Elizabeth Doran, 7-27-1804.³
  Joseph—Elizabeth McCoy. 5-5-1831.³
Lindsley, Thomas G —Charlotte E. Matthews, 3-2-1862.²
Lines, William— Phebe Parker, 9-14-1813.³
Linn, Solomon—Theodosia Elberson, 12-20-1822.³
Linnington, John—Mary Arney, 3-13-1766.¹
Linthicum, Edmund—Meribah Reeves, 9-29-1783.¹
Linton, Benjamin (s. Benjamin)—Hannah Satterthwaite (d. Samuel), 11-21-1764.⁵
  Benjamin, Pennsylvania—Jane Cowgill (d. Ralph), Apr. 19, 1733.⁵
Lippincott, Aaron—Elizabeth Jennings, 1746.⁹
  Aaron—Elizabeth Tomlinson, 1753.⁹
  Aaron—Mary Carr, 10-11-1816.¹³
  Abel—Jemime Evans, 1758.⁹
  Abel—Ann Hammett, 4-19-1797.³
  Ahab—Mary Wills, 11-11-1804.³
  Amasa—Hannah Bishop, 4-6-1827.³
  Amaziah—Hannah Prickett, 10-29-1768.¹
  Amos— ——— ———, 6-30-1814. Bride's name not given.³

Lippincott, Aquilla—Agnes Inskip, 1-15-1784.[1]
   Aquilla (s. Aquilla and Agnes)—Lydia Dudley (d. Joshua and Rachel), 4-11-1822.[12]
   Arney—Rebecca Almon, 3-21-1761.[1]
   Arney—Elizabeth Evans, 1-2-1779.[1]
   Arney—Mary Budd, 9-24-1836.[3]
   Arney—Margaret Oliphant, 11-1-1838.[3]
   Barclay (s. Thomas and Abigail)—Deborah J. Burrough (d. Robert and Mary), 11-18-1824.[12]
   Benjamin (s. Jacob)—Hope Wills, Nov. 11, 1741.[6]
   Benjamin—Hannah Hewlings, 8-10-1783.[1]
   Benjamin—Charlotte Force, 11-21-1824.[3]
   Benjrmin—Emily Herr, Nov. 1899.[2]
   Benjamin H. (s. Moses and Mary) — Martha Collins (wid Arthur; d. Levi and Hannah Ballenger), 1-11-1821.[12]
   Caleb—Hannah Wilkins, 1752.[9]
   Caleb—Jemima Shinn, 3-10-1782.[1]
   Caleb—Ann Thompson, 3-29-1826.[7]
   Charles—Harriet Wiseman, 5-15-1834.[3]
   Crispin—Mary Wilkins, 3-6-1825.[3]
   Crispin—Elizabeth Ann Garwood, 1-15-1832.[3]
   Daniel—Hannah Coles, 11-12-1756.[1]
   David—Mary Chambers, June 26, 1728.[1]
   David—Rebeckah Stockton, June 1, 1731.[1]
   David—Mary McGowen, 4-21-1811.[3]
   David—Anna Holeman, 2-15-1826.[3]
   Elisha—Mary Wooley, 2-23-1819.[3]
   Enos—Elizabeth Doughty, 9-18-1779.[1]
   Ezekiel—Bathsheba Matlack, 1756.[9]
   Francis—Hannah Butcher, 10-14-1812.[3]
   Freedom—Mary Austin, 1680.[6]
   Freedom—Elizabeth Wells (d. John), 1715.[6]
   Freebom—Hannah Rakestraw, 1739.[9]
   Freedom—Elizabeth Ballinger, 1743.[9]
   Freedom M.—Lettis B. Woolston, 1-8-1835.[8]
   George Allen—M. Matilda Kelley (d. James and Mary), 2-6-1879.[4]
   Isaac (s. Josiah and Miriam)—Lydia Matlack (d. George and Sarah), 4-13-1820.[12]
   Isaac—Anna Haines, 5-19-1887.[10]
   Israel—Sarah Shinn, 9-28-1837.[3]
   Jacob—Mary Burr, 1716.[6]

Lippincott, Jacob—Hannah Lippincott, 7-15-1775.[1]
  Jacob—Martha Oliphant (d. John), 9-10-1795.[3]
  Jacob—Elizabeth Stockton, 6-15-1797.[3]
  Jacob C.—Hannah Dorsey, 1-5-1836.[3]
  Jacob W.—Sarah Ballinger, 2-6-1812.[3]
  James—Anna Eves, 1709.[6]
  James—Elizabeth Lippincott, 1751.[9]
  James—Susannah Evans, 1-28-1771.[1]
  James—Hannah Crispin, 9-20-1777.[1]
  James—Ruth Headly, 10-8-1807.[3]
  Jediah—Esse Clifford, 8-14-1812.[3]
  Job—Anna Ogburn, June 25, 1728.[1]
  Job—Sarah Burnes, 3-29-1779.[1]
  Job—Beasely Wells, 2-24-1780.[1]
  Job—Anna Warren, 11-6-1788.[4]
  Job—Bathsheba Evans, 2-24-1794.[1]
  Job—Mary Ridgway, 10-30-1819.[3]
  Job—Mary Stokes, 4-13-1820.[10]
  John—Anne Eves, Mar. 13, 1746.[1]
  John—Abigail Collins, 3-12-1770.[1]
  John—Rachel Hughes, 9-20-1779.[1]
  John—Eiizabeth Elton, 8-1-1782.[1]
  John—Edith Matson, 10-20-1797.[3]
  John—Jane Richardson, 6-16-1814.[3]
  John B.—Mary Fort, 4-17-1838,[3]
  John, Jr.—Mary Lippincott, 6-5-1830.[3]
  John, Jr (s. John and Achsah)—Mary A. Field (d. Robert and Hannah), 10-11-1832.[5]
  John, Jr.—Elizabeth Pittman, 3-17-1838.[3]
  John P.—Annie H. Deacon, 1-25-1870.[2]
  John S —Hannah Albertson, both Gloucester co., 12-13-1821.[3]
  John S., Shrewsbury—Grace Shreve, 12-20-1836.[3]
  Jonathan—Anne Eves, Mar. 12, 1746.[1]
  Jonathan—Edith Zelley, 8-16-1798.[3]
  Joseph—Elizabeth Evans, 1740.[9]
  Joseph—Esther Andrews (d. Samuel, Sr.), 1744.[11]
  Joseph—Anna Ellison, 3-5-1801.[3]
  Joseph—Martha Neale, 4-20-1802.[3]
  Joseph (s. Samuel and Priscilla)—Beulah Conrow (d. Darling and Mary), 9-21-1804.[12]
  Joseph—Rebecca Childs, 2-28-1805.[3]
  Joseph—Keziah Phillips, 12-17-1812.[3]

Lippincott, Joseph—Keturah Haines, 11-16-1815.¹⁰
  Joseph—Elizabeth Brooks, 2-22-1821.³
  Joseph—Hannah Chapman, 5-11-1822.³
  Joseph—Abigail Smith, 9-11-1826.³
  Joseph B. (s. Thomas and Lydia)—Hepsibah Roberts (d. William and Elizabeth), 4-13-1809.¹²
  Joshua—Rachel Dudley, 1756.⁹
  Joshua—Ann Crispin, 2-22-1801.³
  Joshua—Mary Githens, 1-14-1838.³
  Josiah—Merriam Slim, 8-15-1791.¹
  Josiah—Rachel Gaskill, 10-10-1811.¹²
  Judiah—Mary Dugless, 3-27-1762.¹
  Levi—Lettis Wills, 4-12-1773.¹
  Levi—Mary Lippincott, 6-2-1798.³
  Levi (s. Samuel and Priscilla)—Hannah Roberts (d. Samuel and Hannah), 3-18-1813.¹²
  Levi—Hannah Penquite, 12-31-1818.³
  Lewis—Rebecca Lewis, 1-1-1837.³
  Mark—Abigail Evens, 3-23-1843.¹⁰
  Marmaduke—Mary C. Wills, 1-12-1837.³
  Moses—Meribah Miller, 1750.⁶
  Moses—Mary Hewlings, 10-3-1778.¹
  Moses—Sarah Stratton, 2-9-1797.³
  Nathan—Mary Child, 8-9-1815.³
  Noah—Harriet King, 10-13-1822.³
  Noah E. (s. Noah and Mary)—Sarah M. McKelvey (d. Isaac and Sarah, 11-6-1875.⁴
  Preston—Mary Ewan, 3-2-1804.³
  Restore—Martha Owen, 1729.⁶
  Restore—Elizabeth Lippincott, 1-24-1828.³
  Richard—Hannah Clemens, May 1, 1751.¹
  Richard—Jane Nutt, 9-20-1828.³
  Samuel—Hope Wills, Jr., 1708.⁶
  Samuel—Mary Arney, Oct. 29, 1737.¹
  Samuel—Rachel Dobbins, 7-30-1789.⁴
  Samuel—Merian Haines, 3-10-1796.³
  Samuel—Hannah Childs, 3-2-1805.³
  Samuel—Mary Stratton, 9-15-1814.³
  Samuel—Christiana Black, 1-26-1818.⁷
  Samuel—Elizabeth Aaronson, 1-28-1819.³
  Samuel—Elizabeth S. Gauntt, 2-19-1873.⁸
  Samuel H.—Mary Hoffman, 12-30-1793.⁷

Lippincott, Solomon—Sarah Cozens, 1704.[9]
  Stacy—Allis Shinn, 11-26-1806.[3]
  Stacy—Elizabeth Butcher, 9-5-1811.[13]
  Stacy—Sarah Bowne, 12-25-1827.[3]
  Stacy B.—Jane Sapp, 3-12-1835.[3]
  Stephen—Susan Richardson, 2-25-1816.[3]
  Thomas—Nancy Hugg, 1732.[6]
  Thomas—Rebecca Eldridge, 1745.[9]
  Thomas—Elizabeth Haines, 8-13-1767.[1]
  Thomas—Hannah Walker, 4-6-1778.[1]
  Thomas—Rachel Haines, 1-6-1779.[1]
  Thomas—Lydia Burr, 2-6-1782.[13]
  Thomas—Elizabeth Meirs, 7-26-1795.[3]
  Thomas—Hannah Rudderow, 2-3-1831.[3]
  Thomas—Elizabeth Haines, 8-15-1867.[8]
  William—Rebecca Johnston, 6-13-1777.[1]
  William—Rhoda Lishman, 8-9-1779.[1]
  William—Ann Rogers, 9-5-1793.[13]
  William—Hepzibah Gaskill, 9-5-1802.[3]
  William—Grace Bradway, 6-25-1810.[7]
  William—Mergaret Bodine, 5-29-1822.[3]
  William—Sarah Stillwell, 1-15-1824.[3]
  William—Catharine Rudderow, 5-9-1826.[3]
  William—Mary B. Cox, 1-31-1839.[4]
  William C.—Deborah C. Evans. 1-14-1841.[10]
  William P.—Hannah Wright, 6-6-1821.[7]
Lipsett, John—Martha Boyde, 7-4-1839.[3]
  Joseph—Elizabeth Gaskill, 1-15-1803.[3]
Lishman, Henry—Sarah Powell, 5-13-1771.[1]
  Henry—Theodosia Lippincott, 1822.[14]
Liss, Philip—Jane McGinnis, 5-1-1756.[1]
Litman, Peter—Rebecca Dougles, 9-10-1800.[3]
Littit, Samnel—Nancy Mick, 7-18-1801.[3]
Little, Jessy—Ester Wills, 2-20-1823.[3]
  John—Phebe Stevenson, 8-23-1847.[4]
  William—Amy Jobs, 2-17-1758.[1]
  William—Ann Sowden, 9-20-1800.[5]
  William—Ann Pope, 5-27-1815.[3]
  William—Abigail Applegate, 10-23-1828.[3]
Littleton, Bernard—Mary Chipman, Mar. 1, 1685/6.[6]
Livergood, Tobias—Rebecca Gilbert, 9-20-1802.[3]

Lloyd, Archabald—Prescilla Hughes, 4-19-1815.³
 Benjamin—Ann Fortuner, 12-15-1814.³
 Charles—Mary Allen, 11-30-1815.³
 William—Maria Hammell, 3-5-1837.³
Lockwood, Levi—Lettice Fort, 10-29-18)5.³
Lodge, John,* Waterford—Mary Patt.son, Sept. 22, 1747.¹
Lofton, Charles—Anna Wells, 5-18-1822.³
 Thomas—Mary Aaronson, 8-1-1837.³
Lofty, Stephen—Hope Still, 8-31-1811.³
Logan, George—Sarah Cox, 12-26-1807.³
 Israel W.—Hester Scott 12-25-1823.³
 James—Elizabeth Alcott, 5-20-1780.¹
 John—Sarah Welsh, 2-14-1860.⁴
Loker, Samuel—Hannah Kimble, Nov. 5, 1730.¹
Loney, John—Hester Stockton, 9-22-1820.⁸
Long, James—Ann McGowan, 11-22-1830.³
 Martin—Mary Ong, 4-24-1760.¹
 Richard—Mary Whitacre, 1-20-1768.⁸
 Robert—Susan Updike, 4-9-1812.³
 Samuel—Lydia Page, 9-7-1809.³
Longsdale, John—Anna Lee, Bucks co., Pa., 4-12-1819.³
Longstaff, George—Harriet Haines, 4-20-1830.³
Longstreet, John—Margaret Read, 8-13-1886.²
Longstreth, John (s. Isaac and Jane), Philadelphia—Ann W. Thorn (d. Isaac, Jr.), 1-3-1827.⁵
Loofburrow, David—Amy Gaskill, 11-29-1779.¹
Loper, Reuben—Rachel Eztle, 7-1-1821.³
Lord, James, Gloucester co.—Elizabeth Clarke (d. Benjamin and Anne), Somerset co., Mar. 24, 1714.⁵
 John, Gloucester co.—Mary Borton, Jan. 23, 1750.¹
 Joshua, Deptford—Sarah Wills (d. John), Dec. 26, 1721.⁶
 Joshua—Mary Richardson, 9-25-1828.³
 Samuel—Elizabeth Johnson, 5-4-1814.³
 Silas—Elizabeth Bates, 12-5-1774.¹
 William—Achsa Vansciver, 4-2-1829.³
Losey, Peter—Ruth Severs, 11-14-1774.¹
Lott, Charles F., Dr.—Edith Lamb, 10-5-1809.³

*In the marriage bond James Inskeep went security for John Lodge. The marriage record says the license was ifsued to James Inskeep.¹

Louden, Frederick—Elizabeth Hugo, 5-28-1797.³
Lounsberry, Jeremiah—Mary King, Nov. 18, 1745.¹
Love, Richard—Priscilla Johnston, 1690.⁶
   Robert—Rebecca Gaskill, 5-4-1826.³
   Samuel—Elizabeth Monro, 3-19-1824.³
Loveland, Charles—Margaret Grant, 11-6-1823.³
   Clarence Walter—Naomi Mathis, 4-5-1899.²
   Oliver—Mary Cramer (d. Caleb), 3-17-1834.³
   Robert—Harriet Curtis, 12-24-1831.³
   Samuel—Hannah Gale, 2-12-1822.³
Loveless, John—Ann Craft, Nov. 15, 1742.¹
Loveman, John—Martha Grant, 3-24-1796.³
   John—Rebecca Shinn, 12-30-1830.³
Lovett, John— Beulah Hervey, 12-25-1824.³
   Jonathan—Sarah Tantum, May 7, 1741.¹
Lovit, Samuel—Mary Giles, 1703.⁶
Lovitt, Aaron—Liddie Welch, 1730.⁶
   Jonathan—Mary Howard, 1706.⁶
   Nathaniel—Mary Wills, 1729.⁶
Lowden, Dedrick—Rhoda Kimpy, 8-4-1800.³
   George—Belinder Cahoon, 12-4-1800.³
   James—Rebecca Pitman, 9-20-1804.³
   John—Abigail Peak, 5-19-1808.³
   John—Beulah Middleton, 4-14-1814.³
   Joseph—Elizabeth Mingin, 1-24-1819.³
   William—Ann Peacock, 10-13-1785.⁸
   William—Harriet Casteline, 9-8-1820.³
Lowe, Joseph—Rebecca Waite, 1752.⁹
Lowey, John L.—Elizabeth C. Stokes, 3-19-1840.¹⁰
Louthrop, Caleb—Jane Norcross, 2-9-1797.³
Loyd, Joseph A.—Sophia Musgrove, 9-4-1818.³
Luallen, Samuel—Deborah Harvey, 3-7-1795.³
Lubar, Joseph—Sarah Douglass, 10-3-1829.³
Lucas, Edward, Pennsylvania—Bridget Scott, Sept. 3, 1700.⁵
   Gilbert—Marian Ferguson, 1-28-1815.³
   John—Martha Richardson, 3-13-1803.³
   Robert—Rebecca Fennimore, May 18, 1730.¹
   Robert—Sarah Hancock, 11-22-1782.¹
   Seth—Esther Hewlings, 11-24-1760.¹
   Thomas—Susanna Wilkins, 2-4-1819.³
Luch, Jesse—Ann McCollin, 10-8-1795.³

Luckemire, Asa—Mary Force, 1-10-1821.³
Lucus, Benjamin—Sarah Saunders, Nov. 1, 1750.¹
Ludlow, Abraham—Emily Wood, 2-13-1814.³
   Abraham—Lavinia Carter, 9-8-1833.³
Luere, Thomas—Mary Ann Rose, 12-20-1817.³
Luffbury, Abraham—Elizabeth Farmer, 4-11-1810.⁸
Lukas, Daniel—Ann Brown, 9-23-1837.³
Luke, William—Phebe Gilbert, 7-20-1821.³
Lukens, Abraham D.—Mary Hutchinson, 4-7-1836.³
   Clement—Paulina Allen, 1-11-1835.⁴
   Ezekiel—Elizabeth Lippincott, 1825.¹⁴
   George Nicholson—Sara Pennington, 8-28-1889.⁴
Luker, Joel—Mary McKerne, 11-7-1812.³
Lukes, Branson—Elizabeth Gale, 6-25-1839.³
Lutes, Jacob—Rebecca Warrick, 8-20-1777.¹
Lutsey, Caspar—Catharine Weaver, 6-27-1773.¹
Lutts, John—Lydia Cubberley, 1819.¹⁴
Lybrant, Joseph—Maria Moore, 11-30-1815.³
Lycett, William—Elizabeth Archer, 3-14-1831.³
Lynch, William—Catherine Conel, 11-14-1830.⁸
Lyndall, Joseph—Sarah Rowan, 4-17-1778.¹
Lyndon, William—Elizabeth Davis, Dec. 23, 1730.¹
Lyne, John—Anne Hay, Jan. 19, 1748.¹
Lynn, Harry Elder—Amelia Spanner, 12-16-1886.²
Lyons, Adam—Adaline Rogers, 1-6-1838.³
Lytel, William—Ann McElroy, 11-2-1804.⁸
Mackason, John—Anne Hodgkinson, 2-11-1811.⁸
Mackentyar, Silvenious—Hannah Starkey, 11-23-1803.³
Mackfee, Archibel—Bithia Gasouth, 12-13-1807.³
Mackie, John, Philadelphia,—Hannah Butterworth, 8-7-1770.⁸
   Samuel—Mary Ann Long 4-8-1855.⁸
Mackin, Thomas—Jennette Schuyler, 4-25-1824.⁸
Macklane, Charles—Hannah Clifford, 1844.⁰
Mackley, John, Rev,—Abigail L. Morrow, 4-21-1835.³
Macklin, James H.—Anna Henderson (colored), 12-10-1867.⁴
   John Wesley—Martha Ann Chase, 10-29-1868.²
Macurdy, William—Rachel Wilson, 9-25-1853.⁸
Madars, William, Jr.—Hannah Gilbert, 12-16-1838.³
Madden, Henry—Mary Rockhill, 2-22-1798.³
Magaghlen, John—Sarah Havens, 12-3-1814.³
Magee, Michael, Jr.—Elizabeth Whare, 6-11-1797.³

Maggini, Joseph Felix, Philadelphia—Juliet Scount, 9-12-1819.³
Magor, Michael—Mary Edwards, 6-28-1818.³
Magronigle, Nathan—Ellenor Dippold, Trenton, 10-25-1819.³
Maguire, Archibald—Mary Smalley, 12-12-1809.³
    James—Hannah Hughes, 2-24-1789.⁴
    Mathew—Anne Mannington, 4-17-1774.⁸
Mahand, Cornelius—Elizabeth Grant, 10-18-1801.³
Major, Charles—Sarah Taylor, 4-13-1804.³
Malfeson, John Bernard—Rachel Garner, 1826.³
Malone, William—Jane Harris, 8-29-1856.⁸
Maloney, William—Laura Bonsall, 5-14-1896.¹⁰
Malsbury, Benjamin—Jane Cattell, 9-12-1801.³
    Charles—Sarah Rinear, 1-26-1805.³
    Ezekiel— Lettice Sexton, 2-12-1837.³
    Jesse—Abigail Reeves, 8-9-1827.³
    Jesse—Isabella Swaim, 10-31-1836.³
    John—Eliza Platt, 1-23-1820.³
    Jonathan—Dove Rockhill, 3-5-1812.³
    Samuel—Mary Kerlin 5-28-1829.³
Manch, Daniel—Emma Clutch, 2-12-1797.³
Mandy, Richard, Philadelphia—Jane Buff, Trenton, 9-19-1830.³
Manginlay, William—Maria Strangnots, 3-30-1818.³
Mankins, William—Sarah Test, 4-4-1821.⁷
Mannington, William—Sarah Coxe, 2-14-1772.⁸
Manuel, William—Margaret Swainry, 8-14-1813.³
Maps, Reuben—Matilda White, 12-27-1831.³
Marble, James—Mary Goldy, 4-15-1828.³
Marsh, Thomas Edward—Caroline Husband, 6-13-1837.²
Maris, Lewis—Eulalia Katherine Manroy, 8-11-1831.³
Markanney, Samuel—Sarah Hoofman, 4-2-1806.³
Markham, Henry Edward—Harriet Randall, 7-18-1866.²
Markland, John—Elizabeth Beverland, 8-17-1856.⁴
Marles, Charles—Rebekah Folwell, 9-24-1807.³
    Thomas—Hezekiah (?Keziah) Peterman, 12-20-1801.³
Marlin, William—Sarah Garrett, 10-13-1796.³
Marpole, John—Rhode Eayre, 7-10-1805.³
    Joseph—Martha Curry, 5-16-1816.³
Marriner, Edward—Virgin Gaskill, 12-3-1835.²
Marriott, Benjamin—Martha Owen, 1730.⁶
    Benjamin—Sarah Crosby, May 12, 1739.¹
    Isaac—Joice Olive, 1681.⁶

Marriott, Isaac—Sarah White, Aug. 12, 1743.[1]
　Joseph—Martha Nailor, 7-31-1771.[1]
　Philip—Abigail Hall, July 28, 1746.[1]
　Samuel—Ann Miller, July 13, 1738.[1]
Marsh, Samuel Middlesex co.—Ann Middleton, 10-6-1785.[5]
Marshall, James—Elizabeth Sapcutt, 8-15-1811.[3]
　John—Abigail Lines, 8-31-1834.[3]
　Thomas—Rachel Leeds, 4-19-1788.[1]
　William—Esther Wolf, 11-13-1834.[3]
　William H.—Abigail Hodson, 8-27-1836.[3]
Marter, Charles—Hannah Stephenson, 2-6-1820.[3]
　Isaac—Hannah Smith, 5-18-1815.[3]
　John—Susan Kemble, 11-14-1819.[3]
　Lewis—Hannah Blantford, 7-29-1838.[3]
　Michael, Jr.—Rachel Sapcott, 3-21-1805 [3]
　Richard, Catharine Anthony, Apr., 1802.[3]
　Thomas—Margaret Kelley, 9-6-1823.[3]
　Thomas—Martha Seaman, 7-30-1829.[3]
　William—Sarah Schuyler, 12-11-1817.[3]
Martin, Caleb V.—Priscilla Bell, 3-6-1800.[3]
　Charles—Mary Petit, 8-13-1810.[3]
　Elijah—Hannah Shaw, 7-30-1817.[3]
　Horace Edward—Eleanore Jennings Milbine, 7-9-1873.[2]
　John—Anna Bishop, 11-26-1772.[1]
　Stacy—Mary W. Haines, 11-27-1828.[3]
　Thomas—Hannah Marling, 8-6-1781.[1]
　William—Hannah Norris, 8-10-1771.[1]
Mason, Charles—Sarah Walker, 12-28-1834.[3]
　George—Catharine Beck, 2-10-1835.[3]
　Isaac—Rachel Engle, Gloucester co., 7-25-1819.[3]
　Jacob—Rachel Tewksbury, 11-9-1763.[1]
　James—Lida Buzbee, 1718.[6]
　James—Mary Lee, 3-9-1782.[1]
　James—Rebecca Haines, 10-12-1815.[3]
　John—Elizabeth Moore, 4-21-1761.[1]
　John—Charity Borton, 1822.[14]
　Joseph—Hepzibah Eves, 10-29-1787.[4]
　Kemble—Hannah Engle, 2-17-1825.
　Philip (s. Joseph and Mary)—Sarah Woodward (d. Anthony and Increase), 9-8-1808.[5]
　Robert—Mary Ann Parker, 9-13-1836.[3]

Mason, Samuel—Rachel Zelley, 2-9-1786.[13]
  Samuel B.—Mary R. Borton, 7-26-1828.[3]
  Solomon—Anna Kemble, 9-13-1754.[1]
  Solomon—Sarah Davis, 4-4-1788.[1]
  Solomon—Mary Woolston, 1-1-1806.[3]
  Solomon—Mary Brooks, 7-24-1824.[3]
  Thomas—Mary Kitchen, 12-1-1759.[1]
  Thomas—Abigail Pettit, 9-26-1819.[3]
  Thos.—Hannah Hancock, 11-30-1812.[7]
  William—Rebeckah Sharp, 1-9-1786.[1]
Masson, Henry—Barbara Fritze, 10-11-1807.[3]
Mathews, Aaron—Margery Kirkbride, 5-19-1814.[3]
  Daniel—Sophia Gaunt, 1743.[6]
  David William—Ann Maria Gaskill, 7-13-1833.[3]
  John—Mary Small, 10-30-1784.[1]
  John—Sarah Cline, 9-9-1836.[3]
  Mordica—Elizabeth West, 12-24-1817.[3]
  Samuel—Hannah Asa, 12-22-1835.[3]
  William—Sarah Herbert, 7-20-1827.[3]
  William—Elizabeth Lee, 7-20-1833.[3]
Mathis, Caleb—Margaret Horn, 8-10-1815.[3]
  Daniel—Mary Wooley, 10-28-1815.[3]
  Daniel, Sr.—Sophia Gaunt, 1743.[11]
  Eli—Rebecca Borton, 10-3-1816.[3]
  Elihu—Amelia Seaman, 1-11-1816.[3]
  Ellis—Mable Mathis, 10-21-1821.[3]
  Enoch J.—Esther Reeve, 2-15-1842.[4]
  Jeremiah, Jr.—Esther Morse, 5-31-1801.[3]
  Jeremiah, Sr.—Hannah Andrews (d. Samuel), 1747.[11]
  Jesse—Ann Bogin, 2-17-1828.[3]
  Job—Sarah Cosseboon, 2-27-1810.[3]
  Job—Judith Horn, 7-7-1816.[3]
  John (s. Jeremiah, Sr.)—Deborah Grant, 1777.[11]
  Lewis D.—Elizabeth Bareford, 8-21-1817.[3]
  Mahlon—Mahala Andrews, 3-30-1800.[3]
  Micajah—Mercy Shrieve, certificate to marry, 1747.[11]
  Samuel—Patty Mathis, 11-14-1812.[3]
  Samuel—Atlantic Berrey, 1-24-1819.[3]
  Shreve, Gloucester co.—Eliza Mathis, 4-10-1825.
  Stacy—Julia Cramer, 3-1-1827.[3]
  Thomas—Mary Cole, 5-31-1827.[3]

Matlack, George (s. George and Sarah)—Ann Bispham (d. Joseph and Susannah), 11-21-1805.¹²
    Jacob—Ruth Woodoth, Nov. 15, 1733.¹
    Jeremiah—Elizabeth Kinsey, 5-21-1772.¹
    John (s. Joseph and Ann)—Julia Ann Lippincott (d Thomas and Abigail), 3-25-1815.¹²
    Joseph H.—Elizabeth B. Haines, 10-16-1884.¹⁰
    Joshua (s. William and Letitia)—Ann Burrough (d. Reuben and Mary), 1-12-1825.¹²
    Richard—Rebecca Haines, 1721.⁹
    Reuben (s. Reuben and Elizabeth)—Hannah Stiles (d. Isaac and Rachel), 2-13-1817.¹²
    Samuel (s. John and Rebecca)—Mary Stiles (d. Isaac and Rachel), 2-17-1814.¹²
    Timothy—Hester Eldredge, 12-19-1785.¹
    William—Hope Osler, 1827.¹⁴
    William—Rebecca Evens, 3-23-1837.¹⁰
Matlock, George—Mary Foster, 1709.⁶
    Isaac—Abigail Loyd, 2-15-1815.³
    John—Hannah Horner, 1708.⁶
    Jonathan—Mary Indicott, 7-25-1754.¹
    Samuel—Martha Kimble, 4-23-1759.¹
    William—Anne Antrum, 1713.⁶
    William—Letitia Haines, 5-26-1788.⁷
Matson, Benjamin—Susanna Stevenson, 6-4-1764.¹
    John—Elizabeth Tonkins, 10-30-1814.³
Maulsbury, Anthony (s. David and Tillie)—Hattie Applegate (d. Edward and Sarah), 9-2-1876.⁴
    Benjamin—Abigail Gibbon, 8-17-1826.³
Maxfield, James—Sarah Leeds, 6-12-1836.³
Maxwell, Isaac—Rebecca Cole, 1823.¹⁴
    James—Bethier Gale, 1-14-1810.³
    William—Ester Wright, Dec. 22, 1730.¹
May, George—Susannah Thompson, Jan. 34, 1742.¹
    William—Hannah Baker, Sept. 22, 1741.¹
Mayale, William—Roxanna Manering, 10-21-1814.³
Mayberry, Thomas—Mary Spring, Philadelphia, 1-30-1780.¹
Mayhem, Jacob—Elizabeth Garwood, 5-31-1827.³
Mayor, William—Elizabeth Pippet, 11-29-1817.³
Maykand Pash—Hester Leek, 11-24-1825.³
Maynard, Abraham—Rebecca Cole, 8-16-1826.³

Mayoner, Isaac—Rhoda Sheppard, 8-22-1800.³
McAuley, Cornelius—Mary Johnson, 2-1-1784.¹
McCabe, Joseph—Elizabeth Hudson, 7-4-1833.²
   William—Mary Bills, 12-14-1816.²
McCall, Edward—Harriet McKnight, 9-8-1823.³
McCaney, Thomas—Mary Adams, 7-24-1828.³
McCase, Edward R.—Mrs. Eliza Hardenburgh, 9-28-1838.³
McCaul, John—Rebecca Hely, 8-2-1812.⁸
McChesney, Samuel—Sarah English, 5-14-1814.³
McClain, Harry Retson—Mary Malvina Marshall, 1-14-1891.²
McClarkey, James—Anna Maria Mornington, 10-16-1822.³
McClean, Alexander—Mary Snippin, 3-30-1773.¹
McCleese, Cornelius—Mary Pettit, Aug. 13, 1748.¹
McClery, John—Ann Decow, 10-25-1827.³
McClosey, Joseph—Sarah Whitehouse, 10-10-1812.³
McClure, Richard—Elizabeth Green, 8-27-1811.²
   Robert—Mary Thomson, 6-9-1821.³
McClutch, Obadiah—Mary Brooks, 5-3-1784.¹
McCollin, Allan—Rebecca Jolly, 11-25-1771.⁸
McCollister, Charles—Abigail Howard, 1-20-1798.³
McCollum, Hugh—Elizabeth Sucur, 2-21-1800.³
McConaughy, John C.—Ann C. Demuth, 1-17-1855.⁴
McConnell, William—Ann E. Howell, 12-15-1836.⁴
McCormick, John—Jane Fitzgerald, 4-17-1811.³
McCoy, John—Keziah Schooley, 5-27-1830.³
McCoye, John—Margaret Gise, 8-31-1806.³
McCullen, Samuel, Gloucester co.,—Sarah Loveland, 1-9-1823.³
McCulley, William Benjamin—Caroline Rogers Haines, 5-8-1880.⁴
   Joseph—Susan Dolton, 3-23-1830.²
   Samuel—Lydia Esdaile, 11-29-1787.¹
McCully, Joseph—Sarah Gardener, 3-28-1781.¹
McDaniels, William—Rachel Cranmer, 11-16-1833.³
   Jarret, Monmouth co —Mary Rogers, May 11, 1748.¹
McDerman, John—Mary Bryant, 10-30-1803.³
McDermot, John—Hannah Vandegrift, 9-14-1800.³
McDoniel, Augustus—Lydia Morris, 1-10-1776.¹
McDonnell, John—Rebecca Bird, 2-8-1832.³
McDowell, Alexander—Elizabeth Allen, 5-8-1782.¹
   John—Hannah Ashton, 10-1-1808.³
McDowell, Benjamin—Mary Emmons, 2-3-1796.³
McElroy, Charles—Mary Vansciver, 3-13-1831.³

McElroy, John—Sarah Goodman, 11-20-1788.[4]
    William—Elizabeth Ridgway, 11-30-1809.[3]
    Mr., Pennsylvania—Pamelia Vansciver, 3-10-1831.[3]
McFadden, Dennis—Sarah Ireland, 10-8-1812.[3]
McFarlan, Eugene—Elizabeth Sleeper, 9-28-1795.[3]
McFarland, Samuel C.—Susan Plank, 7-20-1837.[3]
    Thomas—Elizabeth Jane Carson, 12-12-1886.[4]
McGailie, Hugh—Christian Ireland (wid.), 10-13-1802.[3]
McGaw Patrick—Amy Cramer, 3-21-1797.[3]
McGee, Charles—Elizabeth Money, 1797.[3]
    Charles—Patty Hedger, 1-6-1815.[3]
    Thomas—Margaret Turner, 2-10-1780.[1]
McGinness, Richard—Mariam Ridgway, 6-20-1775.[1]
McGlockland, Edward—Mary Fisher, 4-4-1795.[3]
McGlocklin, Thomas—Sarah Williams, 3-30-1807.[3]
McGonegal, Henry—Mary Lowden, 4-8-1788.[1]
McGowan, Robert—Mary Cambern, 3-7-1796.[3]
McGraw, Patrick—Catharine Garner, 8-24-1815.[3]
McHelvey, Charles—Jemima Hampton, 8-23-1828.[3]
McHenry, Charles—Rebecca Brighton, 7-13-1814.[3]
    George—Rebecca Shreve, 4-11-1838.[4]
    Mathew—Mary Shinn, 5-23-1805.[3]
McIlvain, James (s. Hugh and Hannah), Philadelphia—Rebecca B. Sterling (d. Thomas and Edith), Trenton, 3-23-1837.[5]
    Thomas Sterling—Mary Zelley, 10-25-1871.[2]
McIlvaine, Charles P., Rev.—Emily Coxe, 10-8-1822.[3]
    Edward S.—Esther Rodman, 10-21-1812.[8]
    William, Dr.—Margaret Rodman, both Bristol, 11-6-1773.[8]
McIlvane, Joseph—Martha Reed, 9-19-1793.[1]
McIntire, John—Lydia Lewis, 2-12-1824.[3]
    William—Eleanor Wilson, 9-23-1821.[3]
McIntosh, Lachlan H.—Anna M. Richards, 2-10-1853.[4]
McKean, Thomas—Mary Reeves, 2-5-1801.[3]
McKean, William—Sarah Vannote, 10-1-1837.[3]
McKee, James—Keturah McCoy, 8-16-1836.[3]
    William—Elizabeth Larzelere, 3-1-1834.[8]
McKeen, Robert—Margaret Burns, 1-8-1818.[3]
McKelvey, Edward—Elizabeth Lucas, 7-5-1813.[3]
    John—Eliza Chambers, 1-16-1825.[3]
McKnight, William—Ann Douglass, 1-3-1805.[3]
McLaughlin, Charles—Mary Shinn, 2-4-1807.[5]

McLynch, William—Eliza McKerney. No date given.*²
McMaster, John—Ella Mitchell, both Roxborough, Pa., 12-24-1891.⁴
　Thomas—Ann Ward, 5-29-1817.³
McMinn, James—Hannah Stratton, 7-7-1800.³
McMinnew, Daniel—Hannah Wiltse, 12-8-1808.³
McMurtrie, William—Elizabeth Coxe, 6-1-1811.⁵
Mears, Joseph, Monmouth co.—Susannah Stewart, 4-5-1764.¹
Meechan, John—Margaret Mannington, 3-14-1814.⁸
Meeks, Aaron—Rebecca Brocks, 7-29-1815.³
　Joseph—Mary Ward, 12-24-1812.⁴
Megargy, George—Ellen Fenton, 3-6-1829.³
Meirs, George—Mary Prickett, May 20, 1751.¹
Mellon, Robert—Susan Hart, 9-25-1823.³
Melowney, Daniel—Nancy Williamson, 1-27-1807.³
Menough, Lewis—Ann Gibson, 2-24-1831.³
Meredith, Thomas—Ruth Williams, 6-29-1755.¹
Meredyth, Thomas—Jane Norcross, 4-8-1740.¹
Merit, Abraham, Garthrey Brooks, 2-12-1785.¹
Merot, Philip—Mary Jobes, 11-8-1860.¹
Merrick, Robert—Achsah Davis, 6-2-1799.³
　Timothy—Sarah Keys, 5-13-1775.⁸
Merril, Isaac—Rachel Ward, 5-22-1823.³
Merriott, Robert—Margaret Brush, 9-26-1812.³
Merrit, Abraham—Rachel Gaskill, 9-28-1757.¹
　Abraham (s. Jacob and Tamson)—Rebecca Lamb (d. Jacob and Elizabeth), 1-31-1802.³
　Thomas S.—Mary Noxon, 2-26-1823.³
Merritt, Absolom—Ester Kindle, 12-18-1831.³
　Charles Ewan, Waynesville, O.—Blanche Rosalie Harker, 6-20-1877.⁴
　Charles Ewan—Mary Josephine Curtiss, 6-1-1889.²
　Ewan—Catharine C. Kempton, 6-7-1853.⁴
　Isaac—Elizabeth Hewlings, 3-21-1782.¹
　Isaac—Alice Wright, 4-13-1784.¹
　Joseph—Mary Rogers, 1-24-1799.³
　Robert—Rosannah Shepherd, 10-27-1827.³
　Theodore G.—Harriet E. Firing, 9-28-1871.⁸
　Thomas—Elizabeth Curtis, 6-28-1770.¹

*Married by Samuel Wright, J. P.

Merritt, Thomas—Jane Gaskill, declaration of intention to marry, 5-8-1817.[13]
Merryman, John—Elizabeth Knott, Monmouth co., 4-24-1779.[1]
Meservy, William—Patty Vansant, 8-4-1802.[3]
Mevis, Joseph, Jr.—Lydia Preston, 3-24-1799.[3]
Meyers, Curtis—Priscilla Laurence, 9-6-1798.[3]
  George Washington—Lydia Gardner, 4-14-1895.[2]
  Jacob, Jr.—Ann Johnstone, 12-16-1800.[3]
  Nathan—Elizabeth Bispham, 10-17-1795.[3]
  Robert—Maggie Cooper, 12-27-1899.[2]
Michner, John R.—Margaret Budd, 8-2-1837.[3]
Mick, Michael—Mary Moore, 12-4-1783.[1]
  Michael, Jr.—Delia Diviney, 3-26-1802.[3]
  Michael, Jr.—Mariah Mathis, 10-20-1827.[3]
Mickle, David (s. William), Gloucester co. — Rachel Wills (d. Moses and Margaret), 4-7-1803.[6]
  John—Lydia Lippincott, 1-11-1822.[3]
  Samuel, Gloucester co.—Mary Stockdal, Aug. 15, 1741.[6]
  Thomas (s. Charles and Matilda)—Ada L. Black (d. Edward), 2-17-1874.[4]
Middleton, Aaron—Isabella Nicols, 11-4-1797.[3]
  Abel—Mary Hews, Somerset co., 12-18-1754.[5]
  Albert (s. Jacob and Sabilla), Philadelphia—Anna S. Middleton (d. Allen and Mary), 1-9-1845.[5]
  Benjamin H.—Eliza English, 3-26-1817.[3]
  Cyrus—Elenor Smith, 12-4-1798.[3]
  Elwood (s. Enoch and Hannah)—Rebecca Ann Potts (d. Samuel and Anna), 10-9-1845.[5]
  Enoch (s. Gabriel and Elizabeth), Philadelphia—Hannah Middleton (d. Asa and Elizabeth), 12-7-1820.[5]
  George S. (s. John and Esther)—Hannah Fowler, Dec. 29, 1743.[5]
  George—Elizabeth Ogbourn, 5-4-1796.[3]
  Gideon—Mary Price, 1-1-1823.[3]
  Howard—Hannah Carr, 3-5-1807.[13]
  Hugh—Mary Fairley, Sept. 25, 1744.[1]
  Jacob—Hannah Tilton, 2-11-1779.[5]
  James—Marian Roberts, 12-7-1828.[3]
  Joel—Sarah Middleton, 12-23-1780.[1]
  Joel—Sarah Warrick, 1-10-1819.[3]
  Joel, Jr. (s. Joseph and Avis)—Amy Bunting (d. Samuel and Deborah), 11-7-1822.[5]

Mideleton, Jonathan—Anne Morris, 1-27-1776.¹
 Joseph (s. Nathan and Lydia)—Avis Holloway (d. James and Rebecca), 4-17-1794.⁵
 Joseph—Sarah Ann Woodrow, 5-9-1833.³
 Mordecai S. (s. Jediah and Anna)—Sarah Furman (d. George M. and Margaret), Trenton, 12-8-1831.⁵
 Nathan (s. George and Hannah)—Lydia Allen (d. Samuel and Mary), 5-14-1767.⁵
 Nathan—Judith Stokes, 7-26-1777.¹
 John—Elizabeth Ellis, 9-14-1826.³
 Nathaniel—Sarah Conrow, 1-21-1790.¹
 Samuel—Sarah Taylor, 2-25-1808.³
 Samuel—Mary Joyce, 1-8-1826.³
 Sheron—Priscilla Sharp, 3-7-1799.³
 Solomon S.—Hannah Wilson, 1-15-1867.²
 Thomas—Patience Tilton, Monmouth co., Jan. 15, 1735.⁵
 Thomas—Esthdr Boreton, 1740.⁹
 Thomas—Jane Nicholson (wid.), 1753.⁹
 Thomas—Mercy Forsyth, 12-14-1780.⁵
 Thomas—Mary Bassett, 8-12-1784.¹
 Thomas—Abigail Brackney, 10-6-1784.¹
 Thomas—Mrs. Delviah Woodward, 3-17-1799.³
 Thomas—Hannah Cox, 4-8-1802.³
 Timothy—Elizabeth Borton, 1740.⁹
 William—Mary Kimble, Oct. 9, 1746,¹
 William—Mary Curtis, 12-7-1824.³
Miers, Abram—Dorcas Andrews, 11-14-1757.¹
 John—Rachel South, 12-8-1763.¹
Millaird, Abraham—Mary Wiles, 8-8-1764.¹
Miller, Abraham—Mary Jane Bell, 6-9-1838.³
 Adam—Martha B. Fowler, 5-21-1836.³
 Charles—Catherine Clevenger, June 26, 1732.¹
 David—Elizabeth McIntire (colored), 10-20-1796.³
 Ebenezer—Hannah Nicholson, 5-26-1788.⁷
 Franklin S.—Mary P. Davis, 12-13-1843.⁴
 Hugh—Charity Mahollen, 11-11-1816.³
 Isaac—Mercy Richards, Aug. 22, 1750.¹
 James—Ruth Lewis, 8-21-1803.³
 James—Sarah Loyd, 9-18-1817.³
 James—Matilda Dodson, 12-31-1835.³
 Johann—Martha Price, 5-20-1761.¹

Miller, John—Anne Millard, Jan. 4, 1728.[1]
  John—Sarah Andrews, 1758.[9]
  John—Hester Tanner, 10-3-1764.[1]
  John—Catharine Bristow, 4-29-1766.[1]
  John—Catherine Rowe, 2-28-1775.[8]
  John, Capt.—Ann Wilson, 4-6-1795.[3]
  John—Mary Gardiner, 2-3-1796.[3]
  John—Mary Simons, 1-2-1804.[3]
  John—Patience Taylor, 1815.[14]
  John—Elizabeth Knowlton, 3-27-1824.[3]
  Joseph—Letitia Matlack (wid.), 5-29-1809.[7]
  Joseph—Susan Thomas, 12-18-1813.[3]
  Joshua—Abigail McCloe, 11-16-1825.[3]
  Joshua—Hannah Mathews, 4-29-1832.[3]
  Samuel—Ann Cooper, 10-14-1812.[10]
  Samuel S.—Martha Wills, 11-28-1830.[3]
  Samuel T.—Rebecca Merritt, 2-7-1833.[3]
  Thomas—Martha Lake, Mar. 11, 1729.[1]
  Thomas—Elizabeth Taylor, 11-1-1825.[3]
  William—Ann Kemble, 4-7-1777.[1]
  William—Susannah Goodwin, 4-24-1797.[7]
  William—Sarah Williams, 11-19-1801.[3]
Milles, James—Sarah Coppuck, 8-19-1761.[1]
  Joshua—Margaret Williams, Nov. 1, 1739.[1]
Milligan, William—Sarah McDole, 9-22-1822.[3]
Milliken, Richard—Rachel Hoskins, 12-18-1759.[1]
Mills, Alexander C.—Mary Anna Sharp, 3-3-1870.[2]
  Aurelius—Beulah Willits, 11-23-1816.[3]
  Francis—Euphemia Smart, 7-29-1782.[1]
  Israel—Ruth Parker, 5-28-1789.[4]
  Joshua—Sarah King, 12-6-1818.[3]
  Joshua—Hannah Gibson, 8-16-1834.[4]
  Royall, Holmesburg, Pa.—Mary Savill, Morrisville, Pa., 12-23-1828.[3]
  William—Hannah Borden, 12-5-1778.[1]
Milner, Nathan—Phebe Swift, 10-18-1810.[3]
Milton, James—Lydia Garwood, 8-1-1761.[1]
  William—Elizabeth Morlan, 1-23-1760.[1]
Mincer, Clayton—Rebecca Kirby, 12-14-1811.[3]
Mingen, Lewis—Mercy Norcross, 2-10-1773.[1]
Mingin, Benjamin—Jane Kell, 1-17-1815.[3]

Mingin, Benjamin—Betsey Rossell, 3-8-1818.³
John—Ann Cook, 8-16-1798.³
John—Mary Foulks, 4-22-1828.³
John, Jr.—Elizabeth Taylor, Monmouth co., 12-21-1820.³
Joseph—Sarah Jones, July 28, 1748.¹
Joseph—Hannah Leeds, 11-20-1777.¹
Lewis—Jane Rossell, 8-29-1824.³
Mingo, Warrant—Dinah Night, 8-21-1795.³
Minor, Lawrence—Elizabeth Platt, 12-8-1760.¹
Minser, Mark—Hannah Burns, 3-10-1784.¹
Mintle, George—Sarah Mintle, 11-26-1795.³
Mires, Aaron—Sarah Butterfield, 8-10-1771.
  William, Jr.—Danos Adams, 5-10-1818.³
Mirs, George—Mary Prickett, May 20, 1751.¹
Mitchel, Daniel—Anne Fort, 10-27-1783.¹
Mitehell, Abraham—Mary Piffets, 1-29-1757.¹
  Abner—Ann Glass, 2-25-1804.³
  David—Sarah Willits, 6-2-1831.³
  George—Ann Croney, 3-2-1782.¹
  Henry—Martha Vanhorne, both Bucks co., Pa., 3-25-1769.⁸
  William—Mary Hutchin, 1-14-1770.⁸
Moffet, Henry—Cecelia Murphy, 3-20-1866.⁸
Moffett, Thomas—Agnes Page, 10-1-1846.⁴
Moller, John—Patience Taylor, 10-1-1815.³
Monday, James—Lydia Malsbury, 8-15-1805.³
Monroe, John—Margaret Mitchell, Aug. 9, 1736.¹
Monrow, George—Rose Sharp, 1-14-1769.¹
  John, Jr.—Sarah Biddle, 6-3-1764.¹
Mons, John—Dorothy Stout, 11-13-1759.¹
Montgomery, Benjamin—Elizabeth Thomas, 11-15-1825.³
  Ross Baines—Elizabeth T. Cooke, 7-16-1825.³
  William—Mary Ellis, 1756.⁹
Moon, Jacob—Ann Adams, 7-27-1815.³
  James—Alice Barry, Aug. 18, 1744.¹
  James—Mary Gipson, 1-17-1807.³
  Jasper—Martha Cripps, 9-1-1773.⁸
Moor, Benjamin, Jr.—Rebecca Fennimore, Oct. 27, 1730.¹
  James—Sarah Ridgway, Dec. 1, 1730.¹
  Joseph—Patience Woolman, 1738.⁶
  Mordica—Alice Walker, Jan. 17, 1731.¹
  Ross—Sarah Cramer, 3-9-1815.³

Moore, Abraham—Martha Rogers, 7-7-1813.³
  Abraham—Elizabeth E. Engle, 1823.¹⁴
  Asa—Katariah Foster, 2-22-1808.³
  Asahel (s. John and Elizabeth), Pennsylvania—Anna Cowperthwaite (d. Job and Anna), 10-11-1810.¹²
  Benjamin—Mary Stokes, 1693.⁵
  Benjamin—Sarah Bowen, 11-17-1878.¹
  Benjamin—Rebecca Ann Moore, 7-15-1820.³
  Bethuel—Ann Austin, 4-18-1805.³
  Bethuel—Mary Mason, 6-22-1813.³
  Bethuel N.—Hannah N. Inskeep, 1825.¹⁴
  Charles—Mary Burr, 12-31-1805.³
  Charles—Sarah Ann Cole, 12-14-1826.³
  David—Cathrine Mount, 4-13-1797.³
  Edward—Susannah Scott, 8-19-1823.³
  Eli—Louisa D. Stricker, 12-25-1823.³
  George—Mary Woodruff, 6-21-1825.⁴
  Gershom—Priscilla Gordon, 6-1-1802.³
  Henry—Sarah Custer, 5-24-1806.³
  Hewlings—Ann Hollingshead, 12-9-1809.³
  James—Ann Bishop, 1744.⁶
  James—Mary Jones, 4-19-1829.³
  Job—Mary Lippincott, 11-26-1766.¹
  John—Bathsheba Ballinger, 5-1-1777.¹
  John—Sarah Lisham, 7-10-1800.¹³
  John—Sarah Fenimere, 11-16-1816.³
  John, Gloucester co.—Nancy Evans, 9-27-1832.³
  Joseph—Mary Hewlings, 5-12-1783.¹
  Joseph—Hannah Eamres, 6-6-1797.³
  Joseph, Jr.—Abigail Woolman, 1-11-1815.³
  Mark—Eliza Moore, 6-18-1825.³
  Mark—Beulah Curtis, 3-27-1830.³
  Robert—Esther Smith, 11-26-1823.⁷
  Samuel—Kesiah Chapman, 12-8-1810.³
  Snowden—Mary Hutchinson, 6-29-1836.³
  Stacy—Sibilla Austin, 2-17-1801.³
  Thomas—Miriam Ridgway, 1741.⁶
  Thomas—Martha Shinn, 10-28-1821.³
  William—Margaret Kerr, 5-18-1775.⁸
  William—Kitturah Wilkins, 12-30-1795.³
  Zebedee—Rachel Githens, 1-14-1819.³

BURLINGTON COUNTY MARRIAGES

Moore, Zebedee—Hannah Newton, 1825.[14]
Morass, William—Mary Johnston, 4-10-1813.[3]
More, John, Jr.—Kitturah Eayre, 10-8-1795.[3]
    Thomas—Mary Wright (d. John amd Hannah), 6-4-1783.[5]
Morehouse, George Y.—Martha Read, 11-21-1820.[4]
Mores, Robert—Jemima Wood, Sept. 15, 1741.[1]
    Robert—Rebecca Cole, 10-17-1813.[3]
Morford, Cornelius—Esther Bryan, 12-21-1761.[1]
Morgan, Benjamin R.—Hannah Haines, 1822.[14]
    Isaac—Sarah Ridgway, 12-8-1785.[13]
    Joseph—Sarah Bispham, 4-6-1786.[13]
    Joseph—Sarah Wallace, 10-24-1808.[3]
    Joseph C.—Margaret Browning, 9-27-1832.[3]
    Joseph, Jr.—Mary Butcher, 2-23-1789.[1]
    Joseph R. (s. Isaac and Sarah)—Mary Burrough (d. William and Achsah), both Waterford, 1818.[12]
    Kimsey—Margaret Simpkins, 1-25-1827.[3]
    Michael—Mary Griffith, 9-1-1808.[3]
    Watson—Margaret Dunn, 10-22-1809.[3]
Mornington, William—Sarah Coxe, 2-14-1772.[1]
Morphett, David—Elizabeth Hedges, Aug. 18, 1735.[1]
Morrel, Samuel—Cathrine Hubbs, 1-2-1800.[3]
Morrell, William—Mary Fennimore, Oct. 28, 1730.[1]
Morrey, John C.—Rachel Camp, 1-13-1819.[3]
Morris, Abraham—Mary Hisler, 2-15-1817.[3]
    Anthony—Sarah Cranmer, 1746.[11]
    Caspar Wistar—Anna P. Milnor, 10-15-1857.[8]
    Daniel—Elizabeth Knight, 4-14-1804.[3]
    George—Elie Fegans, 12-17-1783.[1]
    George—Rebecca Decow, Oct. 14, 1731.[1]
    Isaac—Jemimah Applegate, 4-14-1759.[1]
    Isaac—Amy Sulsey, 9-29-1805.[3]
    John—Rose Ridge, Dec. 13, 1746.[1]
    John—Prudence Butcher, 12-4-1812.[10]
    John—Elizabeth Congle, 5-5-1819.[3]
    John—Rebecca L. Allen, 4-15-1833.[4]
    Joseph—Hannah Asson, Monmouth co., Aug. 21, 1744.[1]
    Joseph—Lydia Wilson, 1-5-1767.[1]
    Joseph—Ruth Shinn, 8-24-1803.[3]
    Joseph—Phebe Yates, 10-27-1812.[3]
    Josiah W. (s. T. E. and Elizabeth) —Carrie Kemble, 12-17-1873.

Morris, Lawrence—Virgin Cripps, 1684.[6]
    Paschall—Anna M. Reeve, 5-29-1873.[10]
    Samuel—Mary Claypool, 6-27-1797.[3]
    Samuel—Elizabeth Beebe, 9-1-1832.[3]
    Stacey—Mary Smith, 2-23-1805.[3]
    Thomas—Ann Ward, 3-29-1779.[1]
    Thomas—Mary Lippincott, 1-31-1811.[3]
    William—Mary Wills, 5-7-1768.[1]
    Wilson—Rhoda Allen, 12-29-1796.[3]
Morrison, Isaac—Sarah Ann Atkinson, 11-16-1828.[3]
Morrow, David—Mary Loveland, 12-6-1784.[1]
    Joseph—Charity Peters, 7-10-1799.[3]
    Samuel—Anna Pharo, 3-20-1764.[1]
Morse, Ephraim—Elizabeth Lippincott (d. Joseph, Sr.), 1772.[11]
Morton, Benjamin—Sarah Roberts, 5-3-1807.[3]
    Benjamin—Hannah Malsbury, 7-7-1833.[3]
    Hezekiah—Margaret Goldy, 2-4-1781.[1]
    Humphrey—Elizabeth Baxter, 1-3-1799.[3]
    Jacob E.—Susan Wainright, 6-8-1835.[3]
    John—Ann Weaver, 8-18-1763.[1]
    John—Abigail Eldridge, 6-9-1807.[3]
    John—Elizabeth Larison, 4-17-1825.[3]
    John—Elenor Sharp, 12-30-1829.[3]
    Joseph—Fanny Headly, 9-14-1805.[3]
    Joseph (wid)—Mary Ann Lippincott, 9-21-1811.[3]
    Restore—Rachel Arey, 11-2-1779.[1]
    Samuel—Rebecca Clinton, 9-28-1805.[3]
    Stacy—Sidney Bishop, 3-22-1829.[3]
    Sylwin—Marian Quann, 11-23-1822.[3]
    William—Rachel Osler, 2-20-1830.[3]
Mott, Asher, Amwell—Ann Biles, Bucks co., 5-10-1769.[8]
    James—Rebecca Rose, both Tuckerton, 6-3-1833.[3]
    Isaac—Lydia Reeves, 3-18-1805.[3]
    John—Phebe Cramer, Aug. 7, 1738.[1]
    John—Patience Austin, 9-15-1777.[1]
    Thomas—Rachel Adams, 12-16-1815.[3]
    William—Jane Jeffries, 3-19-1798.[3]
Mound, Enoch—Lydia Mills, 3-17-1778.[1]
Mount, George Rue—Georgie Collins, 6-23-1892.[2]
    John—Elizabeth Gaskel, 5-16-1835.[3]
    John E.—Ann Archer, 8-9-1834.[3]

Mount, Matthias—Elizabeth Keeler, 8-1-1771.¹
   Michael—Margaret Allen, 3-4-1830.³
   Nicholas D.—Gertrude Raum, 5-2-1823.³
   Nicholas DuBois, Trenton—Mira L. Long, 3-15-1836.³
   Timothy B.—Mary Olden, 2-6-1806.³
   William—Catharine Hoffman, 5-29-1803.³
   William—Sarah Naylor, 10-7-1827.³
Noways, Joseph A., Jr.—Charlotte Bates, 1-9-1796.³
Moyers, William—Martha Watkins, 10-8-1802.³
Mulford, Samuel, Bridgeton—Louisa Rudderow, 1-10-1833.³
   Samuel—Elizabeth Walcott, 3-21-1837.³
Mullin, Edward—Mary Stokes, 1724.⁶
   Edward—Mary Monrow, 10-27-1759.¹
   Edward—Anne Shaw, 11-25-1783.¹
   James—Ann Ostlar, 11-22-1810.³
   John—Druzilla Prickett, Apr. 16, 1751.¹
   John—Hannah Collins, 8-17-1754.¹
   John—Jane Kine, 11-28-1761.¹
   John—Catharine Haines, 3-25-1776.¹
   John—Esther Earl, 1820.¹⁴
   Joseph—Ann Fenimore, Dec. 24, 1748.¹
   Joseph—Hannah West, 11-2-1820.³
   Samuel—Mary Estell, 3-19-1775.¹
   Samuel—Sarah Atkinson, 5-13-1784.¹
   William—Veturia G. Haines, 2-26-1829.³
Mullin, John—Elizabeth Edwards, Sept. 14, 1729,¹
Mingon, John—Sarah Cowgill, Apr. 25, 1738.¹
Munrow, George—Sarah Perkins, Nov. 23, 1737.¹
Murdock, Abraham—Mary Woostall, 10-4-1838.³
   James B.—Hannah Ware, 9-5-1824.³
   Samuel—Mary Black, 5-10-1815.³
Murfin, Thomas—Mary Holland, 9-3-1798.³
   William—Sarah Bunting, Aug. 8, 1704.⁵
Murphin, Thomas—Anne Brelsford, 6-24-1769.³
Murphy, Charles—Elizabeth Jobs, 4-16-1799.³
   David—Sarah F. Taylor, 7-8-1832.³
   Henry—Suzanna Foster, 11-7-1775.⁸
   James—Martha Piper, 1821.¹⁴
   John—Sarah Jones, Aug. 10, 1749.¹
   John—Rebecca Gibbs, 11-9-1815.³
   Joseph—Ann Doltin, 10-3-1816.³

Murphy, Michael—Jenny Ammerman, 3-1-1780.[1]
  Stephen—Esther Fort, Sept. 18, 1729.[1]
Murray, John—Precilla Powel, 8-19-1798.[3]
Murrel, Joseph—Anne Ferguson, 4-14-1758.[1]
Murrell, Joseph—Sarah Scattergood, 7-21-1757.[1]
  Samuel—Rachel Hooper, Mar. 29-1749.[1]
Murrey, James—Mary Dorris, both Pennsylvania, 8-1-1830.[3]
Murrill, William—Sarah Estill, 12-4-1783.[1]
Murry, John—Sarah Beham, 4-30-1800.[3]
  Stacy—Harriet Page, 4-10-1828.[3]
  William—Sarah Bishop, 4-14-1833.[3]
Muscat, Frederick—Mary Thorla 12-5-1768.[1]
Mutt, John—Mary Taylor, 10-8-1809.[3]
Myars, William—Elizabeth Andrews, 3-6-1766.[1]
Myers, John—Sarah Shinn, 10-31-1775.[1]
  John—Ann Bispham, 12-31-1798.[3]
  John L.—Elizabeth Jones, 9-12-1716.[3]
  Joseph—Sarah Bispham, 12-31-1798.[3]
  Moses—Michael Smith, 5-20-1774.[1]
  Samuel—Rebecca Adams, 2-15-1810.[3]
  Thomas—Susanna Shepherd, 5-19-1817.[3]
  Thomas—Anna R. Smith, 5-12-1836.[3]
  William—Abigail G. Garwood, 5-21-1837.[3]
Myller, Joseph—Anne Fenimore, Dec. 24, 1748.[1]
Myres, Aaron—Jannet Vansciver, Dec., 1802.[3]
  Aaron—Amy Warner, 6-4-1826.[3]
  John—Emeline Cook, 11-4-1838.[3]
Nagel, William M.—Viola F. Firing, 9-2-1866.[8]
Nail, James—Mary Cramer, 10-29-1815.[3]
Nailer, Benjamin—Sarah Stockton, 4-13-1778.[1]
  Jacob—Hannah Jones, 1-14-1783.[1]
  Peter—Sarah Jones, 11-1-1804.[3]
  William—Sarah Wills, 4-9-1801.[3]
Nailor, Benj.—Ann Richardson, 12-12-1811.[3]
  Charles—Mary Cattell, 12-4-1828.[3]
  Isaac—Eleanor Richardson, 7-6-1820.[3]
  Joseph—Susan Thompson, 2-13-1800.[3]
  Samuel—Phebe English, 2-12-1812.[3]
  Thomas—Edith Wilson, 9-27-1799.[3]
Nayler, James—Lucretia Rakestraw, 1-9-1777.[1]
  James—Susanna Sharp, 11-28-1787.[1]

Naylor, Charles—Mary Cattell, 12-4-1828.³
  Jacob—Ann Tonkins, 2-6-1819.³
Neal, Benjamin T.—Alice Barrington, 1-13-1820.⁴
Neale, Hugh—Deborah Leeds, Feb. 1, 1748.¹
  John—Eliza Bispham, 12-9-1813.³
  Thompson—Mary Moon, 12-12-1770.⁸
Neall, Thomas—Jemima Rulon, 12-26-1810.²
Negley, James—Mary Barber, 5-30-1808.³
Negus, John—Mary Shreve, 2-16-1779.¹
Nelly, John—Sarah Grimes, Aug. 19, 1742.¹
Nelson, Andrew—Salina Hartman, 3-12-1836.³
  Charles—Rebecca Hooten, 1825.¹⁴
  Michael—Joanna Severn, 2-4-1837.³
  Samuel—Deborah Cubberly, 11-14-1831.³
Nemus, Benjamin—Deborah Higgins, 5-6-1832.³
Netterville, Charles—Rachel Wilson, May 1, 1736.¹
Neviel, Jacob—Margaret Cline, 12-3-1837.²
Nevins, Elisha S.—Margaret Layton, 5-15-1838.³
  Peter—Ann Rodgers, 2-21-1805.³
Newberry, Henry—Sarah Boyes (d. Richard), 1703.⁹
  William—Mary Harker (d. William), 1705.⁹
Newbold, Alexander—Harriet Allen, 12-18-1834.³
  Brazilia—Sarah Core, 1734.⁹
  Charles—Mary Shreve, 1-8-1804.³
  Clayton—Mary Foster, 1759.⁹
  Clayton (s. Clayton and Mary)—Beulah Lawrie (d. Joseph M. and Edith), 10-13-1807.⁵
  Daniel—Rachel Newbold, 7-27-1780.¹
  Daniel—Rachel Lawrie, 1-6-1814.³
  Michael—Susannah Schooley, 1730.⁶
  Samuel—Mary Hough, 11-8-1798.¹³
  Thomas—Edith Coate, 1724.⁶
  Thomas (s. Williams and Susanna)—Mary Taylor (d. Anthony and Ann), 2-19-1789.⁵
  Thomas—Rebecca Shreve, 3-8-1832.³
  William I.—Sarah Collier, 3-17-1831.³
Newbury, John—Mary Dussell, 4-8-1804.³
Newcomb, John—Hope Naylor, 11-7-1833.⁸
Newell, John—Elizann Gordon, 4-5-1823.
  John—Eliza Goreton, 7-5-1823.³
  Joseph—Anna Herbert, 12-5-1813.³

Newell, Robert—Anne Jacobs, 1-20-1822.[8]
   Robert—Elizabeth Wormwood, 5-21-1846.[4]
   Thomas—Jane Pettigrew, Jan. 20, 1740.[1]
   William A., Dr.—Anna Clark Black, 10-1-1879.[2]
Newman, George—Sarah Ann Penn, 10-6-1836.[3]
   Israel—Elizabeth Rockhill, 12-24-1817.[3]
   John, Philadelphia—Hester Heulings, Sept. 12, 1738.[1]
   Richard—Mary Haines, Mar. 23, 1740.[1]
Newport, Benjamin—Anna Walton, 12-28-1799.[3]
Newton, Daniel—Ann Lewis, 2-11-1830.[3]
   Isaac—Dorothy Birdsall, 1821.[14]
   John—Rachel Sharp, 2-12-1807.[3]
   Joseph—Elizabeth Ashburn, 11-29-1775.[1]
   Michael—Mary Rockhill, 2-23-1773.[5]
   Michael—Ann Frazier, 10-17-1822.[3]
   Richard—Hannah Tilton, 1-10-1822.[3]
   Thomas—Jerushe Moore, 3-30-1815.[3]
   William—Ann Vankirk, 12-21-1809.[3]
Nicholas, Joseph, Bucks co., Pa.— Anne Lewis, 5-29-1810.[3]
Nicholson, George—Hannah Woolston, 1706.[6]
   George—Alice Ford, June 6, 1717.[5]
   Isaac—Rebecca Fogg, 7-28-1817.[7]
   Joseph—Catharine Butcher, 1738.[6]
   Joseph—Amy Haines, 11-10-1866.[10]
   Nehemiah—Deborah Ireland, Sept. 3, 1737.[1]
Nicles, John—Sarah Seaman, 3-3-1821.[3]
Niel, James—Abigail Peters, 9-1-1778.[1]
Nightingale, James—Elizabeth Wild, Apr. 17, 1747.[1]
   Arthur David—Lillie Smith, 4-7-1894.[2]
Nippen, Joseph—Ann Willets, 9-21-1824.[3]
Nippins, William—Sarah Gilbert, 8-26-1836.[3]
Nixon, John—Elizabeth Stillwell, 2-26-1819.[3]
   Joseph—Abigail Webb, 12-11-1813.[3]
   Joseph—Ann Ayres, 5-20-1829.[3]
   Mordecai—Anna Southerly, 3-21-1815.[3]
   Samuel—Susan Devinny, 9-6-1815.[3]
Noble, George—Katherine Smith, Nov. 16, 1730.[1]
   John—Mary Smith, 1719.[6]
   Joseph—Mary Ryan, 1747.[6]
Nold, Phillip—Margaret Dyer, 7-25-1774.[1]
Norcross Hudson—Hannah Sharp, 1822.[14]

Norcross, J. L. Franklin—Sarah Ella Taylor, 9-3-1879.[2]
John—Mary Antrom, 1712.[6]
John—Anne Stevenson, 10-4-1756.[1]
John—Rachel King, 9-18-1765.[1]
John—Mary Herbert, 1-2-1776.[1]
Joshua—Jane Strattan, 4-10-1854.[1]
Joshua—Theodosia King, 4-14-1767.[1]
Joshua—Lucas Webb, 5-16-1802.[3]
Joshua—Elizabeth Gaskill, 7-5-1807.[3]
Joshua—Sarah Ann Powell, 9-23-1858.[4]
Levi—Mary Stockton, 3-1-1801.[3]
Nelson—Elizabeth Johnson, 8-29-1824.[3]
  Samuel—Hannah Antram, 3-2-1789.[1]
Samuel—Elizabeth Brittain, 6-18-1817.[3]
Samuel—Priscilla Bowen, 4-4-1833.[3]
Simeon—Lucille Fenton, 5-15-1802.[3]
Simeon—Lucey Fenimore, 3-14-1807.[3]
William—Rebekka Petty, 1720.[6]
William—Mary Johnston, 4-10-1813.[3]
Nordyde, Henry—Rebecca Perkins, Jan. 6, 1731.[1]
Jacob—Anne Betts, 9-3-1770.[8]
Norris, Charles—Keziah Norcross, 12-25-1808.[3]
George—Ann Speechy, 10-19-1800.[3]
Henry—Desire Carter, 11-26-1800.[3]
John—Sarah Cheshire, Apr. 30, 1746.[1]
Thomas—Miriam Branson, 2-25-1788.[7]
North, James—Elinor Quin, 2-5-1778.[1]
Norton, John—Grace Gillum, Aug. 29, 1749.[1]
Joseph—Anne Cozens, Feb. 3, 1727.[1]
William—Mary Clutch, 8-4-1796.[3]
Nove, Thomas—Grace Williams, 7-20-1802.[3]
Nugen, Thomas—Abigall Brittain, 4-29-1772.[1]
Nugent, John—Phebe Andrews, 2-23-1839.[3]
John L.—Margaret Bispham, 1-7-1812.[3]
Nutt, Abraham—Betsey Woodrough (colored), 1-31-1804.[3]
Isaac—Esther Parent, 9-19-1835.[3]
John—Mary Alexander, 5-31-1781.[1]
John—Nancy Munn, 10-12-1805.[3]
John—Allice Rossell, 8-21-1820.[3]
John—Mary Compton, both Monmouth co., 11-17-1827.[3]
Joseph—Yenah Broadhome, Sept. 25, 1750.[1]

Nutt, Joseph—Elizabeth Cliver, 6-24-1804.³
  Joseph—Rebecca Cook, 1-27-1825.³
  Joseph, Jr.—Rebecca Kirby, 6-8-1837.²
  Jonathan—Rachel Myers, 8-16-1774.¹
  Levy—Anne Ivins, Sept. 19, 1748.¹
  Moses—Anne Buffin, 2-3-1772.¹
  Moses—Elizabeth Pope, 10-28-1783.¹
  Moses—Catharine Haley, 4-7-1807.³
  Thomas—Mary Myers, Sept. 27, 1746.¹
  William—Jane Brown, 3-1-1757.¹
  William—Eleanor Bergen, 3-9-1821.³
  William—Sarah Myers, 11-7-1830.³
Oakford, William—Catharine Etris, both Philadelphia, 5-13-1827.³
Oakley, Robert—Mary Reed, both Hunterdon co., 5-22-1823.³
  Thomas—Elizabeth Clayton, 9-1-1773.¹
Obert, George P.—Rebecca Ann Day, 9-13-1828.³
Oblinger, Christian—Mary Horner, 2-25-1832.³
O'Brist, Joseph—Jane Stillwell, 8-19-1824.³
O'Connor, Timothy, Massachusetts—Ann Jones, 7-5-1835.³
Odell, Jonathan, Rev.—Anne Decow, 5-6-1772.⁸
Offley, John N.—Mary Bispham 3-11-1812.³
Ofler, Thomas—Ann Stone, 2-18-1813.³
Ogborn, John—Sarah Shreve (d. Caleb), Mar. 19, 1723/4.⁵
  John—Hannah Warner, 3-23-1769.¹
Ogborne, John—Martha Antram, 1736.⁶
Ogburn, Joseph—Elizabeth Andrews, 11-1-1807.³
  Lewis M., Trenton—Caroline Davis, 4-28-1830.³
  Samuel—Esther Andrews, 11-17-1809.¹⁰
Ogden, Daniel—Sarah Ann Brown, 11-8-1818.¹³
Ogg, John—Abigail Sullivan, 11-19-1761.¹
  Thomas—Elizabeth Earl, 6-30-1818.³
Ogle, Peter—Miriam King, 8-10-1772.¹
Oglee, Henry—Charity Waters, 7-25-1782.¹
O'Harra, Barney—Elizabeth White, 6-2-1806.³
Oldacres, Henry—Elinor Borden, Oct. 11, 1732.¹
Olden, James—Debrough Tallman, 12-25-1802.³
Oldfield, Thomas—Mary Collins, 4-15-1865.²
Oliphant, Benjamin—Rebecca Mullen, 1-2-1812.³
  Eayres—Nancy Mullen, 3-29-1810.³
  Job—Harriet Rogers, 10-20-1835.³
  John—Martha Kirkbride, 12-22-1830.³

Oliphant, Jonathan—Mary Shinn, 6-25-1764.[1]
   Jonathan—Louisa Burr, 11-12-1826.[3]
   Joseph B.—Sarah M. Hulme, 4-25-1854.[4]
   Samuel Duncan, Trenton—Beulah Ann Oliphant (d. Joseph and Sallie, of Medford), Unionville, Pa., 1-23-1877.[4]
   Shinn—Hope Eyre, 11-12-1787.[1]
   Walter Scott (s. Jonathan and Louisa W.)—Augusta Milnor Read (d. James S. and Mary B.), 10-17-1867.[4]
   William—Hannah Prickett, 1-5-1806.[3]
Olive, Thomas—Mary Wills (d. Daniel), certificate to marry, July 8, 1691.[6]
Oliver, Charles—Elizabeth Hooper, 10-25-1810.[3]
   Franklin—Hannah Rockhill, 8-29-1818.[3]
   John—Mary Carman, 4-24-1771.[1]
   Stacy—Achsah Aaronson, 2-28-1804.[3]
O'Neal, James—Catharine Sersson, 8-24-1811.[3]
Ong, Isaac— ——— ———, certificate to marry, 1725.[11]
   Jacob, Jr.—Mary Sprague, 1723.[11]
   Joseph—Tobitha Malsbury, 2-27-1808.[3]
Opdike, John—Sarah Farnsworth, Oct. 7, 1744.[1]
Orr, James—Anne Smith, 6-19-1757.[1]
   John—Sarah Usall, both of Ireland, 2-7-1871.[4]
Osborn, Caleb—Ann Parker, 1783.[11]
   Richard—Christian Belanger (d. Evi, Sr.), 1736.[11]
   Samuel Stratton—Catherine Howell, 11-17-1797.[3]
   Thomas—Rhoda Dunn, 11-24-1788.[7]
Osgood, Thomas—Catherine Steward, June 17, 1732.[1]
Osler, David—Silaney Gaskill, 9-15-1796.[3]
   John, Gloucester co.,—Hannah Land, 1-18-1810.[3]
Overlin, Michael—Elizabeth Parks, 12-19-1795.[3]
Owen, Abraham—Rachel Bunn, 1-24-1784.[1]
   Benjamin—Antey Noline, 9-21-1757.[4]
   David—Esther Douglass, 2-24-1827.[3]
   Humphrey— Ann Mathis, 6-24-1806.[3]
   John—Eleanor Williams, both late of Great Britain, 12-28-1801.[3]
   Joshua—Martha Shinn, 1697.[6]
   Joshua—Mary Butcher, 1730.[6]
   Joshua—Sarah Branson, 1743.[6]
   Rowland—Prudence Powell, 1738.[6]
   William—Rachel Somers, 1-28-1788.[7]

Pack, John—Rhoda Dolton, 11-10-1796.³
Packer, Jonathan (s. John and Christianna Dorothy), Gloucester co.—Elizabeth R. Coleman (d. Samuel and Deborah), Trenton, 11-6-1823.⁵
Padfield, Joseph—Mary Lodge, 10-6-1759.¹
Page, Abner—Elizabeth Folwell, 9-9-1782.¹
    Abner—Nancy Platt, 1-6-1810.³
    Anthony—Lydia Daniels, 12-24-1801.³
    Asa—Amy Evingham, 1-20-1773.¹
    Daniel—Elizabeth Gibberson, 2-19-1802.⁸
    Edward, Pennsylvania—Rebecca VanHagen, May 19, 1726.⁵
    Edward—Elizabeth Groom, May 11, 1741.¹
    Chas. Henry—Mary Anna Hickley, 4-4-1866.⁸
    Edward—Ann Fowler, 3-14-1802.³
    Edward—Elizabeth Hughes, 1-11-1812.³
    Edward, Jr.—Rebeckah Warreck, 9-15-1764.¹
    Francis—Elizabeth Warner, 7-26-1758.¹
    Gilbert—Atlantic French, 3-19-1812.⁴
    Henry—Susanna Stevenson, 11-4-1776.¹
    Henry—Hannah Shinn, 12-5-1806.³
    Henry—Rebecca Woodard, 8-21-1808.³
    Isahel C.—Deborah Ranear, 11-23-1837.²
    James—Ann Hazleton, 10-2-1754.¹
    James—Hannah Everingham, 11-11-1771.⁸
    John—Hannah Irwin, Apr. 6, 1741.¹
    John—Annah Shreve, 3-6-1760.¹
    John—Ruth Ann Sutfield, 12-11-1830.³
    John—Mary Crockford, 11-4-1841.⁴
    Jonathan—Monmouth co.—Rebeckah Budd, 10-10-1799.³
    Joseph—Nancy Skillinger, 12-12-1799.³
    Robert—Mary Tool, 5-5-1761.¹
    Thomas—Alice Scott, 4-20-1767.¹
    William—Mary Williams, Mar. 17, 1742.¹
    William—Phebe Richardson, 4-13-1756.¹
    William—Ann Nixson, 10-10-1812.³
    William—Rebecca E. Coates, 1824.¹⁴
Paget, Ernest Hugh—Laura Anna Phares, 9-13-1893.²
Pain, Guidion—Ann Donnoly, 12-24-1810.³
Paine, Amasa—Deborah Sharp, 9-5-1802.³
Painter, Conrad—Elizabeth Woolston, 10-24-1754.¹
    George—Margaret Ferguson, 10-5-1785.⁸

Painter, George—Jannet Ferguson, 8-13-1789.[1]
  George—Margaret Neale, 10-3-1799.[3]
  John--Hannah Braddock, June 9, 1735.[1]
  John—Susanna Stratton, 1759.[9]
Palmer, Elijah—Sarah Berry, 7-13-1829.[3]
  Elkanah W. Hanna Thompson, both Tuckerton, 10-20-1838.[3]
  John—Rachel Marshall, 1706.[6]
  John—Sarah Tonkin, 10-29-1807.[3]
  John—Ann Henry, 11-15-1826.[3]
  Joseph (s. John and Sarah), Pennsylvania—Elizabeth Watson (d. Levi and Rebecca), Hunterdon co., 4-6-1820.[5]
  Stephen—Hannah English, 2-21-1813.[3]
  Tyrringham—Anne Kemble, 6-15-1769.[8]
Pancoast, Aaron—Cheed, 6-9-1764.[1]
  Adin—Diadema Curtis, 4-22-1762.[1]
  Asher—Elizabeth Irons, 2-3-1839.[3]
  Benjamin—Sarah Hugg, 1741.[6]
  Charles—May Hamell, 3-27-1821.[3]
  David—Sarah Stevenson, 2-23-1815.[3]
  Edward—Hannah King, 8-15-1761.[1]
  George—Mary Hancock, 1-2-1806.[3]
  George Hancock—Eliz. Tomlinson, 8-30-1882.[2]
  James (s Samuel and Sarah)—Sarah Wright (d. Israel and Alice), 12-13-1797.[5]
  John—Anne Snowden, 1682.[6]
  John—Elizabeth Augborn, 1724.[6]
  John—Mary Crosher, 1738.[6]
  Jehn (s. Joseph and Sarah)—Ann Abbott (d. Samuel and Lucy), 1-3-1798.[5]
  John, Jr.—Sarah Griscom, 4-28-1824.[7]
  Joseph—Thomasin Scattergood, 1696.[6]
  Joseph—Unity Shinn, 2-11-1767.[1]
  Joseph Jr.—Mary Ougbourn, 1731.[6]
  Thomas—Sarah Norris, 8-15-1795.[3]
  Thomas M.—Harriet S. Hulme, 10-28-1875.[2]
  William—Hannah Scattergood, 1695.[5]
  William—Meribah Allen, 6-12-1760.[5]
  William—Sarah Lishman, 2-19-1784.[1]
  William—Letitia Sears, 12-28-1820.[3]
  William H.—Elizabeth Read, 12-13-1832.[4]
Pane, Nathaniel—Elizabeth Woolman, 1703.[6]

Pangborn, William—Kethura Hartgrove, 11-28-1822.[3]
Pape Michael—Mary Mackleroy, 3-23-1757.[1]
Parent, Caleb—Elinore Matson, 1-1-1832.[3]
   John—Rhoda Lee, 8-16-1828.[3]
   William—Susannah Jones, 3-20-1802.[3]
Paringer, Peter—Margaret Bleth, 8-31-1763.[1]
Parke, Daniel—Bathsheba Perkins, Feb. 1, 1739.[1]
   Daniel—Hannah Ridgway, July 5, 1746.[1]
Parker, Adam—Margaret Adare, 12-6-1757.[1]
   Adam—Elizabeth Pierson, 2-22-1783.[1]
   Benjamin—Phebe Ogborn, 9-4-1813.[3]
   Boryan—Hannah Conner, 3-24-1795.[3]
   Charles (colored)—Mary W. McClasly, 7-21-1832.[3]
   Ezra—Rebecca Harker, 11-10-1796.[3]
   James—Catherine Rue, Bucks co., Pa., 3-28-1765.[1]
   James—Ann Fenton, 9-19-1813.[3]
   James—Mary Rose, 6-2-1816.[3]
   John—Mary Newberry, Apr. 2, 1734.[1]
   John—Ann Lawrence, 3-24-1789.[1]
   John P.—Elizabeth Ovely, 4-21-1803.[3]
   Jonathan—Ann Denniss, 1-1-1803.[3]
   Jonathan C.—Mary Ann Matlack, 12-7-1834; also recorded as 12-5-1835.[3]
   Jonathan—Hope Ann Stillwell, 1-20-1738.[3]
   Joseph, Shrewsbury—Hannah Adams, 1721.[11]
   Joseph (wid.),—Hannah Osborn (d. Richard), 1739.[11]
   Joseph—Susanna Clifton, 5-31-1759.[1]
   Joseph—Ellionar McIntosh, 9-24-1761.[1]
   Joseph—Mary Meredith, 7-30-1803.[3]
   Joseph—Sarah Cramer, 9-30-1826.[3]
   Joseph—Mary Thomson, 4-6-1824.[3]
   Joseph, Jr.—Edith Andrews (d. Mordecai), 1755.[11]
   Joshua—Agnes Allen, Sept. 5, 1750.[5]
   Marcus—Mary Parker, 5-11-1772.[1]
   Nathaniel, Philadelphia—Mary French, 6-1-1773.[1]
   Peter, Sr.—Elizabeth Seaman (d. Joseph), 1756.[11]
   Samuel—Elizabeth Goldby, May 11, 1741.[1]
   Samuel—Sibilla Atkinson, 4-15-1772.[1]
   Samuel—Amy Burk, 9-30-1806.[3]
   Samuel—Huldy Clevenger, 8-22-1811.[3]
   Samuel—Nancy Titus, 9-6-1832.[4]

Parker, Solomon—Ann Clear, 1819.[14]
   Stephen—Rebecca Linn, 1-17-1824.[3]
   Thomas—Mary King, 3-17-1800.[3]
   Thomas—Ann Ogbourn, 3-16-1822.[3]
   Ward—Hannah Elizabeth Young, 8-23-1821.[3]
   William—Damaris Cole, 1704.[6]
   Wilson—Sarah Wallin, 8-22-1797.[3]
Parkes, George—Elizabeth Johnston, 4-20-1772.[1]
   James, Philadelphia—Mary Stillwell, 4-8-1830.[3]
   Henry—Hannah Dill, 6-6-1832.[2]
Parkson, Andrew—Rosanna Jacobs, 8-11-1839.[3]
Parr, John—Leah Sleeper, 6-5-1788.[1]
   Samuel—Hannah Burroughs, Gloucester co., July 16, 1733.[1]
Parris, Samuel—Dorothy Crispin, 3-3-1828.[3]
Parry, Jonathan (s. Jonathan and Rebecca), Byberry, Pa.—Mary Matlack (d. Reuben and Elizabeth), 3-30-1809.[12]
   Thomas (s. Jacob and Sarah), Bucks co., Pa.—Elizabeth Lippincott (d. Samuel and Priscilla), 12-20-1804,[12]
Parsons, Richard H., M.D.—Eleanor Coppuck Polhemus, 11-18-1885.[2]
   Richard Heller—Elizabeth Ray Cardwell, 6-30-1898.[2]
   William—Susan McAlpin, 10-31-1799.[3]
   William, Bucks co., Pa.—Mary Earle, 5-24-1812.[3]
Passmore, Pennock (s. George and Mary), Pennsylvania—Sarah West (d. John and Elizabeth), Trenton, 6-6-1822.[5]
Paton, James—Ann Wall, 8-24-1804.[3]
Patrick, Owen—Elizabeth Engard, 5-28-1825.[3]
Patterson, David—Elizabeth Donnelly, 8-9-1818.[3]
   Isaac—Phebe Rulon, 3-12-1812.[3]
   Robert—Nancy Taylor, 9-29-1815.[3]
   Thomas—Rebecca Fetters, 11-14-1819.[3]
Paul, Daniel F.—Sarah Penn, 1-20-1830.[3]
   William—Achsah Gee (?), 6-18-1837.[3]
Paxson, Samuel—Beulah Atkinson, 10-5-1786.[13]
   Thomas—Martha Haywood, 5-21-1761.[1]
Paxton, James, Pennsylvania—Mary Horseman (d. Marmaduke), May 28, 1724.[5]
   Henry, Jr.—Mary Shinn, 1739.[6]
Payne, Anthony—Sarah Deacon, 8-31-1768.[1]
   George—Mary Jacobs, 11-3-1799.[3]
   Henry Clay, Milwaukee, Wis.—Lydia VanDyke, 11-13-1867.[4]

Paynton—Robert F., Trenton—Caroline B. Smith, 12-20-1836.³
Peachee, William—Bridget Addiss, Dec. 19, 1733.¹
Peacock, Abner—Isabella McK. Matthis, 3-2-1789.¹
  Adonijah—Sarah Voorhees, 8-15,1782.¹
  Alexander—Mary Sherwin, 8-7-1759.¹
  Alexander—Hannah Sharp, 5-14-1788.⁴
  Alexander—Elizabeth Allcott. 11-25-1809.³
  David—Sarah Hollinshead, 6-16-1801.³
  George—Ann French, 2-25-1788.¹
  John—Mary Brown, 7-14-1784.¹
  John—Sarah Brooks, 7-15-1818.³
  Melchizedeck—Abigail Thorne, 5-21-1767.¹
  Samuel—Hester Rogers, 12-19-1833.³
  Thomas—Mary Chapman, 4-27-1782.¹
  Thomas—Mary Thomson, 2-28-1805.³
  Thomas—Deborah Vansciver, 5-2-1814.³
  William—Catharine Edmonds, 4-14-1811.³
  William—Mary Lord, 9-5-1812.³
Peak, Aaron—Elizabeth Springer, 5-24-1779.¹
  Aaron—Margaret Wooden, 9-9-1832.³
  Freedom—Mary Cony, 8-13-1826.³
  Samuel—Margaret Cox, 1-24-1818.⁵
  Thomas—Elizabeth Nailer 12-21-1768.¹
  Trial—Louisa Hammell, 3-5-1825.³
  William—Elizabeth Butcher, 12-18-1760.¹
Pearce, Edward—Elizabeth Wilkinson, 5-28-1815.³
  Israel—Elizabeth Reeves, 12-16-1818.³
  Moses—Mary Lutts, 11-4-1802.³
  Thomas Atkinson—Levina Shinn, 5-13-1819.³
  Ward—Phebe Ann Brown, 9-12-1833.³
Pearsall, William—Elizabeth Gaunt, 1786.¹¹
  John—Mary Andrews (d. Mordecai, Jr.), 1758.¹¹
Pearson, Aaron—Rachel Ward, 1-27-1807.³
  Anthony—Hannah Adams, 1-1-1830.³
  Isaac—Hannah Gardiner, 1710.⁶
  Isaac—Rebecca Scattergood, Oct. 16, 1746.¹
  Isaac—Elizabeth Smith, 12-7-1761.¹
  James—Elizabeth Arnell, 2-9-1767.¹
  James—Martha Harvey, 1-27-1835.³
  John—Sarah Harnot, Gloucester co., Jan. 3-1736.¹
  John W.—Mrs. Sarah Vannote, 5-15-1827.

BURLINGTON COUNTY MARRIAGES

Pearson, Joseph—Dorothy Stevenson, June 2, 1731.[1]
  Joseph—Hannah Bates, 9-29-1772.[1]
  Joseph—Elizabeth Steel, 10-7-1813.[3]
  Robert—Mary Higbee, 9-12-1764.[1]
  Thomas—Sarah Hoff, Trenton, Jan. 29-1739.[1]
Peart, Richard—Rachel Gibson, 1706.[6]
  Samuel—Mary Brussom, 6-1-1807.[3]
Pechin, George Joseph—Kate Eisenhower Jefferies, 11-15-1886.[2]
Peck, John Benjamin (s. William and Hannah), Elizabeth, N. J.—Leila May Slack (d. Philip F. and Mary F.), Trenton, 6-12-1878.[4]
  Thomas—Susannah Mills, 1-26-1769.[1]
Peddrick, William—Phebe Borton, 1-12-1804.[3]
Pedrick, Isaac—Hannah Osborn (d. Richard, Sr.), 1776.[11]
  Job—Hannah Borton, 1-2-1825.[3]
  Joseph—Maria Gaskill, 12-7-1846.[4]
  Joshua—Elizabeth Fort, 11-21-1819.[2]
  Philip—Hannah Bispham, 1732.[9]
  Thomas— Rebecca Bispham, 1729.[9]
Peet, Abijah—Eliza Clevenger, both Philadelphia, 5-19-1821.[3]
Pemberton, Edward—Sarah Jennings, 1699.[6]
  Phineas—Alice Hodgson, 1699.[6]
Pence, William—Elizabeth Walton, 9-9-1778.[1]
Penn, James—Elizabeth Alloways, Nov. 3, 1749.[1]
  James, Jr.—Margaret Cramer, 2-22-1817.[3]
  John— Martha Kindel, 7-11-1833.[3]
Pennington, Joseph—Phebe Stockham, July 3, 1750.[1]
Pennock, James—Jannetta Keeler, 12-24-1833.[3]
Pennywell David—Mary Ann Laning, 4-10-1813.[3]
Penock, Joseph—Mary Ann Field, 3-13-1822.[2]
Penquite, Gershom—Mary Zilley, 11-6-1780.[1]
Penton, Daniel—Elizabeth Hall, 8-11-1807.[3]
Penuel, Clayton (s. David and Leah)—Anne Buzby (d. Isaac and Hannah), 7-26-1864.[4]
Perence, Edward—Ann Coones, 12-25-1812.[3]
Perkins, Abraham—Mary Simons, Jan. 25, 1730.[1]
  Abraham—Sarah Gardiner, Dec. 4, 1733.[1]
  Abraham—Ann Vansciver, 1-8-1824.[2]
  Benjamin—Susan Vanbrunt, 2-24-1830.[3]
  Benjamin—Ellinor Cox, June 13, 1731.[1]
  Carl—Rebecca Newton, 2-11-1813.[3]

Perkins, David—Tamer Jones, 10-18-1823.³
  Isaac—Jane Vansciver, 3-25-1821.³
  Isaac—Ellener Vanbrunt, 12-19-1822.³
  Isaac—Eliza Vansciver, 7-23-1826.³
  Job—Rebecca Aaronson, 3-13-1833.⁶
  John—Massey Hopkins, 10-30-1804.³
  Joseph—Sarah Adams, 10-6-1814.³
  Thomas—Maria Vansciver, 9-12-1819.³
Perry, John—Maria Thomas, 8-19-1815.³
  Joseph—Hannah Morse, 2-23-1800.³
  Richard—Alice Holms, 9-14-1757.¹
  Samuel—Marthew McConel, 1-17-1771.¹
Peterman, Gasper—Mary Vaughan, 3-5-1761.¹
  Samuel—Amy McDannelly, 10-7-1783.¹
Peters, James—Abigail Fleld, 8-26-1773.¹
  John—Hannah Symonds, May 24, 1736.¹
  John—Mary Seever, 9-11-1788.⁴
Peterson, Daniel—Mary Mathis, 4-30-1826.³
  Jeremiah—Elizabeth Jones, 12-26-1820.³
Petit, James—Keturah Johnson, 9-12-1810.³
  Jonathan, (s. James and Sarah, of Salem co.), Philadelphia—
    Ann Wooley (d. James and Huldah), Hunterdon co., 1-9-1812.⁵
Pettit, ~~Adam~~—Mary Shourds, Nov. 5, 1747.¹
  Benj.—Amelia Uncle, 3-5-1808.³
  Jacob, Rachel Alston, 1-15-1803.³
  John—Rebecca Haines, Sept. 3, 1746.¹
  John—Joanna Simons, 1-2-1768.¹
  John—Catharine Churmley, 9-5-1774.¹
  John—Sarah Mawrane, 1-16-1800.³
  Jonathan—Anna Lamb, 2-22-1779.¹
  Joseph—Hannah Willits, 9-24-1816.³
  Joseph—Sarah Bretton, 7-18-1829.⁵
  Joseph—Ann Mingin, 1-25-1831.³
  Moses—Ann Wainwright, Dec. 14, 1744.
  Samuel—Hannah Sooy, 3-9-1797.³
  William—Charity Stevenson, Feb. 17, 1746.¹
  William—Lydia Shinn, 1-14-1803. (Present, George Wills. But the legality of the marriage is doubtful, as I am informed the said Lydia has a husband living whose name is John Jones, and if she is a widow her nane is Lydia Jones and not Shinn, which was her maiden name. She has since informed me she was married to John Jones by Samuel Read.—Josiah Foster, J.P.

BURLINGTON COUNTY MARRIAGES

Petitt, William—Rosannah McClure, 8-27-1811.³
Petre, John—Barbara Cook, 2-23-1857.⁸
Pettitt, Charles—Elizabeth Brown, 10-31-1816.³
Pevey, Adam—Susanna Shords, Aug. 1, 1741.¹
Pew, John—Jimia Butt (colored), 7-30-1797.³
   Joseph—Hannah Poole, 11-28-1816.³
Phares, Geo. W.—Hannah F. Watts, 11-24-1880.⁴
   James—Hannah Shuff, 3-11-1810.³
   James S.—Catharine Ashmore, 2-4-1835.³
   John C.—Ann Taylor, 11-24-1831.³
   Richard—Alice Thomas, 8-27-1836.³
Pharo, Allen—Phebe B. Willits (d. Thomas, Jr.), 1833.¹¹
   Charles B.—Mary Jones, 11-13-1838.³
   Daniel—Sibilla Sap, 9-8-1822.³
   John—Esther Parker, 3-3-1804.³
   Robert—Anne Collins, 1807.¹¹
   Samuel—Phebe Collins, 1805.¹¹
   Timothy—Hannah Willits (d. James, 3rd.), 1807.¹¹
Phillips, Abraham—Abigail Worden, 10-17-1807.³
   Asher—Rebecca Wechtins, 10-15-1795.³
   Jacob—Sarah Inslee, 9-1-1778.¹
   John—Damaris Parker, 3-5-1762.¹
   Peter—Sarah Sharp, Sept. 11, 1729.¹
   Samuel—Martha Braddock, 9-7-1820.³
   Theodore B.—Harriet Goreman, 1-21-1830.³
Phrampers, David Washington—Martha Ann Adams, 1-1-1837.³
Piard, Xavier—Abigail Pugh, 6-4-1837.³
Pickering, Joseph S.—Rebecca Wright, 3-1-1827.³
Pidgeon, Joseph, Pennsylvania—Anne Bass, June 25, 1727.¹
   Robert, Monmouth co.—Anne Brown, 12-24-1783.¹
   Robert—Esther Sharp, 11-13-1806.³
Pierce, Edward—Catherine Tolbott, Jan. 19, 1730.¹
   Joseph—Elizabeth Laurence, 4-4-1799.³
   Joshua—Ellen Taylor, 7-10-1854.⁸
   Nathaniel—Susanna Sears, 2-11-1812.³
Pierson, Alexander D.—Rebecca Ann Trout, 5-16-1839.³
   David—Deborah Southwick, 10-1-1797.²
   Isaac—Abigail Atkinson, 12-25-1773.¹
   John—Sarah Stout, Monmouth co., 5-15-1766.¹
Pigeon, Robert—Sarah Stillwell, 1-1-1815.³
Pike, Isaac—Jane Thurrell, 3-7-1811.³

Pikes, John—Ann Evans, 12-31-1812.[3]
Pilgrim, Godfrey—Martha Ratford, 2-2-1771.[1]
Pim, John—Lydia Briggs, 1723.[9]
Pine, Joseph—Isabel Alloways, 8-3-1796.[3]
   Joseph—Martha Bacon, 12-25-1815.[7]
   Martin—Kesiah Mires, 11-17-1807.[3]
   Samuel, Gloucester co.—Mary Eves, 1-16-1775.[1]
   Samuel—Hannah Bacon, 3-29-1826.[7]
   William—Judith Lippincott, 5-25-1780.[1]
   William—Hannah Peacock, 4-22-1802.[3]
Pinion, John—Sarah Thompson, 5-31-1790.[7]
Pintard, Samuel, Capt. 25th Regt of Foot—Abigail Stockton, 5-23-1770.[8]
Pinyard, John—Martha Wilkins, 1749.[9]
   William—Mary Young, 1743.[9]
Piper, John—Hannah Pearson, 5-12-1799.[3]
Pipet, Benjamin—Hope Morris, 2-2-1823.[3]
Pippet, Moses—Sarah Ivins, 3-8-1775.[1]
   Moses—Elizabeth Stiles, 4-2-1812.[3]
   Pheanis—Anne Bogart, 11-29-1817.[3]
Pippit, Charles—Hannah Sampson, 10-17-1811.[3]
   John—Lucretia Hooper, 1-26-1784.[1]
   Paul—Abigail Austin, 1-29-1804.[3]
Pippitt, John—Susan Nippins, 3-8-1827.[3]
   Samuel—Rachel Grant, 6-27-1797.[3]
   William—Sibilla Harvey, 2-11-1808.[3]
Pitcher, Reuben—Letitia Hall, 12-27-1832.[3]
Pitman, Abner—Jane Birch, 1-26-1806.[3]
   Caleb—Elizabeth Marloy, 11-1-1798.[5]
   Charles—Rachel Carsner, 1-5-1811.[2]
   Jeremiah—Mary Rodman, 4-20-1809.[3]
   John—Hannah Matson, 3-12-1757.[1]
   John—Theodotia Roberts, 2-8-1762.[1]
   John—Rachel Rainer, 12-31-1835.[3]
   Jonas—Elizabeth Parker, 11-3-1832.[3]
   Jonathan—Susannah Bowen, 3-5-1771.[1]
   Joshua—Sarah Wiles, Aug. 3, 1741.[1]
   Samuel—Eliza Condon, 3-15-1834.[3]
   Samuel—Neome Watson, 3-7-1812.[3]
   Thomas—Margaret Rodman, 3-4-1813.[3]
   Uriah, Middlesex co.—Ann Matson, 3-5-1762.[1]

Pitman, William—Hannah Loker, Nov. 4, 1741.[1]
William—Mary Noble, 12-21-1775.[8]
Pittman, Asa—Elizab. Lanning, 2-23-1801.[3]
John—Mary Saul, Mar. 25, 1731.[1]
John—Charlotte Carter, 3-27-1796.[3]
Plank, Christian—Susan Gibbins, Morrisville, Pa., 11-28-1830.[3]
Platt, Edward—Rachel Reed, 2-5-1839.[3]
Francis—Katherine Brown, 7-2-1797.[3]
George—Lydia Longstreth, 1-2-1810.[3]
Jacob—Rebecca Ann Reaves, 3-12-1843.[4]
John—Phebe Williams, 12-5-1802.[3]
Joseph—Ann McCormack, 3-3-1834.[3]
Samuel—Elizabeth Horner, 3-17-1803.[3]
Samuel—Harriet Rinear, 3-1-1806.[3]
Thomas—Sarah Dennis, Monmouth co., Nov. 1, 1739.[1]
Platts, Levi—Hester Cook, 5-4-1883.[3]
Plum, John—Sarah Kinsey, 4-4-1788.[4]
Plumbly, George—Elizabeth Myres, 4-3-1828.[3]
Plummer, Benjamin—Mary Saylor, 10-24-1825.[3]
Plumstead Clement, Philadelphia—Sarah Righton (d. William and Sarah Biddle), Mar. 14, 1703.[5]
Poinsed, John—Susannah Cross, Sept. 28, 1746.[1]
Poinset, Abner—Ann Hartman, 2-10-1816.[3]
Earl—Beulah Bowker, 1-6-1827.[3]
John—Achsa Ford, 9-25-1829.[3]
Poinsett, Charles—Mary Bailey, 3-19-1837.[3]
John—Nancy Earl, 12-4-1798.[3]
Harris—Mariah Montgomery, 11-22-1828.[3]
Pointset, Benjamin—Parthemia Bowman, 4-6-1816.[3]
Peter—Mary Rockhill 1-10-1818.[2]
William—Allice Branson, 11-11-1820.[3]
Pole, John—Rachel Smith, 1735.[0]
Polemus, Tobias—Parthenia Emley, Dec. 7, 1748.[1]
Polhemus, Clarence Hart—Betsey Chambers Walcott, 6-25-1890.[4]
Garret—Hannah L. Hewlings, 3-2-1831.[3]
Job—Mary Hodgson, 2-16-1832.[3]
Montgomery—Ann Vansant, 1-9-1799.[3]
William Montgomery—Margaret Hollinshead Coppuck, 4-17-1820.[2]
Pollard, John—Amy Crammer, 9-23-1811.[3]
Pond, Anderson—Charlotte Land, 11-5-1818.[3]

Pond, Reuben—Elizabeth Hammell, 3-12-1795.[3]
  Rheuben—Ann Severns, 8-4-1836.[3]
  Robert—Sarah Barton, 1731.[6]
Pool, Abraham—Hannah Jones, 5-12-1796.[3]
  Joseph—Ann Huntly, 8-8-1835.[3]
  Samuel—Charlotte Watkins, 9-13-1798.[3]
Poole, Alexander—Mary Land, 1-3-1811.[3]
  John—Sarah Mead, May 12, 1746.[1]
  John—Eliza Sharp, 12-25-1828.[3]
  Samuel—Eliza Jones, 3-23-1828.[3]
Pope, John—Phebe Fowler, 7-1-1824.[3]
  Nathaniel—Anna Basnett, 1703.[6]
  Samuel—Mary Shinn, 4-14-1830.[3]
  Thomas—Jerusha Goldy, 11-3-1830.[3]
  William—Charlotte Lamb, 6-15-1805.[3]
Porter, Daniel—Elizabeth Blrt, 3-3-1803.[2]
  Joseph—Hannah Knight, 5-19-1771.[8]
  Joseph—Mary Byrne, 10-13-1781.[1]
  Josua—Hope Smith, 6-25-1789.[4]
  Reuben—Elizabeth D. Smith, 11-25-1845.[4]
  Thomas—Mary Wiley, 10-23-1788.[4]
  William—Charlotte Thorn, 7-17-1832.[8]
Potter, James—Deborah Cobb, 9-21-1832.[3]
  Samuel—Martha Horsefield, 11-16-1814.[3]
Potts, Aaron—Mary Harvey, 12-31-1817.[3]
  Aaron—Rebecca Aaronson, 1-27-1824.[3]
  Abraham—Mary Lee, Jan. 1, 1750.[1]
  Joseph—Elizabeth Moore, 12-28-1769.[1]
  Joseph—Elizabeth Allinson, 11-24-1831.[3]
  Nathaniel—Susannah Kallam, Nov. 30, 1741.[1]
  Robert G.—Sarah Stiles, 4-22-1811.[3]
  Samuel—Ann Harvey, 10-20-1814.[3]
  Stacy, Trenton—Esther Pancoast, 4-13-1758.[5]
  Thomas—Sarah Beakes, Oct. 29, 1730.[5]
  Thomas—Rebecca King, 9-13-1777.[1]
  Thomas—Sarah Ashton, 11-20-1777.[1]
  Thomas—Sarah Vansciver, 11-16-1786.[4]
  Thomas, Bucks co., Pa.—Rebecca Wright. No date given.[5]
  William—Louisa Middleton, 11-10-1836.[3]
Pound, Hustin—Elizabeth Atkinson, 6-6-1805.[3]
Powel, Isaac—Elizabeth Perdue, Aug. 10, 1729.[1]

BURLINGTON COUNTY MARRIAGES

Powell, Jeremiah—Mary Ann Wooley, 3-17-1836.³
John—Elizabeth Parker, 1698 ⁶
Allen F.—Lizzie Horner, 2-27-1862.²
Benajah B.—Martha G. Fenimore, 2-9-1832.³
Christopher—Avis Patterson (wid.), 10-11-1801.³
Enos—Hannah Quam, 2-21-1827.³
Henry—Rachel Fowler, 5-21-1814.³
Jacob—Elizabeth Mathis, 4-1-1821.³
James—Mary Kille, Sept. 5, 1740.¹
James—Susannah Lovett, 1-4-1779.¹
Job—Elizabeth King, 2-16-1809.³
John—Virgin Cripps, 1725.⁶
John—Sarah Bateman, 1-1-1770.⁸
John—Susannah Parker, 10-21-1784.¹
John H.—Eliza M. Risden, 10-9-1834.³
Joseph—Anne Bishop, 11-9-1765.¹
Joseph—Mary Butcher, 10-23-1806.³
Joseph—Rebecca Ann Fireing, 2-27-1822.³
Nathaniel—Rebecca Southwick, 9-10-1774.¹
Robert—Mary Roads, Chester, Pa., Nov. 18, 1730.¹
Samuel—Elizabeth Garwood, 9-10-1818.³
Samuel—Abigail Middleton, 2-23-1826.³
Thomas—Sarah Sickells, Aug. 21, 1770.¹
Thomas—Mary Budden, 10-31-1834.³
William—Edith Brown, 1-28-1802.³
William K.—Hannah Alloway, 1-31-1828.³
William S.—Elizabeth Gibbs, 5-17-1834.³
Powelson, Henry—Mary Lippincott, 11-12-1760.¹
Praul, John W., Bristol, Pa., Clara Green, 11-4-1872.⁴
Predmore, John—Mary Hull, Middlesex co., 1-20-1767.¹
Preston, David—Caroline Hopkins, 8-3-1836.³
Richard—Mary Williams, Apr. 5, 1722.⁵
Thomas—Martha Moon, July 25, 1737.¹
Price, Adam—Margaret Stevenson, 3-10-1810.³
David—Rebecca Ballenger, 5-3-1777.¹
Ezekiel—Martha Adams, 2-14-1781 ¹
Francis—Marion Spragg, 6-10-1826.³
Joel—Margaret Brooks, 8-22-1811.³
John—Mary Burne, Gloucester co., Nov. 8, 1737.¹
Joseph—Theodocia Rockhill, 11-16-1779.¹
Joseph—Catharine Johnson, 12-9-1782.¹

Price, Joseph—Caroline Ewin, 2-26-1837.³
  Reese—Mary Reeves, May 16, 1747.¹
  Stephen, Monmouth co.—Anne Lewis, 9-21-1768.¹
  Thomas—Edith Hort, Mar. 4, 1747.¹
  William—Mary Laning, Jan. 1, 1730.¹
  William—Rebecca Church, Mar. 9, 1736.¹
  William—Katharine Holland, 1-9-1788.⁴
  William—Ruth Reylius, Aug. 25. 17—.¹
  William, Jr.—Margaret Butterfield, 9-4-1830.³
Pricket, John—Mary Erwin, 12-14-1768.¹
Prickett, Barzillai—Martha Haines, 5-3-1804.³
  Barzillai—Susannah Brown, 8-2-1826.³
  Budd Frank—Mary Elizabeth Worrell, 9-28-1873.²
  Charles—Hannah Prickett, 1821.¹⁴
  Isaac—Mary Brookfield, Feb. 21, 1739.¹
  Isaac—Hannah Phillips, 12-16-1786.¹
  Isaac—Dolly A. Joyce, 1-21-1813 ³
  Jacob—Mary Parker, July 19-1728.¹
  Jacob—Hannah Bishop, Sept. 20, 1733.¹
  Jacob—Dorothy Springer, May 11, 1745.¹
  Jacob—Sarah Garwood, 1-20-1814.³
  Joab—Mary Buzby, 2-7-1803.³
  Job—Ann Huff, 7-15-1798.³
  John—Jane Garwood, July 12, 1750.¹
  Jonathan—Mrs. Elizabeth Dougherty, 4-28-1831.³
  Joseph—Hepsebe Stratton, 10-16-1800.³
  Joseph—Mary Ann Wisham, 12-6-1826.³
  Josiah—Ann Sharp, 11-22-1804.³
  Levi—Zilpha Austin, 2-27-1775.¹
  Louis L.—Hannah Virginia Patterson, 2-20-1879.⁴
  Samuel L.—Maria Holland, 1-5-1826.³
  Thomas—Mary Reeves, 11-2-1817.³
  William—Harriet Coverley, 6-5-1825.³
  Zachariah—Agnes Stackhouse, 10-6-1783.¹
  Zachariah—Agness Sharp, 8-30-1810.³
Prickingham, Laurence—Jane Lawson, 11-27-1874.⁸
Prickitt, Aaron—Ann Oliphant, 1-24-1788.⁴
  Barzillai—Sarah Sharp, 1759.³
  Barzillai—Rachel B. Lippincott, 4-23-1837.³
  Budd—Elizabeth Prickitt, 1-3-1839.³
  Charles—Atlantic West, 11-19-1834.³

Prickitt, Clayton—Maria Eayre. 11-7-1831.³
   Elwood—Elizabeth H. Middleton, 3-30-1834.³
   Ezra E., Jersey City—Sarah Emeline Patterson, 8-5-1880.⁴
   Ira--Mary Miller, 4-9-1830.³
   Jacob—Elizabeth Phillips, 1758.⁹
   Jacob—Mary Peacock, 5-31-1784.¹
   Jacob, Jr.—Lydia S. Stratton, 10-18-1835.³
   James—Hannah Goldy, 6-18-1814.³
   John—Sibilla Hammit. 1-7-1784.¹
   John—Mary Ann Cramer. 1-21-1836.³
   Levy—Cathern Brown. 5-1-1830.³
   Mahlon—Ann Prickitt, 12-6-1830.³
   Richard—Margaret Crispin, 4-9-1756.¹
   Zachariah—Mary Troth, 1721.⁹
   Zachariah—Margaret Agnew, 12-1-1836.³
Prince, Frederick—Elizabeth Adams, 8-10-1823.³
   Frederick—Ann Leeds, 6-24-1828.³
   Solomon—Belinda Pash, 12-5-1787.⁴
Prior, Georg—Elizabeth Pierce, 3-22-1803.³
Prise. John—Elizabeth Hillier, 12-6-1770.¹
Proud, Abraham—Lucretia Shinn, 10-4-1784.¹
   John—Elizabeth Merriot, 7-23-1774.¹
   Levi—Ann Davis. 10-24-1818.³
   Samuel—Hannah Davis, 5-6-1827.³
   Thomas—Keziah Stratton, 1819.¹⁴
Pryce. Geo. Wm.—Anne Shields. 5-14-1815.⁸
Pryor, Thomas—Mary Large, 1727.⁶
Pullen, James--Eliza Wright, 2-7-1827.³
   Samuel—Mary Mathews, Monmouth co , 10-5-1822.³
Punner, Gabriel—Martha Stebbins, 8-3-1756.¹
Purden, John Bellefonte, Pa.—Anna Putnam, 3-17-1829.³
Purnyea, Abraham VanLieu—Anna Broomhall Curtis, 3-9-1886.²
Putnam, Aaron, Rev.—Mary E. Hodgson, 9-3-1822.³
Quam, George—Mary James, 5-26-1816.³
Quan. Amos—Hester Wilson, 10-26-1826.³
   Charles Rebecca Till (colored), 1814.¹⁴
   Simeon—Hannah Harrison, 1-8-1802.³
   Sipio—Levina Smith. 2-20-1817.³
Quann, Stacy—Grace Vinson (colored), 6-13-1825.³
Queckenbush, Peter—Rachel Starkey, 8-1-1757.¹
Queen, Anthony—Betha Hill, 11-7-1811.³

Queen, Joseph—Sarah Wilson, 1-16-1836.³
Quick, Charles—Sarah Barton, 1-10-1833.³
  Jacob—Catherine Calvin, 6-1-1809.²
  Thomas—Matilda French, 2-16-1826.³
Quicksall, Aaron—Abigail Shreve, 1-18-1801.³
  Aaron—Rebecca Mornington, 9-3-1804.³
  John—Sarah Gardener, 10-9-1800.³
  Jonathan—Anne Taylor, Sept. 17, 1744.¹
  Joshua—Mary Moon, Dec. 13, 1734.¹
  Samuel—Tamar Lippincott, 2-7-1802.³
  Samuel—Ann B. Schenck, Trenton, 4-19-1836.³
  Thomas—Phebe Penton, Oct. 15, 1748.¹
Quigg, Patrick—Mary House, 5-28-1772.¹
Quigley, Daniel—Mrs. Margaret Loyd, 7-28-1799.³
  John—Acsah Bunting, 6-17-1798.³
  John—Hannah Moore, 3-27-1824.³
  John—Elizabeth Creedy, 8-14-1827.³
  Joseph—Susan Pearson, 8-13-1835.³
  Philip—Mary Pearson, Sept. 28, 1733.¹
  Philip—Susan Schuyler, 2-26-1821.³
  Philip—Jane Finch, 12-2-1839.³
  Robert—Mercy Coleman, 6-18-1761.¹
  Thomas—Isabelle Kerlin, 2-11-1832.²
  William W.—Theodosia Pearson, 6-14-1838.³
Quin, George—Silvey Murry, 8-3-1800.³
Radcliffe, Joseph—Catharine Leigh, 2-4-1837.³
Radford, John—Sarah Forsyth, 3-15-1795.³
  Samuel—Elizabeth Baylis, May 11, 1730.¹
  Samuel—Ann Butterfield, 2-24-1768.¹
Rainear, John—Susan Hankins, 8-9-1818.²
  Joseph—Sarah Wood, May 8, 1751.¹
  Parnel H.—Rachel Richardson, 12-28-1828.³
  Samuel—Nancy Stiles, 5-1-1809.³
Rainee, William—Elizabeth Wills, Jan. 7, 1747.¹
Rainer, Anthony—Hannah Pitman, 1-7-1836.³
Rainere, Peter—Eliza Corson, 6-6, 1823.²
Rainier, Caleb—Elizabeth Folwell, 3-14-1807.³
  Edmod—Betsey Butler, 8-4-1781.¹
  Job—Lydia Page, 4-25-1770.¹
  John—Susan English, 12-26-1771.³
  John—Rebecca Gaskill, 9-27-1809.³

Rainier, Thomas—Lydia Hall, 11-27-1804.²
Rakestraw, Thomas—Elizabeth Zanes, 7-4-1757.¹
Lakstraw, Levi—Rebecca Brian, 2-28-1811.³
Ralph, Francis—Mary Stevenson, 9-25-1766.¹
Ramsay, Samuel—Amelia Brown, 1-30-1800.³
Ramsey, Alexander—Anna E. Jenks, 9-10-1845.⁴
   James—Dosha Stogdon, 7-1-1816.³
Rancke, George—Martha Ewing, 4-17-1806.³
Randall, Helme—Mary Hunloke, July 18, 1834.¹
Randolph, Clayton—Eliza Platt, 1-28-1820.³
   John—Margaret Cramer, 3-31-1814.³
   Joseph—Mary Haywood, 10-10-1761.¹
   Robert—Janet Smith, 11-9-1820.³
Raneier, Joseph—Sarah Warwick, 5-24-1780.¹
Raper, Caleb—Mary Coate, 1719.⁶
Ratherwell, John—Mary Ballinger, 1723.⁹
Rawlings, Thomas—Anne Newbold, 1721.⁶
Raybold, Joshua—T. E. Donaldson, 2-26-1856.⁸
Raynolds, Thomas—Mary Bryan, 1-4-1769.¹
Raynor, Jacob—Amanda Whitney, 10-31-1854.⁸
Razier, Charles, Philadelphia—Elizabeth Mitchell, 8-6-1833.³
Read, Elisha—Elizabeth Cox, 7-3-1765.¹
   Elisha—Phebe Austin, 1-15-1803.³
   Jeremiah—Martha Shiras, 12-1-1840.⁴
   Joseph—Martha Rossell, 2-7-1771.⁸
   Joseph—Sarah Butterworth, 2-16-1815.³
   Joseph—Ann Whitelock, 8-12-1820.³
   Joseph S.—Mary Black, 7-3-1839.⁴
   Lewis—Hope Everham, 1-20-1833.³
   Samuel—Amelia Emmons, 11-2-1828.³
   Stacy B.—Anna W. Burrough, 12-3-1840.⁴
   William Logan—Mary Thorp, 5-30-1799.²
Reagers, John—Felitha Peterson, 4-21-1805.²
Reckless, Joseph—Margaret Satterthwaite, Nov. 8, 1716.⁵
   Joseph—Eliza Fowler, Feb. 26, 1740.⁵
Recklys, John—Mary Tallman, 6-12-1781.¹
Reddick, James—Elizabeth Harlem, 2-15-1833.³
Redford, John—Jane Perkins, 3-6-1834.³
Reed, Charles J.—Jane L. Barnhill, 12-25-1838.²
   Doughty—Elizabeth Robertson, 8-18-1839.²
   Edon—Rachel Peterson, 6-20-1807.³

Reed, Francis H.—Pearl Russell Claypoole, 4-20-1898.[2]
  Henry—Mercy Pettit, 11-8-1780.[1]
  Henry—Emily Wood, 10-25-1812.[3]
  Jacob—Sarah Delong, 9-7-1815.[3]
  James—Elizabeth Peacock, 6-16-1778.[1]
  John—Elizabeth Linkin, 2-28-1815.[3]
  John Washington—Mary Fenton, 2-16-1806.[3]
  Obediah—Rachel Jones, 8-7-1822.[3]
  Samuel—Esther Wister, 5-31-1810.[3]
  Samuel—Catharinah Browning, 3-19-1812.[3]
  Thomas—Elizabeth Ready, 6-14-1804.[3]
  William, Jr.—Thirsa Green, 4-7-1799.[3]
Reemer, James—Ann Coward, 7-4-1812.[3]
Reeve, David—Rachel Sharp, 11-16-1823.[3]
  Eber—Patience Folwell, 9-13-1798.[3]
  Henry (s. Henry and Rachel)—Mary Rakestraw (d. Abraham and Mary), 9-21-1804.[12]
  Jacob—Mary Reeve, 1-6-1800.[3]
  John—Rebekkah Satterthwaite, 1741.[6]
  John—Esther Riggents, 3-31-1779.[1]
  John—Sarah Clouts, 1-13-1799.[3]
  John—Annah Shinn, 11-18-1831.[3]
  John, Jr.—Sarah Friedland, 5-30-1814.[7]
  John T.—Mary Elizabeth Fisher, 9-7-1872.[4]
  John Wright, Annie Maria Howell, 6-29-1898.[2]
  Joshua—Hannah Ware, 7-25-1796.[7]
  Joshua—Elizabeth Murdock, 3-28-1813.[3]
  Micajah—Hannah Lee, 3-2-1754.[1]
  Moses—Anne Reeve, 1-17-1776.[1]
  Richard—Sarah Sleeper, 9-6-1804.[3]
  Samuel—Elizabeth Wright, 2-16-1778.[1]
  Samuel—Ann Haines, 1-13-1808.[10]
  Samuel—Elizabeth Proud, 10-26-1815.[3]
  Samuel—Elizabeth Haines, 7-3-1817.[3]
  Thomas—Ann Stratton, 3-24-1831.[3]
  Walter—Anne Powell, Nov. 11, 1682.[1]
  William—Letitia Miller, 4-27-1789.[7]
  William—Eliza Ann Stricker, 11-2-1820.[3]
Reeves, Abraham—Levina Hartman, 6-7-1801.[3]
  Abraham—Hope Stratton, 1-6-1803.[13]
  Abraham—Maria Mahony, 6-13-1813.[3]

Reeves, Abraham—Mary Matlock, 4-5-1821.[13]
Absolom—Abigail Wilson, 10-14-1843.[4]
Allen—Hannah Wright, 1-30-1836.[3]
Benjamin—Abigail Toy, 3-18-1802.[2]
Benjamin—Mary Webb, 8-31-1827.[3]
Biddle (s. Biddle), Gloucester co.—Elizabeth Haines (d. Joseph and Mary), 6-7-1792.[6]
Charles—Hannah Matlock, 12-1-1836.[3]
Clayton—Mary Conllin, 8-13-1834.[3]
David—Grace Rinear, 12-23-1807.[3]
Eli—Mary Carty, 6-10-1798.[3]
George—Eliza Lear, 3-13-1829.[1]
George Benjamin—Laura Eckman, 8-19-1891.
Henry—Abigail Shinn, Feb. 26, 1728.[1]
Henry—Rachel Jess, 3-2-1765.[1]
Henry—Hannah Furnace, 2-23-1772.[8]
Isaiah—Tobitha Maulsberry, 12-6-1795.[3]
Isaiah—Martha Gibson, 1-1-1814.[1]
Joel—Hannah Gaskill, 1-8-1795.[13]
John—Rebecca Huber, 9-29-1770.[1]
John—Hope Jones, 9-23-1798.[3]
Jonathan—Hannah Budd, Mar. 18, 1736.[1]
Joseph—Elizabeth Toy, 8-8-1782.[1]
Joseph—Hannah Quigley, 4-19-1818.[2]
Joseph—Susan Ewing, 10-20-1825.[3]
Mahlon—Agness Vine, 11-10-1816.[3]
Mark—Ann Griffen, 12-26-1805.[3]
Richard—Elizabeth Harker, 11-3-1832.[3]
Samuel—Hannah Hewstice, Jan. 12, 1747.[1]
Samuel—Lydia Tanner, 5-31-1779.[1]
Samuel—Elizabeth Proud, 1815.[14]
Samuel—Achsah Stratton, 5-24-1838.[10]
Samuel—Hope Harbur, 7-24-1784.[1]
Walter—Tabitha Garwood, 2-9-1765.[1]
William—Sarah Bunn, Nov. 21, 1747.[1]
William—Hepsabeth Thompson, 11-1-1801.[3]
William—Elizabeth Newman, 12-14-1826.[3]
William—Mary Parsons, 2-1-1832.[3]
William, Jr.—Eliza Jemson, 11-16-1823.[3]
Refine, Joshua—Zilpah Burnet, 11-20-1813.[2]
Regan—Abigail Whelan, 6-21-1817.[3]

Regar, John— Charlotte Ivens, 12-26-1831.³
Reid, John—Jane Gofogy, 4-4-1764.¹
Reily, Elijah—Susan Price, 6-9-1821.³
  Frank—Margaret Evelyn Watts, 5-18-1887.⁴
  George—Marion Peacock, 11-19-1826.³
  Isaiah—Hannah Anderson, 3-20-1892.³
  John—Mary French, 4-4-1771.¹
Reman, John A.—Rebecca Moore, 9-6-1828.³
Remer, David—Mariah Reubart, 5-24-1818.³
Remine, Benjamin—Sarah Harker, 1-25-1826.³
  John—Ruth Pitman, 10-10-1798.³
  Peter—Lydia Fenimore, 10-18-1830.³
Renear, Elisha—Rebecca Hooper, 7-31-1817.³
  James—Susannah McGuire, 10-17-1778.¹
  Joseph—Anna Malsby, 8-11-1774.¹
Renier, John—Margaret Craft, Dec. 23, 1734.¹
  Joshua—Rosanna Foster, 2-7-1769.⁸
  Peter—Jemima Draper, Feb. 19, 1741.¹
Rennel, Joseph—Catherine Stricker, 7-19-1807.³
Renshaw, John—Martha Shreve, 8-10-1759.¹
Repsher, John—Eleanor Delatush, 10-6-1796.³
Reubart, Thomas—Lydia Stratton, 8-17-1826.³
Reve, Francis—Polly Stratton, 12-24-1806.³
  Joseph—Mary Ashird, 12-7-1809.³
Reves, Henry—Elizabeth Powell, 9-10-1782.¹
Rewbart, Vincent—Elizabeth Stanton, 1-21-1762.¹
Rexineer, Joseph—Amy Vaughn, 7-26-1823.³
Reynear, William—Amy Gaskill, 1-9-1808.³
Reynolds, David—Rhoda Pullen—4-14-1827.³
  Evan—Ann Janney, 6-23-1796.³
  Henry—Prudence Clayton, 1678.⁶
Reynier, Henry, Jr.—Rachel Wills, 3-12-1818.³
Reynolds, Patrick—Austes Rushford, Jan. 29, 1729.¹
  Thomas—Elizabeth Budd, 6-23-1759.¹
  Thomas—Mary Bryan (wid. of Jacob), 1-4-1769.⁸
  William, Monmouth co.—Rebecca Taylor, 4-5-1819.³
Rhine, Daniel—Mary Smith, 10-20-1759.¹
Rhodes, John—Bridget Higgins, Oct. 16, 1738.¹
  John—Mary Caldwell, Oct. 30-1738.¹
Rianeer, John—Ann Pettit, 1-13-1825.³
Rice, Henry—Hannah Ridley, Monmouth co., 4-29-1821.³

BURLINGTON COUNTY MARRIAGES

Richards, Joseph—Anna Rodman, 5-8-1836.²
  William—Margaret Wood, 1-16-1797.³
  William—Constantia Lamand, 2-6-1831.³
Richardson, Benj., Jr.—Nancy Schuyler, 6-18-1815.³
  Caleb (s. Joseph and Dinah), Philadelphia—Sarah Newbold (d. Joshua and Rebecca), Trenton, 1-8-1818.⁵
  Charles—Sarah Ann Johnson, 12-27-1835.³
  David—Elizabeth Kimble, 12-23-1827.³
  Edward—Mary Richardson, 1728.⁹
  James—Mary Beswick, 4-9-1835.³
  Joel—Elizabeth Bavis, 3-7-1805.³
  John—Phebe White, 12-8-1772.¹
  John—Gartery Vansciver, 11-27-1780.¹
  John—Amy Boulton, 8-24-1815.³
  John, Jr.—Rebecca Powell, Aug. 14, 1740.¹
  Jonathan—Ruth Knowles, 3-21-1801.³
  Joseph—Hannah Sphes, 1-18-1785.¹
  Joseph—Abigail Gaskill, 2-15-1788.¹
  Lewis—Rebecca Hancock, 1-13-1833.³
  Rue, Pennsylvania—Abigail Shafer, 4-14-1818.³
  Samuel—Jane Davis, 4-10-1770.¹
  Thomas—Rebecca Gibbs, 1747.⁶
  Thomas—Rebecca Brown, 6-23-1827.³
  William—Sarah Allen, 11-16-1829.³
Rickey, Joseph—Mary Quigley, 8-16-1775.¹
Rider, William—Sarah Jones, 11-23-1823.³
Ridgaway, Solomon—Mary Burr, 1747.⁶
Ridgents, William—Susanna Atkinsor, 1-5-1776.¹
Ridgeway, Barzilla—Edith Haines, 12-28-1775.¹
  Daniel—Emaline Burtis, 2-12-1835.³
  Henry—Mary Wright, 2-25-1771.¹
Ridgley, Thomas—Elizabeth Peacock, 7-23-1828.³
Ridley, Benj.—Nancy Still, 8-31-1823.³
  Charles—Elizabeth Pervin, 10-11-1817.³
Ridgua, Job—Rebekkah Butcher, 1719.⁶
  Job, Jr.—Hannah Bunting, 1739.⁶
  John—Hannah Allen, 1739.⁶
  Joseph—Sarah Butcher, 1727.⁶
  Joshua—Rachel Brown, 1736.⁶
  Richard, Jr.—Mary Crispin, 1714.⁶
  Robert—Hannah Gant, 1736.⁶

Ridgua, Thomas—Ann Ferra, 1699.[6]
Ridgway, Amos—Mary Hubbs, 2-23-1800.[3]
   Amos—Phebe Bartlett, 3-6-1828.[3]
   Aquila—Martha Lippincott, 4-4-1799.[13]
   Delaplaine—Dorothy Reed, 6-25-1803.[3]
   Edward—Mary Delaplaine, 1732.[11]
   Elijah—Ann Rogers, 3-20-1817.[3]
   Jacob—Isabel Schooley, 1750.[6]
   Jacob—Sukey Ellis, 3-29-1780.[1]
   Jacob—Lydia Coates, 1-15-1813.[3]
   James—Nevina Williams, 3-18-1823.[3]
   Job—Mary Tilton, 1744 [6]
   Job—Elizabeth Matthews, 11-25-1766.[1]
   Job—Ruth Belanger (d. James, Jr.), 1767.[11]
   Job, Barnegat—Elizabeth Mathis (d. Jeremiah, Sr.), 1769.[11]
   John—Hannah Brown, May 5, 1727.[1]
   John (wid.)—Phebe Balanger (d. James, Sr.), 1754.[11]
   John—Sarah Whitehouse, 1-2-1806.[3]
   John—Rebecca Olden, 8-23-1806.[3]
   John—Mary McElroy, 2-22-1832.[3]
   Joseph—Prudence Borton, 3-18-1786.[1]
   Joseph—Martha Arney, 1-6-1790.[13]
   Joseph—Unice Garite, 5-11-1800.[3]
   Joseph—Charlotte Sawyer, 1-21-1827.[3]
   Lott—Susannah Peat, Gloucester co., Dec. 3, 1750.[1]
   Lott, Jr.—Deborah Johnson, 4-24-1780.[1]
   Mark—Martha Atkinson, 2-17-1805.[3]
   Noah—Susannah Haddon, 4-8-1779.[1]
   Richard, Philadelphia—Susan R. Shreve, 12-13-1866.[4]
   Robert— ——— ———, certificate to marry, 1735.[11]
   Samuel—Mary Tonkin, 2-15-1797.[3]
   Thomas—Mary Pearsall, 1751.[11]
   Thomas, Jr.—Mary Ong (d. Jacob), 1723.[11]
   Timothy—Sarah Cranmer, 1729.[11]
   William—Betsey Test, 2-25-1788.[4]
   William—Kesiah Burr, 2-26-1815.[3]
   William C.—Mary W. Rosselle, 1-7-1836.[3]
Rigden, William, Pennsylvania—Lydia Thomas, 1-27-1755.[1]
Rigg, Christopher—Rebecca Lavinia Morton, 1-12-1893.[2]
Rigway, John—Phebe Titus, Westbury, L. I., certificate to marry, 1728.[11]

Riley, James—Sarah Phillips, 2-19-1807.[3]
   James—Kesiah Plumby, 6-2-1816.[2]
   Mark (s. Uriah and Rhody)—Ann Taylor (d. Daniel and Miriam Halloway), 4-5-1827.[5]
   Uriah—Rhoda Shourds (d. Daniel), 1795.[11]
Rinear, Isaac—Mary Ann Maulsbury, 7-3-1838.[3]
   Lemuel—Josephine Clark, 8-27-1856.[4]
   Stacy—Elizabeth Ford, 6-24-1820.[3]
Rinier, Ellis—Mary Wilshere, 6-12-1823.[3]
Ripe, Jacob—Jane Kelley, 3-23-1778.[1]
Risdon, John—Mary Peterson, 5-30-1813.[3]
   John, Jr.—Mary Heaton, 5-16-1816.[3]
   Samuel—Jane McGowan, 10-3-1813.[3]
   Thomas—Ellen Hall, 3-4-1835.[3]
   William Mills—Susan Josephine Harker, 6-2-1880.[4]
Risley, Peter, Cape May co.—Ann Carman, Jan. 22, 1736.[1]
Risly, David—Nancy Schull, 12-29-1800.[3]
Rittinger, John—Rachel Fennimore, 10-24-1778.[1]
Roads, Anthony—Mary Dunfee, 4-27-1765.[1]
Robart, John—Mary Jones, 8-18-1765.[1]
Robbins, Antram—Lydia Rogers, 11-3-1802.[3]
   Barzillai W.—Anna Wilson, 10-23-1851.[4]
   Benj.—Catharine Ann Middleton, 2-12-1824.[3]
   Charles—Abigail Davis, 9-20-1801.[3]
   Edward—Mary Bartling, 3-22-1831.[3]
   George—Miriam Sprowls, 9-19-1824.[3]
   John—Sarah Keeler, 4-14-1808.[3]
   Johnson—Elmina Davis, 10-4-1830.[3]
   Johnson—Martha G. Davis, 1-10-1837.[3]
   Joseph—Sarah Johnson, 6-17-1804.[3]
   Nathan—Ann Nutt, 1-1-1839.[3]
   Richard—Ann Race, Mar. 21, 1729.[1]
   Thomas—Elizabeth Page, 11-30-1800.[3]
   William—Mariah Applegate, 1-12-1825.[3]
   Zebidee—Hope Atkinson, 10-23-1766.[1]
Robbinson, John—Rebecca Malsbury, 4-28-1803.[3]
   Robean, Andrew—Isabel Hardin, 3-17-1798.[3]
Roberno, Francis—Ann Thomson, 10-19-1807.[3]
Roberson, Daniel—Elizabeth Wheeler, 8-18-1799.[3]
Robeson, James—Elizabeth Pugh, 5-21-1764.[1]
Roberts, Allen H.—Ida Wilkins, 3-24-1884.[10]

Roberts, Arthur (s. Enoch and Hannah)—Judith Morgan (d. Isaac and Sarah), Waterford, 11-11-1813. [12]
  Asa (s. Samuel and Hannah)—Anna Lippincott (d. Samuel and Priscilla), 10-25-1821. [12]
  Benj.—Charlotte Leeman (colored), 11-15-1821. [3]
  Charles—Prudence Monrow, 1-31-1828. [3]
  Clayton (s. Joshua and Rachel)—Elizabeth S. Pope (d. John and Amy), 2-14-1822. [12]
  David (s. Joseph and Susannah)—Rachel Hunt (d. Joshua and Esther), 2-16-1815. [12]
  Enoch (s. Samuel and Hannah)—Ann Matlack (d. Reuben and Elizabeth), 3-2-1809. [12]
  Enoch (s. Jonathan and Mary), Philadelphia—Rachel French (d. George and Rachel), 10-13-1814. [12]
  Hugh (s. Samuel and Elizabeth)—Lydia Lippincott (d. Samuel and Priscilla), 4-11-1811. [12]
  Hugh (s Samuel and Elizabeth)—Ann Justice (d. Joseph and Esther), 10-13-1825. [12]
  Isaac—Mary Wilkins, 5-19-1887. [10]
  Izzy—Martha M. Rogers, 1-24-1828. [3]
  Jacob—Syllania Evans, 1-12-1824. [10]
  Jacob—Ann Evans, 11-15-1831. [10]
  Jacob—Hannah Roberts, 4-15-1834. [10]
  Jeremiah, Gloucester co.—Elizabeth French, 1-5-1797. [3]
  John—Mary Elkinton, Jr., 1712. [6]
  John—Hannah Newberry, Nov. 24, 1732. [1]
  John—Ann Evans, 11-22-1798 [3]
  John—Ann Huntsman, 3-18-1811. [3]
  John—Mary Hill, 9-30-1824. [3]
  John—Margaret Monrow, 7-14-1832. [3]
  John G.—Sarah Zelley, 10-9-1817. [13]
  Joseph, Philadelphia—Mary Butler, Sept. 21, 1748. [1]
  Joseph—Edith Harrison, 11-13-1770. [1]
  Joseph (s. Jonathan and Mary), Chester co., Pa.—Bathsheba French (d. George and Rachel), 4-24-1806. [12]
  Joseph—Sarah Budden, 11-3-1834. [3]
  Josiah (s. Jos. and Susannah)—Mary French, (d. Robert and Hannah, 3-24-1808. [12]
  Reuben—Rachel Haines, 12-18-1828. [10]
  Samuel H.—Abigail Ann Haines, 10-13-1842. [10]
  William—Hannah Haines, 10-17-1816. [10]

Robins, Benjamin—Ruth Radfield, 3-19-1771.[1]
  Isaiah (s. Benjamin, Jr.)—Sarah Large (d. Samuel), 12-15-1763.[5]
  James—Elizabeth Core, Nov. 2, 1737.[1]
  Moses—Sarah Warner, 8-19-1774.[1]
  Nathan—Joyce Burnett, both Monmouth co., 1-13-1779.[5]
  Nathaniel—Ruth Vanroom, Oct. 7, 1741.[1]
  Nathaniel, Jr.—Mary Swain, 3-26-1779.[1]
  Vanroom—Tabitha Ford, 11-8-1783.[1]
Robinson, Benjamin—Lucy Ann Griffith, 9-4-1833.[3]
  George G —Susan Ransom, 3-3-1836.[3]
  Henry—Mary Ann Morgan, 5-31-1833.[3]
  James—Elizabeth Shirra, 6-11-1806.[3]
  John—Hannah Prickett, 3-31-1829.[3]
  Reter- Edith Williams, 8-27-1797.[3]
  Richard—Maria Fowler, 1-4-1829.[3]
  Thomas—Ann Trenet, 8-15-1757.[1]
Robson, Henry, Philadelphia—Sarah Phillips, 10-17-1782.[1]
  William—Eliza Marsh. 1-23-1830.[3]
Rockhill, Amos—Jerusha Lippincott, Apr. 16, 1751.[1]
  Caleb—Elizabeth Foster, 4-24-1797.[3]
  Clement—Hope Atkinson, 4-13-1797.[3]
  David—Ann Aarison, 8-30-1758.[1]
  Edward—Mary Buffin, 9-10-1763.[1]
  John—Elizabeth Kimelle, 3-23-1822.[3]
  Joseph—Sarah Taylor, May 26, 1728.[1]
  Joseph, Bucks co , Pa.—Sarah Cutler, Apr. 8, 1736.[1].
  Joseph—Ruth Proud. 3-30-1817.[3]
  Joshua—Patience Haines, 12-14-1829.[3]
  Nathan- Frances Pitman, 11-15-1796.[3]
  Robert—Elizabeth Shinn, Nov. 1, 1716.[5]
  Samuel—Hannah Morris, 7-25-1774.[1]
  Samuel—Mary F. Peacock, 1-6-1817.[3]
  Samuel—Ann Wells, 12-21-1817.[3]
  Samuel—Ann Bryan, 2-4-1819.
  Solomon—Susannah Taylor, Aug. 8, 1749.[1]
  Thomas—Lydia Jones, 10-26-1786.[1]
  Thomas C-— Mary Stephens, 12-15-1838.[3]
  William—Deborah Horner. Recorded 9-25-1812.[3]
  William—Theodosia Richardson, 9-29-1816.[3]
Rodman, David—Elizabeth Mead, 11-15-1834,[3]
  Isaac—Margaret Weigand, 3-12-1812.[3]

Rodman, Isaac—Sarah Hoff, 7-29-1821.[3]
   James—Sarah Ann Pittman, 10-11-1835.[3]
   James Smith—Jane Aaronson, 7-3-1887.[3]
   Job—Catherine Williamson, 6-29-1826.[3]
   Samuel—Hannah Antrim, 7-5-1798.[3]
   Samuel—Rachel Cox Stockton, 8-9-1827.[3]
   Thomas—Elizabeth Pearson, 1739.[6]
   Thomas—Elizabeth Fisher, 10-6-1801.[3]
   William—Sarah Ellis, 9-29-1798.[3]
Rodrick, Richard Austin, Martinsburg, Va.—Nellie Shelton Wills 6-15-1892.[4]
Roff, John—Elizabeth McKelery, 12-25-1830.[3]
Roffee, Anthony—Elizabeth Stackhouse, 5-8-1813.[3]
Rogers, Abner—Syllonia Evins, 1-8-1783.[13]
   Asa—Rebecca Field, 3-18-1830.[3]
   Benj.—Sarah Billings, 1-31-1802.[3]
   Benj.—Acsa Kirby, 12-23-1809.[3]
   Charles—Mary Grant, 4-22-1831.[3]
   David—Lydia Evans, 11-13-1833.[10]
   David C.—Sarah Stout, 5-29-1833.[3]
   Elton—Ruth Matlack, 2-1-1810.[3]
   George, Philadelphia—Sarah Stockton, 6-15-1835.[3]
   George W.—Mary M. Smith, 1-26-1837.[3]
   Henry—Rachel Haines, 8-13-1795.[3]
   Henry, Jr.—Louisa Brown, 3-7-1839.[3]
   Isaac—Ann Taylor, 7-6-1765.[1]
   Isaac—Elizabeth Stokes, 10-29-1765.[1]
   Isaac—Elizabeth Lamb, 12-19-1802.[3]
   James—Theophilus Gaskill, 10-10-1786.[1]
   James—Anne Hawkins, 3-14-1799.[3]
   James—Ann Atkinson, 7-30-1829.[3]
   Job—Margery Allen, 1-16-1769.[1]
   Job—Sarah Shinn, 1-25-1823.[3]
   John—Mary Schooley, 1680.[6]
   John—Vesti Austin, 8-6-1754.[1]
   John—Mary Bennett, 4-12-1768.[1]
   John—Anne Norcross, 10-26-1768.[1]
   John (s. Isaac and Ann)—Susanna Forsyth (d. John and Lucretia), 1-14-1796.[5]
   John—Sally Wills, 12-2-1802.[3]
   John—Sarah Norcross, 3-17-1816.[3]

Rogers, John, Monmouth co.—Hannah Hance, 9-11-1822.³
  John—Susan K. Antrim, 12-12-1830.³
  John, Jr.—Mary Daly, 12-27-1796.³
  John Staples (s. Thomas and Ann)—Mary Taylor (d. Samuel), 10-12-1780.⁵
  Joseph—Hester Atkinson, 8-25-1783.¹
  Joseph—Charlotte Cook. No date given.³*
  Joseph K.—Mary Wright, 2-16-1837.³
  Joseph W.—Rebecca Borden, 3-8-1825.³
  Michael (s Michael and Ann)—Ann Shreeve (d. Caleb and Grace), 3-20-1782.⁵
  Michael, Jr.—Mrs. Hannah Harrison, 4-19-1821.³
  Robert, Middlesex co.—Ann Holloway, 12-28-1763.¹
  Samuel—Mary Jones, 11-27-1756.¹
  Samuel—Margaret Thomas, 11-21-1783.¹
  Samuel—Abigail Reeves, 8-27-1796.³
  Samuel—Mary Shinn, 7-26-1825.³
  Samuel, Jr.—Elizabeth Allen, 3-26-1818.³
  Samuel, Sr.—Patience Blackwell, 12-14-1806.³
  Samuel W.—Hannah Antrim, 12-12-1830.³
  Thomas—Ann Staples, Oct. 30, 1736.¹
  Thomas—Elizabeth Craig, 1760.⁹
  Thomas—Jane Chamberlain, 12-29-1825.³
  William—Martha Esturgans, 8-19-1754.¹
  William—Anna Elton, 12-20-1777.¹
  William—Rachel Mathews, 3-1-1797.³
  William—Ann Vinecomb, 5-7-1812.³
  William—Mary Gamble, 6-30-1816.³
Roper, Thomas—Abigail Perkins, 1690.⁶
Rose, Eli—Hannah Jenkins, 4-15-1814.³
  Israel—Rebecca Burtis, 5-27-1816.³
  James—Lucy Ann Fowler, 3-5-1817.³
  Levi—Sarah Burr, 11-13-1800.³
  Samuel—Anne Duckworth, Feb. 26, 1739.¹
  Samuel—Hannah Carman, 6-18-1765.¹
  Samuel—Lydia Moody, 11-21-1788.⁴
  William—Betty W. Clay, 2-16-1812.³
Rosel, Elias—Mary McCabe, 10-5-1816.³

---

*Married by Samuel Wright, J. P.

Rosell, James—Elizabeth Allcott, Apr. 24, 1745.[1]
  Zachariah—Margaret Curtis, Jan. 25, 1748.[1]
  Jachariah—Mary Kemble, 12-24-1783.[1]
  Zebulon—Anne Rosele. Apr. 18, 1746.[1]
Rosnagle, John—Elizabeth Farvour, 4-7-1839.[3]
Ross, David—Mary Covenhoven, 12-1-1799.[3]
  Hugh—Anne Clay, 2-20-1771.[8]
  Jesse—Polly Asay, 1-31-1805.[3]
  John—Anna Sharp, 10-17-1798.[3]
  Joseph W.—Susan Ridgway, 12-3-1837.[3]
  Semor—Martha Diviney, 9-13-1803.[3]
  William, Jr.—Sarah Phillips, 6-16-1799 [3]
Rossel, Michael—Ann Read, 8-18-1799.[3]
  Zachary—Mary Hilliard, 1707.[6]
Rossell, Hezekiah—Elizabeth Bishop, 10-1-1761.[1]
  Job—Huldah Kemble. 5-13-1775.[1]
  Joseph—Nancy Allin, 3-10-1808.[3]
  Joseph Leary—Lottie Mary Lundy, 7-13-1893.[2]
  Samuel—Beulah Starkey, 4-22-1777 [1]
  Walter Howard—Margaret Magee. 5-11-1897.[2]
  William—Rebecca Cox, 12-25-1812.[3]
  William—Harriet Lovett, 11-7-1824.[3]
  Zachariah—Lydia Blakes, 1-25-1815.[3]
Rosswell Samuel—Eliza Diviney, 9-16-1826.[3]
Rouse, John—Abigail Gibbons, 9-1-1814.[3]
Rouze, Joseph—Lydia Asay, 8-26-1882.[2]
Rowan, Joseph—Cathrine Powell, 6-19-1798.[3]
Royal, Wm. Bedford—Eliz Coxe Howell. 10-6-1857.[8]
Roydhouse, Mathew—Elizabeth B. Johnson, 12-26-1840.[4]
Rozell, Benj.—Rachel Applegate, 1-11-1802.[3]
  Joseph—Ann Alcott, Dec. 29, 1737.[1]
  Zachariah—Mary Morgan, Jan. 11, 1739.[1]
Rozester, David—Jane Leonard, 8-25-1807.[3]
Rubart, Daniel—Sarah Leatia (?), 3-3-1832.[3]
  Joseph—Ann Lanning, 1-6-1811.[3]
  Joseph—Rachel Zelley, 11-16-1823.[3]
  William—Nancy Bableton, 3-26-1821.[3]
Rubert, William—Hannah Brown, 4-10-1834.[3]
Rudderow, Benjamin—Ann Allen, 9-15-1813.[3]
  John—Elizabeth Jones, Nov. 2, 1730.[1]
  John—Rachel Bates, Sept. 12, 1747.[1]

Rudderow, Josiah C.—Hannah Kirkbride, 2-14-1833.³
  William—Abigail Spicer, Gloucester co., 5-4-1758.¹
Rudrow, William—Rachel Roweing, 12-27-1797.³
Rue, Vincent, Middlesex co.—Mary Ann Samson, 12-2-1838.³
Rulon, David—Jemima Hankins, 2-12-1781.¹
  John—Mary Borden 12-27-1810.³
  Samuel—Edith Gilbert, 6-26-1830.³
Rundle, William—Hope Wilkins, 1816.¹⁴
Runkle, Ebenezer—Mary Haines, 12-6-1817.³
Runnels, James—Mary Marlin, 9-5-1822.³
Runyon, Chas.—Isabella Pitt Randolph, 1864.⁸
Rush, George—Maria Stockton, 3-10-1825.³
  Samuel—Caroline Stockton, 12-3-1813.³
Russeau, Clet—Eliza Whiley, 1-23-1807.³
Russell, Geo.—Elizabeth Phillips, 12-3-1874.⁸
Rutters, John, Jr.—Phebe Lines, 9-3-1836.³
Ryan, Thomas—Deborah Toner, 9-19-1811.³
Rye, John—Margaret Fairholm, 3-4-1830.³
Ryne, James—Mercy Pearce, 12-19-1799.³
Ryneer, Ezekiel—Deborah Irelan, 3-26-1835.³
Rynegom, John L.—Margaret Ann Dumas, 8-29-1830.³
Ryneir Thomas—Damey Thompson, 1-7-1783.¹
Ryon, Thomas—Sarah Brannin, 10-1-1801.
Sabet, James—Hannah James, Dec. 28, 1736.¹
Sagars, Samuel—Mary Johnson, 3-27-1815.³
Sager, Caleb—Jane H. Clevenger, 1-3-1838.³
Sailer, John A.—Phebe Brown, 11-23-1851.⁴
  Samuel—Sarah C. Bozzel, 1-2-1854.⁴
Sailor, John—Keziah Atkinson, 11-28-1824.³
  Nathaniel—Hannah W. Craft, 9-3-1800.³
Saltor, James, Trenton—Elizabeth Borden, 10-19-1801.³
Sampson, Benjamin—Elizabeth Adams, 7-18-1811.³
  Hasadiah—Rebecca Simson, 3-3-1763.¹
Sanders Jacob Glenn, Albany, N. Y.—Jane Ten Eyck (d. J. C. and Julia), 10-11-1870.⁴
  John—Rebekkah Carlisle, 1732.⁶
Sanderson, Robert—Elizabeth Guy, 4-24-1814.³
Sandoz, Francis—Mary Smitz, 11-6-1802.³
  Francis—Mary Smitz, 12-6-1802.⁸
Sango, Samson—Aihah (?) Leman, 11-18-1798.³
Sands, Christopher—Susannah Tanner, 1-9-1779.¹

Sands, Edmond—Mary Coate, 1720.⁶
　John—Mary Butcher, 1712.⁵
　Richard—Mary Gruff, Jr., 1712.⁶
Sap, Samuel—Elizabeth T. Hamilton, 5-5-1827.³
　Samuel—Mary Sap, 7-24-1801.³
Sapcut, William—Mary Cramer, 9-7-1823.³
Sapcutt, Samuel—Sarah Brown, 3-16-1815.³
Sapp, Charles—Sarah Ann McKee, 2-13-1839.³
　Tanis—Marget Basset, 4-22-1802.³
Sarminto, Ja. C.—Mary Rogers, 7-16-1808.³
Sarish, Stephen—Mary Moore, 2-26-1767.¹
Satterthwait, Aaron (s. Joshua and Ann)—Achsah L. Wright (d. Daniel and Mary Hendrickson), 3-11-1847.⁵
　Joshua (s. Joshua)—Elizabeth Burr (d. Henry), 5-5-1814.¹³
Satterthwaite, Aaron—Abigail Middleton, 1-20-1823.³
　George—Robotha Pattison, June 20, 1727.¹
　Isaac (s. Samuel and Mary)—Hannah Taylor (d. William and Ann), Monmouth co., 2-5-1835.⁵
　Joseph—Eliza Allen, 10-29-1829.³
　Joseph (s. Joseph and Elizabeth)—Elizabeth Fisher (d. Thomas and Elizabeth), 11-14-1816.¹²
　Joshua W. (s. Richard and Elizabeth)—Lydia Middleton, 3-17-1785.⁵
　Nathan—Mary Reckless, 8-24-1820.³
　Richard—Elizabeth Wright, 1752.⁹
　Richard (s. William and Meribah)—Rebecca Wright (d. John and Hannah, 3-5-1812.⁵
　Samuel—Jane Osborn (d. Richard), Nov. 18, 1725.⁵
　Samuel—Susanna Forsyth, May 22, 1745.⁵
　Samuel, Jr.—Mary Cripps (d. John and Mary), 12-14-1757.⁵
　William—Martha Marriot, May 17, 1711.⁵
　William—Mary Osborn, Sept. 7, 1723.⁵
　William—Ann Radford, 11-17-1829.³
Satore, John Baptista—Maria Magdalena Harretta Loffual de Woofin, 3-8-1804.³
Savage, Morris—Hagar VanMater, 10-24-1835.³
Savill, Benjamin—Mary Lindsey, 3-15-1773.¹
Sawyer, David—Sophia Sooy (d. Nicholas), 10-21-1837.³
Saxton, Ezekiel—Achsah Pitman, 1-14-1836.³
Sayles, Samuel—Margaret Jones, 9-14-1773.¹
Sayre, John—Jane Allen, 6-21-1795.³

Scate, Samuel—Nancy Higgins, 9-1-1799.⁸
Scattergood, Benjamin—Hannah Middleton, 2-22-1798.³
　Christopher—Rebekka Powell, 1727.⁶
　David—Sarah Shreaves, 5-4-1768.¹
　Israel—Beulah Ann Woolston, 2-21-1833.³
　John—Mary Heabron, 7-25-1796.³
　Jonathan—Abigail Antram, 2-6-1805.³
　Joseph—Rebecca Watson, Philadelphia, Jan. 11, 1736.¹
　Joseph—Elizabeth Carty, 11-21-1799.³
　Joseph I.—Maria B. Aaronson, 12-3-1835.³
　Joshua—Sarah Miovers (?), 7-21-1805.³
　Samuel (s. Thomas)—Elizabeth Lovitt, 1726.⁶
　Samuel—Rebecca Lovett, Feb. 6, 1730.¹
　Samuel—Mary Stricker, Bristol, Pa., 12-11-1764.¹
　Thomas—Phebe Wetherill, 1694.⁶
　Thomas—Mary Ivins, 2-10-1776.¹
　Thomas, Jr.—Ann Schooley, 1725.⁶
Scoby, William, Gloucester co.—Abigail Johnson, 4-28-1780.¹
　William—Thomazine Johnson, 11-28-1829.³
Schanck, Edmond, Ann Leach, 12-15-1803.³
　Koert—Thitluia Hammett, 1-25-1810.³
Scheetz, Reuben Harvey—Ella Achsah Haines, 11-28-1888.⁴
Schenck, Jacob—Mary VanHarlingen, 2-10-1806.³
　Joseph—Leah Hammett, 10-25-1808.³
Schlagel, Franklin—Sarah Borton, 10-15-1826.³
Schetky, George P., Rev.—Eliza B. Oliphant (d. Jonathan and Leuisa), 1-26-1865.⁴
Scholey, John—Mary Willson, Sept. 14, 1727.¹
　Samuel—Avis Holloway, May 7, 1725.⁵
　Thomas, Jr.—Hannah Fowler (d. John), Monmouth co., May 26, 1720.⁵
Schooley, Asa—Mary Kimble, 1-26-1786.⁸
　Asa W.—Susan S. Ivins, 3-10-1831.³
　John—Rebekkah Bennett, 1697.⁶
　Thomas—Sarah Parker, 1686.⁶
　William—Mary Ann Kelley, 2-1-1823.³
Schuyler, Aaron—Esther Day, 10-9-1784.¹
　Anthony D.- Susan Ridg——, 10-25-1810.⁸
　Arent—Jeneke VanWagener, Essex co., May 19, 1748.¹
　Charles—Rachel Fenimore, 3-21-1822.³
　Daniel—Mary Briggs, 11-30-1833.³

Schuyler, John—Sarah Jacobs, 6-20-1816.³
  Peter—Ann Richardson 5-21-1777.¹
  Peter, Jr.—Deborah Gilbert, 3-14-1811.³
  Philip—Maria Esdell, 11-23-1815.³
  Stacy—Susan James, 3-4-1829.³
Scott, Archibald—Catharine Miller, 11-13-1836.⁴
  Barzilla—Elizabeth Wheeler, 3-25-1765.¹
  Barzilla—Mary Garwood, 5-7-1776.¹
  Barzilla—Mary Carr, 9-8-1791.¹³
  Benj.—Rachel Holland, 11-26-1818.³
  Benjamin—Hannah Kemble, 1683.⁶
  Bethuel—Ann Gibbs, 4-7-1808.³
  Henry—Jane Hancock, Aug. 10, 1728.¹
  Henry—Priscilla Turner, Aug. 7, 1749.¹
  Henry—Thomas (?) Richardson, 10-8-1805.³
  Isaac—Sarah Gibbs, 12-24-1817.³
  Jeremiah—Sarah Simon, 12-7-1800.³
  John—Rebecca Hall, Dec. 13, 1740.¹
  John—Anne Atkinson, 4-29-1754.¹
  John—Mary Berbin, both Bucks co., Pa., 9-25-1811.³
  John—Ann Allen, 1-17-1830.³
  Jonathan—Mary Cassaway, Nov. 4, 1738.¹
  Jonathan—Ann Turner, 11-4-1780.¹
  Samuel—Tamer Scattergood, 5-30-1822.³
Scrogy, Job—Elizabeth Dolton, 3-23-1809.³
  John—Mary Peck, 2-20-1812.³
Scroggy, Budd—Willamina Hulse, 2-9-1822.³
  Isaac—Deborah Fox, 10-30-1817.³
  John—Rachel Butler, Aug. 17, 1748.¹
  Stacy—Mary Cook, 4-2-1812.³
  Thomas—Ann Jones, 3-13-1777.¹
  William—Margaret Early, 2-21-1830.³
Scruby, James—Phebe Johnson, 8-24-1830.³
Scudder, Joseph Rue (s William and Rebecca), Lawrenceville, N. J.—Gertrude McCully (d. Henry B. and Anna L.), 12-2-1891.⁴
Scull, Philip—Priscilla Prickett, 4-1-1777.¹
Seaman, Charles—Elizabeth Cranmer, 6-9-1838.³
  William—Mary Cranmer, 12-30-1830.³
Searles Reuben Rogers—Mary Ella Durand, 1-23-1884.²
Sears, Hammon—Abigail Leek, 1-8-1816.³
  John—Mary Bowers, 1-9-1822.³

Sears, John—Dorcas Adams, 1-19-1827.³
Seeds, Eli—Lydia Conner, 1-31-1828.³
   John—Lydia H. Moore, 4-5-1838.³
   Joseph—Hannah Beliss, 7-11-1795.³
   William—Mary Dunn, Dec. 19, 1739.¹
Seeley, Noah—Rachel Seeley, 7-21-1803.³
Selpath, John—Rebecca Thompson, 8-27-1763.¹
Selva, David, Middlesex co.—Susan Watson, 2-11-1838.³
Serison, Henry—Sarah Eppley, 3-9-1829.³
Sevear, John—Elizabeth Sharp, 12-18-1807.³
Sever, Ashbury—Elizabeth Wills, 9-3-1829.³
   Benjamin—Jane Stratton, 12-29-1783.¹
   Benjamin A.—Elma Allen, 2-2-1837.³
   George—Sarah Tate, 9-27-1818 ³
   George—Anna Birdsall, 3-4-1833.³
   Joseph—Patience Taylor, 3-27-1780.¹
   Peter—Hannah Lewis, 7-16-1757.¹
   Peter—Sarah Jones, 9-24-1801.³
Severnns, William—Kitura Fowler, 11-21-1807.³
Severns, John—Ann Frost, 3-3-1814.³
   John—Elishaby Duglass, 1-28-1816.³
   John—Ann Doughty, 9-15-1836.³
Sevier, John—Sophia Garoiett, 12-25-1809.³
Sewey, William—Rebecca Weeds, Gloucester co., 7-30-1819.³
Sexton, Daniel—Abigail Maxwell, 2-21-1778.¹
   Peter—Catharine Reynolds, 7-24-1813.³
   Samuel—Rebecca Jobes, 6-29-1811.³
   Samuel—Sarah Stiles, 9-5-1811.⁸
Shadiker, Jacob—Mary Cole, 10-25-1798.³
Shaddock, William—Jane Hugh, 1739.⁶
Shafer, Jacob—Mary Toy, 11-20-1796.³
Shamela, William—Mary Anne Johnson, 9-23-1830.³
Shane, John—Anne Eliza Goslin, 5-20-1821.⁸
Sharman, Thomas—Frances Ward, Nov. 1, 1682.¹
Sharmely, Morgan—Margaret Mount, 2-24-1833.³
Sharick, John—Cathrine Conover, 8-31-1800.³
Sharp, Aaron, Jr.—Sarah Garwood, 2-9-1828.³
   Able—Lettice Peacock, 2-22-1821.³
   Abraham—Mary French, Mar. 9, 1735.¹
   Amos—Deborah Haines, May 2, 1751.¹
   Anthony—Rebecca Gaskill, 3-4-1819.¹³

Sharp, Barzilla—Lydia Peacock, 2-15-1785.[1]
  Barzillai—Sarah Evans, 7-2-1824.[3]
  Benjamin—Elizabeth Sharp, Sept. 30, 1728.[1]
  Benjamin—Tamar Austin, 1-11-1773 [1]
  David—Martha Rogers, 9-20-1826.[3]
  Enoch—Susannah Austin, 1-4-1733.[1]
  Enos—Ann Simmons, 12-15-1808.[3]
  Franklin—Elizabeth Braddock, 2-18-1827.[3]
  George—Mary Budd, 6-9-1796.[3]
  George—Amy Reeves, 12-20-1825.[3]
  George—Mary Gibson, 11-12-1838.[3]
  Hugh—Elizabeth Jacquatt, Gloucester co., Apr. 27, 1743.[1]
  Hugh—Anne Stratton, Nov. 1, 1748.[1]
  Hugh—Mary Wilkins, 6-11-1799.[3]
  Isaac—Mary Green, 9-23-1766.[1]
  Isaac—Susannah Peaoock, 8-23-1779.[1]
  Jacob—Mariah James, 7-30-1814.[3]
  Jacob W.—Susanna Folwell, 1-15-1835.[4]
  Job—Phebe Haines, 8-26-1780.[1]
  Job—Elizabeth Green, 12-5-1784.[1]
  Job—Esther Sharp, 1-25-1801.[3]
  John—Elizabeth Paine, certificate to marry June 17, 1688.[6]
  John (s. John)—Anne Haines (d. Thomas and Elizabeth), Nov. 28, 1717.[6]
  John—Rebecca Austin, 4-23-1782.[1]
  John—Mary Peacock, 11-6-1823.[3]
  Jonathan B.—Mary Ann Stewart, 12-12-1833.[3]
  Joseph—Jane Green, 8-8-1774.[1]
  Josiah—Hannah Ingle, 8-16-1770.[1]
  Levi—Rachel Hillard, 10-28-1777.[1]
  Michael—Ruth Cotton, 5-16-1813.[3]
  Noah—Rachel Sharp, 5-27-1817.[3]
  Perry—Ann Green, 3-3-1821.[3]
  Samuel—Elizabeth Haines, 1725.[6]
  Samuel—Elizabeth Peacock, 5-2-1754.[1]
  Samuel—Rosanna Prickitt, 1759.[9]
  Samuel—Rachel Cramer, 8-17-1815.[3]
  Samuel—Elizabeth Sharp, 3-4-1830.[3]
  Stacy—Lydia Wilkins, 3-19-1809.[3]
  Sylvester—Mary Wills, 1741.[9]
  Thomas—Elizabeth Winn, 1701.[6]

Sharp, Thomas—Ruth Stratton, 12-7-1778.[1]
 William—Hannah Austin, May 5, 1735.[1]
 William—Mary Haines, 1752.[9]
 William—Elizabeth Lippincott, 1758.[9]
 William—Elizabeth Green, 5-27-1776.[1]
 William—Hannah Nailor, 10-16-1800.[3]
 William—Lydia Austin, 5-21-1812.[3]
 William—Sarah Morrison, 11-19-1818.[3]
Sharpe, Charles A.—Mariana Shreve, 12-16-1857.[4]
Sharpless, Allen R.—Mary Wills, 5-19-1804.[10]
 Henry J.—Susan Evans, 11-1-1806.[10]
 Jesse—Anna Wills Evans, 3-3-1910.[10]
 Jesse—Katherine Wills, 10-2-1902.[10]
Shatterthwait, William—Ann Burcham, 1685.[5]
Shaver, Jacob—Ann Delan, 9-27-1759.[1]
 John—Margaret Sailor, 1-6-1797.[3]
Shaw, Ezekiel—Mary Adams, 4-10-1825.[3]
 Laurence—Amelia Johnson, 8-1-1833.[3]
 Robert—Ruth Reeves, 1-12-1805.[3]
 Samuel—Lydia Potts, 4-29-1786.[1]
 William—Anna Atkinson, 11-16-1773.[1]
Shearman, Joseph—Ann R. Lewis, 5-21-1835.[3]
Shears, John—Martha O'Brine, 7-5-1797.[3]
Shedaker, Jacob—Rachel Isdall, 4-24-1775.[8]
 Jacob, Jr.—Emma Smith, 9-30-1824.[3]
 Jacob, Sr.—Rachel Boozer, 3-18-1824.[3]
 John—Elizabeth Rodman, 2-8-1824.[3]
Shedeker, David—Anles Vagow, Feb. 22, 1747.[1]
Sheels, James, Grace Mullin, 4-18-1758.[1]
Sheepy, Charles— Elizabeth Davis, Nov. 2, 1695.[1]
Sheermand, Thomas—Alice Brown, 1-24-1803.[3]
Sheffer, Henry—Unice Lukemires, 11-17-1808.[3]
Sheldon, Henry—Hannah Bond, 2-5-1824.[3]
Shemela, Joseph—Mary Ann Reed, 6-8-1833.[3]
Shemely, Samuel—Elizabeth White, 8-5-1824.[3]
 William, Jr—Rachel Fort, 10-2-1828.[3]
Shepherd, Adam—Elizabeth Larzeleer, 7-11-1819.[3]
Sheppard, Charles—Margaret Powell, 6-5-1739.[5]
 Charles—Rachel R. Carpenter, 12-27-1826.[7]
 John—Elizabeth Reeves, 5-16-1776.[1]
 John—Mary Miller, 5-26-1788.[7]

Sheppard, Joshua—Rachel Jones, 8-23-1800.³
  Richard W.—Lydia Foster, 10-11-1797.¹⁰
  Thomas—Hagar Parker (colored), 7-22-1802.³
  Thomas R.—Letitia Miller, 11-30-1812.⁷
Sherman, Bertram Clark—Caroline Sapp, 2-12-1898.²
  Gideon—Elizabeth Cromwell, 6-25-1808.³
Sherro, John Mather—Catharine Burkin, Mar. 21, 1742.¹
Shervell, William—Elizabeth Reeve, 10-14-1756.¹
Sherwin, James—Edith Kemble, Mar. 13, 1748.¹
Shillington, James—Maria Wills, 9-25-1831.³
Shinker, James Keith—Elizabeth Ayres Chambers, 10-13-1886.⁴
Shinn, Aaron—Sarah Cunningham, 3-11-1774.¹
  Aaron—Ann Cunningham, 4-5-1777.¹
  Abel—Allis Parker, 7-2-1803.³
  Abraham—Margaret Wilkins, 12-28-1820.³
  Amos—Anna Carter, 1740.⁶
  Asa—Hannah Gaunt, 11-16-1827.³
  Asa G.—Elizabeth B. Burr, 2-26-1830.⁴
  Budd J.—Artis R. Lacey, 12-21-1831.³
  Buddell—Sarah Bispham, 6-15-1780.¹
  Caleb—Mary Lucas, 12-23-1771.¹
  Caleb—Susan Powell, 5-13-1824.³
  Charles—Rachel Whare, 10-6-1796.³
  Charles C., Trenton—Theodosia C. Lee, 11-22-1830.³
  Clayton—Susan Gaskill, 12-18-1824.³
  Clement—Elizabeth Webb, Aug. 30, 1740.¹
  Curliss—Anna Marriot, 11-15-1777.¹
  David—Hannah Wilkins, 3-16-1898.¹⁰
  Edward—Harriet Hartman, 10-30-1827.³
  Edward—Mary Field, 1-5-1832.³
  Elmer—Sallie Black Asay, 7-24-1878.⁴
  Enoch—Mary Simmons, 5-13-1804.³
  Francis—Elizabeth Atkinson, 1729.⁶
  Francis—Sarah Bell, 5-24-1763.¹
  Francis—Martha Shinn, 12-3-1766.¹
  Francis—Mary Haines, 8-13-1801.³
  Francis—Lettuce Loveman, 12-2-1829.³
  Gamaliel—Beulah Eastwood, 7-21-1797.³
  George—Mary Thompson, 1691.⁶
  George—Elizabeth Lippincott, 1712.⁶
  George—Sarah Owen, 1749.⁶

Shinn, George—Rachel Wright, 9-1-1761.[1]
George—Grace Thomas, 2-13-1805.[3]
George—Barbary Fiffer, 7-20-1816.[3]
George—Hannah Hoaglian, 7-4-1817.[3]
George—Martha Miller, 3-11-1837.[3]
Henry—Anne Fort, 11-13-1770.[1]
Henry—Elizabeth Dillon, 2-9-1828.[3]
Hezekiah—Elizabeth Homan, 3-12-1833.[3]
Irick—Hannah Lynn, 1-15-1837.[3]
Isaac—Martha Jones, 2-14-1805.[3]
Isaiah—Mary Burr, 8-2-1770.[1]
Isaiah—Margaret Rogers, 9-27-1797.[3]
Isaiah—Mary Gaskill, 3-17-1800.[3]
Israel—Hannah Haines, 1-10-1799.[3]
Israel—Sarah Wright, 2-12-1807.[3]
Jacob—Hannah Lippincott, 1745.[9]
James—Abigail Lippincott, 1697.[6]
James—Hannah Shinn, July 18, 1737.[1]
James—Lavinah Haines, 3-7-1768.[1]
Job—Elinor Burns, 11-4-1776.[1]
John—Mary Allen, 6-11-1763.[1]
John—Martha Parker, 10-1-1775.[1]
John—Mary Norton, 1-18-1780.[1]
John—Sarah Jones, 12-6-1780.[13]
John—Ellen Stacy, 1686.[6]
John—Lydia Carter, 1744.[6]
John—Elizabeth Asay, both Monmouth co., 11-26-1809.[3]
John—Mary Frake, 8-13-1817.[3]
John—Eliza Anderson, 12-27-1823.[3]
John W., Columbus, O.—Elizabeth Cox, Philadelphia, 3-19-1835.[3]
Joseph—Mary Lippincott, 1-6-1783.[1]
Joseph L.—Julia Gaskill, 10-23-1828.[3]
Joshua—Ann Gaskill, 11-10-1803.[13]
Kedar— Miriam Willits, 11-11-1798.[3]
Kedar—Mary Chambers, 12-25-1828 [3]
Levi— Hannah Reeve, 1-2-1776.[1]
Levi—Mrs. Hannah McBride, 9-29-1822.[3]
Mahlon—Sarah Church, 10-15-1816.[3]
Moses—HesterDevault, 6-11-1799.[3]
Nathan—Margaret Baxter, 10-6-1797.[3]
Nathaniel—Mrs. Hannah Doren, 3-2-1800.[3]

Shinn, Owen L.—Sarah P. Newlin, 3-10-1839.³
  Peter—Grace Gaskill, 5-5-1779.¹³
  Peter—Rebecca Lippingcott, 1-8-1798.⁴
  Richard—Eliza Bareford, 9-1-1831.³
  Samuel—Provided Gaskill, July 4, 1737.¹
  Samuel—Elizabeth Starkye, 5-6-1766.¹
  Samuel—Christian Wait, 1-4-1769.¹
  Samuel—Mary Colkitt, 12-1-1799.³
  Samuel—Rhody Willsey, 10-11-1804.³
  Thomas (s. John)—Jane Shawthorne, 1688.⁶
  Thomas—Mary Stockdon, 1693.⁶
  Thomas—Martha Earl, 1718.⁶
  Thomas—Jane Austin, 4-15-1782.¹
  Thomas—Abigail Gaskill, 9-24-1797.³
  Thomas (s. Thomas)—Abigail Haines (d. Caleb and Mary), 1-9-1806.⁶
  Thomas—Mary Grant, 6-21-1812.³
  Thomas—Jerusha Goran, 2-20-1825.³
  Thomas—Sarah Anderson, 12-30-1826.³
  Thomas—Mary Newman, 11-16-1828.³
  Thomas—Lydia Frake, 8-7-1831.³
  Vincent—Elizabeth Budd, 9-5-1772.¹
  William—Exercise Corless, June 6, 1739.¹
  William—Sarah Frence, 6-24-1756.¹
  William—Sarah Budd, 1-25-1804.³
  William—Ann Fox, 9-1-1808.³
  William—Elizabeth Reeve, 1-6-1825.³
  William B.—Catharine Goreman, 1-21-1830.³
Shipton, John—Sarah Middleton, May 18, 1732.¹
Shiras, Alexander—Eliza Burr, 6-16-1811.³
  George B.—Joanna Greenman, 4-28-1810.³
  Peter—Rebecca Thomas, 11-11-1770.⁸
Shiring, William—Theodosia Clark, 11-11-1804.³
Shivers, Marmaduke—Abigail Cowperthwaite, both Gloucester co., 2-26-1803.³
  Samuel—Martha Deacon, 1723.⁶
Shoards, Samuel—Maria Brown, 4-26-1810.³
Shoemaker, Allen—Tacy Kirk, 9-5-1809.³
  David—Sarah Bennet, 8-30-1796.³
  Henry—Mabel Ong (d. Jacob Sr.), 1732.¹¹
Sholl—John—Elizabeth Cronin, 6-21-1812.³

Shores, James—Hannah Watson, Aug. 30, 1742.[1]
John—Mary Moore, Feb. 9, 1747.[1]
Shotwell, Hugh—Hannah Coles, 2-20-1821.[3]
Joshua—Sarah Ann Stillwell, 11-13-1834.[3]
Robert—Rebecca Stout, 1-11-1809.[3]
Shourds, Daniel—Christian Belanger (d. James, Jr.), 1761.[11]
John H.—Margaret B. Leek, 10-18-1833.[3]
Joseph—Kesiah Andrews. (d. Mordecai, Jr.)1759.[11]
Joseph—Lydia Ridgway, 10-23-1803.[3]
Samuel—Elizabeth Wever, 6-11-1759.[1]
Samuel (s. Daniel, Sr.)—Hannah Gray, 1788.[11]
Thomas—Amey Buckell, 3-25-1780.[1]
William—Martha Andrews, 2-26-1810.[7]
William—Matilda Reed. 1-20-1829.[3]
Shreeve. Amos—Ann Woolston, Aug. 2, 1737.[1]
Caleb—Mary Hunt. June 4, 1713.[5]
Charles—Rebecca P. Coxe, 10-2-1805.[3]
James—Elizabeth Smith. 12-8-1808.[13]
John—Lucretia Reynolds, 9-17-1818.[3]
Joseph—Hope Harding, June 7, 1711.[5]
Jonathan—Hannah Hunt, Sept. 1, 1720.[5]
Ralph—Sarah Innkeep, 1-23-1826.[4]
Samuel—Mary Stockton, 1-21-1826.[3]
Thomas—Eliza Allison, June 7, 1711.[5]
Shreve, Alexander R. —Ellen C. Shiras, 10-5-1842.[4]
Alfred Ross—Josephine Vasey Haines, 12-30-1864.[8]
Amos—Hannah Peters, Aug. 2, 1750.[1]
Benjamin French—Mary Marion Haywood, 2-17-1857.[4]
Caleb—Ann Jess, 1743.[6]
Caleb—Abigail Antram, 1748.[6]
Caleb D. (s. Caleb and Mary)—Mary L. Slack (d. John and Cornelia), 6-19-1873 [4]
David—Harriet Johnson, 3-5-1834.[3]
Enoch—Eliz. Hough, 1-23-1799.[3]
Isaac—Lydia Talman, 3-29-1781.[1]
Isaac—Abigail Thorn, 4-17-1784.[1]
Isaac—Louisa Green, 9-30-1823.[3]
Job—Rebecca Brown, 8-11-1764.[1]
Job—Elizabeth Gauntt, 11-8-1780.[13]
Joel—Lucy Vanhorn, 8-26-1810.[3]
John—Abigail Ridgway, 9-9-1786.[1]

Shreve, Joseph—Elizabeth Hatch, Aug. 28, 1750.[1]
  Joshua—Susan Ridgway, 11-16-1814.[3]
  Peter—Charlotte Robins, 9-12-1811.[3]
  Ralph—Sarah Inskeep, 1-23-1826.[3]
  Richard—Precilla Wilkinson, 3-19-1808.[3]
  Richard—Rachel Downs, 2-4-1813.[3]
  S. Biddle—Ella Hannah Hulme, 12-21-1865.[2]
  Samuel—Misa Trout, 1-26-1771.[1]
  Samuel—Ann Haines, 10-14-1819.[10]
  William—Anna Ivins, 5-8-1756.[1]
  William—Ann Reckless, 2-17-1779.[1]
  William—Ann Gaskill, 2-7-1808.[3]
  Thomas—Elizabeth Sager, 1-21-1816.[3]
Shrevin, George—Mary Hancock, 2-10-1778.[1]
Shrieve, Joel—Lucy Vanhorn, 8-26-1810.[3]
  William—Sarah Briant, 5-7-1807.[3]
Shults, William—Mary Lewis, 1-8-1830.[3]
Shup, Jacob—Mary Franklin, 11-4-1775.[1]
Shuster, Samuel—Caroline Horner, 3-4-1819.[3]
Shute, John, Waterford—Mary Eastwood, 5-23-1763.[1]
  William—Sarah Jones, 5-21-1775.[5]
Shuts, Jacob—Anne Taylor, 10-21-1765.[1]
Sibbet, Benjamin—Mary Anne Shaw, 5-6-1827.[3]
  Daniel—Elizabeth Swift, 5-29-1817.[3]
Sickles, John W.—Martha Vanzant, 6-30-1812.[3]
Siddol, James—Sarah Bolton, Aug. 31, 1727[1]
Sidman, Jacob—Elizabeth Miller, Trenton, 6-13-1818.[3]
Sidnel, John—Elizabeth Neal, 8-14-1775.[1]
Sill, Michael—Mary Rose, Sept. 11, 1730.[1]
  Thomas—Elizabeth Coward, Monmouth co., 5-27-1754.[1]
Silver, Aaron—Ann Hall, 1749.[9]
  Archibald—Mary Cowgill (d. Ralph), Apr. 14, 1720.[5]
  Archibel—Elizabeth W. Livezey, 10-14-1819.[10]
  Seth, Mannington—Mary Ridgway, 1792.[11]
  William—Lucy Carman, 3-18-1783.[1]
Simmonds, Asa M.—Rachel King, 5-19-1819.[3]
Simmons, David—Mary Pool, 10-5-1826.[3]
  Henry—Mary Glover, 8-9-1834[4]
  John—Hannah Mayo, 1709.[6]
  John—Jemima Perkins, 1-26-1797.[3]
  Thomas—Bathsheba Bozorth, Jan. 6, 1746.[1]

Simmons, Thomas— Abigail Mayove, 12-30-1800.[3]
Simons Eli—Esther White, 6-27-1801.[3]
  Isaac—Mary Ott, 12-15-1825.[3]
  John—Susan Hagaman, 7-23-1837.[3]
  John, Jr.—Sarah Prickett, Dec. 17, 1745.[1]
  Joseph—Roadah Eyley, 11-8-1820.[3]
  Luther M.—Mary Pancoast, 11-2-1858.[4]
  William—Mary Goodwin, 3-22-1828.[8]
Simonson, Simon, New York City—Mary Ferguson, 10-26-1786.[4]
Simpson, Daeid—Elizabeth Carr, 10-3-1813.[3]
  John—Mary Dennison, 9-19-1802.[3]
  Thomas—Rachel Platt, 4-21-1814 [3]
  William—Elizabeth Pearce, 11-14-1825.[3]
Sims, Andrew—Margaret Hutchinson, Jan. 17, 1700/1.[1]
  James—Anna S. Shourds, both Trenton, 11-14-1833.[3]
  John—Mary Neale, 7-18-1797.[8]
Simson, James—Susannah Hammock, 6-17-1774.[1]
Sinclair, Charles—Sarah C. Quicksall, 3-17-1837.[3]
Singleton, John—Elizabeth Shedaker, 10-21-1772.[8]
  Richard—Elinor Gallagher, Sept 20, 1739.[1]
Sitgraves, Wesley—Mary Russell. Recorded 9-20-1828.[3]
  Wesley—Hannah Norcross, 1-20-1839.[3]
  William—Susannah Wooster, 5-28-1795.[3]
Skairm, Samuel—Harriet Johnston, 10-15-1825.[3]
  Thomas—Sarah Hempfield, 10-15-1825.[3]
Skiler, William—Mary Eldridge, 3-23-1816.[3]
Skillington, James W.—Maria Wills, 9-25-1831.[4]
Skelman, Benj.—Mary Nutt, 12-15-1805.[3]
Skendy, Thomas—Lydia Mount, 9-11-1818.[3]
Skiram, Samuel—Mary Harris, 3-18-1826.[3]
Skirm, Abraham (s. Richard and Elizabeth), Trenton—Elizabeth Fowler (d. John and Elizabeth Reckless), May 24, 1750.[5]
  Joseph—Elizabeth Anderson, 7-17-1802.[3]
  Joseph—Susannah Harker, 1-2-1803.[3]
  Richard—Achsah Purdy, 2-28-1820.[3]
Skull, Gideon—Judith Balanger (d. James, Sr.), 1750.[11]
Slack, George Tucker (s. John R. and Cora E.)—Sue Deacon Langstaff (d. James and Harriet), 4-12-1867.[4]
  John—Cornelia E. Tucker, 2-20-1834.[4]
  Mordecai H.—Elizabeth Taylor, 2-2-1832.[3]
  Wesley H.—Annie Longstaff, 12-28-1854.[4]

Slaght, James—Melvina Willits (d. James), 1-13-1838.³
Slawson, William—Louisa Leek, 11-4-1826.³
Sleeper, Benjamin—Sarah Haines, 1814.¹⁴
   Benjamin—Deborah Haines, 5-9-1814.³
   John—Hannah Haines (d. Nehemiah and Ann), Nov. 26, 1754.⁶
   John—Lydia Stratton, 2-27-1812 ¹⁰
   John, Jr.—Sarah Leeks, 3-15-1783.¹
   Jonathan—Sybilla Lippincott, 12-8-1763.¹
   Jonathan (s. Jonathan and Sybilla), Philadelphia — Martha Hance (d. Isaac and Mary), Salem co., 11-19-1807.¹²
   Joseph—Hannah Haines, 1754.⁹
   Joseph—Ann Pitman, 2-26-1815.³
   Mahlon—Jemima Love, 3-11-1813.³
   Vincent—Sarah Logan, Jan 1806.³
Slerman, John—Mary Marter, 1-16-1806.³
Slim—Peter—Christian Houseman, 4-12-1759.¹
   Solomon—Mary Antram, 1739.⁶
   William—Rachel Burling, 2-2-1829.³
Sloan, James—Elizabeth Haines, 11-8-1796.¹³
   Jeremiah H.—Rebecca B. Bispham, 5-6-1824.¹³
   John N.—Helen Eayre, 2-28-1850.⁴
Sluby, Jacob—Jane Williams, 3-5-1830.³
Small, Abraham—Rebecca Pine, 10-30-1812.³
   Israel—Ann Hinchman, 10-13-1763.¹
   Jerard—Levinia Sopers, 5-28-1807.³
   John—Ann Borton, 2-26-1801.³
   Jonah—Rhoda Sexton, 3-21-1778.¹
   Robert—Elizabeth Morris, 12-21-1778.¹
   Samuel—Ann McCone, 11-20-1817.³
   William—Hannah Wheeler, 12-30-1797.³
Smalley, Samuel R.—Elizabeth Budd, 11-26-1822.³
Smallwood, Joseph—Sarah Dodd, 11-16-1805.³
   Thomas—Elizabeth Frankford, 4-7-1831.³
Smart, Isaac— ——— Thompson, 11-27-1797.⁷
   James—Honour Shallick, Apr. 20, 1728.¹
Smick, John—Martha Rose, 6-15-1828.³
   Peter—Grace Trout, 3-25-1804.³
Smiley, Joseph—Ruth Reeve, 10-16-1800.³
Smith, Abraham—Sarah Matlack, 7-28-1807.³
   Absolom—Mary Murphy, 6-1-1825.³
   Anthony—Lydia Willets, Monmouth co., May 16, 1746.¹

Smith, Charles H.—Fannie L. Hauks, 1-14-1877.[4]
Clement—Hannah Tyler, 1-6-1819.[7]
Daniel—Mary Murfin, July 2, 1695.[5]
Daniel—Hannah Thackerell, 12-3-1757.[1]
Daniel—Esther Brooks, 12-22-1809.[3]
Daniel D.—Sarah Wright, 9-14-1803.[8]
David—Hannah Osborn (d. Richard, Jr.), 1778.[11]
Edward—Mary Deacon, 1720.[6]
Edward—Nancy Martin, 1-4-1833.[4]
Elwood E.—Merriam Burr, 6-29-1820.[3]
Ennis—Elizabeth Shee, 1-4-1803.[3]
Enoch—Mary Norcross, 11-1-1798.[3]
Fradcis—Rebekka Woolston, 1714.[6]
Francis—Rachel Zelley, 1728.[6]
George—Hannah Smith, Nov. 15, 1731.[1]
George—Hannah Stockton, 8-9-1768.[8]
Gilbert—Margaret Stillwell, 5-5-1762.[1]
Henry—Sally Kiser, 1-11-1817.[3]
Henry R.—Mary B. Ewen, 2-7-1833.[3]
Hugh—Elizabeth Ashmore, 6-9-1778.[1]
Isaac T.—Mary Ann Gaskill, 3-8-1838.[3]
James—Sarah Lovett, 1742.[6]
James—Mary Atkinson, 1-17-1756.[1]
James—Hilty Heewlinge, 1-13-1772.[1]
James—Deborah Garwood, 2-18-1803.[3]
James—Atty Gardner, 10-5-1813.[3]
James—Mila Lippincott, 12-10-1819.[3]
James—Hannah Quigly, 2-3-1825.[3]
Joel—Elizabeth Brown, 7-31-1814.[8]
John—Elizabeth Ball, Aug. 30, 1685.[1]
John—Mary Cyphars, 10-22-1774.[1]
John—Elizabeth Hodgkinson, 9-23-1730.[1]
John—Rachel Evans, 2-19-1787.[4]
John—Mary Jash, 1-2-1800.[3]
John—Mary Crawford, 12-11-1806.[3]
John—Ann Thompson, 10-18-1809.[3]
John—Susan Rainier, 2-5-1818.[3]
John—Abigail Venable, 11-20-1856.[4]
Jonathan—Hannah Shourds (d. Daniel, Sr.), 1786.[11]
Jonathan—Mary McElvey, 7-13-1831.[3]
Jonathan R—Mary Ann Valentine, 3-20-1833.[3]

Smith, Joseph—Hanah Cornish, 8-1-1764.[1]
  Joseph—Mary Wills, 12-1-1802.[3]
  Joseph—Sarah Lippincott, 11-25-1812.[3]
  Joseph—Elizabeth Murphey, 8-15-1813.[3]
  Joseph—Fallial Wilson, 1-23-1825.[3]
  Joshua, Mary Buffin, 1705.[6]
  Micajah—Mrs. Ann Mathis, 9-20-1819.[3]
  Moses B. (s. Thomas and Latetia), Pennsylvania—Rachel Burrough (d. William and Achsah), 10-15-1818.[12]
  Nathan Allen—Joyce Mannington, 5-3-1776.[1]
  Ralph—Ann Bishop, Nov. 3, 1740.[1]
  Richard—Hannah Douglass, 5-8-1797.[3]
  Richard—Elizabeth Jones, 12-10-1820.[3]
  Richard—Lydia Calvin, 6-17-1821.[3]
  Richard—Naomi Dennis, 11-31-1814.[7]
  Richard, Jr.—Abigail Raper, 1719.[6]
  Robert—Elizabeth Balanger (d. Evi, Sr.), 1720.[11]
  Robert—Elizabeth Wyatt, 1723.[6]
  Robert—Elizabeth Bacon, 1725.[6]
  Robert—Elizabeth Clothier, 4-14-1764.[1]
  Robert—Rebecca Bradley, Philadelphia, 7-1-1830.[3]
  Rowland Piper—Reba Emily Gardiner, 6-26-1926.[10]
  Samuel—Mary Appleton, Nov. 25, 1685.[1]
  Samuel—Dorothy Giles, 1706.[6]
  Samuel—Lewsilla Trusty, 4-28-1816.[3]
  Samuel—Judith Willits (d. Jeremiah, Sr.), 1816.[11]
  Samuel—Margaret Parker, 2-19-1838.[3]
  Samuel, Jr.—Susannah Hewlings, 1-14-1801.[3]
  Seth—Mary Pancoast, 1682.[6]
  Seth (s. Thomas)—Martha M. Lawrence (d. Richard), 12-10-1814.[13]
  Solomon—Mary Raper, 1715.[6]
  Solomon—Sarah Smith, 1723.[6]
  Stephen (s. Stephen and Phebe), Bucks co., Pa.—Catherine Olden (d. Samuel and Mary) Middlesex co., 10-7-1801.[5]
  Tallman—Ann Anderson, 4-27-1756.[1]
  Thomas—Mary White, Aug. 7, 1738.[1]
  Thomas—Rebecca Shreeve, Nov. 22, 1738.[1]
  Thomas—Rebekkah Wood, 1740.[6]
  Thomas—Elizabeth Sharp, Nov. 25, 1744.[1]
  Thomas—Elizabeth Pettit, 3-23-1773.[1]

Smith, Thomas—Meribeth Rockhill, 11-6-1775.¹
  Thomas—Frances Haldan, 11-4-1778.¹
  Thomas—Betsey Cramer, 6-3-1802.³
  Thomas—Elizabeth Downs, 4-14-1808.³
  Thomas—Mary Parker, 4-13-1818.³
  Thomas—Mary Stokes, 4-13-1818.³
  Thomas S.—Elizabeth H. Roberts, 1-8-1886.³
  Tolman—Ann Marter, 5-25-1811.³
  Waters, M.D.—Hannah Cora Nicholson, 7-7-1834.³
  William—Mary Compton, Feb. 22, 1728.¹
  William—Mary Wild, 1-22-1761.¹
  William—Michael Aldridge, 10-28-1761.¹
  William—Rebecca Sherrin, 1-22-1776.¹
  William—Hannah Lawrence, 3-19-1784.¹
  William—Mary Botenhouse, 8-26-1780.¹
  William—Mary Ridgway, 9-6-1803.³
  William—Elizabeth Nordike, 11-25-1820.³
  William—Martha Grant, 11-14-1825.³
  William—Sarah Lenning, 9-30-1827.³
  William—Hannah Jones, 4-28-1831.³
  William—Achsah White, 2-19-1834.³
  William Lovett—Elizabeth Lacy, 2-25-1800.³
Smither, William—Mary Catharine Jeakey, Aug. 5, 1734.¹
Snape, John—Anne Clark, May 12, 1685.¹
Snowden, Elisha—Hannah Taylor, 10-24-1822.³
  John—Anne Barret, Apr. 30, 1692.⁵
  William—Hannah White, July 15, 1728.¹
  William—Rachel Reed, 1-3-1771.¹
Snuffen, George, Jr.—Keziah Marpole, 12-12-1796.³
Snyder, Amos—Merion ———, 1-7-1817.³
  Christopher—Ann Eliza Penquite, 9-9-1838.³
  James—Sybilla Copperthwaite, 1820.¹⁴
  Joseph—Rebecca Johnson, 7-29-1823.³
  Levi—Alice Riley, 8-9-1815.³
  Samuel—Elizabeth Brown, 11-9-1812.³
  William—Susan Mariner, 11-25-1818.⁸
Somers, Jacob—Ann Osborn (d. Richard, Jr.), 1778.¹¹
  James—Rebecca Steelman, 7-20-1759.¹
  John—Mary Austin, 4-1-1761.¹
  Samuel—Mary Leeds, 1726.¹¹
Somerville, James—Anne Bath, July 19, 1740.¹

Sooy, Archabold—Bethiah Cramer, 12-26-1816.³
   Eben—Caty Loveland, 5-28-1811.³
   Daniel—Jemima Loveland, 7-15-1824.³
   Josephus—Sarah Thomas, 1-30-1820.³
   Luke—Rebekah VanGuilder, 12-8-1786.¹
   Noah—Rebecca Johnson, 11-15-1835.¹
   Samuel—Catharine Leek, 5-3-1827.³
Souder, Joseph—Ann Reed, 1-15-1829.³
Southard, Abel—Louisa Hopkins, 3-29-1817.³
   Able, Jr.—Mary Hopkins, 5-29-1824.³
   Benjamin—Abigail Coleman, 1-10-1838.³
   John—Hannah Faulkinburg, 3-25-1767.¹
   William—Mary Taylor, 12-10-1795 ³
Southwick, Charles—Mary Wolcott, 1-9-1833.³
   James—Rachel Dawson, 1737.⁶
   James—Hannah Powell, 5-4-1778.¹
   Jonathan—Elizabeth Green, 8-20-1772.¹
   Josiah—Elizabeth Parker, Apr. 23, 1728.¹
   Maham—Hannah Parker, June 3, 1737.¹
   Solomon—Ann Shreve, 1749.⁶
   Solomon—Rebecca Rossel, 4-14-1759.¹
   Solomon—Mary Hill, 7-23-1809.³
   William—Eliza Vandegrift, both Trenton, 11-10-1816.³
Soy, Moses—Mary Huntsman, 7-7-1809.³
Spain, Edward—Sarah Church Hall, 12-27-1821.⁸
Spachling, Philip—Prudence Wright, 10-22-1763.¹
Spencer, James—Sarah Borton, Aug. 1, 1737.¹
   John—Elizabeth Tauntum, 5-26-1825.³
   Richard—Mary Birch, 3-17-1805.³
Spenser, Wm.—Amey Mathews, both Monmouth co, 6-1-1822.³
Spicer, Jacob, Jr.—Elizabeth Donaldson, 9-23-1805.³
Spining, Ichabod—Mary Person, 3-2-1779.¹
Sprag, Aaron—Abigail Havens, 12-21-1826.³
Spragg, James—Elizabeth Ann McIntosh, 10-1-1836.³
   Jesse—Miriam Hackney, 6-12-1831.³
   Jonathan—Mary Rulong, 1-29-1822.³
   Timothy—Ann F. Wray, 12-4-1836.³
Spraggis, Joseph—Elizabeth Wiles, Dec. 11, 1736.¹
Sprague, James—Elizabeth Johnson, 3-30-1798.³
   John—Mary Key, 12-22-1786.¹
Spraul, Andrew—Rebecca Robins, 11-6-1831.

Springer, Benjamine--Jerusha Tyler, Mar. 9, 1747.[1]
   Dennis—Ann Prickett, Nov. 29, 1736.[1]
   John—Elizabeth Bozworth, Sept. 24, 1733.[1]
   William—Sarah Roberts, 9-17-1825.[3]
Sprouls, William—Elizabeth King, 11-9-1765.[1]
Sreve, Caleb, Jr.—Mary Hunt, 1713.[5]
   Caleb, Jr.—Mary Atkinson, 1718.[6]
   Jonathan—Hannah Hunt, 1720.[6]
   Joseph—Hope Harding, 1711.[6]
   Thomas—Elizabeth Allison, 1711.[6]
Sruggy, Budd—Lavina Letts, 11-3-1813.[3]
Stackhouse, Amos—Mary Powell, 1-13-1779.[1]
   Charles—Hannah Rosell, 12-22-1833.[3]
   Ebenezer—Martha Gosling, 2-13-1802.[3]
   John—Elizabeth Pearson, 1702.[6]
   John—Mary Ernest, 6-2-1783.[1]
   Joseph—Elizabeth Branning, 2-12-1818.[3]
   Samuel—Hester Penquite, 1-4-1779.[1]
   Samuel—Hannah Keller, 1-17-1813.[3]
   Samuel—Elizabeth Crow, 12-5-1830.[3]
   Samuel—Harriet Both, 9-18-1834.[3]
   Samuel—Elizabeth Prickett, 6-4-1894.[2]
   William—Elizabeth Benezet, 4-5-1820.[8]
   William—Hannah Ellison, 10-11-1827.[3]
Stacy, John—Alice Jones, 1687.[6]
   John—Ann Cahoon, 4-12-1787.[1]
Stafford, Joseph—Kesiah Morgan, 8-22-1822.[3]
Standley, Michael—Martha Jones, 7-30-1767.[1]
Stanhope, Mayew—Elizabeth Hart, 10-23-1828.[3]
Stanley, Samuel G.—Sarah Hudson, 9-13-1818.[3]
   William—Rebecca Budd, 1686.[6]
Stanton Edward—Amy Child, 1686.[6]
Stapes, Ellis—Mary Burns, 9-27-1803.[3]
Staples, Thomas—Mary Rogers, Mar. 25, 1738.[1]
Stapleton, Andrew—Mary Reeves, 6-21-1782.[1]
   George—Rhoda Wheatcraft, 11-17-1784 [1]
Stark, James—Mary Middleton, 11-11-1822.[3]
Starkey, Asher—Clarissa Haight, 2-3-1838.[3]
   John—Elizabeth Jacobs, 11-10-1799.[3]
   Nathan—Elizabeth Platt, Nov. 1, 1736.[1]
   Nathan—Edith Willson, Oct. 17-1749.[1]

Starkey, Samuel—Rebecca Kerlin, 2-7-1805.³
Starling, Archiby—Mary Ann Robeson, 11-21-1818.³
Starn, Charles—Elizabeth Downes, 3-16-1826.³
  Eli D., Gloucester co.—Mary Ann Albertson, 3-20-1839.³
  Samuel—Deborah Wilson. 8-3-1834.³
Staunton, John—Dinah Gale. Oct. 6, 1732.¹
Stead, Joseph Elwood—Mary Matilda Frake, 9-15-1900.²
Steadling, William M. (s. Jesse and Mary)—Alice Rouge (d. Edward), 1-1-1874.⁴
Stealman, Elias—Ann Little, 11-21-1785.⁴
Stebins, William—Jane Cribbs. 12-7-1770.¹
Steen, Hezekiah—Alice Mount, 1-21-1832.³
  Joseph—Betsy Morris, 6-30-1808.³
  William—Christine Balantine, Philadelphia, 8-15-1838.³
Stephens, David—Mary Jones, 9-25-1834.³
Stephenson, Samuel—Rebecca Gaskill, 4-5-1804.¹³
  Samuel—Ann Rudderow, 5-16-1833.³
  Seth—Mary Ann Welch, 4-11-1826.³
Sterling, Benjamin—Rebecca Elkinton, 1-2-1817.³
  Benjamin—Elizabeth Elkinton (d. Enoch), 1819.¹⁴
  Budd—Eliza Wright, 5-22-1817.³
  James—Rebecca Budd, 11-9-1785.¹
  James—Caroline E. Fenimore, 12-1-1830.³
  James Hunter—Eliza Fielding. 10-29-1824.⁵
Stern, Isaac—Sarah Lear, 2-12-1829.³
  Samuel—Rebecca Browning. 9-17-1897.³
Sterne, Joseph—Martha Maraback, 12-28-1814.³
Stetton, John—Mary Brown, 11-17-1801.³
Stevens, Charles—Wilhelmina Lintz, 10-4-1865.²
  David—Mary Jones, 9-25-1834.³
  John—Levinia Waterman, 1820.¹⁴
  Peter—Martha Bennett, 2-5-1807.³
  Samuel—Rebecca Truax, 9-11-1836.⁴
Stevenson, Benjamin—Sarah Fenimore, 5-4-1763.¹
  Caleb—Mary Stockton, 1-8-1804.³
  Charles—Rachel Hilliard, 12-9-1818.⁷
  Cornel (s. Cornel)—Ann Haines (d. Joseph and Mary), 5-13-1790.⁶
  Cornwell—Patience Morton. 10-4-1804.³
  Elnathan—Mary Riley, 10-21-1756.¹
  Elnathan—Bathsheba Norcross, 10-25-1767.⁸
  George—Sarah Tindall, 12-24-1836.³

Stevenson, Isaiah—Edith Webb, 10-25-1821.³
  John—Mary Jennings, 1706.⁶
  John—Martha Walton, Apr. 21, 1739.¹
  Jahn—Amelia Lawrie, 11-23-1786.⁵
  John—Anna W. Brick, 12-5-1821.⁷
  Jonathan—Mary Allen, July 17, 1684.¹
  Jonathan—Elizabeth Proud, 7-18-1805.³
  Joseph (s. Cornel and Anna A.)—Anna Satterthwaite (d. John W. and Ann), 11-4-1819.⁵
  Joseph—Catharine Cross, 6-12-1834.³
  Josiah—Ann Groff, 10-28-1829.³
  Peter—Mary Burne, 6-8-1774.¹
  Thomas—Sarah Pennington, 1704.⁶
  Thomas— Experience Cheshire, Sept. 17, 1733.¹
  Thomas—Alice Shinn, 1740.⁶
  William—Ann Jennings, 1699.⁶
  William—Sarah Kimbal, Apr. 19, 1740.¹
  William—Persilla Lippencot, 6-26-1798.³
  William—Jane King, 12-3-1813.³
  William—Emeline Cornelius (colored), 7-12-1834.³
Steward, Aaron, Monmouth co.—Lydia Steward, 3-20-1822.³
  Aaron—Hannah Woodward, 2-20-1780.¹
  Abner—Mary Rockhill, 10-24-1777.¹
  Isaac—Sarah Green, 2-4-1837.³
  John—Margaret Carman, 5-12-1773.¹
  John—Rhoda Shinn, 9-22-1783.¹
  John—Mary Ann Barcalow, 2-13-1834.³
  Joseph—Ann Rubins, 5-6-1767,¹
  Joseph—Sarah Rogers, both Allentown, 2-1-1818.³
  Josiah—Martha Browne, Jan. 21, 1728.¹
  Samuel—Susannah Antram, 5-7-1774.¹
  Samuel—Rachel Malcom, 10-31-1833.³
  Thomas (s. Joseph)—Mary Allen (d. Samuel), 3-11-1784.⁵
  William—Elizabeth Robinson, Dec. 31, 1739.¹
  William (s. John and Elizabeth)—Rebecca Taylor (d. Samuel and Anne), Nov. 28, 1751.⁵
  William—Mary Major, 5-12-1788.⁴
  William—Catharine Carter, 4-19-1827.³
  Wilson—Ann Vansant, both Bucks co., Pa., 1-28-1819.³
Stewart, Alexander—Rebecca Ann Winton, 11-13-1825.₇
  Daniel—Lucy King, 11-13-1801.³

Stewart, Daniel—Mary Cliver, 3-26-1821.³
　Furman—Elizabeth Kirling, 12-11-1813.³
　John—Mary Scott, 8-14-1828.³
　Joseph—Martha Down, 11-12-1756.¹
　Joseph—Martha Vaughn, 9-24-1808.³
　Lewis—Maria Allen, 2-6-1823.³
　Robert—Sarah Moon, 5-2-1796.³
　Thomas—Elizabeth Wallings, 9-1-1795.³
　Thomas—Hannah Winters, 2-14-1822.³
　Thomas—Charity Stockton, 6-28-1829.³
　William—Maria Johnson, 4-21-1853.⁸
Sticket, Adam—Adelia Veliak, 5-28-1836.³
Stidpole, Joseph (s. William and Sarah)—Georgianna Dennis (d. Barton and Lydia), 8-18-1875.⁴
Stien, Hinchman—Lydia Ann Lippincott, 4-27-1834.³
Stiles, Benjamin (s. Isaac and Rachel)—Martha Matlack (d. Reuben and Elizabeth), 1-11-1816.¹²
　Clayton—Mary Thomas, 12-13-1818.³
　Edward—Martha Bishop, 3-14-1761.¹
　Ephraim—Mary Lippincott, Apr. 3, 1749.¹
　Henry Roberts—Anna L. Evans, 10-26-1829.¹⁰
　Isaac—Grace Price, 10-28-1776.¹
　Jacob—Elizabeth Rainier, 4-16-1804.³
　James—Sarah Dobbin,, 12-16-1830.³
　Jesse—Sarah Willits, 1-7-1816.³
　John Blakely—Rachel English, 2-18-1836.³
　Joseph—Elizabeth Stiles, 2-3-1819.²
　Joseph R.—Rebecca L. Atkinson, 12-10-1831.³
　Joshua—Ann Rynear, 9-10-1795.³
　Levi—Elizabeth W. White, 2-12-1832.³
　Martin—Sarah Sopers, 9-21-1826.³
　Nicholas—Elizabeth Sherwin, Jan. 23, 1750.¹
　Robert—Hannah Burrough, 1743.⁹
　Samuel—Jane Dobson, 6-26-1771.⁸
　Stacy—Priscilla Stiles, 10-21-1824.³
　Thomas—Ann Brown, 10-19-1772.¹
　Thomas—Judith Roberts, 3-17-1825.³
　William—Elizabeth Vandergrift, 1-23-1821.³
Still, Anthony—Mary Ficher, 4-8-1821.³
　Clayton—Sarah Jane Harris, 3-9-1836.³
　Daniel—Mary Dawson, 11-4-1783.¹

Still, Freeborn—Harriet Morris (colored), 8-31-1835.³
  Henry—Pamela Fenton, 12-9-1777.¹
  James—Mary Cromwell, 6-25-1807.³
  Lewis—Margaret James (colored), 8-29-1822.
  William—Eliza Sharp, 7-6-1833.³
Stille, Freeborne—Grace Sulsy, 10-6-1804.³
  Ishmael—Mary Lewis, 5-12-1800.³
Stillwell, John—Penolipe Wkite, 11-19-1772.¹
  Joseph—Hannah Stillwell, 1-26-1804.³
  Joseph—Hannah Jones, 7-17-1824.³
  Lias—Hope Ann Jones, 11-4-1825.³
  Obadiah—Rachel Owen, 4-2-1798.³
Stines, Elisha—Ann Dennis, 3-5-1831.³
  George—Beulah Morris, 11-16-1834.³
  Isaac—Mary Richardson, 12-7-1800.³
  James—Jerusha Rockhill, 12-6-1834.³
Stockham, George, Sarah W. Long, 11-9-1835.³
  William—Susannah Paine, 8-29-1778.¹
Stockins, Israel—Grace Conover, 1753.¹¹
Stockton, Abraham—Susannah Kemble, 6-6-1774.¹
  Abraham—Mary Louisa Lamard, 6-15-1832.⁸
  Benjamin—Hannah Cowperthwaite, 11-29-1789 ¹
  Charles—Martha Hough, 4-3-1800.³
  Daniel—Hannah Fisher, July 1, 1728.¹
  Daniel—Jane Peake, 1-8-1780.¹
  David—Ruth Lippincott, Oct. 3, 1733.¹
  David—Elizabeth Ireton, 3-7-1761.¹
  David S.—Lydia Stockton, 11-28-1827.³
  Job—Hannah Jones, Feb. 4-1760/1.¹
  Job—Anne Munrow, 6-9-1757.¹
  Job—Polly Bates, 2-28-1780.¹
  Job—Nancy Ridgway, 11-23-1791.¹
  Job—Amelia Clark, 2-22-1809.³
  Job—Amy Branson, 1-28-1831.³
  John—Mary Gardner, 10-11-1777.¹
  Richard—Sarah Stockton, 1-22-1768.¹
  Richard—Hannan Crispin, 5-2-1768.³
  Richard—Sarah Peake, 10-20-1814.³
  Richard H.—Elizabeth Thomas, 11-19-1828.³
  Samuel—Abigail Burr, 3-5-1777.¹³
  Samuel—Hannah Gardiner, 6-11-1784.¹

Stockton, Samuel—Vasty Gardener, 8-30-1819.³
  William—Hannah Elkinton, 9-5-1775.¹
  William—Ann Boozer, 11-2-1806.³
  William, Philadelphia— Maria Cox, 10-19-1829.³
  William, Jr.—Abigail Hollinshead, 11-31-1802.³
  William W —Sarah Butterworth, 10-25-1829.³
Stockwell, Nelson, Gardner, Mass.—Ella (Lane)Clark, Derry, N. H., 4-14-1884.⁴
Stocton, John B.—Ellen A. Beatty, 11-9-1853.⁴
Stondard, Benjamin—Jane Davis, 2-2-1833.³
  Israel—Sarah Woodward, 10-25-1823.³
Stogden, William—Mary Bryan, Jr., 1736.⁶
Stokes, Aquilla—Sarah Borton, 11-14-1806.¹⁰
  Asher—Martha Hollinshead, 10-22-1829.³
  Barzillai—Elizabeth Gibbs, 2-26-1798.³
  Bezelia—Elizabeth Gibbs, 3-4-1795.³
  Caleb—Ruth Shinn, 11-25-1802.³
  Charles—Amy C. Wille, 10-3-1842.¹⁰
  Daniel, Salem co.—Ann Ridgway, 4-5-1810.³
  Ellis (s. Samuel and Sarah), Philadelphia—Hannah Morgan (d. Isaac and Sarah), Waterford, 11-10-1815.¹²
  Ezra—Martha N. Shreve, 11-14-1850.¹⁰
  Hezekiah—Frances Braddock, 12-21-1815.¹⁰
  Isaac—Lydia Collins, 10-18-1809 ¹⁰
  Israel (s. Daniel and Anna)—Sarah Borton (d. Joshua and Elizabeth), 12-22-1808.¹²
  Jacob, Waterford—Hester Wilkins, 2-1-1774.¹
  Jacob, Gloucester co.—Hannah Hains, 4-28-1779.⁵
  Jarvis—Elizabeth Rogers, 11-27-1773.¹
  John—Elizabeth Woolman, 1-17-1799.³
  John—Lydia Evans, 3-15-1804.¹⁰
  John, Jr.—Hannah Stockdill, 1740.⁶
  John W.—Elizabeth Lippincott, 5-22-1834.³
  Joseph (s Thomas and Sarah) Philadelphia—Rachel Matlack (d. Reuben and Elizabeth), 2-19-1807.¹²
  Joseph—Harriet Stockton, 11-26-1812.³
  Josiah—Hope Borton, 12-12-1794.¹⁰
  Joshua—Elizabeth Burrough, 3-29-1838.¹⁰
  Levi—Deborah Haines, 5-15-1828.¹⁰
  Nathan H.—Rebecca Rogers, 11-21-1839.³
  Thomas—Sarah Inskeep, 1764.⁹

Stokes, Thomas—Mary Chambers, 2-9-1797.³
 Thomas, Jr. Deliverance Horner 1704.⁶
 William—Hannah Hatcher, 4-8-1798.³
 William—Anne Watson, 11-11-1813.¹⁰
Stokesberry, Jacob—Charity Reeves, 3-20-1775.⁸
Stone, William—Sarah Moore, May 10, 1741.¹
Stoops, Eliakim—Mary Phares 9-27-1754.¹
Storrow, William—Mary Vann, 12-20-1780.¹
Story, John—Mary Ann Fisher, 6-21-1827.³
 Joseph—Margaret Pestel, 6-16-1802.³
Stout, David—Margaret Vollow, Bergen co., Jan. 1, 1743.¹
 Joseph—Sarah Hancock, 10-28-1771.¹
 William—Elizabeth Hutchinson, 12-27-1780.¹
Stradling, John J. (s. Jesse H.)—Frances E. Presno (d. Francis) 6-26-1879.⁴
Stratan, Isaac—Ann Adams, Great Egg Harbor, 6-30-1810.³
Straton, Manuel—Mary Joyce, Feb. 20, 1741.¹
Strattan, Daniel—Mary Sharp, May 1-1739.¹
 Isaac—Mary Prickett, 3-4-1778.¹
 Isaac—Mary Bullen, 12-25-1782.¹
 John S.—Phebe Inman, 7-14-1779.¹
 Josiah—Mary Brady, 9-15-1777.¹
 Josiah—Sarah Alloways, 2-20-1784.¹
 William—Hannah Antram, 7-28-1777.¹
Stratton, Benjamin—Sarah Bishop, 2-14-1811.³
 Caleb—Mary Collins, 5-20-1802.³
 Charles—Elizabeth Bishop, 12-11-1816.³
 Daniel—Mary Evans, 10-26-1823.³
 David—Edith Page, 8-13-1795.³
 David—Margaret Cathcart, 5-4-1828.³
 Elias—Ellen Norcross, 4-10-1836.³
 Emanuel—Hannah Hancock (d. Timothy), 1713.⁹
 Enoch—Amy Elkinton, 1746.³
 Enoch (s. Enoch and Hannah), New York City—Amy Thorn (d. Jona.), 11-5-1828.⁵
 George—Hannah Cox, 6-18-1814.³
 Hosea—Jane Austin, 8-28-1800.³
 Isaiah—Esther Borton, 4-27-1828.³
 Israel—Priscilla Gale, 10-22-1836.³
 John—Ann Prickett, Nov. 13, 1744.¹
 John—Ann Cline, 2-5-1808.³

Stratton, John—Mary S. Branson, 2-23-1823.[3]
   John L.—Ann Newbold, 12-26-1816.[3]
   John L. N.—Caroline E. Newbold, 9-14-1842.[4]
   Joseph—Naomi Guinn, 3-30-1765.[1]
   Manuel—Martha Joyce, Feb. 20, 1741.[1]
   Mark—Ann Hancock (d. Timoth)y, 1713.[9]
   Mark—Hannah Simons, 7-24-1799.[3]
   Owen—Mary Shinn, 6-4-1808.[3]
   Reuben—Rebecca Barret, 3-4-1802.[3]
   Samuel—Elizabeth Price, 8-24-1771.[1]
   Samuel—Abigail Borton, 6-19-1823.[10]
   Thomas—Sarah Matlack, 2-23-1777.[1]
   William—Margaret Camp, 4-4-1835.[3]
Streaker, Elias—Mary Blair, 10-14-1779.[1]
Street, Benj.—Hannah Stiles, 2-15-1810.[3]
Stretch, Joseph—Mary Jones, 5-2-1811.[3]
Stricker, Philip, Jr.—Sarah Wilkins, 12-31-1829.[3]
   Philip—Anna Hays, 2-9-1839.[3]
Strickland, Isaac—Sarah Jones, 6-16-1832.[3]
Stringer, Benjamin—Anne Budd, Dec. 29, 1731.[1]
Stroles, William—Catharine Horner, 6-6-1817.[3]
Sturtevant, Chester—Margaret Vandusen, 9-19-1829.[3]
Sudrick, Solomon—Rhoda Smith, 10-15-1815.[3]
Suffrins, David—Deborah Morrit, 1-7-1786.[1]
Suiter, Thomas—Mary Pippitt, 11-15-1826.[3]
Sullivan, Thomas—Beulah Hollinshead, 3-22-1827.[3]
Sulsey, Joseph—Mary Ann Sulsey, 1-4-1815.[3]
Sulsum, James—Maria Shores, 3-19-1824.[3]
Super, Jacob—Jane Brooks, 8-22-1802.[3]
Surly, Francis—Mary Reeves, Mar. 22, 1737.[1]
Surley, Lawrence—Mary Vanhorn, 6-14-1738.[8]
Surridge, William—Mary Witcliff, 1681.[6]
Sustis, Enoch—Elizabeth Fish, 7-31-1813.[3]
   John—Ann Hiles, 1-13-1813.[3]
Sutcliff, Charles—Elizabeth Cox. No date given.[3*]
Sutton, Charles Wesley—Mary E. Stoddart, 11-15-1882.[2]
   Daniel—Agnes Carre, Apr. 10, 1688.[1]
   Daniel—Mary Jackson, Mar. 14, 1732.[1]
   James—Sarah Dilks, 5-31-1818.[3]

---

*Married by Samuel Wright, J. P.

BURLINGTON COUNTY MARRIAGES

Sutton, John—Susannah Ivins, 3-27-1784.[1]
  Reuben—Edith Nixon, 4-18-1837.[3]
  Robert—Elizabeth Hardeman, Mar. 24, 1729.[1]
  Robert—Mary Sands, Nov. 11, 1747.[1]
  Robert I.—Abigail Lione, 11-25-1813.[3]
  Thomas—Letitia Harris, 10-4-1798.[2]
Sutvan, Jacob—Ann Holland, 1822.[4]
Swaim, Benjamin R.—Maria Davidson, 4-3-1828.[4]
  Isaiah, Jr.—Mary L. Rogers, 1-18-1817.[3]
  James—Elizabeth Turner, 2-27-1816.[3]
  Thomas—Mary Budd, 3-3-1807.[3]
  Thomas—Phebe Kerr, 8-11-1837.[3]
Swain, Gabriel—Hannah Brown, 3-2-1778.[1]
  Samuel—Isabell Brown, 10-2-1763.[1]
  Samuel—Hannah Borden, 3-30-1780.[1]
Sweet, George—Lucy Ann Pearson, 11-29-1818.[2]
  John—Martha Rose, 6-15-1828.[3]
  Joseph—Hannah Nailor, 8-14-1798.[3]
  Joseph, Jr.—Telphul (?) Weeb, 8-24-1837.[3]
  Peter—Sarah Smith, 4-5-1834.[3]
  Samuel—Mary Moore, 6-12-1835.[3]
Sweeton, John—Gertrude Vansciver, 6-11-1801.[3]
Sweney, John—Ruth Yard, both Trenton, 5-26-1811.[2]
Swem, Anthony—Nancy Marll, 8-10-1834.[3]
  Daniel—Esther Bowen, 12-27-1801.[3]
  Dahiel—Lewis (?) Grant, 3-9-1836 [3]
  Matthias—Elizabeth Brayman. No date given.[2]*
  William—Exercise Rulon, 1-21-1802.[3]
Swift, Robert—Sarah Swift, 8-31-1800.[3]
  Samuel—Ann Hancock, May 20, 1738.[1]
  William—Hannah Shreve, 11-18-1772.[1]
  William—Mary Smith, 1-2-1804.[3]
Swiger, Jacob—Hannah Patterson, 9-18-1758.[1]
  Jacob—Elizabeth King, 9-7-1766.[1]
Sykes, John—Johanna Murfin, Oct. 19, 1704.
  Thomas (s. Anthony and Mary)—Mary Lawrie, Monmouth co., 4-16-1801.[5]
Symmons, Peter—Sarah Sidnaham, 8-8-1763.[1]
Symons, Richard—Mary Nail, 2-11-1759.[1]

---

*Married by Samuel Wright, J. P.

Sysom, Joseph—Margaret Specule, 12-25-1796 ³
Samuel—Margaret Elborne, 12-16-1832 ³
Tagg, Edward—Patience Wainwright, Jan. 3, 1739.¹
Taggart, Jacob, Salem co.—Rachael Marshall, 6-24-1775.¹
Tait, Ephraim—Abigail Leconey, 2-16-1826.³
Talbert, William—Rachel Antram, 2-13-1767.¹
Talbot, William—Jennet Smith, Mar. 31, 1741.¹
Tallman, Augustin—Susan Atkinson, 5-4-1820.³
   Benjamin—Ruth Taylor, 12-21-1815.³
   Joseph—Margaret Taylor, 12-25-1815.³
Tantum, David K.—Susannah Havens, 11-22-1838.³
   Hartshorn (s. Joseph and Mary)—Miriam Killey (d. David and Hannah), 9-10-1795.⁵
   John—Elizabeth Bacon, Nov. 25, 1702.⁵
   Joseph (s. Joseph and Mary)—Sarah Killey (d. David and Hannah), 11-5-1795.⁶
   Joseph—Elizabeth Wooly, 8-18-1838.³
   Samuel—Sarah Bunting, 3-24-1808.³
   Samuel—Amy Toner, 7-24-1826.³
   Warren—Ann Elizabeth Parent, 1-5-1832.³
Tarbus, Martin—Madaline Paxson, 11-16-1835.³
Tash, Samuel—Mary Powell, 7-25-1796.³
Tasso, Philippo—Phebe Springer, Mar. 6, 1732.¹
Tatam, Samuel—Elizabeth Berdin, 12-7-1805.³
   Samuel—Betsey G. Archer, 3-15-1842.³
Taylor, Aaron—Abigail Nutt, 7-25-1768.¹
   Abel, Jr.—Elizabeth ———, 8-10-1824.³
   Alfred N.—Mary N. Newbold, 4-2-1829.³
   Allen—Julian Brown, 9-3-1801.³
   Allen—Mary Antrim, 11-30-1825.³
   Amos (s. James and Ann)—Rebecca H. Troth (d. James and Rebecca), Trenton, 2-6-1845.⁵
   Anthony N.—Mary I. Newbold, 4-2-1829.³
   Benjamin—Rachel Taylor, Apr. 11, 1751.¹
   Beriah—Keziah Gaskill, 3-12-1767.¹
   Caleb—Hannah Springer, 11-4-1812.³
   Charles—Rachel Horner, June 15, 1736.¹
   Charles M. (s. Isaac and Susan), Philadelphia—Anna E. Sterling (d Thomas and Edith), Trenton, 10-15-1845.⁵
   Charles P.—Mary I. Brown, 12-31-1772.⁸
   Daniel—Mary Davis, 2-21-1778.¹

Taylor, Eber—Sarah Ferguson, 4-21-1769.[8]
Eber—Ann Shreve, 9-9-1802.[3]
Edward, Jr. (s. Edward and Sarah)—Esther E. Wright (d. Caleb and Catharine), both Monmouth co., 1-5-1815.[5]
Ezra—Mary Potter, 12-19-1768 [1]
George—Mary Stuart, Jan. 3, 1742.[1]
George—Susannah Clarke, Dec. 14, 1845.[1]
George—Annie Carman, 10-10-1785.[1]
George—Fanny Johnston, 11-26-1800.[3]
George—Amey Carson, 2-3-1839.[3]
Gisbert—Elizabeth Proud, 3-6-1825.[3]
Henry—Keziah Wills, 3-31-1764.[1]
Henry—Julia French Shinn, 6-29-1905.[10]
Holbert, Newark—Catherine Louisa Lehman, Philadelphia, 2-7-1861.[1]
Isaiah—Sarah Hall, 7-5-1812.[3]
Israel—Sarah Ann Kilkeade, 7-30-1835.[3]
Jacob—Hannah Lame, 3-27-1781.[1]
James—Joanna Bowen, 11-16-1805.[3]
James—Caroline W. Yates, 4-20-1833.[8]
Jared—Lucy Springer, May 11, 1751.[1]
Jediah—Nancy Estelow, 12-30-1820.[3]
Joel—Ann Vanderbake, 10-11-1780.[1]
Joel—Abigail Taylor, 1-16-1824.[3]
John—Deliverance Robins, Nov. 24, 1739.[1]
John—Sarah Quicksell, May 10, 1748.[1]
John—Amey Moss, 8-9-1810.[3]
John—Sarah Cliver, 3-7-1818.[3]
John—Esther Crammer, 9-16-1819.[3]
John Mary Brannin, 1820.[14]
John—Lydia Wooley, 10-30-1823.[3]
John, Sr.—Ann Thorn (d. Thomas and Susanna), 11-6-1800.[5]
Jonathan—Ann Clifton, Feb. 12, 1740.[1]
Jonathan—Mary Shourds, 6-3-1772.[1]
Joseph—Elizabeth Dean, May 8, 1751.[1]
Joseph—Dorothy Moulton, 4-29-1773.[8]
Joseph—Hester Vandegrift, 1-26-1810.[3]
Joseph—Merriam Chamberlain, 9-27-1819.[3]
Joseph—Ann Heisler, 3-24-1831.[3]
Joseph S., New York City — Hannah Hendrickson, 3-10-1836.[3]

Taylor, Mahlon (s. Bernard), Hunterdon co.—Mary Horner (d. Joseph), Middlesex co., 1-12-1777.[5]
Nathan—Susan Garwood, 9-25-1831.[3]
Nicholas, Waterford—Elizabeth Brooks, Dec. 21, 1747.[1]
Robert—Sarah Woodward, May 14, 1728.[1]
Robert—Jane Birdsall, Apr. 11, 1751.[1]
Robert—Susannah Tonkin, 5-10-1762.[1]
Robert—Fanny Poinset, 2-22-1812.[3]
Robert—Sarah Whirl, 10-31-1818.[3]
Robert—Hannah Dillen, 11-28-1819.[3]
Samuel—Susanna Horseman, Apr. 14-1786.[5]
Samuel—Mary Holloway, 2-6-1760.[1]
Samuel—Hannah Peacock, 8-23-1779.[1]
Samuel—Mrs. Neome Ferrall, 12-9-1798.[3]
Samuel (s. James and Abigail)—Achsah Decow (d. Isaac and Mary), 3-7-1805.[5]
Samuel—Mary Laily, 3-6-1823.[3]
Samuel—Mary Hankins, 1-11-1829.[3]
Samuel, Jr.—Anne Folks (d. Thomas and Elizabeth), Nov. 29, 1716.[5]
Samuel, Jr.—Rebecca Field, Oct. 3, 1741.[1]
Stacy—Bribget Stewart, 1-7-1802.[3]
Stacy—Elizabeth Collins, 10-15-1814.[3]
Thomas—Ahna Lippincott, Aug. 6, 1746.[1]
Thomas—Elizabeth Bird, 1-20-1789.[4]
Thomas—Hannah Brown, 6-23-1813.[3]
Thomas—Esther Loveland (d. Charles), 3-28-1819.[3]
Thomas—Mary King, 3-19-1825.[3]
Thomas—Mary Ann Gaskill, 1-1-1839.[3]
Thomas J.—Hannah B. Haines, 2-4-1832.[2]
Wesley—Hannah N. Carson, 3-28-1833.[3]
William—Anna Savlor, 6-24-1754.[1]
William—Abigail Carter, 9-18-1768.[8]
William—Marietta Mooney, 9-22-1789.[4]
William (s. Daniel and Hannah)—Ann Holloway (d. Samuel and Miriam), 2-4-1808.[3]
William—Rachel Henry, 3-9-1819.[3]
William—Amelia Lewallen, 4-6-1822.[3]
William—Mary Willits, 11-31-1828.[3]
William, Jr.—Mary Shinn, Jan. 14, 1745.[1]
William S.—Phebe Ann Rogers, 2-14-1839.[3]

Taylor, Zephaniah—Rachel Kelley, 10-25-1785.[1]
Tenbell, Michael—Martha Clutch, 5-22-1767.[1]
Tennet, Edward—Margaret Smith, Nov. 3, 1741.[1]
Terry, William—Mary Shaw—12-17-1809.[3]
Test, John—Hannah Allen, 4-1-1793.[7]
  William—Mary Stephenson, 9-3-1826.[3]
Thomas, Aaron—Mary Hutchinson, 7-16-1854.[4]
  Absolom—Mary Springer, Apr. 28, 1750.[1]
  Andrew—Mary Woolstone, 5-27-1798.[3]
  Benjamin—Rebecca Sexton, 10-23-1825.
  David—Margaret Lucas, Oct. 27, 1746.[1]
  Enrich—Mary Davis, 4-11-1803.[3]
  Ephraim—Elizabeth Garwood, 10-2-1807.[3]
  George—Achsa Rogers, 11-28-1829.[3]
  Isaac—Margaret Bullock, 12-23-1801.[3]
  Isaac—Mary Ann Chambers, 10-6-1831.[3]
  Isaiah, Trenton—Mary Smith, 7-31-1800.[3]
  James—Bridget Fitzgerald, Aug. 21, 1731.[1]
  Jesse—Sarah Beckett, 1769.[9]
  John—Sarah Wood, June 7, 1746.[1]
  John—Abigail McLoe, 7-8-1802.[3]
  John—Lydia Farmer. No date given.[3]
  Jonathan—Sarah Gaskill, 10-27-1832.[3]
  Joseph—Sarah Mullen, 12-21-1809.[3]
  Joseph L.—Maria Leeds, 7-2-1825.[3]
  Martin—Ann Nut, 4-26-1779.[1]
  Nathaniel, Monmouth co.—Ann Leeds, Oct. 23, 1738.[1]
  Peter—Mary Coward, 6-9-1799.[3]
  Samuel—Hannah Bisbop, 3-9-1795.[3]
  Samuel—Julian Cummings, 7-27-1815.[3]
  Seth—Susanna Pratt, 2-21-1799.[3]
  Solomon—Ann Cooper, 3-18-1808.[10]
  Timothy—Elizabeth Lucas, Nov., 1744.[1]
  Timothy—Bathsheba Gardiner, 8-21-1774.[5]
  Thomas—Mary Grimes, 2-20-1783.[1]
  William Henry, Philadelphia—Annie M. Newton, 2-22-1871.[2]
Thompson, Abel—Jemima Kemp, 9-28-1778.[1]
  Andrew—Rebecca Abbott, 5-28-1818.[7]
  Arthur—Elizabeth Sooy, 5-11-1797.[3]
  Bevis—Elizabeth Alloway, 6-13-1838.[3]
  Charles—Deborah Adams, 9-25-1825.[3]

Thompson, Charles Thorn—Abigail Bozorth, 9-4-1833.[3]
  George—Jane Perkins, 3-4-1800.[3]
  Henry—Mary Taylor, 8-31-1754.[1]
  Henry Anthony—Julia Zelina Machelot, 6-13-1827.[8]
  John—Elizabeth Staples, June 11, 1730.[1]
  John—Jehoshebah Schooley, 8-22-1759.[1]
  John—Rebecca Allen, 5-27-1793.[7]
  John—Rebecca Ryness, 3-23-1800.[3]
  John—Beulah Pangburn, 3-11-1817.[3]
  John—Elizabeth Meyers, 12-18-1823.[3]
  John—Margaret Woodrow, 4-29-1830.[3]
  Joseph—Hannah Turner, 2-9-1830.[3]
  Joseph S.—Harriet Herbert, 12-27-1835.[3]
  Joshua—Mary Shourds, 6-29-1812.[7]
  Joshua, Jr.—Susannah Mason (wid.), 12-29-1788.[7]
  Michel—Mary Severs, 10-4-1811.[3]
  Nelson—Sarah Shinn, 5-25-1831.[3]
  Pemberton, Gloucester co.—Margaret Dobbins, 9-6-1834.[3]
  Samuel—Charity Inglin, 2-17-1816.[5]
  Samuel—Susan Reeves, 1-24-1828.[3]
  Stacy—Martha Burroughs, 11-16-1818.[3]
  Sooy—Elizabeth Sooy, 2-1-1824.[2]
  Thomas—Mary Spragg, 12-29-1759.[1]
  Thomas—Phebe Fenton, 9-26-1814.[3]
  Uriah—Elinor Fagan, 9-28-1771.[1]
  William—Mary Foster, 9-13-1815.[3]
  William—Hannah Weeks, Gloucester co., 7-6-1820.[3]
  William D.—Alice Morris, 12-24-1812.[3]
Thomson, Able—Mahala Still, 6-8-1826.[3]
  Elias—Rachel Wills, 3-19-1801.[3]
  John—Ann Gifford, 4-7-1802.[3]
  Uriah—Elizabeth Allen, 5-20-1809.[3]
Thorn, Anthony—Phebe Sansinger, 11-28-1828.[3]
  Asher—Elizabeth English, 1-22-1809.[3]
  David—Sarah Sharp, 2-6-1824.[3]
  Enoch—Rebeccah French, 9-30-1804.[3]
  Enoch—Lucretia Horner, 5-5-1834.[3]
  George (s. Thomas and Susanna)—Mary Fields (d. Benjamin and Tabitha), 4-9-1801.[5]
  Isaac (s. John)—Mary Schooley (d. Joseph), 10-12-1780.[5]

Thorn, Isaac (s. Isaac and Mary)—Mary Wooley (d. James and
Hulda, Trenton), 1-8-1807.[5]
Isaac—Hulda Wooley, 9-9-1818.[5]
James C.—Hope S. Force, 10-5-1820.[3]
John—Ann Borllen (?), 5-4-1815.[3]
John—Mary Thomas, 11-14-1816.[3]
John, Jr.—Tace Skirm, 3-29-1785.[1]
Joseph—Ann Beck, 4-17-1802.[3]
Langhorn—Mary Warren, 11-15-1815.[3]
Mahlon—Zeuriah Page, 2-23-1761.[1]
Pearson—Mary Hesler, 10-14-1834.[3]
Richard—Deborah Herbert, 10-7-1821.[3]
Samuel—Mary Ivins, 7-21-1827.[3]
Thomas—Mary Robins, 1-16-1764.[1]
Thomas—Ann Falkingburg, 2-24-1805.[3]
William—Achsah Hill, 12-14-1803.[3]
William (s. Thomas and Abigail), Waterford—Hannah Dudley
(d. Joshua and Rachel), 10-28-1813.[12]
Thorne, Benjamin—Sarah Bunting, Apr 14, 1704.[1]
Benjamin (s Thomas and Abigail)—Ruth Dudley (d. Joshua
and Rachel), 3-23-1809.[12]
Joseph, Jr.—Sarah Rogers, 1-29-1807.[3]
Joshua—Hannah I. Rogers, 11-16-1826.[10]
Samuel—Hannah Clay, Oct. 22, 1730.[1]
Samuel—Sarah Collins, 3-12-1794.[10]
Thornton, Edward C.—Adelaide Deacon, 2-17-1864.[2]
James (s. Joseph and Hannah), Pennsylvania—Rebecca Stokes
(d Dr. John H. and Anne), 9-24-1818.[12]
Thomas—Martha Smith, June 2, 1735 [1]
Throckmorton. Craig—Rhoda Fagans, 3-5-1835.[3]
Isaac—Hannah McCoy, 4-29-1837.[3]
Thurston, Moses—Hannah Parker, 7-29-1815.[3]
Tibbetts, John R.—Mary Ann Russell, 1-15-1874.[8]
Tice, Benjamin—Mary Birdsall, 12-4-1831.[3]
Joshua— Lydia Moore, both Gloucester co., 11-28-1835.[3]
Tiswell, Brooke—Louisa Eddleman, 4-4-1897.[2]
Tilgman, Lloyd—Louisa Hugg, 6-12-1824.[3]
Tillson, Apollo M.—Elizabeth Lippincott, 12-2-1839.[3]
Tilton, John—Anne Banks, 9-15-1784.[1]
Abraham—Elizabeth Rogers, 1-15-1781.[1]
John—Elizabeth Vanse, 3-7-1758.[1]

Tilton, Judiah—Hannah Allen, 11-9-1775.[5]
William, Monmouth co.—Esther Middleton, 3-1-1770.[5]
Tindall, David—Abigail Britton, 6-2-1799.[3]
    Isaac—Bulah Ann Gifford, 1-7-1832.[3]
Titus, Charles—Phebe Townsend, 4-24-1808.[3]
Tod, Samuel—Rhoda Peacock, 3-16-1797.[3]
Todd, James—Anna Horner, 3-23-1815.[3]
    John—Mary Rosell, 9-28-1834.[3]
Tolman, Henry, Bloomsbury—Elizabeth Pitt, Newton, 11-31-1818.[3]
    Job—Sarah Scattergood, Feb. 25, 1736.[1]
    Joseph—Mary Woodward, May 18, 1736.[1]
    Thomas—Hannah Austin, 8-18-1763[1]
Tolmer, Jacob—Margaret Sutton, 9-2-1797.[3]
Tomlin, Barzillai—Anne Heritage, 10-17-1799[3]
Tomlinson, Benjamin—Frances Haines, 12-6-1804.[13]
    Isaac—Rebecca C. Lippincott, 1-24-1836.[3]
    John—Margaret Mugglestone, 1689.[6]
    Joseph—Ollinda Lloyd, 12-20-1825.[3]
    William, Gloucester co.—Rebekkah Wills (d. John), Oct. 13, 1731.[6]
Tonkin, Edward—Mary Cole, Gloucester co., May 7, 1733.[1]
    Edward—Hepziah Ridgeway, 3-18-1777.[1]
    Richard—Martha Stiles, 9-5-1830.[3]
    Samuel—Elizabeth Inskeep, 5-10-1765.[1]
Tonkins, Jacob—Máry Sikes, 2-11-1778.[1]
    John—Elizabeth Fox, 10-7-1804.[3]
Tool, Peter—Mary Wagner, 2-17-1772.[1]
Toole, John—Susanna Leland, Sept. 22, 1740.[1]
Topham, Mathew—Catherine McKeaman, Mar. 18, 1731.[1]
Topping, Joshua—Elizabeth Brooks, 11-11-1778.[1]
Torn, John—Sarah Bennet, 4-19-1778.[1]
Torr, William H.—Elizabeth H. Kelly, 6-25-1866.[8]
Tourtelot, Francis—Mary Heppard, 11-7-1805.[3]
Town, Vincent—Hannah L. Southwick, 4-5-1830.[3]
Townsen, John—Mary Jane Burns, 10-30-1852.[4]
Townsend, Furman—Amy Taylor, 12-23-1830.[3]
    Joseph—Elizabeth Scull, Mar. 6, 1735.[1]
    Reddock—Mary Covenoven, Dec. 9, 1736.[1]
Toy, Daniel—Sarah Bennet, 12-29-1756.[1]
    Jacob—Mary Merrill, 10-17-1777.[1]
    John—Sarah Maxfield, 9-3-1780.[1]

Toy, John—Mary Wallace, 3-21-1825.³
 Thomas—Rachel Hartshorn, 2-21-1821.³
 Thomas—Anna Maria Shinn, 12-1-1825.³
Tradway, Henry—Anne Driver, Dec. 8, 1685.¹
Treat, Samuel—Agnes Hollinshead, 10-3-1774.¹
Trevillon, John—Elizabeth Crawford, 5-17-1835.³
Tribet, Simon—Elizabeth Hawkins, 8-12-1770.⁸
Troth, Isaac—Atlantick Phillips, 12-14-1799.³
 Isaac—Sarah A. Jones, 10-25-1832.³
 Joseph E.—Rebecca Stratton, 1-8-1839.³
 Joseph G.—Isabella Murrell, 2-31-1830.²*
 Paul—Sibbillah Ballinger, 2-13-1799.¹⁰
 Samuel—Edith Lippincott, 3-6-1806.³
 William—Esther Borton, 1757.⁹
 William—Elizabeth Phillips, 2-6-1787.¹
Trotter, Joseph—Ann Hough, 9-11-1809.¹³
 Nathan (s. Daniel)—Susanna Hough (d. Samuel), 10-7-1813.¹³
 William—Mary Kempton, 7-27-1797.³
Trout, Christopher—Ann Fisher, 10-22-1796.³
 Christopher—Margaret Jackway, 12-3-1809.³
 James—Mary Reeves, 12-29-1836 ³
 John—Anne Rockhill, July 31, 1750.¹
 Samuel Borden—Rebecca Brittenham, 10-9-1821.³
 William Reeves—Mary Jane Haines, 7-22-1871.⁴
Truax, Charles—Mary Ann Kelley, 6-10-1832.³
 Joseph—Hannah Burr, 2-23-1789.⁴
Trueax, Solomon—Betsey Hambleton, 7-30-1814.³
Trulon, William—Hannah Wright, 10-24-1812.³
Trumis, Benjamin—Jane Kelly, 2-24-1764.¹
Trusty, William—Ann Still, 2-18-1821.³
Tucker, Major—Sarah Quicksell, 6-6-1754.¹
 Reuben D.—Elizabeth Lippincott, 7-12-1809.³
 Wesley—Sarah McNeelie, Nov., 1829.³
Tuckney, Henry—Ann Vaughn, Oct. 16, 1733.¹.
Tudor, John—Elizabeth Rowlan, 9-20-1769.¹
Tully, Daniel—Dorothy Stratton, 3-31-1816.¹⁰
 Francis—Margaret Cheamealy, 7-7-1797.²
Tuly, Jonathan—Martha Brown, 6-22-1758.¹
 Thomas—Margaret Scott, Sept. 13, 1729.¹

---

*February 31, 1830 in record.

Tunis, Benjamin—Dorothy Higginbottom, Aug. 23, 1745.[1]
Turner, Apollo—Catharine Cook, 2-25-1813.[3]
  Benjamin—Allice Emley, 2-18-1821.[8]
  James—Elizabeth Page, 9-13-1801.[3]
  John—Rebecca Sweim, 12-25-1810.[3]
Tussley, George—Eliza Heaten, 8-3-1825.[3]
Tuttell, Daniel—Elizabeth Rogers, 7-29-1761.[1]
Tyley James—Elizabeth Sreve, 1740.[6]
Tyson, George—Mary Rue, 12-2-1763.[1]
Twining, William—Rebecca Riley, 1826[11]
Updike, John—Diademia Jackway, 2-26-1815.[3]
  Joseph—Elizabeth Wilson, 6-27-1832.[3]
Updyke, Solomon—Hannah Poore, both Bucks co., Pa., 5-26-1822.[3]
Uston, Josiah—Mary Worrel, 5-23-1813.[3]
Valentine, John—Ann Cross, 6-23-1808.[3]
Van, Jonathan—Esther Rah, 12-23-1813.[4]
VanArminge, William S., New York—Susan B. Sterling, 10-7-1818.[3]
Vanarsdall, Lawrence—Tabitha Curry, 10-22-1809.[3]
VanBrunt, Hendrick—Amelia Adams, 2-21-1830.[3]
  Henry—Thomasen Fennimore, 7-24-1797.[3]
  Henry—Ann Emmons, 12-24-1834.[3]
VanCampen, Rachel Johnson, Hunterdon co., 8-29-1763.[1]
VanCourt, Lewis C.—Harriet Flemings, 4-6-1837.[3]
Vanderbilt, Samuel Browne—Sarah Talman, 12-27-1798.[3]
Vanderbeck, Benjamin—Rachel Curtis, 11-8-1786.[5]
  Benjamin—Susan Torn, 11-16-1811.[3]
  Benjamin—Eliza Bailey, 7-15-1824.[3]
Vandegraft, Garret, Philadelphia—Agnes Harris, Bristol, Pa., 8-14-1767.[8]
Vandergrift, Edward—Jane Stiles, 4-7-1825.[3]
  Jacob, Bucks co., Pa.—Elizabeth Matlack, May 10, 1746.[1]
  Jesse—Rebecca Middleton, 10-25-1808.[3]
  Joseph—Lydia Brelsford, Bristol, Pa., 8-18-1769.[8]
  Josiah—Hannah Connan Herbert, 12-30-1830.[3]
  Leonard, Bucks co., Pa.—Charity Haines, Oct. 23, 1750.[1]
Vanderplank, William—Maria de la Mercede Macomb, 2-25-1833.[8]
Vandeventer, Josiah—Rachel White, 7-31-1831.[3]
Vandeveer, Daniel—Margaret Alcott, Dec., 1824.[3]
  Foster—Ann Bates, 9-21-1837.[3]
  John—Mrs. Ann Smith, 2-14-1833.[2]

Vandike, Charles—Elizabeth Phipps. June 27, 1752.[1]
  Peter—Catharine Jackson, 3-26-1818.[3]
  Thomas—Mary Osburn, 6-18-1770.[1]
Vandivere, David—Elizabeth Morris, 11-17-1801.[8]
Vandyke, Cornelius—Elizabeth Yerkes, both Bucks co., 6-7-1770.[8]
  Richard—Lydia Wood. Oct., 1796.[3]
Vanharlingen, John—Mary Stiles, 4-16-1797.[8]
Vanhart, James, Trenton—Eliza Gulick, 8-4-1819.[3]
Vanhise, Abram, Middlesex co.—Eliza Ann Butcher, 7-30-1825.[3]
Vanhorn, Amos—Harriet Britton, 1-1-1814.[3]
  Bernard—Lavinia Bogart, 12-29-1767.[1]
  James, Monmouth co.—Alice Dennis, 5-9-1831.[3]
  John—Eliza Winnnr, 1-16-1830.[3]
  Samuel—Keziah Mitchell, 11-2-1814.[3]
  William—Sarah Rudderow, 5-21-1757.[1]
  William—Margaret Ellis, 8-17-1780.[1]
Vanhorne, Abraham—Elenor Stout, 3-17-1813.[3]
  Barret—Levina Bogart, 12-30-1867.[8]
  Gabriel—Susannah Ashton, both Bucks co., Pa., 11-18-1767.[8]
  Isaac—Sarah Fury, 8-5-1770.[8]
  John—Mary Tomlinson, 3-22-1804.[3]
  Lewis—Caroline Consolly, 3-10-1833.[3]
  Peter—Sarah Mode, both Bucks co., Pa., 9-4-1771.[8]
  Peter—Rebecca Selpath, 5-27-1798.[3]
  William—Mary Ann Cattell, 1-14-1802.[3]
VanHussars, Volkert—Elizabeth Bennett, 4-9-1797.[3]
VanKirk, Israel—Sarah England, 4-24-1828.[3]
  Thomas (s. Bernard and Rebecca)—Lillie Claypoole (d. Abraham and Emmeline). 4-27-1865.[4]
  William—Prudence B. Rice, 1-9-1812.[3]
VanLaw, Preston—Judith Ann Marot, Apr. 15, 1746.[1]
Vann, John—Nancy Harker, 2-25-1827.[3]
VanNasdoll, Garret—Ann Taylor, 12-30-1824.[3]
Vannest, Peter—Charlotte Stanton, 4-1-1810.[3]
Vanote, Wilbur F. K. (s. Daniel and Susan)—Mary Anna Smith (d. Daniel and Mary), 5-19-1867.[4]
Vansant, George—Margaret Grant, 5-19-1816.[3]
  John Bucks co, Pa.— ——— ———, 6-26-1811.[3]
  Nicholas—Mercy Davis, 12-23-1808.[3]
Vanschoik, John, Rev.—Eliza L. Bunting, 6-30-1813.[3]
VanScbuyver, Joseph—Martha Belford10-29-1776.[1]

Vansciver, Abraham—Sarah Fort, 10-19-1801.³
  Abraham—Achsah Deacon, 11-25-1813.³
  Asa—Rebecca Bee, 8-17-1805.³
  Barnabas—Elizabeth Warner, 3-24-1825.³
  Franklin—Elizabeth Kale, 6-13-1832³
  Jacob—Elizabeth Cole, 5-17-1754.¹
  James—Mary Luck, 8-15-1805.³
  Jeremiah—Mary Borden, 3-26-1781.¹
  John, Jr.—Janett Fenimore, 10-11-1804.³
  Levi—Ofpy Warner, 12-21-1823.³
  Nathan—Sarah Ann Still, 4-3-1838.³
  Richard—Agnes Vankirk, 10-22-1820.⁵
  Robert—Sarah Ann Austin, 8-12-1838.³
  Samuel—Sarah Booze, 7-25-1817.³
  Samuel—Elizabeth Shimella, 2-11-1826.³
  Solomon—Martha McLaughlin, 7-23-1815.³
  Solomon—Rachel Ann Read, 9-6-1816.³
  William—Sarah Vankirk 10-17-1865 ³
Vanskiver, John—Mary Cross, 4-3-1769.⁸
Vanskyver, Walter—Elizabeth Thorn, 10-2-1769.¹
Vanseveer, Abraham—Hannah Lippincott, 11-20-1782.¹
Vansandt, Clifford Shreve—Nettie Maude Triplette, 12-16-1891.²
Vanzant, Christopher—Anne Turner, 11-7-1770.¹
Vantilburgh, Henry—Sophia Latimore, 3-6-1806.³
Vaucan, William—Lydia Ann Wooley, 3-7-1839.³
Vaughan, David—Mary Renier, 1-31-1768.⁸
  George, Gloucester co.—Hannah Smith, June 30, 1735.¹
  John—Patience Vaughan, Freehold, 4-6-1764.¹
Vaughn, James—Sarah Gibbins, 6-27-1765.¹
  John—Mary Berredale, 3-9-1809.³
  John—Nancy Harker, 12-29-1825.³
  John—Lucy Ann Norcross, 11-4-1836.³
Velve, Levy—Hannah Crones, 4-6-1797.³
Venable, Arthur—Mary Ann Stratton, 2-10-1825.³
  Job—Hannah Hooten, 1-13-1803.³
  John—Ann Crusher, 5-16-1795 ³
  John—Abigril Ann Hancock, 1-1-1839.³
  Joseph—Susannah Jenkins, 9-5-1778.¹
  Joseph—Eliza Fish, 3-14-1832.³
  Peter—Mary Briggs, 4-30-1818.³
  Thomas—Sarah Wallis, Jan. 10, 1729.¹

BURLINGTON COUNTY MARRIAGES

Venable, Thomas—Hester Borrodail, 8-2-1756.[1]
   Thomas—Sarah Pearson, 4-10-1806.[3]
Vennable, Arthur—Rebecca Shin, 5-24-1783.[1]
Vennel George—Deborah Field, 10-27-1808.[3]
Vernon, Eli H.—Elizabeth Dennis, 12-22-1836.[3]
   Jackson—Mary Perry, 1-25-1837.[3]
   James—Esther Colbreath, 11-13-1756.[1]
Vickery, Thomas Gilbert—Lizzie Beaber Worth, 9-9-1890.[4]
View Peter—Lydia Ward, 11-26-1831.[3]
Villette, Dennis—Ann Veno (French), 10-9-1800.[3]
Vinicomb, Francis—Rachel Lippincott, 1739.[6]
   William—Sarah Jones, 1706.[6]
Vogt, Edward LeClerc—Emma Adelia Robinson, 1-28-1874.[8]
Voorhees, Daniel J. Capt.—Mary Ann Bishop, 10-31-1826.[3]
   Elias—Martha Joyce, 5-16-1799.[3]
   Elias—Elizabeth McKarson, 10-31-1832.[3]
   Gilbert—Charlotte Allen, 12-6-1821.[3]
Vordyke, Thomas—Sarah Gaskin (?), 10-21-1798.[3]
Wainwright, John—Mary Johnson, 2-1-1830.[3]
   Thomas—Mary Bossom, 2-7-1835.[3]
   Wincent—Rebecca Potts, 6-10-1802.[3]
Wake, Baldwin—Mary Syphers, 10-23-1774.[3]
Walker, Abraham—Rebecca Chambers, July 15, 1736.[1]
   Isaac—Mary Horner, Dec. 4, 1728.[1]
   John—Judith Land, Sept. 5, 1746.[1]
   John—Mary Lees, 9-28-1788.[4]
   John—Elizabeth Craig, 1-9-1805.[3]
   John—Ann Hackney, 4-8-1813.[3]
   Robert—Ann Bates, 10-25-1798.[3]
   Thomas—Elizabeth Gaskin, 8-7-1783.[1]
   William, Gloucester co.—Ann Austin, 9-20-1773.[1]
   William—Hope Venable, 5-2-1816.[3]
Waling, Thomas—Elizabeth Bevis, 7-10-1760.[5]
Wall, Humphrey, Monmouth co—Elizabeth Tilton, 8-25-1763.[1]
Wallace, Archibald—Florence Glass, 10-1-1898.[2]
   Benjamin—Sibilla Marter, 12-27-1835.[3]
   Charles—Rebecca Marter, 11-6-1836.[3]
   David—Ann Garwood, 2-11-1801.[3]
   John M—Rebeka McIlvaine, 12-28-1805.[3]
   Joyn—Rebecca Wallace, 12-25-1816.[3]
   Samuel—Elizabeth Fish, 1-6-1830.[3]

Wallace, Shippen—Laura Christina Barclay, 6-15-1871.[8]
William—Martha Jones, 3-30-1797.[3]
William Henry, England—Mary Anna Heisler, 2-13-1873.[4]
Wallen, Thomas—Anna Lipencott, 12-4-1783.[5]
Wallets, Ebenezer—Elizabeth Gilbert, 5-20-1818.[3]
Wallin, Thomas—Hope Dawson, 5-23-1755.[8]
Walling Thomas—Hannah Wallace, Nov. 12, 1740.[1]
Wallins, John—Lydia Andrewson, 11-21-1816.[3]
Wallis, Edward—Mary S. Hess, 9-20-1837.[3]
  Thomas—Hope Lippincott, July 12, 1750.[1]
Walne, James—Martha Adams. Oct. 13, 1746.[1]
Walsbey, William—Rachel Rynear, 10-14-1780.[1]
Walsh, John—Margaret Norton, June 16, 1739.[1]
Walter, Benjamin—Phebe Plalke, 1739.[6]
Walters, Harry Lincoln—Janey Bunting Parsons, 11-3-1885.[2]
Walton, Benjamin—Mary Swift, 10-4-1808.[8]
  Jeremiah—Elizabeth Clark. 11-27-1803.[3]
  Lewis, Philadelphia—Elizabeth Stockton, 9-16-1824.[3]
  Robert C.—Abigail Woolston, 8-26-1813.[3]
  Thomas—Anne Bower, Monmouth co., 6-14-1766.[1]
  William—Micha Swem, 6-2-1760.[1]
Waney, John—Patience Moore, 9-22-1775.[1]
Ward, Hezekiah—Beulah Pearson, 11-17-1796.[3]
  Jacob—Hannah Bowker, 12-3-1784.[1]
  Jacob—Rhoda Boulton, 1-4-1808.[3]
  James—Harriet Ivins, 3-9-1839.[3]
  Peter—Hannah Hollinshead, Feb. 28, 1745.[1]
  Peter—Ahne Barkenof, 12-14-1763.[1]
  William—Mary Brown, 2-16-1830.[3]
Wardell, Parker—Phebe Trueax, 6-9-1830.[3]
  Anthony—Elizabeth Page, 5-5-1808.[3]
  John—Margaret Tucker, Shrewsbury, 10-26-1761.[1]
  Joseph (s James), Monmouth co.—Hannah Bunting (d. John), 11-28-1761.[5]
  Samuel—Hannah Pancost, 5-23-1763[1]
Wardelle, Samuel—Sarah Ivins. 1-27-1777.[1]
Warden, Jeremiah, Jr —Hannah Moore, 3-8-1780.[13]
Ware, Job—Grace Thompson, 11-30-1789.[7]
  Job—Susannah Smith, 6-30-1794.[7]
  Job—Mary Bagley, 4-25-1808.[7]
  Joel—Martha Stillwell. 10-24-1807.[3]

BURLINGTON COUNTY MARRIAGES

Ware, John—Sarah Buffin, 1750.⁶
John (s. John)—Catharine Titus, 6-16-1779.⁵
Warner, David—Susan Brinker, 7-13-1830.³
  Francis B.—Beulah Gaskill, 11-21-1822.³
  George W.—Eliza Rogers, 5-11-1839.³
  Isaac—Mary Austin, 12-28-1825.³
  Jaconias—Sibella Eldridge, 3-1-1770.¹
  James—Sarah Favis, 8-29-1767.¹
  John—Eliza Kester, 8-30-1821.³
  John H.—Lydia Ford, 2-26-1820.³
  Morris M.—Eliza Laton, 7-5-1834.³
  Moses—Elizabeth Gardner, 2-4-1782.¹
  Nathaniel—Mary Chapman, 11-13-1756.¹
  Obadiah R.—Artemesia A. Pierce, 2-21-1839.³
  Salaways—Susannah Conder, 12-5-1760.¹
  Samuel—Hepzibah Matlack, 8-3-1784.¹
  Steven—Abigail Jones, 6-17-1819.³
  Thomas—Jane Wood, 7-6-1809.³
  Wilbert Rose—Grace Matilda Hannon, 4-20-1884.⁴
  William—Ann ———, 12-21-1815.³
  William—Beaulah Hooper, 11-7-1824.³
Warren, Jacob—Rebeckah Mount, 2-2-1768.¹
  James—Phebe Alloways, 1-15-1800.³
  John—Joan Sykes (wid. Samuel), Jan. 9, 1689.⁵
  John—Rebeckah Fretwell, 1706.⁶
  John—Sarah Wilkinson, 12-5-1796.³
  John—Henry (?) Mattson, 11-29-1797.³
  John—Elizabeth Reynolds, 3-30-1801.³
  John—Mary Dennis, 2-10-1830.³
  John—Sarah Leuallen, 12-25-1823.³
  Jonathan—Sarah Allen, 4-4-1801.³
  Robert (s. Gamaliel and Meribah)—Hannah Wright (d. Ebenezer), Middlesex co., 1-4-1810.⁵
  Thomas—Sarah Brown, 8-2-1807.³
  Thomas (s. James)—Martha Webb, 5-27-1819.³
Warring, Adam—Susannah Platt, 3-19-1808.³
Warrington Benjamin (s. Joseph and Rebecca)—Hannah Thompson (d. John and Keziah), 12-18-1806.¹²
  Enoch—Rachel Pierson 10-29-1795.³
  Henry (s. Joseph and Rebecca)—Anna Lippincott (d. Thomas and Lydia), 11-15-1804.¹²

Warrington, John (s. John and Mary)—Deborah Zane (d. Simeon
and Sarah), 4-18-1805.[12]
   John—Ann Atkinson, 3-12-1835.[3]
   Thomas (s. Henry and Rebecca)—Hannah Lippincott (d. Josiah
and Miriam), 2-13-1817.[12]
Warters, Amos—Mary Carragin, 9-7-1809.[3]
Washington, George—Mary Boling, 7-22-1824.[3]
   George—Mary Lee, 1-4-1826.[3]
   Jacob—Ann Martin, 12-31-1846.[4]
Waterman, Anthony—Tobitha Green (colored), 1813.[14]
   Henry—Mary Godfrey, Apr. 12, 1727.
   Henry—Jane Lippincott, 11-9-1831.[3]
   Jesse—Elizabeth West, 7-7-1796.[13]
Waters, Daniel—Mary Welks, 11-14-1807.[3]
   William—Anne Munrce, 1-31-1757.[1]
Watkins, Abijah—Phebe Field, 10-1-1773.[1]
   Eleazer—Elizabeth Scott, 5-5-1773.[1]
   John—Martha Leeds, 1-27-1800.[3]
   Solomon—Mary Brayman, Mar. 20, 1734.[1]
Watkinson, George—Anna King, 1-19-1837.[3]
   John—Abijah Monear, Nov. 4, 1745.[1]
   John—Margaret Leland, 7-24-1776.[1]
   Richard—Martha Ewing, 4-18-1771.[1]
Watson, Benjamin—Martha Evans, 2-11-1767.[1]
   David—Mary Jane Platt, 8-12-1832.[3]
   James—Hannah Estill, 1-5-1774.[1]
   Joel—Mary Gale, 2-27-1822.[3]
   John—Hannah Marriott, Nov. 7, 1823.[5]
   John—Mary Everingham, 8-16-1766.[1]
   John, Jr.—Ruth Biles, 4-23-1771.[1]
   John—Elizabeth Gibbs, 11-25-1800.[3]
   Marmaduke—Elizabeth Pancoast, 1718.[6]
   Matthew—Hannah Pancoast, Jr., 1725.[6]
   Richard—Mary Howard, 8-13-1756.[1]
   William—Bridget Bingham, 1687.[6]
   William—Mary Welch, 1735.[6]
   William—Sarah Smith, 1-13-1802.[3]
   William I.—Frances Shippen, 4-7-1825.[8]
Watt, David S., Virginia—Mary Riley, 9-9-1830.[3]
Wayman—Henry—Patience Chapmar, 6-20-1763.[1]
   Henry—Sarah Burtis, 6-20-1767.[1]

Weart, Eli—Mary Munrow, 5-26-1819.³
Weatherby, Benjamin—Sarah Mathis, 8-1-1802.³
Weaver, Edward—Mary Staples, 1729.⁶
  Jesse—Hephzebah Troth, 3-7-1795.³
  Joseph—Rachel Robinson, 1-21-1770.⁵
  Thomas—Sabilla Duval, 4-26-1826.³
Web—John—Sabella Hartman, 12-3-1817.³
Webb, Daniel—Grace Malsbery, 2-17-1812.³
  Isaac—Mary Penrow, 2-15-1783.¹
  James—Mary Antram, 12-16-1783.¹
  James—Susan Maria Horner, 7-7-1824.³
  John—Rebecca England, June 5, 1740.¹
  Robert—Mary Gaunt, 1713 ⁶
  Robert, Jr.—Barthia Crammer, May 9, 1751.¹
  Samuel—Rhoda Bowker, 4-7-1812.³
  Samuel—Sarah Perine, 9-17-1818.³
  Stacy—Catharine Parker, 8-4-1825.³
  Zebulon—Edith Lowder, May 26, 1740.¹
  Zebulon—Ezabel Pearson, 7-4-1762.¹
Webber, Jacob—Ann Cripps, 1741.⁶
  John Cristen—Anna Meria Burkins, 8-5-1806.³
Webster, Isaac—Sarah L. Cowperthwaite, 2-27-1834.³
  Joseph—Deborah Vansciver, 4-29-1838.³
  Lawrence—Hannah Hugg, 3-22-1764.¹
  Levi—Lydia Coxe, 2-19-1799.³
  Thomas (s Samuel), England—Sarah Vinicomb (d. William), Jan. 31, 1732.⁶
Weeks Henry—Elizabeth Morris, 5-21-1814.³
  Job—Sarah Pettitt, 7-10-1815.³
  James, Galloway—Mrs. Phebe Wilson, 1-20-1820.³
Weems, William L.—Mary Kinsey, 5-13-1803.³
Weester, Samuel—Ann Sweet, 5-18-1820.³
Weigand, Samuel—Hannah Adams, 3-8-1818.²
Weldermuth, John—Elizabeth Wiseman, 11-9-1825.³
Weller, Amos—Rebeckah Wright, 12-22-1776.¹
  Marick, Monmouth co.—Mary Wright, 1-3-1767.¹
Welmerton, Abraham—Mary Marter, 2-15-1816.³
Wells, Abraham—Neomy Whitcraft, 10-16-1800.³
  Amos—Hannah Moore, 5-27-1807 ³
  Asa—Elizabeth Nippins, 10-3-1833.³
  Carrol—Martha Bright, 12-14-1838.³

Wells, Charles—Abigail Renear, 1-28-1827.³
  David—Mary Leeds, 2-13-1801.³
  Herbert T.—Mary E. Jackson, 6-10-1872.⁸
  James, Philadelphia—Rachel Lovele, Oct. 23, 1750.¹
  John—Jane McCormick, 1-11-1825.³
  John—Ann Garner, 9-18-1836.³
  Joseph—Elizabeth Force, 12-29-1811.³
  Joseph C. (s. Charles and Hannah)—Mary Rickey Cox, 6-11-1875.⁴
  Joshua—Sarah Cross, 7-25-1811.³
  Moses—Rebecca Black 12-17-1818.³
  Samuel—Sarah Cheesman, 6-11-1837.³
  Samuel T.—Emla Lippincott (d. Joseph), 2-21-1877.⁴
  William—Hannah Coleet, 12-24-1806.³
  William—Hezekiah (?) Atkinson, 3-5-1822.³
Welsh, Darley—Sarah Leed, 9-17-1757.¹
  David—Sarah Larrison, 7-21-1803.³
  Isaac—Ann Marie Oby (colored), both Trenton, 4-12-1836.³
  Isack—Ellen Quire, 12-6-1832.⁴
  John—Ruth Stackhouse, Pennsylvania, 10-5-1776.¹
  John—Martha Quigley, 7-5-1780.¹
  Patrick—Jane Flanigan, Mar 11, 1734.¹
  Peter—Anna Burns, 6-3-1778.¹
Wentling, Jacob—Elizabeth Townsend, 1-4-1801.¹
West, Bartholomew—Susannah Shinn, Oct. 5, 1727.¹
  Daniel—Elizabeth Arned, June 5, 1736.¹
  David—Charlot Wood, 9-13-1838.³
  George—Mary Clark, 2-2-1768.⁸
  George—Amy English, 1-21-1802.³
  John—Mary Ash, Oct. 19, 1728.¹
  John—Mary Reynolds, 7-19-1759.¹
  Joseph—Jennet Neal, 4-22-1802.³
  Mahew—Sophia Blain, 12-30-1800.³
  Marmaduke—Elizabeth Paxon, declaration of intention to marry, 12-8-1785.¹³
  Matthew—Margaret Rossell, 1-1-1784.¹
  Morgan—Elinor Conklin, 6-26-1819.³
  William—Anne Stout, 3-26-1778.¹
  William—Beulah Rodman, Nov., 1797.³
  William—Jane Osburn, 9-10-1808.³
  William—Martha Sickles, 7-11-1819.³

West, William—Atlantic Stokes, 9-28-1822.[3]
Westcoat, Jonathan—Sarah Keeler, 1-2-1807.[3]
Westcote, Richard—Margaret Lee, 3-18-1761.[1]
Westley, John—Alse Harman, 11-27-1817.[3]
Wetheral, Thomas—Rebecca Lippincott, 1-18-1810.[3]
Wetheril, Thomas, Jr. (s. Thomas and Anne)—Catherine Sykes (d. John and Joanna), May 16, 1744.[5]
   William—Isabella McComb, 7-6-1825.[8]
Wetherill, Alexander P.—Elizabeth Rogers, 2-24-1836.[8]
   Christopher—Elizabeth Pope, 1690.[6]
   Christopher—Mary Whisten, 1705.[6]
   Isaac—Rebecca Deacon, 5-16-1776.[1]
   John—Sarah Burradall, 1700.[6]
   John—Thomasine Scattergood, 1734.[6]
   Joseph—Mercy Ridgway (d. Job), 1789.[11]
   Joseph, Jr.—Rebecca Aaronson, 1-22-1800.[3]
   Thomas—Ann Fearson 1703.[6]
   William—Rebecca Haines, Bucks co., Pa., Nov. 2, 1748.[1]
   William—Arvolina Haines, 3-21-1844.[10]
   William Delaney (s. Robert and Phebe), Philadelphia—Louisa Stratton, 6-4-1874.[4]
Wever, John H.—Emma M. Risdon (d. J. N. and Matilda), 11-22-1870.[4]
Whaineright, James—Mary Mullin, 1-11-1801.[3]
Whare, James—Mary Taylor, 3-29-1817.[3]
Wharton, C. H., D.D.—Anne Kinsey, 11-28-1799.[8]
   Loyd—Mary Rogers, 4-6-1797.[3]
   Reynold—Beulah Burr, 5-27-1782.[1]
   Thomas—Arabella Griffith, 9-10-1817.[8]
Wheatcraft, Edward—Elizabeth Weston, Monmouth co., July 18, 1732.[1]
   Samuel—Sarah Carter, May 7, 1736.[1]
   Samuel—Ann Hill, 5-26-1773.[1]
Wheatley, Caleb—Sarah Scholey, Dec. 10, 1696.[5]
   William—Ann Warren, 11-5-1760.[1]
Wheeler, Jacob—Jerusa Batselor, 8-25-1801.[3]
   Patrick—Mary Johnston, 1-10-1800.[3]
   Robert—Rebekkah Kenner, 1692.[6]
Whistler, Thomas—Mary Harris, 3-19-1770.[1]
   Thomas—Sabilla Wilks, 1-27-1803.[3]
Whitall, Benjamin Gilbert—Rachel Newbold, Jr., 10-27-1823.[3]

Whitall, Joshua—Sarah Ann Rogers, 10-1-1835.[10]
White, Aaron S.—Elizabeth Lukemires, 11-25-1849.[4]
  Benjamin—Margaret White, 12-25-1824 [3]
  Crawford (s. Robert and Esther), Monmouth co.—Anna Taylor (d. Joel and Anna), 12-9-1819.[5]
  Edward—Rebecca Wright, 12-30-1824 [3]
  Edward—Mercy Rainier, 7-10-1831.[3]
  George—Mary Williams, Bucks co., Pa., Dec. 25. 1732.[1]
  George—Jane Pigen, Monmouth co., 6-20-1818.[3]
  George—Elizabeth T. Newell, 3-2-1837.[3]
  Hezikah—Mary Fenimore, 8-10-1805.[3]
  James—Ann Gilbert, 8-27-1828.[3]
  John—Mary McDermott, 11-19-1816.[3]
  John B.—Rebecca Coleman, 1-16-1833.[3]
  Joseph—Rebecca Smith, 12-11-1807.[13]
  Joseph—Elizabeth Clark, 4-18-1819 [3]
  Joseph—Sarah Hornor, 11-15-1827.[3]
  Joseph—Mary Parent, 9-2-1805.[3]
  Joseph—Elizabeth Shiras, 3-12-1828.[3]
  Joseph, Philadelphia—Elizabeth C. Maylan. Gloucester co., 1-22-1832.[3]
  Joseph—Elizabeth Atkinson, 3-11-1849.[4]
  Josiah—Rebecca Foster, 1734.[9]
  Josiah—Catharine Ridgway, 3-7-1805.[13]
  Michael—Lydia Jones, 8-4-1831 [3]
  Philip—Hannah Southard, 8-16-1777.[1]
  Reuben—Hannah Brown, 8-30-1817.[3]
  Thomas—Isabella Friend, 4-16-1787.[4]
  Thomas—Sarah Scott, 9-21-1805.[3]
  William, Bristol, Pa.—Mary Stockton, 3-22-1821.[3]
  William—Ann Ingling, 11-20-1823.[3]
  William—Fanny Early, 3-7-1830 [3]
Whitehead, John—Mary Peachee, July 27, 1738.[1]
Whitehouse, Job—Olivia McCulley, 11-27-1773.[1]
Whitiss, John—Elizabeth Topping. Mar 7, 1741.[1]
Whittaker, Elam—Anseline Fowler, 9-15-1835.[3]
Whitten, Thomas—Lydia Williams, July 14, 1740.[1]
Whitton, William—Mary Hammett. Mar. 27, 1738.[1]
Whitworth, Allen W., Jr.—Mary L. Crockford. 3-20-1882.[4]
Wiart, Thomas—Hannah Rubart, 4-6-1815.[3]
Wickard, Philip—Rachel Bishop, 3-29-1758.[1]

Wicker, Daniel M.—Sarah Dunyon, 3-17-1825.³
Wiikward, John A.—Rebecca Wilson, 11-11-1837.³
   Samuel—Sarah Buzby, 1741.⁹
Wiggins, William Ashley, Trenton—Deborah Bunting, 7-16-1818.³
Wilcocks, Hugh—Sarah Alburtice, June 5, 1727.¹
Wilcox, John—Elizabeth Elkinton, Apr. 3, 1728.¹
   Joseph—Sarah Iredell, 1752.⁹
   Samuel—Eliza S. Osborn, 11-14-1824.⁴
Wildes, Tilton—Lydia Brown, 5-27-1824.³
Wiler, Tanner—Kessiah Johnson, 8-29-1801.³
Wiley, John—Lydia Lippincott, 8-29-1780.¹
Wilgus, James—Hannah Titus, 4-17-1799.³
   John—Diademia Danielly, 1-26-1806.³
   William, Hunterdon co.—Nancy Reed, 3-30-1819.³
Wilkason, John—Mary Sanders, 7-10-1759.¹
Wilkerson, George—Susan Wood, both Trenton, 8-20-1818.³
Wilkins, Abel (s. Samuel and Elizabeth)—Phebe Virginia Shreve
   (d. Samuel and Mary), 12-18-1866.⁴
   Amos—Sarah Haines, 6-17-1756.¹
   Amos—Ann Hewlings, 10-26-1815.³
   Benjamin Mariah Sharp, 11-21-1816.³
   Booze—Hannah Wilkins, 1822.¹⁴
   Charles—Grace M. Collins, 8-30-1828.³
   Henry H.—Deborah C. Prickett, 3-21-1872.¹⁰
   Isaac—Emma Stricker, 12-28-1823.³
   Jacob—Rachel Braddock, 10-2-1825.³
   Joy—Rachel B. Evans, 9-28-1905.¹⁰
   John—Hannah Gwinnall, 5-19-1761.¹
   John—Mary Stokes, 8-24-1776.¹
   Jonathan—Hannah Haines, 3-24-1809.³
   Joseph—Sarah Norton, 1-17-1784.¹
   Josiah—Hester Sharp, 7-13-1788.⁴
   Joshua—Rebecca Ballenger, 10-28-1812.³
   Nathan—Mary E Troth, 11-23-1826.³
   Richard—Elizabeth Ann Coats, 3-26-1829.³
   Samuel—Mary Eldridge, 10-16-1783.¹
   Samuel—Martha Borton, 8-6-1815.³
   Samuel—Sarah French, 1-7-1819.³
   Thomas—Mary Core, 1727.⁹
   Thomas—Elizabeth Miller, 2-11-1798.⁴
   Thomas—Rebecca Haines (d. Isaac), 1-29-1829.³

Wilkins, Uriah—Elizabeth Eyre, 10-18-1792.¹
  Uriah—Ann Eliza Foster, 11-26-1835.³
  William—Hannah Austin, 1820.¹⁴
Wilkinson, Amos Hannah Martindale, Bucks co., Pa., 2-13-1822.³
  John—Levinah Wilson, Jan. 10-1748.¹
  John—Amy Small. 11-30-1784.¹
  Nathaniel—Rachel Fenton. Dec. 1, 1735.¹
  Thomas—Elizabeth Early, 1-31-1773.³
  Winson—Sarah Rickets, 1-30-1781.¹
Willets, Amos, Monmouth co.—Abigail Cook, Aug. 17, 1743.¹
  Amos—Charity Engle, 5-9-1778.¹
  Hope—Mary Buck. Cape May co., June 20, 1730.¹
  John—Hannah Thompson, 3-11-1819.³
  Joshua—Rebecca Parker, 3-31-1801.³
  Lewis—Sarah Morris. 2-17-1768.¹
  Stephen—Mary E. Oliphant, 1-15-1835.²
Willger, Edmond—Susanna Donoly, 2-16-1804.³
Williams, Asher—Mary Beck, 11-10-1763.¹
  David—Ann Buffin, 6-6-1806.³
  Erwin. Jr.—Mary Hugg, 1726.⁶
  George, Monmouth co.—Mary Ellis (d. John and Anna), Nov. 12, 1730.⁵
  George, Jr.— Monmouth co.—Eliza Abbott (d. John and Anne) May 18, 1738.⁵
  George—Mary Gloster, 3-7-1833.³
  Henry—Emeline Phillson (colored), 9-26-1883.⁴
  Hezekiah (s. George), Monmouth co.—Sarah Abbott (d. John and Anne), May 22, 1740.⁵
  Isaac—Mary Marriott, 1720.⁶
  James—Ann Swift, 7-22-1777.¹
  Jesse—Sarah Cornelius, 8-18-1818.³
  John—Ann Coperthwait, 6-10-1798.³
  John—Sarah Randolph, 4-18-1804.³
  John—Mary Berryman, 3-14-1812.³
  John—Sarah Moore, 3-24-1825.¹⁰
  John—Hannah Knight (colored), 12-8-1831.³
  John—Emeline Kelley, 8-1-1833.³
  Joseph—Margaret Blair, 10-14-1795.³
  Joseph—Sarah Franklin, 11-24-1803.³
  Joseph—Ann Mick, 5-7-1826.³
  Josiah D.—Mary McClary, 3-4-1838.³

Williams, Lewis S.—Rebecca Ann Moore, 4-14-1832.³
  Oliver H.—Elouisa Blake, 4-24-1832.³
  Richard—Rachel Burr, 7-29-1831.³
  Samuel—Ann Ballinger, 8-7-1831.³
  Samuel S.—Sarah Hutchinson, Bucks co., Pa., 9-11-1834.³
  Smith—Mary Stevenson, 2-13-1830.³
  Solomon—Jane Penquite, 5-7-1802.³
  Solomon—Mary Burrows, 11-8-1829.³
  Theophilus—Ann Mulligan, 3-10-1821.³
  Thomas—Sarah White, 7-10-1814.³
  William—Margaret Kelley, 5-6-1832.³
Williamson, Esau—Ann Covey, 11-8-1831.³
  Francis—Hannah Wilkins, 4-30-1795.
  Jacob—Rebecca Curtus, 2-28-1798.⁴
  Joseph—Mary Fox, 11-15-1800.³
Willis, Amos—Merribe Wells, 3-2-1767.¹
  Daniel, Jr.—Mary Shinn, Mar. 12, 1695.¹
  John—Elizabeth Wood, June 25, 1743.¹
Willits, Archelaus—Mary Haines, 1816.¹¹
  Benjamin Hew—Robecca Howard, 4-13-1798.³
  Henry—Phebe Osborn, 1770.¹¹
  Horatio N.—Elizabeth M. Biddle, both Philadelphia, 1-16-1839.³
  Hosea—Lydia Hults, 9-22-1814.³
  James (s Richard, Sr.), 1715.¹¹*
  James. 2nd—Ann Ridgway (d. Thomas, Jr.), 1740.¹¹
  James. 3rd—Marjorie Belanger, 1813.¹¹
  Jeremiah—Mary Bartlett (d. Nathan, Sr.), 1783.¹¹
  Joseph—Mary Halloway, 5-26-1768.³
  Joseph—Charlotte Langdale, 1-1-1812.³
  Micajah—Elizabeth Baker (d. John, Sr.), 1740.¹¹
  Micajah—Mary Shamela, 1-16-1830.³
  Micajah, Jr.—Judith Crammer, 1777.¹¹
  Parker—Phebe Willits (d. John, Sr.), 1820.¹¹
  Richard—Elizabeth Ridgua, 1704.⁶
Richard, Monmouth co.—Sarah Overton (d. Samuel and Hannah), Sept. 28, 1732.⁵
Richard, Jr.—Sarah Barton, 1732.¹¹
  Richard, Jr—Patience Butcher, 1734.⁶
  Richard, Jr.—Rachel Birdsall, 1801.¹¹

*Married out of meeting. Bride's name not given.

Willits, Samuel (s. Henry)—Elizabeth Gray, 1793.[11]
Willitt, Edward—Bethena Calvin, 12-7-1816 [3]
Wills, Abraham—Hester Garwood, 1-16-1800.[3]
  Ahab—Mary Snuffin, 1-12-1796.[3]
  Amos—Rebecca Haines, 4-22-1802.[3]
  Benjamin H.—Elizabeth E. Wills, 12-21-1826.[10]
  Charles—Sarah Johnson, 12-14-1801.[3]
  Charles—Hannah Leeds, 9-5-1836.[3]
  Daniel (s. John)—Elizabeth Woolston (d. John), 1714.[6]
  Daniel—Margaret Eayre (d. Richard), 1719.[6]
  Daniel—Elizabeth Stratton, 1-31-1805.[3]
  Daniel, Jr.—Margaret Newbold, Dec. 30, 1686.[1]
  David—Martha Crispin Jan. 21, 1750.[1]
  David—Mary Sharp, 8-27-1796.[3]
  George—Sarah Paschall, 3-3-1787.[1]
  George Augustus—Beulah Scattergood Brown, 10-12-1898.[2]
  Henry W. Lydia Stokes, 5-13-1841 [10]
  Howard H—H. Rosa Stokes 6-11-1868.[2]
  Isaac—Anne Hollingshead, 4-14-1796.[3]
  John—Hope Delefoss, 1682.[6]
  John—Elizabeth Frampton, 1701.[6]
  John—Hannah Circuit, Aug. 2, 1722.[6]
  John—Abigail Lippincott, 1732.[9]
  John—Bethnia Cox, 8-19-1763.[1]
  John—Hope Gaskill, 3-4-1778.[1]
  John—Catty Wynds, 7-7-1790.[1]
  John—Sarah Alloways, 4-29-1820.[3]
  Joseph—Virgin Powel, 11-6-1794.[13]
  Joseph—Rebecca Garwood, 10-16-1800.[3]
  Joseph—Rebecca Master, 5-7-1801.[3]
  Joseph—Hannah Ballinger, 10-4-1812.[3]
  Joseph P.—Mary Ballenger, 11-6-1823.[13]
  Joseph—Rhoda McCollister, 7-21-1825.[3]
  Joseph—Ann Rogers, 7-17-1826.[3]
  Mark E.—Elizabeth M. Ballinger, 2-13-1890.[10]
  Micajah—Margaret Stockton, 1-7-1807;[3] also recorded as 1-13-1807.[3]
  Moses—Margaret Wills, 3-31-1764.[1]
  Moses—Elizabeth Wills, 4-5-1787.[13]
  Moses—Rebecca Black, 1818.[11]
  Philip—Mary Fieles, 1-11-1800.

Wills, Samuel—Jane Buil, 3-27-1801.[3]
  Samuel—Sarepta Reeves, 5-7-1801.[13]
  Samuel—Abigail L. Shinn, 12-20-1837.[3]
  Seth—Phebe Hubbs, 12-16-1813.[3]
  Silas—Elizabeth Kain, 3-7-1805.[3]
  Thomas—Kiziah Murfin. 12-25-1807.[3]
  Thos —Margaret Hackney, 11-18-1813.[3]
  William—Ann Craig, 1765.[9]
Willson, Ezekiah—Christian Atkinson, Feb. 1, 1727.[1]
  Joseph—Lydia Browh, 3-27-1802.[3]
  Matthew—Anne Guilliam, Sept. 12 1728.[1]
  Matthew—Hannah Scroggy, 8-24-1771.[1]
  Michael—Sarah Blackburn, May 4, 1730.[1]
  William—Mary Ashton, Monmouth co., Aug. 29, 1730.[1]
Willow, Moses—Beulah Still, 1-8-1818.[3]
Willey, Daniel—Ann Boozerth, 8-21-1806.[3]
Wilmer, William H., Rev —Marion Cox, 1-23-1812.[4]
Wilmerton, John—Sarah Jones, 11-28-1811.[3]
  Rich'd F.—Emmeline H. Kirk, 2-3-1875.[8]
Wilse, Eli—Sarah Meritt, 3-27-1806.[3]
Wilson. Abraham —Grace Kerlin, 8-16-1814.[3]
  Ahab—Ann Pike, 9-23-1813.[3]
  David—Penelope Worley, July 15, 1748.[1]
  David—Martha Heuston, 10-22-1829.[3]
  Edward—Sarah Bennett, 1724.[6]
  Henry—Eliza Nickles, 11-3-1829.[3]
  Henry L.—Amy Wright, 11-9-1824.[3]
  Hezekiah—Beulah Pippet, 1-12-1796.[3]
  H. Joseph—Beulah Smith, 10-25-1813.[7]
  Isaac, Philadelphia—Phebe Middleton, 10-10-1793.[5]
  Isaac—Rebecca Haines, 11-22-1830.[3]
  Isaac, Jr.—Hannah Jones, 1-14-1836.[3]
  Isaac P.—Ann Chamberlin, 1-10-1839.[3]
  James—Mary Joyce, 1-4-1781.[1]
  James—Leanora Sears, 4-13-1809.[3]
  Jesse—Elizabeth Mason, 1-26-1801.[7]
  John—Catharine Eslo, 9-11-1778.[1]
  John—Esther Shinn, 1820.[14]
  John—Elizabeth H. Taylor, 4-3-1798.[3]
  John—Mary Taylor, 3-15-1808.[3]
  John—Sarah Fenimore, 4-29-1819.[3]

Wilson, John—Sarah (colored). 3-2-1827.³
  John—Elizabeth Hile, 12-4-1831.³
  Joseph—Lydia Updike. 11-18-1800.³
  Joseph—Margaret Woolston. 9-10-1825.³
  Levy—Mary Weeks, 1-17-1808.³
  Michael—Acksah Forsythe, 1-25-1823.³
  Nathan B.—Lydia Pitman, 2-14-1833.³
  Richard - Sarah Priestly, 5-15-1831.³
  Samuel—Rebecca Heritage, 11-26-1801.³
  Samuel—Marg't Ann Huggins, 4-12-1861.⁸
  Stacy—Sarah Bareford, 7-23-1812.³
  Thomas—Hannah Berry. 5-4-1759.¹
  William—Abigail Smith, 12-16-1800.³
  Zebedee—Elizabeth Vandegrift, 2-20-1827.³
Wiltse, Henry—Martha A. Haines, 3-10-1842.⁴
Wiltshire, Chalkley—Hannah Batso, both Gloucester co , 2-9-1837.³
  Charles—Louisa Jones, 3-29-1832.³
Winchell, Ira—Ann Boltenhouse. 1-27-1805.³
Wineright, Joel—Charity Cook, 8-10-1805.³
Winmore. Stephen—Lavina Quan. 5-6-1821.³
Winner, Abraham—Mary Thatcher, 9-13-1769.⁸
  Amos—Mary Brackney, 9-16-1805.³
  Jacob—Elizabeth Hellings, 9-24-1774.⁸
  John—Hannah Carr, 4-1-1776.¹
  Richard, Trenton—Elizabeth Rosman, 10-27-1832.³
  Thomas, Jr. (s Thomas and Sarah), Caldwell, N. J.—Hannah Williams (d. George and Margaret), 3-6-1823.⁵
  William—Mary Horner, 7-15-1808.³
Winter, David—Elizabeth Howard 12-27-1799.³
Winters, Joseph M.—Catharine W. Hickman. 11-23-1837.³
Wiseman, James—Harriet Burr, 11-11-1804.³
Wisener, Stephen—Mary Whitcraft. 6-25-1809.³
  William—Sarah Little, 9-5-1829.³
Wisham, George S.—Elizabeth E. Williams, 12-24-1831.³
  Samuel—Elizabeth English, 12-30-1830.³
Wisner, William Henry—Ellen B Horner, 12-27-1836.⁴
Wistar, Casper—Rebecca Bassett. 6-28-1817.⁷
  Clayton—Mary Stevenson, 10-31-1814 ⁷
  Clayton—Martha Reeve, 11-26-1827.¹⁰
Wister, John (s. Richard and Sarah)—Charlot e Newbold (d. Clayton and Mary), 10-17-1781.⁵

Witchart, Philip—Mary Critch, 2-27-1781.[1]
Witchell, Samuel—Ann Blouk, 7-9-1779.[1]
Witcraft, Charles—Mary Reeves, 2-24-1821.[3]
    Samuel—Mary Butler, 12-25-1808.[3]
    Theodore—Sarah Ann Allen, 12-23-1838.[3]
Withers, Joseph Sarchett—Elizabeth Woolman Deacon, 4-29-1861.[2]
Wirts, Henry—Emeline Nixon, both Bristol, Pa., 8-9-1838.[3]
Witt, Francis—Abigail Stevenson, 1-18-1766.[1]
Wolard, Benj.—Phebe Elbertson, 2-1-1811.[3]
Wonderlin, Aron—Hannah Rockhill, 8-5-1809.[3]
    John—Phebe Doughty, 2-4-1822.[3]
    Peter—Hester Anderson, 1811.[3]
Wood, Abraham—Elizabeth Wooley, 10-7-1837.[3]
    Alexander—Massy Adams, 12-10-1822.[3]
    Alexander—Mary Braddock, 11-24-1834.[3]
    Alfred (s. John and Elizabeth)—Emily Jane Snowball (d. John, Jr. and Hannah)— 3-6-1871.[4]
    Allen—Mercy Lownsbury, 10-22-1796.[3]
    Amos S.—Elizabeth G. Myers, 9-16-1832.[3]
    Benj.—Sarah Anderson, 1-3-1808.[3]
    Caleb—Naomi Ridgway, 6-24-1816.[7]
    Edward—Bridget Early, 12-2-1834.[3]
    Hezekiah—Mary Kenton, 3-14-1771.[1]
    Hezekiah—Sarah Moore, 5-4-1823.[3]
    Hudson—Rebecca Dilling, 8-30-1834.[3]
    Isaac—Sarah French, 1695.[6]
    Isaac—Mary Rossell, 1-25-1770.[8]
    John—Susannah Furniss, 1716.[6]
    John—Matilda Luttz, 11-28-1828.[3]
    John—Jane Norcross, 1-21-1830.[3]
    Joseph—Mary Carman, 8-8-1812.[3]
    Joseph—Elizabeth Trout, 4-1-1832.[3]
    Robert—Elizabeth Smith, 3-11-1818.[3]
    Samuel—Sarah Carr, 7-29-1805.[3]
    Thomas—Mary Howle, Nov. 3, 1685.[1]
    Thomas—Elizabeth Wills, 10-23-1800.[3]
    Thomas—Margaret Blakeley, 11-19-1828.[3]
    Thomas—Lucy Shreve, 10-28-1838.[3]
    William—Mary Parnell, 1682.[6]
    William—Elizabeth Branson, 3-6-1819.[3]
    William—Rebecca Ann Pilgrim, 11-14-1830.[3]

Woodin, William—Mary Mingin, 3-14-1816.[3]
Woodnutt, Jonathan—Mary Goodwin, 4-30-1810.[7]
Woodrow, Joseph—Jemima Leeds, 10-31-1765.[1]
   Joseph—Rebecca Jones, 1-14-1838.[3]
   William—Margaret Kirkland, 7-23-1837.[3]
Woodruff, Abraham Ogden—Mary Ann Foster, 8-28-1825.[3]
   David—Ruth Bird, 9-2-1796.[3]
   Robert—Elizabeth Mitchell, 8-11-1810.[3]
Woodward, Aaron—Margaret Grant, 12-27-1820.[3]
   Anthony, late of Long Island—Hannah Folkes (d. Thomas), Feb. 14, 1685.[5]
   George—Margaret Mount, 8-31-1780.
   George—Jemima Shinn, 1-22-1800.[3]
   Henry—Mrs. Rozanna Luckmeier, 10-27-1799.[3]
   James (s. Anthony and Keziah), Monmouth co.—Lydia Bullock (d. Joseph and Lydia), 4-10-1806.[5]
   John E.—Rebeckah Lippincott, 12-10-1795.[13]
   Joseph—Hannah Warner, May 30, 1727.[1]
   Joseph—Susan Deacon, 11-4-1824.[3]
   Josiah—Rebekah Woodward, 1-7-1801.[3]
   Ralph—Mary Brock, 5-18-1758.[1]
   Samuel—Rachel Cowgill, Sept. 16, 1728.[1]
   Samuel—Ann Vaughn, 9-1-1821[3]
Woodwero, Samuel—Rebecca Jones, 1-1-1797.[3]
Woolcott, Bloomfield—Sarah Reeves, 6-11-1814.[3]
Wooley, James—Abigail Middleton, 12-13-1770.[5]
   James—Huldah Skirm, 12-18-1776.[5]
   John—Hannah Potter, 2-8-1806[3]
Woolly, Nathan—Abigail Stewart, 10-20-1810.[3]
   Samuel—Ann Corless, 3-2-1807.[3]
Woolhell, Benjamin—Elizabeth Cripple, 7-2-1829.[3]
Woolman, Aaron Aaronson (s. Samuel and Jane), Salem co.—Mary Warrington (d. John and Mary), 8-15-1816.[12]
   Abner—Mary Aaronson, 1752.[9]
   Abraham—Elizabeth Newton, 11-23-1765.[1]
   Abraham—Julian Richardson, 5-7-1818.[3]
   Burr (s Judah and Martha)—Rachel Hollingshead (d. Edmund and Hannah), 3-22-1810.[12]
   Charles—Mary Merit, 2-11-1802.[3]
   Geo. Haines—Lavinia Forgus, 3-31-1870.[8]
   John—Elizabeth Bourton, certificate to marry, Oct. 8, 1684.[6]

BURLINGTON COUNTY MARRIAGES 251

Woolman, John, Pennsylvania, Elizabeth Shadger, Nov. 14, 1749.[1]
  John—Sarah Ellis, 1749.[6]
  John—Mary Gorden, 4-29-1799.[3]
  John L.—Mariah Stokes, 1-18-1824.[3]
  Joseph—Mary Haines, 3-28-1805.[3]
  Josiah H.—Martha Rodgers, 11-9-1837.[3]
  Reuben—Mary Mason, 11-22-1803.[3]
  Samuel—Elizabeth Burr, Jr., 1714.[6]
  Samuel—Jane Ware, Pennsylvania, 11-23-1771.[1]
  Samuel (s. John and Martha)—Rebecca Wills (d. James and Elizabeth), 6-15-1799.[5]
  Samuel—Deborah S. Evans, 4-13-1879.[10]
  Thomas B.—Elizabeth M. Haines, 8-4-1825.[3]
  William—Sarah Burr, 3-4-1796.[3]
  William—Elizabeth Bishop, 3-16-1837.[3]
  William A.—Maria Clifton, 12-27-1832.[3]
Woolson, Samuel W.—Ann Cooper, 10-3-1795.[3]
Woolston, Abel—Rachel Woolston, 9-11-1819.[3]
  Abraham—Ann Miller, 2-19-1809.[3]
  Cornwell—Hannah Arison, Apr., 1762.[1]
  George—Abigail Ellis, 11-29-1787.[4]
  George—Rebeckah Stockton, 4-5-1810.[3]
  Hinchman—Louisa Miller, 2-5-1832.[3]
  Jabez—Esther Bozell, 12-5-1767.[1]
  Jacez—Mary Stratton, 10-6-1785.[13]
  Jacob—Sarah Gosling, 2-27-1759.[1]
  Jacob—Hannah Lippincott, 12-1-1796.[3]
  John—Hannah Cooper, 1681.[6]
  John—Hannah Tencher, May 23, 1738.[1]
  John—Lydia Burdsall, 4-23-1795.[3]
  John—Mary Woolston, 11-30-1826.[3]
  John, Jr.—Lettice Newbold, Dec. 6, 1683.[1]
  Joseph—Jane Topping, Dec. 22, 1737.[1]
  Joseph—Mary Eayres, 6-21-1781.[1]
  Joseph—Martha Joyce, 1-3-1839.[3]
  Joshua—Hannah Birdsel, 5-18-1767.[1]
  Joshua—Tamar Ewing, 9-29-1770.[1]
  Melintus—Charity Eldridge, 5-30-1764.[1]
  Michael—Anne Chemaly, 3-5-1774.[1]
  Michael—Charlotte Haines, 2-13-1798.[3]
  Newbold—Mary Bowlby, 4-7-1775.[1]

Woolston, Samuel, Jr.—Celena Woosltcn, Dec. 25, 1749.[1]
  Samuel—Marty Shinn, 6-30-1824.[3]
  William—Hannah Eayre, 2-11-1771.[1]
  William—Hannah Assa, 12-14-1809.[3]
Wooster, William—Tacy Davidson, 4-30-1795.[3]
Wooston, Isaac—Hope Rogers, 10-30-1817.[3]
Woorace (?), Noah—Nancy Williams, 7-10-1803.[3]
Worden, Benajah—Mary Sears, 12-16-1815.[3]
Worinton, John—Mary Hesher, 4-11-1772.[1]
Worrell, William—Elizabeth Hunter, 2-6-1812.[3]
Worriel, William—Sarah Lee 10-2-1784.[1]
Worth, Giles (s. Joseph and Sarah), Middlesex co.—Elizabeth Tantum (c. John and Eliza), Oct. 22, 1724.[5]
  Joseph—Elizabeth Risdon, 1-24-1822.[3]
  Josiah S.—Hannah H. Bruere, 5-9-1822.[3]
  Peter—Hannah Rossell, 4-10-1834.[3]
  William—Mary Smith, 1687.[6]
  William—Joan Woolcott, 1695.[6]
Worthington, Thomas B.—Rebecca Howell, 3-3-1830.[3]
Worthy, Waldo—Elizabeth Ann Purdy, 12-28-1826.[3]
Wour, James—Sarah Kemble, 3-26-1779.[1]
Wright, Aaron—Elizabeth Satterthwaite, 4-1-1779.[1]
  Aaron W.—Elizabeth Smith, 8-28-1838.[3]
  Abner (s. Amos and Ann)—Sarah Harrison (d. Thomas and Sarah), 12-19-1776.[5]
  Adam—Hannah Gaskill, 5-29-1802.[3]
  Amos—Mary Wright, 11-29-1810.[3]
  Andrew—Mary Ann Cook, 6-6-1830.[3]
  Benjamin—Mary Page, May 10, 1732.[1]
  Benjamin—Ruth Harrison, 1-17-1759.[1]
  Benjamin—Elizabeth Stackhouse, 11-11-1771.[1]
  Benjamin—Charlotte Zelley, 1-12-1832.[3]
  Caleb—Catharine Gardiner, 5-5-1779.[13]
  Daniel—Achsah Hutchinson, 11-2-1832.[3]
  David—Elizabeth Curtis, 9-25-1812.[3]
  Ebenezer—Elizabeth Steward, 6-8-1780.[6]
  Ellis—Ann Shaw, 10-1-1776.[1]
  Empson—Amy Wood, 11-30-1772.[8]
  Ezekiel—Mercy Holbard, Nov. 1, 1739.[1]
  Fretwell—Margaret Ellis, Aug. 2, 1738.[1]
  George—Rebecca Hartshorne, Middletown, Mar. 17, 1729.[1]

Wright, Isaac, Jr.—Mary Arney, 3-9-1796.[5]
Isaiah—Rody Jonson, 7-23-1784.[1]
Israel—Alce Stackhouse, 2-10-1773.[1]
Jacob—Sarah Wright, 6-2-1836.[3]
Joel—Harriet Potts, 10-20-1808.[3]
John—Persilla Garwood, 4-4-1772.[1]
John—Esther Austin, 7-23-1772.[1]
John—Ann Fowes, 4-18-1800.[3]
John—Rachall Jones, 12-2-1802.[3]
John—Elizabeth Shinn, 3-20-1816.[3]
John—Ann Wells, 11-18-1831.[3]
John—Elizabeth Budden, 3-12-1838.[3]
John Lew—Sarah Fennimore, 12-24-1796.[3]
Jonathan—Mary Inskeep, June 15, 1747.[1]
Jonathan—Mary Ireton, 3-18-1754.[1]
Joseph—Rebecca Scholey, 1747.[6]
Joseph—Rebecca Bunting, 5-26-1799.[3]
Joseph—Sarah Lucas, 4-16-1800.[3]
Joseph L.—Jane R. Miller, 11-10-1830.[3]
Joshua—Sarah Mitchell, both Bucks co., Pa., 4-26-1770.[8]
Joshua—Jane Owin, 1-18-1818.[3]
Josiah—Elizabeth Brock, 1720.[6]
Josiah—Prudence Paulin, Feb. 23, 1730.[1]
Josiah—Anne Watson, June 5, 1750.[1]
Jotham—Mary Hollingshead, 5-30-1803.[3]
Mahlon—Ann Willguss, 6-24-1798.[3]
Mathew—Penelope Jones, Jan. 17, 1742.[1]
Robert—Elizabeth Hierton, 1711.[6]
Robert (s. David and Sarah)—Ann Harrison (d. Thomas and Sarah), 2-13-1783.[5]
Robert W.—Eliza H. Bishop, 6-20-1816.[3]
Robert H.—Sarah A. Scattergood, 3-31-1825.[3]
Samuel—Elizabeth Haines, 1747.[6]
Samuel—Jane Allen (d. William), Bucks co., Pa., 11-15-1768.[5]
Samuel—Mary Shinn, 12-1-1784.[1]
Samuel—Euphemia Rogers, 3-19-1806.[3]
Samuel—Sarah Bowman, 11-13-1824.[3]
Samuel B. (s. William and Mary—Fanny Wells (d Noah and Ellen), 1-25-1868.[4]
Samuel G. (d. Caleb and Catherine), Philadelphia—Sarah Wright (d. Robert and Ann), 9-5-1805.[5]

Wright, Stacy—Sarah Baker, 6-8-1768.¹
  Thomas—Margaret Hopkinson, Sept. 18, 1729.¹
  Thomas—Charity Thompson, 8-26-1756.¹
  Thomas—Rebecca Inskeep, 5-10-1798.³
  William—Sarah Lovett, 10-10-1769.¹
  William—Mary Abraham, 1797.³
  William—Rebecca Silvers, 2-25-1799.⁷
  William—Mary Scuyler, 3-10-1839.³
Wylie, Samuel Semple—Elizabeth Shreve Gaskill, 5-4-1881.²
Yard, William K.—Priscilla Robins, 5-27-1837.³
Yardley, Joseph (s. William and Mary), Philadelphia—Sarah Field
  (d. Isaac and Mary), 11-8-1798.⁵
Yates, George—Peggy Johnson, 12-4-1803.³
  George Henry—Elizabeth May Strouse, 6-18-1892.
  Joseph—Abigail Wiggins, 11-7-1802.³
Yearling, Eli—Rachel Maulsbury, 1-23-1819.³
Young, Alexander A.—Elizabeth Budd, 10-4-1821.³
  Charles—Mary Foster, 7-29-1826.³
  George—Elizabeth H. Ellis, 11-6-1838.³
  James—Martha Fish, 7-1-1803.³
  John—Mary McVey, 3-17-1768.¹
  John—Liticia Hancock, 4-9-1807.³
Youngman, Charles K.—Helen Louise Gaskill, 6-9-1895.²
Zane—James—Mary Ellis, 2-6-1800.³
  Robert—Alice Alday (an Indian girl) Apr. 10, 1679.⁶
Zelley, Aaron—Rhoda Case, 3-9-1826.³
  Abraham—Rebecca Lippincott, 12-13-1815.³
  Benjamin—Martha Gaskill, 11-4-1802.¹³
  Benjamin—Elizabeth H. Lippincott, 11-8-1818.¹³
  Daniel—Damaras Butcher, 1725.⁶
  Enoch—Sarah B. Ashead, 3-22-1849.¹⁰
  Job—Elizabeth Richardson, 1-4-1816.³
  John—Hannah Taylor, 1-7-1773.¹
  John—Hannah Stockton, 3-10-1818.³
  John—Mary Dudley, 7-4-1839.³
  Ridgway—Rebecca Gaunt, 3-17-1833 ³
  Silvanus—Bathsheba Butcher, 3-10-1796.¹³
  William—Ann Reeves, 2-23-1815.³
Zillay, Abraham—Sarah Croshaw, 10-19-1773.¹
Zilley, Chalkley—Rachel Dudley, 1-29-1835.
  Daniel—Hannah Southwick, 3-21-1776.¹

BURLINGTON COUNTY MARRIAGES 255

Zilley, Richard—Mary Sweet, 7-20-1834.³
——— Samuel—Martha Green, 3-6-1781.¹
——— Silvanus—Elizabeth Matlack, 2-27-1808.³
Zook, John Trimble—Mary B. Evens, 2-18-1875.¹⁰
——— William T.—Abbie L. Evans, 3-18-1879.¹⁰
———tution—Sarah ———, 11-13-1798.³
———, Andrew—Rebecca Nichols, 9-8-1815.⁸

MARRIAGES OMITTED IN THE FOREGOING

Allen, Nathan—Martha Davenport, July 6, 1721.⁵
Applegate, Liscom—Eliza Ewin, 2-3-1856.⁸
Archer, Howard Kirkbride—Mary Britton, 11-23-1898.²
Atkinson, Mahlon Stacy—Beulah Lippincott, 1-13-1809.¹⁰
Barracliff, William—Anne Burgis (wid. Samuel), Dec. 4, 1718.⁵
Bickley, Abraham Wharton—Laura Virginia Vail, 5-15-1861.⁸
Borden, Samuel—Elizabeth Cruson, 1-31-1802.³
Bowker, Rodman Whortman—Ida Louisa Wiseman, 11-24-1880.²
Brutton, Joseph—Bridget Kelley, both Bristol, Pa., 8-30-1767.⁸
Bullock, William W.—Mary C. Davis, Monmouth co., 11-3-1837.³
Canady, James—Dorothy Throgmorton, 8-16-1801.³
Carson, Thomas C.—Mrs. Mary Ernshaw, 8-30-1872.⁸
Chew, Contine—Mary Ewen, 7-29-1787.⁴
Christopher, Charles—Rebecca Lippincott, 10-29-1815.³
Collins, John—Hester Earle, 2-27-1800.³
Cook, John Middleton—Margaret Reynolds, 2-1-1803.³
——— John Middleton—Elizabeth Hartman, 1-23-1806.³
Cox, Asa—Martha Huston, 4-27-1815.³
Dangerfield, William—Esther Foster, 4-6-1778.¹
Darlington, William, Dr.—Catheran Lacey, 6-1-1808.³
Davis, Clayton—Mary McKenny, 11-2-1811.³
Disborough, Henry, M.D—Henrietta Nottnagle (wid. of Leopold), Bristol, Pa., 6-1-1820.⁸
Dobbins, Micajan—Mary Brock, 11-13-1830.
Dunn, Lot, Trenton—Elizabeth Swaime, 8-9-1817.³
Dyer, John—Kesiah Lee, 8-10-1820.³
Earlin, Daniel—Mary Sutvan, 9-30-1815.³
Engard, William, Jr.—Prudence Major, 5-3-1824.³
Estell, John—Sarah Eggnew, 10-21-1817.³
Estilow, Christopher—Sarah Snowden, 11-14-1827.³
Everham, Daniel—Abigail Malsbury, 11-16-1823.³
Falkenburgh, Timothy, Tuckerton—Elizabeth Parker, 9-19-1838.³

Haggins, Harmon—Marjory Rubart, 3-24-1821.[3]
Haines, Isaac—Elizabeth Butcher, 3-19-1794 [10]
   Joseph H.—Anna Wills, 5-17-1875.[10]
Hobson, George—Hannah Kinnison, Pennsylvania, Aug. 8, 1732.[1]
Hough, Samuel—Rebecca Philips, 1820 [14]
Hutchens, Alfred—Susan Edgar, 12-17-1835.[3]
Kaighn, Levi L.—Hannah Mason, 12-17-1827.[3]
Kimsey, Abraham—Rhoda Stockton, 9-27-1779.[1]
Lippi, Anthony—Rebeckah Briggs, 1-9-1800.[3]
Lippincott, George M.—Anna Haines, 8-15-1866.[10]
Matlack, Thomas—Abigail West, 2-17-1766.[1]
Nailor, John—Lydia Austin, 10-10-1802.[3]
Patrick, Owen—Elizabeth Engard, 5-28-1825.[3]
Peacock, John—Susannah Ballinger, 1758.[9]
Pero, William—Ruth Plumbe, 11-14-1819.[3]
Plat, John—Phebe Williams, 12-5-1802.[3]
Prawl, James—Elizabeth Shreve, 6-11-1835.[3]
Robbins, Caleb, Philadelphia—Hannah Shreve, 11-19-1818.[3]
Richet, William—Sarah Allen, 11-16-1829.[3]
Sharp, Joseph—Annie Willits (d. James, 2d), 1772.[11]
Sheene, John—Katherine Gale, Mar. 3, 1745.[1]
Shinn, Isaac—Frances Vaughn, 12-1-1825.[3]
Smith, John—Rebecca Borden, 9-13-1874 [8]
Stratton, Stacey—Hannah Lippincott, 2-20-1796.[3]
Taylor, John B.—Susan D. Woolman, 9-27-1832.[3]
   John Gardiner—Rebecca H. Ballinger, 3-22-1849.[10]
Thomas, Seth—Elizabeth Borton, 2-28-1774.[1]
Till, John—Anne Banks, 9-16-1784.[1]
Varnon, James—Anne Enoch, 4-12-1783.[1]
Weitzel, John—Tabitha Morris, both Philadelphia, 12-25-1771.[8]
Willhouse, George—Mary Hill, Nov. 9, 1685.[1]
Woodrow, Thomas—Sarah Muckelvane, 1-30-1800.[3]
Woolston, Daniel—Martha Ridgway, 12-8-1814.[3]

CORRECTIONS

Bartlett, Joseph—Ann P. Willits (d. Thomas, Jr.), 1826.[11]
Bishop, Andrew—Margaret Sutton, Oct. 20, 1738.[8]
Branson, William White, Rev.—Mary Isabelle Clark, 8-5-1855.[8]
Burton, William—Emelia Troth, 8-24-1821.[3]
Carwood (top of page 90) should be Garwood.
Consolly, Barney A.—Harriet Smith, 4-25-1833.[3]
Stockton, Benjamin—Hannah Cowperthwaite, 11-29-1789.[3]
Taylor, Robert—Hannah Dillen, 12-28-1819.[3]
  Samuel—Susanna Horseman, Apr. 14, 1686.[5]
  William—Anna Taylor, 6-24-1754.[1]

INDEX TO BRIDES

Aarison—Ann, 193.

Aaronson—Achsah, 169; Eliza, 98; Elizabeth, 144; Hope, 123; Jane, 194; Louisa E , 106; Maria B., 199; Mary, 146, 250; Mary Ann, 14; Phebe Ann, 13; Rebecca, 176, 180, 241; Sarah, 13; Sarah P., 5.

Abbey—Ann. 95.

Abbott—Ann, 50, 171; Eliza. 244; Elizabeth, 52; Hannah, 8; Helena, 64; Jane, 38; Mary, 71; Rebecca, 227; Sarah, 244.

Abliven—Hope, 136

Abraham—Mary, 254; Sarah, 60.

Acey—Jemima, 41.

Ackley—Mary, 116.

Adams—Amelia, 232; Amy P., 140; Ann, 13, 67, 80, 159, 221; Barbara, 133; Bettina, 81; Charlotte, 137; Danos, 159; Deborah, 227; Diadame, 30; Dorcas, 201; Elizabeth, 9, 95, 183, 197; Hannah, 86, 141, 173, 174, 239; Levise, 29; Martha, 181; Mary, 19, 30, 57, 84; 91, 153, 203; Margaret Ann, 83; Martha, 236; Martha Ann, 177; Massy, 249; Mercy, 83, 113; Phebe, 31, 140; Rachel, 162; Rebecca, 164; Sarah, 176; Susanna, 133; Susannah, 98.

Adare—Margaret, 172.

Addams—Clarissa, 86; Margery, 25.

Addis—Ann, 72.

Addiss—Bridget, 174.

Adeir—Mary, 63.

Adinson—Sarah, 110.

Agnew—Margaret, 183.

Albertson—Hannah, 143; Mary Ann, 216.

Alburtice—Sarah, 243.

Alcot—Hester, 25.

Alcott—Ann, 196; Elizabeth, 146; Jane, 22; Margaret, 232; Meribah, 47; Rebecca, 79; Sarah, 47.

Alcutt, Mary, 113; Rebecca Ann, 28

Alday, Alice, 254.

Aldridge, Michael, 213.

Alexander—Mary, 167.
Alkman—Elizabeth, 116.
Alkut—Hannah, 9.
Allcot—Martha, 27.
Allcott—Elizabeth, 174, 196.
Allen—Agnes, 172; Ann, 33, 48, 84, 109, 134, 196, 200; Anne, 140; Augusta, 47; Betsey, 9; Catharine, 35; Charlotte, 235; Deborah, 14; Eliza. 63, 198; Elizabeth, 8, 32, 195, 228; Elma, 201; Emeline, 54; Hannah, 80, 111, 189, 227, 230; Harriet, 165; Jane, 198, 253; Lydia, 157; Margaret, 30, 163; Margery, 194; Maria, 218; Marietta, 95; Mary, 23, 45, 84, 94, 146, 205, 217; Mary A., 20; Massey, 88; Mercy, 16; Meribah, 171; Paulina, 148; Rachel, 256; Rebecca, 49, 228; Rebecca L., 161; Rhoda, 162; Sarah, 60, 237, 25; Sarah Ann, 249.
Allin—Nancy, 196.
Allingbury—Sarah, 113.
Allinson—Elizabeth, 45, 180.
Allison—Eliza, 207; Elizabeth, 215; Mary, 14, 121; Phebe, 72; Sarah, 72.
Alloway(s)—Elizabeth, 97, 175, 227; Hannah, 181; Isabel 178; Judith, 45; Martha, 31; Phebe, 237; Sarah, 221, 246; Taressa, 28.
Almon—Rebecca, 142.
Alston—Rachel, 176.
Alton—Sarah, 51.
Ambruster—Elizabeth, 55.
Amish—Martha Ann, 121.
Ammerman—Jenny, 164.
Anderson—Ann, 109, 212; Eliza, 106, 205; Elizabeth, 27, 31, 102, 111, 209; Hannah, 188; Hester, 249; Lydia, 117; Margaret, 8; Maria, 20; Mary 97, 98; Matilda, 53; Phebe, 119; Sarah, 10, 105; 206, 249; Sara A., 69.
Andrews—Amy, 25; Dorcas, 157; Edith, 8, 172; Elizabeth, 74, 164, 168; Esther, 143, 168; Hannah, 151; Lydia, 29; Kesiah, 207; Mahala, 151; Martha, 207; Mary, 16, 57, 174; Mary A., 122; Matilda, 94; Phebe, 167; Prudence, 20; Sarah, 158.
Andrewson—Lydia, 236.
Andries—Catharine, 73.
Annan—Sarah Anne, 137.
Anthony—Ann, 40; Catharine 15'; Matildy Ann, 24.
Antram—Abigail, 199, 207; Bathsheba, 17; Elizabeth, 83; Hannah, 167, 221; Kesiah, 140; Martha, 163; Mary, 51, 210, 239; Patience, 102; Rachel, 224; Sarah, 120; Susannah, 217.

Antrim—Abigail, 13; Bethia, 105; Hannah, 19, 194, 159; Hannah V., 90; Jane, 52; Martha, 10; Mary, 71, 131, 224; Rebecka, 52; Rebekah, 54; Susan K., 195.

Antrom—Mary, 167; Sarah, 59.

Antrum—Anne, 152; Elizabeth, 71, 89; Margaret, 61; Mary, 21; Rachel, 59; Rebecca T., 77.

Applegate—Abigail, 145; Achsah, 97; Hattie, 152; Jane, 107; Jane Ann, 97; Jemimah, 161; Lydia, 126; Mariah, 191; Rachel, 196; Sarah, 26, 81, 123.

Appleton—Ann, 18; Mary, 212.

Archer—Ann, 162; Betsey, 224; Elizabeth, 148; Mary, 81; Rebecca, 11.

Arey—Rachel, 162.

Arison—Hannah, 251; Mary, 13; Mary Ann, 92; Sarah, 13.

Armstrong—Ann, 38; Elizabeth, 116; Mary, 101, 108.

Arnal—Hannah, 97.

Arned—Elizabeth, 240.

Arnel—Amey, 137.

Arnell—Elizabeth, 174; Mary, 132.

Arney—Mary, 141, 144, 253; Martha, 190.

Arnold—Betsey, 83; Martha, 85; Rebecca, 51.

Asa—Hannah, 151.

Asay—Elizabeth, 205; Lydia, 196; Mary, 30; Sallie Black, 204.

Asey—Hepzibah, 35; Mary, 78; Polly, 196; Susan, 65.

Ash—Mary, 240.

Ashard—Ann, 101.

Ashbrook—Hannah, 97; Mary, 16.

Ashburn—Elizabeth, 166.

Ashead—Eleanor, 39; Sarah, 254.

Ashird—Mary, 188.

Ashmore—Ann, 30; Catherine, 177; Elizabeth, 211; Jane, 96; Mary Ann, 113.

Ashton—Elizabeth, 113; Hannah, 153; Jemima, 107; Mary, 51, 247; Sarah, 180; Susannah, 233.

Ashwood—Ester, 28.

Assa—Hannah, 252.

Asson—Allice, 134; Hannah, 161; Mercy, 47.

Atkinson—Abigail, 13, 71, 177; Alice, 29; Ann, 66, 194, 238; Anna, 129, 203; Anne, 200; Beulah, 173; Christian, 247; Cora Anna, 67; Elizabeth, 79; 129, 180, 204, 242; Hannah, 42, 51, 54, 137; Hannah Ann, 93; Hester, 195; Hezekiah, 240; Hope, 82, 191, 193; Jane, 127;

Atkinson—Keziah, 197; Leonia, 131; Lydia, 130, 138; Martha, 190; Mary, 29, 32, 63, 100, 113, 126, 211, 215; Mercy, 106; Rachel, 48, 71, 95, 131; Rebecca, 35, 60, 111, 218; Sarah, 12, 107, 163; Sarah Ann, 162; Sibilla, 172; Susan, 224; Susanna, 189.

Aucker—Mabelle, 34.

Augburn, Eveline, 94.

Austin—Abigail, 67, 178; Ann, 7, 160; 235; Eliza, 102; Elizabeth, 101, 103, 171; Esther, 253; Hannah, 14, 40, 92, 203, 230, 244; Hester, 105; Jane, 206, 221; Judith, 14; Lydia, 6, 203, 255; Martha, 115, 120; Mary, 142, 213, 237; Patience, 162; Phebe, 109, 185; Rebecca, 292; Sarah, 8, 101, 102, 116; Sarah Ann, 28, 234; Sibilla, 160; Susannah, 202; Tamar, 202; Vesti, 194; Zilpha, 182.

Ayres—Ann, 166; Phebe Ann, 36; Sarah, 54.

Babcock—Margaret, 70.

Babbleton—Jane, 127.

Bableton—Nancy, 196.

Backster—Mary, 7, 121.

Bacon—Eleanor, 101; Elizabeth, 212, 224; Hannah, 178; Martha 178.

Baggesgaard—Christine, 98.

Bagley—Mary, 236.

Bailey—Eliza, 232; Mary, 179; Rhoda, 136.

Bain—Margaret Little, 135; Mary Elizabeth, 86.

Barid—Martha, 120.

Baker—Ann C., 15; Elizabeth, 41, 121; Hannah, 47, 86; Rachel, 125; Sarah, 25, 254.

Balanger—Elizabeth, 212; Judith, 209; Marjorie, 99; Phebe, 190.

Balantine—Christine, 216.

Baldin—Prudence, 11,

Ball—Annie Odenheimer, 98; Elizabeth, 211.

Ballanger—Rebecca, 102.

Ballenger—Charity, 70; Elizabeth, 14; Mary, 40, 246; Rebecca, 181, 243.

Ballinger—Ann, 245; Bathsheba, 160; Elizabeth, 103, 125, 142, 246; Esther, 32; Hannah, 246; Mary, 90, 97, 185; Phebe Eliz, 109; Rebecca, 256; Sarah, 61, 143; Sibbillah, 231; Susannah, 256.

Balm—Mary Taylor, 133.

Banks—Anne, 256

Barbarouse—Eliza, 56; Frances, 23.

Barber—Margaret, 92; Mary, 165; Sarah, 135.

Barbiss—Margaret, 25.

Barcalow—Mary Ann, 217.
Barclay—Laura Christine, 236.
Bard—Catherine, 44; Mary, 120; Mary Martha, 41.
Bareford—Eliza, 206, Elizabeth, 151; Rachel, 137; Sarah, 248.
Barkenof—Anne. 236.
Barker—Esther, 82; Patience, 48.
Barklay—Rachel, 59.
Barnes—Lydia, 76; Phebe Ann, 17.
Barnhill—Jane, 185.
Barns—Elizabeth, 80.
Barrenhart—Betsey, 27.
Barret(t)—Anne, 213; Mariah, 76; Rebecca, 222; Sarah, 7.
Barrington—Alice, 165; Susan. 70.
Barris—Margaret, 74.
Barry—Alice, 159; Mary, 81.
Bartlett—Elizabeth, 12; Mary, 245; Phebe, 190; Sarah, 68; Susannah, 118.
Bartling—Mary Ann, 191.
Barton—Margaret, 33; Mary, 23, 81; Rachel, 63; Sarah, 180, 184, 245; Sarah Ann, 23.
Bass—Anne, 177; Catharine, 19; Jane, 6; Mary, 133; Rebecca, 48; Sarah, 91.
Basnett—Anna, 189; Elizabeth, 88.
Basset(t)—Hannah, 43; Marget, 198; Mary, 157; Rebecca, 248.
Bateman—Sarah, 181.
Bates—Achsah, 84; Adaline, 134; Ann, 231, 235; Charlotte, 163; Elizabeth, 28, 146; Hannah, 133, 175; Judith, 28; Lydia, 29; Mary, 81; Polly, 219; Rachel, 196; Sarah, 12, 86.
Bath—Anne, 213.
Batselor—Jerusa, 241.
Batso—Hannah, 248.
Battison—Susannah, 75.
Batton—Mary, 55.
Baughman—Annie, 52.
Bavis—Elizabeth, 189.
Baxter—Ann, 116; Elizabeth, 162; Margaret, 205; Priscilla, 42; Sarah, 96.
Bayley—Sarah, 80.
Baylis—Elizabeth, 184.
Beakes—Sarah, 180
Beaman—Elizabeth, 42.

Beats—Rosity, 13.
Beatty—Elizabeth, 62; Ellen, 220; Lilla, 83.
Beck—Ann, 229; Catharine, 150; Elizabeth, 87; Hannah; 93, 98; Mary, 244.
Becket(t)—Mary, 116; Sarah, 227.
Bee—Rebecca, 234.
Beebe—Elizabeth, 162.
Beham—Sarah, 164.
Belange—Mary, 56.
Belanger—Christian. 169, 207; Marjorie, 245; Ruth, 190.
Belford—Martha, 233.
Bell—Mary Ann, 43; Mary Jane, 157; Priscilla, 114, 150; Sarah, 204; Tabitha, 106.
Bellford—Rebecca, 124.
Belliss—Hannah, 201.
Benezet—Elizabeth, 215; Susan, 19.
Bennet(t)—Charity, 54; Deborah, 82, 120; Elizabeth, 46, 64, 65, 81, 108, 233; Martha, 88, 216; Mary, 96, 131, 137, 194; Rebekkah, 199; Rhodia, 122; Ruth, 42; Sarah, 54, 113, 206, 230, 247; Susan, 36; Susannah, 70, 77; Thankful, 22,
Benneworth—Sarah, 14.
Benton—Mary, 122.
Berbin—Mary, 200.
Berdin—Elizabeth, 224.
Bergen—Eleanor, 168.
Berredale—Mary, 234.
Berrey—Atlantic, 151.
Berry—Elizabeth, 21; Hannah, 248; Sarah, 13, 171.
Berryman—Margaret, 16; Martha, 106; Mary, 244.
Beswick—Mary, 189; Priscilla, 119.
Betts—Anne, 167; Elizabeth, 45.
Beverland—Elizabeth, 149.
Bevington—Elizabeth, 67.
Bevis—Elizabeth, 235.
Bickham—Anne, 31, 33.
Bickly—Dorothy, 137.
Biddle, Elizabeth, 245; Charlotta, 23; Rebecca Ann, 99; Sarah, 159.
Bidelle—Achsah, 102.
Bigelow—Rebecca, 135.
Billings—Sarah, 95, 194.

Biles—Ann, 162; Ruth, 238.
Bills—Mary, 153.
Bingham—Bridget, 238; Mary, 71.
Binney—Florence, 134.
Birch—Jane, 178; Mary, 214.
Bird—Deborah, 42; Elizabeth, 226; Rebecca, 163; Ruth, 250.
Birdsall—Abigail, 57; Anna, 201; Dorothy, 166; Jane, 226; Mary, 223; Rachel 245.
Birdsell—Hannah, 251; Mary, 129.
Birdsill—Ann, 68.
Birn—Mary, 9.
Bishop—Abigail, 87; Ann, 160, 212; Anna, 150; Anne, 181; Catharine, 141; Charlotte, 137; Diadema, 62; Eliza, 253; Elizabeth, 76, 99, 128, 196, 221, 251; Emeline, 123; Hannah, 141, 182, 227; Hester, 76; Lovinia, 15; Martha, 218; Mary, 13, 14, 27, 34, 35; Mary Ann, 235; Rachel, 120, 242; Rebecca 79; Rebeckah, 29; Sarah, 7, 71, 85, 164, 221; Sidney, 162.
Bispham—Abigail, 70; Ann, 152, 164; Anna, 44; Eliza, 165; Elizabeth, 22, 101, 108, 156; Hannah, 175; Harriet, 24; Margaret, 38, 167; Martha, 38; Mary, 168; Mary Chetwood, 140; Rebecca, 175, 210; Ruth, 79; Sarah, 161, 204.
Bittle—Lydia, 118.
Birt—Elizabeth, 180.
Black—Achsah, 5; Ada, 156; Ame, 134; Amy, 5; Anna Clark, 166; Charlotte, 23; Christina, 144; Julia, 19; Margaret, 20; Mary, 163, 185; Rebecca, 240, 246.
Blackwell—Patience, 195.
Blackwood—Elizabeth, 37.
Blake(s)—Elizabeth, 85; Elouisa, 245; Lydia, 196.
Blakely—Margaret, 249.
Blain—Sophia, 240.
Blair—Margaret, 244; Mary, 222.
Blanchard—Mary Ann, 118.
Blantford—Hannah, 150.
Blantley—Sarah, 119.
Bleth—Margaret, 172.
Blouk—Ann, 249.
Bodger—Elizabeth, 80.
Bodine—Abigail, 52, 121; Ann, 49; Ann Maria, 84; Margaret, 145; Mary, 39, 105; Sarah, 8.
Bogar—Sarah, 117.

Bogart—Annie, 178; Levina, 233; Lydia, 70; **Rachel, 41.**
Boger—Mary, 27.
Bogin—Ann, 151..
Bowling—Mary, 238.
Bolsworthy—Patience, 64.
Bolten—Mary, 131.
Boltenhouse—Ann, 248; Mary, 213.
Bolton—Elizabeth, 127; Sarah, 208.
Boman—Parthenia, 179.
Bond—Hannah, 203; Harriet, 41; Jane, 17.
Bonnalt—Mary, 47.
Bonney—Frances, 103.
Bonsall—Laura, 149; Sarah, 108.
Boody—Mary, 56.
Boone—Ann, 66.
Booy—Hannah, 101.
Booze—Sarah, 234.
Boozer—Ann, 220; Rachel, 203.
Boozerth—Ann, 247.
Borden—Abigail, 19, 28; Achsah, 44; Amy, 16; **Amye, 23; Ann Eliza, 88;** Caroline, 108; Elinor, 168; Elizabeth, **67, 110, 135, 197;** Hannah, 118, 138, 158, 223; Innocent, 26; **Jane, 82; Margaret, 8;** Mary, 54, 138, 197, 234; Patience, 8; Phebe, 88; **Rachel, 138;** Rebecca, 85, 195, 256; Sarah, 18.
Boreen—Sarah, 8
Borllen, **Ann,** 229.
Borrodail—Hester, 235; Rebecca, 15; Sara, 29.
Borton—Abigail, 222; Ann, 26, 85, **125, 210; Charity, 150;** Elizabeth, 157, 256; Esther, 157, 221, 231; Hannah, 14, 61, **175;** Hope, 220; Lydia, 31; Martha, 115, 243; Mary, 26, 68, 74, 146, **151; Phebe, 175;** Prudence, 190; Rachel, 25; Rebecca, 151; **Sarah, 199, 214, 220.**
Bossom—Mary, 235.
Bostido—Judith, 69.
Both—Harriet, 215.
Boulton—Amy, 189; Mary, 133; **Phebe, 29; Priscilla, 33; Rhoda, 59, 236.**
Bounds—Charity, 122.
Bourton—Elizabeth, 68, 250; Esther, 109.
Boutenhouse, Mary, 213
Bowen—Esther, 223; Joanna, 225; Mary, 40; Priscllla, 167; **Sarah** 106, 160; Susannah, 178.

BURLINGTON COUNTY MARRIAGES

Bower(s)—Anne, 236; Margaret, 44; Mary, 200; Sarah, 22; Sarah Ann, 11.

Bowker—Ann, 31, 130; Beulah, 179; Elizabeth, 6, 101; Fanny, 109; Hannah, 236; Harriet, 92; Hope, 82; Margaret, 88; Mary, 86, 125, 138; Rhoda, 239; Tamar, 45.

Bowlby—Mary, 251.

Bowles—Sarah, 59.

Bowman—Isabella, 137; Mary, 119; Sarah, 253.

Bowne—Abigail, 110; Eleanor, 117; Sarah, 145.

Boyd(e)—Hannah, 122; Martha, 145; Mary, 7.

Boyer—Grace, 80; Ruth, 24.

Boyes—Margaret, 111; Sarah, 165.

Boynton—Esther, 36.

Boys—Jane, 31.

Bozarth—Barbara, 104.

Bozell—Esther, 251.

Bozorth—Abigail, 228; Bathsheba, 208; Cybelah, 82; Mary Ann, 5.

Bozough—Agness, 70.

Bozworth—Elizabeth, 215; Mary, 137.

Bozzel—Sarah, 197.

Brackney—Abigail, 127; Ann, 126; Elizabeth, 20; Janet, 130; Mary, 248.

Braddock—Ann, 100; Elizabeth, 202; Frances, 220; Hannah, 49, 94, 171; Jemima, 25, 29, 107; Martha, 177; Mary, 25, 249; Phebe, 102; Rachel, 25, 68, 243.

Bradley—Rebecca, 212.

Bradshaw—Rachel, 56.

Bradway—Grace, 145; Hannah, 28; Sarah, 51.

Brady—Mary, 221.

Bragg—Mary Eliza, 106.

Brailsford—Letitia, 111.

Braithwaite—Agnes, 24.

Brandenburg—Margaret, 114.

Branin(g)—Abigail, 45; Martha, 8; Penniah, 104.

Brannen—Theodosia, 93.

Brannin(g)—Elizabeth, 12, 215; Isabella, 93; Martha, 7; Mary, 225; Sarah, 197.

Branson—Allice, 179; Amy, 219; Ann, 45; Elizabeth, 249; Mary, 54, 222; Mirian, 167; Nancy, 132; Sarah, 169.

Brass—Rachel, 133.

Brayman—Eliza, 111; Elizabeth, 223; Mary, 238; Rachel, 32.

Brazington—Olive, 87.
Breeds—Mary, 58.
Brelsford—Anne. 163; Lydia, 232.
Brethwaite—Mary Ann, 10.
Breton—Elizabeth, 47.
Bretton—Sarah, 176
Brewer—Ann. 49, 57; Hannah, 61; Lucy, 104.
Brian—Margaret, 54; Rebecca, 185.
Briant—Mary, 10; Rachel, 10; Rebecca, 43; Sarah, 70, 208.
Brick—Anna, 217; Rebecca, 119.
Bride—Deborah, 83.
Brigs—Ann, 140.
Briggs—Emelia, 9; Hannah, 30; Lydia, 178; Mary, 72, 199, 234; Rebecca, 58; Rebeckah, 256; Sarah, 12, 101, 116; Sarah Ann, 94; Theodocia, 134.
Bright—Martha, 239.
Brighton—Rebecca, 154.
Brinker—Susan, 237.
Bristow—Catharine, 158; Phillis, 53.
Britain—Susanna, 26.
Brittain—Abigall, 167; Elizabeth, 51, 167.
Britten—Mary, 133.
Brittenham—Rebecca, 231.
Brittin—Sarah, 54.
Britton—Abigail, 230; Charlotte, 62; Harriet, 233; Mary, 255.
Broadhome—Venah, 167.
Brock—Abigail, 66; Ann, 94; Deborah, 32; Elizabeth, 253; Hannah, 55; Martha, 9; Mary, 32; 250, 255; Rebecca, 105; Sophia, 22.
Brockhay—Rachel, 56.
Brockney—Mary, 30.
Bromley—Martha, 17.
Brookfield—Mary, 182.
Brooks—Elizabeth, 28, 128, 144, 226, 230; Esther, 211; Garthvey, 155; Jane, 222; Margaret, 181; Mary, 85, 151, 153; Rebecca, 155; Sarah, 174; Sarah Ann, 18.
Brown(e)—Alice, 134, 203; Amelia, 185; Ann, 59, 74, 148, 218; Anna, 83; Anne, 177; Bathsheba, 26; Beulah, 105; Beulah Scattergood, 246; Catherine, 117; Cathern, 183; Charity, 15; Edith, 181; Elizabeth, 99, 103, 135, 177, 211, 213; Euphemia, 118; Hannah, 190, 196, 223, 226 242; Isabell, 223; Jane, 168; Jemima, 61, 68, 101; Julian, 224; Katherina, 179; Leah, 72; Louisa, 194; Lydia, 97, 243,

247; Margaret, 47, 88; Maria, 206; Mariam, 102; Martha, 51, 217, 231; Mary, 33, 108, 128, 174, 216, 224, 236; Mary Ann, 66; Mary Jane. 55; Nancy. 115; Neomy, 132; Pamelia. 126; Phebe, 197; Phebe Ann, 174; Prudence, 53; Rachel, 42, 189; Rebecca, 20, 123, 189, 207; Rody, 52; Ruth Ann, 54; Sarah, 17, 41, 65, 93, 127, 198. 237; Sarah Ann. 168; Susan, 41, 128; Susanna, 26; Susannao, 182.

Browning—Catharinah. 186; Margaret, 161; Rebecca, 216.

Bronson—Mary, 111.

Bruce—Anne, 116.

Bruere—Hannah, 252.

Brundidge—Jemima, 122.

Brush—Ann, 6; Lorina, 6; Margaret, 155.

Bruson—Ann, 126.

Brussom—Mary, 175.

Bryan—Ann, 193; Elizabeth, 100; Esther, 161; Hannah, 53; Mary, 118, 185, 188, 220; Rebecca, 10, 26; Sarah, 132.

Bryant— Mary, 153; Minnie Emma, 61; Rebekkah, 10, 106; Sarah, 80.

Buchanan—Elizabeth, 122.

Buck—Ann, 85; Mary, 244.

Buckell—Amey, 2)7.

Buckman—Phebe, 131; Ruth, 108.

Budd—Anna, 51; Anne, 222; Elizabeth, 63, 69, 206, 210, 254; Hannah, 187; Harriet Watson, 132; Lydia, 91; Margaret, 22, 156; Maria Burr, 19; Martha, 45; Mary, 142, 202, 223; Rachel, 28; Rebecca, 51, 136, 170, 215, 216; Sally Ann, 22; Sarah, 35, 96, 98, 206; Susan, 41; Theodosia, 130.

Budden—Deborah, 34; Mary, 181; Sarah, 192.

Buil—Jane, 247.

Buff—Jane, 149.

Buffin—Ann, 33, 244; Anne, 168; Grace, 135; Lavinia, 94; Margaret, 32; Mary, 43, 193, 212; Rebecca, 33; Sarah, 237.

Bugbee—Lida, 150.

Bugbie— Elizabeth, 67.

Bull—Sarah, 51.

Bullen—Mary, 221.

Bullers—Ann, 72.

Bullock—Lydia, 250; Margaret, 50, 227.

Bulong—Hannah, 32.

Bunting—Acsah, 184; Amy, 156; Deborah, 243; Eliza, 233; Elizabeth, 50, 81; Hannah, 138, 189, 236; Louisa, 130; Lydia, 36; Mary

Louisa, 24; Phebe, 79; Rebecca, 13, 253; Sarah, 94, 109, 120, 163, 224, 229.
Bunn—Rachel, 169; Sarah, 187.
Burcalow—Ann, 122.
Burcham—Ann, 203; Annie, 45.
Burden—Hannah, 106.
Burdin—Mary, 23.
Burdsal(l)—Avis, 84; Eleanor, 131; Elizabeth, 50; Lydia, 251; Phebe, 36.
Burdsell—Ruth, 50.
Burge—Rejoice, 107.
Burgess—Ann, 98.
Burgis—Anne, 255.
Burk—Amy, 172; Ann, 102; Anne, 44.
Burkee—Sarah, 65.
Burkin(s)—Anna Meria, 239; Catharine, 204.
Burling—Rachel, 210.
Burne(s)—Mary, 181; Mary, 217; Sarah, 143.
Burnet(t)—Joyce, 193; Zilpah, 187.
Burns—Anna, 240; Elinor, 205; Hannah, 159; Margaret, 154; Mary, 113, 215; Mary Jane, 230; Sarah, 124.
Burr—Abigail, 219; Achsah, 38, 52; Ann, 16, 63; Beulah, 241; Edith, 17; Eliza, 206; Elizabeth, 112, 198; 204; 251; Hannah, 231; Harriet, 248; Keziah, 190; Louisa, 169; Lydia, 145; Martha, 102; Mary, 23, 69, 107, 142, 160, 189, 205; Matilda, 122; Merriam, 211; Parthenia, 37; Priscilla, 131; Rachel, 6, 245; Rebecca, 34, 128; Sarah, 31, 100, 105, 195, 251.
Burrodall—Sarah, 241.
Burrey—Jane, 122.
Burrodail—Elizabeth, 33.
Burrough(s)—Ann, 152; Anna, 185; Deborah, 142; Elizabeth, 220; Esther, 21; Grace, 31; Hannah, 93, 173, 218; Martha, 228; Mary, 161; Rachel, 212; Rebecca, 55; Sarah, 76, 93 112; Susanna, 110.
Burrows—Mary, 25, 245.
Burtall—Mary, 56.
Burtis—Emaline, 189; Mary, 115; Rebecca, 195; Sarah, 238; Susannah, 78.
Burton—Ann, 110; Mary, 9.
Busby—Elizabeth, 63.
Buson—Charlotte, 124.
Busson—Achsah, 15.

Bustil(l)—Ann, 127; Mary, 64.

Butcher—Ann, 18; Bathsheba, 254; Catharine, 166; Damaras, 254; Eliza Ann, 233; Elizabeth, 145, 174, 256; Esther, 10; Frances, 10; Hannah, 142; Margarat, 35, 109; Mary, 25, 161, 169, 181, 198; Patience, 245; Prudence, 161; Rebekkah, 189; Sarah, 12, 189; Susannah, 25.

Butler—Ann, 38, 120; Betsy, 184; Eliza, 65; Elizabeth, 127; Mary, 74, 117, 192, 249; Phebe, 126; Rachel 200; Sarah, 105, 131.

Butt—Jimia, 177.

Butterfield—Ann, 184; Margaret, 132; Sarah, 13, 159.

Butterworth—Anne, 59; Hannah, 148; Mary, 112; Sarah, 185, 220; Sophia, 125.

Buttler, 115.

Buzby—Anne, 175; Elizabeth, 102; Esther, 102; Hannah, 40; Jane, 37; Lidya, 79; Mary, 43; Mary, 57, 58, 182; Rebecca, 53; Sarah, 243; Sarah Ann, 59; Vashti, 134.

Byles—Elizabeth Anna, 72.

Byrne—Mary, 180.

Caffary—Sarah Ann, 11.

Cahoon—Ann, 215.

Caldwell—Mary, 188.

Calvert—Mary, 42, 80.

Calvin—Jane, 96; Lydia, 212.

Cambern—Mary, 154.

Cameron—Sarah Lydia, 98.

Cammel—Eliza, 15; Hope, 84.

Camp—Ann, 77; Margaret, 222; Rachel, 161.

Campbell—Esther, 137; Hannah, 26, Rachel, 84.

Campion—Sarah, 41, 117, 128.

Cannon—Marg't, 31.

Cardiffe—Mary, 138.

Cardwell—Elizabeth Ray, 173.

Carlisle—Rebekkah, 197.

Carll—Hannah, 16.

Carman—Ann, 191; Anre, 35, 225; Edith, 132; Hannah, 195; Levina, 68; Lucy, 208; Margaret, 217; Mary, 110, 120, 169, 249; Sarah, 134; Sarah Ann, 118.

Carns—Lydia, 68.

Carpenter—Mary, 18; Rachel, 203.

Carr—Ann, 41; Elizabeth, 209; Hannah, 156, 248; Isabella, 10; Issabel, 124; Margrit, 86; Mary, 141, 200; Naomi, 134; Rhoda, 72;

Sarah, 8, 101, 249.
  Carragern—Nancy, 31.
  Carragin—Mary, 238.
  Carre—Agnes, 222.
  Carry—Elizabeth, 136.
  Carslake—Ann, 132.
  Carsner—Jane, 178.
  Carson—Amy, 225; Brazilla, 16; Eliza, 184; Elizabeth Jane, 154; Hannah, 226; Rachel, 80; Sarah, 30; Susanna, 9.
  Carter—Abigail, 226; Acsah, 29; Ann, 39; Anna, 204; Catharine, 217; Charlotte, 179; Desire, 167; Elizabeth, 35, 127; Ellen, 95; Hannah, 61; Jane, 60; Lavinia, 148; Lydia, 205; Mary, 36, 38, 49, 64; Parmelia, 51; Sarah, 134, 241; Susanna, 20.
  Carty—Elizabeth, 34, 199; Hannah, 123; Mary, 104, 187; Sarah, 66, 104.
  Cary—Mary, 120.
  Case—Rhoda, 254.
  Caskey—Hannah, 42.
  Cassada—Mary, 120.
  Cassaway—Mary, 200.
  Cassel—Diana, 76.
  Cassida—Mary, 67.
  Casteline—Harriet, 147.
  Castle—Susannah, 48.
  Cathcard—Rebecca, 134.
  Cathcart—Margaret, 221; Rebecca, 21.
  Cattel(l)—Jane, 149; Mary, 87, 103, 164; Mary Ann, 233.
  Cattle—Beulah 131; Hope, 134.
  Cavaleer—Ann, 65; Hester, 88; Mary, 140.
  Cawen—Elizabeth, 23.
  Cawman—Mary, 69.
  Cesar—Hannah, 44.
  Chamberlain—Jane, 195; Keturah, 85; Meriam, 225; Mary, 73; Sarah, 133.
  Chamberlane—Anne, 122.
  Chamebrlin—Ann, 247; Sarah, 12.
  Chambers—Ann, 124; Eliza, 154; Elizabeth Eayres, 204, Frances, 12; Lydia, 78; Martha, 129; Mary, 63, 118, 142, 205, 221; Mary Ann, 227; Rebecca, 235; Sarah, 96, 123.
  Channell—Lydia, 76.
  Chapman—Ann, 55; Elizabeth, 124; Hannah, 144; Kesiah, 160;

Mary, 174, 237; Patience 238; Rebecca, 46.
  Charles—Martha, 63.
  Charlton—Nancy, 37.
  Charmelee—Sarah Ann, 126.
  Chase(y)—Martha Ann, 148; Sarah, 33.
  Cheamealy—Margaret, 231.
  Cheed—Hannah, 171.
  Cheeseman—Mary, 28, 73.
  Cheesman—Cecelia, 12; Sarah, 240.
  Chemaly—Anne, 251.
  Chemilly—Susannah, 48.
  Chequvine—Mary, 123.
  Cherrington—Mary, 76.
  Cheshire—Ann, 123; Experience, 217; Sarah, 167.
  Chester—Basheba, 76; Hannah, 14.
  Chew—Sarah, 5.
  Child(s)—Amy, 215; Beulah Ann, 133; Eliza, 95; Hannah, 144; Mary, 144; Rebecca, 143.
  Chipman—Christian, 35; Mary, 145.
  Chub(b)—Ann, 58: Martha, 34.
  Chumelea—Hannah, 50.
  Church—Rebecca, 118, Rebecca, 182; Sarah, 205.
  Churchman—Emma, 112.
  Churmley—Catharine, 176.
  Ciger—Elizabeth, 44.
  Circuit—Hannah, 246.
  Clackberen—Catharine, 124.
  Clair—Hannah, 32.
  Clanagan—Mary Ann, 12.
  Clark(e)—Amelia, 219; Anne, 53, 213; Elizabeth, 146, 236, 242; Ella, 220; Emeline, 72; Hannah, 34, 35, 79; Josephine, 191; Josephine Kille, 133; Mary, 70, 93, 240; Mary Isabelle, 29; Mary Jane, 59; Nancy, 132; Olive, 46; Phebe, 104; Rachel, 46; Rebecca, 54; Sarah, 97, 104; Susan, 95; Susannah, 225; Theodosia, 206.
  Clay—Anne, 196; Betty, 195; Hannah, 229.
  Claypool(e)—Deborah, 32; Hannah, 15; Lllie, 233; Mary, 162; Pearl Russell, 186.
  Clayton—Ann, 41; Catharine, 94, 111: Charlotte, 96; Content, 28; Elizabeth, 186; Hannah, 90; Honour, 32; Joanna, 126; Prudence, 185.
  Clear—Ann, 173; Edith, 120; Margaret, 95.
  Clemens—Hannah, 144.

Clement—Mary, 33; Ruth, 104.
Clevenger—Catherine, 157; Eliza, 175; Elizabeth, 13; **Emma, 14**. Hannah, 68, 131; Huldy, 172; Jane, 197; Mary, 128; **Rebecca, 52**; Sarah, 21; Ursilla, 141.
Clifford—Esse, 143; Hannah, 148.
Clifton—Ann, 225; Maria, 251; Susannah, 172.
Cline—Ann, 116, 221; Elizabeth Atkinson, 130; **Margaret, 165**; Mary, 66, 70 89, 114, 121; Rachel, 8; Sarah, 151.
Clinton—Eliz., 42; Phebe, 11; Rebecca 162.
Cliver—Elizabeth, 42, 168; Mary, 123, 218; Sarah, 61, 225.
Cloin—Deborah, 111.
Clothier—Elizabeth, 212; Sarah Jane, 59.
Clouts—Sarah, 186.
Clutch—Martha, 227; Mary, 28, 167; Sarah, 89, 121, 128.
Clymer—Elizabeth, 117.
Coal—Hannah, 43; Sarah, 103; Susan, 11.
Coata—Hannah, 53.
Coate(s)—Catharine, 18; Edith, 103, 165; Elizabeth Ann, 243; Hannah, 112; Josephine, 92; Lydia, 190; Mary, 100, 185, 198; Rebecca, 170; Sarah, 103, 107, 139.
Cobb—Deborah, 180.
Cock—Kitturah, 83.
Cogall—Rachel, 104.
Cohn—Hannah, 119.
Colbreath—Esther, 235.
Cole(s)—Ann, 103; Charity, 106; Damaris, 173; Eliza, 62; Elizabeth, 37, 234; Hannah, 26, 142, 207; Harriet, 33; Kesiah, 140; Lucy, 57; Martha, 82; Mary, 50, 151, 201, 230; Mary Greenleaf, 69; Rachel, 124; Rebecca, 152, 161; Sarah, 126; Sarah Ann, 103, 160; Susan, 116; Susanna, 35.
Coleet—Hannah, 240.
Coleman—Abigail, 214; Elizabeth, 170; **Mary Ann, 58**; Mercy, 184; Rebecca, 242.
Colket—Hannah, 42.
Colkitt—Mary, 206.
Collier—Margaret, 139; Sarah, 165.
Collins—Abigail, 143; Anne, 177; Elizabeth, 132, 226; Esther, 76; Georgie, 162; Grace, 21, 243; Hannah, 163; Lydia, 220; Jane, 81; Martha, 142; Mary, 26, 76, 135, 168, 221; Phebe, 177; Ruth, 16; Sarah, 18, 48, 112, 229; Susannah, 66, 89; Sybella, 92.
Colvin—Bethena, 246; Catherine, 184.

Combes—Rebecca, 99.
Compton—Ella, 45; Mary, 167, 213.
Conaro—Mary, 17.
Conder—Susannah, 237.
Condon—Eliza, 178.
Conel—Catherine, 148.
Coney—Jane, 108.
Congle—Elizabeth 161.
Conklan—Sarah, 86.
Conklin—Elinor, 240.
Conllin—Mary, 187.
Connar—Eleanor, 99.
Connaro—Elizabeth, 30.
Connarro(e)—Lydia, 62; Rebecca, 122; Sarah, 122.
Conner—Hannah, 172; Lydia, 201; Rachel, 58.
Conover—Catharine, 104, 201; Deleh, 123; Grace, 219; Phebe, 126.
Conrad—Evaline, 77.
Conrow—Abigail, 60; Beulah, 143; Eleanor, 21; Mary, 77, 115; Rebecca, 62, 116; Sarah, 103, 157.
Consolly—Caroline, 233.
Cony—Mary, 174.
Cohoon—Belinder, 147.
Cook(e)—Abigail, 244; Acksa, 73; Ann, 53, 159; Barbara, 177; Catharine, 232; Charity, 248; Charlotte, 195; Eliza, 140; Elizabeth, 159; Emeline, 164; Faith, 78; Hester, 179; Maria, 11; Mary, 62, 200; Mary Ann, 252; Plovine, 12; Rebecca, 82, 168; Sarah, 97.
Coombes—Rebecca, 99.
Coombs—Rebecca, 52.
Cooms—Susan, 125.
Coones—Ann, 185; Cloe, 52
Cooper—Ann, 158, 227, 251; Elizabeth, 53, 76; Hannah, 251; Jane, 46, 104; Maggie, 156; Mary, 13; Priscilla, 18; Rachel, 56; Sarah, 141.
Cope—Hannah, 91.
Coperthwaite—Rebecca, 89.
Copperthwait(e)—Ann, 244; Deborah, 54; Sybilla, 213.
Coppuck—Elizabeth, 46; Ellen Virginia, 128; Hannah, 26; Margaret Hollinshead, 179; Mary, 132; Rebecca, 140; Sarah, 158.
Core—Elizabeth, 193; Hannah, 85; Mary, 71, 243; Rebecca, 126, 139; Sarah, 165.
Corey—Alice, 140.

Corin—Lydia, 57.
Corless— Ann, 250; Exercise, 206.
Cornelius—Elizabeth, 98; Emeline, 217; Sarah, 244.
Cornish—Hanah, 212; Mary Ann, 105.
Corr—Mary Lavina, 95.
Corwine—Abigail, 59.
Coshell—Mary, 81.
Cosseboon—Sarah. 151.
Costill(e)—Hannah, 101; Rebecca, 39.
Cotten—Mary, 117.
Cotton—Ruth, 202; Susan, 82.
Coulson—Naomi, 118.
Cousins—Mary, 84.
Covenhoven—Martha, 113; Mary, 196, 230.
Coverley—Harriet, 182.
Coverly—Margaret, 105.
Covey—Ann, 245.
Coward—Alice, 32; Ann, 186; Elizabeth, 111, 208; **Mary, 227**; Rebecca, 21.
Cowgill—Jane, 141; Janett, 13; Mary, 208; Rachel, 250; Rebecca, 93; Sarah, 163.
Cowperthwaite—Abigail, 206; Ann, 8; Anna, 160; Ester, 87; Hannah, 219, 257; Martha, 8; Mary, 123; Phebe, 120; Sarah, 239.

Cox(e)— Amy, 54; Ann, 54; Anne 51, 111; Barbara, 138; Bythnia, 246; Eliza Smith, 30; Elizabeth, 51, 80, 127, 129, 155, 185, 205, 222; Ellinor, 175; Emily, 154; Fanny, 34; Hannah, 99, 157, 221; Ida Eliz., 89; Kesiah, 60; Kitty, 8, 53; Lavinia, 112; Leah, 126; Lydia, 239; Margaret, 174; Maria, 220; Marion, 247; Martha, 96, 141; Mary, 123, 145; Mary Rickey, 240; Mercy, 87; Meriam, 72; Naomi, 118; Pamy, 12; Patienbe, 38; Rebecca, 196, 207; Sarah, 34, 100, 104, 146, 149, 161.
Coyne—Mary, 130.
Cozens—Anne, 167; Sarah, 145.
Crachow—Mary Ann, 79.
Craft—Ann, 147; Charity, 51; Franklina, 7; Grace, 137; Hannah, 197; Margaret, 188; Mary, 74; Rebecca, 98.
Craig—Ann, 247; Ellzabeth, 195, 235; Mary, 59.
Cramer—Amy, 154; Ane, 27; Anna, 9; Bethiah, 214; Betsey, 213; Charlotte, 45; Elizabeth, 49; Julia, 151; Levina, 87; **Lydia, 88**; Margaret, 175, 185; Margarette, 126; Mary, 17, 43, 124, 147, 164, 198; Mary Ann, 183; Nancy, 83; Phebe, 162; Rachel, 139, 202;

Sarah, 56, 57, 109, 159, 172.

Crammer—Amy, 179; Ann, 90; Barthia, 239; Elizabeth, 35, 102; Esther, 225; Hope, 88; Josephine, 50; Judith, 245; Mary Adelaide, 69; Rebecca, 83; Sarah, 8, 19.

Crane—Ruth, 14.

Cranmer—Elizabeth, 200; Esther, 49; Grace, 52; Mary, 200; Mary Ann, 50; Meriah, 104; Rachel, 153; Sarah, 52, 161, 190.

Crawford—Eliza, 95; Elizabeth, 231; Mary, 60, 211; Rhoda, 64.

Creedy—Elizabeth, 184.

Creeley—Rebecca, 30.

Crevier—Ida Josephine, 65,

Cribbs—Jane, 216.

Cripple—Elizabeth, 250.

Cripps—Ann, 239; Hannah, 40; Martha, 159; Mary, 63, 69, 198; Sarah, 134; Theophila, 92; Virgin, 162, 181.

Crispen—Rebecca, 105; Sarah, 71.

Crispin—Abigail, 138; Ann, 28, 144; Dorothy, 37, 173; Hannah, 219; Margaret, 183; Martha, 246; Mary, 21, 189; Phebe, 122; Priscilla, 121; Rebecca, 19; Sylvia, 28.

Critch--Mary, 249.

Crocket—Margaret, 44.

Crockford—Hannah, 29; Mary, 170, 242.

Crockfort—Margaret, 106,

Cromwell—Deborah, 34; Elizabeth, 204; Euphemia, 34; Jane 32; Lydia, 97; Mary, 219.

Croner—Sarah, 41.

Crones—Hannah, 234.

Croney—Ann, 159.

Cronin—Elizabeth, 206; Mary, 18.

Crosby—Mary, 80; Rebekka, 90; Sarah 149.

Croshaw—Ann, 12; Rachel Price, 99; Sarah, 35, 254.

Crosher—Mary, 171.

Cross—Ann—232; Catharine, 217; Elizabeth, 113; Mary, 85, 138, 234; Sarah, 32, 240; Susannah, 179.

Crossby—Susannah, 19.

Crossley—Martha, 6.

Crow—Elizabeth, 215.

Crozier—Rachel, 97.

Crumwell—Eliza, 125.

Crushaw—Rebecca, 66.

Crusher—Ann, 11, 85, 234; Mary Ann, 125.

Cruson—Elizabeth, 255.
Cubberly—Lydia, 148; Deborah, 165; Sarah, 62.
Cummings—Julian, 227.
Cunningham—Ann, 204; Charlotte, 7; Elizabeth, 39, 97; Jemima, 79; Sarah, 204.
Curel—Elizabeth, 79.
Curlis—Hannah, 118.
Currey—Sarah, 26.
Curry—Tobitha, 232.
Curtis(s)—Ann, 114, 122; Ann Eliza, 75; Anna Bromhall, 183; Beulah, 160; Diadama, 171; Elizabeth, 14, 63, 82, 135, 155, 252; Harriet, 109, 147; Hester, 106; Jane, 45; Jerusha, 96; Margaret, 196; Mary, 109, 157; Mary Josephine, 155; Rachel, 103, 138, 232.
Curtus—Rebecca, 245,
Cushman—Mary, 51, 33.
Custer—Elizabeth, 97; Mary, 85; Sarah, 160, 193.
Cyphars—Mary, 211.
Dagworthy—Elizabeth, 79.
Daily—Mary, 65, 226.
Daly—Mary, 195.
Danally—Susannah, 20.
Daniels—Silva, 108.
Daniells—Lydia, 170.
Danielly—Deidamia, 243.
Darby—Ann, 56; Elizabeth, 54.
Darets—Louisa, 166.
Dark—Emily, 98.
Darling—Mary, 82.
Davenport—Anne, 64; Martha, 255; Mary, 90; Rebecca, 130.
Davidson—Christian, 9; Elizabeth, 38; Maria, 223.
Davis—Abigail, 191; Acsah, 155; Ann, 80, 183; Caroline, 168; Elizabeth, 54, 148, 203; Elmina, 191; Esther, 55; Hannah, 26, 97, 183; Jane, 189, 220; Lydia, 113; Martha, 25, 191; Mary, 35, 38, 104, 110, 114, 157, 224, 227, 255; Mercy, 233; Sarah, 53, 151; Susannah, 66, 93.
Davison—Catherine, 75; Mary, 121.
Dawson—Hope, 236; Julia, 81; Mary, 33, 89, 218; Rachel, 214.
Day—Esther, 199; Louisa, 26; Rachel, 125; Rebecca Ann, 168; Sarah, 18.
Daymond—Mary, 137.
Dayton—Ann, 67.

Deacon—Achsah, 234; Adeline, 229; Ann, 52; Annie, 143; Bathsheba, 127; Catharine, 56; Deborah, 30; Edith, 22; Elizabeth 117; Elizabeth Woolman, 249; Emily, 6; Jane, 88; Lydia, 131; Martha, 106, 206, Mary, 49, 56, 211; Mary Ann, 50; Meriam, 106; Rachel, 104; Rebecca, 241; Rebecca Zelley, 101; Sarah, 173; Susan, 55, 250.

Dean—Elizabeth, 225.

Deberd—Catherine, 25.

DeCamp—Charlotte, 73; Lydia, 108; Susan, 73.

Decker—Catherine, 124; Eliz, 87.

DeCow—Achsah, 226; Ann, 153; Anne, 168; Elizabeth, 64; Nancy, 123; Rebecca, 61, 161; Susan, 81.

Dalan—Ann, 203.

Delaplain(e)—Mary, 95, 190.

Delatush—Eleanor, 188; Elizabeth, 83; Sarah, 95.

Delong—Sarah, 186.

Demuth—Ann, 153.

Dennett—Mary, 40.

Dennis(s)—Alice, 233; Ann, 172, 219; Elizabeth, 235; Georgeanna, 218; Grace, 24; Mary, 90, 237; Naomi, 212; Rachel, 43; Sarah, 179.

Dennison—Mary, 209.

Denton—Theodosia, 9.

Departeone—Catherine, 25.

Depuy—Laura, 84.

Devault—Hester, 205.

Devenny—Abigail, 102.

Devinney—Leah, 90; Phebe, 57.

Devinny—Mary, 91; Susan, 166.

Dicks—Mary, 90; Rhoda, 82; Sarah, 222.

Dill—Hannah, 173.

Dillen—Hannah, 226, 257.

Diliing—Rebecca, 249

Dillon—Cora Lucinda, 122; Elizabeth, 205; Rachel, 89; Sarah Eliz., 43.

Dippold—Ellenor, 149.

Diviney—Delia, 156; Eliza, 196; Martha, 196.

Divinny—Sarah, 73.

Dobbins—Abigail, 124; Lettice, 140; Lucy, 132; Margaret, 228; Martha, 38; Mary, 95; Rachel, 144; Sarah, 35, 115, 218; Susan, 45.

Dobson—Mary, 40.

Dodd—Sarah, 210.

Dodson—Mary, 27; Matilda, 157.
Dokon—Jane, 218.
D'Olivares—Adrianne, 79.
Doltin—Ann, 163; Mary, 50.
Dolton—Elizabeth, 200; Rhoda, 170; Sarah, 129; Susan, 153.
Donaldson--Elizabeth, 214; T. E., 185.
Donally—Ruth, 91.
Donielly—Susan, 9.
Donley—Mary, 57.
Donnell(y)—Mary, 46; Elizabeth, 173; Emma Louisa, 21.
Donnoly—Ann, 170.
Donoly—Susan, 244.
Doran—Elizabeth, 141.
Dorce—Sarah, 7.
Doren—Hannah, 205; Mary, 15.
Dorman—Jane, 116.
Doron—Rebecca, 99.
Dorris—Mary, 164.
Dorsey—Hannah, 143.
Doster—Rebecca, 45.
Dotey—Anne, 133.
Dotson—Christiana, 17.
Dougherty—Elizabeth, 182; Letitia, 132; Margaret, 134; Rebecca, 41.
Doughty—Ann, 43, 201; Elizabeth, 72, 142; Mary, 128; Phebe, 249; Rebecca Ann, 44; Sarah, 120.
Douglas(s)—Ann, 154; Hannah, 212; Mary, 50; Rebecca, 145; Sarah, 147.
Dowers—Nancy, 79.
Downes—Elizabeth, 216.
Down(s)—Elizabeth, 213; Hannah, 70; Martha, 218; Priscilla, 12; Rachel, 208,
Draper—Jemima, 188; Mary, 20.
Drexall—Hannah, 88.
Driver—Anne, 231; Jane, 60; Mary, 25; Sarah, 53.
Droew—Anna, 102.
Drummond—Mary, 84.
Dubal—Susan, 126.
Dubble—Mary, 98.
Duby—Josephine, 34.
Duckworth—Anne, 195; Mary, 108.

Dudley—Hannah, 220; Lydia. 142; Martha, 106; Mary, 25, 254; Priscilla, 15; Rachel, 144, 254; Rebecca, 45; Ruth. 229.

Duglass—Elishaby. 201; Mary, 144.

Duley—Pamelia Ann, 100.

Dumas—Margaret Ann, 197.

Duncan—Jane, 64.

Dunfee—Mary, 191.

Dungan—Lettice, 39; Maria. 41.

Dunlap—Margaret, 62.

Dunn—Margahet. 161; Mary. 201, Rhoda, 169.

Dunphy—Penelope. 117.

Dunum—Mary, 27.

Dunyon—Sarah, 243.

Durand—Mary Ella, 200.

Durell—Elizabeth, 117; Hannah, 21, 26; Sarah, 92.

Dussell—Mary 165.

Dutton—Mary. 126; Priscilla, 124; Rhoda, 95.

Duval—Sibilla, 239.

Dye(r)—Ann, 44; Margaret, 166.

Eakin—Ann, 31.

Eamres—Hannah, 160.

Earl(e)—Edith, 112; Effe Norcross, 24; Elizabeth, 67, 168; Esther, 163; Hannah. 110; Hes er 255; Martha, 206; Mary, 25, 72, 136, 173; Mary Sykes, 89; Mercy, 93; Nancy, 179; Sarah, 35.

Earley—Lydia, 135; Mary, 103.

Earlin—Rachel Ann, 106; Rebecca Ann, 106; Susan. 57.

Early—Bridget, 249; Elizabeth, 244; Fanny, 242; Margaret, 200; Mary, 32

Easely—Dorothy, 58.

Eassland—Abigail, 37.

Eastlack—Elizabeth, 61.

Eastland—Amanda, 14.

Eastwood—Beulah, 2 4; Mary, 208.

Eavs—Rebecca, 77.

Eayre(s)—Anne, 99; Elizabeth, 70, 139; Hannah, 63, 66, 252; Helen, 210; Keziah, 55; Kitturah, 161; Margaret, 246; Maria, 183; Martha, 101; Mary, 251; Mary Ann, 54; Priscilla. 100; Rachel, 53; Rhode. 149; Sallie, 123; Sarah, 113, 127; Sarah Ann, 70.

Ebert—Catherine, 17.

Eckman—Laura, 187.

Ecret—Mary, 107.

Eddleman—Louisa, 229.
Edgar—Susan, 121, 256.
Edge—Mary, 29.
Edmond(s)—Catharine, 174; Martha, 78; Mary, 24; Elizabeth, 84; Margaret, 52.
Edward(s)—Ann, 18, 137; Diana, 55; Elizabeth, 26, 163; Mary, 16, 43, 149; Matilda 20; Sarah, 50.
Eggnew—Sarah, 255.
Elberson—Elizabeth, 82; Jane, 110; Lucy, 85; Theodosia, 141.
Elbertson—Phebe, 249.
Elborne—Margaret, 224.
Eldridge—Abigail, 162; Ann, 68; Charity, 251; Elizabeth, 88, 127; Hester, 152; Mary, 24, 34, 66, 100, 209, 243; Rachel, 76; Rebecca, 145; Sarah, 107, 140; Sibella, 237.
Elkenton—Jemimah, 87.
Elkington—Ann, 137; Mary, 192.
Elkinton—Amy, 221; Ann, 31, 104; Elizabeth, 16, 216, 243; Hannah, 220; Rebecca, 15, 216; Sabillah, 108; Sarah, 52.
Ellet—Sarah, 18.
Elliott—Martha, 33.
Ellis—Abigail, 55, 251; Ann, 99; Elizabeth, 60, 107, 157, 254; Jane, 26; Leah, 74; Margaret, 233, 252; Mary, 9, 126, 159, 244, 254; Meribah, 46; Sarah, 39, 75, 194, 251; Sukey, 190.
Ellison—Anna, 143; Hannah, 215; Sarah, 109; Susannah, 71.
Elmor(e)—Mary, 6; Sarah, 64.
Elsden—Hannah, 66.
Elton—Ann, 56; Anna, 195; Elizabeth, 14, 143; Hannah, 63; Mary, 132, 133; Rebecca, 22; Susannah, 88.
Elwell—Mary, 58.
Emley—Alice, 120; Allice, 242; Elizabeth, 73, 123; Lydia, 119; Martha, 73; Mary, 115; Parthenia, 179; Sarah, 56.
Emly—Ann, 88.
Emmand—Sarah, 130.
Emmins—Eliza Ann, 86.
Emmons—Amelia, 185; Ann, 92, 232; Charity, 67; Mary, 153.
Endicott—Ann, 71; Sarah, 90.
Engard—Elizabeth, 256.
Engham—Mary, 132.
England—Rebecca, 239; Sarah, 233.
Engle—Charity, 244; Deborah, 102; Edith, 100; Elizabeth, 160; Esther, 34; Hannah, 30, 119, 150; Jane, 48; Lucy Ann, 102; Rachel,

150; Rachel Ann, 74; Sarah, 50.
  Englind—Elizabeth, 140.
  English—Abigail, 74; Amy, 240; Ann, 7, 122; Eliza, 156; Elizabeth, 67, 77, 228, 248; Hannah, 171; Lydia, 130; Mary, 56, 106, 110; Phebe, 164; Rachel, 23, 218; Sarah, 71, 80, 105, 153; Susan, 94, 184.
  Enoch(s)—Anne, 256; Mary, 90, 92.
  Enocks—Abigail, 79; Martha, 78.
  Entosh—Hannah, 11.
  Epley—Margaret, 108.
  Eppley—Sarah, 201.
  Ernest—Mary, 215; Sarah, 90.
  Ernshaw—Mary, 255.
  Ervin(e)—Elizabeth, 59; Mary, 140; Rebecca, 34.
  Erwin—Eliza, 11; Mary, 182.
  Esdaile—Lydia, 153.
  Esdall—Mary, 41; Sarah, 32.
  Esdel(l)—Jane, 33; Maria, 200.
  Eslick—Rebecca, 140.
  Eslo(n)—Catharine, 247; Mary, 17.
  Estalow—Susanna, 10.
  Estelo(w), Ann, 17, Nancy, 225.
  Estel(l)—Elizabeth, 13; Leuraney, 41; Mary, 163.
  Estill—Hannah, 238; Mary, 95; Rhoda, 126, 136; Sarah, 164.
  Estlow—Sarah, 22.
  Esturgans—Martha, 195..
  Evans—Abbie, 255; Ann, 99, 178, 192; Anna, 218; Anna Wills, 203; Bathsheba, 143; Deborah, 145, 251; Elizabeth, 16, 100, 142, 143; Esther, 14; Hannah, 58; Hepsibah, 31; Jane, 87, 119; Jemima, 141; Lydia, 53, 194, 220; Mabel Bartram, 90; Martha, 238; Mary, 60, 62, 221; Mary Ann, 138; Nancy, 160; Priscilla, 19; Rachel, 18, 211, 243; Rebecca, 87; Sarah, 16, 129, 202; Susan, 77, 203; Susanna, 133; Susannah, 143; Syllania, 192.
  Evens—Abigail, 144; Elizabeth, 77; Esther, 50; Hannah, 128; Mary, 102, 255; Rachel, 101; Rebecca, 152; Sarah, 76, 101; Susannah, 19.
  Everham—Hope, 185.
  Everingham—Elizabeth, 123; Hannah, 123, 170; Mary, 238; Rachel, 108.
  Eves—Anna, 143; Anne, 143; Dorothy, 112; Elizabeth, 112; Hepzibah, 150; Mary, 58, 178; Rachel, 105; Sarah, 63.
  Evingham—Amy, 170.

Evins—Rachel, 94; Syllonia, 194.
Ewan—Bulah, 70; Letitia, 126; Mary, 144; Rebecca, 18; Susannah, 42.
Ewen—Keziah, 64; Mary, 211, 255.
Ewin(g)—Anne, 136; Caroline, 182; Eliza, 255; Jane, 212; Martha, 185, 238; Mary, 49, 98; Susan, 187; Tamar, 251.
Eullock—Susan, 5.
Extle—Rachel, 146
Eyley—Roadah, 209.
Eyre(s)—Ann, 6, 112; Elizabeth, 244; Hannah, 103; Hope, 169; Martha, 96; Mary, 41.
Fagan—Elinor, 228.
Fagins—Rebecca, 125.
Fagons—Rhoda, 229.
Fairholm—Margaret, 197; Rachel, 133.
Falkenburg—Hannah, 35.
Falkingburgh—Ann, 6, 229; Mary 10.
Fann—Martha, 44.
Fanning—Thankful, 40.
Farley—Sarah, 89; Susanna, 29.
Farmer—Elizabeth, 148; Lydia, 227; Sarah, 46.
Farnsworth—Sarah, 169; Susannah, 70.
Farnum—Mary, 95.
Farra—Ann, 190.
Farren—Sarah, 110.
Farrow—Elizabeth, 71; Hope, 7; Martha, 139.
Fatchett—Catherine, 93.
Fauley—Mary, 156.
Faulkenburg—Phebe, 133.
Faulkinburg—Hannah, 214.
Favis—Sarah, 237.
Fearson—Ann, 241.
Fegans—Elie, 161.
Felton—Ann, 90.
Fenemore—Merium, 38.
Fenimore—Ann, 124; Anne, 163, 164; Caroline, 216; Elizabeth, 53, 68, 79, 80, 131; Hannah, 121; Hope, 82; Janett, 234; Lucey, 167; Lydia, 188; Martha, 45, 53, 82, 181; Mary, 34, 242; Rachel, 24, 29, 199; Rebecca, 75, 103; Sarah, 62, 79, 160, 216, 247.
Fennimore—Ann, 118; Anna, 105; Hope, 46; Joan, 63; Mary, 161; Rachel, 191; Rebecca, 80, 141, 159; Sarah, 253; Thomasen, 232.

Fenton—Ann, 172; Elizabeth, 114; Ellen, 155; Hannah, 126; Lucille, 167; Lydia Ann, 92; Mary, 12, 127, 186; Pamela, 219; Phebe, 228; Rachel, 244; Sarah, 11; Sarah, 80, 125; Vashti, 122.

Feorigin—Elizabeth, 138.

Ferguson—Anne, 164; Isabella, 81; Jannet, 171; Margaret, 170; Mary, 209; Sarah, 87, 225; Sarah Ann. 115.

Ferrall—Neome, 226.

Ferris—Martha, 57; Polly, 19.

Fetters—Mary, 72; Rebecca, 173.

Field(s)—Abigail, 176; Anne, 137; Deborah, 235; Eleanor, 114; Eliza, 137; Elizabeth, 108, 128; Mary, 143, 204, 228; Mary Ann, 175; Phebe, 238; Rachel 69; Rebecca, 194, 226; Sarah, 118, 254.

Fielding—Eliza, 216.

Fieles—Mary, 246.

Fiffer—Barbary, 205; Susannah, 57.

Filer(s)—Rachel, 106; Sarah, 70.

Finch—Jane, 184.

Fireing—Rebecca Ann, 181.

Firing—Harriet, 155; Viola, 164.

Fish—Eliza, 234; Elizabeth, 222, 235; Grace, 34; Martha, 254; Mary Ann, 130; Rebecca, 121.

Fisher—Ann, 231; Elizabeth, 194, 198; Hannah, 219; Margaret, 74; Mary, 120, 140, 154; Mary Ann, 221; Mary Elizabeth, 186; Rebecca, 14.

Fitzgerald—Bridget, 227; Jane, 153.

Fitzhugh—Mary, 113.

FitzRandolph—Charity, 26.

Flanagan—Elizabeth, 46.

Flanigan—Jane, 240.

Fleanard—Catharine, 95.

Fleet—Charlotte, 100.

Flemings—Harriet, 232.

Flicher—Mary, 218.

Flinn—Susan, 37

Flint—Margaret, 6.

Flitcraft—Mary, 65.

Flood—Lydia, 137.

Foard—Hester, 24; Martha, 58.

Fogg—Hannah, 28; Rebecca, 166.

Folkes—Hannah, 250; Mary, 36.

Folks—Alice, 27; Anne, 226.

Folwell—Ann, 53; Elizabeth, 170, 184; Hannah, 5, 69; Hope, 5; Patience, 186; Rebecca, 75; Rebekah, 149; Sarah, 13, 108; Susanna, 202; Unity, 61

Folwlen—Sarah, 106.

Force—Charlotte, 142; Elizabeth, 240; Hope, 229; Mary, 114, 148.

Forcyth—Grace, 136.

Ford—Achsa, 179; Alice, 166; Anne, 59; Elizabeth, 117, 191; Hannah, 97; Lydia, 237; Margaret, 109; Rebecca, 45; Sarah, 15; Tabitha, 193.

Fordham—Elizabeth, 78.

Forgison—Margaret, 115.

Forgus—Lavinia, 250.

Forguson—Marian, 147.

Forker—Hannah, 71.

Forman—Effe, 20; Louisa Caroline, 74; Mary, 42; Phebe, 24; Sarah, 85.

Forsyth(e)—Achsah, 248; Elizabeth, 111; Mercy, 157; Rebecca, 93; Sarah, 59, 62, 184; Susanna, 194, 198.

Fort—Ann, 80; Anne, 75, 159, 205; Bessie, 17; Elizabeth, 20, 48, 71, 175; Esther, 164; Hannah, 75; Jane, 128; Johanna, 139; Kiturah, 47; Letitia, 13; Lettice, 131, 146; Mary, 143; Rachel, 203; Rebecca, 88; Sarah, 7, 234.

Fortiner—Eliza, 6.

Fortuner—Ann, 146.

Farvour—Elizabeth, 196.

Foster—Abigail, 22; Ann, 5; Ann Eliza, 244; Elizabeth, 37, 86, 193; Esther, 45, 60, 255; Hannah, 106, 130; Katariah, 160; Lettice, 135; Lydia, 131, 204; Martha, 106; Mary, 26, 94, 152; 165, 228, 254; Mary Ann, 250; Rebecca, 128, 242; Rebekka, 103; Rebekkah, 103; Rosanne, 183; Sarah, 13; Suzanna, 163.

Foulks—Ann, 27; Elizabeth, 134; Mary, 159.

Four—Rebecca, 107.

Fowes—Ann, 253.

Fowler—Abigail, 66; Ann, 170; Anseline, 242; Caroline, 82; Eliza, 185; Elizabeth, 17, 60, 72, 209; Hannah, 112, 156, 199; Kiturah, 201; Lucy Ann, 195; Maria, 193; Martha, 157; Mary, 66, 94; Phebe, 80, 180; Rachel, 181; Rebecca, 125.

Fox—Ann, 206; Anne, 66; Deborah, 200; Elizabeth, 230; Marla, 12; Mary, 35, 245.

Frake—Harriet, 111; Lydia, 206; Mary, 205; Mary Matilda, 216.
Frampton—Elizabeth, 246; Sarah, 24.
Frankford—Elizabeth, 210.
Franklin—Hester, 125; Mary, 208; Sarah, 86, 244; Winefred, 34.
Franks—Fanny, 133.
Fraser—Elizabeth, 73.
Frasher—Margaret, 128.
Frazer—Ann, 21; Frances, 91.
Frazier—Ann, 166; Elizabeth, 131; Hannah, 30; Rachel, 96; Sarah, 112.
Freaze—Marche, 125.
Freeman—Isabella, 17; Susan, 62.
Fregam—Ruth, 111.
French—Ann, 21, 134, 135, 174; Atlantic, 170; Bathsheba, 192; Elizabeth, 192; Hannah, 40, 76; Hope, 139; Jane, 104; Jemimah, 25; Lydia Ann, 103; Margaret, 116; Mary, 33, 40, 103, 123, 172, 188, 192, 201; Matilda, 36, 184; Rachel, 192; Rebeccah, 228; Sarah, 63, 206, 243, 249; Susannah, 115.
Fretwell—Rebekkah, 237.
Friedland—Sarah, 186.
Friend—Isabella, 242.
Frieze—Tabitha, 60.
Fritze—Barbara, 151.
Fromberger—Anna, 44, 118.
Frost—Ann, 201.
Fuffmon—Ann, 48.
Furman—Sarah, 157.
Furnace—Hannah, 187; Lucretia, 22.
Furniss—Flizabeth 44; Susannah, 249.
Fury—Catherine, 94; Sarah, 233.
Gabitas—Deborah, 98.
Gale—Anne, 77; Bethier, 152; Dinah, 216; Elizabeth 148; Hannah, 147; Katherine, 256; Mary, 66, 88, 96, 108, 238; Meribah, 49; Priscilla, 47, 221; Rebecca, 69; Sarah, 24.
Gallagher—Elinor, 209.
Gamble—Deborah, 48; Jane, 75; Mary, 195; Rebecca, 134.
Canfac—Mary Ann, 136.
Gant—Elizabeth, 75.
Gard—Mary, 72.
Gardener—Sarah, 153, 184; Vasty, 220.
Gardiner—Bathsheba, 227; Catharine, 252; Elizabeth, 20, 87, 138;

Hannah, 77, 174, 219; Hester, 69; Lydia, 18, 156; Mary, 21, 136, 158; Priscilla, 99; Reba Emily, 212; Rebecca, 133; Susannah, 82.

Gardner—Atty, 211; Elizabeth, 237; Jane, 107; Mary, 120, 219; Phebe, 45; Rachel Shemar, 92; Rebecca Ann, 51; Sarah, 175;

  Garite—Unice, 190.
  Garner—Ann, 240; Catharine, 154; Rachel, 149.
  Garoiett—Sophia, 201.
  Garret—Catherine, 75; Hannah, 43; Parthena, 134; Sarah, 149.
  Garrish—Bloomey, 20.
  Garrison—Ann, 56; Hannah, 12.
  Garrottel—Martha, 67.
  Garvey—Susannah, 92.

Garwood—Abigail, 164; Amey, 34; Ann, 116, 235; Deborah, 211; Elizabeth, 16, 64, 181, 227; Elizabeth Ann, 142; Grace, 27; Hester, 246; Hope, 28; Jane, 182; Lydia, 158; Martha, 62; Martha Jane, 59, Mary, 129, 200; Mary Ann, 211; Patience, 140; Persilla, 253; Priscilla, 119; Rebecca, 13, 103, 246; Rosamond, 112; Ruth, 131; Sarah, 22, 61, 63, 70, 182, 201; Susan, 226; Susannah, 31; Tabitha, 187.

  Gaskel(l)—Eliza, 5; Elizabeth, 162; Sarah, 20.

Gaskill—Abigail, 189, 206; Amelia, 6, 47; Amy, 146 188; Ann, 75, Ann, 80, 205, 208; Ann Maria, 151; Beulah, 69, 237; Bithia, 148 Charity, 90; Elizabeth, 6, 145, 167; Elizabeth Shreve, 254; Grace, 206; Hannah, 83, 187, 252; Helen Louise, 254; Hepzibah, 145; Hope, 246; Jane, 156; Julia, 205; Keziah, 224; Lavinah, 92; Lydia, 127; Maria, 175; Miriam Epley, 8; Martha, 84, 91, 254; Mary, 42, 48, 56, 65, 205; Mary Ann, 35, 226; Patty, 59; Provided, 206; Rachel, 144, 155; Rebecca, 147, 184, 201, 216; Rhoda, 27; Ruth, 100; Sarah, 87, 140, 227; Silaney, 169; Susan, 204; Susanna, 96; Theodotia, 127; Virgin, 149.

Gaskin(s)—Catherine, 112; Elizabeth, 235; Hannah, 75; Lydia, 8; Sarah, 235.

  Gaugh—Mary, 65.

Gaunt(t)—Achsah, 29; Anna, 83; Elizabeth, 81, 144, 174, 207; Hannah, 88, 189, 204; Mary, 239; Phebe, 114; Rebecca, 27, 254; Sarah, 140; Sophia, 151.

  Gee—Achsah, 172.
  Geer—Betsey, 26.
  Gibberson—Ann, 39; Elizabeth, 170.
  Gibbins—Rachael, 120; Sarah, 234; Susan, 179.
  Gibbon(s)—Abigail 152, 196; Charlotta, 132.
  Gibbs—Adeline, 114; Ann, 15, 200; Anna, 84; Bathsheba, 15;

Gibbs—Bersheba, 7, 41;Elizabeth, 61, 132, 181, 220, 228; Hannah, 19; Jane, 24, 64; Lydia, 43; Martha, 76; Mary, 23, 81, 82; Mercy, 34; Phebe, 31, 136; Rebecca, 8, 54, 123, 163, 189; Sarah, 77, 121, 129, 200; Susannah, 111.

Giberson—Hannah, 21, 44; Mary, 57; Rebecca, 122.

Gibson—Ann, 13, 96, 155; Elizabeth, 43, 132; Hannah, 158; Harriet, 114; Martha, 187; Mary, 202; Rachel, 43, 175; Sarah, 69, 140.

Gifford—Ann, 228; Bulah Ann, 230; Catherine, 16; Esther, 94; Hannah, 59; Jemima, 50; Mary, 111.

Gilbert—Ann, 242; Hannah Ann, 63; Bula, 136; Deborah, 200; Edith, 197; Elizabeth, 236; Hannah, 148; Lydia, 106; Mary, 77, 130; Phebe 148; Rebecca, 145; Sarah, 166.

Giles—Dorothy, 212; Hannah, 35; Mary, 147; Mary Ann, 125.

Gilkinson—Esther, 114.

Gillam—Ann, 122.

Gillingham—Lydia, 65; Rachel, 52.

Gillman—Anne, 113.

Gillum—Grace, 167.

Gilman—Elizabeth, 20.

Gilmer—Mary, 121.

Gilmore—Elizabeth, 79.

Gingling—Mary, 29.

Gipson—Mary, 159.

Gise—Margaret, 153.

Githens—Ann, 94; Mary, 37, 43, 104, 144; Melissa, 134; Rachel, 160.

Githerson—Mary Eliz., 112.

Giveson—Lydia, 95.

Glading—Mary, 41.

Glass—Ann, 159; Florence, 235; Margaret, 69.

Gloster—Mary, 244.

Glover—Mary, 208.

Glynn—Ann, 122.

Goaldy—Sarah, 108.

Goddas—Sarah, 44.

Godfrey—Mary, 238.

Godly—Susan, 33.

Goff—Mary, 11.

Gofogy—Jane, 188.

Goforth—Martha, 97.

Goheen—Elizabeth 96.

Goldby—Elizabeth, 172.
Goldy—Dority, 47; Elizabeth, 116; Hannah, 183; Jerusha, 180; Margaret, 162; Mary, 149; Sarah, 102.
Gongo—Mary, 113.
Gooby—Lettice, 126.
Gooldy—Jarasa, 59; Mary, 35; Sarah, 53.
Good—Ann, 15.
Goodman—Sarah, 154.
Goodwin—Mary, 209, 250; Susannah, 158.
Goran—Jerusha, 206.
Gorden—Mary, 32, 251; Priscilla, 160.
Gordon—Hannah, 30; Olivia, 194; Elizann, 165.
Goreman—Catharina Ann, 206; Harriet, 177.
Goreton—Eliza, 165.
Goslin(g)—Ann, 83; Anne Eliza, 201; Martha, 215; Mary, 50, 122; Sarah, 251.
Gould—Hester, 91.
Grant—Catherine, 99; Deborah, 151; Elizabeth, 149; Lewis, 223; Margaret, 147, 233, 250; Martha, 147, 213; Mary, 194, 206; Rachel, 77, 91, 178; Sarah, 43; Susan, 110; Susanna, 91.
Grapevine—Catherine, 58.
Gray—Elizabeth, 246; Hannah, 207; Mary, 78.
Green—Ann, 202; Clara, 181; Elizabeth, 46, 99, 113, 153, 202, 203, 214; Hannah, 14; Jane, 122, 202; Louisa, 207; Martha, 255; Mary, 138, 202; Rachel, 130, 140; Rebecca, 34; Sarah, 20, 217; Susan, 85; Thirsa, 186; Tobitha, 238.
Greenman—Joanna, 206.
Greenwood—Lena, 18.
Gragg—Elinor, 60.
Gregory—Christiana, 38.
Grey—Mary, 42.
Griffin, Ann 187; Margaret, 72; Rebecca, 76.
Griffith(s)—Arabella, 241; Elizabeth, 27; Esther, 140; Louisa, 15; Lucy Ann, 193; Mary, 19, 91, 161; Sarah, 50.
Griffy—Martha, 106.
Grimes—Martha, 45; Mary, 227; Sarah, 165.
Griscom(e)—Hannah, 13; Mary, 124; Mary Ann, 81; Rachel, 36; Sarah, 171.
Grissom—Emeline, 133.
Groff—Ann 217.
Groom(s)—Elizabeth, 170; Mary, 51, 60; Saran Ann, 68.

Grosvenor—Mary Smith, 64.
Grover—Martha, 30; Rebecca Borden, 96.
Grubb—Mary, 113, 198.
Guest—Ann, 48.
Guilliam—Anne, 247.
Guinn—Naomi, 222
Guinnell—Hannah, 31.
Gulick—Eliza, 233.
Gunnels—Rebecca Ann, 46.
Guy—Elizabeth, 197.
Guyan—Elizabeth, 61.
Gwin—Esther, 27.
Gwinnall—Hannah, 243.
Gyberson—Mary, 56.
Hackney—Abigail, 58; Agnes, 115; Ann, 235; Elizabeth, 89, Keziah, 76; Kiturah, 89; Margaret, 247; Martha, 31; Niriam, 214; Rebecca, 22; Susannah, 85.
Haddon—Hannah, 40; Susannah, 190.
Haely—Phoebe, 127.
Hagaman—Susan, 209.
Hagerman—Rachel, 45.
Haight—Clarissa, 215.
Haigus—Pleasant, 117.
Haines—Abigail, 69, 206; Abigail Ann, 192; Achsah, 71; Amey, 89; Amy, 166; Ann, 35, 50, 102, 138, 186, 216; Anna, 57, 68, 85, 142; Anne, 202, 256; Arolina, 241; Aseneth, 69; Caroline Rogers, 153; Catharine, 49, 163; Charity, 232; Charlotte, 65, 251; Deborah, 128, 201, 210, 220; Edith, 101, 189; Eliza, 44; Elizabeth, 33, 47, 60, 71, 91, 145, 152, 186, 187, 202, 210, 251, 253; Ella Achsah, 199; Elma, 128; Emeline, 113; Emily, 48; Esther, 14, 62, 76, 115, 121, 132; Frances, 230; Grace, 113; Guiielma, 40; Hannah, 23, 29, 51, 55, 161, 192, 205, 210, 226, 243; Harriet, 137, 146; Henrietta, 25; Hester, 89; Hope, 52; Jane Eves, 15, 77; Jerusha, 22; Josephine Vasey, 207; 38; Keturah, 144; Lavinah, 205; Letitia, 152; Lucretia, 134; Lydia, 60, 136; Margaret, 37, 40, 48, 71, 73; Marian, 85; Martha, 88, 182, 248; Mary, 24, 34, 50, 61, 63, 68, 72, 74, 75, 81, 86, 100, 102, 103, 112, 115, 150, 166, 197, 203, 204, 245, 251; Mary Ann, 16; Mary Jane, 231; Merian, 144; Patience, 58, 130, 193; Phebe, 202; Priscilla, 76; Rachel, 21, 112, 145, 192, 194; Rebecca, 18, 62, 90, 107, 150, 152, '176, 241, 243, 246, 247; Ruth, 16; Ruth Ann, 29; Sarah, 99, 103, 113, 118,, 136, 210, 243; Veturia, 163.

Hains—Hannah, 105, 220; Ruth, 111.
Haldan—Frances, 213.
Hale—Maria, 124; Susan, 94.
Haley—Catharine, 168; Mary, 75; Sarah, 47.
Hall—Abigail, 150; Ann, 208; Elizabeth, 175; Ellen, 191; **Ester,** 69; Letitia, 178; Lydia, 185; Mary, 22; **Martha,** 86, 93; **Sarah, 41,** 225; Sarah Church, 214; Rebecca, 200.
Halloway—Ann, 226; Mary, 226.
Hambleton—Betsey, 531; Ellen, 123; Phebe, 23.
Hamilton—Anne, 11; Elizabeth, 198; Kathariue, 114; **Margaret;** 60; Sarah, 46.
Hammel(l)—Ann, 119; Deborah, 180; Elizabeth, 74, 89, 110; 180; Gartree, 89; Hannah, 6, 116; Harriet, 109; Maria, 146; **Mary, 120,** 171; Sarah, 18, 19; Theodosia, 123.
Hammett—Amelia, 30; Ann, 141; Leah, 199; Mary, **224; Thit-**luia, 199.
Hammick—Elizabeth, 112.
Hammit(t)—Esther, 101; Hester, 40; Sarah, 135; Sibilla, **183.**
Hammock—Hannah, 60; Susannah, 209.
Hampton—Elizabeth, 131; Jemima, 154.
Hance—Eliza, 84; Hannah, 19; 125, 195; **Martha, 210; Sarah, 6,** 19.
Hancock—Abigail Ann, 234; Ann, 37, **222, 223;** Ann Eliza, 11; Elizabeth, 33, 115; Hannah, 58, 151, 221; **Jane, 105, 135, 200;** Leticia, 254; Lydia, 56; Martha, 37; Mary, 5, 63, **109, 138;** 171, 208; Rebecca, 189; Sarah, 124, 147, 221.
Handcock—Constant, 115.
Hane(s)—Jane, 22; Rebecca, 121.
Hankins—Ann, 106; Caroline, 181; **Jemima, 197; Mary,** 226; Susan, 6, 184..
Hankinson—Ella, 23.
Hanse—Mary, 93
Harber—Hannah, 96.
Harhur, Hope, 187.
Hardeman—Elizabeth, 223.
Hardenburg—Eliza, 153.
Hardin(g)—Ann, 50; Hope, 207, 215; Isabel, 191; **Mary, 16;** Mercy, 116; Sarah, 128.
Hark—Ann, 92
Harker—Amy, 109, 109; Blanche Rosalie, 155; **Elizabeth, 91;** Hester, 85; Mary, 117, 165; Nancy, 233, 234; **Rachel, 123; Rebecca,**

172; Rhoda, 93; Sarah, 188; Susan Josephine, 191; Susannah, 209.

Harlem—Elizabeth, 185.

Harman—Alse, 241; Grace Matilda, 237.

Harnot—Sarah, 174.

Harris—Abigail 128;. Achsah, 42; Agnes, 232; Eleanor, 105; Hannah, 210 Harriet, 44; Jane, 51, 149; Letitia, 223; Lucy Virginia, 82; Margaret, 125; Martha, 97; Mary, 106, 209, 241; Mercilah, 132; Rachel, 15; Rebecca, 127 Rhoda, 96; Sarah Jane, 218; Susan Ann, 111.

Harrison—Ann, 253; Edith, 192; Hannah, 183, 195; Margaret, 41; Mary, 20; Ruth, 252; Sarah, 252.

Harsems—Letty, 32.

Hart—Edith, 182; Eliza, 81; Elizabeth, 215; Lydia, 116; Mary Anna, 38; Susan, 155.

Hartgrove—Kethura, 172; Rebecca 66.

Harthorn—Elizabeth, 48.

Hartman—Ann, 179; Elizabeth, 255; Emeline, 47; Harriet, 204; Levina, 186; Sabella, 239; Salina, 10, 165.

Hartshorne—Lenah, 135; Rachel, 231; Rebecca, 252.

Hartsman—Susannah, 99.

Harvey—Ann, 180; Beulah, 147; Deborah, 147; Elizabeth, 39, 77; Harriet, 69; Lydia, 5; Martha, 174; Mary, 39, 102, 180; Sarah, 23, 36; Sibilla, 178.

Hatch—Elizabeth, 208.

Hatcher—Hannah, 221; Mary Emma, 22.

Hatkinson—Elizabeth, 39; Mary, 61.

Hauke—Fannie, 211.

Havelon—Elizabeth, 84.

Havens—Abigail, 62, 214; Hannah, 55; Mary, 84; Mary Ann, 99; Sarah, 148; Susannah, 224.

Haverland—Mary, 92.

Haverson—Abbie Mary, 46.

Hawk—Charlotta, 11.

Hawkins—Anne, 194; Elizabeth, 231; Juliana, 51.

Hay(s)—Amy, 61; Ann Eliza, 130; Anna, 222; Anne, 148; Anne Mary, 112; Elizabeth, 78; Hannah, 92; Harriet, 110; Margaret, 78; Maria, 60; Mary, 49, 67; Rebecca, 42.

Hayne—Lydia, 72.

Haywood—Martha, 173; Mary, 71, 185; Mary Marion, 207; Melinda, 19.

Hazelton—Abigail, 132; Ann, 170.

Heabron—Mary, 199.
Head—Suffiah, 79.
Head ey—Ann. 76; Eliza, 87.
Headly—Fanny, 162; Ruth, 143.
Heaton—Eliza, 232; Harriet, 25; Mary, 125, 191.
Hebbarn—Ann, 54.
Hebberth—Catherine, 113.
Hedge(s)- Deborah, 26; Elizabeth, 161.
Hedger—Patty. 154.
Heisler—Ann, 225; Mary Anna, 236.
Heivin—Eliza. 55.
Helberson—Elizabeth, 140.
Hellings—Elizabeth, 248.
Helson—Anne, 12.
Helverton—Martha, 65.
Hely--Rebecca, 153.
Hemp—Ann, 119.
Hempfield—Sarah, 209.
Henderson—Anna, 148.
Hendricks—Mary. 37.
Hendrickson—Ann, 29; Cornelia, 135; Hannah, 225; **Margaret**, 13.
Henry—Ann, 171; Rachel, 226.
Heppard—Mary, 230.
Herber(t)—Anna, 165; Anne, 8; Deborah, 36, 229; Elizabeth, 107; Hannah Connan, 232; Harriet, 107, 228; Mary, 167; Phebe, 85; Rebecca, 69; Sarah, 151.
Herd—Alice, 83, 119.
Heritage—Anne, 230; Sarah, 41.
Herr—Emily, 142.
Herritage—Rebecca, 248.
Hesher—Mary, 252.
Hesler—Mary, 229.
Hess—Mary, 236.
Heulings—Bathsheba, 44; Eliz., 60; Hester, 166; Sarah, 49.
Heustis—Tamar, 118.
Heuston—Martha, 247.
Hewes—Mary, 156; Sarah, 46.
Hewit—Anne, 118; Charlotte, 75.
Hewlinge—Hilty, 211.
Hewling(s)—Ann, 243; Elizabeth, 71, 155; Esther, 147; Hannah,

63, 142, 179; Lydia, 122; Mary, 144, 160; Sarah, 85, 102; Susannah, 212.
  Hews—Elizabeth, 86; Phebe, 75.
  Hewson—Elzy, 20.
  Hewstice—Hannah, 187.
  Hickley—Mary Anna, 170.
  Hickman—Catharine, 248; Theodosia, 132.
  Hierton—Elizabeth, 253
  Higbee—Abigail, 139; Alice, 137; Mary, 175; Sarah, 7, 124.
  Higby—Mary, 112.
  Higginbottom—Dorothy, 87, 232.
  Higgins—Agnes, 39; Bridget, 188; Deborah, 165; Elizabeth, 43, 46, 111; Matilda, 70; Nancy, 199; Sarah, 62, 95, 116.
  Higgs—Anne, 32.
  Hilberson—Nancy, 15.
  Hilderman—Ann, 97.
  Hile(s)—Ann, 222; Elizabeth, 248; Rachel, 51.
  Hill—Achsah—229; Ann, 241; Betha, 183; Elizabeth, 121, 130; Frances, 55; Hannah, 60; Mary, 192, 214, 256.
  Hilliard—Lydia, 97; Martha, 95; Mary, 196; Rachel, 202, 216; Rebekah, 97.
  Hillier—Ann, 135; Hannah, 54; Elizabeth 183.
  Hillyer—Mary, 13.
  Hilsee—Hannah, 128.
  Hinchman—Ann, 210; Elizabeth 82; Sarah, 22.
  Hise—Ann Eliza, 118.
  Hisler—Ann, 47; Mary, 161.
  Hoar—Catherine, 137.
  Hodge—Elizabeth, 130.
  Hodgins—Ann, 113.
  Hodgkinson—Anne, 148; Elizabeth, 211.
  Hodgson—Alice, 175; Mary, 179, 183.
  Hodson—Abigail, 150; Anne, 131; Margaret, 83; Rebecca, 108.
  Hoff—Hester, 100; Letitia, 35; Sarah, 175, 194.
  Hoffman—Catharine, 163; Mary, 144.
  Hogelan(d)—Hannah, 20, 205.
  Hoiles—Elizabeth 53.
  Holbard—Mercy, 252.
  Holden—Lacy, 61.
  Holeman—Anna, 142; Elizabeth, 86.
  Holl—Hannah, 86.

Holland—Amanda Elizabeth, 114; Ann, 85, 223; Jerush, 105; Katharine, 182; Margaret, 69; Maria, 182; Mary, 6, 163; Rachel, 61, 200.

Hollins—Jane, 129.

Hollinshead—Abigail, 200; Agnes, 231; Ann, 160; Anne, 38, 246; Beulah, 222; Eleanor, 54; Hannah, 94, 236; Hope, 18; Jerusha, 115; Lydia, 112; Martha, 220; Mary, 253; Rachel, 250; Rebecca, 107; Sarah, 174; Zelas, 115.

Holloway—Ann, 195; Avis, 157, 199; Hannah, 126; Mary, 132, 245; Rebeck, 5.

Holman—Agnes, 67; Eliz., 109.

Holmes—Sarah, 34.

Holms—Alice, 176.

Holt—Catharine, 112.

Homan—Elizabeth, 205.

Hoofman—Sarah, 149.

Hooper—Ann, 91; Anne, 59; Beaulah, 237; Elizabeth, 169; Lucretia, 178; Margaret, 7; Phebe, 117; Rachel, 164; Rebecca, 188.

Hooten—Elizabeth, 71; Hannah, 234; Mary, 25; Rebecca, 165.

Hopewell—Elizabeth, 53, 56; Martha, 34; Mary, 71; 109.

Hopkins—Catherine, 19; Emma, 109; Eliza, 24; Elizabeth, 51; Louisa, 214; Mary, 123; Mary, 214; Massey, 176; Sarah, 96.

Hopkinson—Margaret, 254.

Hoppnagle— Mary Louisa, 16.

Horn(e)—Esther, 57; Jean, 122; Judith, 151; Margaret, 151; Sarah Vansciver, 89.

Horner—Achsa, 73; Ann, 110; Anna, 230; Caroline, 208; Catharine, 106, 222; Deborah, 193; Deliverance, 47, 221; Elizabeth, 89, 107, 179; Ellen, 248; Hannah, 89, 152; Isabella, 140; Lizzie, 181; Lucretia, 22:; Mary, 77, 168, 226, 235, 248; Mary Ann, 97; Phebe, 136; Rachel, 120, 224; Rebecca 25; Susan Maria, 239.

Hornor—Elizabeth, 49, 75; Mary, 61; Rachel Ann, 49; Sarah, 242.

Horsefield—Martha, 180.

Horseman—Abigail, 37; Christian, 210; Mary, 173; Susanna, 226, 257.

Hoskins—Abigail, 98; Rachel, 158.

Hotten—Abigail, 85.

Hough—Ann, 231; Eliz., 207; Martha, 219; Mary, 58, 111, 165; Susannah, 231.

House—Mary, 184.

Houston—Elizabeth, 126.
Howard—Abigail, 153; Demaris, 79; Elizabeth, 248; Harriet, 127; Mary, 147, 233; Rebecca, 245.
Howell—Ann, 107, 131, 153; Anne, 186; Annie Maria, 186; Catherine, 169; Deborah, 28; Eliz. Coxe, 196; Elizabeth, 102; Ella Nora, 118; Euphemia, 113; Mary, 48, 249; Rebecca, 252.
Hoy—Mariah, 84.
Hubbs—Cathrine, 161; Elizabeth, 44; Hannah, 44; Mary, 190; Phebe, 90, 247.
Huber—Rebecca, 187.
Huddleston—Katherine, 50; Rebecca, 6.
Hudson—Elizabeth, 153; Hannah, 105; Mary, 77; Susan, 215.
Hueston—Hester, 58.
Huff—Ann, 182; Eliza, 90.
Hufman—Nancy, 112.
Hufty—Catherine, 7.
Hugg—Ann, 111; Hannah, 12, 239; Lettice, 27; Louisa, 229; Martha, 8; Mary, 244; Nancy, 145; Phebe, 97; Sarah, 171.
Huggins—Margt. Ann, 248; Jane, 201.
Hughes—Ann, 60; Anna, 18; Dorothy, 9; Elizabeth, 170; Esther, 54; Hannah, 81, 149; Mary English, 65; Prescilla, 146; Rachel, 143; Susan, 32
Hugo—Elizabeth, 147.
Hull—Mary, 181.
Hulme—Ella Hannah, 208; Harriet, 171; Sarah, 169.
Hulse—Rebecca, 141; Willmina, 200.
Hults—Lydia, 245.
Humphrey(s)—Rachel, 80; Sarah, 137.
Humphries—Anna, 72.
Humpner—Mary, 65.
Hun—Elizabeth, 109.
Hungerford—Mary, 100.
Hunloke—Martha, 119; Mary, 185.
Hunt—Beauler, 125; Edith, 124; Elizabeth, 25, 72; Esther, 52; Hannah, 207, 215; Mary, 207, 215; Rachel, 141, 192; Sarah, 97; Susannah, 6.
Hunter—Allis, 99; Ann Eliza, 102; Elizabeth, 252; Hannah, 100, 127; Lydia, 110; Mary, 52, 82; Susan, 109.
Huntly—Ann, 180.
Huntsman—Ann, 192; Mary, 214.
Hurley—Hannah, 49.

Husband(s), Caroline, 149; Rachel, 114.
Husted—Catharine, 97; Sarah, 90.
Huston—Martha, 255; Mary, 46.
Hutchin(s)—Achsah, 63; Alice, 85; Margery, 72; Mary, 79, 159; Rebecca, 47.
Hutchinson—Achsah, 252; Agnes, 58; Elizabeth, 73, 221; Emily, 100; Margaret, 209; Mary, 23, 108, 121, 148, 160, 227; Mary Ann, 65; Phebe, 83; Sarah, 63, 245.
Hutton—Eleanor, 109.
Hyle—Margaret, 47.
Imlay—Margaret, 44; Thomasin, 34.
Imley—Parthena, 55.
Indlcott—Ann, 95; Mary, 22, 152.
Inger—Catherine, 128.
Ingersoll—Rachel, 87.
Inglan(d)—Deborah, 197; Jane, 7.
Ingle(r)—Elizabeth, 6; Hannah, 202; Sarah, 99.
Inglin(g)—Ann, 242; Charity, 228.
Ingram—Mary, 70.
Inman—Elizabeth, 48, 123; Phebe, 12, 96, 221.
Innion—Rachel, 85.
Inskeep—Anne, 74; Elizabeth, 37, 230; Hannah, 160; Mary, 253; Rebecca, 254; Sarah, 136, 207, 208, 220.
Inskip—Agnes, 142.
Inslee—Sarah, 177.
Iredell—Elizabeth, 66; Sarah, 8, 243.
Ireland—Anna, 124; Christian, 154; Deborah, 166; Mary, 111; Ruth, 105; Sarah, 154.
Ireton—Elizabeth, 219; Hannah, 72; Mary, 253; Mercy, 104; Susanna, 44.
Irick—Ann, 35; Mary, 49.
Irons—Elizabeth 171; Hannah, 170.
Isdall—Rachel, 203.
Ivins—Achsah, 119; Anna 208; Anne, 168; Beulah, 51; Charlotte, 188; Deborah, 73; Elizabeth, 123; Harriet, 236; Lydia, 11; Mary, 199, 229. Rachel, 62, 99; Sarah, 17, 131, 178, 236; Susan, 199; Susannah, 223.
Jack—Isabel, 38.
Jackson—Catharine, 233; Frances, 119; Margaret, 118; Maria, 53, 117; Mary, 222, 240
Jackway—Diademia, 232; Margaret, 231.

Jacobs—Ann, 25; Anne. 166; Elizabeth, 215; Hannah, 75; Mary 173; Rosanna, 173; Sarah, 200.

Jacoby—Elizabeth, 64.

James—Diana, 99; Hannah, 197; Joanna, 27; Margaret, 219; Mariah 202; Mary, 104, 116, 183; Susan, 200.

Jameson—Elizabeth, 9; Mary, 67.

Janney—Ann. 188.

Jaquatt—Mary, 137.

Jaques—Frances, 23.

Jash—Mary, 211.

Jeakey—Mary Catharine, 213.

Jefferies—Jane, 162; Kate Eisenhower, 175.

Jemson—Eliza, 187.

Jenkins—Hannah, 195; Mary, 102; Susannah, 234.

Jenks—Anna, 185.

Jennet—Alice, 120.

Jennings—Ann, 217; Elizabeth, 141; Jane, 64; Mary, 217; Rhoda, 16; Sarah, 175.

Jervis—Elizabeth, 68; Patience, 78.

Jess(e)—Ann, 21, 207; Rachel, 62. 187.

Jobes—Ann, 125; Mary, 155; Rebecca, 201.

Jobs—Amy, 145; Elizabeth, 163; Mary, 112; Tobitha, 79, 85.

John—Alice. 75.

Johnson—Abigail, 199; Amelia, 203; Ann, 90; Buley, 39; Catharine, 181; Catherine, 66; Deborah, 190; Delia, 107; Dorothy, 119; Eleanor, 10; Elizabeth, 48, 75, 139, 146, 167, 196, 214; Ella, 48; Ellen, 48; Esther, 53; Hagar, 30; Harriet, 207; Isabella, 110; Kesiah, 14, 27; Kessiah, 243; Keturah, 176; Letitia, 53; Maria, 218; Mary, 55, 62, 86, 116, 153, 197. 235; Mary Ann, 201, Peggy, 90, 254; Phebe Ann, 121; Rachel, 88, 232; Rebecca, 213, 214; Rhoda, 73, 92; Sarah, 64, 70, 123, 191, 246; Sarah Ann, 189; Thomazine, 199.

Johnston(e)—Ann. 156; Elizabeth, 111, 173; Fanny, 225; Hannah, 67; Harriet, 209; Jane, 140; Keziah, 51; Mary, 64, 66, 97, 161, 167, 241; Priscilla, 147; Rebecca, 19, 145; Rhoda, 28; Sarah, 11, 125.

Joice—Mary, 41.

Jolley—Deriah, 20.

Jolly—Hannah, 124; Rebecca, 153.

Jones—Abigail, 237; Abigail Ann, 29; Alice, 215; Ann, 61, 102, 168, 200; Eliza, 6, 180; Elizabeth, 8. 48. 55, 98, 102, 108, 125, 132, 139, 164, 176, 196, 212; Emeline, 95; Hannah, 45, 68, 164, 180, 213, 219, 247; Henrietta, 53; Hope, 187; Hope Ann, 219, Isabell, 78;

Jane, 110; Lavina 22, 78; Lydia, 77, 193, 242; Keturah, 41; Louisa, 248; Margaret, 78, 139, 198; Martha, 205, 215, 236; Mary, 24, 33, 41, 69, 99, 107, 122, 126, 160, 177, 191, 195, 216, 222; Meribah, 76; Penelope, 253; Phebe, 200; Rebecca, 57, 122, 250, 253; Rebeckah, 75; Rachel, 48, 186, 204; Rachell, 253; Sarah, 159, 163, 164, 189, 201, 205, 208, 222, 231, 235, 247; Sarah Anderson, 141; Susan, 131; Susannah, 172; Tacy, 114; Tamer, 176.

Jonson—Edith 48; Rody, 253.

Jordan—Jerusey, 25.

Jorman—Sarah, 85.

Jourdan—Mary, 88.

Joyce—Dolly, 123, 182; Martha, 222, 235, 251; Mary, 157, 221, 247; Rachel, 8.

Jupiter—Margaret, 124.

Justice—Ann, 192.

Kain—Mary, 44; Elizabeth, 247.

Kale—Elizabeth, 234.

Kallam—Susannah, 180.

Karlin—Hannah, 24.

Kay—Jemimah, 24; Mary, 100; Sarah, 116.

Kearns—Catherine, 122.

Keeler—Ann Eliza, 32; Elizabeth, 163; Hannah, 7, 215; Jannetta, 175; Sarah, 21, 191, 241; Theodosia, 68.

Keen(e)—Elizabeth, 134; Lucy Ann, 135; Margaret, 11.

Kele—Elizabeth, 32

Kell(e)—Jane, 158; Hannah, , 11.

Kelley—Abigail, 5, 91; Beulah, 86; Bridget, 255; Deborah, 65, 114; Elizabeth, 60, 105; Emeline, 244; Jane, 191; Margaret, 150, 245; Mary Ann. 199, 231; Matilda, 142; Rachel, 227; Rebecca, 88; Sarah, 55.

Kelly—Elizabeth, 230; Margaret, 87; Jane, 231; Mary, 62; Mary Stella, 72; Nancy, 60.

Kelts—Sarah, 138.

Kemble—Abigail, 100; Ann, 158; Anna, 151; Anne, 171; Carrie, 161; Edith, 204; Hannah, 200; Huldah, 196; Margaret, 24; Mary, 20, 129, 196; Sarah, 252; Susan, 150; Susannah, 219.

Kemp—Jemima, 227.

Kempton—Catharine, 154; Fanny, 130; Mary, 231.

Kendall—Jane, 45.

Kendle—Sarah, 132.

Kennedy—Anne, 124.

Kenner—Rebekkah, 241.
Kent—Rebecca, 80.
Kenton—Mary, 249.
Kerlen—Ann, 93.
Kerlin—Grace, 247; Isabelle, 184; Mary, 149; Rebecca, 216; Susanna, 122.
Kerr—Margaret, 160; Phebe, 223.
Kester—Eliza, 237.
Key(s)—Mary, 214; Sarah, 155.
Kilkeade—Sarah Ann, 225.
Killday—Bridget, 106.
Kille(y)—Catharine, 137; Elizabeth, 88; Mary, 181; Mary Lippincott, 137; Miriam, 224; Sarah, 224.
Killingham—Jane, 47.
Kimbal—Sarah, 217.
Kimber, Mary, 66.
Kinelle—Elizabeth 193.
Kimble—Ann, 84; Elizabeth, 189; Hannah, 146; Martha, 152; Mary, 39, 157, 199.
Kimpson—Susannah, 39.
Kimpy—Rhoda, 147.
Kindall—Elizabeth, 81,
Kindel(l)—Achsah, 119; Martha, 175; Mary, 20.
Kindle—Ann, 91; Ester, 155; Mary, 31; Rebecca, 17.
Kine—Jane, 163.
King—Achsah, 122; Ann, 8; Anna, 238; Anne, 62; Beulah, 41; Catharine, 125; Caroline, 121; Eliza, 77; Elizabeth, 86, 100, 181, 215, 223; Hannah, 15, 35, 87, 171; Harriet, 144; Jane, 217; Lucy, 217; Mary, 40, 90, 114, 173, 226; Miriam, 168; Rachel, 167, 208; Rebecca, 62, 110, 180; Sarah, 73, 84, 97, 139, 158; Susan, 120; Theodosia, 167.
Kingdon—Anna, 65.
Kinison—Mary, 75.
Kinnison—Hannah, 256.
Kinsey—Anne, 241; Elizabeth, 78, 152; Hannah, 42; Mary, 137, 239; Polly, 109; Sarah, 179.
Kirby—Acsa, 194; Alice, 79; Ann, 73, 115; Beulah, 90; Charlotte, 38; Elizabeth, 99; Helenah, 133; Lydia, 94; Mary, 47, 147; Rebecca, 158, 168.
Kirk—Emmeline, 247; Tacy, 206.
Kirkbride—Hannah, 197; Margery, 25, 151; Martha, 168.
Kirkland—Elizabeth, 50; Margaret, 250.

Kirkpatrick—Elizabeth, 58.
Kirling—Elizabeth, 218.
Kiser—Sally, 211.
Kithcart—Pheby, 107.
Kitchen—Mary, 151.
Klimpton—Ann, 33.
Klingle—Mary, 99.
Knapp—Mary, 67.
Knight—Eleanor, 84; Elizabeth, 161; Hannah, 180, 244; Mary Ann, 34; Sarah, 83.
Knott—Elizabeth, 156.
Knowles—Ruth, 189.
Knowlton—Elizabeth, 158.
Knox—Charlotte, 136; Elizabeth, 22.
Krantz—Mary Tilton, 42.
Kunlass—Hannah, 108.
Lacy—Artis, 204; Catheran, 255; Elizabeth, 213.
Lain—Catharine, 83.
Lake—Ann, 7; Martha, 158.
Lamand—Constantia, 189.
Lamand—Mary Louisa 219.
Lamb—Anna, 176; Anne, 139; Charlotte, 180; Edith, 146; Elizabeth, 24, 55, 194; Lydia, 112; Margaret, 10, 100; Mary, 107; Rebecca, 55, 155; Sarah, 70, 91; Susanna, 62; Thirza, 84.
Lambert—Charity, 12.
Lame—Hannah, 225; Mary, 27; Sarah, 53, 75.
Land—Abigail, 82; Ann, 6; Charlotte, 179; Hannah, 169; Jane, 68; Judith, 235; Mary, 134, 180.
Lane—Anne, 141; Eliza, 85; Mary, 40; Priscilla, 127; Sarah, 82.
Langley—Elizabeth, 105.
Langstaff—Annie, 209; Sue Deacon, 209.
Laning—Hannah, 36; Mary, 182; Mary Ann, 175; Matilda, 132.
Lannen—Elizabeth, 60.
Lannin(g)—Abigail, 21; Ann, 196; Elizab., 179; Hannah, 9, 22, 56; Mary, 56; Phebe, 123; Sarah, 24.
Large—Jane, 37; Mary, 36, 183; Sarah, 193.
Larison—Elizabeth, 162; Sarah, 240.
Larzalere—Sarah, 137.
Larzelere—Elizabeth, 154, 203.
Lascal—Hannah Ann, 68.
Latas—Mary, 68.

Lathbury—Experience, 61.
Latimore—Sophia, 234.
Laton, Eliza, 237.
Laurence—Elizabeth, 177; Priscilla, 156.
Lawkie—Ann, 116.
Lawrence—Ann, 172; Catharine, 87; Elizabeth, 130; Eva, 118; Hannah, 27, 85, 213; Martha, 212; Salamy, 65; Sarah, 95.
Lawrie—Amelia, 217; Beulah, 165; Eliza, 41; Hannah, 46, 58; Helena, 5; Lydia, 36; Mary, 46, 64, 223; Rachel, 165.
Lawson—Jane, 182.
Layton—Margaret, 165.
Lazilere, Jane, 7.
Leach—Ann, 199.
Lear—Abigail, 104; Barbary, 128; Eliza, 187; Hannah, 20; Rebecca, 122; Sarah, 216
Leatia, Sarah, 196.
Leconey—Abigail, 234.
Lee(s)—Abigail 126; Anna, 116; Elizabeth, 12, 36, 81, 151; Hannah, 63, 186; Kesiah, 255; Lavinia, 133; Margaret, 241; Mary, 27, 150, 180, 235, 238; Patience, 128; Rachel, 138, Rebecca, 13; Rhoda, 172; Sarah, 252; Theodocia, 13, 204.
Leach- Elizabeth, 23; Mary, 112.
Leeds—Ann, 17, 56, 58, 133, 183, 227; Anna, 133; Charlotte, 100; Deborah, 165; Elizabeth, 133; Hannah, 57, 70, 159, 246; Jemima, 250; Keziah, 14; Latisha, 57; Mariah, 227; Martha, 238; Mary, 213, 240; Mercy, 119; Rachel, 150; Rebecca, 10; Sarah, 66, 67, 152, 240; Sybilla, 68.
Leek—Abigail, 200; Catharine, 214; Eliza, 90; Hester, 152; Louisa, 210; Margaret, 207, Pnebe, 11; Rachel, 83; Sarah, 43, 210.
Lehman—Catherine Louisa, 225.
Leigh—Catherine, 184.
Leland—Margaret, 238; Susanna, 230.
Leman—Aihah, 197.
Leeman—Charlotte, 192.
Lemas—Carrie, 13.
Lemon—Ella, 47·
Len—Ann, 131.
Lenning—Sarah, 213.
Leonard—Anne, 138; Jane, 16, 196; Mary, 102; Rhoda, 99.
Letts—Lavina, 215, Lydia, 126; Mary, 96; Nellie Blanche, 47.
Leppingcott—Rebecca, 206.

Leuallen—Sarah, 237.
Levine—Mary, 74.
Lewallen—Amelia, 226.
Lewis—Ann, 166, 203; Anne, 166, 182; Hannah, 201; Elizabeth, 134; Emeline, 95; Lydia, 154; Mary, 126, 128, 208, 219; Rebecca, 6, 144; Ruth, 157; Sarah. 127; Tina, 113.
Libby—Joanna, 84.
Light—Elizabeth, 43.
Likins--Sarah, 39.
Lincum—Ann, 126.
Lindon—Sarah, 33.
Lindsey—Mary, 198.
Lines—Abigail, 150; Elizabeth, 117; Phebe, 197.
Linkin—Elizabeth, 186.
Linn—Rebecca, 173.
Linsey—Ann, 68; Elizabeth, 133.
Lintz—Wilhelmina, 63, 216.
Lione—Abigail, 223.
Lippincott—Abigail, 76, 139, 205, 246; Ann, 79, 92, 101, 130; Anna, 105, 192, 226, 236, 237; Anne, 138; Anner, 38; Beulah, 255; Edith, 231; Elizabeth, 10, 14, 15, 25. 38, 40, 53, 61, 91, 143, 144, 148, 162, 173, 203, 204, 220, 229 231, 254; Emile, 129; Emla, 240; Encrease, 120; Fanny, 127; Grace. 40; Hannah, 8, 35, 40, 120, 132, 143, 205, 234, 238, 251, 256; Hannah Ann, 49; Harriet, 68; Helen, 77; Hope, 79, 95. 100. 101, 236; Jane, 115, 71, 238; Jerusha, 193; Judith, 178; Julia Ann, 152; Laura, 33; Leah, 81; Letitia, 71; Lucy Ann, 84; Lydia, 24. 30. 68. 156, 192, 243; Lydia Ann, 218; Martha, 190; Mary, 20, 23. 28, 49, 60, 66, 71, 78, 91, 110, 111, 143, 144, 160, 162, 181, 205; 162; Mercy, 218; Merion, 79; Mila, 211; Neziah, 50; Parham, 76; Patience, 10, 88; Persilla, 217; Rachel, 58, 125, 182, 235; Rebecca, 45, 49, 53, 66, 82, 90, 112, 230, 241 254, 255 Rebeccah, 105; Rebeckah, 250; Rhoda, 105; Ruth, 28, 219; Sarah, 32, 40, 103, 212; Susan, 68; Sybilla, 210; Tamar, 184; Theodocia, 87, 145; Vashti, 41.
Lipsay—Ann, 45.
Lishman—Rhoda, 145; Sarah, 160, 171.
Little—Ann, 216; Hannah, 37; Mary, 139; Sarah, 57, 67, 137, 248; Susan, 78.
Littlejohn—Mary, 7.
Livezey—Elizabeth, 208.
Lloyd—Olinda, 230.
Loakinson—Julian, 124.

Lodge—Mary, 170.
Lofton—Ann, 130.
Logan—Mary, 47; Sarah, 210.
Loker—Hannah, 179.
London—Joanna, 12.
Long—Mary Ann, 148; Mira, 163; Sarah, 219; Theodosia, 79.
Longcusp—Anna, 107.
Longdale—Charlotte, 245.
Lonstow—Anne Lindsey, 124.
Longstreet--Lucy Ann. 33.
Longstreth—Hannah, 92; Lydia, 179; Mary, 11, 104.
Looker—Anna, 73.
Loper—Sarah, 78; Theodotia, 41.
Lord—Anne, 85; Mary, 174; Rachel, 119.
Loten—Catharine, 33.
Louman—Eliza, 51,
Lounsberry—Marcy. 137.
Love—Elizabeth, 103; Jemima, 210.
Loveland—Caty, 214; Esther, 226. Mary, 162; Ruth, 57; Sarah, 153.
Lovele—Rachel, 240.
Loveman—Lettuce, 204; Mary, 134.
Loverman, Ann, 83.
Lovett—Harriet, 196: Mary, 123; Rebecca, 199; Sarah, 111, 211, 254; Susannah, 181.
Lovit(t)—Elizabeth, 199; Nancy. 36.
Lovland—Jane, 121; Jemima, 8, 214;
Lowden—Elizabeth, 138; Mary, 84, 154; Sarah, 75.
Lowder—Edith, 239.
Lownsbury—Mercy, 249.
Loyd—Abigail, 152; Margaret. 184; Sarah, 157.
Lucas—Ann, 93; Elizabeth, 117, 154, 227; Hester, 66; Margaret, 227; Mary, 7, 88, 125, 204; Sarah, 104, 253.
Luck—Mary, 234.
Lucking—Ann, 45.
Lucus—Rebecca, 79.
Ludrick—Rachel, 91.
Ludy—Rebecca, 54.
Luffbury—Elizabeth, 121.
Luckmeier—Rozanna, 250.
Luckmiers—Mary, 138.

Luke—Caroline, 67.
Lukemire(s)—Elizabeth, 127; 242; Hannah, 129; Unice, 203.
Lukens—Anna, 136; Martha, 31.
Lundy—Lottie Mary, 196.
Lutts—Eliza, 69; Mary, 70, 133, 174.
Luttz—Matilda, 249.
Lycans—Elizabeth, 29.
Lykens—Gertrude, 126.
Lynch—Katharine, 32.
Lynn—Hannah, 205.
Lyons—Mary, 81.
Machelot—Julia Zelina, 228.
Mackleroy—Mary, 172.
Macolm—Eliza Monkton, 97,
Macomb—Maria Theresa, 59; Maria de la Mercede, 232.
Macpherson—Christian, 94.
Maddocks—Elizabeth, 119.
Magee—Margaret, 196.
Mahan—Elizabeth, 96; Margaret, 7.
Mahollen—Charity, 157.
Mahony—Maria, 186.
Mairs—Margaret, 8.
Major—Mary, 217; Prudence, 255.
Malcolm—Rachel, 217.
Mallen—Mary, 115,
Malone—Ada, 37
Malsberry—Grace, 239; Rachel, 138.
Malsbury—Abigail, 255; Elizabeth 22; Hannah, 162; Lydia, 96, 159; Rachel, 90; Rebecca, 43,191; Thomasine, 43; Tobitha, 169.
Malsby—Anna, 188; Elizabeth, 82.
Manering—Roxanna, 152.
Mann—Elizabeth, 97.
Mannery—Rachel, 97.
Mannington—Ann, 18; Anne, 149; Joyce, 212; Margaret, 155.
Manroy—Eulalia Katherine, 149.
Manus—Mary, 29.
Maraback—Martha, 216.
Marett—Sarah, 39.
Marian—Mary, 74.
Marice—Abigail, 104.
Margerum—Rachel, 137.

Marjoram—Sarah Amy, 38.

Marlin(g)—Elizabeth, 3; Hannah, 150; Lucretia Mary, 51; Mary, 197.

Marll—Nancy, 223.

Marloy—Elizabeth, 178.

Marls—Rebecca, 79.

Marot—Judith Ann, 233.

Marpole—Keziah, 213; Mary, 7.

Marriot(t), Anne, 5; Elizabeth, 84; Hannah, 238; Martha, 198; Mercy, 31; Sarah, 97; Susanna, 79, 90.

Marrow—Sarah, 106.

Marsh—Eliza, 193.

Marshall—Elizabeth, 98; Mary Melvina, 153; Rachel, 171, 224, 88; Sallie, 99; Vinice, 11.

Marter—Abigail, 68; Ann, 6, 213; Catharine, 68; Hannah, 14, 79; Mary, 210, 239; Mary Ann, 134; Rebecca, 235; Sarah, 30; Sibilla, 235.

Martin—Ann, 115, 238; Bulah, 94; Elizabeth, 97; Hannah, 119; Nancy, 211; Pamela, 66; Priscilla, 14; Rebecca, 131.

Martindale—Hannah, 244.

Mason—Alice Anna, 101; Ann, 11; Anne, 26; Elizabeth, 247; Grace, 82; Hannah, 256; Lydia, 14, 25; Maria, 106; Mariam, 53; Martha, 33; Mary, 52, 160, 251; Rachel, 56; Rebecca, 14; Susanna, 18, 228.

Master—Rebecca, 246.

Matlack—Elizabeth, 232; Hepzibah, 237; Keziah, 97; Letitia, 158; Mary, 77, 122, 173; Rachel, 75; Ruth, 194; Sarah, 100, 210, 222.

Matlock—Ann, 192; Bathsheba, 142; Elizabeth, 225; Hannah, 187; Lydia, 142; Martha, 218; Mary, 50, 187; Mary Ann, 172; Rachel, 92, 124, 220; Rebecca, 22, 115; Ruth, 73; Sarah, 100.

Mather—Phebe, 83.

Mathews—Amey, 214; Anne, 77; Charlotte, 95, 141; Elizabeth, 190; Hannah, 89, 158; Hester, 16; Isabella, 174; Margaret, 114; Mary, 183; Rachel, 51, 195.

Mathis—Adeline, 39; Ann, 57, 169, 212; Dorcas, 10; Eliza, 151, 181; Elizabeth, 190; Esther, 94; Esther Jane, 48; Gartrightfredis, 114; Grace, 24, 111; Hannah, 87, 139; Mable, 151; Mahala, 65; Maria, 49; Mariah, 49, 156; Mary, 176; Naomi, 147; Patty, 151; Phebe, 57, 87; Sarah, 140, 239; Susan, 48.

Matson—Ann, 178; Edith, 143; Elinore, 172; Hannah, 178; Rachel, 24; Susannah, 56.

Mauliverer—Anne, 5.
Maulsbury—Mary Ann, 191; Rachel, 254; Tobitha, 187,
Mauris—Elizabeth, 104.
Mawrane—Sarah, 176.
Maxfield—Bridget, 98; Sarah, 230.
Maxwell—Abigail, 201,
Mayhew—Elizabeth, 29.
Maylan—Elizabeth, 242.
Mayo—Hannah, 208.
Mayove—Abigail, 209.
McAlpin—Susan, 57, 173.
McBride—Hannah, 205.
McCabe—Ann, 121; Mary, 195.
McCarty—Ann, 39; Mary, 70.
McChever—Analiza, 85.
McClain—Elizabeth, 97.
McClang—Ellen, 91.
McClary—Mary, 244; Mary Ann, 47.
McClasly—Mary, 172,
McClean—Elizabeth, 11.
McCloe—Abigail, 158.
McClong—Ann, 47.
McCloskey—Anna Maria, 92.
McClure—Rosannah, 177.
McClurg—Elizabeth, 97.
McCollin—Ann, 147; Rachel, 10.
McCollister—Rhoda, 246.
McCollum—Mary, 126.
McComb—Isabella, 241; Martha, 65.
McConacal—Mary, 89.
McCone(l)—Ann, 210; Marthew, 176.
McCormack—Ann, 179.
McCormick—Jane, 240.
McCoy—Elizabeth, 141; Hannah, 229; Hester, 47; Keturah, 154.
McCully—Gertrude, 200; Mary, 95; Olivia, 242.
McDaniel—Penelope, 131.
McDermott—Mary, 242.
McDevitt—Ann, 70.
McDole—Sarah, 158.
McDonald—Mary, 37; Mary Rambo, 89.
McDannelly—Amy, 176.

McDowell—Jane, 59.
McElroy—Ann, 148; Mary, 190.
McElvey—Mary, 211.
McEvarry—Isabella, 137.
McFarland—Ann Jane, 62.
McFarlin—Joyce, 80.
McGallard—Elizabeth, 19.
McGinnis—Jane, 145.
McGlocklin—Sarah, 41.
McGowan—Ann, 146; Harriet, 140; Jane, 191; Mary, 142; Rebecca, 13.
McGuire—Ann, 21; Mary, 34; Susannah, 188.
McHenry—Mary, 119.
McIlvaine—Ann, 6, 67; Rebeka, 235.
McIntire—Elizabeth 157.
McIntosh—Elizabeth Ann, 214; Ellionar, 172; Rosanna, 74.
McKarson—Elizabeth, 235.
McKeaman—Catherine, 230.
McKee—Sarah Ann, 198;
McKelery—Elizabeth, 194.
McKelvey—Sarah, 144.
McKenny—Barbary, 76; Mary, 255.
McKerne(y)—Eliza, 155; Mary, 148.
McKilley—Margaret, 109.
McKnight—Harriet, 153.
McLaughlin—Martha, 234.
McLealand—Rachel, 117.
McLeary—Mary, 69.
McLoe—Abigail, 227.
McMann—Bridget, 82.
McMasters—Mary, 121.
McMichael—Eliza, 125.
McMinn—Jane, 32.
McMullen—Hester, 41; Juliann; Sarah, 97.
McMurren—Wrightstell, 117.
McNeelie—Sarah, 231.
McNeill—Anna, 61.
McVay—Rachel, 21.
McVey—Mary, 254.
Mead—Elizabeth, 193; Sarah, 180.
Medcalf—Anne, 38.

BURLINGTON COUNTY MARRIAGES 309

Meek—Mary, 133.
Megonagle—Catharine, 118.
Meirs—Elizabeth, 145.
Meredith—Mary, 172; Sarah, 29.
Merrill—Mary, 230.
Merret—Anna, 10.
Merrit(t)—Ann, 136; Levina, 132; Mary, 23, 250; Rebecca, 158; Sarah, 247.
Merriot(t)—Any, 46; Anne, 204; Elizabeth, 183; Mary, 244.
Meyer(s)—Elizabeth, 228; Lydia, 109; Martha, 130; Mary, 81; Sarah, 59.
Micholson—Prudence, 106.
Mick—Ann, 244; Mary, 57, 96; Nancy, 145.
Middleton—Abigail, 181, 198, 250; Ann, 42, 72, 129, 150; Anna, 156; Beulah, 147; Catharine, 64; Catharine Ann, 191; Deborah, 53; Elizabeth, 87, 118, 183; Ester, 230; Hannah, 74, 87, 102, 111, 132, 140, 156, 199; Increase, 114; Izabella, 102; Louisa, 180; Lucy, 53; Lydia, 44, 198; Margaret, 83; Maria, 134; Martha, 90; Mary, 119, 215; Mary Ann, 100; Meribah, 85; Miriam, 72; Naomi, 104; Phebe, 129, 247; Rachel, 28; Rebecca, 232; Rebecka, 25; Ruth, 112; Sarah, 8, 77, 156, 206.
Miers—Ann, 81.
Milbine—Eleanore Jennings, 150.
Miles— Sarah, 11.
Millard—Anne, 158.
Miller—Ann, 53, 87, 150, 251; Anna Maria, 118; Catharine, 106, 200; Elizabeth, 71, 73, 127, 208, 243; Esther, 107; Esther Ann, 86; Euphamia, 118; Hannah, 89; Jane, 253; Letitia, 186, 204; Louisa, 251; Lydia, 101; Martha, 205; Mary, 9, 106, 183, 203; Meribah, 144; Rebecca, 46; Ruth, 18; Sarah, 6.
Milligan—Elizabeth, 52.
Mills—Ann, 95; Florence, 5; Jemima, 27; Lydia, 162; Margaret, 124; Mary, 47; Phebe, 73; Sarah, 48; Susannah, 175.
Milnor—Anna, 161; Maria, 72.
Milton—Anna, 10.
Mingin(g)— Ann, 176, Anne, 59; Elizabeth; 147; Mary, 117, 250; Rebecca, 110.
Minion—Lydia, 63.
Minnick—Maria, 141.
Mintle—Hope, 105; Sarah, 159.
Miovers—Sarah, 199.

Mires—Kesiah, 178.

Miskelly—Mary, 32.

Mitchel(l)—Anna, 39; Catherine, 49; Elizabeth, 19, 185, 250; Ella, 153; Ellen, 27; Keziah, 233; Margaret, 159; Mary, 49; Sarah, 253.

Mode—Sarah, 233.

Moffett—Frances Craig, 65.

Moll—Bathsheba, 33.

Mollikan—Rachel, 75.

Monear—Abijah, 238.

Money—Elizabeth, 154.

Monro(w)—Abigail, 34, 148; Elizabeth, 55, 147; Margaret, 192; Mary, 163, 239; Prudence, 192; Sarah, 68, 78.

Montgomery—Mariah, 179.

Monyon—Sarah, 107.

Moody—Lydia, 195.

Moon—Jane, 65, 112; Letitia, 70; Martha, 181; Mary, 165, 184; Saran, 218.

Mooney—Marietta, 226.

Moore—Eliza, 160; Elizabeth, 24, 43, 119, 150, 180; Hannah, 21, 86, 96, 134, 236, 239; Jerushe, 166; Lydia, 38, 201, 229; Lucrecy, 27; Maria, 148; Martha, 64, 79; Mary, 40, 86, 156, 198, 207, 223; Nancy, 99; Patience, 236; Priscilla, 38; Rachel, 100; Reb., 98; Rebecca, 129, 188; Rebecca Ann, 160, 245; Sarah, 107, 132, 221, 244, 249; Valeria, 51.

Moran—Elizabeth, 73.

Mareton—Mary, 124.

Morford—Elizabeth, 17, 20; Rachel, 16.

Morgan—Basheba, 17; Eliza, 67; Hannah, 220; Judith, 192; Kesiah, 215; Mary, 196; Mary Ann, 193; Rachel, 96.

Morlan—Elizabeth, 158.

Mornington—Anna Maria, 153; Rebecca, 184.

Morriel—Sarah, 82.

Morris—Alice, 228; Anne, 157; Betsy, 216; Beulah, 219; Elizabeth, 210, 223, 239; Hannah, 193; Harriet, 219; Hope, 178; Lydia, 123, 153; Martha, 68; Mary, 12, 84, 139; Mary Emma, 96; Nancy, 81; Patience, 117; Rachel, 54; Sarah, 137, 244; Theodosia, 116; Tobitha, 256.

Morrison—Sarah, 203.

Morrit—Deborah, 222.

Mortimer—Elizabeth, 68.

Morse—Elizabeth, 67; Esther, 151; Hannah, 176.

Morton—Elizabeth, 11; Esther, 75; Lavinia, 89, 126; **Mary, 94;** Meribah, 75; Patience, 216; Rachel, 95; Rebecca, 33; **Rebecca Lavinia, 190.**
Moses—Mary, 109.
Moss—Amey, 225; Hannah, 87.
Mott(e)—Anna, 78; Desire, 21; Eleanor, 114; Elizabeth, 94; Hannah, 54; Louisa, 116; Mary, 12.
Moullton—Dorothy, 225.
Mount—Alice, 216; Ann, 108; Annie, 27; Chatrine, 160; Elizabeth, 44, 114; Hannah, 116; Lydia, 209; Margaret, 201. 250; Phebe, 11; Rebeckah, 237; Susan, 83.
Muckelvane—Sarah, 256.
Mugglestone—Margaret, 230.
Mulford—Susanna, 104.
Mullen—Ann, 113; Baulah, 116; Elizabeth, 50; Jerusha, 127; Keziah, 34; Lydia, 117; Mary, 37 38, 104; **Nancy, 168; Rebecca,** 168; Sarah, 134, 227.
Mulligan—Ann, 245.
Mullin—Elizabeth, 103; Grace, 203; Mary, 241.
Munn—Nancy, 167.
Munroe—Anne, 238.
Munrow—Anne, 219; Sarah, 35.
Munyan—Hannah, 15.
Murdock—Elizabeth, 186; Sarah, 108.
Murfin—Ann, 138; Johanna, 223; Katherine, 19; Kizia, 247; **Mary, 137, 211.**
Murphey—Elizabeth, 212.
Murphy—Cecelia, 159; Elizabeth, 111; Mary, 210; Rachel, 67, 121.
Murray—Ann, 32.
Murrel(l)—Isabella, 231; Mary, 17, 40, 66.
Murry—Prudence, 16; Rachel, 53; Silvey, 184.
Musgrove—Elizabeth, 97; Mary, 61; Sophia, 147.
Meyers—Catherine, 66; Elizabeth, 121, 179, 249; Hannah, 130; Mary, 168; Rachel, 168; Sarah, 74, 168.
Nail—Mary, 223,
Nalier—Elizabeth, 174; Hannah, 203; Hester, 84.
Nailor—Ann, 24; Hannah, 223; Jane, 27; Lydia, 15; Martha, 150.
Nalk—Carrie Edna, 95.
Naylor—Hope, 165; Sarah, 163.
Neal(e)—Elizabeth, 58, 208; Jennet, 240; Margaret, 171; Martha, 143; Mary, 209; Tennel, 120.

Nebb—Elizabeth, 141.
Nelson—Mary, 59.
Neven—Amelia, 29.
Newberry—Hannah, 192; Mary, 172.
Newbold—Alice, 121; Ann, 222; Anne, 5, 185; Caroline, 222; Charlotte, 248; Helen Earl, 111; Lettice, 251; Lydia, 23; Margaret, 246; Martha, 69; Mary, 38, 113, 224; Rachel, 165, 241; Sarah, 7, 23, 38, 189; Susanna, 135.
Newbould—Mary, 45.
Newbury—Elizabeth, 56, 104.
Newell—Ann, 43; Elizabeth, 242; Hannah, 61; Jane 28; Sarah, 80; Sarah Ann, 32.
Newlin—Sarah, 206.
Newman—Catharine, 33, 113; Elizabeth, 187; Mary, 206.
Newton—Ann, 7; Annie, 227; Eliza, 70; Elizabeth, 250; Hannah, 161; Martha, 87; Mary, 80, 126; Rebecca, 175; Sarah, 34.
Nicholas—Lydia, 79.
Nichols—Elizabeth, 106; Poeby, 119; Rebecca, 255.
Nicholson—Hannah, 64, 157; Hannah Cora, 213; Jane, 157; Mary, 18; Sarah, 44.
Nickles—Eliza, 247; Florence, 59.
Nicols—Isabella, 156.
Night—Dinah, 159.
Niglee—Hannah, 139
Nippins—Eliza, 239; Hannah, 123; Susan, 178.
Nixon—Edith, 96, 223; Elizabeth, 24; Emeline, 249; Mary, 9; Rebecca, 62; Sarah, 70, 126.
Nixson—Ann, 170.
Noble—Mary, 169; Phebe, 82.
Noline—Antey, 169.
Nolton, Rachel, 118.
Norcross—Abigail, 18; Anne, 194; Bathsheba, 216; Beuley, 86; Drucilla, 92; Elizabeth, 28, 50; Ellen, 221; Hannah, 209; Harriet 60; Jane, 147, 155, 249; Keziah, 167; Lucy Ann, 234; Mary, 32, 56, 130, 211; Mercy, 158; Sarah, 69, 194; Sarah Barns, 8.
Nordike—Elizabeth, 213.
Nordyke—Ann, 135
Norris—Hannah, 150; Sarah, 171.
North—Lizzie, 85.
Norton—Ann, 97; Anne, 73; Margaret 236; Marian, 14; Martha, 122; Mary, 205; Sarah, 243.

Nott—Anne, 125.
Nottaway—Ann, 9.
Nottnagle—Henrietta, 255.
Noxon—Mary, 155.
Nugent—Rhody, 106,
Nummock—Sarah, 56.
Nut(t)—Abigail, 224; Amy, 36; Ann, 121, 191, 227; Hannah, 73; Jane, 144; Mary, 33, 209.
Oakley—Mary, 84.
O'Brine—Martha, 203.
Oby—Ann Maria, 240.
Odell—Elizabeth, 120.
O'Donley—Bridget, 90.
Oen--Nancy, 92.
Ofttar—Margaret, 129.
Ogborn—Mary, 74; Phebe, 172;
Ogbourn—Ann, 173; Elizabeth, 159.
Ogburn—Ann, 39; Anna, 143.
Ogden—Jane, 68.
Okeley—Ann, 124.
Oldale—Grace, 33; Sarah, 7.
Olden—Annie, 46; Catherine, 212; Hannah Ann, 46; Mary, 163. Rebecca, 190; Sarah, 72.
Olding—Rebecca, 83.
Oldman—Ann, 135.
Oliphant—Ann, 182; Beulah Ann, 169; Eliza, 199; Jerusha, 115; Margaret, 120, 142; Martha, 113, 143; Mary, 244; Mary Louise, 115.
Olive(r)—Joice, 149; Mary, 77; Sarah, 121.
O'Neal—Tabitha, 7.
Ong(e)—Esther, 68; Hannah, 30; Mabel, 206; Mary, 146, 190; Phebe, 134; Rachel, 29; Sarah, 10, 64.
Orr—Helen, 88; Mary, 122
Orsburn, Jane, 240.
Osborne—Ann, 55, 125, 213; Eliza, 243; Hannah, 172, 175, 211; Jane, 198; Lydia, 46; Martha, 29; Mary, 139, 198; Palmyra, 21; Phebe, 245.
Osburn—Mary, 233.
Osler—Hope, 152; Rachel, 162.
Ostlar—Ann, 163.
Ostler—Elinor, 89.

Ott—Mary, 209;
Otway—Elizabeth, 66.
Ougbourn—Mary, 171.
Ovely—Elizabeth, 172.
Overton—Sarah, 245.
Owen—Hannah, 91; Jane, 253; Margaret, 58; Martha, 26, 144, 149; Mary, 37; Mercy, 25; Rachel, 219; Rebekkah, 76; Sarah, 204; Susanna, 45.
Packer—Rebecca, 35; Rhoda, 105.
Pacock—Priscilla, 26.
Page—Agnes, 159; Amy, 117; Edith, 221; Elizabeth, 191, 232, 236; Haney, 47; Harriet, 125, 164; Lydia, 146, 184; Margaret, 117; Maria 5; Mary, 32, 57, 252; Priscilla, 123; Ruth, 112; Sarah, 129; Sarah Etta, 5; Zeriuah, 229.
Pain(e)—Elizabeth, 202; Martha, 110; Sarah, 99, 103; Susannah, 219.
Paiste—Elmina, 130.
Pall—Hannah, 38.
Palmer—Ann, 132; Elizabeth, 75; Esther, 137; Priscilla, 117.
Pancoast—Elizabeth, 238; Esther, 180; Hannah, 236, 238; Latice, 36; Mary, 19, 34, 90, 209, 212; Rebecca, 33; Sarah, 19, 23, 24, 65; Susannah, 55.
Pangburn—Rachel, 228.
Parent—Ann Elizabeth, 224; Esther, 167; Mary, 242.
Parke—Margaret, 85.
Parker—Alice, 16; Allis, 204; Ann, 113, 169; Catharine, 239; Charity, 80; Charlotte, 134; Damaris, 177; Dasey, 30; Dorothy, 126; Elizabeth, 15, 78, 139, 178, 181, 214, 245, 255; Esther, 177; Florence Coleman, 13; Frances, 86; Hagar, 204; Hannah, 10, 152, 214, 229; Harriet, 108; Margnret, 31, 212; Maria Ross, 86; Martha, 91, 107, 205; Mary, 7, 31, 39, 78, 121, 130, 172, 182, 213; Mary Ann, 50, 150; Phebe, 141; Rebecca, 110, 244; Ruth, 7, 158; Sarah, 109, 141, 199; Susannah, 181.
Parks—Elizabeth, 169; Rosanna, 97.
Parmer—Hannah, 13; Sarah, 85.
Parnell—Mary, 249.
Parrot—Elizabeth, 56
Parson(s)—Elizabeth, 114; Janey Bunting, 236; Mary, 187.
Paschall—Sarah, 246.
Pash—Belinda, 183.
Patterson—Adelaide, 103; Ann, 136; Avis, 181; Hannah Virginia,

182; Hannah, 223; Lydia, 8, 137; Sarah Emeline, 183; Susan, 81.
Pattin—Hannah, 141.
Pattison—Hannah, 108; Mary, 146; Robetha, 198.
Paul—Elizabeth, 120; Lydia, 94.
Paulin— Prudence, 253.
Paxon—Elizabeth, 240; Madaline, 224.
Peachee—Mary, 232.
Peacock—Abigail, 129; Aliceina, 73; Ann, 147; Elizabeth, 73, 186, 189, 202; Hannah, 96, 178, 226; Isabella, 87; Lettice, 201; Louisa, 63, Lydia, 21, 202; Margaret, 13, 120; Marion, 188; Mary, 119, 183, 193, 202; Rachel, 101; Rhoda, 230; Ruth, 25; Sarah, 76; Susannah, 202.
Peak(e)—Abigail, 147; Deborah, 102; Elizabeth, 105; Jane, 219; Rebecca, 14; Sarah, 117, 219.
Pearce—Elizabeth, 209; Hannah, 65; Mary, 43; Mercy, 197; Rachel, 79; Rebecca, 20; Rebecka, 49; Rhoca, 140.
Pearsall—Mary, 190.
Pearson—Beulah, 236; Elizabeth; 8, 121, 195, 215; Ezabel, 239; Grace, 94; Hannah, 178; Lucy Ann, 223; Margaret, 120; Mary, 61, 121, 184; Rachel, 67; Rebecca, 15; Sarah, 115, 235; Sibilla, 104; Susan, 184; Theodosia, 184.
Peat—Susannah, 190.
Peck—Mary, 200.
Pedrick—Charity, 130; Esther, 40; Grace, 95; Izilah, 96; Jane, 43.
Pendergrass—Fame, 129.
Penier—Susan, 97.
Penn—Elizabeth, 45; Hannah, 18; Sarah, 173; Sarah Ann, 166.
Pennington—Sara, 148; Sarah, 217.
Penquite—Ann, 28; Ann Eliza, 213; Hester, 215; Jane, 245; 57, 144.
Penrow—Mary, 239.
Pensor— Frances, 221.
Penton—Phebe, 184.
Perdue—Elizabeth, 180.
Perine—Sarah, 42, 239.
Perkins—Abigail, 195; Ann, 80; Bathsheba, 172; Esther, 5; Jane, 185, 228; Jemima, 208; Mary, 98; Rebecca, 62, 167; Sarah, 57, 112, 163.
Perrin(e)—Maria, 98; Sarah, 71.
Perry—Mary, 235; Sarah, 92.
Person—Mary, 214.
Pervin—Elizabeth, 189.
Pes—Ann, 21.

Pestel—Margaret, 221

Peters—Abigail, 166; Charity, 162; Elizabeth, 65; Hannah, 207; Rachel, 71.

Peterman—Edith 21; Hezekiah, 149; Prudence, 85.

Peterson—Ann, 19; Catharine, 89; Elizabeth, 15; Felitha, 185; Mary, 20, 191; Rachel, 185; Sarah, 84.

Petit—Mary, 150.

Pettigrew—Jane, 166.

Pettit(t)—Abigail, 151; Amy, 57: Ann, 188; Elizabeth, 212; Johannah, 84; Judith, 6; Lucretia, 103; Lydia, 43; Mary, 103, 153; Mercy, 186; Rachel, 19; Rebecca, 26, 134; Sarah, 239.

Petty—Rebekka, 167.

Phagens—Elizabeth, 97.

Phares—Hannah, 132; Laura Anna, 170; Mary, 221.

Pharo—Ann, 52; Anne, 162; Hannah, 57, 139; Keziah, 117; Rebecca, 62; Sykes, 50.

Philips—Hannah, 86; Jane, 61; Martha, 101; Rebecca, 256.

Phillips—Ann, 135; Atlantick, 231; Catharine, 42; Eliza, 139; Elizabeth, 19, 84, 183, 197, 231; Hannah, 129, 182; Julianna, 44; Keziah, 143; Lydia, 28; Mary Ann, 46; Sarah, 191, 193, 196.

Phillson—Emeline, 244.

Phipps—Elizabeth, 233.

Pierce—Artemesia, 237; Elizabeth, 183; Sarah, 97.

Pierson—Elizabeth, 172; Rachel, 237; Rebecca, 46; Theodosia, 120.

Piffets—Mary, 159.

Pigen—Jane, 242.

Pike—Ann, 247; Sophia, 95.

Pilgrim—Rebecca Ann, 249.

Pincock—Rose, 139.

Pindel—Mary, 79.

Pine—Rebecca, 210.

Pinear—Rosanna, 64.

Piper—Hannah, 72; Martha, 163; Rebecca, 66.

Pippet(t)—Abigail, 33; Beulah, 247; Claria, 70; Elizabeth, 152; Mary, 6; Rachel, 84.

Pippit(t)—Hannah, 45; Margaret, 134; Mary, 222; Phebe, 90; Rachel, 53; Sarah, 15, 56, 95.

Pitman—Achsah, 198; Ann, 210; Anna, 183; Deborah, 13; Elizabeth, 106; Frances, 193, Francis, 133; Hannah, 184; Lydia, 248; Martha, 79; Rebecca, 147; Ruth, 188; Sarah, 6, 8.

Pitt—Elizabeth, 230; Hester, 42; Jane, 80.

Pittman—Elizabeth, 143; Isabella, 51; Mary, 80; Sarah Ann, 194.
Plalke—Phebe, 236.
Plank—Susan, 154.
Plasket—Margaret, 135; Mary Jane, 61.
Platt—Ann, 84; Anna, 88; Eliza, 185; Elizabeth, 159, 215; Harriet 7; Jane, 47; Mary, 13; Mary Jane, 238; Matilda, 117; Nancy, 170; Rachel, 209; Rebecca, 87; Sarah, 67, 123; Susannah, 237.
Plum(b)—Mary, 21, 134.
Plumbe—Ruth, 256.
Plumby—Flora, 68; Keziah, 191.
Plummer—Jane, 18; Keziah, 130.
Poinset(t)—Fanny, 226; Jane, 73.
Pointset—Ann, 91.
Pointsway—Sarah, 96.
Pointzell—Elizabeth, 29.
Polhemus—Eleanor, 173.
Polk—Hannah, 54.
Ponarro—Sarah, 129.
Pool(e)—Hannah, 177; Mary, 47.
Poore—Hannah, 232.
Pope—Ann, 145; Elizabeth, 55, 74, 168, 192, 241; Hannah, 93; Mariam, 127.
Porter—Elizabeth, 28; Rachel, 137.
Potter—Hannah, 250; Jane, 79; Mary, 225; Parthenia, 30;
Potts—Anne, 82; Harriet, 253; Lydia, 104, 203; Mary, 117; Rebecca, 235; Rebecca Ann, 156; Sarah, 105.
Powel(l)—Catharine, 196; Dorothy, 70; Elizabeth, 13, 33, 44, 88, 129, 188; Grace, 91; Hannah, 214; Hope, 119; Levinia, 9; Lydia, 91; Margaret, 203; Mary, 132, 208, 215, 224; Precilla, 164; Prudence, 169; Rebecca, 107, 189; Rebekkah, 199; Sarah, 145; Sarah Ann, 167; Susan, 133, 204; Theodocia, 139; Virgin, 246.
Power—Mary, 5.
Pratt—Jane, 34; Mary, 43; Susanna, 227.
Preston—Eliza Ann, 64; Lydia, 156; Susanna, 23.
Price—Elizabeth, 74, 129, 222; Grace, 218; Hannah, 114; Martha, 157; Mary, 156; Rebecca, 129; Ruth, 61; Sarah, 42; Susan, 188.
Prickett—Ann, 7, 129, 183, 215, 221; Deborah, 22, 243; Druzilla, 163; Elisha, 22; Elizabeth, 135, 215; Esther, 37; Hannah, 48, 69, 141, 169, 182, 193; Josephine, 66; Lizzie, 27; Lois, 91; Lydia, 66; Mary, 9, 62, 84, 155, 159, 221; Patience, 102; Priscilla, 18, 200; Rachel, 69, 90; Roxanna, 67; Sarah, 119, 209.

Prickitt—Elizabeth, 182; Roxanna, 202.
Priestly—Sarah, 248.
Prince—Martha, 133.
Prior—Rebecca, 74.
Probasco—Drucilla, 30.
Proud—Elizabeth, 92, 187, 217, 225; Ruth, 193.
Purdy—Elizabeth Ann, 252.
Ptule—Sarah, 70.
Pugh—Abigail, 177; Elizabeth, 191.
Pullen—Rhoda, 188.
Punner—Elizabeth, 46.
Purdy—Achsah, 209; Rachel, 30.
Quam—Hannah, 181; Lavina, 248; Marian, 162.
Quest—Dinah, 127.
Quick—Margaret, 37.
Quickmire—Mary, 88.
Quicksal(l)—Elizabeth, 21; Keturah, 99; Sarah, 209, 225, 231.
Quig—Elizabeth, 129.
Quigley—Elizabeth, 36; Hannah, 187, 211; Jane, 30; Lydia, 125; Martha, 240; Mary, 78, 189; Sarah, 135.
Quigmore—Susan, 131.
Quin(n)—Catherine, 20; Elinor, 167; Sarah, 127.
Quire—Ellen, 240.
Race—Ann, 191.
Radfield—Ruth, 193.
Radford—Ann, 198; Mary, 20; Rebecca, 23; Sarah, 108.
Rah—Esther, 232.
Rainar—Zeiruiah, 42.
Rainear—Lydia Ann, 81.
Rainer(e)—Charlotte, 107; Rachel, 178; Sarah, 118; Susan, 86.
Rainier—Elizabeth, 218; Mercy, 242; Susan, 211.
Raker—Rachel, 98.
Rakestraw—Hannah, 99, 142; Lucretia, 164; Mary, 186; Rachel, 117.
Ramsey—Charlotte, 109.
Randall—Charlotte Evelyn, 119; Harriet, 149; Rebecca, 59.
Randolph—Isabella, 197; Sarah, 244.
Ranear—Deborah, 170.
Ransom—Susan, 193.
Raper—Abigail, 212; Martha, 17; Mary, 118, 212.
Rapp—Mary Emma, 133; Sarah Lizzie, 11.

Ratford—Martha, 178.
Rato—Rhoda, 89.
Raum—Gertrude, 163; Mary Ann, 59.
Raynels—Margaret, 9.
Read—Ann, 97, 196; Augusta Milnor, 169; Charlotte, 57; Elizabeth, 129, 171; Lucy Ann, 116; Martha, 66, 161; Mary, 97, 108; Rachel Ann, 234; Sarah, 66.
Ready—Elizabeth, 186.
Reaves—Rebecca Ann, 179.
Reckless—Ann, 73, 208; Mary, 198.
Rekford—Deborah, 105.
Redman—Rachel, 46; Tabitha, 24.
Reed—Abigail, 128; Ann, 50, 214; Dorothy, 190; Elizabeth, 31, 96; Fanny, 59; Margaret, 146; Martha, 108, 154; Mary, 41, 168; Mary Ann, 80, 203; Matilda, 207; Nancy, 243; Rachel, 179, 213; Rebecca. 99; Rhoda, 27; Thirza, 124.
Reese—Mary, 71.
Reeve(s)—Abigail, 149; 195; Amisa Ann, 10; Amy, 30, 202; Ann, 22, 104, 113, 254; Anna, 162; Anne, 186; Charity, 221; Elizabeth, 13, 58, 101, 174, 203, 204, 206; Esther, 71, 151; Hannah, 114, 135; 205; Henrietta, 23; Hope, 102; Isabella, 98, Jane, 114; Louise, 131; Lydia, 162; Martha, 15, 119, 248; Mary, 72, 81, 97, 101, 102, 105, 154, 182, 186, 215, 222, 231, 249; Mary Ann, 61; Meribah, 141; Rachel, 30; 115; Rebecca, 97; Ruth, 203, 210; Sarah, 250; Sarepta, 247; Susan, 228.
Regions—Margaret, 28.
Reily, Anna, 6.
Remer—Ann, 132.
Renear—Abigail, 240; Margaret, 5; Mary, 234.
Renner—Hannah, 47.
Reubant—Sarah, 97.
Reubart—Mariah, 188.
Reves—Rebecca, 104.
Reylius—Ruth, 182.
Reynear—Rachel, 236.
Reynolds—Ann, 32; Anne, 122; Catharine, 201; Elizabeth 237; Florence, 98; Lucretia, 207; Margaret, 22, 255; Mary, 240.
Rhodes—Sarah, 84.
Rice—Prudence, 233.
Richards—Ann, 22; Anna, 154; Bathsheba, 132; Elizabeth, 118; Grace, 121; Mercy, 157.

Richardson—Achsa, 85; Amy 105; Ann, 164, 200; Eleanor, 164; Elizabeth, 26, 43, 54, 254; Esther, 27; Hannah, 74; Jane, 62, 107, 143; Julian, 250; Lucia, 65; Martha, 106, 147; Mary, 26, 52. 105, 146, 189, 219; Nancy, 34; Phebe 170; Rachel, 184; Sarah, 124; Susan, 145;Susanna, 31; Tabitha, 10; Theodosi7, 193.

Rickets—Sarah, 244.

Rickey—Ann, 5; Jane, 121.

Rider—Kesiah, 10.

Ridge—Rose, 161.

Ridgeway—Hepziah, 230; Lucy, 22; Phebe, 92.

Ridgua—Elizabeth, 245; Jane, 10; Mary, 16.

Ridgway—Abigail, 24, 207; Ann, 38, 40, 65. 92; 95, 138, 220, 245; Catharine, 88, 242; Elizabeth, 10. 31, 55, 60, 67, 76, 91, 154; Esther, 56; Hannah, 54; 172; Harriet, 56; Jane, 31; Lydia, 63, 207; Lucia, 72; Martha, 256; Mariam, 154, 160; Mary, 57, 135, 143, 208, 213; Mercy, 17, 241; Nancy, 219; Naomi, 249; Sarah, 13, 42, 97, 159. 161; Susan, 196. 208; Susannah, 66.

Ridg—— —Susan, 199.

Ridley—Hannah, 188; Miriam, 27.

Rigane—Lorena, 9.

Riggents—Esther, 186.

Righton—Sarah, 179.

Rigua—Abigail, 48.

Riley—Alice, 213; Jane, 8; Mary, 216, 238; Rebecca, 232; Sally, 113; Susannah, 86.

Rinear—Emily, 9; Harriet, 179; Grace, 187, Sarah, 149.

Rinold—Ann, 16.

Ripp—Johanna, 23.

Risdon—Bertha, 71; Clara, 11; Eliza. 181; Elizabeth, 106, 252; Emma, 241; Juliana, 83; Sarah, 141; Theodora, 140.

Ritchie—Mary, 34; Sarah Ann, 32.

Rite—Jane, 36.

Rizar—Polly, 97.

Roads—Mary, 181.

Robbins—Ann 35, 112; Elennor, 11; Elizabeth, 131; Mary Ann, 60; Nancy, 57; Rebecca, 23; Sarah, 138; Susan, 25.

Roberts—Abigail, 39; Ann. 40; Elizabeth, 135, 213; Hannah, 136, 144, 192; Hepzibah, 144; Judith, 218; Keziah. 7; Marian, 156; Mary, 52, 113, 125, 131; Mary Ann, 23; Sarah, 75, 77, 162, 215; Theodotia, 178.

Robertson—Elizabeth, 185; Mary, 37.

Robeson—Mary, 15; Mary Ann, 216.

Robins—Abigail, 175; Ann, 45; Charlotte, 208; Deliverance, 225; Deoshe, 26; Margaret, 32; Mary, 32, 229; Priscilla, 254; Rachel, 239; Rebecca, 214.

Robinson—Adelaide, 126; Emma Adelia, 235; Elizabeth, 217; Lydia, 65, 66; Martha, 113; Mary, 48.

Roche—Catherine, 118 Joanna 50.

Rochelle—Ann, 78.

Rockhill—Abigail, 42; Acsah, 36; Ann, 68, 75; Anne, 231; Dove, 149; Elizabeth, 75, 139, 166; Hannah, 169, 249; Jemima, 77; Jerusha, 219; Margaret, 56; Mary, 110, 148, 166, 179, 217; Mercy, 107; Merebeth 213; Regina, 23; Sarah, 13, 23, 25, 56, 74; Susannah, 123; Theodocia, 181; Tobitha, 81.

Rodgers—Abigail, 111; Ann, 44, 165; Martha, 251; Mary, 98; Sarah, 28.

Rodman—Anna, 48, 180; Beulah, 240; Elizabeth, 203; Esther, 154; Margaret, 94, 154, 178; Mary, 178.

Roe—Mary, 37.

Rogers—Abigail, 29, 73, 129; Achsa, 227; Adaline, 148; Ann, 18, 28, 43, 87, 119, 145, 190, 246; Augusta, 52; Beulah, 15; Eliza, 237; Elizabeth, 63, 135, 220, 229, 232, 241; Esther, 71; Euphemia, 253; Fanny, 140; Hannah, 21, 44, 229; Harriet, 168; Hester, 174; Hope, Hope, 252; Lettis, 128; Lydia, 191; Margaret, 205; Martha, 20, 60, 138, 160, 192, 202, 223; Mary, 65, 87, 132, 135, 153, 155, 198, 215, 223, 241; Mehitable, 63; Phebe Ann, 226; Prudence, 39; Rebecca, 29, 70, 220; Sarah, 6, 122, 138, 217, 229; Sarah Ann, 242; Sebiny, 55; Vashti, 101.

Rolly—Fanny, 97.

Rose—Eliza, 98; Elizabeth, 92; Martha, 210; Mary, 24, 172, 208; Mary Ann, 148; Matilda, 12; Rebecca, 162; Susan, 105.

Rosel(e)—Anne, 196; Louisa, 136.

Rosman—Elizabeth, 248.

Ross—Mary, 54; Mary Ann, 28; Polly, 131; Sophia, 46.

Rossel(l)—Allice, 167; Betsey, 159; Elizabeth, 84; Grace, 84; Hannah, 215, 252; Hope, 90; Jane, 159; Margaret, 240; Martha, 185; Mary, 230, 249; Mary Ann, 44; Meribah, 16; Rebecca, 214.

Roselle—Mary, 190.

Rossill—Mary, 123.

Roth—Rebecca, 38.

Rouge—Alice, 216.

Rouse—Rebecca, 51; Susannah, 137.

Rowan(d)—Elizabeth, 53; Sarah, 148.

Rowe—Catherine, 158.
Roweing—Rachel, 197.
Rowlan—Elizabeth, 231.
Roy—Martha, 54.
Roydhouse—Sarah, 37.
Rubart—Hannah, 242; Margery, 256.
Rubins—Ann, 217.
Rudderow—Ann, 43, 81, 216; Catharine, 145; Hannah, 145; Louisa, 163; Sarah, 233; Sarah Ann, 52.
Ruder—Ann, 28.
Ruderon—Hannah 115.
Rudrow—Ester, 91.
Rue—Catherine, 172; Mary, 232.
Rulins—Mary, 110.
Rulon(g)—Exercise, 223; Jemima, 165; Mary, 214; Phebe, 173.
Runyan—Rebecca, 130.
Rushford—Anstes, 188.
Russell—Ann, 115; Mary, 209; Mary Ann, 229; Rebecca, 42.
Ryan—Mary, 166.
Rydan—Sarah, 88.
Rymar—Jane, 54.
Rynear—Ann, 218.
Ryner—Mary, 6.
Ryness—Rebecca, 228.
Sabborne—Elizabeth, 86.
Sage(r)—Ann, 51; Elizabeth, 208; Hannah, 58.
Sailer—Mary Laura, 133; Ray, 116.
Sailor—Margaret, 203; Mary, 123; Rebecca, 92.
Saint—Elizabeth, 42.
Salar—Barbara, 56.
Saltar—Lucy, 127.
Salter—Elizabeth, 108, 120.
Sampson—Hannah, 178.
Samson—Mary Ann, 179.
Sanders—Rachel, 77.
Sands—Mary, 223.
Sansinger—Phebe, 228.
Sap(p)—Caroline, 204; June, 145; Margaret, 83; Mary, 198; Sibilla, 177.
Sapcott—Rachel, 150.
Sapcutt—Elizabeth, 150.

Sargible—Sarah, 133.
Satterthwaite—Anna, 217; Deborah, 43; Dorothy, 97; Elizabeth, 252; Elizth, 101; Hannah, 141; Jean, 92; Margaret, 185; Mary, 6, 109; Rebekkah, 186; Sarah, 73.
Saturday—Kate, 133.
Saul—Mary, 179.
Saunders—Elizabeth, 77; Mary, 243; Sarah, 60, 148.
Saundes—Sarah, 18.
Savill—Mary, 158.
Sawyer—Charlotte, 190; Cynthia, 126.
Saxton—Ann, 35; Elizabeth, 73.
Saylor—Hannah Ann, 127; Mary, 179.
Scattergood—Elizabeth, 9, 29, 80; Hannah, 171; Judith, 86; Maria, 105; Rebecca, 5, 174; Sarah, 19, 87, 164, 230, 253; Tamer, 200; Thomasine, 171, 241.
Schenck—Ann, 184; Mary, 78; Sabina, 22.
Schofield—Rebecca, 109.
Scholey—Mary, 194; Rebecca, 253; Sarah, 241.
Schooley—Ann, 123, 199; Frances, 140; Isabel, 190; Jehoshebah, 228; Keziah, 153; Mary, 18, 228; Susannah, 165.
Schull—Nancy, 191; Ruth, 81.
Schuyler—Elizabeth, 108, 133; Emily Ann, 63; Jennette, 148; Nancy, 189; Sarah, 150; Susan, 184.
Scoby—Mahaley, 107.
Scott—Alice, 170; Ann, 18; Anna, 125; Bridget, 147; Elizabeth, 141, 238; Hannah, 23, 26, 70; Hester, 125, 146; Lydia, 16; Margaret, 136; Margaret, 231; Mary, 89, 218; Patience, 17; Priscilla, 131; Rebecca, 66; Sarah 242; Susannah, 160.
Scount—Juliet, 149.
Scroggins—Jane, 11.
Scroggy—Abigail, 127; Elizabeth, 7, 80; Hannah, 247; Mary 91.
Scull—Elizabeth, 230.
Scuyler—Mary, 254.
Seal—Judith, 23.
Seaman—Amelia 151; Elizabeth, 172; Lydia, 55; Martha, 150; Sarah, 166.
Seamons—Phebe, 7.
Searle—Grace, 62.
Sears—Eliza, 26; Leanora, 247; Letitia, 171; Mary, 252; Rebecca, 9; Susanna, 177.
Sedgwick—Elizabeth, 74.

Seed—Mariah, 17; Mary, 37.
Seeley—Rachel, 201.
Seever—Mary, 176.
Selpath—Rebecca, 233.
Sersson—Catharine, 169.
Sesen—Agnes, 117.
Severn(s)—Ann, 180; Elishaba, 120; Elizabeth, 74; Joanna, 165; Mary, 80.
Severs—Anna, 130; Elizabeth, 128; Mary, 15, 228; Ruth, 146.
Sevill—Mary, 7.
Sexton—Lettice, 149; Rebecca, 227; Rhoda, 210.
Shadager—Elizabeth, 251
Shafer—Abigail, 189.
Shaffer—Charlotte, 18.
Shallick—Honour, 210.
Shamaley—Elizabeth, 70.
Shamela—Mary, 245.
Sharoe—Katherine, 131.
Sharp—Abigail, 127; Agness, 30, 182; Ann, 182; Anna, 54, 196; Beulah, 99, 139; Charlotte, 114; Deborah, 8, 170; Elenore, 162; Eliza, 180, 219; Elizabeth, 27, 36, 103, 128, 201, 202; 212; Esther, 13, 105, 177, 202; Hannah, 30, 102, 166, 174; Hester, 243; Jemima, 15; Julian, 86; Lavinia, 47; Lydia, 141; Margaret, 31; Maria, 57; Mariah, 243; May, 69, 90, 130, 221, 246; Mary Anna, 158; Mary Augusta, 78; Priscilla, 18, 21, 157; Rachel, 39, 110, 166, 186, 202; Rebecca, 76, 103; Rebeckah, 151; Rebekkah, 49; Rose, 159; Sarah, 21, 105, 177, 182, 228; Susannah, 164.
Shaver—Sarah, 78,
Shaw—Ann, 252; Anne, 163; Hannah, 150; Mary, 227; Mary Anne, 208; Sarah, 6; Susannah, 67.
Shawthorne—Jane, 206.
Shealds—Mary, 61.
Shedaker—Elizabeth, 209.
Shee—Elizabeth, 211.
Shemely—Elizabeth, 111; Mary, 126.
Shemerwas—Elizabeth, 108.
Shephard—Lucy Ann, 52.
Shepherd—Margaret, 26; Mary, 15; Rosannah, 155; Susannah, 164.
Sheppard—Rhoda, 153.
Sherman—Elizabeth, 88; Maria, 98.
Sherrard—Abigail, 77.

Sherrin—Rebecca, 213.
Sherwin—Elizabeth, 218; Mary, 174; Rebecca, 8.
Shields—Ann, 65; Anne, 183; Mary, 125.
Shimela—Elizabeth, 234,
Shinn—Abigail, 35. 108, 127, 187, 247; Alice, 217; Allis, 145; Amy 24; Ann, 61; Anna Maria, 231; Annah, 186; Anne, 123; Beulah, 24;' Catharine, 136; Elizabeth, 9, 11, 28, 83, 123, 127, 136, 193, 253; Emily, 45; Esther, 16, 247; Frances Maria, 55; Hannah, 13, 70, 79, 85, 133, 170, 205; Hope, 14, 19; Ida, 24; Jane, 91; Jemima, 142, 250; Julia, 225, Lavinia, 128, 174; Lucretia, 183; Lydia, 31, 128, 176; Margaret, 119; Martha, 92, 160, 169, 204; Marty, 252; Mary, 9, 16, 58, 77, 123, 124, 136, 154, 169, 173, 180, 195, 222, 226, 245, 253; Mehitable, 67; Rachel, 12, 29, 38, 39; Rebecca, 28, 45, 147, 235; Rhoda, 217; Ruth, 161, 220; Sarah, 20, 93, 128, 139, 142, 164, 194, 228; Susanna, 14; Susanah, 240; Unity, 171.
Shippen—Frances, 238.
Shippy—Ann, 116.
Shiras—Elizabeth, 242; Ellen, 207; Martha, 185.
Shires—Anna, 48.
Shirra—Elizabeth, 193.
Shivers—Ann, 42; Hope, 42.
Shoemaker—Mable, 104.
Shords—Hannah, 68; Su2anna, 177.
Shores—Maria, 222; Sarah, 44.
Shourds—Anna, 209; Hannah, 211; Mary, 176, 225, 228; Rhoda, 191; Sarah, 138.
Shreaves—Sarah, 199.
Shreeve—Ann, 195; Rebecca, 212; Sarah, 168,
Shreve—Abigail, 97, 184; Acsah, 138; Ann, 214, 225; Annah, 170; Elizabeth, 256; Grace, 143; Hannah, 223, 256; Hope, 55; Keziah, 69; Lucy, 249; Lydia, 43; Mariana, 203; Martha, 30, 188, 220; Mary, 101 113, 120, 165; Merab, 34; Phebe, 94; Phebe Virginia, 243; Rachel, 14; Rebecca, 78, 88, 154, 165; Sarah, 21, 28; Susan, 190.
Shrieve—Mercy, 151.
Shubb—Elizabeth, 132.
Shuff—Hannah, 177.
Shute—Rachel, 31.
Sickells—Sarah, 181.
Sickles—Martha, 240.
Sinmans—Jane, 83.
Sidnaham—Sarah, 223

Signet—Mary, 106.
Sikes—Johannah, 34; Mary, 230.
Sile—Mary, 21.
Sill—Catharine—48.
Silver(s)—Lydia, 62; Rebecca, 254; Ruth, 125; Susan, 103.
Sinclear—Hannah, 48.
Simpkins—Margaret, 161.
Simmons—Ally, 55; Ann, 252; Deborah, 35; Mary, 204.
Simon(s)—Amey, 10; Keziah, 44; Bethenie, 12; Elizabeth, 134; Hannah, 222; Joanna, 176; Kitty, 5; Mary, 158, 175; Sarah, 134, 200.
Simson, Ann, 87; Rebecca, 197.
Singer—Rebecca, 30.
Sirman—Rachel, 106.
Skillinger—Nancy, 170.
Skirm—Elizabeth, 65; Huldah, 250; Mary, 46; Tace, 229.
Slack—Leila May, 175; Mary, 92, 207; Nina, 92.
Sleeper—Edith, 39; Elizabeth, 154; Leah, 173; Sallie, 7; Sarah, 186.
Slim—Merriam, 144.
Sloan—Mary, 103.
Small—Amy, 244; Hannah, 78; Hope, 73; Margaret, 88; Martha, 126; Mary, 151; Sheba, 134.
Smalley—Mary, 149.
Smallwood—Mary, 99.
Smart—Abigail, 58; Alley, 50.
Smick—Mary, 116.
Smith—Abigail, 26, 62, 69, 144, 248; Alice, 111; Amy Matilda, 27; Ann, 17, 28, 41, 75, 232; Anna, 164; Anne, 94, 169; Artis, 140; Barbara, 130; Beulah, 247; Catharine, 40; Caroline, 63, 174; Dorothy, 20; Eleanor, 89, 156; Eliza, 99, 189; Elizabeth, 14, 26, 28, 94, 104, 113, 118, 174, 180, 207, 249, 252; Emma, 203; Esther, 160; Euphemia, 158; Frances, 40; Hannah 40, 55, 58, 71, 98, 150, 211, 234; Harriet, 52, 357; Hope, 180; Jane, 138; Janet, 185; Jannet, 224; Joan, 139; Joyce, 55; Katherine, 166; Lillie, 166; Levina, 183; Lucretia, 111; Margaret, 6, 57, 227; Maria, 96; Marjorie, 19, 96; Martha, 229; Mary, 7, 37, 57, 71, 76, 78, 94, 114, 122, 141, 162, 166, 188, 194, 223, 227, 252; Mary Ann, 52; Mary Anna, 233; Mercy, 27, 84; Nancy, 9, 25; Rachel, 131, 179; Rebecca, 49, 71, 91, 125, 242; Rhoda, 133, 222; Ruth, 72; Sarah, 7, 14, 22, 31, 100, 127, 212, 223, 238; Susannah, 236
Smitz—Mary, 198; Michael, 164.

Smygrum—Nancy, 92.
Snippin—Mary, 153.
Snow—Eva, 130.
Snowball—Emily Jane, 249.
Snowden—Anne, 171; Ruth, 112.
Snuff—Elizabeth, 82.
Snuffin—Mary, 246.
Snyder—Margaret, 127, 129.
Sogers—Ann, 68.
Somers—Hannah, 10; Judith, 17; Rachel, 169.
Sooy—Elizabeth, 17, 227, 228; Esther, 127; Hannah, 176; Mary, 20; Parnel, 16; Rebeckah, 139; Sophia, 198.
Sopers—Levinia, 210; Lydia, 47; Mary, 94; Sarah, 218.
Souder—Sarah, 124.
South—Rachel, 167.
Southard—Hannah, 242; Phebe, 78.
Southerly—Anna, 116,
Southwick—Ann, 27; Elizabeth, 84; Hannah, 125, 230, 254; Henrietta, 10; Jane, 91; Mary, 56, 98; Priscilla; 116; Rebecca, 181; Ruth, 57.
Sowden—Ann, 145; Elizabeth, 55; Sarah, 255.
Spachus—Mary, 54.
Spacius—Phebe, 116.
Spanner—Amelia, 148.
Sparkurn—Catherine, 87.
Sparks—Mary, 67.
Speachy—Ann, 167.
Specule—Margaret, 224.
Sphes—Hannah, 189.
Spicer—Abigail, 197.
Spike—Catharine, 82.
Spragg—Marion, 181; Mary, 228.
Sprague—Mary, 169.
Spring—Mary, 152.
Springer—Amy, 27; Dorothy, 182; Elizabeth, 174; Hannah, 224; Lucey, 225; Mary, 227; Phebe, 224.
Sprowls—Marian, 191.
Squan—Charlotte, 124; Robert, 53.
Sreve—Amy, 91; Elizabeth, 232.
Ssheriper—Catharina, 140.
Stacey—Ann, 139.

Stack—Susan, 118.
Stackhouse—Abigail, 135; Agnes, 182; Alce, 253; Ann, 67, 115; Bathsheba, 90; Elizabeth, 194, 252; Jane, 61; Margaret, 61; Ruth, 240; Sarah, 10.
Stacy—Ellen, 205
Staffon—Martha, 16
Stainbrook—Anna, 110.
Stancie—Ann, 32.
Stanhope—Ruth, 59.
Stanton—Charlotte, 233; Elizabeth, 188.
Staples—Ann, 195; Elizabeth, 128; Martha, 128; Mary, 239.
Stapleton—Mary, 30.
Starkey—Anna, 28; Beulah, 196; Elizabeth, 118; Hannah, 148; Matilda, 64; Nancy, 136; Rachel, 183; Ruth, 50: Sarah, 9, 111.
Starkye—Elizabeth, 206.
Stebbins—Martha, 183.
Stedford—Emaline, 13.
Stee(l)—Elizabeth, 175; Lydia, 98; Lydia Catharine, 45.
Steelman—Elizabeth, 85; Rebecca, 213.
Steinson—Dinah, 128.
Stephens—Hannah, 94; Mary, 193.
Stephenson—Ann, 36; Hannah, 150; Lizzie, 92; Mary, 227; Priscilla, 80.
Sterling—Anna, 224; Margaret, 126, 127; Mary, 115; Rebecca, 154; Susan, 232.
Stern—Sarah, 130.
Stevens—Elizabeth, 24; Phebe, 133.
Stevenson—Abigail, 249; Alice, 31, 93; Ann, 47; Anna, 136; Anne, 167; Bernice, 108; Charity, 131, 176; Dorothy, 175; Elizabeth, 41, 80, 89; Harriet, 49; Margaret, 181; Mary, 44, 103, 185, 245, 248; Phebe, 145; Sarah, 110, 131, 135, 171,; Susanna, 152, 170.
Steward—Catherine, 169; Elizabeth, 36; Hannah, 132; Lydia, 217; Mary, 66; Rebecca, 43; Sarah, 73.
Stewart—Abigail, 250; Ann, 70, 98; Anne, 37, 79; Bridget, 54, 226; Elizabeth, 36, 83, 252; Martha, 44; Mary Ann, 202; Rebecca, 138; Susannah, 155.
Stile(s)—Ann, 101; Dinah, 17; Elizabeth, 137, 178, 218; Emma, 65; Grace, 100; Hannah, 95, 152, 222; Jane, 232; Martha, 12, 230; Mary, 49, 63, 132, 152, 233; Nancy, 184; Priscilla, 218; Rebecca, 83; Sarah, 180, 201; Susannah, 94.
Still—Abigail, 141; Ann, 231; Beulah, 247; Fanny, 119; Hope, 146;

Lavinia, 42; Mahala, 228; Mary, 56; Nancy, 189; Sarah Ann, 234; Vilet, 6.

Stillwell—Ann, 83; Eleanor, 58; Elizabeth, 166; Hannah, 131, 219; Hope Ann, 172; Jane, 168; Margaret, 211; Martha, 236; Mary, 173; Sarah, 145, 177; Sarah Ann, 207.

Stinmitz—Rachel, 114.

Stockdal—Mary, 156.

Stockdill—Hannah, 220.

Stockdon—Hannah, 139; Mary, 206.

Stockham—Phebe, 175.

Stockton—Abigail, 72, 91, 178; Anna, 58; Anne, 41, 132; Caroline, 197; Charity, 218; Dorothy, 16; Elizabeth, 58, 104, 134, 143, 236; Hannah, 7, 11, 12, 39, 40, 86, 122, 211, 254; Harriet, 220; Hester, 146; Hope, 112; K., 39; Louisa, 111; Lydia, 219; Margaret, 45, 246; Maria, 197; Maria Ann, 52; Martha, 117; Patience, 9; Mary, 12, 22, 49, 92, 97, 100, 125, 167, 207, 216, 242; Mary Ann, 104; Nancy, 113; Rachel, 139, 194; Rebecca, 118, 119; Rebeckah, 142, 251; Rhoda, 119, 256; Sarah, 62, 91, 164, 194, 219.

Stoddart—Mary, 222.

Stogdon, Dosha, 185.

Stokes—Ann, 101; Anna, 18; Atlantic, 121, 241; Bathsheba; 76; Deliverance, 52; Elizabeth, 23, 63, 99, 103, 120, 147, 194; Frances, 50; Hannah, 50, 101; H. Rosa, 246; Judith, 157; Lydia, 133, 246; Maria, 22; Mariah, 251; Martha, 99; Mary, 87, 119, 143, 160, 163, 213, 243; Priscilla, 10; Rebecca, 123, 229; Sarah, 11, 103, 139; Susanna, 78.

Stokesberry—Rebecca, 78.

Stone—Ann, 168; Rebecca, 18.

Story—Dority, 64; Elizabeth, 136.

Stout—Achsa, 130; Anne, 240; Catharine, 59, 63; Dorothy, 159; Elenor, 233; Hannah, 67; Lucy, 67; Penelope, 78; Rebecca, 57, 207; Sarah, 177, 194.

Stoutenburge—Margaret, 42.

Strallein—Rebecca, 48.

Strangnats—Maria, 149.

Strattan—Hannah, 58; Jane, 167.

Stratten—Martha, 16.

Stratton—Abigail, 18; Achsah, 187; Alice, 24, 26; Amy, 98; Ann, 129, 186; Anne, 202; Dorothy, 231; Elizabeth, 21, 246; Hannah, 105, 155; Harriet, 29; Hepsebe 182; Hester, 120; Hope, 186; Jane, 201; Keziah, 183; Louisa, 241; Lydia, 183, 188, 210; Martha, 55, 95; Mary, 62, 103, 121, 141, 144, 251; Mary Ann, 234; Neomy, 102;

Polly, 188; Prudence, 14; Rebecca. 231; Ruth, 203; Sarah, 65, 144; Susanna, 171.
  Streatrer—Achsa, 82.
  Stretch—Hannah, 10; Mary, 28; Rebecca, 116; Sarah, 5,, 70.
  Stricker—Catherine, 188; Eliza Ann, 186; Emma, 243; Louisa, 160; Mary, 199; Priscilla, 135.
  Striker—Ann, 31; Caroline, 35.
  Stringer—Hannah, 88.
  Strouse—Elizabeth May, 254.
  Stuart—Elly, 114; Mary, 225; Rachel, 98.
  Sucur—Elizabeth, 153.
  Sulcey—Deborah, 18; Rachel, 76.
  Sullivan—Abigail, 168; Elinor, 30; Elizabeth, 12.
  Sullyvan—Suzanna, 17.
  Sulsey—Amy, 161; Mary Ann, 222.
  Sulsy—Grace, 219.
  Sutfield—Ruth Ann, 170.
  Sutphin(e)—Catharine, 65; Elizabeth, 98.
  Sutton—Ann, 52; Elizabeth, 187; Hannah, 65; Margaret, 21; 230, 257.
  Sutts—Ann, 17; Mary, 56.
  Sutvin—Bulah, 109.
  Swaim—Isabella, 149; Mary, 193.
  Swainry—Margaret, 149.
  Swame—Lydia, 63.
  Swanson—Mary Ann, 94.
  Sweem—Elizabeth, 20; Mary, 140.
  Sweet—Ann, 239; Hannah, 111; Julian, 44; Keziah, 44.
  Sweeney—Susanna, 51.
  Sweim—Rebecca, 232.
  Swem(m)—Alexia, 109; Elizabeth, 52; Micha, 236.
  Swift—Ann, 244; Elizabeth, 208; Mary, 236; Phebe, 158; Rachel, 141; Sarah, 223.
  Sydenham—Elizabeth, 57.
  Sykes—Catherine, 241; Edith, 69; Elizabeth, 117; Hannah, 135; Joan, 237; Mary, 33; Rebecca, 89.
  Symonds—Hannah, 176; Sarah, 26.
  Symons—Lottie, 75.
  Syphers—Mayr, 235.
  Talbott—Catherine, 177.

Talman—Lydia, 207.
Tallman—Deborough, 168; Elizabeth, 139; Hannah, 40; Martha, 81, 138; Mary, 185; Sarah, 20, 54, 232.
Tamper—Sarah, 137.
Tanner—Hester, 158; Lydia, 187; Susannah, 197,
Tantum—Ann, 112; Elizabeth, 252; Sarah, 147.
Tarker—Catherine, 107.
Tash—Mary, 38; Sarah 75.
Tate(m)—Patience, 49; Sarah, 201.
Tauntum—Elizabeth, 214.
Taylor—Abigail, 117, 225; Achsah, 64; Amy, 230; Ann, 77, 101, 114, 177, 191, 194, 233; Anna, 226, 242, 257; Anne, 184, 208; Catherine, 25, 94; Clara, 124; Dorothy, 139; Edith, 136; Eleanor, 53; Eliza, 90; Elizabeth, 7, 26, 65, 73, 114 158, 159, 209, 247; Ellen, 177; Hannah, 198, 213, 254; Hepsebee, 129; Jane, 40; Jannet, 110; Kesiah, 78; Lydia, 87; Lydia Ann, 136; Lucretia, 83; Margaret, 43, 64, 224; Maria, 48; Martha, 29, 101; Mary, 9, 10, 27, 72, 80, 81, 104, 164, 165, 195, 214, 228, 241 247; Miriam, 64; Nancy, 173; Patience, 12, 158, 159, 201; Phebe, 67, 72; Rachel, 122, 224; Rebecca, 36, 86, 188, 217; Ruth, 224; Sarah, 33, 60, 109, 117, 118; 121, 149, 157, 163; 193; Sarah Ella, 167.
Tayror—Sarah, 11.
Tearney—Ann, 43.
Tencher—Hannah, 251.
Ten Eyck—Augusta, 55; Jane, 197; Julia, 113.
Terry—Elizabeth, 129; Sarah, 37.
Test—Ann, 97; Betsey, 190; Hope, 8; Sarah, 149.
Tewksbury—Rachel, 150.
Thackerell—Hannah, 211.
Thatcher, Mary, 248.
Thimble—Elizabeth, 70.
Thomas—Alice, 177; Anne, 42; Elizabeth, 31, 132, 159, 219; Grace, 205; Hannah, 15 131; Hope, 51; Jane, 15; Margaret, 195; Maria, 176; Mary, 37, 66, 81, 218, 229; Prudence, 112; Rebecca, 206; Sarah, 10, 214; Susan, 158; Susanna, 9, 15, 66, 74; Unity, 41.
Thompson—Ann, 97, 142, 211; Charity, 254; Damey, 197; Dinah, 116; Elizabeth, 22, 33, 38, 58, 104; Grace, 236; Hannah, 171, 237, 244; Hepsabeth, 187; Julia Ann, 17; Laomia, 99; Martha, 113; Mary, 9, 24, 55, 204; Prudence, 94; Rebecca, 64, 98 201; Sarah, 57, 178; Susan, 30, 164; Susanna, 152; S. Lavinia, 135; Ruth, 15.
Thomson—Ann, 191; Lydia, 190; Martha, 60; Mary, 153, 172, 174,

Thorla—Mary, 164.
Thorne—Abigail, 174, 207; Amy, 33, 221; Ann, 146, 225; Charlotte, 180; Diademia, 39; Elizabeth, 234; Jane, 127; Jemima, 47; Lydia, 11; Margaret, 92; Mary, 105, 109; Nancy, 76; Tacy, 28.
Thorp—Mary, 185.
Throgmorton—Dorothy, 255.
Thurrell--Jane, 177.
Tidiagot—Bath, 11.
Tilton—Charlotte, 60; Elizabeth, 235; Hannah, 156, 166; Lucy, 38; Mary 81, 129, 190; Patience, 26, 157.
Tindal(l)—Joanna, 114; Lydia, 39; Sarah, 216.
Tindell—Elizabeth, 118.
Titus—Catharine, 237; Hannah, 243; Nancy, 172; Phebe, 190.
Toal—Mary, 7.
Tolbert—Rebecca, 51.
Tool—Mary, 170.
Tolman—Elizabeth, 88.
Tomlin--Hannah, 40.
Tomlinson—Eliz., 171; Elizabeth, 98, 141; Mary, 233; Naomy, 52; Rebecca, 76.
Toner—Amy, 223; Deborah, 197; Elizabeth, 123.
Tonkan—Elizabeth, 39.
Tonkin(s)—Ann 165; Elizabeth, 27, 152; Mary, 42, 190; Sarah, 171; Susannah, 226.
Topping—Elizabeth, 242; Jane, 251.
Torn—Susan, 232.
Towey—Sarah Jane, 86.
Townsend—Elizabeth, 240; Phebe, 230.
Toy—Abigail, 187; Ann, 96; Elenor, 9, 139; Elizabeth, 117, 187; Mary, 18, 35, 201.
Treat—Elizabeth, 39; Martha, 117.
Trendwell—Margaret, 123.
Trenet—Ann, 193.
Trenton—Anne, 77.
Trimbless—Ann Jane, 112.
Triplette—Nettie Maude, 234.
Troth—Ann, 56; Anna, 49; Emelia, 257; Esther, 49; Hephzebah, 239; Jane, 90; Lucy Ann, 37, 136; Mary, 100, 183, 243; Rebecca, 99, 224; Susannah, 16.
Trout(h)—Ann, 92; Elizabeth, 249; Emelia, 39; Grace, 210; Misa, 208; Rebecca Ann, 177.

Truax—Hannah, 78; Julian, 104; Phebe, 236; Rebecca, 216.
Truckniss—Ann, 43.
Trusty—Lewsilla, 212; Lucida, 67.
Tucker—Cornelia, 209; Eliza, 124; Hannah, 32; Margaret, 236; Sarah, 121; Susan, 22.
Tuley—Hannah, 98; Mary, 27.
Tulley—Ann, 9, 106; Martha, 11; Mary, 69, 94; Margaret, 74.
Turner—Ann, 200; Anne, 234; Dinah, 136; Elizabeth, 223; Hannah, 228; Margaret, 154: Priscilla, 200; Theodosia, 37.
Tyler—Annie, 65; Bathsheba, 83; Hannah, 211; Jerusha, 215; Mary, 15; Tryphena, 119.
Uncle(s)—Amelia, 176; Latetia, 42; Susannah, 88.
Underhill—Rebecca, 121.
Unkel—Rebeccah, 93.
Updike—Lydia, 248; Mary, 105; Susan, 146.
Usall—Sarah, 169.
Vagow—Anles, 203.
Vail—Laura Vir6inia, 255.
Valentine—Mary Ann, 211; Phebe, 57; Philay, 118.
Vanbrunt—Ellener, 176; Susan, 175.
Vanderbake—Ann, 225.
Vanderbeck—Elizabeth, 126; Rachel, 29.
Vandegrift—Eliza, 214; Elizabeth, 124, 248; Hannah, 153; Hester, 225.
Vandergrift—Elizabeth, 218; Mary, 34; Mary Ann, 67; Rebecca, 119; Sarah, 59.
Vandeveer—Elizabeth, 138; Mary, 112.
Vandusen—Margaret, 222.
Vandyke—Catharine, 72; Cornelia, 46; Lydia, 74, 173.
VanGuilder—Rebeckah, 214.
VanHagen—Rebecca, 170.
VanHarlingen—Mary, 199.
Vanhise—Elizabeth, 31.
Vanhorn(e)—Lucy, 207, 208; Martha, 159; Mary, 5, 40, 222 Rebecca, 72; Sarah, 32, 80.
Vankirk—Agnes, 234; Ann, 166; Sarah, 234.
VanMartyr—Mary Ann, 116.
VanMater—Hagar, 198.
Vanneman—Ann, 126,
Vannote—Sarah, 154, 174.
Vanroom—Ruth, 193.

Vansant—Ann, 179, 217; Patty, 156.

Vansciver—Abigail, 75; Achsa, 146; Ann, 77 94, 117, 175; Deborah, 129, 174, 239; Eliza, 176; Gartery, 189; Gertrude, 223; Harriet, 83; Jane, 176; Jannet, 164; Maria, 176; Mary, 52, 153; Pamelia, 154; Sarah, 124, 180.

Vanse—Elizabeth, 229.

VanWagener—Jeneke, 199.

VanWyck—Susan, 35.

Vanzant—Elizabeth, 61; Martha, 208.

Vaughan—Catherine, 65; Mary 176; Patience, 234.

Vaughn—Amy, 188; Ann, 231, 250; Frances, 256; Martha, 218; Rhody, 110.

Vaun(n)—Hester, 43; Lydia, 94; Mary, 221.

Veal—Rebecca, 75.

Veliak—Adelia, 218.

Venaball—Elizabeth, 114.

Venable—Abigail, 211; Anne, 54; Hope, 235; Mary, 116.

Venicomb—Rachel, 102.

Veno—Ann, 235.

Vernon—Susan, 32.

Verree—Mary, 107.

Victory—Elizabeth, 133.

Vinicomb—Ann, 61, 195; Rachel. 122 Sarah, 239.

Vine—Agness, 187,

Viscombe—Zilpha, 22.

Vollow—Margaret, 221.

Voorhees—Sarah, 174.

Voto—Sarah, 58.

Vreeland—Susannah, 105.

Wager—Emma, 136.

Wagner—Mary, 230.

Wagoner—A., 96.

Wainright—Hope, 50; Rebecca, 110; Susan, 162.

Wainwright—Ann, 176; Lydia, 109; Mary, 88; Patience, 224.

Wair—Isabella, 28.

Wait(e)—Christian, 206; Rebecca, 147.

Walberth—Catherine, 113.

Walcott—Annie, 118; Betsey. 179; Elizabeth, 163; Mary, 214.

Walker—Alice, 159; Ann, 16, 23; Benjamina, 67; Hannah, 145; Martha, 54; Sarah, 150.

Wall—Ann, 173; Edith, 111.

Wallace—Hannah, 236; Mary, 231; Rebecca, 235; Sarah, 138, 161; Susan, 50.
Wallen—Levine, 31; Mary, 94; Sarah, 123, 173.
Walling(s)—Elizabeth, 218; Mary, 20.
Wallis—Jane, 128; Rachel, 14; Sarah, 234.
Waln—Elizabeth, 34.
Walsh—Sarah, 64.
Walton—Ann, 127, 166; Elizabeth, 175; Martha, 108, 217; Mary, 21; Mary Ann, 74; Rachel, 130.
Wanderlin—Hope, 125.
Ward—Abigail, 127; Ann, 24, 155, 162; Frances, 201; Hope, 45; Lydia, 235; Maria, 121; Martha, 61; Mary, 155; Rachel, 155, 174; Rebecca, 47; Sarah, 56.
Wardell—Elizabeth, 15, 73.
Ware— Ann, 112; Elizabeth, 12; Hannah, 163, 186; Jane, 251.
Warner—Amy, 164; Elizabeth, 170, 234; Hannah, 168, 250; Mary, 90; Ofpy, 234; Rebecca, 74; Sarah, 75, 193.
Warren—Achsah, 108; Ann, 41, 241; Anna, 143; Eliza, 6; Emeline, 31; Hannah, 41; Lydia, 140; Mariah, 136; Meribah, 58; Mary, 69, 82, 229; Peniah, 104; Rebecca, 92; Susanna, 136.
Warrick—Mary, 11, 26, 52; Rebecca 148; Rebeckah, 170; Sarah 112, 156.
Warrington—Elizabeth, 48; Lydia, 100; Mary, 139, 250; Rebecca, 101.
Warris—Nancy, 59.
Warwick—Frances, 121; Sarah, 185.
Washington—Mary, 138.
Waterman--Levinia, 216; Tabitha, 10.
Waters—Charity, 168; Catherine, 138; Elizabeth, 38.
Watkins—Charlotte, 180; Martha, 163.
Watkinson—Charlotta, 19; Margaret, 136; Martha, 98.
Watmough—Mary, 95.
Watson—Abigail, 71; Anne, 253; Elizabeth, 171; Esther, 41, 43; Hannah, 207; Neome, 178; Rebeeca, 135, 199; Sarah, 17, 84; Susan, 201; Theodosia, 75.
Watts—Hannah, 177; Margaret Evelyn, 188.
Weatherby—Aan, 62; Elizabeth, 34, 43; Hannah, 74.
Weaver—Ann, 162; Catharine, 148; Dorothy, 59; Mary, 90; Mehitable, 78; Susanna, 10.
Webb—Abigail, 166; Anna, 136; Bethiah, 89; Edith, 217; Elizabeth, 21, 53, 204; Grace, 105.

Webb—Lucas, 167; Martha, 237; Mary, 44, 187; Ruth, 10; Sabilla, 129; Sarah, 42, 111, 125.
Weber—Ann, 54.
Webster—Catharine, 10; Hannah, 39; Hester, 128.
Wechtins—Rebecca, 117.
Weeb—Telphu, 223.
Weeds—Rebecca, 201.
Weeks—Elizabeth, 18, 43; Hannah,, 228; Mary, 248.
Wehronz—Leah, 28.
Weigand—Margaret, 193.
Weiley—Elizabeth, 113.
Weister—Ann, 128.
Weldon—Eliza, 23.
Welks—Mary 238.
Wells—Ann, 193, 253; Anna, 146; Beasley, 143; Bulah, 71; Elizabeth, 39, 120, 142; Fanny, 253; Hannah, 67; Mary, 40, 139; Merribe, 245; Rebecca 82.
Welsh—Esther, 96; Liddia, 147; Mary, 238; Mary Ann 216; Sarah, 73, 146.
West—Abigail, 256; Atlantic, 182; Elizabeth, 151, 238; Hannah, 32, 163; Martha, 52; Mary, 109, 134; Phillis, 86; Rachel, 58; Rebecca, 97; Sarah, 68, 173; Sophia, 97; Susanna, 86.
Westervelt—Deborah, 109.
Weston—Elizabeth, 241.
Wetherby—Ann, 128.
Wetherill—Ann, 22; Anna, 69; Deborah, 40; Elizabeth, 127; Mary, 69; Phebe, 199; Sarah, 122.
Wever—Elizabeth, 207
Whare—Elizabeth, 148; Rachel, 204.
Wheat—Mary, 68.
Wheatcraft—Rhoda, 215.
Wheeler—Elizabeth, 8, 191, 200; Hannah, 210.
Whelan—Abigail, 187.
Whildon—Experience, 83.
Whiley—Eliza, 197; Hannah, 58.
Whirl—Sarah, 226
Whisten—Mary, 241.
Whitacre—Emily, 17; Marion, 99; Mary, 146.
Whitaker, Amey, 64; Esther, 12; Mary, 111.
Whitcraft—Elizabeth, 86, 110; Mary, 218; Neomey, 239; Rhoda, 136.
White—Achsah, 213; Elizabeth, 99, 119, 168, 203, 218; Esther, 209;

Hannah, 69, 213; Lydia, 86; Margaret, 14, 242; Maria, 41; Mary, 29, 34, 47, 98, 77, 98, 212; Matilda, 149; Nancy, 82; Penolipe, 219; Phebe, 189; 232; Rebecca, 35; Sarah, 150, 245.
Whiteall—Sarah, 111.
Whitecraft—Elizabeth, 79; Lydia, 89; Meribah, 89·
Whitehouse—Elizabeth, 91; Hannah, 51; Sarah, 153, 190.
Whitelock—Anne, 185.
Whitiker—Anne, 114.
Whitton—Hannah, 59.
Whodo—Mary, 9.
Whye—Nancy Ann, 62.
Wickers—Rebecca, 29.
Wiegan(d)—Hannah, 80; Sarah, 90.
Wiggins—Abigail, 254.
Wild—Elizabeth, 166; Mary, 213.
Wilder—Margaret, 89.
Wildman—Mary, 12,
Wiles—Elizabeth, 214; Mary, 157; Sarah, 178.
Wiley—Mary, 180.
Wilguss—Ann, 253.
Wilkerson—Achsah, 48.
Wilkins—Ann, 45; Anne, 78; Elizabeth, 12, 84, 93; Hannah, 49, 142, 204, 243, 245; Hester, 220; Hope 133, 197; Ida, 194; Kitturah, 160; Lydia, 76, 202; Margaret, 204; Martha, 178; Mary, 35, 142, 192, 202; Rachel, 68; Sarah, 222; Sarah Ann, 90; Susan, 70; Susanna, 147; Theodocia, 103.
Wilkinson — Anne, 32; Elizabeth, 174; Ellen, 137; Mary, 80; Precilla, 208; Sarah, 37, 237.
Wilks—Sibbilla, 241.
Willets—Ann, 166; Deliverance, 21; Hannah, 17, 177, Lydia, 210; Sabilla, 78.
Willguss—Elizabeth, 44.
Williams—Ann, 27, 140; Blance, 118; Edith, 193, Eleanor, 169; Eliza, 131; Elizabeth, 31, 72, 248; Grace, 167; Hannah, 248; Hester, 59; Jane, 210; Lydia, 242; Margaret, 158; Maria, 121; Mary, 16, 30, 119, 134, 170, 181, 242; N., 107; Nancy, 252; Nevina 190; Phebe, 246; Phillis, 33; Rebecca, 135; Ruth, 155; Sarah, 41, 89, 154, 158.
Williamson—Ann, 19; Catherine, 194; Elizabeth, 9; Mary, 80; Nancy, 155.
Willis—Esther, 63; Mary, 138.
Willits—Abigail, 56; Ann, 17, 131, 257; Annie, 256; Beulah, 158;

Elizabeth, 73; Hannah, 176; Hepsibah, 48; Judith, 212; Mary, 36, 226; Melvina, 210; Miriam, 205; Phebe, 177; Phebe, 245; Sarah 159, 218.

Wills—Amey, 220; Ann, 47, 135; Anna, 256; Elizabeth, 23, 38, 49, 53, 116, 184, 201, 241, 249; Ester, 145; Hannah, 126, 129; Hope, 142, 144; Jane, 77; Katherine, 203; Keziah, 225; Lydia, 76; Letis, 27, 144; Margaret, 246; Maria, 204, 209; Martha, 158; Mary, 16, 20, 37, 40, 101, 141, 144, 147, 162, 169, 202, 203, 212; Nellie, 194; Priscilla, 28; Rachel, 49, 156, 188, 228; Rebecca 76, 251; Rebekkah, 230; Sally, 194; Sarah, 76, 83, 100, 102, 146, 164; Thaney, 69.

Willsey—Rhody, 206.

Willshire—Atlantic, 30.

Willson—Eleanor, 81; Elizabeth, 97; Mary, 199.

Wilmerton—Rachel, 14.

Wilsey—Ann, 86; Hannah, 85; Sophia, 17.

Wilsford, 106; Rebekkah.

Wilshere—Mary, 191.

Wilson—Abigail, 87, 187; Ann, 34, 71, 80, 103, 158; Anna, 191; Anne, 221; Catherine, 128; Christian, 107; Deborah, 216; Edith, 164, 215; Eleanor, 154; Eliza, 111; Eliza Jane, 79; Elizabeth, 58 100, 232, Fallial, 212; Hannah, 107, 157; Hester 183; Levinah, 244; Lydia, 161; Mary, 93, 110; Mary Ann, 134; Phebe, 239; Rachel, 148, 165; Rebecca, 125, 243; Sarah, 27, 29, 109, 115, 126, 184, 248; Tryphena, 74.

Wiltse(y)—Hannah, 155; Rebecca, 58.

Wiltshire—Elizabeth, 98.

Winan—Susan, 51;

Window—Mary, 83.

Winkelspecht—Annie, 25.

Winn—Elizabeth, 202.

Winner—Eliza, 233; Susannah, 95.

Winnick—Elizabeth, 36.

Winters— Hannah, 218.

Winton—Mary, 45; Rebecca Ann, 217.

Wirt—Elizabeth, 113.

Wiseman—Elizabeth, 239; Harriet, 142; Ida Louisa, 255.

Wisham—Mary, 103; Mary Ann, 182.

Wissing—Margaret, 94.

Wistar—Esther, 186; Hannah, 19; Laura, 23; Mary, 61.

Witcraft—Diedemia, 56; Levina, 59; Rhoda, 65; Rhodia, 136.

Wolf—Esther, 150,

Wood—Amy, 252; Anne, 136; Atlanah, 67; Charlot, 240; Deborah,

19; Edith, 36; Effy, 19; Elizabeth, 91, 46; Emily, 148, 186; Hannah, 36, 112; Jane, 237; Jemima, 161; Lydia, 233; Margaret, 189; Maria, 86; Mary, 10, 23, 37, 48, 96; Rachel, 17; Rebecca, 39; Rebekkah, 212; Ruth, 115; Sarah, 60, 184; 227; Susan, 243.

Woodard—Kesiah, 12; Rebecca, 170.
Wooden— Margaret, 174.
Woodhouse—Elizabeth, 37.
Woodington—Annetta 10; Mary, 26; Ruth, 80.
Wooomansee—Ann, 51.
Woodnutt—Eliz., 104; Han., 17.
Woodoth—Ruth, 152.
Woodrow—Margaret, 228; Mary, 129; Sarah Ann, 157;
Woodruff—Mary, 160.
Woodward—Anna, 107; Delviah, 157; Elizabeth, 26, 134; Hannah, 217; Mary, 141, 230; Rachel, 66; Rebeccah, 81, 250; Rhoda, 30; Sarah, 150, 220, 226.
Woofin—Maria Magdalena Henrietta, 198.
Woolcott—Joan, 252.
Wooley—Ann, 176; Lydia Ann, 234; Corstant, 47; Edna, 135; Elizabeth, 249; Hulda, 229; Lydia, 225; Mary, 142, 229; Mary Ann, 181; Sarah, 62; Susan, 140.
Woolman—Abigail, 160; Ann, 35; Anne, 66; Edith, 100; Elizabeth, 171, 220; Ellen, 42; Grace, 59; Hannah, 63, 92; Jane, 135; Kaziah, 31, 101; Macy, 31; Mary, 120; Patience, 159; Sarah, 72; Susan, 256.
Woolston(e)—Abigail, 236; Ann, 44, 50, 207; Anne, 30; Beulah, 63; Beulah Ann, 199; Celena, 252; ElizaAnn, 31; Elizabeth, 170, 84, 246; Hannah, 19, 45, 50, 166; Jean, 38; Lydia, 33; Lettice, 30, 142; Margaret, 67, 100, 248; Mary, 22, 35, 36, 128, 129, 151, 227, 251; Mary Ann, 102; Matilda, 17; Martha Virginia, 113; Rachel, 251; Rebekkah, 211; Ruth, 35; Sarah, 41.
Wooly—Elizabeth, 224; Mary, 151.
Worth—Elizabeth, 129; Lizzie, 235.
Woostall—Mary, 163.
Wooster—Hannah, 9; Mary, 129; Susannah, 209.
Worden—Abigail, 177.
Worley—Mary, 114; Penelope, 247.
Wormwood—Elizabeth, 166.
Worrel(l)—Hannah, 100; Mary, 232; Mary Elizabeth, 182; Nancy, 81.
Worster—Hannah, 45.
Wright—Abigail, 110; Acsah, 198; Alice, 155; Amelia, 95; Amy,

247; Ann, 8, 88, 214; Catharine; 63, 73; Charity, 89; Edith, 108; Eliz., 15; Eliza, 91, 183, 216; Elizabeth. 12, 75, 79, 186, 198; Elinor. 52; Esther, 152, 112, 225; Hannah. 12, 17, 58, 131, 145, 161, 187, 231, 237; Jane, 114; Levisa, 117; Margaret. 21; Martha, 189; Mary, 47, 68, 71, 189, 195, 239. 252; Nancy. 130; Paudence, 214; Rachel, 205; Rebecca, 45, 176, 180, 198, 242; Rebekah. 239; Ruth, 40; Sarah, 46, 82, 171, 205, 211, 253; Sarah Ann, 7; Susannah, 95; Theedosia, 14; Thomesin, 74.

Wyatt—Elizabeth, 212.

Wynds—Catty, 246.

Wynn—Mary, 36.

Yard—Elizabeth, 42; Ruth, 223; Susanna, 23.

Yarnall—Alice, 14.

Yates—Caroline, 225; Phebe, 161.

Yerkes—Elizabeth, 233.

Young(s)—Hannah Elizabeth, 173; Jane, 88; Martha, 49; Mary, 109, 178; Rachel, 11.

Zane(s)—Beulah. 9; Deborah, 238; Elizabeth, 96, 185; Lurania, 74; Martha, 89; Rebecca, 71; Sarah, 140.

Zelley—Annie. 63; Bathsheba Ann, 43; Charlotte, 252; Edith, 143; Elizabeth, 36; Florence, 59; Hannah, 25; Mary Louisa, 154; Rachel, 151, 196, 211; Sarah, 11, 49, 192.

Zilley—Elizabeth, 36; Mary, 175,

www.ingramcontent.com/pod-product-compliance
Lightning Source LLC
Chambersburg PA
CBHW020639300426
44112CB00007B/172